NELSON'S RELIGIOUS SERIES

General Editors

LUTHER A. WEIGLE
ROBERT SENECA SMITH

FAITHS MEN
LIVE BY

FAITHS MEN LIVE BY

JOHN CLARK ARCHER

Hoober Professor of Comparative Religion
Yale University

New York
THOMAS NELSON AND SONS
1934

PRINTED IN THE UNITED STATES OF AMERICA

TO

C. C. A. A.
A. A.

AND

V. C. A.

PREFACE

This book was written primarily to provide the author's students with a coherent, comprehensive guide to their study of the living faiths.

It seeks to serve college upper classmen, theological students and general students of religion. A bold venture into many baffling fields, it represents materials which the author has used for many years in the class-room and on the public platform. Many of the materials have been gathered at first-hand in foreign, especially Asiatic, lands in which he has lived and studied. Other sources are far more numerous than those gratefully acknowledged.

The approach to each faith is deliberately, but cautiously, contemporary. For each there is an appraisal, with some description of current forms and symbols, since this is a book of faiths which men *now* live by. The approach differentiates this from similar books, and is the chief basis on which it claims to be a new contribution to the subject. The method discovers the persistent elements in each faith which demand attention; these have been sufficiently presented.

Each religion is viewed both in its cultural setting and in itself, with regard for interactions when meeting other faiths. The treatment is objective, with the author's own prejudices reduced to a minimum. Many of the criteria of judgment are indicated throughout the volume, but especially in the *Conclusion*.

Some inconsistencies appear in spellings, in transliterations, and in punctuation. In transliterating Oriental terms, the author has sometimes avoided appropriate phonetic signs for the sake of forms more familiar or intelligible to the general student. The omissions need not annoy the specialist, and the presence of technical terms should help rather than hinder students.

The student's edition includes a list of references arranged mostly by topics, whereby major subjects may be amplified; and a list of questions for discussion which will serve to clarify and emphasize various aspects of the study. The Bibliographies are sufficiently full, and the ample Index should make easy the location of any important item.

The author is under obligation to a host of scholars, but must rest content to specify a few: his teachers, Elmer Ellsworth Snoddy, of Hiram and Transylvania Colleges, George Foot Moore and William Ernest Hocking, of Harvard, and Edward Washburn Hopkins and Charles Cutler Torrey, of Yale; and his colleagues, the consulting editors of this series, Dean Luther Allan Weigle and Professor Robert Seneca Smith.

J. C. A.

New Haven, Connecticut
June 25, 1934

CONTENTS

NELSON'S RELIGIOUS SERIES

General Editors

LUTHER A. WEIGLE

ROBERT SENECA SMITH

FAITHS MEN
LIVE BY

CHAPTER I

An Introduction to the Study of the Living Faiths

Twelve great faiths are living still: Primitivism, Taoism (pronounced as *dow*ism), Confucianism, Shinto, Hinduism (including Brahmanism), Jainism, Buddhism, Parsiism (or Zoroastrianism), Sikhism, Judaism, Islam, and Christianity. They claim the total population of the globe, some seventeen hundred million souls, but we may properly suppose that the sum of the really "faithful" falls far short of such a figure. However, if their total is a billion only, as someone has reminded us,[1] we still find substantial evidence that religion is a vital factor in the human world. Even if men today are questioning religion, or are in revolt against it,[2] their attitude enlists our interest, and provides good ground of inquiry as to what religion is and what may be its value to society. We may be able, as we pass from faith to faith, to separate what is essential from the forms which have been more conspicuous, and to discover why religion has been throughout history co-terminous with human life. Religion is historical, and certain forms may be inseparable from faith. But forms are variable. History indicates that the twelve faiths alive today will change and that some of them might even disappear. But man's record indicates that religion in some form must continue as an agency of human progress.

The twelve great religions, in spite of their disdain of barriers, fall into several groups—if we except the primitives, who are widely scattered. Three major "racial" stems, so-called, are represented: (1) the Turanian, for example, Taoism, Confucianism, and Shinto; (2) the Indo-European, for example, Hinduism, Parsiism, Jainism, Buddhism and Sikhism; and (3) the Semitic, Judaism, Christianity, and Islam. They are, of course, not mutually exclusive, for "race" is difficult of definition. Certainly no one religion is itself a racial unit. Furthermore, each has its own divisions doctrinally, which have sometimes followed racial

---

[1] See P. Hutchinson, *World Revolution and Religion*, N. Y., 1931.
[2] *Op. cit.*

I

alterations. Indo-European Buddhism took on Turanian culture in China and Japan. Semitic Christianity moving into Europe took on the likeness of the Indo-European West. Sikhism was in part an effort to unite the Indo-European cult of Hinduism and Semitic Islam. And yet one may detect, in spite of cultural transfusions, a certain racial grouping and a general racial character, even as one may find within the many subdivisions of whatever faith something of common creed and practice.

According to the latest (1933) estimates of their respective numbers the religions might be classed as follows:

1.	Christianity	about	625,000,000
2.	Confucianism	"	250,000,000
3.	Islam	"	235,000,000
4.	Hinduism	"	220,000,000
5.	Primitivism	"	160,000,000
6.	Buddhism	over	140,000,000
7.	Taoism	"	40,000,000
8.	Shinto	"	17,000,000
9.	Judaism	"	15,000,000
10.	Sikhism	"	3,000,000
11.	Jainism	"	1,000,000
12.	Parsiism	about	100,000

These are "round" numbers, and each total might be cut by nearly half, if one would count the "faithful" only. Moreover, the title now and then is doubtful. For example, "Confucianism," or "Shinto," is a *name* to cover an indefinite condition. In connection with the former, a Chinese might be of several faiths at once (*cf.* the "three religions," p. 51, below). And although a Japanese may be a Buddhist, there is a form of Shinto to which he must be loyal, also. The terms Hindu and Primitive cover culturally much more than mere religion.

In *age* the faiths might rank as follows: prehistoric and immemorial Primitivism, Judaism, Hinduism, Parsiism, Taoism, Jainism, Buddhism, Confucianism, Christianity, Shinto, Islam, and Sikhism. The order is in a measure meaningless. Primitivism lies back of all forms and lives on in many of them. Its age is twenty thousand years, at least, for *homo sapiens* has been on earth that long. Back of Taoism and Confucianism lies early Sinism, or the "way" of ancient Sinim (China). Behind both Hinduism and Parsiism lies a common heritage of early Indo-European culture. Nor was the Jewish faith original. It rests upon a common ground with several faiths now gone. Shinto had a prehistoric origin, but as an organized religion it is comparatively late. Christianity and Islam had a common Jewish heritage, and both became heirs of other sources of religion. It is easier to determine order, if we think in terms of "founders." Then we have this list: the Hebrew Moses'; Iranian Zoroaster; the Taoist Lao-tze; the Jainist Mahavira; Buddha; Confucius; Jesus; Mohammed; and the Sikh Nanak. Hinduism, Sinism, and Shinto had no early "founders." Such a figure as the Hindu Krishna appeared in the very *midst* of Hinduism. These three religions must be viewed at once as movements rather than as bequests of rites and dogmas from well-known individuals. Still Judaism with its Moses and Hinduism with its Krishna must be deemed the very oldest of the living faiths.

The *distribution* of the religions is interesting and at once suggestive—suggestive of even more than merely aspects of the interplay of cultures. Five, the Primitive, Jewish, Buddhist, Christian, and Islamic, might be called international. Primitive peoples may be found in every land while Jews and Christians are almost everywhere. Buddhism is more restricted, but touches India, Ceylon, Burma, Tibet, Siam, and all the regions eastward. Islam stretches in a wide, irregular belt from Morocco eastward to the Philippines. Others are somewhat more than national, for example, Chinese Confucianism in Japan, and Persian Zoroastrianism in India. Others still are possibly somewhat less than national. At least, Hinduism, Jainism, and Sikhism are virtually confined to India, except for adherents temporarily abroad as merchants, soldiers, students, and officials. Taoism is practically limited to China, although there are Taoists in Japan. Shinto is peculiarly the spirit of Japan, but in so far as it has expressed itself in sects it claims a mere minority of the total population.

Perhaps some faiths are by nature international, while others are by nature national. Primitivism seems international on a certain level. Hinduism once seemed destined to be international. It had an era of expansion into mainlands and islands lying east of India, but soon Buddhism, later on, Islam, checked and defeated it. However, such a congeries of faiths as one finds in Hinduism contains ideas of universal value. The world has long been debtor to the Hindu in the realm of thought. One might judge that India, so self-contained, is really international.

Such observations as we have made regarding numbers, age,

and the distribution of the several faiths might furnish us at once
good ground for many questions, such as these:

1. Why does primitive religion (we mean by this something
more, perhaps, than the religion of *primitive peoples*) still survive
so widely throughout the world?

2. *Why* have some religions "died"? In what *manner* did they
die? To what *degree?*

3. To what degree may the survival of a faith be an indication
of essential quality? What quality?

4. Have "dead" religions any longer any following? If so, why?
What of their sacred scriptures as a means to their survival?

5. When faiths have lived long and spread with vigor, what
factors beyond their own essential qualities have aided them, and
how?

6. Are some living faiths by their essence universal; Are
others more provincial, even national?

7. Does nature ever set the bounds of a religion? (Has Islam
been limited by geographical and economic factors?)

8. Is there any fundamental relation between the spiritual and
moral qualities of a religion and its physical environment?

9. Is there any causal connection between the numbers of
adherents of a faith and its qualities as a religion?

10. What motives have impelled large groups of men to
change their faith? (To what extent has the motive been religious
hunger?)

11. Why have certain faiths (the Buddhist and the Christian)
met with more success in other lands than those in which they first
arose?

12. What of the future of these many faiths? Should any one
expect to be eventually victorious over all? What are the qualities
of a "final" faith? Do the living twelve have any things in common? To what extent is any one of them religion in the full
sense of the term?

It is not possible to meet these questions adequately at this stage
of our study. The answers lie, in fact, beyond the scope of the
inquiry we may rightly make directly in our course. The questions
would inevitably lead us into the fields of history, psychology,
philosophy, economics, geography, and sociology. Nevertheless,
we may gradually find pertinent answers as we travel the highways of our study. In any case, the questions may serve to open
up our minds and to free them of any false, embarrassing assumptions we may hold with reference to any faith or all of

them. We may indeed gain certain subjective values in the end, but at the outset we must undertake our study with an experimental and objective mind.

Change and Essence in Religions.—Let us return then to the theme we interrupted. We said that not one of the twelve religions is a unit. Keep this fact in mind. It will tend to qualify our final judgment of each of the religions. We may not pass on any one a final, comprehensive judgment. Nearly every faith knew at its beginning the influence of at least one other faith. Each has divided with the years. Granted that there was a time when its adherents were unanimous, this single-mindedness was transient. With several religions the cleavage grew so deep that history alone preserves the memory of their unity. Perhaps a faith is really known today by one of its divisions. Yet even when we find a conspicuous and powerful division—perhaps, with but a single party name—as among the Buddhists (for example, Mahayanists), the Moslems (*e.g.,* Sunnites), and the Christians (*e.g.,* Roman Catholics), we may yet detect within it evidences of many minds. The largest single Christian group, the Roman Catholic,—in itself the largest distinguishable religious body in the world—is by no means one in matters of belief, whatever be its uniformity of ritual and its ecclesiastical compactness. The Parsis, although they constitute the smallest communion, are divided both in religious thought and ritual behavior. If uniformity be looked for among the twelve religions, the nearest approach both in the state of mind and the method of behavior may be found among the primitives. In contrast with their low estate of uniformity, we may see among the sects of higher culture some value in division. Divisions may be evidence of life and vigor and the will to grow, while uniformity may show inevitably inertia and decay.

And yet no faith is ever altogether static. Among the lowest orders, where custom seems to set insuperable barriers and to fix unbending standards, changes in religion have occurred. If in any tribe there have been men old enough or strong enough to introduce an innovation, it has often been accomplished.[3]

Or perhaps some extraordinary event has brought the change. Let us cite an illustration of what, no doubt, has often happened in primitive religion. John Rave, a Winnebago Indian, learned while on a visit to a distant tribe in Oklahoma to eat *peyote,* a

---

[3] See Spencer and Gillen, *The Arunta,* Vol. I, pp. 11–12; R. H. Lowie, *Primitive Religion,* pp. 200–204; F. E. Williams, *Orokaiva Magic,* p. 6.

species of small cactus used by Oklahoma Indians in their religious ceremonial. Returning to the Winnebagos, John continued
to eat peyote. To his surprise the peyote cured him and his wife
of a disease from which they had long suffered. Many Winnebagos
took to peyote-eating, whether for medicine or ritual, and a new
cult of the peyote was established, which in the end completely
modified and almost superseded the former Winnebago ritual.

On every plane of human culture changes both of creed and
ritual are frequently occurring, although it may be creed is readier
to change than ritual. Professor Radhakrishnan says of his own
faith, "There has been no such thing as uniform, stationary,
unalterable Hinduism whether in point of belief or practice." [4]

We might apply this view to all faiths. Often while a faith was
unaware of it, change was in the making—to be verified later on
by history. Take an illustration, that of caste peculiar to the
Hindu. Certain features must have crept in unawares. Even now
the system is not altogether rigid. Or take the God-idea. No
human concept has been changed more often, nor is changing now
more rapidly, than man's God-idea, especially on the higher levels.
The great religions, after all, are movements not positions, processes not results, growing revelations and not fixed traditions.
Religion is a journey rather than a destination.

Nevertheless, in spite of frequent change, one may find in
almost every faith a main idea, a dominant tradition, or a ruling
tendency. An essence seems at last, whatever strength it might
have had to start with, to have been distilled within and by each
faith. This gives it its distinctive character and defines it not only
in relation to another faith, but to the whole of life. We may thus
justly call one system Buddhist, another Moslem, another
Christian. For, even if psychological experiences have much in
common, such other elements as these determine a distinctive
essence: (1) historical events, (2) conspicuous and influential
personalities, (3) the major customs of peculiar peoples, and
(4) the local qualities of lands and climates. Nature speaks to men
a various language, whether of land or sea, torrid or temperate
zone, ominous, dense jungle or smiling plains, of the hard, open
desert or forbidding mountain ranges. Once the essence is established, all changes while the faith endures are so controlled
that we might say the faith runs "true to form."

But we should bear in mind a further high consideration, lest
we miss the woods by looking at the trees. There may be some-

4 *The Hindu View of Life*, p. 129.

thing which at least is larger than the twelve faiths all together—greater in degree, if not in quality. We might affirm that anything in its totality is larger than the sum of all its parts. Certainly this theory accords with what we know of this expanding universe. And it was held by some before we knew the universe is growing. At any rate there is for us something larger than the sum of twelve religions. We mean Religion. If this be so, no one faith quite fully represents *as such* the whole field of religion. One may therefore be religious with a double meaning. He may hold to one religion and be numbered with the faithful, and yet may look beyond with open-mindedness for growing revelation. One need not hold the view which Gandhi seems to hold, that all religions have validity in equal measure, and that a man is loyal to his own through sheer tradition. He seems to think that any faith will do full service as Religion.

Definitions.—Religion as such is abstract, intangible, strictly indefinable, and yet existent. One might liken it to time and say, "Everyone knows time, feels conscious of it, recognizes that man exists in time," and further add, "yet who can define time properly, or say that it ever began or never began?" [5] We must, however, get a working definition of religion, and a norm of judgment. What is this "whole," some parts of which we know—or are to know? What the full orb whose "broken lights" we see?

We may appeal first to several Western students who from their several points of view are qualified to tell us what religion means. The word itself is Latin, *religio.* It may be traced, however, from two important sources in the language: (1) Cicero drew it from *relegere,* which means to "gather up, consider," that is, the assembling and consideration of what concerned the worship of the gods,—or more simply, reverence and respect toward the gods. (2) Certain early Christian writers, following the Roman Lactantius, derived it from *religāre,* meaning "to bind to or back, to restrain," that is, restraint under divine power, or for fear of God.[6]

Cicero was a Roman pagan under the influence of Greek philosophy, a popularizer of Greek ideas, much inclined toward eclecticism. He was incurably optimistic in politics, and tolerant in temper toward religion. Those early Christian writers, on the other hand, were advocates of one peculiar faith, holding the present world, its politics, and all its other faiths in deep con-

[5] E. W. Hopkins, *The History of Religions,* p. 1.
[6] Mohammed called the Christian monk a *rahib,* or "one who *fears* his God."

tempt. They counselled men to fear the one true God, keep His commandments, and be forever saved.[7] There were other views than these, but for the most part religion in the Roman world was early associated with ideas and practices of *reverence,* on the one hand, and with elements of *fear* on the other. But religion is vastly more than reverence or fear. There are elements of awe and a feeling of dependence, a sense of moral good, a touch of reason, and a sense of mystery. Above all else is the awareness of the presence and superior power of some mysterious and infinite Being who orders the universe of men and things. But any definition which seeks to take into account all phases and functions of religion must seem too theoretical, and to fall short of the final whole. Each student passes judgment in the light of all the facts he can command. Every definition represents the student's own experience and his own impression; it indicates his point of view, whether as philosopher, psychologist, anthropologist, or other.

Plato, for all his high philosophy, voiced for all time one of the lowest concepts of religion, namely, that religion is "a science of begging and getting" gifts from the gods. He recognized the "gods," but was merely feeling after God. His notion of religion is scarcely higher than that of a modern primitive who barters with his god in this wise, "I give to you that you may give to me." Some students of our time connect religion with man's quest of surety in a world of flux, his eagerness for certainty amidst change. Says one such, "Religion is society's adjustment to that which is, in any age, beyond knowledge—to the aleatory (*i.e.,* "chance") element, as personalized, through the long ages of human evolution, in the spirit-environment."[8] That is, there are personified spirits to whom the menace of chance may be referred, and spirits from whom surety may be found from mischance. Somewhat in contrast at the basic point, Levy-Bruhl declares that primitives never think of such a thing as "chance." But even if we build our definition upon chance, we might deny that men when they have won a sense of surety have forfeited religion. At least one master of religion has declared that faith is the "assurance of things hoped for, the evidence of things not seen."[9] The assurance of a man of faith is one of the most striking

---

[7] Augustine adopted the idea derived from *religāre,* which dominated the theology of the Middle Ages.

[8] A. G. Keller, *Science of Society,* p. 1430.

[9] The Christian apostle Paul, at any rate, the writer of the *New Testament* letter to the *Hebrews,* 11:1.

features of religion. The above definition indicated the important presence of something personal in the spirit-environment—a more significant observation than the reference to "chance." Mason says that "in a general sense, religion is what is thought or believed about a spirit world and what is done in consequence of such thinking." [10]

On this plane of *thought* as an element of religion, another adds, "Religion is the conception man forms of his relations with the superhuman and mysterious powers on which he believes himself to depend." [11]

Matthew Arnold indicates the place of *feeling* and of moral good, when he says "Religion is morality touched with emotion." Schliermacher, the philosopher, found the very essence of religion in "the feeling of absolute dependence" of man on the Divine.[12] This further emphasizes the *individual* character of religion (in contrast with "society's adjustment," in the phrase of Keller, above). Professor William James used the word religion to cover "the feelings, acts and experiences of individual men in their solitude, so far as they apprehend themselves to stand in relation to whatever they may consider the divine." Professor Whitehead, mathematician and philosopher, follows James in one respect, at least, by saying that "religion is what a man does with his solitariness." Martineau is more explicit than James about what he calls "the Divine." Religion, says he, is "a belief in an everlasting God, that is, a divine mind and will ruling the universe and holding moral relations with mankind."

These selected definitions by men of different minds indicate these elements in what is called "religion": (1) man, whether as an individual alone or in the group, over against a world of mystery and spirit; (2) the moods of men, whether of fear, or awe, or humility; (3) man's effort to adjust himself to the spirit world, whether by gifts, by thought, or righteous living; and (4) a heightening appreciation of the spirit world where dwells a dependable, eternal God. In general, they establish for religion the two worlds, human and divine, and the task of harmonious adjustment on man's part.

Oriental Definitions.—Even more germane to our investigation is an acquaintance with Eastern sources which give us something of a meaning for "religion." We should not expect to find exact

10 Mason, *Woman's Share,* p. 241.
11 D'Alviella, *The Conception of God,* p. 63.
12 See his *Discourses on Religion.*

equivalents for our word "religion." [13] And within the words we do find are differences of meaning, for the Eastern scriptures were often centuries in composition, and words may change their meaning from one age to another.

Among the Chinese ideographs for what we call "religion" are such terms as *chiao, tao,* and *hsiao. Chiao* is "teaching, or doctrine," used mainly in the concrete. It is applied to a teacher of religion, the doctrine he teaches, a schoolmaster, a lesson, a church, a disciple, a Roman Catholic, a Buddhist. *Tao* means "nature, way, or reason." It is often more abstract than *chiao,* although it, also, may be used (in combination) concretely, for such objects as a road, a gentleman, a Taoist priest, and a college of theology. *Hsiao* (it sounds like *shiao*) means "dutiful, obedience, or filial devotion." It, more than the other two, has something of the very meaning of our word "religion." At least, it has meant at times to Chinese what our own word means to us. But we may look in vain for Chinese terms, or Chinese definitions, of religion, save what may be implied in *chiao* and *tao* and *hsiao.* They indicate a tendency to think of filial devotion to a set of teachings in accord with nature,—or with reason. The Taoist Lao-tze thought about "the way (*tao*) of nature, and of man's practice of this way." The sage Confucius was overcautious in matters spiritual. He went no further than to urge *"respect* for spirits" (departed human spirits and various nature powers) and the worship of them. He urged this as a part of "wisdom" (*chih*).[14]

Among the Hindus of India the word in most common use is *dharma,* which in itself has many meanings, such as "religion, doctrine, ordinances, piety, duty, righteousness, law, quality, nature, and idea." It runs this way, with variations, through the whole range of India's sacred writings, and when associated with the God-idea or the divine, it has the meaning of "religion." The importance of the word is great, for the orthodox Hindu has given extraordinary place to the divine. To the Hindu who is a pantheist, *dharma* has meant to him the realization of the essential oneness of the divine soul within him and the divine universe about him. To the theist, *dharma* has meant loving devotion due from him to a personal god. If he has been, with the masses generally, a polytheist, *dharma* has meant his doing of the works divinely ordained of the various gods to save men's souls. Buddha also

---

13 Furthermore, a word alone is no credible proof of the existence of a concept, nor is absence of a word proof of the lack of the concept. There is a language of the heart as well as of the tongue.
14 *Analects,* VI, xx.

used the term, but gave it his own meaning. Giving scant place to the divine, he taught the need of "goodness," of "fellowship with what is lovely," and "of walking uprightly in accordance with the Law." His later followers, in contrast with himself, became far more "religious." They had regard for things divine. While the Indian Moslem also employs the Hindu *dharma,* he has words for "religion" peculiarly his own. His *madhhab* means "religious opinion or creed," and his *iman,* "faith or devotion." But his strictly religious vocabulary is naturally Arabic.

When the Moslems mean religion they usually say *din* (pronounced as *deen*),—unless they say *Islam. Din* chiefly means "observance," that is, observance of the divine injunctions, or obedience to Allah. It occurs with great frequency in the Koran, where the reference is always to Islam. Islam itself primarily is "resignation," to Allah. Both Arab and Persian Moslems think of religion as "observance."

The Jewish Scriptures contain at least two special terms, *yirath,* "fear, or fear of God" [15] and *daath,* "knowledge, or consciousness" (of God, that is). There is a larger, if implicit definition of religion in the famous declaration of the Jewish prophet Micah, "What doth the Lord require of thee, but to do justly, to love mercy, and to walk humbly with thy God?" [16] And the prophet Jeremiah indicated that God's law is written not in books but on the hearts of men.[17] To him religion was not outer form but inner character.

Neither the ancient Greek nor the Roman had a comprehensive term for "religion." One had *hieros* to apply to what was "holy," and the other had *sacer* to apply to what he deemed "sacred." Both terms and their cognates (*e.g.,* the *hiereus* or *sacerdos,* the "priest") reflected much of an original content of what we may call *mana* or *orenda,* supernatural potency (see p. 30, below).

Christians, while believing in divinity, did not at first attempt a thoroughgoing definition of religion. Although in their Scriptures (specifically the Greek *New Testament*) religion is the major theme, it is seldom defined explicitly. No writer seems to have found religion simple enough to be reduced to definition. The word *threskeia,* for example, is used five times only, and its adjective *threskos,* only twice. It means "the fear of God and the worship of God" and is applied to man's bridling of his unruly tongue,

---

[15] *Cf.* the Koranic *taqwa,* "godly fear, or piety."
[16] *Book of Micah,* 6:8.
[17] *Jeremiah,* 31:33.

his care of the fatherless and the widowed in their distresses, and his aloofness from "the world." [18]

When sacred books themselves discuss religion, they usually do so in terms of a *particular* religion. Religion *as such* is seldom alluded to. The attitude of any sacred writer is frequently that the religion of which he treats is itself religion, either actually at the time, or in process of becoming, the full and final manifestation. Other religions to him are simply "imperfect," "incomplete," or altogether "false." Zoroaster admitted that other religions than his own might have good qualities, including righteous men, but that his own was "superior." Buddha recognized other faiths, but, preached his own as the final Way. Moses recognized other gods (or idols), but enjoined Israel to have no god but Yahweh. Mohammed tolerated certain other faiths, but held Islam to be their consummation. He said, "if they [the followers of these other faiths] believe as you [Moslems] believe then have they the *true* guidance."

Religion, then, in general has been measured by religion in particular. Thereby one has meant the Jewish, Christian, Moslem, or some other faith. If, however, we return to our theory that Religion as a whole is something greater than religions all together, we might formulate a working definition as follows: *Religion is man's whole and developing reaction within and upon life, "the expression of his summed-up meaning and the purport of his whole consciousness of things," such reaction, meaning, and consciousness implying the recognition of things spiritual and superhuman.* This may serve us for a time, until we gather further outward facts, discover further inner secrets of human emotions, and further learn about the operations of men's minds. Meanwhile, we may assume that Religion is for man the most comprehensive of all terms, that Religion is a *fact* of life, whether of inner experience or outer observation.

More immediately we seek to know religions. And in viewing each of the twelve we shall approach it through what it seems to be today. Its history to which we ultimately appeal becomes an explanation of its enduring character. Among the things we seek to know are these: (1) its forms; (2) its leaders—and, perhaps, its founders; (3) the causes it has advocated; (4) its effects upon man's life and mind; (5) its attitude toward other faiths; and (6) to what extent it is religion. Like a tree, a religion may be known by its fruits.

[18] See *Epistle of James*, 1:26–27.

Ritual and Worship.—Worship inevitably tells us much at the outset. This active side of faith is more effective, picturesque, and demonstrable than the side of sheer belief, and may tell us more than creed can. Some faiths may be more tolerant in worship than in creed—or quite the contrary, as in Islam, or any "close communionists." The prayers of some religions are directed to an exclusive, jealous, perhaps a national, God. The gifts of money which the faithful bring may be devoted to exclusive propaganda—or, in certain instances, may be freely used for any worthy cause or enterprise. At any rate, worship, or to be more specific, ritual, is a more constant element than creed. It is the continuing bond which holds the faithful together from one generation to another. Rites may arise in connection with belief, but often continue long after their original meaning has been lost or modified. Old formulas of prayer and sacrifice may continue in the ritual when new gods have taken the places of the old. Although the Buddha served no god at all, the ancient Hindu Indra was carried on to China by the Buddhist ritual. It is probable that ritual, more than creed, allows the interchange of ideas among strange cults. Faiths have sometimes spread by ritual rather than belief. Ritual emerged before men phrased belief, and changes in the ritual have sometimes brought about a change of creed. Ritual is the fruit of man's emotion, and rites stir men's souls far more than creed. On every plane mankind has found in ceremony the more agreeable expression of faith and the more effective means of harmony with its environment. When faiths have met for common worship their differences of creed have been obscured.

Where there are priests—and every faith has priests, except Confucianism, Sikhism, and Islam—they are the leaders of the worship. They are the "elders" of the people.[19] As is the priest so is the faith itself, for better or for worse. With the priest sprang up a lore of worship and a calendar of festivals, with the priest as editor of one and the expert in guidance of the other. Men have looked to him to do what they had neither time or skill to do, and for learning which he alone had opportunity for getting. He was vested with authority, demanding and providing precision in religious exercises. Under his hand the faith was organized and men subjected to its authority—to *his* authority in fact. For ages the priest administered the law which regulated human life. He has ordained the chieftain and the king—and he has deposed them in the name of the divine. He has been the officer of sacrifice

---

[19] The word "priest" comes down to us from the Greek *presbyteros,* an "elder."

and the custodian of holy places. These are universal elements in religion. He has lead men in their prayers, and in times of war and peace has been the chief interpreter of the will of God.

Every faith has its prophets, though not in such close succession as the priests. Priests are constant; prophets are occasional. The history of religion shows the tendency of priests to be conservative and of sacerdotalism to prevail. On the other hand, the prophet arises in conflict with the priest and "utters forth" fresh words of God with newer emphases in faith. He also is an interpreter of God's will, although unlike the priest, he may be self-appointed. In theory he has heard the "call" of God, or seen a "vision" of a transformed order. Perhaps he is a priest turned prophet, for priests may be prophetic, as prophets may be ultimately priestly. A certain priest of ancient India grew prophetic when in connection with the ritual sacrifice he declared that worship might be properly performed without the slaughter of an actual horse, and that instead men might meditate upon the horse's image: the sky its body, the sun its eye, the streaming cloud its mane; and that he might do this in any place in which his mind was free and fit for meditation. He meant, of course, by implication that *some* men might worship truly thus. A modern Indian prophet has voiced the same prophetic mood: "Utter Kali's [that is, the Goddess's] name, and sit in meditation. . . . What is thy gain from images of metal, stone, or earth?" The Hebrew prophets said that God was not most pleased with mere grain offerings, nor pleased with animals slain in sacrifice. Jesus said, "Enter into thine inner chamber and when thou hast shut the door, pray to the Father who seeth in secret." But the priestly office has never fully lapsed, nor has the priestly ministry ever grown dispensable.

Religion stands in frequent need of prophets to challenge its ceremonial, to scrutinize its creed, and to remind men that God at times must speak to men directly,—incidentally, to free the priest ofttimes from the very system for whose welfare he has been responsible. The prophet's weakness is isolation. He stands apart from the current tradition, although his lips may have been touched by coals from off the altar of the established order. He stands conspicuously alone, whether as judge or inspiration. He has his day and passes on. Then the priest takes upon himself the constant burdens of the faith. The "elders" furnish continuity, and bear their testimony that religion cannot live by "vision" only. What the prophet sees must take on body and become an institution before becoming true reform. So the house of prayer is renovated, not destroyed, the high places of pure worship reconstructed and newly dedicated. Forms and ceremonies then revised become the marks and agencies of man's inner spirit of devotion. Both the prophet and the priest are men of God. True religion is a spirit. It is also an order. Religion must be orderly, if it be effective, at whatever level.

A religion has its symbols also, which may catch the ranging eye and call for comprehension. They are more than signs. They signify the faith to those who hold them dear. What the symbols stand for had been long accumulating. They represent a multitude of scenes and varied feelings and ideas, whether primitive or advanced, gross or refined, formal or vital, genuine or perverted, individual or social. They are the fruitage of the varied fortunes of the faithful and the signs of their devotion. Each faith has its own peculiar shrines whose familiar symbols satisfy its worshipers. But symbols represent to some degree division, misunderstanding, and antipathy. Often, faiths with much in common in creed hold aloof in their worship—Jewish, Christian, and Islamic, for example. When one faith has imposed its symbols on another, it has assumed the other faith's conversion. For its own integrity a faith has usually declined to tolerate the symbols of another. Each body of believers has been reared according to its own peculiar symbolism, and has often made no effort to understand another. The cross, the crescent, the swastika, the mirror, the trident and the tilak are examples of this divisive symbolism. The Christian cross was to the Jew a "stumblingblock" and to the Greek pagan "foolishness," observed St. Paul. A Hindu idol is an outrage to the Moslem. To the Protestant the Catholic mass is "mummery," and the Catholic finds no satisfaction in the "services" of the Protestant.

Obviously the student of a religion must seek to understand its symbols. To that end he must view them all with sympathy, first of all. There is no warrant for division between religion and religion on the basis of mere symbol. An interchange of symbols —at least the *use* of one another's symbols—may be a way of common understanding among the twelve religions. Each people might to some extent determine for itself the meaning of another people's symbols. The words themselves which peoples use in worship or in statements of their creed are really symbols,— for example, T'ien, Krishna, Brahmā,[20] Ahura Mazdah, and Allah. "God" itself is a name derived from roots which mean "to

20 This form is personal. Brahma and Brahman refer to the impersonal All.

worship," to "pour a libation," or "the worshipful." [21] While each
of these words for God may represent to men a cherished heritage,
no word is fully comprehensive of Reality. Even Nanak's "True
Name" (*Satnam*) falls short of *Truth*. Any name may represent
a growing body of belief and a ripening experience, whether of
religion or of God. The *tao,* said Lao-tze, which can be named is
not the *Tao*.

As we view men worshiping, as we visit their sanctuaries, observe
their ritual acts, read their books, interview their ministers, and
ask the causes which they advocate, we put ourselves in the way
of understanding what their faith is. It is, first of all, a formidable exterior we must penetrate, whether of books and buildings, or prophets, priests, and ritual. We must get behind the
realistic to the real, discriminate between the signs and what they
signify, and let the mind identify at last what the eye sees super-
ficially.

A Religion is a Quest.—A religion has been called a journey.
It is a quest. It is a two-fold quest. (1) It seeks for God and
Truth. (2) It seeks adjustment to environment, including God.
Men would "organize experience into some form or other of
coherent totality." [22] Religions through long periods, at least have
grown by integrations, whether of instinct, custom, reason, or
moral insight. In the highest stages of man's quest nature is one,
reason is one, the human mind is one, God is one, and man is one
with God, Various religions have all looked for human good.
Usually this human good has been referred to God. By whatever
name it has been called—the theologian has said "salvation"—
man has sought a great release and a great realization, the truest
happiness and the highest good. One faith has looked forward to
the earthly conquest of the evil by the good, has offered men a
share in this conquest, and his pictured "heaven" as the good life
in a good world. One old faith has thought that its God would
establish it as an independent nation and then send it His messiah
through whom justice would reign throughout the earth and all
nations be brought ultimately under its own sway. Some faiths
have enjoined men singly to turn from evil and do well, thus
insuring their safety and happiness in this world and the next.
One ancient faith has offered many ways to the great goal, by
works, by knowledge, and by personal devotion. And every faith
has had its mystics who might say, with a Moslem saint,

---

[21] *Cf.* the Sanskrit *hŭ* and *hū*. "God" is related to the "good." *Cf.* the Teutonic
gut and *Gott.*
[22] John Murphy, *Primitive Man,* p. 24.

"As the birds fly in the air, as the fishes swim in the sea, leaving no trace behind, so even is the pathway of God traversed by the seeker of the spirit."

Religion has been the mightiest force within the minds of men throughout the history of mankind and the human social order.

CHAPTER II

THE RELIGION OF THE PRIMITIVES

About nine percent of the peoples of the earth today are "primitives." One hundred and sixty millions, in round numbers, possess those qualities and maintain those institutions which characterized mankind near the beginning of human life. It is an amazingly large proportion of the human race which still speak and feel and think as children. They must be accounted for, and there is no easy solution. Their religion must be studied closely. Perhaps it has values of its own which the student of religion should recognize in making his appraisal of the total, permanent spiritual element in man.

We cannot call them uncivilized, for many of them have a certain culture. Many of them make pottery by *throwing,* that is, by the turning of a wheel, something no genuinely primitive folk have ever done. Nor are they racially homogeneous; they are of many widely scattered stocks, of varied tongues and customs. They live in "culture zones," whether of development or retardation. We cannot set them off from peoples we call "civilized," if our judgment be according to religion. For among the members of the so-called higher faiths are multitudes whose religious theories and practices are still comparatively primitive.

On the lower levels culturally are these:

the Negritos of the Philippine Islands;
various tribes of Micronesia and Polynesia;
the Papuans of New Guinea;
the black Aruntas of Australia;
the Andaman Islanders in the Bay of Bengal;
the Kols and Pariahs of Central and South India;
the Pygmies and Bushmen of the Central African Congo basin;
the Caribs of the West Indies; and
the Yahgans of the extreme south of South America.

On a higher plane are these:

the Samoans and Hawaiians;
the Kalmuks of Siberia;

the Veddas of Ceylon;
the Todas of the Nilgiri Hills, South India;
the Bantu of south central and southern Africa;
the Eskimos and the Amerinds (American Indians).

Primitives, although most numerous in Africa, are found throughout the whole world. They live in the remote places, on the distant islands of the seven seas, along or near the edges of the mainlands, in interior pockets of habitation, cut off by the trackless deep, often pressed off the continents onto coastal islands by the expansion of abler peoples, or thrust into still centers on the mainlands as the tides of higher culture have ebbed and flowed about them. They provide pathetic evidence of the dreadful hurt of isolation.

Their names bring images to mind of huts of straw, fire lit by friction, tattooed and cicatrized bodies, bead ornaments, flint arrowheads, leathern shields, bows and arrows, boomerangs, dug-out canoes, out-rigger sailboats, masks and the ritual dance, zimbas and tomtoms, magic and shamans, demons, priests, and nature spirits. These are elements of a primitive order and the peoples fall into a convenient whole, regardless of the fact that they are widely scattered and speak many different and mutually unintelligible tongues.

1. *Sociologically,* they are still in the stage [1] of the *sib* or tribal organization of family units. The family rather than the individual is the constituent unit. Though an individual acquire goods by reason of his special skill, they are shared by all his relatives. The family is sponsor for its separate members, and its members rely ultimately upon it for aid, defense, vengeance, and livelihood. It arranges marriages for its younger members, and oversees the education of its children. It exploits in the interest of the group the strength, the skill, and the relationships of every individual. We can imagine the religious implications of such a social organization, religion being coterminous with life, and its manifestations related to the whole round of social forms.

2. *Psychologically,* primitives yield to custom, and give to the common usage only a minimum of critical attention. They live on the plane of action more than reason; they give way to emotion rather than to thought. The group is dominant, providing sanctions and prohibitions for itself and for its members. Personality is

---

[1] The use of the word "stage" does not justify the inference that the social order and religion have developed by distinct stages in a consistently progressive series, as, for example, from promiscuity to the family, to the tribe, and to the nation, or from "animism" to polytheism and later to monotheism.

seldom more than germinal or potential, and whenever manifested in a conspicuous manner is usually deemed hurtful to the group. It is suppressed in the end, save in the case of strong elders whose determination may bring on change. Ordinarily, primitives lack the force of intellect by which their religion might be lifted out of its low estate. What small demand is made by reason is satisfied by *myth* [2]—among primitives myth creates facts from mere ideas, writes thereby the record of tribal origins and history, and explains the constitution of nature and the universe. Primitives, to be sure, have keen faculties and unusual skills; so also have birds and animals! The thoughts of primitives are simple, and their thought-processes are often not far removed from "those simplest nervous reflexes of the human body which are merely the antecedents and rudimentary forms of thinking." Their thought as well as feeling depends largely upon sensation; primitives are impressionistic. Concepts are few, for primitives lack the power to generalize effectually. Distinctions are seldom clearly drawn, as, for example, between one man "alive" and another "dead." Judgments are based upon scanty evidence, often on fewer facts than are readily available. Deductions are often most erratic, conclusions being reached at times much after the manner of the grasshopper that jumps, flies and lights at random. Primitives are deficient in coördination and control. Analogy is their logic, and whatever moves is thought to be "alive." In the primitive view, if an acorn falls upon a sleeper's head, it *meant* to hurt him, or to arouse him to a sense of danger; if a man drowns in a stream or lake, the water *meant* to take his life. Nature is a realm of action and of will, but the primitive's magical notions of nature often blind him to facts that should be obvious.

Their mental constitution gives them a peculiar view of their world. It gives them a *small world*, for the immediate is the limit of their practical interest, and their "universe" is but a duplicate of their own situation, including beings that are alive as men themselves are alive. The realm of mystery is subject to whatever "controls" are valuable in the realm of sight. A man treats the spirits as he treats his human neighbors—the spirits are *like* his neighbors. The spirit-world is humanized and socialized after the pattern of the more immediate world, and is deemed to operate as this world operates, not according to uniform laws and principles, but by the will of specific parts and persons. It is a realm

---

[2] A legend has some basis in fact, but a myth is born of sheer imagination.

of concrete events, of accident, exception, and miracle. The bounds
of their small world and of their scarcely larger universe are seldom
broken by theoretical speculation about origins and destiny. It is
enough for them that some great spirit or some culture hero made
the world and all its contents, and they give little thought to what
and why is God. They talk of soul and spirit, but give slight notice
to questions of the nature of either or the after-life.

3. The world of the primitive is *not an actually different world*
from our own, although we can by no means assume that it is the
same world. Nor is primitive mentality to be distinguished absolutely from our own,[3] even though we may not hold the opposite
theory that the human mind is everywhere essentially the same.
To hold the view, even as a working hypothesis, that "civilized"
and "uncivilized" mentalities differ radically would seem, incidentally, to be an admission that civilized man cannot enter
into the way of thinking and feeling of the uncivilized. Any serious
student admits that he finds it difficult to understand the primitive
mind, quite apart from the difficulties of language and the physical environment. He would find it difficult, as an American, to
enter into the ways of thought and feeling of the higher Hindus
and Chinese, but it would not prove a fundamental difference of
mentalities. One might insist that a purely objective description
of the primitive state is possible even without entering into
primitive thought and feeling; upon such a one rests a formidable
burden of proof that his account is both purely objective and true.
To hold, on the other hand, the theory of the fundamental identity
of the human mind and the view that human nature is everywhere
the same is not to find an easy way of understanding primitive
mentality, for such a theorist pursuing his studies among living
primitives themselves becomes aware of actual differences. Primitives do not think and act as he assumes they should think and
act, nor can he imagine himself as behaving under the circumstances as the primitives behave.

4. What then may we properly assume? The mind of the
primitive uses a primitive type of brain with certain centers un-
developed or untried. The primitive has a retentive memory, great
powers of observation, of limitation and of adaptation. He practices
many of the higher human virtues, but he knows less about the
world than men of higher culture know; has had neither clear
opportunity nor long-sustained inducement to resolve the incon-

[3] As some investigations have insisted—for example, L. Levy-Bruhl. See his
Primitive Mentality, N. Y., 1923.

sistencies and contradictions in his ideas and acts; has never sought to be logical; indeed has never been consistently troubled by contradiction and disorder. The primitive is nearer than any other living man to the point where man began really to be man. In his religious character he stands nearest to what religion must have been at the beginning of the human story, when religion was inherent, instinctive, spontaneous, and mystical. This is not to say that the primitive mind and primitive religion are utterly simple in contrast with the complexity of things amongst us. Even slight acquaintance with the vocabulary of primitives shows an amazing complexity, an indication of the baffling intricacies and ramifications of the primitive order.

5. Why, then, are primitives as they are? Why have they remained nearest the primal state of things? Will they ever get on? Is there any basis of improvability? They are after all at a certain general level, and have not succeeded in rising above it. The Bantu never thought to make a wheel, but continued to bear their heavy burdens on their heads. To the Polynesians lightning is still the menace of an angry deity, and meteors are missiles of divine vengeance. Although human history discloses cycles of advance and decay, it is difficult to think of living primitives as having fallen from a higher state. Civilizations have grown from crude beginnings; and may fall. But the primitives of today have never risen. Their sense organs are not inferior as such; nor were the primitives handicapped by an inferiority of *original* endowment which held them back while other men made progress. It would be well to look for some valid explanation in connection with: (1) the food supply (if food lies near at hand no effort need be made to get it); or, (2) the climate (which may be enervating); or, (3) repeated catastrophe of various sorts (by which men are discouraged with respect to goods and institutions and even life itself); or, (4) belief in magic (which arrests intelligence); and we might add (5) illiteracy and the absence of written documents (by which the primitive is denied a knowledge of what civilized men have done, or even a record of what his own abler kindred may have done). Whatever our conclusion, we are confronted immediately by millions of living men in what we may as well call a state of arrested development. We shall view and describe their religion as it is today.

To select any primitive group for detailed study is somewhat arbitrary, considering the great numbers and wide distribution of the stocks. It is manifestly impossible to find any *lowest* and *most primitive* tribe, although there might be fairly common agreement that the Australian blacks (the Aruntas and others), the African bushmen, and the South American Patagonians and Fuegians are the lowest we now know. But, furthermore, it is unsound procedure to draw from any one of these small, isolated and diminishing groups conclusions with reference to the whole field of primitive religion. We may with more propriety select a great Negro tribe of Africa. Much patient and exhaustive study has been of late devoted to various aspects of Negro life in Africa. If we can anywhere see the childhood of the human race it is there, —speaking culturally and not racially. There in the world's most promising human laboratory for the study of primitivism we may learn at last whether the mind of the primitive is really quite distinct, what are the effects of higher upon lower culture, and whether extinction, or transformation and development, will be the lot of primitive religion.[4]

In Africa are both Negroes and Negroids. The former are the truest, purest type of blacks, although the latter represent the black men at their primitive best in culture. The *Negroes* are found mostly in the forests of the Congo River basin, and about the lakes and waterways inland from the coast of Guinea. There in the west, out of easy communication with other folk, they have maintained their own faith and customs. They number many millions, let us say forty. They go by many names, the most familiar being Ashanti, Dahomi, and Yoruba, to mention only three language groups. Among the *Negroids* the most familiar name is Bantu, meaning "the people." They number fully fifty millions and stretch through the congo region and through eastern, central, and southern Africa. Bakongo, Barotse, Baganda, Mbunda, Bechuana, and Zulu are among the more prominent of the negroid Bantu subdivisions.

The Ashanti Negro.—The *West African Negro* is strong and sturdy. He is an agriculturist, and works with a hoe with an iron blade. He eats all manner of available food, save only what may be *tabu*. His principal food is yam and manioc (both introduced into Africa from America, they say). If he is a Dahomi Negro, he may eat human flesh. His clothing is bark-cloth, his bow has a chord of cane-fiber, and his shield is made of wood or wickerwork. He knows the language of the "talking drums." His face and body are marked by conspicuous, tattooed lines and ridged scarifications. His teeth are filed or chipped. He belongs to a secret

---

[4] Certain primitives have vanished almost before our eyes, *e.g.*, the Tasmanians before 1876. The Bantu may not disappear, but their religion may.

society and wears *jujus* (amulets).[5] On ceremonial occasions he has use for masks, man-like figures, and wooden and iron gongs. He is an "animist" and a polytheist and practices "fetishism." In the food, the *cane* bow-string, the *heavy* scars, and the *juju*, there is something distinctive of the pure Negro. Let us look particularly at the religion of the Negro of Ashanti, part of the so-called "Gold Coast" over which Great Britain holds sway, whose native population is about 400,000.

There is in Ashanti the *Afahye* ceremony, an annual festival (*afa*) held in connection with the eating of the first fruits of a crop, for example, yams. Part of the ceremony has reference to ancestral spirits (*samanfo*), and part is concerned with the gods. There is the *Baya* ceremony in homage to departed ancestors. There is the more elaborate *Adae* ceremony during which the spirits of the departed rulers of the clan are propitiated, their deeds recalled and extolled and requests made of them for boons. There is, also, the *Apo* ceremony, an annual ritual of tribal purification and restoration, by which, in the words of an early observer, "the Devil is banished from all their towns." In former days the *Odwira* ceremony was held annually in the capital town of Coomassie. Its purpose was to honor and propitiate the spirits of deceased Ashanti kings—and the dead, generally; to celebrate the ingathering of the first-fruits of the crops (yams, specifically); to purify the shrines of ancestral and other spirits and of the gods; and to cleanse and restore the nation. There was much display and unrestrained indulgence. Among the bloody sacrifices were twelve human victims. The soberest motive of the rite was to enhance the prestige of the king and to augment the consciousness of national and religious solidarity. When, however, British rule began in 1896, this ceremony became politically unnecessary. Likewise the British banned the repulsive aspects of the celebration. The Odwira disappeared. The other ceremonies which are still observed include rites of various sorts in connection with tabus, fetishes, the higher gods (with the great god Tano, or Ta Kese), and 'Nyame, the Ashanti Supreme Being.

The Apo Ceremony.—We may take the *Apo* as a type. It is suggestive of almost every important element in Ashanti religion.[6] It may serve, also, as concrete evidence of almost the whole range and content of primitive religion. The custom is several centuries old, at least, and has presumably remained substantially unchanged.

[5] French *joujou*, or "doll."
[6] See R. S. Rattray, *Ashanti*. Oxford, 1923. Captain Rattray witnessed this ceremony at Tekiman, Northern Ashanti, in 1922.

The word *apo* probably means "speaking roughly." Other designations for the rite mean "to insult," and "to cleanse." The total meaning might be expressed as freedom to speak out frankly in complaint or even vilification of anyone, for the sake of unburdening the mind, cleansing the soul (*sunsum*), and doing good to the community. The ceremony lasts eight days each year.

On the first day, priests (*akomfo*) and priestesses (*akomfo mma*) with their attendants and followers, bearing the brass pans, or shrines of various gods (*abosom*), keep arriving from neighboring regions. Toward evening, all who have arrived, along with the local priests, priestesses and residents, parade up and down the main street, in no particular order, but mingling in cheery groups. The shrines of the various gods, containing assortments of sacred objects and covered with colored silk handkerchiefs, are borne on the heads of their respective priests under gorgeous, huge umbrellas of plush and velvet. The blackened stools of deceased priests and priestesses are carried about, suspended from the necks of certain bearers. The face, neck, shoulders, arms and chest of each priest and priestess in procession are smeared with white clay-powder, while attendants bear plates of this white powder for further sprinkling (much in the manner of flour-throwing at our Hallowe'en).

The second day, the people sit about their houses or outside the big temple of Ta Kese (the Ashanti *earth* god Tano, who in Tekiman is called Ta Kese, or elsewhere Ta Kora). In the afternoon bands of women run up and down the main street singing *apo* songs, with such passages as these:

"The God, Ta Kese, says if we have anything to say, to say it,
For by doing so we take away misfortune from the nation.
O King, you are a fool . . . you are impotent, O King. . . .
We take today the victory from out your hands . . .
Had the Ashanti known about guns,
Would they have let the white man seize King Prempeh and
        Ya Akyaa [the Queen Mother] . . . ?
Oh, Buabasa [the British representative] is a proper fool,
He causes the nation to be destroyed. . . .
Ashanti, what do you here? [the Ashanti conquered Tekiman]
Do you tabu your own country? . . .
We are casting stones at Ati Akosua [a god] . . .
The Ashanti people may be the children of slaves,
The King of Ashanti may have bought them, but not us.

All is well today.
We know that a Brong [7] man eats rats,
But today we have seen our master, Ansah, eating rats [Ansah was Captain Rattray's secretary] . . .
Do you people know the *child* who is head of this town? . . ."

On this second day a crier, beating an iron gong, goes about with a proclamation that the chief welcomes abuse, and that if anyone has cause of quarrel with another, if any man's wife is seduced by his friend, if anyone should be insulted, and does not keep his temper, but lodges a complaint, he is bound by the oath and liable to a penalty. That is, a man is free during the *Apo* ceremony to commit offences and no one must complain, but *after* the ceremony is concluded he may be prosecuted and fined as usual!
. . . The fourth day the priests and priestesses, stripped to the waist and holding swords or cow-tails in their hands, heavily powdered with white clay-dust and most of them adorned profusely with charms (*suman,* fetishes), dance throughout the morning to the accompaniment of drums and singing. The priestesses wear loose cloth skirts of gay design, and the priests kilts of palm-leaf fiber. In the afternoon a sort of durbar is arranged near the chief's "palace." The chief and state officials seat themselves in a great semi-circle under their huge umbrellas, surrounded by sword-bearers, heralds, executioners, and others. The villagers congregate as they will. From the direction of the temple of the god Ta Kese comes a long priestly procession. In it the high priest of Ta Kese is carried aloft in a basket hammock, while the chief priestess of Ati Akosua is borne on the shoulders of one of her attendants. The procession swings past the royal semi-circle from left to right, exchanging greetings and hand-shakes, and sprinkling powder. Then the high priest and priestess and their companions fill out the circle, sitting under great umbrellas opposite the royal party. The priests dispose themselves beside the circle. The sub-chiefs of outlying districts salute the chief. Before him the priests dance, one of whom may imitate a leopard. There may be, also, a humorous performance by an executioner. Among the songs of the day is one that runs, "Is today not a good day! The god who is our king has risen up. He removes misfortune from his people." One may notice that the priestess falls into a trance under her umbrella, with her attendant sprinkling her with powder. In mid-afternoon the durbar ends and the people all disperse.

[7] A Congo tribe.

Toward evening the shrines of all the gods (these shrines had not been displayed this afternoon) are again paraded, each under its umbrella, the chief priest himself bearing on his head Ta Kese's shrine and reeling in an ecstasy. Priests walk behind their chief in readiness to catch the shrine if it should fall. It had been blessed when first it left Ta Kese's temple by a medicine man, who, waving a pot of water three times before it, inverted the pot quickly and placed it on the ground as the shrine went by. Again in the evening the black stools of dead priests and priestesses are slung from the necks of carriers holding big umbrellas.

Dancing, singing and processions fill the days. Take an illustration of how the various participants may prepare. At the edge of the town about a tree are gathered a group of men, women, and boys. Beside the tree stands a small table or chair on which rest a stool and a god-shrine with a pair of sandals on it. Beside the tree are also a couple of drums, a plate with powdered clay, a plate of eggs, and a priest's dress. These objects belong to a [visiting?] priest, and the people are his attendants. Here comes the priest to "work up the spirit of his god upon him" in preparation to take part in the dance and procession in the main street of the town. He dons the dress, powders himself, and decks himself in charms. He smashes an egg on the ground to avert any ill which another priest might will against him or his god. Then he dances to the accompaniment of drums and singing. Sometimes he holds the god-shrine on his head; sometimes he passes it to his attendants. At last the spirit is upon him and he sets off for the town, with his god upon his head, and his followers behind him. He joins the priest of another god and both dance together. Both make their way to the temple of Ta Kese, greeting there the chief priest and entering the temple for a moment. On coming out again they dance. They throw eggs into the air and intercept them on their heads as they fall. Or, each holds aloft a pair of dolls (*juju*), male and female, the "speedy messengers" of the gods. Now each holds a mirror, now a sword, again a spear, as they dance. At intervals they walk round and round shaking hands with everybody. They dance late into the night, perhaps. They are ready for tomorrow's ceremony.

. . . On the sixth day, still more dancing, by priests and priestesses who had not performed before. And then before the following dawn many of the visiting gods are taken back to their villages, where they are sprinkled with the water of their own localities and reëstablished among their own peculiar people. They are taken back for fear that if left until the conclusion of the Tekiman ceremonial, they may have so enjoyed their outing as to be unwilling to return to their proper temples. Are there not empty shrines in every village whose gods one time did not return?

On the seventh day in the evening the gods of Tekiman, in particular, are taken to the river Tano, the lesser gods leading the procession, followed by Ta Kese and Ta Kwesi (prominent in Tekiman), each god on a priest's head under his umbrella. With the gods are priests, priestesses, executioners, a herald, a soul-washer, stool-carriers, and drummers. Some marchers carry guns and cow-tails. The way is lighted by torches of palm-leaf stalks. In the beginning a herald had been sent to the chief to say that the end of the festival was at hand, and to ask permission for the visit to the river. The chief had said, "Go. May no misfortune happen in the new year now approaching. May still another year come round again." He and his chief wife may or may not attend the river-ceremony. At the river each shrine is set down on its own stool or head-pad, and the priests stand by. One of Tano's servants draws water from the river in a basin, meanwhile saying:

"O Sky God [*i.e.*, 'Nyame, the Ashanti Supreme Being], upon whom men lean and do not fall, O Goddess of Earth [*i.e.*, Asase Ya], O thou Being that rules the underworld, O Leopard that owns the forest, O Tano River, by your kindness the edges of the years (*i.e.*, the old and the new) have met, and we have brought here all the shrines of the gods to sprinkle them with water. May you all stand behind us with a good standing. Let no bad thing whatsoever overtake us. We give our children, we give our wives, we give ourselves into your hands. Let no evil come upon us."

White clay and *odwira* leaves are now mixed with the water. Then a spokesman with a branch of the sacred *summe* tree in each hand addresses Ta Kese and the other powers, summoning them to attend and be sprinkled. He thereafter sprinkles each shrine in turn, beginning with Ta Kese's, and saying:

"We beg you for life; when hunters go to the forest, permit them to kill meat; may child-bearers bear children; life to the chief; life to all hunters; life to all priests; we take the *apo* of this year and put it in the river."

Water is sprinkled on the stools and upon all persons present. Guns are fired and everyone shouts, "Farewell! Farewell!" The shrines are scrubbed with sand and water and the outside of each is marked by lines of wet clay, two sets of three lines each, crossing each other at right angles. The silk handkerchiefs are again placed over the shrines and the procession starts for the temples. The chief priest and the spokesman take three long branches of the *summe* tree, and after the last man has left the river bank, place them across the path, with a handful of clay and sand on top. This precaution prevents any evil from following into the town. The shrines are placed in their respective temples, the temple of Ta Kese being the main repository. There they are uncovered, and yams are placed upon them. No songs are sung during this solemn evening rite; only the drums beat occasionally.

The eight day is the first day of the New Year for the people of Tekiman. It is celebrated by a simple service at the temple of Ta Kese. Branches of *summe* are laid in front of Ta Kese's house to mitigate any evil that might come from breaking one of his tabus. The chief priest, the priests, and the elders officiate; no women take part. In the house of Ta Kese the chief takes his stand on a raised platform at the left of the altar, while the chief priest and two men holding a sheep stand beside him. He offers thanks to Ta Kese that no one acted wantonly during the festival, and a prayer on behalf of the people, himself and the government. Then as the sheep is held above the altar, he cuts its throat, allowing some blood to drop on Ta Kese's shrine. Next the bloody sheep is held over the other shrines in turn, the blackened stools, and the shrine of the special messenger and watchman of all the gods. It is then carried out into the temple court and held dripping above the drums. The carcass is cut up in the yard, small bits of meat and entrails are distributed, some on the floor before the altar, some in the shrine-pans, some on the stools, and some to the worshipers. The chief says in a loud voice from his platform, "We invoke blessings"; to which all reply, "Farewell; blessings upon all, farewell; we invoke blessings upon the chief." Later in the day these offerings are removed, some of the bits to be roasted and eaten by the chief and the high priest.

What is the meaning of this *Apo* ceremony? Consider its major elements: soul (*sunsum*); dolls, charms, or "fetishes" (*suman*); shrines and temples (*abosom* and *kuduo*); clay powder, gongs, stools, holy water, sacred plants and trees, and the dance; tabu and purification; priests (*akomfo*), priestesses (*akomfo mma*), messengers, gods (*abosom,* meaning shrines, also), Ta Kese (chief earth god), and 'Nyame (Sky God, the Supreme). This is a fairly complete list of the ingredients of primitive religion. We need only two other major elements, and these, also, may be found in other ceremonies in Ashanti: spirits (*samanfo,* especially ancestral spirits), and "totemism" [8] (probably the Ashanti *ntoro*). Such elements as "potency" [9] and magic inhere in the *suman* and the dance, respectively. The terminology of religion in Ashanti may be taken, therefore, as providing close equivalents to the terms used among all primitives.

The Elements of Primitive Religion.—1. The originally basic element in primitive religion was the sense or notion of a potency which fills and moves all things. This is still the most fundamental aspect of the primitive religious consciousness. This potency is a weird, mysterious, supernatural something in the presence of which the primitive stands in awe and fear,—possibly more fear than awe. It has been given many names. It is *njomm* to the African Ekoi, *n'gai* to the African Masai, *pi* to the Indo-Chinese Moi, *maxpé, manitu, wakan,* and *orenda* to various Amerinds (American Indians). Let us call it *mana,* as the Polynesians do, amongst whom this potency as such was first discovered by modern investigators.

Mana is everywhere, intangible and all-pervasive as the ether. All things have it; rather, each separate thing is *manaized,* for *mana* is not a spiritual *entity* in a physical body; it is a dynamism which permeates, tones and colors the whole object. It is, for example, *of* the arrow, *of* the poison on the arrow-head; and that which kills is *not* the poison or the arrow. but *mana. Mana,* however, is not a universal something, a portion of which imbues each object,—for the primitive has not risen high enough to generalize a prime and universal reality. He acts in response to immediate, concrete things and situations—to objects *mana-saturated,* whether stream, stone, mountain, cloud, plant, or animal. Furthermore, *mana* itself has no moral quality; rather, it may be good or bad, favorable or dangerous, according to the time or place; it may do good or evil, according to the agent's will. It may be seen in operation when a man, attempting the strange and "impossible," succeeds; when a chieftain falls in battle. or is taken by an enemy. When a warrier falls, either he has lost his *mana,* or his *mana* was less potent than that of his antagonist.

---

[8] Totemism means, roughly, the religion of the group which is *in itself* divine, and is symbolized by a "totem" plant or animal.
[9] Known generally as *mana,* or *orenda.* See below.

While *mana* is ascribed to all objects, those persons are peculiarly imbued with it, who behave in a strange and striking manner. Some persons, furthermore, have it more effectively than others. Or, they know better than others how to recognize, control, and use it for a special end. These are the shamans (the *akomfo* in Ashanti), medicine men, and witches (fox-women, or what not).[10] They have a "higher" knowledge and a greater skill, which may have come by chance, or through a course of training. While the common man may exercise at times his own "control," he leans upon these special agents in emergencies, whereby to find favor or escape an injury. *If* the common man acts for himself, he does so doubtless by the aid of "power" which a special agent has supplied him. He has a private fetish, or a charm, perhaps.[11]

Charms and their use illustrate an early application of *mana* to the actual life of man. They may be *talismans* by which some wonderful and (*telos* in Greek) or *good* luck may be brought about. They may be *amulets* by which men are protected from *ill*-luck, accident, or witchcraft. Charms are in most cases objects easily handled or carried on the person. They may be natural objects, such as shells or twisted roots, which have gained men's notice by some peculiar property or shape, or by some unwonted show of "power." They may be objects manufactured or "doctored" by a special process or agent. The owner may himself have found them, or he may have got them at some cost from a shaman. The faith reposed in them is absolute. If they fail to work, or if they work feebly, they may be cajoled, or cuffed, or thrown away as hostile to their owner. They are objects of hope; their proper power is that of blessing; they should not disappoint their owners.

While charms have been used throughout the primitive world, they have enjoyed peculiar prominence in Negro Africa, possibly greatest prominence in West Africa where "fetishism" is conspicuous. Fetishism is not religion; it is only a phase of religion, although the "fetish" has come to be regarded by the native as in itself potent, conscious, and willing. He distinguishes between the *suman* and the god, or shrine (*abosom*). The *suman* is usually

---

10 *Cf.* p. 40, below.
11 If from charm one draws the inference of magic, let him understand that *mana* is itself essentially *religious*. The charm, of course, may be used as magic. The "fetish" (*suman* in Ashanti) gets its name from the Portuguese *fetiço*, a "medallion, image, or other sacred object" having magical virtue. Portuguese sailors applied the term to all sorts of objects with reputed efficacy, which they found along the West African coast. Unfortunately they found through a loose parallelism with their own experience *too many fetiços* in Africa. Consequently, West African religion has been too widely known as "fetishism."

the owner's private object. The *abosom* is god of the many, the
family, the clan, or the nation. It is of higher origin and power,
coming, in fact, from the Supreme God. *Mana* is the power of the
suman, which comes from plants, animals, fairies, or witches.
A *suman* is inferior to an *abosom,* and may be considered by
the priest of an *abosom* a hindrance to "true" religion.[12] Among
primitives generally, however, charms and the gods are intimately
associated. In fact, the religion of the common man, whether in
Ashanti, or on the lower levels elsewhere, is scarcely more than
magic and dependence upon charms [13] whatever be the "higher"
views and practice of the priests.[14]

2. Not only has the primitive the sense of "potency" (*mana*) ;
he is an "animist." This means that *some* primitives are above
the stage of *mana.* They attribute to all objects life in the form of
a living soul, or *anima,* and believe this soul to be distinct and
separable from its object. They believe in souls, whether natural
or human, and worship them. Animism [15] gives us an innumerable
multitude of beings. With reference to natural phenomena they
are *spirits;* with reference to animals and humans, they are *souls.*
If the primitive distinguishes between soul and spirit he applies
the former term to the living and the latter to what we should call
the dead, or the inanimate. When a man "dies," his soul becomes
his spirit. This distinction need not be emphasized, however, while
we are intent upon understanding the primitive notion that *man
is alive in a world alive,* and that there is a continued existence
after death. Worship is accorded souls and spirits because they
have religious value. They have religious value because of their
close connection with the fearful and mysterious.

Souls and spirits, then, are higher forms, a development beyond
the fundamental primitive-consciousness which feels the potency
that fills and moves all things. Out of man's reaction to this
primal sense come what we know as "nature-worship," on the one
hand, and the "worship of ancestral spirits," on the other, as
man's mind frames these higher and more definite concepts of
soul and spirit. In any one community there may exist a mixture
of ideas. In one man's view, a charm may be itself alive, saturated
with potency, while in another's view it may possess a soul. In

12 Rattray, *Religion and Art in Ashanti,* pp. 9–24.
13 With reference to certain ethical and political aspects of charms, see Hopkins,
op. cit., pp. 38, 39.
14 For his view of "magic and religion," see J. G. Frazer, *The Magic Art,* Vol. I,
pp. 220–243. See also pp. 39–40, below.
15 The anthropologist, E. B. Tylor, introduced the term "Animism" as descriptive
of primitive religion and as accounting for the origin of religion. See his *Primitive
Culture.*

still another view, the charm may simply be a symbol that represents an object which is potent. There may be objects worshiped by one man as if they were sentient and able to act on man's behalf —charms, for instance, of the *mana* type. There may be objects which a man addresses as if there were spirits in or near them, such as a star or a tree.[16] There may be disembodied spirits, the souls of departed kindred, or of dead priests and chieftains. Indeed, any one man may have within himself this confusion of ideas. Seldom, in fact, is any worshiper free from such confusion. It need not surprise us, then, if we find among the primitives no clear-cut conception of the *anima*, although we find among them "animistic" consciousness and practices.

No primitives have done any systematic thinking on the nature of the souls and spirits which they worship.[17] If they use many terms for *soul*, this is evidence of confusion of thought rather than proof of thoughtful differentiation, or proof of the existence of multiple souls. Their distinction between the soul of the living and the spirit of the dead is not speculative, nor is their query whether the soul is life, or blood, or breath, or wind. It is natural for even primitives to have various terms to express various characteristics and operations of one vitality. It is natural, also, to personify these vital forces.

To the primitive the human soul is separable from the body. It may leave the body when one dreams or swoons, but it returns. It leaves permanently at death. It may be taken from the body by a shaman and put away somewhere for safety in a time of danger. It may direct itself. When a child is born its soul may actually take up residence in a plant or tree which must thereafter be carefully tended for the very life of the child. A soul may reside in any one of several parts of the human body, in the liver, or the heart, or the skull—or in all at one time, for variety of function. Some Africans contend that the child receives one soul from its mother and another from its father, but not two separate souls. In a similar vein, some Amerinds declare there is a soul which at death goes to the spirit-world, and one which lingers about the body, or the grave. One man may get another's soul. If he eat the flesh of an enemy, his heart, his liver, or his brain, he may acquire his courage, patience, or wisdom. These and other hasty theories tend to show that to the primitive what we call

[16] Tree-worship is widespread with many varied rites. See J. G. Frazer, *The Magic Art,* Vol. II, pp. 7–96.
[17] W. C. Willoughby, *The Soul of the Bantu,* p. 9; E. W. Smith, *Ila-speaking Peoples,* pp. ii and 100ff.

personality is highly complex and that his personality is intimately identified with the world about him. Thus the many forms and many names of one vital principle. Thus the soul as that vital principle operating in and through the human body. Thus man's shadow as his soul's extension.[18] So, also, the view that a man's name is himself, and if another has, or knows his name, he controls his soul thereby. A man may not pronounce his name before a stranger or an enemy, for this might be to give his soul away. Then he would die.

When, therefore, we read or hear it said that certain primitives hold, or have held, a theory of many souls, internal souls, external souls, shadow souls and ghost souls, we may take this multiplicity as nothing more than fiction. The primitive imagination has invented them. Or in his naïve thinking in the concrete, the primitive has thus accounted for the one soul, a counterpart of his own body, a miniature of himself, yet known in its varied operations.

To what extent the primitive worships *nature* spirits distinct from the souls of living men and things and the spirits of dead men, is difficult to say. Negro African religion has much to do with the veneration of the spirits of the dead (*cf.* the Ashanti *samanfo*). It shows little regard for nature spirits as such, although some attention without doubt is paid to certain spirits, not ancestral, which live in trees, rivers, rocks, and mountains. The North American Indians, on the other hand, had high regard for nature-spirits, for the spirits of trees—the cottonwood especially. They seem to have had no place for an ancestral-cult. The Tami Islanders of Melanesia "clearly distinguish the spirits of the departed from supernatural beings of other categories." [19] But most Melanesian supernatural beings seem derived from the souls of the deceased. Among many primitives, spirits which at first might be considered nature-spirits, certain tree-spirits, in particular, prove on closer view to be the spirits of the dead, which have taken up their residence in trees. It is a primitive trait to personify the objects of his world, to create a spirit-world in duplicate, and to people it with the spirits of his family, clan, and nation.

3. To what extent do primitives have gods? If gods, what kind? Obviously a god is something higher than mere potency, powers, and spirits. Are there, then, stages of development in religion? Doubtless there *is* progress in man's thoughts of the divine. His experience widens and new needs appear, and his

---

[18] *Cf.* the theory of some primitive-minded people that another's shadow, if it touch them, will pollute or harm them.
[19] Lowie, *op. cit.*, p. 61.

regard increases for natural and supernatural forces. We find gods
in primitive religion, although when the gods arrive the half-gods,
powers and spirits do not altogether disappear. There is increased
confusion. The gods are comprehended and served by the more
rationally sensitive members of the group, while the common man
continues his devotion to the spirits. We discovered in Ashanti
the *abosom,* with their slightly higher powers, priests, tabus, sacred
days, and shrines. We even found a "High God," 'Nyame, of whom
a myth recounts that all the gods were made by him. There were, it
says, four sons of 'Nyame (created "out of nothing"?), whom he
sent down to earth (whence came the earth? presumably from 'Nyame) for the good of men ('Nyame's creatures?) and for the good
they might receive from men. Rivers and lakes now bear the names
of these four sons. That is, the waters of Ashanti are looked upon
as containing the spirit of the divine Creator, 'Nyame. Tano
(Tekiman Ta Kese), the chief Ashanti earth-god, resides near
the source of the Tano River. His temple there, we may suppose,
is fairly free of *suman* (charms), such as usually adorn Ashanti
temple walls. He is represented not by an image (idolatry is more
than primitive) but by a shrine, a brass pan containing objects
and "medicine" of various kinds: clay from the sacred river;
roots of medicinal plants; bark, tendrils, and leaves of sacred
trees; a white bead and a nugget of virgin gold. All were assembled
by one on whom god Tano's spirit came, and consecrated by a
formal ceremony of incantation, prayer, and sacrifice. There are
gods like Tano throughout the primitive world. They constitute
a natural polytheism, often quite distinct from anything ancestral
(that is, they are gods whose origin is *natural*). They may be
supernatural. They are superhuman. They are, however, humanized, personified, and are therefore moral. They are not vague
like the "powers" (or *mana*), nor capricious like the spirits. They
are dependable, if man can only know their will. There are gods
of plenty, war-gods, gods of death, and so on. There is usually a
locality, perhaps remote, where they make their "home."

The presence of a High God raises questions of origin and
significance. Whence the conception? What the character and
function of such a deity? What relation can he sustain to spirits,
other gods, and men? That there are supreme deities among certain primitives cannot be doubted. Nor can one doubt that they
are worshiped. There are, in addition to 'Nyame, Nzambi of the
Lower Congo; the Bakwena "Supreme Spirit"; the Zulu "Lord of
Heaven," who alone can send rain; Tilo, or Heaven, of the

Thongas; the Algonkin Indian "Great Spirit" (*Kichi Manitu*), the Andaman *Puluga,* and many more. Some students [20] claim that they are merely authors, originators, or "culture-heroes," by whom creation is explained, who made men and things from pre-existent elements. If this is so, these gods have no religious significance. Other students [21] claim to find true High Gods, even, in fact, the One God, who is altogether good, the author of good, and who created *ex nihilo*. This God, whatever be his local name, is worshiped, but not frequently.

It is not necessary to assume that the conception of a Supreme is due to missionary influence, whether Christian, Moslem, or Jewish. There is no valid objection to the assumption that the idea is innate, as that of Yahweh of the Kenites.[22] Probably we should look toward the sky and the sun for an explanation. Among certain nomads the sky itself early became the greatest god, for it alone continued with them on their journeys, while local gods were left behind. To peoples in the agricultural stage both the sky and the sun have extreme importance. Both are powers which prosper or undo them. Consider 'Nyame once again. In spite of spirits and the lesser gods, he is widely worshiped. Almost every village contains an altar to him in the shape of a forked tree-branch ("God's tree") holding a basin with a neolithic celt ("God's axe"), and prayers and sacrifices are made to him. The *abosom* are his intermediaries. Ordinarily, 'Nyame is considered too remote to be concerned directly with the affairs of men. He is active for men's sake through his delegated agents. Man is devoted to these lesser powers, for they are near. In his simple-minded attempt to realize the presence of deity through worship it is easier and more availing to call on what is near.

To recapitulate, primitive man believes in the existence of various powers and beings upon whose favor his welfare is dependent; he believes these powers and beings to be actuated by motives like his own, or higher. Having personified them, he can comprehend them. He believes it to be possible for him to work upon them to keep them from doing harm and to make them do good. In so far as he *acts* upon these beliefs he is religious and a seeker of religious knowledge and experience (mere belief itself does not constitute religion). How he deals with these beings is

---

[20] *E.g.,* Archbishop Söderblom, of Upsala. See also C. Clemen *Religions of the World,* p. 28.
[21] *E.g.,* Andrew Lang, and more recently, Professor W. Schmidt, of Vienna. See the latter's *High Gods in North America.* Oxford, 1933. See also A. Le Roy, *The Religion of the Primitives,* pp. 128–131.
[22] *Book of Exodus,* 6:3.

determined partly by what he thinks of them, but more by what he desires them to do, what he wants to get from them. Experience sooner or later indicates what means to use to accomplish his desires. In time, common experience combines into an accepted body of ritual upon whose exact performance the welfare of the group depends.

4. Ritual is a consequential factor, as the *Apo* ceremony has already indicated. We have now to examine more closely the elements, the character, and the ministers of it. It is not always religious; there are certain ceremonial customs in connection with birth, marriage, death, and other episodes, which may or may not be religious, although they frequently include some religious element. But ritual at certain times is definitely religious, as in recurring seasons when men are most aware of their physical needs and of their dependence upon climatic influences, or on special occasions arising from danger or disaster.

Ritual at first must have been spontaneous and instinctive, the outgrowth of isolated responses to such influences as accidents, diseases, perils, times of hope, hunger and awe. Men tried to find out what to do about it. They did something about it, if possible, and when a like situation arose again, they repeated any act that might before have been effective. A man in flight from danger might have stumbled on an odd-shaped stone, have picked it up and fled to safety. Thereafter, his plea in time of danger was to the stone, his benefactor. The simplest forms, both individual and social, are found among unsettled peoples, while more elaborate forms, mostly social, are found among agricultural folk. In fertile areas where life is settled and complex, ritual also is complex. Most primitives are agricultural; there are few who still linger in the hunting and fishing stage. In agricultural ritual, more than in nomadic, there is representation, personification, and anthropomorphism, with emphasis upon the seasons. Nature is a prime concern, and the gods are in process of being humanized and civilized.

The primitive's objective in the use of ritual is to realize the presence of his god, or gods, and to work on the divine for certain human ends. On its lower level, ritual may be merely a method of control, or of coercion—this is magic. On its higher side, it may be or provide a mystical union and comprehension of the divine.

One of the commonest ritual exercises is the dance. It exhibits the primitive man in a many-sided rôle. In some instances the dance is nothing more than man's expression of animal joyousness, like the caperings of quadrupeds, except that it exhibits the human feeling of rhythm, with the movements measured as well as graceful. The rhythm is that of the man of action, the endless repetition of acts, sounds, and words of the same general level,[23] rather than the rhythm of the thinker who in recital and dramatization craves for logical coördination and integration of events. Often the dance has such serious purposes as providing animal and plant food, guaranteeing victories in war, initiating youths into full membership in the tribe, expelling demons and cleansing from evil, and invigorating the tribe. The dance itself is considered as having peculiar, sacred power. Men put forth to sea, and their womenfolk sing and dance upon the beach to bring them safely back again. Men die and the dance is performed to bring them back to life, or at least to secure their aid in further ventures. If during the dance a spirit or a god is called upon, the exercise is definitely religious and counts as worship, although its predominant value even then is magical.

The Hopi Snake Dance, the most famous of all American Indian dances and one of the most famous religious ceremonies of primitive peoples, was the climax of a rain-making ceremony. The snakes used during the nine-day performance were the embodiment of the spirits of their ancestors, from whom came the knowledge of making rain. This dance was the essential element of Hopi religion. The Sun Dance of the Crow Indians was a prayer for vengeance. A particular brave is thirsting for revenge. He visits a medicine man, the possessor of a sacred doll whose power is expected to grant his prayer. He and the medicine man arrange a drama that takes on the color of a war-expedition, and involves the entire tribe for several months, perhaps. Young braves fast and torture themselves during the ceremony, while old braves proclaim their prowess and recite their deeds. It becomes a tribal event, even though for particular members there are personal, intimate motives. Among the Cheyenne Indians the Sun Dance was more an individual affair, the fulfilment of a vow. Having escaped some frightful danger, the warrior gives a dance before his tribe. It not only pays his vow, but it energizes his people, for all the tribe takes part, at least, as sympathetic witnesses.

Whatever the details and the locality, the story of the dance is essentially uniform. All primitives are fond of music, singing,

[23] P. Radin, *Primitive Man as Philosopher*, pp. 234 ff.

and drama. They have their needs, and they implore their spirits and gods to fill them. The dance is magical movement and the symbol of movement. It takes the place of thought; it is emotional rather than reflective. As the primitive gives his body to exciting dances, he calls upon his gods for what he wants; he moves in order to move them. Here is movement set to music and singing to affect the living and the dead, to make the family, the fold and the field productive, and to win a multitude of individual and social goods.

5. Belief in *magic*—is this the basis of primitive religion? Is it magic which holds the religion of primitive peoples to such low levels? Magic is something coercive rather than persuasive; religion is persuasive. The magical act is something effective in itself; persuasion recognizes something else as the real seat of power. Magic and religion may have the same motive of self-preservation, and both may seek to influence to that end the powers on which men lean, but religion is very different from magic in the quality, at least, of its ideas and practices. Religion recognizes powers superior to man, before whom man must bow in awe and godly fear. Magic would compel the powers to do man's will. The charm is magical, the dance is magical. At times magic, acknowledging its failure, has called upon religion for aid; at times religion has stooped to take aid from magic, thus insuring failure. Magic and religion often have been intimate, but we must distinguish between the two. Magic may be religious and religion may be magical, but the more magical religion is, the less it is religion.

The religion of all primitives is full of magic, of which there are two kinds, black and white. Black magic has to do with demons; white magic, with friendly powers. Black magic is much the lower type and stands distinctly apart. White magic may rely upon good gods for help and come very near religion. It is black magic which has been prevalent among primitives. It works by two principles, that like produces like, and that two objects once in contact are always in contact. Take the case of like producing like. The medicine man draws the figure of a person in sand, ashes, or clay, or shapes an image in clay, straw, or wood. He considers that thus he has the person in his power, to do him good or ill, as he may wish. By pricking a certain spot, for example, in the image or figure he affects the corresponding part of the person. To kill an enemy he might run a needle into the head or heart of the enemy's likeness. To cure a friend of illness, he might prick the friend's image and let the demon out. We are familiar with the process of "burning in effigy," by which an enemy may be injured or destroyed. Or, take the case of contact magic. The Malay charm illustrates this. The charm, a contact-magic charm, is made of nail parings, eyebrows, hair, spittle, and other parts of an intended victim. These parts once of his body are still of his body, and so may be used for magical effects. Simpler still is the magic of stabbing a man's foot-print for the sake of laming him, like the huntsman who drives a nail into the fresh hoofprint of the fleeing deer, believing that this will halt the animal.

The prevalence of magic in primitive religion is nowhere better seen than in the place and power of the magician. By whatever name he is known—doctor, sorcerer, shaman, witch, exorcist, medicine man, or priest—the magician is the greatest figure among primitives. He is greater than the chief, unless the chief be also a magician. He is the custodian of all the lore of magic, the authority on all the usages. He has "knowledge" of mysteries and "control" of hidden forces. Special circumstances may have made him conspicuous in relation to the natural and spiritual order, giving him extraordinary power. Or he may have come by heredity or special training into his position. By whatever means he obtained it, power is undoubtedly his; and men have fearful faith in him. The magician—or, let us say the priest—is the mediator between men and the unseen. He gives "thought" to the causes of events, hits upon effective "methods" of procedure to gain desired results, and makes himself indispensible to all men in their time of need. He thrives on men's misfortunes, and feeds upon men's hopes, whether he be mere charlatan or in some measure sincere. He is the interpreter of belief and the chief custodian and administrator of religious ritual.

6. In worship the two constant elements are offering and prayer, or better, offerings and prayers. These elements are more prominent among the higher primitives who recognize ancestral spirits and nature powers as gods. Worship is eminently practical. Men desire escape from evil, and of the realization of good. The most primitive offerings were probably things to eat; man liked food and knew his dependence upon it, and so gave it to his gods.[24] He still gives offerings of food, but with mixed motives. Some primitives give gifts to win the favor of their gods, or to appease them; some seem merely intent upon sheer homage and devotion, or in

[24] *Cf.* Rattray, *Ashanti,* p. 191.

demonstration of self-denial. Some seem to think the gods, because they are men's saviors, must be fed to be kept alive, or to be kept strong against old age. Sometimes the offering is of blood in expiation, to cleanse the people of their sins. When the flesh of the slaughtered animal is consumed in part by priest and people, it strengthens the whole tribe; and when portions of the offering are burnt, the odor rising on high is pleasing to the nostrils of the gods. Sacrifice is not a simple, but a complex rite, even among primitive peoples. It may have some lofty intent; it may be little more than magical. Its efficacy depends on the exactness of the performance, whether it be magical or religious, but especially if it be religious. Priests, whose office grows in importance with the development of the sacrificial rite, preserve the tradition and see that sacrifice is done exactly. From this it is only a step to become ministers of the will and purpose of the gods.

Offerings are accompanied by prayers; man voices his intent before the gods, telling his simple needs. Now prayer, and possibly sacrifice, is, strictly speaking, on a higher than magical level, for prayer is a recognition of superhuman powers which must be petitioned, not coerced. Primitive prayers are, however, scarcely more than declarations, praise, and petitions. They are for the most part extempore, but since the occasions of prayer are more or less constant, the prayers often assume apparently fixed forms. Requests of various sorts are made: for escape from a present or a dreaded evil, opportunity and power to obtain revenge, a chance to get another's goods without detection, a chance to kill an enemy, fertility and increase of flocks, skill in hunting, and— in the case of a recorded Navaho Indian's prayer [25]—to be made clean and whole, swift and courageous. But they are mainly requests for material blessings. Man's usual attitude in prayer is one of due humility; if he takes to drama as an offering and for the sake of acting out unspeakable religious thoughts which clamor for expression, postures showing humility are most common. But drama that is purely magical acts out spells, not prayers. Words men utter then are threats, not humble petitions, although frequently even in religious ritual, words are used as charms, as in "calling on the name" of the god.

7. Primitives are not only "animists," polydemonists, and polytheists; some of them are "totemists," as well. "Totemism" in itself is not uniform. There is no totemism in the Andaman islands,

[25] G. H. Turnbull, *Tongues of Fire*, pp. 100-101.

for example; African totemism is a modified sort (the Bantu do not sacrifice their totems) ; and the Amerind's totem is scarcely more than a guardian spirit. By "totemism" strictly speaking, we mean a theory of human descent from a natural object—a plant or an animal, usually—and of kinship established through such common descent. The word *totem* comes from the Ojibwa Indians, but the classical example of totemism among living primitives is that of the Australian Blacks. Among them each clan bears a plant or animal name—at times, even the name of an inanimate thing— and professes descent from the ancestor whose name is borne. Intermarriage of men and women of the same totemic group is prohibited. The living totem representing the original ancestor is sacred and tabu to its own group except at times of religious cere- monial. What pertains to the totem and to the group is sacred and tabu. It is not the totem as such, but the totem as symbol which is sacred and tabu, and since the totem is the symbol of the group, the group symbolized is sacred. Their religion, there- fore, is a matter of group experience, and since the group is a comprehensive religious unit, it is virtually its own god, and its totem is the symbol of the group inherently divine.[26] Too much, however, has been made of totem and totemism, but we must reckon with such phases of religion as "totemism" may properly represent. No kind of totemism is general, and what there is is far from being strictly primitive. Aside from totemism, there are sufficient explanations of the wide prevalence of animal and plant names, with the worship of animals and plants. The outstanding fact is that many primitives claim kinship in small groups through plant or animal ancestors, and that many groups merely sym- bolize themselves through a "totem" for social and political solidarity. The real religion may still be "animism," possibly ancestor-worship.[27] To the American Indian the totem may be an individual rather than a group sign, the guardian spirit re- vealed to the young brave as he keeps his lonely vigil in quest of a vision. This spirit may remain the brave's own private secret for life (such it is in the Crow vision-quest), or it may become the spirit of the clan or sib.[28]

[26] Lowie. *op. cit.,* Chap. VI: Rattray, *Ashanti,* Chap. II; *Religion and Art,* p. 318.
[27] See Willoughby, *op. cit.,* p. 339.
[28] The totem pole is, in Australia, a tree carved with simple geometric lines, in New Zealand and among the Amerinds, very large, elaborately carved and colored tree-trunks. The pole bears carvings of the totem of the owner and episodes from tribal mythology. The totem pole should be distinguished from the burial post of Borneo, or the poles erected after a head hunt (see *Customs of the World,* pp. 234, 206), or Burmese spirit-posts (*ibid.,* p. 289), or the memorial images and sacred drums of the Solomon Islands (*ibid.,* p. 99), and the masks of various peoples.

8. Primitive religion designates and insists upon the enforcement of many tabus. The Polynesian says *tapu*, the Hawaiian, *kapu;* we say "taboo." Equivalents of the word are found among all primitives, for the notion is common, thus, *yila*, "everything prohibited," among the South African Thongas; *akyiwadie*, "something you turn your back upon," in Ashanti. The theory is that any object, any act, or any person that implies a danger to any individual or to the community is under a kind of ban. The ban may be artificially imposed, as in the case of protection for crops or private property,[29] or it may inhere in corpses, human blood, sacrificial offerings, strangers, murderers, magicians, priests, and kings. There is no universal system of tabu but the theory is universal. Primitive religion everywhere is tabu-ridden. Some of the commonest tabus have to do with eating and drinking, for these acts are dangerous, since at these times a man's soul may escape from his mouth, or be extracted by his enemy. Certain savages eat behind closed doors. Other savages will not let even their own womenfolk see them drink. Some kings will allow neither man nor beast to see them at their meals. No man may drink from the king's cup, lest power go out of the king and his life be endangered. Specifically religious, many spirits and gods have their own tabus. The names of gods, at times, are known only to themselves, or, if known to their followers, may not be spoken by them. Temples, shrines, holy days, and objects associated with spirits and gods are tabu, except at certain times and to special persons.

Tabu is negative magic. Whereas positive magic says, "Do this, and such a result will follow," tabu, or negative magic says, "Do not do this, for fear that such an issue will result." Fundamentally persons and things are tabu because considered mysterious, and hence sources of potential injury. The notion tends to differentiate between what is impure and therefore to be shunned, and what is holy and therefore to be avoided, but the primitive never quite makes the distinction clear between what is "devilish" and what is "godly." Penalty for the breach of a tabu ranges from the automatic discharge of magico-spiritual potency which visits its own punishment upon the offender, to the wrath of offended spirits and gods visited directly or administered through priests.[30] Tabu serves certain useful, protective purposes, but obviously (to us) tabus are characteristic of victims of imagination. Since tabus

---

29 Cf. *Customs of the World*, p. 209.
30 *Customs of the World*, p. 214, shows trussed up to die naturally a sacred crocodile which has killed a man.

are chiefly negative, the evils avoided are imaginary, and the goods acquired by restraint are also imaginary.

9. In some quarters, primitive religion is predominantly, if not exclusively, regard for and the worship of ancestral spirits.[31] This is not so among the North American Indians, but it is remarkably true of the African blacks who constitute the bulk of living primitives. We have referred to the *samanfo,* or ancestral spirits, recognized in the *Afahye, Baya,* and *Adae* ceremonies of Ashanti. Whereas in Ashanti there are deities other than ancestral spirits, among the Bantu (some fifty millions), says Willoughby, ancestor-worship is "always normative to thought," [32] and "the aspect of religion which has gripped their interest most firmly is that ancestral spirits are active in the affairs of men." [33] The Bantu pay little attention to other powers than the spirits of the dead. The great Unkulunkúlu of the Bantu Zulus was originally an ancestor who became God. But 'Nyame was first God, then the creator and ancestor of all. The mausoleum of the royal spirits of Ashanti at Bantama, distinct from the temple of 'Nyame, became the center and prototype of the cult which throughout Ashanti venerates the spirits of ancestors.

The primitive is like men of all ages in that he has intuitive convictions that (1) there is an existence after death, not differing radically from the scenes and experience of this bodily life, (2) the dead, still near, are interested in the lives of the living, especially their own descendants and relatives, and (3) the welfare of the dead depends upon the behavior of the living. There is no absolute difference between the highest and the lowest of men, and even the primitive refuses to draw a clear line between life and death, or between the divine and that which is not divine. The primitive mind tends to fashion and hold ideas of permanence, continuity, and unity, be they never so rudimentary, and he acts in various ways upon these notions. Customs vary, but more in content than in motive and interpretation. Where fear is unrelieved, the dead are "worshiped" to prevent them from molesting the living. The dead body may be loaded with stones, or a pyramid built over it, or it may merely be bound with cords, or thrust through with a stake to fasten it to the ground. Some Congo races strew thorns about the grave to prick the feet of the dead should they try to return to the midst of the living. The Nicobar islanders close the eyes of the dead to keep them from seeing the way back. Such

[31] Willoughby, *op. cit.,* pp. 90–379.
[32] *Op. cit.,* p. 1.
[33] *Op. cit.,* p. 76.

customs indicate not only that the dead retain the powers they had in life, but that they are hostile toward the living. It follows that means must be employed to placate them; whereas, if those who died were friendly, means must be used to keep them so. It is also thought that by dying they gained other powers, such as ability to move with lightning-like rapidity, and to enter other bodies, whether of men, animals, or inanimate objects. Somewhat contrariwise, but with little meaning to allay men's fears, it is thought that the soul by dying becomes a pale and unsubstantial ghost, at least until it "finds itself" in the spirit-world and has been nourished by the offerings of the living. Not only, then, are the dead as powerful as though they were alive, but they now know what the living do and say and experience,—although the living do not assume that the dead are omnipotent. In particular, the religious obligation is between the living and their own deceased relatives, especially their fathers and the paternal ancestral lines,[34] although there is recognition of the ancestral spirits of the tribes.

Ancestor-worship assumes two forms: private and public. For private boons, for protection against dreaded ills, and for deliverance from personal foes and misfortunes, the primitive relies upon the spirits of his own family. Offerings are made to the family gods during the routine of the day: a little food to the spirits before commencing a meal; a few drops of water before the drinker quenches his own thirst; greetings to the spirits at the dawn of a new day and when night closes in. There are unusual ceremonies for unusual occasions, such as child-birth, marriage, illness in the family, or among the cattle. Certain spots about the hut may be sacred to the spirits, such as the central pole or the uprights of the doorway, and a family may have its own priest to perform, with ancestral images and symbols, the major sacred rites.[35]

The worship of the tribal spirits differs from private worship,[36] but one should never draw too distinct a line between family gods and tribal gods. The tribal gods are usually the gods of some outstanding family, or the gods of many great and powerful families which have flourished during the centuries. There may be, as in Ashanti, a headquarters of the spirits of the ruling house. Tribal

[34] Since worship of the common Father is often the bond which binds the clan in one, ancestor-worship is found in patriarchal rather than in matriarchal societies.

[35] Cf. Clemen, op. cit., pp. 27, 28, showing ancestral figures from the Philippines and from Easter Island.

[36] See Willoughby, op. cit., pp. 179–202, for Bantu family worship, and pp. 202–265, for the tribal cult of ancestors.

gods are the objects of worship on all great tribal occasions, such as the time of sowing, harvest-time, the offering of the first-fruits, and times of war. When there is need of rain, they alone are implored, unless, as in some instances, there is one great Lord who controls the rain (*cf.* p. 35, above). Among agriculturists water is always needed, and water is commonly supplied by the ancestral spirits or through their intercession, as in the case of the Hopi Snake Dance. Says Rattray of the cult of ancestral spirits in Ashanti, "it is intimately bound up with the predominating desire for the fertility of man and the fertility of nature. 'Give us children; give us good hunting; give us a good harvest'; such is the basis of every prayer, whether to the gods or to the ghosts." [37] Gods and ghosts are the two basic elements in ancestor-worship. The conception of spirit was first gained through death, presumably the death of one's own kinsfolk. This conception being applied by some peoples to other objects than man, there came to be for the living nature spirits as well as spirits of the dead. As worship developed there came to be nature-worship [38] and ancestor-worship. The two are related, but not identical, save in the case of an ancestral spirit taking up its abode in a natural object, even in the sky. All gods were not first human spirits. All ancestor-worship is religion, but religion is not entirely ancestor-worship. How one may merge into another may be seen by a close examination of the Taro cult of Papua. What began as the worship of the taro spirits (the spirits of the corn, or *ba,* the staple food of the Orokaiva) became by a significant change the placation of the spirits of ancestors or departed relatives, believed to control the growth of the taro. This is at once a fertility cult and a cult of the dead.[39]

10. A *summary* of "primitive" religion:

A. Some aspects may be said to be *common to the whole field,* either inherently and potentially, or explicit in stated beliefs and concrete rites:

(1) The sense of Power and Mystery in an active, willing environment.

(2) This sense is not the conception of something universal or of abstract reality, but the notion that there is potency in every object to which man's attention is given.

(3) More specifically, belief in spirits ("animism")—a belief

---

[37] *Religion and Art,* p. 120.
[38] That is, where the nature power was at first an ancestral spirit.
[39] F. E. Williams, *op. cit.,* pp. 7–9ff.

which has religious value not in itself, but through the association of spirits with the Mysterious.

(4) Myth, in satisfaction of man's easily satisfied queries as to how he and things came to be as they are.

(5) Belief in magic, and the employment of magical processes for the satisfaction of human needs, especially through magicians.

(6) Tabu, what is hateful, feared, or to be avoided, any breach of which calls for an act of purification.

(7) Belief in gods conceived mainly in man's own image and character.

(8) Reaction, chiefly emotional and ritualistic, to the world of Power and Mystery, in general, and to spirits and gods in particular; offerings and prayers.

B. Some phases are *less than common* throughout the whole field:

(1) "Fetishism" and idolatry, the "fetish," strictly speaking, being West African, and the idol, or graven image, being of very limited use in worship.

(2) "Totemism," very limited in the sense of human descent from a totem, and not universal in the sense of group consciousness through the totem as a religious symbol.

(3) Ancestor-worship, with the concurrent notion that souls are transmissible, and that the spirits of men and animals may interchange.

CHAPTER III

AN INTRODUCTION TO RELIGION IN CHINA

In China, in contrast with the wholly "primitive" fields, we find both civilization and a homogeneous social order.[1] Nevertheless, Chinese religion of today contains particulars not far from primitive. In fact, the eminently practical Chinese have laid stress on the earthly life, and it may be truly said that they have consistently possessed "the feeblest religious sense to be found in any great nation."[2] They have, indeed, their "three religions" and others, also, but have registered toward them recently a mood of open opposition, in addition to their traditional religious unconcern.

Religion Today.—China yields place to the Soviet Union alone in her open and official hostility toward the age-old faiths. During the Revolution in 1911 the great god *T'ai Shan* (*cf.* p. 104, below) was "slain" in Foochow, along with hundreds of gods, goddesses, and demons who lived in his temple, and the temple itself was sealed against its further use for worship. Similar acts of anti-religious violence were committed elsewhere, although such incidents may at times have been at the hands of "communists" beyond any governmental control. The Foochow temple, however, was later reopened and restored, and the image of *T'ai Shan* paraded publicly in recognition of his lordship over men.[3] In recent years, 1928–1931, multitudes of images and idols were officially destroyed excepting, ironically, the images of the god of loyalty to friends and of the god of loyalty to nations. The "Government," and in particular, the Kuomintang, or "nationalist" party, have called the religions of the country "superstitions," and have set about to "regulate" them. Scores of temples have been demolished by official action. Some have been converted to other than religious usages.

Many Chinese leaders, intellectuals, and governmental officials have protested against allowing religion any place in the building

---

[1] *Racial* homogeneity, especially.
[2] C. H. Toy, *Introduction to the History of Religions*, p. 325.
[3] *Chinese Recorder*, 1923, pp. 465–6.

of the new society and state of China. The father of the Chinese Revolution, Dr. Sun Yat Sen, made no reference to religion in his *San Min Chu I,* or the "Three Principles of the People." His three proposals for national reconstruction were nationalism, democracy, and livelihood.[4] He, however, advocated vigorously the "old morality," in association with which were certain elements of religion. Said he, "As for China's old moral standards, they are not yet lost sight of by the people. First come loyalty and filial devotion, then kindness and love, then faithfulness and justice, then harmony and peace. The Chinese still speak of these ancient qualities of character.[5]

China has been much stirred from without.[6] Russian influences have been powerful. Probably the anti-religious movement among Chinese radicals has been stimulated most by Communism. But China's temper today is nationalistic, and the current scepticism toward religion is not universal. What has been typically Chinese throughout the centuries may be counted on to play its part in the direction of national integrity, for the Chinese have been too long a stable and culturally independent people lightly to toss aside their heritage. Moreover, it is an established principle, verifiable throughout the history of the world, that any major cultural reconstruction, especially by means of revolution, ultimately requires a revival of religion. The ancient Chinese ideals still have survival value. Many leaders of today are turning once again to the ancient Chinese *Classics* as their sufficient ground for "the conservation of the excellent," "the renovation of the deficient," and the "innovation" which true development demands. In contrast with recent governmental "regulation" of Chinese "superstitions," several monuments to the sun have been erected by the state, and there have been indications that neither the Government nor the people have any mind to create or to tolerate a void in faith and worship. The Kuomintang, at least, or, the "national" party, is as a whole not hostile to religion. The president, Chiang Kai Shek, was recently baptized as a Christian. A former president of China, General Li Yuan Hung, who died in 1928, was not buried until April, 1933. His body rested while certain seers following ancient custom determined the auspicious time for the funeral ceremony and the auspicious place for burial.

As for Confucius, while there has been of late a tendency to

---

[4] *Cf. Chinese Recorder,* 1928, p. 47. For the *San Min Chu I,* see translation by F. W. Price. Shanghai, 1927.
[5] *San Min Chu I,* trans. Price, p. 126.
[6] See C. S. Braden, *Modern Tendencies in World Religions,* pp. 87–134.

discredit him,[7] many "men of vision and moral insight still consider him the mainspring of Chinese civilization," and presumably a standard for the newer day, as China appropriates what alien values she requires and "renovates" her society and institutions. The cult of Sun Yat Sen has many followers, especially in South China.[8] A noble monument to him has been erected in Nanking. But Dr. Sun's foundation was Confucian,[9] and Confucius is the greatest Chinese name in three millenniums.

Religions.—There are five formal religions, or "teachings," (*chiao*) in China today:

1. *Ju-chiao,* or "Scholar-teaching," referring to Confucianism. The character *ju* means "learned, or a scholar." Confucius is known as the "head, or beginning," (*shou*) of the *ju-chiao,* which is known also as the "sacred teaching" (*sheng-chiao*).

2. *Tao-chiao,* or "Way-teaching," referring to Taoism. The character *tao* meant first a "road," but has acquired many other meanings. It enters today into terms for morality, moral philosophy, etc. "Taoism," in an exclusive sense, refers to the doctrine of the *tao,* supposed to have been formulated by Lao-tze (sixth century, B.C.).

3. *Fo-chiao,* or "Buddha-teaching," known also as the "Buddha-way" (*fo-tao*), the "Buddha-gate" (*fo-mën*), and the "Great-Vehicle-teaching" (*ta-ch'eng-chiao*).[10] The character *fo* is composed of a symbol for "man" and a symbol for "not," suggesting things beyond human life, or, as Chinese Buddhists say, the deeper understanding of oneself and the universe.

4. *Hui-hui-chiao,* or "Return-teaching," referring to Islam, or Mohammedanism. *Hui* (pronounced as hway) may refer to the common Moslem expression, "to thy Lord is the *return* of all," "unto him shall all *return,*" e.g., Koran, 96:8. Or, it may be the *hui* of "association." Other titles for Islam in China are the "exclusive teaching" (*ko-chiao*) and the "pure, true teaching" (*ch'ing-chen-chiao*), the latter obviously its own designation.

5. *Ya-chiao,* or "Jesus-teaching," Christianity, known also as the "Christ-teaching" (*chi-tu-chiao*). Christians are called "teaching-people" (*chiao-min*).

In a somewhat arbitrary fashion we may apportion the four hundred millions of Chinese among these five groups, unless we attempt to cut across all five to find the primitive strain, or unless

---

7 *Chinese Recorder,* 1930, pp. 164–5. *Cf.* Z. K. Zia, *The Confucian Civilization.* Shanghai, 1928.
8 Confucius was a North Chinese.
9 *Cf.* "All my best thoughts were stolen by the ancients."—R. W. Emerson.
10 E. Morgan, *New New Terms,* p. 315, *i.e.,* Mahayana, the "Great Vehicle."

we attempt the almost equally impossible task of numbering the people unwilling to be classified under any traditional "teaching." Difficulties and contradictions abound in the Chinese scene, but for our purposes the general situation is understandable, and we need not be annoyed by what is vague or intangible. The Christians represent a fairly distinct group in comparison with the other groups. Christianity first entered China in the seventh century with the Nestorians. Roman Catholicism has had a footing in China for more than three centuries. The Eastern Orthodox Church entered in 1685. Protestant missions began in 1807. The total Christian community came to number between two and one half and three million baptized persons, of whom about four-fifths were Roman Catholics, about one-fifth Protestants, and about 5,000 Eastern Orthodox. There was a threefold increase in the grand total after 1900, but it is probable that the Christian community has diminished very perceptibly during the last few years. Moslems first entered China in the seventh century, and are now found in every province, although they are mostly in the far-inland regions. Estimates vary widely; the total is probably between ten and fifteen millions. There is no sufficient ground for believing that the total has diminished recently. Chinese Moslems and Christians, combined, number probably less than four per cent of the total population. The *Ju-fo-tao* combination, therefore, represents the bulk of the people. Of these three, Confucianism and Taoism are indigenous, while Buddhism has been so intimately adopted that we might say, "If one wishes to understand China, one must see China in the light of Buddhism." [11] although one hundred millions may be the actual total of Chinese Buddhists, while Confucianists may number two hundred and fifty millions. Taoists number forty-five.

Giving this preponderance to Confucianism is after all an estimate. In general culture China is without doubt Confucian, but in religion she is Buddhist. Most Chinese, exclusive of the Moslems and the Christians, profess and practice the *san-chiao,* or "three religions," that is, the *ju-fo-tao.* The average Chinese may be Confucian, Buddhist, and Taoist—and an "animist," as well—without much sense of inconsistency. An ancient proverb says "the three religions are all one." This Chinese trait may be accounted for in part by their indifference to religion, and in part to toleration. The layman has not found in any one a full religion. Nor has he been eager usually to fight for any faith,

11 K. L. Reichelt, *Truth and Tradition in Chinese Buddhism,* p. 311. Shanghai, 1927.

or lose his life for his religion. There have been religious persecutions in China, but without the bigotry and armed severity often shown in the Near East and in Europe. In contrast with the laity, however, there has been a priesthood both in Taoism and in Buddhism which has been loyal in each instance to its Church. There is no priesthood in Confucianism.

Chinese Characteristics.—Chinese religion must be viewed in the light of its physical setting and the racial fiber and mental qualities of the people.

1. The Chinese are *pacifists,* all signs to the contrary, notwithstanding. Exceptions might be likened to the legendary *chi,* a species of large deer found in western China, said to have long tusks, feet like a dog's, and to be fond of fighting! The Chinese claim their love of peace to be a natural disposition—not a reaction against war. Some of them sincerely expect to surpass the people of other lands in this moral quality.[12] Confucius seems to have suggested a precautionary military training for all the people,[13] but to have insisted that militarism[14] was contrary to "benevolence." The Chinese, in fact, have a natural indisposition toward war, and a lack of capacity for war as a definite campaign toward definite ends. The professional soldier is by tradition a man of low estate—a brigand? But beyond this fact, the fighting, when wars have occurred,[15] has been of more importance than the consequences. By a Chinese military code, leaders and men might change from side to side, while fighting, without disgrace or charge of treason, so long as they were loyal to the fighting. Chinese tactics always left the [Chinese] enemy one chance of escape,[16]—to save his "face"—and surrender was not necessarily disgraceful, unless to a foreign foe. Even warfare in China has been—among the leaders, at least—of the category of ceremony and polite intercourse, although in recent years the situation has slightly changed. We hear today a little less of "face."

2. The Chinese, are *practical,* yet not utilitarian. It is not the result but the process itself to which they devote their thought and labor. Perfection is an aim, but not an end; perfection is of the process itself,—"fulfilment is deception." China has had the creative spirit, but has had little interest in the thing created. She

---

12 *San Min Chu I,* p. 133.
13 *Cf. Hsiang Chuan,* an appendix to the *Li Chi,* or *Book of Changes.*
14 *I.e.,* a standing army, etc.
15 Wars have by no means been infrequent. Armies have been maintained by Chinese rulers, for example, the ancient emperor Wu, whose maneuvers have been a theme of Chinese drama. See *Shu Ching,* Part V.
16 E. T. Williams, *Short History of China,* p. 71.

has invented (*e.g.,* gunpowder, paper, and the mariner's compass), but with small concern for the use of things invented. She has given scant attention to details, or to the particular application of ideas, for the sake of their improvement, but, rather, has been more concerned with the formulation and acceptance of a general idea, position, or program. The Chinese "have said black and white but have not distinguished between white objects and black." Their very character for "idea" is "thinking elephant," *i.e.,* exercising the imagination, inferring an elephant which one has never seen, from a tusk or a bone which he has seen. This appraisal of Chinese practicality, needless to say, is made by comparison with Western utilitarianism, with no assumption, however, that the Chinese thereby are necessarily morally discredited.

3. The Chinese are *agnostics*. At least, they have never professed to know much about God and the human soul. Their agnosticism seems not to be the result of any great social revolution or intellectual crisis which made faith fade into doubt, nor due to the commingling of many distinct faiths which sometimes takes the edge off each one of them, nor yet is it the result of any crowding of the people into great cities, for China is an agricultural land. Their agnosticism, like their pacifism, seems to be part of the general temper as manifested throughout the centuries. It is akin to China's characteristic conservatism which in part is sheer indisposition to advance, rather than a product of reaction against radicalism.

4. Indeed, the Chinese have been characterized by some observers as unemotional nerveless *quietists*. They seem to be made of fiber that defies disease and insures immunity to a remarkable degree; physical distresses have not destroyed their native optimism. Yet with their quietism the Chinese have emotion. *Æstheticism* has provided them an outlet. The æsthetic temper has been acute, persistent, and inclusive. Music, poetry, and the fine arts have flourished to a predominant degree. The Chinese, in fact, may be called æsthetic rather than religious. Certainly religion has provided them no such outlet for their emotions as it has provided for Hindus, Moslems, and others who have not been specialists in the universality of art. The Chinese might even be called at times æsthetic rather than moral. Their pacifism is less moral than æsthetic. And the emphasis which Confucius put on music as an aid to government is typical of the artistic temper. This temper may be further seen in Chinese picture writing and the Chinese disposition to revere the inventor of it.

5. However, one may never deny the high *moral character* of the Chinese people, even though among them as with others, also, the pursuit of moral truth has been one thing and the application of it still another. Nor may one who knows the Chinese intimately deny that *religion* such as we shall find among them has had a strong hold on them. We might say the Chinese *religion is moral,* or even that their morality is their religion. But we may not say with equal justification that their morality is religious. We shall examine more closely the relation in China between morality and religion.

Spiritism.—China has had her own interesting and influential conceptions of Heaven and Nature, of the human spirit, and of the relation of human character and conduct to the natural order and Heaven's will. She has further exhibited her religious attitude by welcoming alien faiths from without and by her appropriation from them of solutions they had to offer of the problems of life. There has been throughout the centuries among the masses of China such a sense of mysterious potency as we find characteristic of the primitive peoples. There is no general term, or ideograph for it in their language—no symbol corresponding with *mana,*[17] but the vague conception or undefined assumption of such potency is and has been manifest in various aspects of the people's life. The pilgrim to Mt. Omei may rub a copper cash on an ancient bronze pagoda and carry the coin away with the conviction that it will protect one from demons and disease; or, at Chengtu, the devotee may seek to cure an ailment by rubbing a bronze goat at the part of the goat's body which corresponds with the diseased portion of his own body; or, again, a Szechuan coolie whose back aches from the heavy burdens borne may seek relief by placing sticks in the crevices of certain rough and curious stones.[18] Charms are everywhere in use: printed or written characters pasted by doorways, or in the rooms of houses, pinned on bedding, or sewed to the clothing; the stamps of seals belonging to temples, gods, and priests; and many other sorts. There is mock-money for the dead, dispatched to them in some temple brazier. There is divination by coins and sticks, auguries from entrails, portents and geomancy by means of "wind and water." There are many such practices resting upon the notion of an all-pervading potency within the universe. There are spirits, also, without number, and gods, besides. China is still full of temples,

---

[17] Unless it be *ch'i,* πνε͂υμα.
[18] *Cf. Chinese Recorder,* 1929, pp. 235–7.

and in the temples are images both numerous and of great variety in size and appearance. Many Chinese have regarded these images as no more than material objects, whether of clay, or wood, or bronze, and of no spiritual value. Others, on the other hand, have thought of them as symbols, or as suggestions of the actual presence of the beings represented. Most of the common people have regarded them as gods, or powers, knowing, willing, and able to do for men what men crave. Many officials and priests have held this same view. To such and to the common people the power, or god, is present in the image as the soul is present in the human body.[19]

Chinese religion of recent years represents a survival of beliefs and practices from very ancient times,[20] in spite of agnosticism on the one hand, and rationalism on the other. We may detect in it two major original and persistent factors, nature-worship and ancestor-worship, with possibly the greater emphasis upon the latter. It is eminently fitting, in the case of a homogeneous people who have always lived in the land they now occupy[21] that we consider the whole history of their spiritual attitudes and activities, especially since throughout most of their traceable existence, devotion to the dead has been the outstanding characteristic. "Filial piety" (the filial attitude toward one's living elders and superiors, which extends itself in worship of their spirits after they have died) has been the ruling idea in religion. It is this element more than any other which has made for Chinese conservatism; the faces of the living have been set toward the past, in so far as life has been controlled by the will of the departed.

The Past.—China's past runs back into the third millennium, B.C. Where there is so much culture one expects to find much social history, even as one infers a long geologic era from such stalactites as were found in the Carlsbad Caves. What the Chinese writings call "history" (*shu,* to write) began with the accession of the emperor Yao (known while alive as Fang hsün) in 2356 B.C. to rulership over the people of the ancient basin of the Yellow River (the *Huang-ho*)[22] when it flowed from the vicinity

---

[19] The Chinese notion of the relation of soul and object might be illustrated by an incident from the writer's own experience, sailing from China on the S.S. *Monteagle,* with Chinese stewards. A friend had given him at the pier a photograph of a group which included several Chinese. The picture, left exposed in the cabin, was appropriated by the cabin-boy—*rescued* from the foreigner who had in his possession as long as he had the picture the souls of several Chinese!

[20] The very gods of today are expressions of elements of the ancient faith.

[21] There is no tradition that the real Chinese were not indigenous.

[22] *Ho* is the word for "river" in North China; in the south they say *kiang.*

of the present-day city of K'ai-feng southeastward to the Yellow
Sea. The first verifiable date in Chinese history is 842 B.C.,[23] as
we reckon, but this does not mark the boundary between fancy
and fact in Chinese records. We may trust the general facts preserved from the fifteenth century, B.C., at least. Before the end
of the pre-Christian era the great Chinese historian Ssu-ma-Ch'ien
had carefully weighed the records from the earliest times of which
anything was known. Even before the end of the sixth century,
B.C. Confucius had begun the editing of all the ancient classics.
It is tradition that as early as the era of Yao, and of Shun, who
followed him, democratic institutions flourished along the Yellow
River: government was "by the people." By 1000 B.C. four definite
classes of society had formed: scholars, husbandmen, mechanics,
and merchants—their relative ranking in the social scale being
indicated by the order given. The high character of early Chinese
civilization is further indicated by the fact that the ceremonies of
marriage and the burial of the dead, the institution of writing,
and the calculation of chronology are so ancient that the Chinese
cannot account for them.

The beginnings of Chinese religion lie within the realm of conjecture, but by the aid of available sources and by comparison with
the general history of religion, we may reconstruct the early
form. We have no good ground for believing that the origin and
development of religion in China is essentially different from the
story of religion in any other major field. What difference there
is lies in the quality and comprehensiveness of Chinese religion.
We have no name to give the early Chinese form, unless we call
it "Sinism," or the Sinæan religion (the Greeks called China
Sin and her people Sinai). Such a term may be used for convenience for the pre-Confucian era, say until 600 B.C. The Sinæan
era provided what is basic for all time in China, especially as this
base was modified into the two indigenous orders, Taoism and
Confucianism. Confucius, it should be remembered, professed
merely to transmit what he found by "looking into antiquity."
Sinæan religion consisted of the two major aspects to which
reference has already been made, nature-worship and ancestor-
worship, both of which, in China, are immemorial, and not always
separable.

Nature.—*Sinæan nature-worship.* As in India and Greece, although in a far less personal character than in these lands, so
also in China the overarching *sky* is the first great early object

---

[23] An eclipse of the sun occurred in 775 B.C.

of worship. It is the sky-god, or the sky-as-god, become universal. In Greece, Zeus as god of the sky, or god in the sky, became supreme and the head of a pantheon of separate, conspicuous gods, including Apollo, who rose to the position of sun-god. In India the early sky-god, "Father Sky," gave way to gods of wind, sun, storm, and the dawn. In China, on the other hand, the sky maintained its high place and never became subordinated to other nature powers. This is in part the clue both to Chinese morality and Chinese religion. Heaven is supreme as father, governor, and pattern of mankind. As the rationalist philosopher, Chu Hsi, said in the 12th century, A.D., "Heaven is God and God is Heaven."

The "inverted bowl they call the sky" is known as *T'ien*. This term has yielded various meanings, such as the material heavens, nature, the eternal principle of right, and God. We might say with Chu Hsi, *T'ien* is *Heaven*. It is a very ancient term; how ancient is a matter of surmise.[24] There is evidence that the early Chinese recognized also a high god *Shang-ti*,[25] and a divine being, *Ti*, but it is difficult to understand what relation *T'ien, Shang-ti*, and *Ti* sustained to one another. The view has been advanced that the three separate terms came from three separate sources,— three tribal sources,—and that each represented the supreme deity. The great Taoist Chuang-tze used the three terms as equivalents. Another view is that *Shang-ti* is "the Most High God" whose dwelling place is Heaven (*T'ien*), and that *Ti* is a deified ancestor-god. It is probable that *Shang-ti* (or simply *Ti*, for the character *ti* is the same in both cases) represents the more intimate, personal and active aspect of divinity, and *T'ien* the more remote and passive. Chu Hsi observed this distinction in his use of the terms. In general, however, we may assume for Chinese religion what we shall discover to be true of religion in certain other lands, that these and other terms are many names for one God. If then we associate the terms together under the one title "Heaven" we may offer the following descriptive definition of the Chinese conception of the Supreme—a definition true of the pre-Confucian era as well as of subsequent times,

Personal, loving, fatherly, the Creator, spiritual without form, omnipresent, omniscient, eternal, supreme, moral, moved by virtue, compassionate to the people, the dethroner of tyrants,

---

24 As early as 1000 B.C., at least.
25 Concerning *T'ien and Shang-ti*, see P. J. Maclagan, *Chinese Religious Ideas*, pp. 15–43.

who has attached his law to every faculty and relationship, and will give effect to what the people properly desire.[26]

We must take this definition, however, for less than what it seems to mean, for the meaning of "God" in early Chinese religion is not so clear and consistent as our definition indicates. China has had no theologians in the strict sense of the term to gather up the fragments of phrases and the scattered ideas with respect to Heaven as God, and to mould them into a consistent whole. At best, we are left in some doubt as to God's personality, and as to his essential moral character. At times we scarcely know whether he is more than Law, or a Name to cover and symbolize all the component elements of human experience, or yet a Unity whose reality after all inheres in the parts which make it.

Next to Heaven, Earth (*Hu*)[27] was held in highest regard in ancient China. Indeed, from about 1000 B.C. the worship of Earth enjoyed an equal place with that of Heaven. Heaven and Earth were the "parents of all creatures." As the heavenly bodies had their place in the worship of Heaven, so the spirits of the mountains, rivers, and seas, and of the soil and the crops had their place in the Earth-cult. It was the function of the State to offer annually at the capital sacrifices to Heaven at midsummer, and to Earth at midwinter, and otherwise to administer the nature-cult at various times and places.

The development of the relation of Heaven and Earth, and especially the early association of the two on equal terms, seems to have furnished ground for an interesting dualism which has characterized Chinese thought and religion for three thousand years. We might say it is a dualism against a background of the One, for Chinese philosophy is monistic, with emphasis upon the good life in a good world. It exhibits the earliest Chinese attempt at speculation about the physical universe. The One which constitutes this background is the *Tao,* the Absolute, the First Cause, Nature-in-itself. The *Tao* is essentially of two parts, a heavenly, positive, active, aggressive part, and an earthly, negative, passive, receptive part. Heaven and Earth, then, become products and

[26] The ancient records tell us of other nature powers, such as the sun, the North Star, the five planets, the constellations of the Zodiac, the moon, and weather gods (clouds, thunder, wind, and rain). These powers were all worshiped on the altar of Heaven at Peking until 1912 A.D. Since 1928 they and their shrines everywhere have all been banned by the Kuomintang—whose authority is effective only in portions of China.

[27] *Ti,* also,—not the *ti* for spirit,—is a common term for "earth."

aspects of the *Tao*. In fact, the creation of Heaven and Earth and all that they severally contain took place through the alternate motion and rest of the *Tao;* and every object in the universe, whether animate or inanimate, is possessed of these two qualities of motion and rest in interaction. These are the two principles through whose interaction all things have been evolved, and which are in eternal operation. This is a materialistic philosophy, and a philosophy of impermanence; [28] the early Chinese thinkers were impressed by Nature and by the changes, often momentous, which were constantly occurring in Nature.

This dualism, known as the *Yang-Yin* theory, is the explanation of all things in the created universe. *Yang* is the heavenly, active, and aggressive principle; *Yin* is the earthly, passive, and receptive principle.[29] The two principles might be conceived as male and female. In inanimate nature *yang* operates as the sun, light, heat, growth, etc., and *yin,* as the moon, darkness, cold, decay, etc. In the moral realm, in each individual person, *yang* operates as good, and *yin* as evil. Every person has two natures which conflict in life and separate in death. In religion, *yang* is God, the gods, and what is godly; and *yin* is God's enemy, demons, and what is devilish. More specifically, the gods and godly forces are called *shen;* demons and things devilish are *kuei* (pronounced as kway).[30] The universe is thus divided into two great, opposing camps, the good opposed by what is evil, the *shen* obedient to *yang,* and the *kuei* obedient to *yin.*

The Manes.—*Sinæan ancestor-worship.* As early as the reign of Shun (23rd century, B.C.), Man was worshiped in the triad with Heaven and Earth. The worship of Man was the worship of one's own ancestors. There was thus combined the ancestor and the nature cults, with their three rituals and a "usual form" of sacrifice. This was true of the state religion, in particular. The common people worshiped indirectly. Sacrifices, under the state's direction, to the ancestral-natural Heaven [31] and Earth—and to lesser nature powers [32]—were made in the open upon uncovered altars. Heaven being everywhere could be worshiped anywhere under its vast expanse. Ancestor-worship as such, however, was

---

28 We shall have occasion later to realize how congenial to the Chinese was the Buddha's doctrine of impermanence.

29 The Taoist Chuang-tse devoted thought to identifying such contraries.

30 The *kuei* at first were spiritual beings—at least, they threw no shadow. A *kuei* was both good and bad, or it might be either good or bad. Chinese superstition, however, made *kuei* altogether vengeful ghosts and evil spirits. The *shen* have been altogether good. In time Catholic missionaries in China called Christian angels *t'ien shen,* "divine messengers." The term has been used for God.

31 *I.e.,* Heaven as Father. Heaven was *not,* however, first an ancestral spirit.

32 Ancestral spirits might be recognized during nature-worship.

performed in *miao,* or temples. The temples mentioned in the
oldest *Classics* are dedicated to ancestors, imperial especially.

There was one national ancestral temple, that of the ruling
dynasty, where the imperial [33] spirits were worshiped. In addition,
vassal princes and officials had their temples, where they worshiped their own ancestors. The common people had no temples,
for their ancestors were all *kuei.*[34] They had their household
shrines. Ancestor-worship was for the ordinary family purely
a domestic ritual. The Great Temple of the ruling house was a
composite of several structures. During the Chou (pronounced
Jo) dynasty (12th–3rd centuries, B.C.), there were seven. A
"seven-shrined" Chou temple included: the shrine of the "Great
Ancestor," on the north, facing south, with a row of three shrines
on either hand extending south. On the right, the west, and
facing east, the shrines successively of Wen, the founder of the
Chou dynasty; the great grandfather of the ruling king; and
the father. On the left, the east, and facing west, parallel with
the western row, the shrines of Wu, the son of Wen; the great-
great-grandfather of the ruling king; and the grandfather. In these
seven buildings reposed the spirits of the ruler's lineal ancestors
(all, of course, were *shen*), each of which was represented, not
by an image, but by a tablet (*shen chu*). At least, at a time of
worship the souls of the deceased were "called" to reside in their
respective tablets.[35] The ordinary family had its own commemorative tablets, but they were set up within the private home.

The soul and the distinction between soul and body is fundamental to Chinese religion. The earliest literary records indicate
that man was composed of a compound, intelligent spirit which
at death ascends "on high," [36] and a compound body which then
descends to earth, *i.e.,* a material body and a knowing mind, or soul.
The soul in life becomes the spirit after death. It was believed
that when man sleeps his soul departs to come back voluntarily
when he wakes, that when he swoons, it has gone further and
must be helped back again, and at death it is permanently separated. But "no one knows the exact location of the spirits at any
time. They may be here or they may be there; they may be near
or far." Usually, it was thought, they lingered in indefinite prox-
imity, retaining power to help or harm, to occupy and control

[33] As early as this there was no Empire, however. There was no Emperor until
after Confucius' time.
[34] *Kuei* then were simply "powers," indifferently good or evil.
[35] A *shen chu* is, ordinarily, a thin, narrow, flat, rectilinear slab, or double-slab of
lacquered wood bearing an appropriate inscription.
[36] Not to Heaven, for Heaven was not conceived of as a Paradise.

inanimate objects, such as ancestral tablets or a dead body, to enter the bodies of living animals (a girl's soul in a rat), or to enter human bodies as disease. They had power to assume any shape, and to act accordingly.

Worship.—*Sinæan ritual.*[37] Sacrifices and prayers were offered to *all* the spirits. China vies with India and Palestine in the complexity and splendor attained by the sacrificial system. Public ceremonies at the Temple of Heaven were noteworthy in ancient China, although not until later times did they become extremely elaborate. The great annual sacrifice to Heaven was held in midsummer at the capital. An act of thanksgiving, it welcomed the arrival of the longest day. The sun on this occasion was the seat of Heaven's Spirit. It was the emperor's prerogative to offer this Great Sacrifice, as the religious head of the nation, reigning by Heaven's appointment (not otherwise by divine right, for China entertained no theory of imperial divinity). The sacrifice was offered in the open on ground swept for the purpose in the southern suburb. The offering burnt was at first a single bull calf (ignorant of sex) which had been kept in a clean stall nearby for three months. The emperor, in ceremonial robes, rode to the place of worship "in the plain carriage." Not the costliness of the sacrifice, but the spirit of the worshipers was regarded. In time elaboration set in. Soon an ox, a sheep, and a pig were offered; in Chou times, a horse, dogs, and hens were included. Along with Heaven, the other powers upon which depended the welfare of the whole empire were worshiped. Not only was there the Great Sacrifice at the capital, but secondary sacrifices were offered by deputies throughout the land to all inferior deities.

At midwinter there was offered by the emperor in the northern suburb of his capital, and by princes and officials elsewhere, the annual official sacrifice to Earth: to the four quarters of the sky; to the four mountains and the four rivers; to the spirits of the soil and the crops; to Shen-nung, the Father of Husbandry; and to the royal guardians of the door, the kitchen, the court-yard, the path, and the gate.

The worship of Heaven and Earth was performed *for* the people, not *by* them. It was state ceremonial. Private religion required merely the worship by each family of its own ancestors, save as each household had its guardian spirit of the door and its kitchen-god. Beyond this, the worship of the commoners was confined to the attendance of their representatives at clan sacri-

[37] See J. Ross, *The Original Religion of China*, pp. 229–291.

fices to the spirits of the clan fields, and at village sacrifices to the local spirits of the soil. Officers of state performed the sacrifice.

Ancestor-worship was essentially private, except as Heaven was regarded not only as Supreme Ruler, but also as Great Ancestor, and save as the spirits of the deceased in the imperial line were included in the ritual of the Great Sacrifice. The rites performed in the ancestral temples differed only in scale and impressiveness. Sacrifices were offered at the four seasons of the year and at times such as the installation of a new tablet. On stated occasions sacrifice was made to all ancestors of a given line or household; those taking part prepared themselves by fasting and purification. The offerings might be cereal, vegetable, animal, ardent spirits, or precious stones—something valuable, although sincerity was highly regarded. "The incense of good conduct was more agreeable than the most costly spices burnt in a censer." The sacrifice was a family feast, a communion. The fat of a victim was first burnt as fragrance, and music was played to induce the spirits of the dead to come and share the feast. The common people, having no ancestral halls, carried on their worship in their homes, in simpler and less costly manner, but with the motives of the upper classes.

Both nature- and ancestral-worship were accompanied with prayer, music from flutes, drums, and stringed instruments, chanting, and a solemn dance. A favorite dance showed the maneuvers of Wu's army the night before his victory over Shang.[38] Four hymns of the ancient ritual are preserved in the *Shih Ching,* or *Book of Odes.*[39] Prayer was not for pardon, but to ask the spirits to "regard" the offering. There was in the sacrifice nothing expiatory, no indication of penitence, or desire for the remission of sins. Its motive was rather the information of Heaven or the spirits, to acknowledge relationship and dependence, and to give thanks. If, on the other hand, the will of Heaven and the spirits was sought, it could be learned by divination, by drying ink in a tortoise-shell (and reading the lines), or by casting lots. The sacrifice was performed with dignity and precision, for irregularity indicated lack of reverence, and might produce disorders.

Morals.—*Sinæan morality.* Ancient China had high ideals in morals, as the *Shu Ching,* or *Book of History,* shows. According

---

[38] Wu, the son and successor of Wen who founded the Chow dynasty. He vanquished the lawless king of Shang. See *Shu Ching,* Pt. V, bk. 1, sec's. 2, 3 (*Sacred Books of the East,* III, pp. 127–130), and *Shih Ching,* Sacrificial Odes of Chow, 2nd decade, No. 10 (S.B.E., III, p. 328).

[39] *Cf.* S.B.E., III, pp. 303ff.

to this "honorable" classic, Heaven [40] is moral, loves the people, is mercifully just; may be "moved with indignation" and "roused to anger"; sends down happiness or misery according to the people's conduct; blesses the doer of good and sends calamities upon the evil-doer; and confers a moral sense upon the high and the low. A doctrine of original human goodness is displayed: "All things have their origin in Heaven, men have their origin in their ancestors"; "what Heaven bestows is called nature (*hsing*), what accords with nature is called the way (*tao*)," and if man follows the way he is in harmony with Heaven's nature; "people are born good, they are made bad by circumstances which cause them to follow their own desires." "The mind of man is prone to err, its affinity to what is right is scant"; humility exalts, but pride debases; "being vain of one's ability is the way to lose the merit it might win"; "it is not the knowing but the doing that is difficult."

The ancient code enjoins men against excess in pleasure, "confusion" of the senses (as with drink), forsaking what is right to win men's praise, neglect to align their purposes with reason, "officiousness in sacrifice," and denial of the equality of others with themselves. It warns men that "calamities sent by Heaven may be averted, but from those brought by men upon themselves there is no escape." The ruler—the code was meant primarily for him—is reminded that when he exercises virtue, good government is realized; when he does not, disorder comes. He is cautioned not to oppress, to be gentle but strict, and to promote harmony (*ch'êng*) by forbearance. The minister is reminded that he is to promote virtue in relation to his sovereign, and seek the good of all the people. The cardinal virtue was *jen* (pronounced *ren*), an inward and spiritual love for all mankind, of which *i* (pronounced *ee*), what is right to do, is the outward and visible manifestation. Since to the Chinese, as someone has said, "religion is an extension of moral relations into the world of spirit," the emphasis upon *jen* seemed to meet their greatest need.

Woman's place in the ancient order provides a useful commentary on the moral code. From the first the Chinese have been polygamous, but the "wife," even in early times, held a higher place than concubines, or "wayside wives." In theory, the wife enjoyed equal honors with her husband. Her tablet, usually, was placed beside her husband's in the ancestral temple, or on the family shelf. But practically her place was secondary. She was

[40] *Cf.* the definition of "Heaven," p. 57f, above.

subject to divorce. She and her children were "like clothes," they could be replaced. "Rich men easily find wives," and more easily concubines. The Chinese have been no more sensual than other peoples, but woman's function has been biological and practical; she has been the mother of men's sons, the cook, and seamstress. She had nothing to do, in general, with religion, and as for morals, she was to be neither good nor evil, nor to cause her parents sorrow. Obviously Sun Yat Sen, commending "old morality," [41] was not immediately concerned with woman's status in it.

Ceremony.—Propriety, or ceremony (*li*) is an ancient and persistent element. Nowhere has it been more highly esteemed. It early came to command the attention and the talent of the national leaders,—in particular, the scholars, who even before 1000 B.C. were the highest of the social classes. Twenty-five hundred years before the Christian era, there was a Minister of Ceremony, an authority on Propriety. Propriety was the key to individual conduct. Every man knew his duties in relation to other men. It was the index of character, and the endurance of the nation was related to propriety and the exactness of ceremonial observance. One may understand neither the leaders nor the people who disregards the rôle of ceremony.

Do not suppose that *li* merely represents externalism, mere observance of rules of etiquette for various occasions. It represents an inner quality, expressing itself in outward conduct. "*Li* has a root and a flower." Its root is sincerity, reverence, and precision of speech; its flower is rites and ceremonies, harmonious social relationships, and good government. "Of all methods for the regulation of mankind the most important is *li*." The ideograph for *li* is a compound of three simple characters, meaning essentially, "grain over a vessel held up by two hands," that is, the two hands of the worshiper holding aloft before Heaven and for Heaven's "information" the sacrificial vessel filled with stalks of grain. *Li* must have meant originally the ritual of sacrifice, with the view of Heaven as the source of all. *Li* would thus properly become the symbol of the way of life and conduct for mankind, with the implication that since Heaven is moral, man's mind and conduct must be moral to accord with Heaven's will and way.

The major terms in any people's language, particularly in their vocabulary of religion, and the meanings which they carry furnish

---

[41] It might be of interest to recall Dr. Sun's political morality. "Chosen [Apr. 7, 1921] by the fag-end of a Parliament that no longer had any right to sit, and by a vote that lacked more than three hundred of the necessary majority, Dr. Sun nevertheless accepted the office and called himself the 'Constitutional' President of China."— E. T. Williams, *op. cit.*, pp. 574-5.

ready insight into the national character. In broad outline the religious mind of China has from the first [42] operated upon such basic principles as these:

1. *T'ien,* Heaven the over-arching sky, the Ultimate, the Source of nature, man, and morals.

2. *Tao,* or Way, the "way of Heaven" (*T'ien tao*), the "way of Earth" (*Ti tao*), the "way of benevolence" (*Jen tao*), etc.; perhaps, as a speculative principle, either the Ultimate itself, or derived from a Primal Ultimate, or from Chaos,[43] thus being antecedent to Heaven; the source of the contending forces, *yang* and *yin,* which came from its spontaneous bifurcation and have operated both in nature and in morals.

3. *Ch'êng,* Harmony, conformity of man with *Tao* and *T'ien,* expressing itself inwardly in man as *jen,* and outwardly as *i* and *li.*

4. *Jen,* Love, Benevolence, the supreme virtue among moral values, ranging from good thought to universal love.[44]

5. *Chung,* Fidelity, or Conscience, "fidelity to one's better self." Compare Shakespeare, "First to thine own self be true, and 't will follow as the night the day thou canst not then be false to any man."

6. *Shu,* Consideration, due regard for other men, and actual forgiveness, when the need arises.

7. *Li,* Propriety, of which *hsiao,* or "filial piety," "reverence," is a chief expression.

These are not all. We shall view others with them, later, as we investigate the formal systems of thought and religion.

Two systems came directly out of the Sinæan era, the "Confucianist" (the *ju-chiao*) and the "Taoist" (*tao-chiao*). Both were in process of development during many centuries, each awaiting the coming of the great person who would unify whatever consistent tendencies he could find and favor in the best thought and conduct of the ages, would give them a coherent philosophy, and stamp the issue with an enduring name. Two great persons came at last, within one century, Lao and K'ung (Lao-tze and K'ung-fu-tze). The latter transmitted in *concrete* terms the preponderant tendencies he discovered and sealed the vast bulk of national tradition with his name. The former specialized in an *exceptional*

---

42 *I.e.,* from the first known to history (*shu*).
43 *Cf.* Lieh-tze, below.
44 Thus interpreted by Mo-ti (Meh-tze). See below.

condition of the national mind, and expounded it as worthy of universal sway. He made capital out of Chinese quietism, and proposed passive, mystical accord with Heaven as the highest good. Confucius stressed the practical and proposed that human conduct regulate itself in active harmony with Heaven.

CHAPTER IV

CONFUCIANISM

THE *JU CHIAO:* CONFUCIUS AND HIS SCHOOL

Chinese thinkers and reformers of today who are seeing visions of a new China are subjecting the ancient "Confucian" system to the closest scrutiny, and the world must await the issue with more than academic concern. It is a matter of serious consequence, morally, politically, and otherwise, not only to China but to the world, what the Chinese may decide about Confucius and what solution they may apply to their present problems. Whatever the immediate solution, Confucianism must stand as a monumental contribution to the world's thought on human conduct and to its theories of human nature. Confucianism likewise, no matter what the issue, has a claim on China. It must be recognized as having been in an unusual degree "the maker of the Chinese people."

Confucianism Today.—China has been exalted through Confucius. "The glory of a state may arise from one man," says the last sentence of the *Shu Ching.* The Sage may not be cast aside "like clothes." He has reigned for more than twenty centuries, and whoever seeks to know the mind of China must look behind today with its fruits of alien thought and movements and view with penetration the tokens of his reign. Confucianism [1] is the only ancient culture of magnitude which has maintained itself until today in an unbroken sequence in the life of a great people. We therefore undertake to penetrate the inner character of China by the *ju-chiao,* or "scholar's way," in spite of adverse factors in the distracted present.

While Confucianism to a marked degree in modern times has suffered from general neglect and from its association with debased forms of religion,[2] the reaction from which it suffers today may be traced in bold outline, or by such a graph as a swinging pendulum might make. From its position of neglect, although it

---

[1] The term "Confucianism" is of Western origin and not found in the writings of Chinese scholars prior to the latter part of our seventeenth century, when the Jesuits began to use it. *Ju-chiao* is the Chinese term, historically.

[2] E. Faber, *Doctrines of Confucius,* pp. 110–115.

was the state religion, it swung into new prestige toward the close of the last century. The Christians had been declaring their faith to be the only true religion, thus placing the "three teachings" [3] in the category of false religions. During the 1880 decade the aroused Chinese made numerous attacks upon Christian missionaries and institutions. An alarming situation developed. The Confucianists especially were incensed. Through reaction against Christianity, Confucius who had ranked eight hundred years as "Emperor," was elevated on Dec. 31, 1906, by Imperial Rescript to equal rank with Heaven. The triad was restored which had been worshiped four thousand years before,[4] save that at last there was in it a concrete Man. In spite of the Revolution of 1911, by which the Chinese "Republic" (1911–1927) was inaugurated, and notwithstanding the fact that the *Classics* were eliminated as a required subject in government elementary and primary schools, Confucianism was continued as the state religion. The worship of Confucius was maintained by the first president of the Republic, Yuan Shih-k'ai. There was even some republican thought of making Confucianism compulsory.

The Revolution, however, meant more than the overthrow of the alien Manchu dynasty [5]; it gave occasion for the introduction of experimental theories and methods. Confucianism itself was ultimately challenged. In 1917 its influence was diminished by a thoroughgoing public criticism in the journal *La Jeunesse* by Chen Tu-hsiu and his associates. The young men of China, and not a few young women, for the most part the product of Western education, found among the old Confucian theories many which they deemed intolerable. As the "youth movement" grew, opposition was registered against not only all religions, but against religion itself as deserving no consideration from earnest, practical people. In 1928 the Minister of Education, of the Kuomintang, with its capital in Nanking, ordered the cessation of the annual sacrifices to Confucius. But, a year later, a day was again set for these annual ceremonies. And recently, the Confucian Temple in Nanking has been dedicated as a Memorial Hall to Confucius. In contrast, the Government Memorial to Dr. Sun Yat Sen is assuming proportions larger than the Great Confucian Temple and above any ever accorded even an Emperor's tomb.

---

3 Confucianism, Taoism, and Buddhism. The last two were then semi-official religions, with state subsidies.

4 Heaven-Earth-Man. *Cf.* p. 59, above.

5 See Williams, *Short History*, pp. 472–6. The dynasty has been restored (1934) in Manchukuo. See news of March 1, 1934.

Chinese conservatives cling with tenacity to a comparatively unmodified Confucianism, but their views have little weight. The day, however, is not entirely in the keeping of the radicals, for many moderate progressives are exerting influence. Progressives organized in Peking a "Confucian Church," an attempt not only to renovate the Confucian heritage, but to organize Confucianism into a separate cult. But this does not seem the way out for China. There is small prospect for the success of a sectarian movement. Many progressive Chinese are taking the long look, both backward and forward. The day may be theirs in the end. They are analytical and critical, disposed to distinguish between the religious and the moral elements in Confucianism, and to reconstruct Confucian morality to modern needs. They may at least induce their people to do new things by showing them they have been doing them all along. We may follow them respectfully in their processes, if not in their conclusions, for they are our surest guides to an understanding of the present.

Objections.—The major objections lodged by various Chinese against Confucianism are that it:

(1) is old, of the ancient past, and is therefore presumably decayed;

(2) is feudal and not democratic; at least, it recognizes social classes, with the intelligensia outranking others, and with tradesmen lowest of all;

(3) is not scientific, whether in psychology, politics, or economics;

(4) is suppressive in its conservatism, veritably Victorian in its stress upon honor for one's parents, elders and what is of the past;

(5) is negligent and disdainful of women, children and slaves, withholding from them a just equality of rights with freemen;

(6) has been manifestly impotent in modern times, failing, for example, to prevent the outrage of foot-binding;

(7) is pacifistic in the extreme, making no provision for the use of force even as a means to peace and government;

(8) is primitive in its religious aspects, tolerating sheer superstition in both belief and ritual;

(9) is palpably limited in those positive aspects which at first glance seem valuable, for example, its advocacy of knowledge— knowledge which proves to be something for its own sake.

We may understand the objections of militarists—of whom there are many active in China—to Confucianism, without granting their validity. Are they correct in their assumption that Confucianism is absolutely pacifistic? The revolting youth of China found that Mencius, the great pupil of Confucius, had provided for revolution against unjust rule (see p. 99, below). Is not militaristic objection this, that Confucianism insists upon government for the good of the people, and not for any party? We understand, also, the modern spirit which abolished the old classical examinations as a means of political preferment. The system seemed based upon learning for learning's sake, or, at most, provided knowledge of slight use for government. The memorization of the *Classics* for examination was irrefutable evidence of the theory of knowledge for its own sake. The old examination stalls could no more stand before the presence of modern Western educational method than Alexander I's Great Cathedral of Moscow could stand before the Soviet theory of religion.

We might grant the force of other objections, for example, that Confucianism has kept womanhood in unwonted subjection, and that Confucian morality is embarrassed by association with crude forms of religion. We should be over-hasty, however, were we to grant the cogency of all the objections which we have noticed, without examining patiently the essential meaning of the forms assailed. We might find ourselves denying not only Confucianism, but wider reaches of morality and religion. We are not prepared to do so without closer study. We look, therefore, for whatever permanent and recreative power there is among the many elements we must examine.

The Writings.—1. The "Confucian" *Classics* (five *Ching* and four *Shu*). It is inconceivable that a self-respecting people would destroy [6] its precious source books and greatest literary treasures. Sacred books have proved more durable than nations themselves. While a nation lives, its sacred books endure; when it perishes, the world preserves its literary monument. A people may be indifferent to their sacred writings, but in preserving them, they cherish, even though unwittingly, opportunities for men to reconsider the sources and to recommit themselves to the old ideals. The Chinese are not disposed to destroy their sacred *Classics*. They have pride in them as evidence of early Chinese culture, a national monument. Once indeed there was an attempt to destroy them. The first Emperor,[7] Shih Huang-ti, who con-

---

[6] Milton said that to kill a book is worse than the killing of a man.
[7] That is, the first to assume the title *Huang*, "Emperor," from *Wang*, or "King."

structed the Great Wall, built a new capital city, and sought to consolidate an empire, finding his political reforms blocked by the scholars, ordered (213 B.C.), the destruction of the *Book of History* (*Shu Ching*) and the *Book of Odes* (*Shih Ching*), whose authority was quoted against reform. He decreed capital punishment of all persons who quoted them. His purpose was not fulfilled though copies were burned, and several hundred scholars put to death. The books were in the minds of multitudes left alive. As if in answer to the futile effort, a later emperor in 195 B.C. visited the tomb of the Sage and offered a sacrifice, thus beginning the national cult of the worship of Confucius. The *Classics* returned to favor. They have survived imperial wrath, historical criticism, rationalistic philosophy, popular neglect, and attacks from followers of other faiths.

There are nine of these sacred writings, according to the canonization begun in the time of Confucius. The number has been fixed since 1000 A.D. They are in two sets, one of five, and one of four, and cover a period of time from *c.* 2000 B.C. to the 2nd century, A.D. It is apparent that they are "Confucian" in only an indirect sense.

The "Five" (*Wu Ching*):

1. The *Book of History* (*Shu Ching* [8]), believed to belong to the period from 2000 to 700 B.C. This book is a collection of state papers, memoranda of the speeches of early rulers, and records of conversations between rulers and their ministers. Confucius used *shu* to designate all the "historical" remains of antiquity, in distinction from poems, descriptions of rites, and works on divination, medicine, agriculture and horticulture. An English translation extends to about 250 *octavo* pages.

2. The *Book of Poetry,* or *Odes* (*Shih Ching*),[9] consisting of 305 pieces and the titles of six others. Five "sacrificial odes of Shang" are very ancient, and may be dated about 1800 B.C. There are eleven sacrificial odes of the early Chou dynasty. The rest, odes of various sorts, songs and ballads rather than of a religious character, may be dated within the Chou dynasty as late as *c.* 600 B.C. The whole is equivalent to about one hundred *octavo* pages in English.

3. The *Book of Changes* (*I* [10] *Ching,* or *Yi Ching*), containing a fanciful system of philosophy deduced from the combinations

---

8 In English, *Ching* or *king,* and pronounced as *jing* or *ging,* according to the locality.
9 See *Analects*, XVII, ix, 1–7 for Confucius' comment on some values of the *Odes*.
10 Not to be confused with another "*I*" character, meaning "right."

of the eight Diagrams,[11] each representing a power of nature, such as water, fire, thunder, virtually a book of divination. It is said that Confucius studied the Book of Changes so persistently that the leather strap around the bamboo slips broke three times. The Diagrams are said to have been invented bofore 2000 B.C. by Fu Hsi, who copied the lines from the back of a tortoise. The Book based upon the Diagrams is of uncertain date, but it is pre-Confucian. It is of about the size of the *Shih Ching*.

4. The *Book of Rites* (*Li Chi*[12]), consisting of things to be "remembered" and done precisely at ceremonies, with rules for individual conduct on various occasions. The bulk of its contents dates from before the time of Confucius, although the work took final form in the 2nd century, A.D. It is eight times the size of the *Shih Ching*.

5. *Spring and Autumn* (*Ch'un Ch'iu*), or the *Annals of Lu*. Lu was the native state of Confucius. The book contains the history of the state from 722 to 481 B.C. Confucius himself probably wrote the narrative portions, but a disciple probably wrote the commentary.

The "Four" (*Ssu Shu,* altogether about two hundred *octavo* pages) :

1. The *Analects* of Confucius (the *Lun-Yü,* or Discourses"), a collection of sayings of the Sage and of conversations between him and his disciples. This is the chief source-book for descriptive details of the habits and qualities of Confucius. In its present form it represents the collation of several early editions.

2. The *Great Learning* (*Ta Hsüeh*), a small work once a chapter of the *Li Chi.* It contains some sayings of Confucius, and some commentary. It seems to have been intended for the guidance of a ruler; it is politico-moral philosophy: "to illustrate illustrious virtue, to renovate the people, and to rest in the highest excellence."

3. The *Doctrine of the Mean* (*Chung Yung* or the *Conduct of Life,* a small work, larger than the Great Learning, once a part of the *Li Chi*[13]; the contents, including sayings of Confucius, are attributed to his grandson. The work treats of the human mind as it is in itself, and of its proper expression in accordance with its correct, Heaven-bestowed nature.

4. The *Book of Mencius,* the work of the greatest of the successors of Confucius, who died 289 B.C. He commented upon the

---

[11] See below.
[12] Or *Li Ki.* This is our best source for the religion of the ancient Chinese.
[13] *Cf. Li Chi,* XXVIII.

proper qualities of the righteous ruler, laid down the essentials of a rightly governed state, and entered into controversy with prominent philosophers holding contrary or divergent views of human nature, duty, and government.

These, then, are the *Nine Classics* which bear in some form or other the stamp of Confucius. They are the most important of the vast literature of China. In every generation to come, as in every generation past, leaders of China will draw upon them as a permanent store of Chinese characteristics.

2. Confucius. It seems inconceivable that the personality of the Great Sage should utterly fade from memory and honor, so long as China endures. He is not merely a man; he is an institution. In every city, even the smallest, there is a temple dedicated to him, with a wooden tablet to his memory. While he is not now of official rank as in days gone by, and while many do not worship him today, he is the object of sincere regard, the only man revered by all Chinese. While Confucianism is no longer an imperial cult, or even the official faith of the new Republic, it is still the embodiment of Chinese culture and morality. It exists without organization as a spirit, an idea, a norm, in the social consciousness. To many genuinely religious Chinese it is still their only faith.

Confucius [14] (551–479 B.C.) was born in the petty state of Lu, in the fruitful Shantung section.[15] At that time China was comparatively small, and "barbarians" [16] encroached upon its borders; it consisted of many loosely related states in the eastern basin of the Yellow River; there was no semblance of an "empire" until the 3rd century, B.C. The boy's father, a conspicuous military leader, was very old, but strong and brave. His mother was very young, a second wife which the old soldier had married for the sake of a son to carry on the family name and to worship the ancestral spirits. When the lad was three years of age his father died. He was reared, therefore, by his mother, who lived until he was twenty-two, or twenty-four years old. She had a very religious nature, and the son also seems to have been grave and reverent. As a boy he liked to play at ritual instead of at such games as were then common. He was humane, and especially fond of dogs and horses. Once, for a dead dog of his, he dug a

---

14 As the custom was, he had a "milk-name" when he was a baby, a "school name" later on, and as a youth he was called Chung-ni. A fourth name, K'ung, or K'ung Ch'iu, was given him when he had become great; *k'ung* means "great."

15 This lies between the old and the new mouths of the Yellow River. He was thus a Northerner. *Cf. Doctrine of the Mean*, X, 1–5.

16 See *Analects*, III, 5; *Great Learning*, X, 15.

grave and provided a shroud of silk lest the ground pollute the body.[17] He was accustomed to fish with a line and never a net, and he shot at birds only on the wing (*Ana.* VII, xxvi). He was fond of asking questions, and had a retentive memory. He was honest, earnest, and dependable; punctilious in social relations, and precise in the discharge of his duties.

The Life of Confucius.—His education was begun with a local magistrate. At the age of fourteen or fifteen he had mastered what his teacher had to offer, and had developed a decided "bent toward learning." He was a learner all his life, and looked on all men as his teachers. At the age of seventeen he was forced by poverty in his home to take a post in Lu, his native state, as clerk of revenue. At nineteen he married a bride selected by his mother for him from a family in the neighboring state of Sung. He had one daughter, and a son named Li.[18] He was advanced in public office, given charge of the Lu state granaries, with some such power as the Hebrew Joseph had in Egypt.

Sometime between Confucius' twenty-second and his twenty-seventh year, while yet a state official, he opened his home to pupils and became a teacher. For about a decade he had many pupils who, in spite of the rigor of his requirements and the severity of his methods, seem to have been quite devoted to him. He never refused admission to a pupil even though the proffered fee was merely a bundle of dried fish (*Ana.* VII, vii). He allowed all pupils to remain who were eager for learning and the development of their mental powers (*Ana.* VII, viii). He gave instruction in history, social propriety, literature, science, music, and government; or, in his own words, in "letters," "ethics," "devotion of soul," and "truthfulness" (*Ana.* VII, xxiv).

At thirty-five, Confucius gave up his work for the state to devote the next fifteen years to education and research. He probably gave up his family also, at least, he separated from his wife, for his studies. During this period ancient music and its composers constituted a major line of study. At fifty—when, as he says, he "knew the decrees of Heaven"—he took public office once again in his own state of Lu. There is some indication that he may have been challenged to put his political and moral theories into practice. If not for this reason, he may have sought office to test his views. At any rate, his interest was always in living issues, and whatever he advocated had a bearing upon real life.

---

[17] We scarcely think this may have been a sacrifice to Earth.
[18] This *li* means "carp."

He was successively assistant-superintendent of public works and chief justice of the state. Remarkable things are said (by his partisans) to have been achieved by his administration, such as the utter security of private property. Nevertheless, his administration finally came to grief. Some say that his success had aroused the enmity of neighboring states, and that one of them at least (the state of Ts'e) took measures to undermine his influence (*cf. Ana.* XVIII, iv). Or, was the failure due to the ineffectiveness of some major theory, or to the inability of the man as a practical administrator? One of his theories was that the chief business of the state is not revenue, but the proper "functioning" of all the citizens (*Ana.* XII, xi; *cf. Great Learning,* X, xxii, xxiii), a theory which may have been slightly idealistic. There was, indeed, some lack of proper functioning; internal discord arose, and Confucius found himself after four or five years in office an exile from Lu. He went to a neighboring state,[19] where he asked for a trial of his program, promising complete reform in three years. Given a year's trial as he requested, his program seems to have been even less successful than in Lu, and his official connection with this state was broken. He became a wanderer for a dozen years, preaching rather than practicing reform. It may have been asking too much of any program that it prove itself effective in a generation so marked by political confusion and low ideals.

In spite of adversity, however, Confucius never lost his supreme confidence: in himself as Heaven's agent; in the power of his doctrines to produce good government; and in the power of good government to produce order in society and the reformation of human nature itself. At the age of sixty-eight he was recalled to his native state, there to spend his remaining four years and to complete editing five of the nine *Classics* (the "five" in the list above). The Wise Man "withered away like a plant." He died in great discouragement, not on his own account, but with regret that no ruler had taken him as his master. He died without fear, and his confidence was justified by succeeding centuries. The details of his career are difficult to establish precisely —there are contradictions and discrepancies in the records—but we have before us the gist of the story and have no need to depend upon exact details beyond those given incidentally in the records. The final place of any great man in history may properly depend, at last, upon the vividness of imagination and the power of will of the men who come after him. The past, if it have enduring

[19] Probably Ts'e.

qualities, inevitably gets a wealth of meaning from the centuries succeeding—and including always the living present.

Confucius gave his attention to the actual situation in which he found himself. The political confusion of the times gave him a dominating interest in this life rather than the next (on the other hand, it made his contemporary, Lao-tze, other-worldly). In his day luxury and debauch were rife and the nobles stronger than the Emperor.[20] With a primary concern for practical living, he sought harmony among the petty states, and their unification into a harmonious empire. He sought what Justinian, Mohammed, and Akbar later sought, namely, unity of empire; but, unlike them, he lacked the necessary political authority and force. He was, as a legendary "prophecy" had it at his birth, only "a throne-less king."

In place of political authority, conquest of arms and legislation, he offered a philosophy of government and life, a system of politics and ethics. He formulated an ethical code for men and rulers alike. Human conduct was his primary concern. He included a touch of religion, but not as a separate consideration. Religion to Confucius was scarcely other than "moral law reduced to a system" (*Chung Yung,* I, i.). Religious objects were included on prudential grounds and viewed indirectly through the living present. Confucius had a profound belief in an all pervasive and all controlling moral law, which was at once "the ordinance of Heaven" and "the law of our being." This moral law was not so much of a separate, divine origin, as in man by reason of human nature's heavenly origin; it was an element within man's own original consciousness, which human experience might verify. Such was the philosophy by which men were to live, whereby the confusion of the times might be resolved into complete order.

At the death of Confucius,[21] his disciples, who had never lost faith in him, mourned for him the customary three years. Mencius records that one of them remained *six* years at the grave (*Book of Mencius,* 3:1). In due time they and new disciples set about the preservation of his works and exaltation of his name. His sayings were collected (the Book of *Analects*) and commentaries written on his doctrines (the *Great Learning,* the *Mean,* and *Mencius*). No doctrine of divine verbal inspiration of scripture was evolved by this Confucian "school"; the books made their way to preëminence on other grounds. The process of "canoniza-

20 *Cf.* the time of Charles V in Europe.
21 *Cf. Li Chi,* I, ii, 20.

tion," as we have said, was slow. The admission of the *Book of Mencius* was long delayed; but ultimately the "four" books took their place beside the "five" which the Sage himself had edited.

In spite of indication that Confucius had an humble (or self-depreciatory) estimate of himself (*Ana.* V, xxvii), his followers thought him extraordinary. He claimed to be only a learner, a "transmitter, not an author" or creative thinker (*Ana.* VII, i, ii). His confidence was in his mission (*Ana.* XIV, xxxvii, 2). He acknowledged certain personal deficiencies (*Ana.* VII, iii, xxxii, xxxiii; IX, xv), such as inability to put wisdom into practice, to alter evil, to do his duty fully toward his elders and the dead, and to shun excess in wine.[22] He said he "had not reached the level of the ideal man." In the *Chung Yung* is a record that he denied intention of so acting as "to be mentioned with honor in future ages" (XI, 1). While he remarked that "wealth and honor obtained unworthily are as a fleeting cloud" (*Ana.* VII, xv); and that a "noble man is pained over his own incompetency, but not pained that others ignore him" (*Ana.* I, xvi); he held that if virtue is the root of man's conduct, wealth and fame [23] are among the fruits.

His followers esteemed Confucius because "he had no foregone conclusions, no arbitrary predeterminations, no obstinacy, and no egoism (*Ana.* IX, iv). They deemed him far above the appreciation of ordinary men: "The wall of the Master is several fathoms high. . . . They are few who find the door" (*Ana.* XIX, xxiii, 3, 4); "Our Master cannot be attained to," any more than the heavens can be climbed (*Ana.* XIX, xxv, 3). They thought if he had been a *ruler*,[24] he would have established the people, won their loyalty, and made them happy and harmonious (*Ana.* XIX, xxv, 4). The *Chung Yung* (XXX, 2; XXXI, 1–4) ascribes to Confucius certain qualities ascribed in the *Li Chi* (XXVIII, 49–56) to the Ideal Man, and the Master thereby becomes endued with far-reaching intelligence and all-embracing knowledge; a generous, mild, energetic, enduring, self-adjusted, correct individual, the "equal of Heaven." To Mencius, he was a full-rounded combination of strength and wisdom, and a model of propriety. "There never was another Confucius" (*Mencius,* Bk. II, 5). Later centuries further honored him, first as "emperor" and last as virtually "divine." As early as 195 B.C. (Han dynasty) he

---

22 Although a disciple called him "temperate" (*Ana.* I, x, 2).
23 By "fame" is meant distinction, not notoriety (*cf. Ana.* XII, xx, 4).
24 Most "sages" were rulers also.

was officially worshiped.[25] The distinguished social reformer would have been amazed, and perhaps reproachful at the sacrificial ceremonies attending his commemoration, but he might agree in principle, at least, with the manifest intention of the present Nation to honor him as a sage and moralist.

Confucian Teachings.—3. Confucian *Morality*. From among a number of philosophies, concerning which he kept silent, Confucius "looking to antiquity" formulated his own system of practical morality and polity, which became in time the classic standard of the state. The Han dynasty (206 B.C.–221 A.D.) declared the *Ju-chiao* to be the sole permissible doctrine and the embodiment of the national view of man and the world. By its adoption virtually as the state religion, it doubtless suffered some depreciation as a moral code; yet China has had no other system of morality.

Confucian morality is characterized by a keen sense of *duty* in accord with the *law* of man's *nature*. "He upon whom a moral duty (*jen*) devolves, should not give way" to anyone (*Ana.* XV, xxxv), for duty is "a personal affair requiring personal performance." In the *Chung Yung* it is declared that if we would fulfill the law of our being, we must follow the moral law; that it is a law whose operation we cannot escape; that our moral being is the great reality of existence, and moral order is the universal law of the world; and that when true moral being and moral order are realized, the multiplicity of things becomes a cosmos, and all parts attain their full growth and development.[26] Confucianism recognizes the moral obligation as the fundamental basis of the social order, and makes the perfection of moral conduct its greatest, if not its only, aim. This purpose gives to the system a high degree of durability. It is fundamental to Confucian theory that man by nature is good, that through obedience to the moral law man maintains his natural goodness, and that by concentric waves of influence, men effect through self-development the control and welfare of the family, the community and the state (*Great Learning,* especially *paragraphs* 7–10).[27] In this view the moral law issues first in "the cultivation of the person."

Virtues.—*Jen.* The Confucian symbol for the moral law is the

---

25 An emperor in the 17th century sustained the Jesuit missionaries' contention that the worship of the Sage was merely *honorific.*—Williams, *op. cit.,* p. 235.

26 Ku Hung Ming, *The Conduct of Life,* pp. 14ff.

27 Compare this with Emerson's statement, that "the moral law lies at the center of Nature and radiates to the circumference; it is the pith and marrow of every substance, every relation and every process."

pre-Confucian *Jen* (*cf.* p. 63, above). The ideograph represents a man from whom extend horizontally two parallel lines,— he is "on the level." If the *Analects* alone were drawn upon,[28] this might be a just composite view of *Jen,* or "Virtue." *Jen* is perfect virtue (VII, vi, 3), love for all men (I, vi; XII, xxii, 1), the very foundation of the unselfish life (I, ii, 2), the quality which a man of honor never disregards (IV, v, 2, 3). It is accessible (VII, xxix), personal (XV, xxxv), more than skill at one's tasks (XIX, xv), or mere loyalty (V, xviii), or success (VI, xx). One who loves virtue esteems nothing above it, and whoever has it finds in it strength sufficient for the day's work (IV, vi, 1, 2). He is cautious and slow of speech (XII, iii, 2) avoiding artful words and an ingratiating manner (I, iii). One may rest in virtue (IV, ii), free of anxiety (IX, xxviii; XIV, xxx), while without virtue he is soon crushed by adversity (IV, ii). One who has his mind on virtue does no evil (IV, iv); he does not do to others what he would not have them do to him (XII, ii).[29] *Jen* is the sum of all good qualities, for example, gravity of demeanor, earnestness, firmness, kindness, magnanimity, dependability, modesty, simplicity, and sincerity (XVII, vi; XIII, xix, xxvii; XIX, vi). It should be exercised in humility (XIV, ii), with caution and prudence (VI, xxiv; *cf.* XVII, xxi, 2); yet there are occasions when life itself is better sacrificed than virtue (XIV, xvii, xviii; XV, viii). It was possibly sly humor when Confucius said he had never seen a man die in virtue's path (XV, xxxiv). Several sayings directly indicate how hard the Sage deemed it to be virtuous: he mentioned a disciple who could obey virtue three months at a time (VI, v), and yet commended anyone who could be perfect for a single day (XII, i, 1). Yet virtue in the Confucian view is something which a man has and exercises naturally (that is, through *teh,* "moral excellence" shown spontaneously, without one's being able to restrain it). One saying bears upon religion, indicating that a virtuous man is worshipful (III, iii, "A man who is not virtuous, what has he to do with worship . . . and with temple music?").

Jen, as the sum of all the virtues, includes in formal analysis

---

28 While it is said that *Jen* was a subject of which the Master seldom spoke (IX, i), the *Analects,* especially Bk. XII, include over half a hundred references to it. Wei Liaoweng (1178–1237) suggested a solution of the contradiction by making *two* sentences of *Ana.* IX, 1, instead of one. We should get this translation, as a result, "The Master rarely spoke of profit (*li*). But he expounded the appointments (*ming*) and perfect virtue (*jen*)," instead of Legge's translation, "The subjects of which the Master seldom spoke: profitableness (*li*), the appointments [of Heaven] (*ming*) and perfect virtue (*jen*). See *JAOS,* 53–4, pp. 347–351.

29 This is the so-called "Silver Rule," yet often Orientals state things positively through the negative.

jen-i, "benevolent justice," *jen-chih,* "benevolent understanding,"
jen-hsin, "benevolent heart," etc. It includes:

(1) *I,* that which is right to do, duty toward one's neighbor,
loyalty to rulers and the state, faithfulness to one's family, and
justice to mankind. *I* is the outward manifestation of *Jen.* It represents the standard of right (I, xiii; XII, x, 1; XIV, xiii, 2; XV,
xvi, xvii) [30] which to see and not do is cowardice (II, xxiv, 2; *cf.*
VII, iii). One on the side of *I* "has neither predilections nor
prejudices" (IV, x). Knowledge of *I* is a quality of the wise man
(IV, xvi), one of the four characteristics of "the Ideal Man"
(V, xv), and a prerequisite to general esteem (XII, xx, 5).
Possessed by a ruler it insures the submission of the people (XIII,
iv, 3). "The noble man takes the right (*I*) as his foundation principle, reduces it to practice with all courtesy, carries it out with
modesty, and renders it perfect with sincerity" (XV, xvii). *I* is
of more worth than courage, for courage without *I* brings rebellion
on the part of men of the superior class, and makes men of the
lower order robbers (XVII, xxiii). *I* requires service to one's
fellows, the acceptance of public office (*cf.* XVII, i), and the
doing of what one's station demands of him, although he may be
"aware that right principles have ceased to make progress"
(XVIII, vii). The first thought of a servant of the state in the
presence of personal gain should be prompted by *I,*—"whether it
be right" (XIX, i).

(2) *Chih,* knowledge, perception, understanding, experience,
wisdom, and insight. *Chih,* is, in particular, knowledge of men
(XII, xxii; IV, vii; *cf. Chung Yung* XX, 7.) Of himself Confucius said, "I will not grieve that men do not know me; I will
grieve that I do not know men" (I, xvi; *cf.* IV, xiv). At fifty he
claimed to have knowledge of the laws of Heaven (II, iv). The
acquisition and exercise of *chih* affords pleasure—this is the first
saying of Confucius recorded in the *Analects.* True knowledge is,
"when you know a thing to recognize that you know it, and, when
you do not know, to know that you do not" (II, xvii). It amounts
to wisdom when one takes account of his surroundings (IV, i).
It is wisdom to "devote oneself earnestly to one's duty to humanity, and, while respecting the spirits (the *kuei-shen*), to avoid
them" (VI, xx). Those who possess *chih* are free from doubt, as
the brave are from fear (IX, xxviii; XIV, xxx; *cf.* XII, iv).
The man of *chih* is willing to impart his wisdom to those who can
profit by it, and to deny it to those who cannot be enlightened

---

[30] All references are to the *Analects,* unless otherwise specified.

(XV, vii), for possession of it gives him an obligation to teach it (cf. II, xi). *Chih* without moral character is of no permanence or value (XV, xxxii). *Chih* gained in study is better than mere speculation (XV, xxx), for "love of knowledge without a love to learn finds itself obscured by loose speculation" (XVII, viii).

(3) *Hsin* (pronounced shin), truth, especially truth in speech (cf. I, vi; XIV, xxxiii), confidence, fidelity, reliability, belief, sincerity.[31] The character *hsin* is composed of one for "man" and one for "word,"—man and his word. He uses no second, or double word. Confucius had much to say about *hsin* (VII, xxiv). He insists that a scholar must have it (I, viii, 2), and examined himself daily to see if he had exercised it in his intercourse with friends (I, iv). *Hsin* is indispensable for all, as necessary as the yoke-bar to the ox-cart, and the horse-collar to the carriage (II, xxii). In government it goes with attention to business, economy in expenditure, love of the people, and their employment on public works[32] at the proper seasons (I, v). Consistent with his optimistic view of human nature, he deemed it a fairly common quality of men (V, xxvii). He had confidence that "the man of unwavering sincerity and love of moral discipline, will keep to the death his excellent principles" (VIII, xiii, 1); that *hsin* as a ruling principle of life will beget sincerity in others (XII, x, 1; XIII, iv, 3; XX, i, 9); and that with *hsin* one might get on even with "barbarians" (XV, v). *Hsin* will make perfect what is right, *i.e., I* (XV, xvii), but has no value as mere affirmation (XIX, ii). Steadfastness is its sign, as development is in itself evidence of virtue. The *Chung Yung* says of *ch'êng* (=*hsin*), "It is the way of Heaven, is man's objective; who has it, hits the right mark without effort and apprehends intuitively. . . Who attains to it chooses what is good and holds it fast" (XX, 18). *Ch'êng* is that by which self-completion is accomplished, "a most excellent thing" (*ibid.*, XXV, 1, 2; XXVI, 1). *Ch'êng* never faileth. Whoever has it may expect to "assist the powers of Heaven and Earth and make himself a third with them (*ibid.*, XXII).

(4) *Li* bulks large in the *Nine Classics,* especially the *Li Chi* and the *Analects.* "The observances of *Li*" was one of the three subjects, with History and the Odes, on which Confucius "frequently discoursed" (*Ana.* VII, xvii; cf. XVI, xiii, 1–5). He inti-

---

[31] A synonym *Ch'êng* is used in the *Chung Yung* for "sincerity." See also p 65.

[32] The C.W.A. program of President F. D. Roosevelt has an ancient Chinese precedent.

mated that a man could have "no standing" unless he studied the
Li Chi (*Ana.* VIII, ii, 1, 2).

Li has a wide variety of meaning: politeness, propriety, ceremony, reverence, ritual temper, worship—not merely outward
form but inner character. *Li* is properly an expression of inner
jen; it is *i* (duty) done with *chih* (insight) and *hsin,* sincerity.
Both the symbol and the quality are ancient (*cf.* p. 64, above).
In Sinæan times it had, perhaps, a more religious connotation. Confucius took it to express a moral quality and exercise.
He seems to have spared no pains either to ignore or to suppress
religious elements which preceded him.[33] By a sort of destiny,
however, the times which followed took revenge by making *Li* less
moral and more formal than he had intended. History would
indicate that bare morality is neither self-sufficient nor all-suf-
ficient. While Confucius attempted[34] to balance the outward, appropriate expression and the inner, benevolent, and respectful
spirit, he disregarded a behest of Heaven, and Li became too
easily politeness and convention. Before the canon of the *Classics*
closed, *Li* had become the supreme and all-inclusive virtue, with
a pronounced tendency as formal "propriety" to ignore both
religion and the moral law. Confucius advocated ceremony for its
morally beneficial effects on human character. He talked of "man,
the ideal man, in perfect adjustment to the universe of men and
things"; but in effect the adjustment which he advocated was
attained through ceremony. By his own disposition, lacking in
imagination, by the vagueness of his program for society, by his
failure to provide religion for his people, he gave to formalism
unimpeded opportunity. *Li* triumphed over *Jen.*

According to the *Li Chi,* which, of course, the *Ju-chiao* edited,
here are materials for a view of *Li:*[35] "Always and in everything
let there be reverence; with the deportment grave as when one is
thinking, and with speech composed and definite. . . . Pride
should not be allowed to grow; the desires should not be indulged; the will should not be gratified to the full; pleasure
should not be carried to excess. Men of talents and virtue can be

---

[33] Confucius "deliberately omitted from his teaching a considerable part of the
ancient religious faith of his people."—F. E. A. Krause in Clemen, *op. cit.,* p. 85.

[34] His own view is set forth in the *Analects,* where he emphasizes: naturalness,
provided it be not self-conscious (I, xii); simplicity (III, iv); the spirit of reverence
(III, xxvi); respect consistent with good taste (I, xiii; VI, xxv; VIII, ii); restraint
upon individual conduct (IX, x). He commends *Li:* as indispensable in the formation
of human character (VIII, viii; XII, i; XIV, xiii: XV, vii; XX, iii); as the means
of good government (II, iii; XIII, iii, iv; XIV, xliv; XV, xxxii): and as the means
of brotherhood among men "within the four seas" (XII, v),—four imaginary seas!

[35] It is a symbol of religious import. The oldest Chinese dictionary represents *Li*
as "an act whereby we serve spiritual beings and obtain happiness." The sign for
"spiritual beings" entered into the ideographs, also, for spirits, sacrifices, and prayers.

familiar with others and yet respect them; can stand in awe of others and yet love them. . . . Do not seek for victory in small contentions; do not seek for more than your proper share. . . . In observing the rules of propriety, what is right should be followed. . . . To cultivate one's person and fulfill one's words is called good conduct. . . . The course of duty, virtue, benevolence, and righteousness cannot be fully carried out without the rules of propriety . . . nor can the duties between ruler and minister, high and low, elder brother and younger, be determined. . . . nor can majesty and dignity be shown in assigning the different places at court, in the government of the armies, and in discharging the duties of office so as to secure the operation of the laws; nor can there be the proper gravity and sincerity in presenting the offerings to spiritual beings on occasions of supplication, thanksgiving, and the various sacrifices. Therefore, the superior man is respectful and reverent, assiduous in his duties and not going beyond them, retiring and yielding, thus illustrating the principle of propriety." [36] To read further would be to learn of the multitudinous details of *Li's* bearing upon life and conduct: for example, giving gifts in return for gifts; warming the parents' bed in winter and cooling it in summer; carrying a stool for an elder to sit on, if one goes to ask the elder's counsel; keeping the eyes cast down when entering a door; never touching a woman's hand in greeting; not marrying a wife of the same surname with himself (but *cf. Ana.* VII, xxx); not to make a noise in eating; if presenting cooked food, taking sauce and pickles for it; while fasting, not to listen to music; solicitude always for parental welfare (*cf. Ana.* IV, xxi), such as inquiries about their health, instant obedience, encouragement to eat, admonishing them, if necessary, with bated breath, bland aspect, and gentle voice (*cf. Ana.* IV, xviii); innumerable items, besides, extending throughout the range of private and public life, possessing values great and small, even trivial, save among people to whom propriety as such is highly regarded.

Filial Devotion.—*Hsiao.* The keen sense of duty which characterized Confucius (see p. 78, above) and which the Chinese in general have possessed found its chief expression in what is known as "filial piety" (*hsiao;* this symbol is composed of a sign for "young man" and, above it, a sign for "old man,"—the aged supported by the young, and forefathers reverenced by the living sons). The social inequalities observed in China since 1000 B.C.,

---

[36] *Li* is the key word in each of these expressions.

at the latest, furnished fruitful ground for the development of
hsiao. The performance of filial piety became primarily a matter
of the obedience of this individual or that to some person or
power above him (*cf. Ana.* II, v). There was on the part of the
superior persons or powers the reciprocal responsibility of con-
descension and justice toward those beneath them. It was a
matter of relations between persons and powers, and the duties
devolving upon persons and powers in view of their station.
Filial piety is discussed in terms of five (or, six, or, seven) "reciprocal" relationships, namely,

(1) Emperor-subject, or administrator-citizen,
(2) Father-son (mother-daughter is only implicit, not ex-
     pressed),
(3) Elder brother–younger brother (sisters are not men-
     tioned),
(4) Master-servant (man-servants and maid-servants),
(5) Friend-friend (the nearest approach to equality, but with
     probable differences of age, with their implications),
(6) Husband-wife, and
(7) Host-guest.

The first five constitute the traditional, or classical, relationships
(but *cf. Chung Yung,* XX, 8). In a sense, the root of *hsiao* is the
family and the home, where one is expected "to serve well one's
father and mother." It begins with respect for one's parents, devotion to them, and the care of the body which they have given, and
extends, by the regulation of oneself and the attainment of true
character and unselfishness, to all the relationships of life (*cf.
Ana.* I, ii, and commentary). The son is "filial" who while his
father lives, marks his tendencies, and when his father is dead,
marks his conduct, and who does not change from his father's
ways for three years (*Ana.* I, xi),—the season of morning. Once
in direct reply to the question of the meaning *hsiao,* Confucius said
it is "not being disobedient," adding "While parents live, serve
them with decorum; when they are dead bury them, and sacrifice
to them, with decorum" (II, v). *Hsiao* required of the young that
they assume the burden of anything to be done (II, viii), especially
the providing of food for the family.

It is natural that filial devotion to the living should find extension in continued regard and homage toward those who have
died. Confucius recognized the propriety of filial offerings to

the spirits of the departed (*Ana*. VIII, xxi). To this extent, at least, he encouraged the continuance of the worship of ancestral spirits, which had prevailed in China from the earliest times. In fact, this type of religion was the only type left by him for the common people of China. He formulated a *state* cult of morality and of the imperial ancestors, and ordained for the *common people* filial piety and the worship of their family spirits.

The claims of filial piety are adequately set forth in many of the *Classics,* including the *Analects* to which we have already referred. In the *Book of History* (*Shu Ching*) mention is made of Shun, *c*. 1000 B.C., the successor of the great king Yao, who, although the son of "an obstinately unprincipled father," with an insincere step-mother and an arrogant half-brother, was able, by filial piety, to live in harmony with them, and to lead them gradually to self-discipline and goodness. This character commended him to Yao, who only—says Confucius—responded to the standard of Heaven, and he (Shun) became an ideal ruler (*cf. Ana*. VIII, xx). But among all the writings there is one in particular devoted entirely to filial piety. This is the *Hsiao Ching,* or *Book of Filial Duty,* consisting of eighteen short chapters, culled out from various sources and arranged soon after the death of Confucius. Some Chinese have contended that it really antedates Confucius and that he styled it a "classic" (*ching*). There can be no question that it represents ancient ideals; *hsiao* is one of the oldest ideographs. The book has been a favorite with emperors. It describes the "perfect virtue" of the ancient kings as "filial piety," and calls it "the root of all virtue, out of which grows all moral teaching." It carries its subject throughout all the classes of society and variations of human station, applying the virtue to kings, princes, ministers, and the common people, in their respective dealings with the "three powers" (Heaven, Earth, and Man), government, and the family.

Very late in Chinese history (say *c*. 1500 A.D.) there were composed twenty-four stories in illustration of filial virtue as described in the *Hsiao Ching* and elsewhere. These "twenty-four examples" became a part of the instruction thereafter given in Chinese schools [87] (until the recent order of the Kuomintang that they be no longer taught). The stories began with the "preëminent" Shun and ran in point of time down to 1200 A.D. Among the paragons of piety were the emperor Wên who during a three-year illness of his mother never left her bedside, and tasted first all the soups

[87] See Ivan Chen, *The Book of Filial Duty.*

and medicines prepared for her; Yen, who disguised himself in deer-skin and endured hardship in the forests in search of deer's milk for his parents; Chiang Ko, who hired himself out as a common laborer to support his widowed mother; Huang Hsiang, who cooled his father's bed in summer, and in winter warmed the bedding with his own body; Wang Hsiang, who melted the lake-ice with the heat of his own body in order to procure fish for his step-mother, who had no affection for him; and the lad, Wu Mêng, who went to bed early and allowed legions of mosquitoes to attack him, thereby diverting them from his parents, who, too poor to buy a net, slept in peace, nevertheless. A fairly full and complete description of filial duty is attributed to Confucius himself by the canonical edition of the *Hsiao Ching:* "The service which a filial son does to his parents is as follows,—in his general conduct toward them he manifests the utmost reverence; in his nourishing of them he seeks to give them the utmost pleasure; when they are ill, he feels the greatest anxiety; in mourning for them when they are dead, he exhibits every demonstration of grief (*cf. Li Chi,* II, 19); in sacrificing to them, he displays the utmost solemnity."

While the obligation of "filial piety" pertains to the whole round of social relationships, it pertains primarily and most of all to the family itself,[38] particularly to the relation of a son to his parents (*cf. Ana.* II, vii). It can be seen, therefore, that *hsiao* is the principle of family solidarity, whose value the fundamental place of the family as the unit in the Chinese social system tended to exaggerate. It tended, furthermore, to make the virtuous man an ideal *son* rather than an ideal *man.* This lent enhanced value to *hsiao* in comparison with *jen:* jen, the "perfect virtue" of the *man,* and *hsiao,* the "perfect virtue" of the *son.* Chinese of the present day, especially the leaders of the Kuomintang, see, therefore, in *hsiao* a handicap in any scheme of moral renovation. They blame China's backwardness upon "filial piety," which, however virtuous once under certain circumstances, lost its virtue and became a force for conservatism, reaction and stagnation.

The Superman.—There are other aspects of Confucian morals. These are, however, not separate and independent items, but explicit signs,—"small virtues,"—of the moral substance represented by benevolence (*jen*), duty (*i*), knowledge (*chih*), sincerity (*hsin*), propriety (*li*), and filial piety (*hsiao*), which themselves

---

38 "The great exercise of virtue is in serving one's relatives."—*Chung Yung,* XX, 5.

constitute the body and spirit of Chinese traditional morality and religion.[39] Filial piety itself was in essence merely man's supreme duty (i), even as duty, knowledge, sincerity, and propriety were all component parts or manifestations of *jen*. Confucius himself meant no more than this when, in reply to the question, "Is there one word which may serve as a rule of practice for all one's life?" he said, "Is not *reciprocity* or sympathy (*shu*) [40] such a word? What you do not want done to yourself, do not do to others" (*Ana.* XV, xxiii; V, xi; XII, ii; *Grt. Lrng,* X, 2; *Chung Yung,* XIII, 3; *Li Chi,* XXVIII, 1, 32). Reciprocity was *jen* applied especially to the "five relationships" (see p. 22, above), and these again are the fields of operation of *hsiao*. When he speaks of bravery, he conditions it with right and propriety (*Ana.* XVII, xxiii; VIII, ii), and he associates loyalty with reciprocity (*Ana.* IV, xv, "conscientiousness to self and consideration for others" are "one all-pervading principle").

In a composite picture of the *Superior Man* (the virtuous, ideal, perfect man) we may behold the virtues in their proper combination. Such a person is referred to at least eighty-eight times in the *Analects* alone. In him nature and training are proportionately blended (VI, xvi); he takes the right as his foundation principle, reduces it to practice with all courtesy, carries it out with modesty, and renders it perfect with sincerity (XV, xvii); he seeks in himself what he wants (XV, xx); upholds his dignity without striving (XV, xxi); in his bearing he avoids rudeness and heedlessness; in his expression he is sincere, and in the tone of his conversation he keeps aloof from vulgarity and impropriety (VIII, iv); he is widely versed in letters (VI, xxv) and qualified in music (XI, xxv), stands unshaken by any emergency (VIII, vi), is free from anxiety, doubt and fear (XIV, xxx), bears want unshaken (XV, i; *cf.* VI, ix) because his mind is not on eating, nor on poverty (XV, xxi), is not lustful, nor quarrelsome, nor covetous (XVI, vii); he holds in awe the divine will, the great, and the precepts of the sages (XVI, viii), observes distinctly, apprehends clearly, is kindly in appearance, respectful in manner, conscientious in speech, earnest in the discharge of duty, ready to take advice, curbs his anger, and takes no gain without right (XVI, x); has concern for filial piety and brotherly love (I, ii), enhances his humanity by friendship (XII, xxiv), is broad-minded and not partisan (II, xiv), practices what he preaches (II, xiii), is not

[39] Confucius distinguished between great and small virtues (*Ana.* XIX, xi; *Chung Yung,* XXX, 3).
[40] *Cf.* p. 65, above.

an automaton (II, xii), never disregards virtue (IV, v), does not meddle in other men's private affairs (XVII, xxiv), helps the needy (VI, iii), and holds all men as his brothers (XII, v, because he is reverential).

The *Chung Yung* adds several elements to this composite, showing that the Superior Man is also watchful over himself when alone, has no stirrings of pleasure, anger, sorrow, or joy, but rests in mental equilibrium, embodying the course of the mean; feels no regret, though he be unknown and unregarded by the world; corrects himself and seeks for nothing from men; reposefully awaits destiny; cherishes the past, knows the present, properly evaluates propriety, is not proud in high position, nor insubordinate in low; does what is proper to the station in which he is (how incomparable as a short definition of a gentleman— one who knows his place and keeps it!); dislikes to speak of men's faults, dislikes underlings who slander their superiors (*cf. Ana.* XVII, xxiv); does not abandon his course mid-way; and his way is that of Heaven and Earth and all things. In simpler phrase, this hero, sage and *uebermensch* embodies benevolence, duty, knowledge, sincerity, propriety, filial piety, and reciprocity; repays injury with justice, and kindness with kindness (XIV, xxxvi).[41] He stands in the center of things and does not lean; is in harmony with the universe. The *Chung Yung,* which is equivalent to Book XXVIII of the *Li Chi,* is virtually an essay on the Superior Man, and is an admirable summary of Confucian doctrine.[42] Indeed, the conception of the Superior Man is the one specific formulation of the Confucian ethical ideal. It is the center and circumference of morality.[43] The self is the first consideration, but self-development and self-realization are attainable only when the individual is poised, with Heaven, Earth, and all things in perfect adjustment. This is all very ideal indeed,[44] and perhaps a trifle theoretical.[45]

The Sage Evaluated.—Confucius, in spite of his theoretical idealism, accommodated his moral code to many of the conditions prevailing in his day. Although he accepted distinctions of class

[41] Lao-tze, an older (?) contemporary of Confucius, urged men to "repay injury with kindness," to return good for evil.—*Tao Teh Ching,* 30, 63.

[42] See J. Legge, *Confucius,* pp. 282–320; L. A. Lyall, *The Chung Yung;* M. M. Dawson, *The Ethics of Confucius,* pp. 1–47.

[43] *Cf.* "Illini" (whence Illinois) which, according to Hennepin, signified "a complete, finished and perfect man, imbued with the spirit and bravery of the men of every nation that ever lived."

[44] *Cf. Li Chi,* VII, 1, 2.

[45] Possibly for this reason the Chinese have confused—or identified?—two expressions, "a very virtuous individual" and "an idle fellow." At any rate, the two differing ideographs *sound* alike on a Chinese tongue (*cf.* Giles, *Chinese Dictionary,* No. 4344).

and rank in the social structure (*Ana.* I, viii; XII, xi; XIII, xx; *Chung Yung,* XIV, 1–3; XIX, 4), he seemed to imply that they might be abolished by means of learning (*Ana.* XV, xxxviii). He may have edited or composed a work, Bk. VII, of the *Li Chi,* describing an ideal, brotherly republic in actual operation during the days of primitive simplicity, but he held that inequalities of lot have their proper basis in the moral law. He certainly provided, contrary to antiquity, for something other than government by the voice of the people (*Ana.* VIII, ix, xiv), and held that some men could not learn (VI, xix; XVII, iii). He described the inferior man in contrast with the superior. In general, he took the ancient view of woman as an inferior in both station and capacity, as intended to "follow the man," whether father, elder brother, husband, or son, as circumstances might successively determine. His family ideal tolerated polygamy and concubinage (the Oriental "family" is more comprehensive than the Western), thus establishing distinctions and a double standard of morality within the household. Actual marriage, however, was to this extent a mutuality, that the wife received her husband's rank and was to be the object of his respect and love.[46] Active virtue, as Confucius said, roots in the relations of the sexes.[47]

Confucius held a very interesting theory regarding the place of music and poetry in life and government. It was to him normal and fitting that man should be moved by "the concourse of sweet sounds," and thus be prevented from "treasons, strategems and spoils." The symbol for "pleasure," or "joy" (*lo*) is a big drum with a small drum on either side of it, and all three resting on a frame. A certain tone or reading of this symbol signifies "music" (*yüeh,* or *yo*). Music is thus linked with pleasure. The foundation of all music, according to the Sage, is "harmony," in the absence of which chimes, strings, bells, and drums produce only "noise" (*cf. Ana.* XVII, xi). Propriety (*li*) and music are "brothers," since both depend upon harmony. When the two symbols, "propriety and music," are used together, they may be understood to mean "civilization," or the "arts" (*Ana.* XI, i). Confucius once indicated the process of character education as beginning with the Odes, or *Book of Poetry* (*cf. Chung Yung* IX, i), being established by propriety and perfected by music (*Ana.* VIII, viii; XIV, xiii). He recommended music as valuable

---

46 In China, love *follows* marriage; marital love is an achievement; traditionally, the man's wife was chosen for him by his parents.
47 See Westermarck, *Origin and Development of the Moral Idea,* Vol. I, Chap. V, for the view that morality arose from the sexual relation.

toward good government, whether in a small town or in the larger centers. He commended the commandant of little Wu for bringing the people to exchange their mail and helmets for stringed instruments and singing (*Ana.* XVII, iv). In every case, music to be beneficial must be harmonious (*Ana.* III, xxiii) and rendered by men of virtue (*Ana.* III, iii). Confucius himself studied music in his youth, and later made the subject of music and of musical instruments a matter of intense research. He played the flute with some skill, and on occasion joined in singing (*Ana.* VII, xxxi). Having established the details of ancient practice, he sought to bring about thereby reform in government.

So much has been said about Confucius' reference to the past for principles necessary for man's complete development—in fact, as containing adequate examples of perfection in character and government—that it might seem irrelevant now to ask, Did Confucius provide for *change?* The word for "change," or "reform" (*kai*) was certainly in his vocabulary.[48] He told men not to hesitate to "change" when in the wrong (*Ana.* I, viii) and lamented his own inability to correct his imperfections (VII, iii; but *cf.* VII, xxi). He said, "It is amendment that is of value" (IX, xxiii), and "to err and not reform may indeed be called error" (XV, xxix). On so scanty a basis, however, we are scarcely justified in thinking of Confucius as an experimentalist. His mind was bent upon reform to this extent, that the present seek correction in terms of ancient principles and precedents. His nation has thus understood him through the centuries. It is against this understanding of him that his people are in revolt today, and on the face of it, their revolt seems eminently justified. We question, nevertheless, the imputation of an utter absence of a sanction for reform.[49] Confucius is, after all, less than his system, and his system perpetuated inconsistencies, and displayed some flexibility. The larger question is, Does Confucianism provide for change? Did Confucius indicate high principles which, though ancient, are eternal and ideal? Did he err in the *manner* of application of them to some aspects of his times? May not his people follow his ideals, if not himself? It has yet to be demonstrated that Confucianism as an institution does not provide within itself for change. Possibly the theory of Mencius (see p. 99, below) by which the right of rebellion is maintained is in itself suggestion of the need and value of perpetual experiment. Confucius paints

---

[48] *Kai* is still in use for "change, reform."—Evans, *op. cit.*
[49] Confucius editorially sanctioned revolution (*Shu Ching,* IV, bks. 1, 2: V, bks. 1, 2, 13).

a very clear and compelling portrait of the Ideal Man, but himself renders the ideal innocuous by undue emphasis upon propriety, —amenities and conventions. He sketched a ground in *Jen* for an individualism which, although subject to some disapproval in China today, may ultimately prove to be sufficiently sound for permanent progress. It calls for supplementation, rather than rejection. Confucius failed, as we have said, to lay sufficient emphasis upon the only valid and effective agency by which he could keep men in mind of the proper goal of their own enlightened wills, namely religion. This failure left unchallenged a number of discriminations, and left practically uncharted the course of human brotherhood which he himself proclaimed.

The Agnostic.—Confucius was a sincere and insensitive *agnostic*. He did not attempt to solve in any way the why and wherefore of man's existence, nor to postulate and explain a future life. He dealt with things mundane. He was simple, non-speculative, and even childish with regard to things spiritual. Any attention to the spiritual world did not "serve his main purpose." He would not inquire into death until he fully understood life (*Ana.* XI, xi). He gave himself "earnestly to the duties due to men," honored the gods, but refrained from familiar intercourse with them (*Ana.* VI, xx). To use his own figure, he would not shoot at a mark so distant he could not tell whether he hit it or not. He may have thought religion valuable for the weak and inferior, but of no avail for scholars and strong men. He would not say, even, whether the dead have consciousness, for fear that filial sons might neglect the living for the sake of the dead. On the other hand, he did not say the dead are not conscious, lest unfilial sons give up burying their dead and sacrificing to them.

He recognized invisible Power and powers,—Heaven and the spirits (*Ana.* XI, vii). He felt that Heaven "knew him" (*Ana.* XIV, xxxvii), had entrusted him with his mission, and would sustain him against his enemies. He thought it possible that Heaven might "strike him dead," if he did wrong. Concerning the spirits he said, "How surpassing great are they; looking, we cannot see them; listening, we cannot hear them; embodying themselves in things, they are not to be neglected; they make all men breathe, fast, put on sacrificial clothing, and worship them; vague and yet pervading, they seem to be above and all around us" (*Chung Yung,* XVI, 1–5). He declared that if men sinned against Heaven, they had nowhere to direct their prayers (*Ana.* III, xiii). He himself was in the habit of praying, and he sanctioned prayer on his own behalf (*Ana.* VII, xxxiv). He commended sacrifice as the chief method of approach to Heaven and the spirits. However impersonal Heaven was taken to be in later times, Confucius thought of Heaven as personified and personalized, able to see and hear, and to take delight in offerings and in the homage and servìce rendered by men; compassionate and the author of man's moral sense; the rewarder of those who obeyed his will and the punisher of offenders against his laws; giving seed to the sower, and blessing all who toiled virtuously; so jealous of the people's welfare as to remove rulers from office who neglected or abused their subjects; whose will was absolute and whose highest concern was the moral conduct of mankind. Confucius, therefore, was a *qualified* agnostic. He seems to have accepted the general view which antiquity held of Heaven. He may have been more religious in private than he publicly admitted, holding it a fault to be demonstrative. Yet he sacrificed to his forefathers and to the gods (*Ana.* III, xii), and observed scrupulously the religious proprieties.

The religious result, however, of Confucius' public attitude and opinion was that the God-idea of the *Classics* lost something of its developing power and became dim and vague. Confucius' followers since his day have often been inclined to consider the ancients rather stupid in theology and, living in an unintelligible world, over-religious. They have thought that religion may have had formerly through the fear of divine wrath and the hope of divine reward certain values for social control, but that for scholars who know the universe there is no need of any other than the religion of humanity. Their use of "Heaven" has been as a term for nature and natural law. Chu Hsi,[50] in the 12th century, A.D., put this final stamp upon the term. In other words, posterity accepted generally the judgment of the Sage, and, incidentally, gave no place to priests or nuns, monks or ascetics, and religious sects or orders,—save by remote association with other faiths.

To conclude our estimate of Confucius himself we may observe that:

(1) He was a purist in culture and institutions at a time when his country was encroached upon by various "barbarians" with foreign customs. He was a patriot, born an aristocrat, and serving as a scholar.

---

[50] *Cf.* p. 105, below.

(2) He was exclusive, content to deal with what he could know immediately in his situation, and applying to it what Hegel called a "religion of measure." He excluded or minified the rest. True, he looked into the past, but without imagination—the past was only real with reference to the present. The system he expounded was virtually a shadow world, closed but not complete, which shadowed forth a world familiar to his consciousness. Nor did his consciousness include references to experience as a whole. He was not lured by rainbows—he *might* have thought of rainbows as merely the measurable vibrations which create them. There was nothing truly venturesome within him. These words of the neo-Confucianist Wang Yang Min (1472–1528) might be made a reference to him, "What has been seen and heard exists; what has not been seen or heard does not exist." But, strange to say, along with what the Sage excluded of reality (*cf. Ana.* VII, xx; IX, i) went himself. That is, not only did he rate himself imperfect, save, perhaps, in eagerness to learn (*cf. Ana.* V, xxvii), but he gave himself no meaning for religion. He claimed no insight in the realm of spirit. His has been the great name in matter practical, but he has provided his followers no spiritual satisfaction.

(3) Nor was he as a "scientist" (for he emphasized research and knowledge) the equal of men almost contemporary with him: for example, the utilitarian Mo-ti, who proposed a system of values or ends as the basis of conduct and judgment;[51] and the Taoist Chuang-tze, who proposed a theory of the reconciliation of opposites as the means to social harmony.[52] Confucius was not only not speculative, but was set in opposition to philosophy. The emphasis on philosophy by the rival school of Taoists may, indeed, have moved him to greater emphasis on moral realism than he might otherwise have given it.[53]

(4) He brought to bear upon the tasks at hand too much of theory. He was indefinite, and inconsistent. He strove for the acceptance of his general position (*e.g.,* the ideal man, and virtue), without due regard for the application of deductions to the needs of men (*cf. Ana.* XV, iv),—a frame of mind which is expected of a *prophet,* but Confucius was no prophet. Success was, after all, a "secondary motive" (*Ana.* XII, xxi). He would have men put duty first, as if the result of duty done was not itself

---

[51] Mo-ti, says Hu Shih, is "the only Chinese who can truly be said to have founded a religion."
[52] See pp. 127–129, below.
[53] "Reaction" often *has* affected theories of thought and conduct.

a criterion of duty. He was opposed to government by legislation
(*cf.* Mencius, also, p. 96, below), holding law ineffective as an
agency of reform (*Ana.* II, iii). He minimized thinking (thob-
bing?) and commended "learning" (*Ana.* XV, xxx), and insisted
that "the wise man aims at truth, not at a living" (*Ana.* XV, xxxi;
cf. IV, viii; XVIII, vii, 5). Definitions and the concrete could
not apply to truth! He urged men to be moral for morality's own
sake (*cf. Ana.* IV, xvi). While conceding that virtue is a means
to happiness (*Ana.* IV, ii), he nowhere defines happiness. He has
no theory of human goodness (*cf. Ana.* VI, xvi, xvii), save that it
is Heaven-given. And even so, some men cannot be touched by
education, like wood "too rotten to be carved." He had no theory
of evil, except that it is absence of the good—evil was not real to
him. Perhaps his vague theory of self-expression might warrant
social tyranny. And his theory of "no profit" (*Ana.* IX, i) has
never yet been tried.

Human Nature.—The great problem occupying the minds of
Confucian scholars for centuries after the Great Sage was that
of human nature. We have said that the Sage did not press his
inquiry beyond the realm of human conduct. His theory of man
was, doubtless, merely that of the "five" *Classics,* that "man is the
product of interaction of the dual forces of nature, *yang* and *yin,*
a union of an intelligent and an animal soul, the heart and mind
of Heaven and Earth, the embodiment of the five elements"
(*Li Chi,* Bk. VII, sec. iii) ; and that man has, "without learning
them," the "seven feelings, joy, anger, sadness, fear, love, disliking,
and liking" (*ibid.,* sec. ii). He evaded questions about souls and
spirits, while using words to designate them. There were many
words for soul, although it is difficult to say just what their early
content was. There are: *kuei shen, i.e.,* good and evil spirits, separable from bodies; *hun,* half *yang,* half *yin,* an *anima,* or subli-
mated self, which goes to heaven at death (distinct from *p'o,*
that part of man which goes to earth at death) ; and *hsing,* the
nature, temper, faculty of man (*cf. Ana.* V, xii; XVII, ii). The
Sage acknowledged: that man is a creature of desire, liking food,
drink, and sexual pleasure, and greatly disliking poverty, suffering,
exile, and death; that by some faculty he deems some things right
and advantageous, and other things the opposite; that he has a
moral sense which urges him to obey the moral law, and to keep
himself in harmony with nature; that men have by nature (*hsing*)
high and low propensities, and tend in practice to fall apart in
grades and classes; and that all (?) men may, if they will, attain

to virtue and accord with nature. In a word, it seems the Sage's view that "man is good by nature." [54] We can say little more.

The "Second" Confucian.—Mencius (372–289 B.C.), the greatest of Confucianists, first extended the Master's naïve view that man is good by nature, and formulated the doctrine of man's original and essential goodness. This doctrine ever since, along with that of the inequality of men, has been Confucian orthodoxy: essential goodness manifest in class. Confucius in his own class was a democrat, but in the total situation an aristocrat. His view, therefore, that all men might reach perfection if well educated, had the net result of education for the exceptional individual and of neglect for the ordinary and inconspicuous. Mencius pointed out that some men work with their hands and others with their minds, and frankly said that to banish such distinctions (or forms of inequality) would mean return to barbarism (*Mencius, VI,* Pt. II, 5, 6).[55] Hsün-tze (*c.* 300–235 B.C.; pronounced *schwinze*), a Confucianist inclined to make human evil positive, held it fundamental that man makes distinctions and expresses them in class divisions which grow from human desire and its proper satisfaction. The nearest approach to a Confucian reconciliation of the aristocratic theory of distinctions and the democratic theory of natal goodness has been the implicit theory of more or less *goodness*. Do the two theories, however, stand in need of merging?

Mencius virtually kept the system flexible by directing it toward optimism [56] and democracy, toward democracy by his theory that the welfare of the people is the end of government, that rulers are of less importance than their subjects (Bk. VII, pt. II, xiv), that unjust rulers may be overthrown by rebellion morally justified. As an optimist, Mencius may have got his cue from passages like *Chung Yung,* XXVI, 5, 6, where men are made partakers of the "entire sincerity," or "absolute trustworthiness." [57] That is, the virtue of the natural order and of men's hearts is one. Otherwise, how could man evolve goodness from himself? Mencius rests his doctrine of human nature on such ground, and shows that man tends to goodness even as water tends to flow downhill (Bk. VI, Pt. I, ii, 2); that the evil which men do represents not an absence but a corruption of good; that human nature does not have to be forced from without to goodness, but

---

[54] H. A. Giles, *Confucianism,* p. 84.
[55] References following are from the *Book of Mencius,* unless otherwise indicated.
[56] Optimism in the technical sense.
[57] This passage bristles with difficulties—incoherencies?

that *jen,* benevolence, *i,* justice, *chih,* understanding, and *li,* propriety, are among inherent qualities (Bk. IV, Pt. I); that these virtues are developed by superior men seeking to be perfect (Bk. IV, Pt. II); that "benevolence is man's mind, and righteousness is man's path" and the "four principles" (*jen, i, li* and *chih*) belong to man as naturally as his four limbs. Legislation was to Mencius a phase of external discipline futile in the making of morality. To live naturally is to achieve virtue. He recognized the ancients, and acknowledged that a few of them were perfect (*cf.* Bk. IV, Pt. I, 4), but he insisted that men—himself, at least —could do without them, for of what value, said he, were they, if virtue lies within you? His theory is clearer-cut than anything Confucius had proposed; wherein he makes a weighty contribution. Before we look more closely at other details of his doctrine, let us see the man himself.

Life of Mencius.—Mencius, whom the Chinese rate second only [58] to the Sage, was born of a noble family in the state of Lu. He was contemporary with such foreigners as Aristotle, Epictetus, and Demosthenes, and with the Chinese Chuang-tze. His mother [59] was remarkable, extremely careful in her habits. She "taught him when he was yet unborn," and protected him in early childhood by living in a proper neighborhood. She had lived at first beside a cemetery, and the imitative lad acted out the funeral ceremonial, like Confucius, with its all-too-formal grief. Thinking this harmful for her son, she moved to the market-place. But there the lad began to think that life is noisy bartering and deceitful boasting. So she moved again, and took up residence beside a school, where the pupils were being taught Confucian standards. Even there she was not content with his merely "doing well enough" in school, as he said indifferently one day. She gave him on the occasion an object lesson by dramatically slashing the threads she was weaving into cloth, saying that he by not attending to his studies was doing so with the threads of life. The lesson stimulated his exertion, and he excelled thereafter. She was equally solicitous for him in all relations, winning his undying reverence and love. She continued his advisor in family and public matters, urging him always to do as right dictated. Such was "the mother of Mencius," whom China honors as the ideal mother. We know him by knowing her. Otherwise we know little of his first forty

---

[58] In 1330 A.D. this rank was officially assigned to him.
[59] We may accept the legend that his father died in his infancy.

years. To know her is to account for many of her son's opinions.

Mencius studied the "five" *Classics,* especially the *Shu* and the *Shih,* and Confucius became to him the greatest mortal. While he could not have known the Sage's grandson, he acknowledged his indebtedness to him. He lived in a day more turbulent than Confucius knew: the Chou dynasty was in decay, and loyalty to government was weakened; the authority of Confucius was questioned; by some he was disowned.[60] Mencius entered into spirited controversy with opponents, and gave counsel to the princes on government and morals. He probably spent a quarter of a century (after forty years of age) in public life, journeying among the petty states, urging their rulers to "be strong to do good," and combating doctrines which he held to be inimical to personal character and the public welfare. He, like Confucius, had a sense of mission. Although he felt that "Heaven did not yet wish the empire to enjoy good order and tranquillity," he had no doubt that he could bring such end about. His last twenty years were spent in the congenial company of his disciples and in compiling his *Works* for posterity.

Work of Mencius.—Mencius contended with opponents and commented upon his predecessors. Kao, a contemporary, declared that man was neither good nor bad by nature. He likened human nature to a willow tree, and man's duty to a willow bowl, saying that duty is got from man's nature as the bowl is chiselled from the tree. Again, he likened human nature to running water which, without "bias" in itself, might be deflected easterly or westerly. Mencius in reply contended that cutting bowls from trees does damage to the trees, and by this figure duty is injurious to the doer; that water really has a "bias," it tends to seek its level. Kao must have seen that men did not necessarily hurt or kill themselves by doing good. He may have thought, like Locke, that ideas are not innate; that—again, like Locke—morality depends on Heaven, not on man.[61] Or, he may have meant to say that good and evil are not essentially distinct, but only what they are thought to be. Mencius sought to show that duty did not harm the doer, but rather enlarged him,—although he declared that a man's moral sense *might* suffer loss, as the tree suffers from the axe. He seems not to have thought of the bowl as al-

---

[60] As soon after Mencius as 213 B.C. an imperial attempt was made to destroy many of the *Classics.*

[61] We know Kao only through Mencius. See *Mencius,* Bk. XI: see also Bk. VI, Pt. I, i, ii, vi.

ready existing in the tree before the chisel is applied, or of the tree's existence in the bowls carved out of it: yet he said that Nature and men's hearts are one.

Another contemporary whose "words filled the empire," as Mencius said, was Yang Chu, pessimist, egoist, anarchist, and cynic, who preached a doctrine which Mencius phrased as "every man for himself." He was cynical because, he declared, he *had* seen men perish walking in the path of virtue, and rulers flourishing in wickedness. He did not recognize the legitimacy of any ruler or governmental authority. He lived in a self-created atmosphere of gloom, despairing of the effectiveness of any remedial measures for mankind. When asked if he would not be willing to spare a single hair if that might save the world, he sneeringly replied that "merely plucking hairs from one's head could not save it." He had no faith in other men, nor in spirits—if there are spirits, he said, they know nothing of men's needs and praises. He would live his life and yield at last to annihilation. But he was an advocate of fortitude, and not surrender. He would endure life and get what he could from it. He did not count on life for pleasure. He calculated that if man should live a hundred years, there would be little margin above infancy, sleep, pain, sorrow, distresses, toil, and the increasing weaknesses of old age. He declined to worry, even over death. Mencius was disgusted with him. Nor have many Chinese followed him.

Chuang-tze, the great Taoist,[62] was probably contemporary, but Mencius does not mention him. Could there have been a bond of sympathy between them? Or might Mencius have feared him for his greatness?

Among the predecessors whom he criticized was Mo-ti,[63] who had proclaimed a doctrine of universal *jen,* love to all men equally in bonds of brotherhood. Mencius thought this meant a disregard of the special and proper claim of parents upon their children, a weakening of loyalty to virtuous rulers, and a guarantee that men, lacking true charity of heart and a true sense of duty, would become as "beasts devouring one another." Mo-ti had indeed struck at some of the roots of Confucianism, and was "unorthodox." By Confucian standards both Yang Chu and Mo-ti were extremists. Mencius won the day against them both. The Chinese on the whole assented to his doctrines and have retained the institutions which sustained them.

62 See the chapter on Taoism.
63 See below.

Mencius: Major Doctrines.—These, in conclusion, are his major doctrines:

1. Human nature is originally, essentially, and incorruptibly [64] good (see p. 94, above).

2. The people are Heaven's great concern. "They are the country's most important element."

3. The state is born of the people and on occasion may be modified or overthrown by them. It is intended as a means to facilitate the development of men, so that every individual in all human relations may rest in the highest excellence. The good state deserves men's loyalty.

4. Rulers are intended to be Heaven's agents, but should "see according as the people see, and hear according as the people hear" (Bk. V, Pt. I, v.) If they outrage the benevolence and righteousness proper to their nature and their office (*cf*. Bk. I, Pt. II, viii), they may be deposed. Government should be benevolent; not contentious, wasteful, or oppressive; should insure the prosperity of the people, and provide them education (Bk. VII, Pt. I, xxiii; *cf*. Bk. VI, Pt. I, vii). Prosperity, however, is futile without virtue, and education avails little in the midst of grinding poverty.

Rulers must have both personal and official virtue (although Mencius seems not to have dwelt as Confucius did upon the ruler's personal need of virtue). If a ruler is benevolent, righteous, and correct, his acts will be conducive to a firmly settled state (Bk. IV, Pt. I, xx).

5. The "minister of Heaven" is a special agent whom Heaven nominates on occasion (presumably through the voice of "the people"), not for *rebellion,* but for "righteousness" (*cf*. Bk. I, Pt. II, iii, 7), that is, for the reëstablishment (through force?) of equity and truth.

6. Pomp and display are "despicable." To be a duke, or a minister, or a high official is an honor, but the "heavenly dignities" are to have charity of heart, to do one's duty toward one's neighbor, to be loyal to the state, and to speak the truth. Magnificent buildings, rich viands, pleasure and wine are to be avoided— nor, on the other hand, are men to be allowed to "eat the bread of idleness" (Bk. VII, Pt. I, xxxii), or live in want.

7. Men make and observe "distinctions." There are princes and workers (*cf*. Bk. III, Pt. IV), and necessarily a division of labor among them. This is by the ordinance of Heaven, as nature

---

[64] Bk. VI, Pt. II, xv, "Men constantly err, but are afterward able to reform."

gives itself expression. Government is the prerogative of "scholars," [65] for the "thinker" must direct the toiler (in Mencius' day there were no "thoughtful" toilers?).

8. The individual self is the moving factor in social welfare (in this regard Mencius is more emphatic and more exclusive than Confucius).[66] His balancing of parental obligation and self-concern is very delicate, with the suggestion of over-emphasis on self. He contended that the "superior man" would bring back the unchanging standard of truth and duty" (Bk. VII, Pt. II, xxxvii). That the superior man did *not* bring about the perfect order in Mencius' day was due, Mencius said, to the fact that Heaven was not ready for it—which seems a commentary on man's own power. Yet, in effect, Mencius' exaltation of the individual minified the power of Heaven. His view was further harmful to religion, beyond the damage which the Sage had wrought. Nor was it altogether helpful to morality. It tended to exclude at least as much as Confucius had excluded, especially of things spiritual. His indifference toward ancestral spirits was of one piece with his slighting of the ancients. He seemed to think, however, that his own spirit would deserve commemoration. With man alone the object of one's faith, too great a faith may be reposed in man, thereby taking too little account of the inconsistencies of human conduct and the evils which men do. Mencius' optimism may have made somewhat unreal for him the hatred, strife, unfilial acts, and perverted attitudes which displayed themselves about him. With Confucius, attention to one's self brought a certain measure of humility,[67] but with Mencius it brought pride and self-sufficiency. Who, after all, is the genuine Confucian, Mencius, or his Master?

Hsün-tze.—Hsün-tze [68] (possibly 318–235 B.C.) was a young man when Mencius died in 289, but his prominence began when he was fifty years of age—when he first began to spread his teachings in Shantung. The historian says—and this suggests the time of Mencius—that Hsün-tze "belonged to a generation of evil and

---

65 In Confucianism: culture keeps its own identity; the cultured man best understands nature, for culture is a part of nature, is nature's supreme manifestation; but "scholarship" needed widening.

66 While Mencius' character was above reproach, he seemed disposed to countenance deception as a means to private good. He was a man of pride, and possibly some aspects of his view of human nature (he was at heart an aristocrat) may be reflections of himself. He thought himself "the genial heat" of the garden of princes, while other men were a numbing cold (Bk. VI, Pt. I, ix).

67 Humility is a fundamental *religious* virtue.

68 See H. H. Dubs, *Hsün-tze*, but use the work with care. *Cf. Journal of the American Oriental Society*, 49–51, March, 1929, pp. 88ff.

foul governments, of dying states and evil princes, who did not
follow the great *Tao,* or Way, but attended to magic and prayers,
and believed in omens and luck; a generation of low scholars and
worthless fellows." In contrast, he suggests that Hsün-tze was a
high scholar, "a compendium of all the learning of the age," a
respected exemplar of virtue, who embodied the Confucian virtues,
and warned against the doctrines of Mo-ti and other non-Con-
fucianists. Hsün-tze was, perhaps, the leading scholar of his
generation. He is at once Confucian in his theory that vice must
lose and virtue conquer (*cf. Ana.* XV, xxxiv). He expects that
propriety,[69] benevolence, justice, sincerity, and loyalty[70] will
conquer, but he criticizes freely the standard theory of human
nature. He took more consistent account of the facts of life
than either Confucius or Mencius had done, and, more utilitarian
than his predecessors, he seemed more eager to deal with those
factors which made for "doing things properly" and right, and
for the spread of teachings which advanced the right (*cf.* his
Works, XVII, 13). He considered futile any discussion of Heaven,
except as Nature round about man and natural law operating
upon man; and discussions of the *Tao,* except as the "Way" in
which man himself acts. He was interested in man as part of
the immediate, social order, rather than an object of speculation. Eliminating prayer, providence, spirits, divination, and the
supernatural, he placed man fundamentally upon his own resources.

Hsün-tze's Theories.—(1) Man is "a crooked stick" in need
of straightening, "a blunt knife" in need of sharpening; by birth
he is "small-minded," prone to think only of profit, his own advantage; he is naturally susceptible and imitative, and, if he
meets an evil age, will be affected by bad customs; he will repeat
the smallness of the small, and acquire evil from the evil-minded.

(2) Man stands in need of good example in order to develop.
"The nature of man being prone to evil,[71] must be submitted to
teachers and laws to make it correct." "Without a teacher, or a
set of principles, he can only think of profit." He must depend,
at least indirectly, upon the examples of ancient times, known
through the *Classics,* even as one must use a long rope to draw
water from a deep well.

69 Hsün-tze seems to put the virtue of propriety (*li*) first in order. For the relation
of *li* and *jen* in former times, see Dubs, *op. cit.,* pp. 111–132.
70 Hsün-tze puts loyalty where in the categories of Confucius knowledge (*chih*)
appears. Mencius had emphasized loyalty, and Hsün-tze follows him.
71 That is, not altogether evil, as some interpreters have said. Hsün-tze held at least
a *modified* doctrine of "original sin."

(3) Man can observe and discriminate. He "is not truly man more particularly in that he has two feet and no feathers, but rather in that he makes distinctions." He distinguishes times, seasons, men, and values. He observes grades of virtue in the social classes: (*a*) in the common man who follows custom, seeks gain, and filially supports his parents, (*b*) in the "high scholar" of firm will, who allows no selfish desires to confuse his learning, (*c*) in the "solid, superior man," who attends to the self-correction of his deficiencies in speech, action, knowledge, and thought, who reveres the sages, and instructs inferiors, and (*d*) in sage rulers who adjust themselves easily to the principles of rulership, carry out spontaneously the rules of propriety, treat the people naturally according to ceremony, and bind the people together by the goodness and justice of their administration.

(4) Man is a member of society.[72] The essence of humanity is social organization in which occupations differ for the sake of getting work done easily. The rights of all the classes are harmonized through social distinctions. When society is harmonious, it is strong, controls all things, and enjoys universal goodness.

(5) Man is in a measure self-dependent. Good and evil, fame and fortune, are from within him. That is, he need not depend on *Heaven,* for of itself Heaven can neither impoverish nor enrich men. Both Heaven and Earth have their functions, as have also *Yang* and *Yin:* they perform their great mutations, as they have done from the beginning, and man may observe them and act accordingly to his advantage.

(6) The ideal human virtue is Propriety (*Li*). It is virtually the sum of all the virtues; it is *Tao,* the Way of the universe; it is *Teh* (or *Tê*), morality. It is proper conduct, rites, and ceremony, all of which are indispensable in human intercourse. It is the inner quality of the human mind and heart, by which man may train himself for his proper place in the social order.

(7) Every man, even "the man on the street," may become a sage, *if* he learns and practices the virtues. Men have the capacity to be sages, but some *do not* take advantage of it.

Hsün-tze has not wholly been accepted. His theory of human nature was "heretical." He may be compared with Mencius, although both seem to have given emphasis in partial manner. Hsün-tze's view was more specific, that man is *prone* to evil and

---

[72] Hsün-tze says that society, rather than nature or virtue, is the standard of authority. This is "heresy," although Confucius said, "It is the moral character of a neighborhood which constitutes its excellence" (*Ana.* IV, i).

must *attain* to positive and complete virtue. Mencius said that evil is merely the temporary corruption of original goodness. Hsün-tze said that men had actually corrupted goodness and had *thereby* disposed human nature to corruption. Mencius said that virtue is the development of what is altogether innate, thus making man quite self-dependent. Hsün-tze observed that men stood in need of external guidance, were not really independent, and therefore needed the good example of the ancients. He admitted that the ancient sages had first to *become* ideal, but that, nevertheless, they still had value; they predisposed mankind to goodness. The Chinese preferred Mencius' optimistic assumptions about human nature to Hsün-tze's logical deductions. Hsün-tze insisted that Mencius had ignored a host of vital facts in man's experience and the world about him. Perhaps they both ignored some vital facts. Neither one accounts quite fully for goodness as a moral factor, and neither one assigns a place to Heaven as the religious object of man's dependence, and the source of spiritual insight and direction. After them, Confucianism had to reckon with other faiths in competition with it. Perhaps man is not naturally as good as Mencius thought him. Perhaps he is not naturally as prone to evil as Hsün-tze thought him.

Confucianism through the Centuries.—Our story carries us now rapidly over thirteen centuries, especially through the interesting and notable T'ang Era (620–907 A.D.), when China was the most highly civilized nation on the earth.[73] The feudal system known to Confucius, Mencius, and Hsün-tze gave way about 236 B.C. to a semblance of empire and imperial control; and soon thereafter the first Emperor, Shih Huang-ti, ordered most of the Confucian *Classics* burned,[74] because, he said, they blocked the way of progress. China was, however, unwilling to surrender them; they were restored in time, and progress went on with them. The *Ju-chiao* was kept alive mainly by the educated classes. The masses continued the worship mainly of their ancestral spirits. At times during this long period the higher Taoism of Lao-tze and Chuang-tze influenced both rulers and philosophers. Lower Taoism, with its magic, spiritism, and "medicine of immortality," was influential with the masses. Buddhism by that time affected all classes. The Emperor himself had welcomed the new faith during the first century, B.C., and had sent messengers to India to inquire further into it. For five hundred years Indian Buddhist mis-

[73] See Williams, *op. cit.*; K. S. Latourette, *The Chinese: Their History and Culture*, N. Y., 1934.
[74] *Cf.* p. 71, above.

sionaries had come to China, after which monks from among the Chinese were trained to carry on. Buddhism, or the *Fo-chiao,* took its place as one of the "three teachings" and must be reckoned with if one accounts for modern thought and faith in China.

The worship of Mt. T'ai was a conspicuous feature of the period. T'ai was the most important of the five sacred mountains, which, along with the sun, moon, rivers, hearth, and the ancestral spirits, were objects of prayer and sacrifice. With the formation of the Empire, T'ai Shan, the mountain of the east (in Shantung), had become its guardian. As the east is of the spring, the source of life, T'ai Shan became the "source" and ruler of men's lives, determined their station, fixed their life's-span, measured out happiness and misfortune for them, and ruled over their spirits and the "seven hells" after death. Both the state and the people worshiped holy T'ai. Favors especially sought of T'ai were: (1) rain, or fine weather, according to the people's need, and (2) protection from earthquakes, violent storms, and dangers attendant upon comets, eclipses, and other natural phenomena. The worship of T'ai was regularly a springtime ceremony, preferably on the mountain-top, but allowed from a distance if one faced the mountain. The earliest sacrifices were laid upon square altars under the open sky. Later, temples were built and used, both on the mountain and elsewhere. The worship of T'ai spread in fact to every part. The Emperor would announce to T'ai his accession to the throne, and ask T'ai's blessing on his reign. He would ask his aid in a distant campaign, or if he were desirous of a son. On occasion he would make a pilgrimage to the mountain-top and worship there. T'ai was not only guardian of the state, but god of the people. In time any worshiper might worship in T'ai's temples anywhere. T'ai's temples and his images have suffered much since the Revolution (1911), but among the masses he is still lord of the seventh hell.

During the T'ang era, the "Golden Age," religious toleration prevailed, and two other foreign faiths came into China, Islam and Christianity. Christians and Moslems both came in the seventh century, but were not widely influential, especially in the north. Ultimately Islam spread widely among the masses of the west, and Christianity exerted its influence intensively in eastern centers of learning and leadership. All the faiths combined failed, however, to save the Golden Age from dissolution. Moral laxity and religious superstition prevailed. By 1000 A.D., the Mongols were pressing upon China, and it was destined to become tributary to their sway. The emperors, as a rule, had been Confucian, although some had given aid to Buddhism or to Taoism. Although in 955 the Emperor closed thirty thousand unauthorized Buddhist and Taoist monasteries, both faiths endured. Taoism of the lower type was a nursery of magicians, while Buddhism was corrupted by a discipline of self-torture. A few of the Buddhist monks and several higher Taoists were worthy scholars, and both faiths exerted lasting influences on Chinese literature. The era needed its great man, and Chu Hsi came.

Neo-Confucianism.—Chu Hsi,[75] or Chu Fu-tze (1130–1200 A.D.), is the great philosopher of the *Ju-chiao,* thirteen centuries after Hsün-tze. He was born in Fukien, where his father held office. He also held office several times, once as governor of a province. He was a diligent and competent scholar. He studied Buddhism [76] and Taoism, but became an ardent Confucianist. He represents the re-awakening of Chinese philosophy, and the dawn of the neo-Confucian era. He revolted against Taoism and Buddhism, and strove to restore the *Ju-chiao* to its ancient supremacy. But neither Taoism nor Buddhism could be disregarded by the neo-Confucianists. They both had their influential metaphysics, and their teachings had become an aspect of the general mind. The Confucian scholars had to meet them on their own ground. In consequence, neo-Confucianism became highly philosophical— quite in contrast with the traditional system which had ignored things metaphysical in favor of the socio-political and ethical. Chu Hsi did not neglect the weighty matters of social organization, politics, and morals, but he wrought out a theory of the universe, and especially a philosophy of human nature. He established thus a newer type of "orthodoxy." His literary method thereto was by commentary on the ancient *Classics.* He reduced the *Classics* to consistency.

Chu Hsi found in the *I Ching* and the *Li Chi,* especially, passages useful for his philosophic purposes. He used the *Great Learning (Ta Hsüeh)* for its theory of politics and its suggestion of logical method. He and the entire neo-Confucian school took as their task "the investigation of things." [77] Note this passage in the *Ta Hsüeh,*[78] which represents the simple thesis of the work, and served as inspiration to Chu Hsi,

[75] Pronounced *ju shee.*
[76] It has been said that once he was a Buddhist monk.
[77] Assuming that everything had a "reason," they sought to find the reason, thus to understand and control it.
[78] *Ta Hsüeh,* para. 5.

Connects mind & matter.

"By investigation knowledge becomes complete. When [rulers'] knowledge becomes complete, their thoughts become sincere; through sincere thoughts their hearts are rectified; their hearts being rectified, their persons are cultivated; through the cultivation of their persons their families are regulated; by the regulation of their families their states are rightly governed; and with right government in the states the whole empire enjoys tranquillity and happiness."

The system [79] of Chu Hsi, the most important element in neo-Confucianism, is the "orthodoxy" which, in reality, has been assailed in recent years by restless and revolutionary China.

Chu Hsi's Theory of the Universe.—The universe is a dualism, the two elements of which are matter (*ch'i*) and law (*li*).[80] *Ch'i* permeates all things and makes them what they are. *Ch'i*, therefore, is not confined to "matter" in the sense of being tangible and perceptible to the senses. It is rather the primordial substance, intangible and invisible, from which spring all phenomena, not only material (in a strict sense), but also psychical and spiritual. He put the greater emphasis upon the material aspect of *ch'i,* and thus may seem a "materialist," but he did not disallow the term a spiritual meaning. We are not unfamiliar with theories which make matter and spirit two manifestations of one element, for example, ether, and demonstrate the constant interaction of the two, whereby matter becomes spirit and spirit, matter. The "matter" (*ch'i*) of Chu Hsi seems to have been in its primordial form pure spirit. Pure spirit is set in motion (by law, *li*); it rotates; by its rotation, two modes are produced, energy and inertia (*yang* and *yin*); following these two modes the "five agents" (water, fire, wood, metal, and earth) [81] are developed; beyond these come the two principles which become the male and female elements, ultimately giving rise to creation; universal production and reproduction follow in an unending stream.

Ch'i is the underlying substance in all stages, and the ground of all phenomena, both physical and psychical. *Li* is the law, or principle, of existence and operation. It is the "reason" for existence. Every thing has its own *li*. The movement of *ch'i* [82] depends upon *li*. *Li* has both energy and inertia, which is why

---

[79] See J. P. Bruce, *Chu Hsi and His Masters,* and his translation of Chu Hsi's *Philosophy of Human Nature;* Le P. S. Le Gall, *Le Philosophe Tchou Hi.*
[80] This ideograph is *not* the same *li* with which we were already familiar, and which means rites, ceremony, propriety, worship, etc.
[81] "Agents" or "ethers," rather than specific substances, effective through their qualities, such as humidity, hardness, etc.
[82] Lieh-tze's *ch'i,* also, is generated from motion; *cf.* p. 125, below.

ch'i has both motion and rest. *Li* can form nothing, because it has no content; *ch'i* is the content. *Li* may induce motion, but is more a regulative principle than a principle of activity. *Li* depends upon *ch'i* for the *extent* to which it manifests itself. *Li* and *ch'i* come near to what we generally mean by the familiar speculative terms, mind and matter. There is no *li* apart from *ch'i*, and no *ch'i* apart from *li*. The two elements are mutually dependent and inseparable. They are eternal, co-existent, but *ch'i* is subordinate to *li*.[83] Matter is subordinate to mind, or reason.

Chu Hsi is the great Chinese monistic rationalist. To him the material is subject to the immaterial, and the immaterial is the moral, that is, the material is subject to the moral. He is not, therefore, a thoroughgoing "materialist." To him *li* is reverence, wisdom, righteousness, and love. He does not divide his universe; he is not an actual dualist; he is a monist. He looks to a Supreme Ultimate (*T'ai Chi*, primal unity), or the "Law of the Universe," the source of all laws and of all things. The "Supreme Ultimate" is not thought of as a separate entity, but is identified with *Li* as both natural law and moral law (*tao*). Reason and Morality stand highest in his philosophy, and things which come into being by the action and interaction of *li* on *ch'i*, must for the sake of the highest good obey the law of their being. He is saying what Confucius said, and proving it by the constitution of the universe, as well as by appeal to human nature and the rational soul.

If every event and everything has its own *li*, it has its own *tao*, or "moral law," within it, for *li* operates as *tao*. There is this right in everything, and its "rightness" is the same for all things. *Li* indicates that everything has its own rule of existence; *tao* expresses the fact that everything conforms to one moral law. Right (*tao*) is in everything and is at the heart of the universe; it has a real existence in actual connection with men and things, and is not merely something transcendent beyond the reach of man. There is identity between *tao* and *li*, and *tao*, as the all-pervading and all-comprehensive moral law, is the source of all things, and in all things.

Chu Hsi's Philosophy of Human Nature.—What is man's nature? Whence comes it? What is its character? It is said in the *Chung Yung, Doctrine of the Mean,* that "the decree of Heaven is what is termed our nature," or, "the ordinance of God is what we call the law of our being." In other words, what is in the universe as law is in man as his nature; what is universal and all-

---

[83] *Li* is prior "in dignity."

pervading is individualized in man. This is his view, and it is a clear indication of divine law over against man's will. It is, therefore, man's duty to obey the divine law, his essential nature. Chu Hsi's word for "nature" is composed of the signs for "birth" and "heart," and may be taken to mean that man from his birth has the moral law within his heart. Nature, however, is more than law; it is life; it is consciousness.[84] It is man's duty, therefore, consciously to live according to the moral law, which is the law of his being and the concrete manifestation of the Ultimate.

In his view, as in that of Mencius, the nature of man is good. He predicated good of human nature, while allowing for the presence of evil. He knew that men have evil thoughts and do evil but he explains the evils in man's mind and conduct as the development of what was potential, and points out that the term "good" is relative and implies a contrast with what is potentially evil. He runs no risk of losing the distinction between good and evil. Human nature was "constituted for the practice of what is good," that is, the virtues of benevolence (*jen*), or love (*ai*), righteousness (*i*), wisdom (*chih*), sincerity (*hsin*), and propriety (*li*).

It was Chu Hsi's aim to transmit the Confucian *Classics* with a philosophical interpretation of their major teachings. He finds, therefore, as much place for religion as the *Classics* themselves allow. He found Heaven (*T'ien*) used in three senses: (*a*) the over-arching sky, (*b*) the Supreme Ruler, a personal Power that governs mankind, rewarding their goodness and punishing them for doing evil, and (*c*) the moral Law, or *li*. He "affirms the spirituality and ethical perfection of the Divine Being." [85] "There is a man, *as it were,* above us commanding things to come to pass; [86] 'great Heaven who has conferred upon the people below a moral sense,' is taught by the *Odes* and the *Records.*" He did not rule out God entirely, although he left Him scarcely more than a bare abstraction. He did not rule religion out; he advised men against images and idolatry, and not to bother themselves about the spirits; but he declared that the breath of man at his death leaves his body, mingles with the *ch'i,* and may return again at times of worship. He recognized ancestor-worship, but finding no *proof* of God, he ignored certain elements within the human con-

---

[84] Not the mind, but nature, is the seat of consciousness.
[85] Bruce, *Chu Hsi,* p. 296.
[86] Note "as it were." He avoids an anthropomorphic meaning by declaring elsewhere that the *Odes* and *Records* refer to *Law.* Chu Hsi was concerned to counteract the too literal anthropomorphism of his day.

sciousness, and rested in the characteristic Confucian agnosticism, with certain forms of faith as measures of expediency.

Chu Hsi raised Confucianism again to the place of preëminence and made it the state religion. Every other faith was required to recognize it by erecting in their temples and mosques and on their altars tablets of loyalty to the Emperor. His philosophy shaped the thinking of Chinese scholars for eight centuries. His commentary upon the *Classics* was officially recognized as orthodox. Nevertheless, Taoist mysticism and magic, Buddhist ritual and ideals of contemplation, Moslem testimony to the unity and omnipotence of God, and the Christian view of the divine Christ, continued to affect the Chinese and to promise the Chinese seeker after God something not found in Confucian orthodoxy.

CHAPTER V

Taoism

THE *TAO-CHIAO*: LAO-TZE AND OTHERS

The naturally endowed, temporal-minded Chinese surprise us by the extent to which they have been given both to mysticism and to magic—yet often they have sought practical ends thereby. Mystical and magical elements have entered largely into Chinese character and religion in the guise of Taoism. Confucianism is perhaps the one prevailing mood of human nature, especially in general culture. It is in essence an expression of the Chinese moral consciousness. "Taoism" represents another mood, quite as truly Chinese. It has its moral connotations, but is mainly either mystical or magical—with sometimes no clear line between the two. While the Sage refrained from mentioning "wonders" and the supernatural (*Ana.* VII, xx), having little taste for mysticism, his country has been a land of wonders and of wonder-workers, of divination, witchcraft, exorcism, and geomancy, as well as the home of mystics, dreamers, and ascetics. China has been both "Confucianist" and "Taoist" from her earliest days.

Primitive Taoism.—As early as Shun (from 2224 B.C., according to the *Shu Ching*), orders were taken for the conduct of affairs, and indications were received of mortal destiny, from "the great tortoise." The tortoise-shell was perhaps the earliest instrument of divination. The hollow surface of an upper shell was smeared with ink; then held convex side down above a flame until the coating dried and cracked—into lines directed by the spirits of the unseen world. Those skilled in reading the meaning of these lines (and there were treatises by which one could be schooled) announced the spirits' will and guidance in the matter. For example, Duke Wen of Chou (*c.* 1100 B.C.) used the tortoise-shell (*Shu Ching*, V, vi, 9) and learned that his beloved brother Wu, at the point of death, might yet be spared.

Stalks of the yarrow plant (the *shih*) were also used in divination. Pieces of varying length were jostled and allowed to fall, forming haphazardly a diagram (by spiritual direction) from which the omen might be read. Another early avenue to the world of spirit was the "personator" of the dead. From the Chou Dynasty (twelfth to the third centuries, B.C.), it was customary at the funeral feasts for personators imbued with the spirits of the dead (which had been invoked to dwell within them for the time) to act as mediators between the departed and their kinsmen. These actors sat solemnly at the feasts, and solemnly ate and drank. They listened to the prayers of the bereaved, and in reply revealed the will of the deceased, giving their blessing to the living for their filial devotion.

Divination by tortoise-shells and yarrow-stalks early went out of use, but other methods took their place. "Personators" had disappeared by 300 B.C., but mediums have been employed ever since. In recent times a favorite method has been that of lots. Many lots, each marked with its clear (or cryptic) answer, are thrown into an urn, from which one is drawn out by a person guided by the spirits in control. During many centuries since the third century, B.C., a common method has been to use two marked or shaped pieces of stone, wood, or, perhaps, two coins. These are thrown down and read from the positions into which they fall. Also persons known as *wu* (*wu* means witch, magician, magic), have served from early times as mediums (comparable with the medicine-men and shamans of all primitives). They have spoken for the dead, uttered oracles from the spirits, read men's minds, forecast the future, traced lost articles, written the strangely beautiful ideographs of the spirit-world, and worked all sorts of miracles. They have been able, so it is said, actually to make visible the spirits of departed ancestors.

Perhaps the magical—and the mystical—although not peculiar to the Chinese, has been among them more seriously reduced to system than elsewhere. As a *system* it is Taoist. The *Book of Changes,* the *I Ching,* has its mysterious diagrams which Confucius and his school tried hard to rationalize as the summary of all knowledge. In spite of them, the *Book of Changes* stands a senseless monument to China's easy faith in magic numbers. It is a Confucianist concession to a universal "Taoist" temper of the people which has held its own till now, a temper in favor always with the masses and often with rulers and the literati. Likewise there has been a *mystical* aspect of this temper of the common mind. This, too, has been reduced to system. When Buddhism brought from India near the dawn of the Christian era its own peculiar mysticism, its own ascetic theories and practices, and its own methods and formulas of magic, it had to *take* as well as give, so deep implanted were the Taoist ways. It fused with Taoism, but did not supplant it. While Buddhism did become the *real religion* of the people, it was one of "three." Confucianism held its place in morals, while Taoism reigned supreme as the one effective system of intercourse between the world of mystery and man.

In other words, the Chinese are *taoistic,* and the system, whether on its higher or its lower side, known as Taoism is the formulation of elements inherent in the common mind and conduct. Taoism as mysticism was "founded" by Lao-tze (6th century, B.C.), as religion, by Chang Tao Ling (2nd century, A.D.), and as philosophy, by Ko Hung (3rd century, A.D.). In one form or another the entire life of China has been permeated with its ideas and its imagery; in the poetry and art of every age. China's drama is peculiarly, profoundly Taoist, and Taoist fancy runs riot in her folklore, myths, and legends. Chinese medicine is Taoist, whence charms and incantations; the potencies of precious stones and rare, mysterious herbs; and drugs concocted of strange and horrible ingredients.[1] At least one memorable demonstration with grave international consequences was Taoist both in origin and temper—the "Boxer" uprising of 1900.[2] Although the Taoist pope (see below) was lately driven by the Kuomintang from his seat in Kang-su, although many Taoist shrines have been destroyed and certain Taoist rites put under ban, Taoism both as form and spirit still defies the modern reformation. The system stands intact in those larger areas where the National forces have not conquered. In its lower form, especially, it administers in many regions the spirit forces which play mysteriously upon the life of millions of the common people.

The Tao Association.—Taoism has been *organized* as magic and religion since the second century, A.D., with a pope or Master of Heaven at its head. The founder of this order was an able man of that century, named Chang Tao Ling, who lived on Dragon Tiger (Lung Hu) mountain in the province of Kiang-si, south of Po-yang lake and the city of Nan-chang-fu. Descendants lived on Lung Hu mountain and served as popes until recently, each

---

1 Cf. *Journal American Oriental Society,* Vol. 53–3 (Sept., 1933), pp. 215–250.
2 The "Boxers" concocted a magical immunity, they thought, against the weapons of the "foreign devils" whom they ruthlessly attacked and slew. They knew (?) how to prevent foreign blades from *cutting* them.

head of the Chang family being known as T'ien-tze, or "Heaven Master." Tradition says there was passed on to each successor a sword of the founder, at once the symbol of the papal office and the instrument of miracle. Visitors at the Dragon Tiger lodge have reported various evidences of the Heaven Master's power, for example, a court-yard full of jars in each of which some hurtful demon is held prisoner. The Taoist order has been known since the days of Chang Tao Ling as the *Tao Chiao Hui,* or the "Way Teaching Association." It came in time to have branches in different parts of China, most of which acknowledged the Heaven Master as their head. While many branches were established and many priests took office without the Master's knowledge, many of the priests and heads of local branches received their commissions directly from the Master's own hands at Lung Hu mountain. In 1015 A.D. the large estates were added to the pope's possessions, which the Chinese Nationalists have lately confiscated. They were given to him by the Emperor Chen Tsung, whose capital was the then beautiful and spacious city of Hangchow, which Marco Polo visited and praised (*cf. Travels* of Marco Polo, ed. Cordier). It was this same weak-kneed Chen Tsung who allowed his country to become tributary to the rising empire of Cathay. The Mongol vassals of Cathay in their turn got control of China in the thirteenth century. But the Taoists did not suffer from the change. The Mongol Kublai Khan invited in 1276 the pope to visit him in his showy capital of Peking (called today Peiping), where he built a great temple of the Taoist order. Many emperors of China were patrons of the Taoist popes, and many of these noble rulers put their trust in Taoist divination and geomancy. Taoist alchemists and geomancers described a fairy island of the Eastern sea where grew, they said, the herb of immortality. The Emperor, Shih Huang-ti,[3] actually sent an expedition in search of the fairy island and its magic herb. These alchemists pretended to make "medicine of immortality" and to prepare elixirs of life. In the ninth century, A.D., five emperors in succession, each eager for long life, died from elixirs prepared by Taoist priests. Taoism as magical religion enjoyed then a golden age.

Taoist Worship.—Modern Taoism is, to some extent, an order, but one not closely articulated nor immediately visible. Its

---

[3] The first to use the title *Huang-ti* or "Emperor," 3rd C, B.C., instead of the formerly long used title, *Wang,* or "Monarch."

heads and priests are exclusively its own, it has some rites and doctrines of its own, and a truly Taoist temple has its own peculiar character; but its forty million members mingle somewhat indistinguishably among the masses, and in some respects a Taoist and a Buddhist are alike. By outward signs alone the casual observer might be unable to distinguish between a Taoist and a Buddhist fane, for they are often similar in design, and both are filled with images of all sorts. Both faiths have been ready to accept any goods among their own. There are, however, about two thousand truly Taoist temples, many of them notable.

Outside the East Gate of Anking (An-king-fu), in An-hwei province, on the Yang-tze river above Nanking, stands the Taoist temple of the "Eastern Peak" (Tung Yo),[4] that is, the holy Mt. T'ai, in Shantung. Its walls are done in red in imitation of state (Confucian) temples. The entrance faces southward, whence the *yang* influences, and above it rests a stage for theatrical performances. The ten Taoist hells, five on a side, impressively portrayed, appear along the eastern and western walls of the first court-yard. At the northern end of each row stands the heroic image of a god; on the right, or east, Tsung Kuan, "Controller of the Universe," and on the west, Wen Shen, "Disease God." Within the main hall rest the images of three more gods: in the center stands Tung Yo (Mt. T'ai), with gilded face, and wearing robes and a head-dress which show his rank; at one side of him stands his minister, the Civil Judge, at the other, his second minister, the Military Judge. Tung Yo has long been worshiped as a natural divinity (see account of Mt. T'ai, p. 104, above), but the Taoist version is that Tung Yo was originally a general of the Emperor Wu Wang, who lost his life in battle. His temple in An-king was founded prior to 900 A.D. There was a reconstruction in 1656 A.D. Tung Yo is worshiped for protection generally, and for the gift of children—although his popularity with respect to children is not so great as that of the Buddhist goddess Kwannon, or Kwanyin. His birthday is celebrated as a public festival. His son, also, has been deified, and his grand-daughter is a popular goddess in Shantung. The Taoists claim that Tung Yo of An-king governs the entire province of An-hwei, but others dispute this claim, some scoffers saying that his power is no more than local, perhaps only suburban.

---

[4] Many details of this temple are taken from J. Shryock, *The Temples of Anking*. Paris, 1931 (MS. dated 1924).

On the walls within the temple are inscriptions such as these:

> The shelter is wide and large,
>   Dreadful, famous, clear, and effective,
> Shines upon the hearts of men.
>   The Tao of Heaven both rewards and punishes.

*   *   *   *   *

I am more awful than the rest of the Five Mountains. When you enter my temple, your good and your evil deeds are separated. If you try to deceive when you stand before me, you are as the proverb, 'although he has eyes, he cannot tell T'ai shan from other mountains.'

*   *   *   *   *

No matter how deceitful you may be, or how bad, or how much you act against your conscience, Heaven is always watching you.

*   *   *   *   *

You must know that I am a just god who rewards the righteous and who punishes the wicked.

*   *   *   *   *

My power is used to punish and reward. My grace o'erspreads a million men.

*   *   *   *   *

. . . When you look upon the rewards of the chaste and the punishments of adulterers, you will wash your face and clean your heart; you will believe in Tao and turning your boat about will reach safe harbor.

There are no congregational services in any Taoist temple. The temples are headquarters for the priestly ritual on seasonal occasions, in times of emergency, and for private worship. A society of men, numbering between five and six hundred, has flourished in connection with the An-king temple. It has kept in close communication with the Heaven Master at Lung Hu, and lately raised $7000 to defray the cost of a month's visitation in An-king. It admits men to membership by first assigning them apprenticeships to various members. One may become a priest by way of the society. If the candidate for orders is literate, he pursues a course of study for three years; if illiterate, for six.

The course includes the *Confucian Classics*. All members are monks known as *tao-shih,* "patrons, or followers, of the Tao." [5] Celibacy is not a rule, and many of the monks live with families in their own homes. Ascetic monks may live apart within a monastery.

The Ministry.—When a novice, or apprentice, is ready for admission, he burns a prayer before the picture of the Heaven Master, and learns in some way the ideographs which will represent his spiritual name thereafter. He thereupon begins his course of study. Once it was the custom for the candidate becoming a monk to wear his hair long, coiled as a top-knot. Many nowadays shave their heads, as the Buddhist priests have always done, although the Taoists do not sear their scalps with burning incense, as the Buddhists after ordination. The priest in preparation for a ritual service dons a special robe and a high, round hat. Masses for the dead are his usual service, and his chief means of support. If he be sincere, he knows that what he does gives comfort to the simple-minded who employ him. He has small regard for creeds as such. He knows that common men are unable to understand and cherish the abstractions of higher Taoism (see pp. 118 ff., below), and so he gives himself to aid them through images, festivals, and ritual. He may be insincere, and then—?

There are many irregular and insincere (?) Taoist monks and nuns. Some are self-appointed. These are not rightly priests and priestesses, but magicians, exorcists and geomancers. There are many "professors of *fêng-shui,*" or interpreters of "wind and water." There are many "Taoist dames" (Tao Nai-nai), or "Taoist witches" (Tao-nu), sometimes connected with a Taoist sect or order and operating where priests of any sort are seldom seen. These "magic Grannies" [6] all profess ability to cure diseases, and their employment for "cures" is their means of livelihood. They pretend to get their power from intercourse with weasel- and fox-demons. Sometimes the "dames" have been recruited in the first place from women cured by demons, thus bearing in their own bodies the evidence of power. Although the farmer-folk hold these magic dames in slight repute, they still have recourse to them in illness for want of better service. Each dame has in her house a simple demon-shrine at which she worships and which she may use in working her cures. Or she may perform her

---

5 There are also Taoist nuns, for there are societies of women, sometimes attached to local men's societies.
6 *Cf.* Doré *Researches,* Vol. V, pp. 546 ff.

ceremony at some "temple of the immortals," a demon-shrine found in almost every rural village. She has been known to make her ministry contingent upon human sacrifice to the demon power.

The modern priest is a wind-and-water expert, a "professor of *fêng-shui.*" He knows the "way of heaven" (*T'ien Tao*) which means also "the weather." He is a geomancer. *Geomancy* is the science of accord between the acts of man and the processes of nature, or, the reading of these natural processes in order to determine what the acts of men should be on various occasions. For example, the location of a grave must be exactly calculated, for the soul of the deceased may remain disquieted if his body (near which the soul remains) is not interred in the place and at the time which the experts in *fêng-shui* determine. The expert also exorcises, or "casts out" evil spirits. He may exorcise a demon of disease. If so, he frightens it away with the noise of gongs, drums, and fire-crackers, or to lure it off by an offering of pork, deemed more attractive to the evil spirit than the sick man's lungs, intestines, or what not. He may cast out evil spirits from men's houses. He may purge *new* houses so that men may live safely in them. He may "protect" all dwellings from danger and their inhabitants from ill fortune. He has all sorts of magic potions, instruments, and formulas for such purposes. He "cures" disease? He might as well *prevent* it. If he can prevent *disease,* why not also death? Taoists priests have claimed the power of thwarting death.

While modern Taoism, through its strange practices strangely primitive, is in general of the "lower" sort, a nobler aspect is in evidence, although the higher and the lower forms both have historical and psychological connection. Elixirs of immortality, ascetic practices, and mysticism have common ground in origin, lineage, and destination. Taoists early divided their teachings into Inner and Outer, the inner, mystical which dealt with the cultivation of man's nature, and the outer, magical which dealt with acts and ceremonies. The higher Taoists, Lao-tze, Lieh-tze, and Chuang-tze, put their emphasis upon the Inner, which they called the All. Later, when the Buddhists came to China, the Outer got the greater emphasis. Taoists borrowed wantonly from Buddhist sources, formed a Triad of divinities, organized a pantheon, fabricated images, constructed monasteries, initiated monks and nuns, imagined hells and heavens, and adopted the Buddhist-borne Indian theories of "ages" (*kalpas*) and transmigration. Thus

Taoism *revived* its ancient Sinistic magic, and "naturism," which had been interrupted by Confucianism and the higher Taoists. Higher, mystical and philosophic, Taoism was a brilliant interlude, and an exalted reformation.

The Higher Taoism.—The classical *Tao-chiao,* or "the teaching of the Way." Its story opens in antiquity, but its truths are timeless. The first expounder of the teaching was Lao-tze—if, indeed, there was an actual man who bore this name. He was born in 604 B.C., somewhere in the little China of that time, the basin of the Hwang-ho, or Yellow River. We know little of his life-story, yet we need not dismiss him as a myth. Nor should we treat him merely as a name to cover lesser persons otherwise unknown. The scanty records assign his birth to a date fifty-three years prior to Confucius, suggest that he may have known the Sage, and tell us that he lived to the ripe old age of eighty-seven. They tell us he held office as keeper of the public records at Lo-yang, the capital of the Chou dynasty (Lo-yang is now Honan-fu, near the Yellow River, west of Kai-feng-fu). They tell us that he resigned his office toward the close of his life to fulfill in himself the doctrines he had advocated; that he wandered off toward the "barbarous" frontier, toward the unknown land of the Beyond in which to lose himself forever; that he tarried long enough at the boundary, at the border-officer's behest, to compose in writing the paragraphs transmitted as the *Tao Teh*[7] *Ching,* or "classic of the Way and Morals"; and that he rode away immediately thereafter on a "black ox" and disappeared.

He seems not to have claimed to be the founder of a faith. Like Confucius, he pointed to the ancients. He said they had "practiced the *Tao*" and had used it to "make men simple and natural." [8] He claimed but to have taught what others had taught before him. His followers have said that "Taoism" is really the philosophy of the *I Ching* and the *Li Chi,* two of the "five books" (*wu ching*) of the Confucian canon. Lao-tze was most engaged with the ancient symbol *Tao,* appropriated it as the central concept of the ancient teachings and his own, and gave to China higher Taoism.

The Writings.—The book he left must have been a compromise for expediency's dear sake, for symbols written on a page were not reality to him. The *Tao Tê Ching* is very small in size, some five thousand Chinese ideographs, and scarcely longer

---

[7] We may use indifferently the transliterations Tê and Teh, since both are widely used.

[8] *Tao Tê Ching,* para. 65.

in an English free translation. It is a curious assortment of arresting aphorisms, a series of suggestive hints thrown out in disregard of sequence. Tradition has arranged the miscellany in eighty-one titled chapters, such as Form's Completion, The Function of Emptiness, Practicing Placidity, Returning to Simplicity, Humility's Increase, Non-assertion, The Disease of Knowledge, and The Root of Order. Lao-tze's teachings on *Tao* and *Tê* had become a Chinese "classic" (*ching*) before the Christian era, and brought with it to the West some ideas strangely similar. Its place was further established in 666 A.D., when the author was canonized and made a member of the royal line. During the entire period of the national examinations it was included in the course of study. Its text was cut in stone at the capital of each province. It is essentially Chinese.

Perhaps the *Tao Tê Ching* was the product of old age, when disillusionment had set in and the earth had become a realm of vanities. Or, it may be the proper summary of a long life's wide experience, whose author had seen much of human nature, high and low, had exercised a good, discriminating mind, and had separated form and essence; who amid political confusion, license and corruption, had made an honest effort to account for virtue; who amid the poverty and hardship of the masses had sought in earnest how to cure their ills. He professed to have found a higher life than this, which men might come to know by returning in this life good for evil, and to be able to tell men what is good. It may appear that rejection rather than participation and control was Lao-tze's way of life. To some his teachings seem a counsel of despair by one who seeks oblivion in terms of "a return home to the Absolute." Lao-tze, indeed, seems not to have given himself steadfastly to meeting squarely the arduous issues of mortal life. And yet he may be credited with a distinct, valuable contribution toward the solving of the mystery of living, in this world and the next. We may dismiss the thought that he was either sceptical or pessimistic; he merely did not take the world for granted. He had schooled himself in the *Book of Changes,* and sought to find amid a world of change the enduring values of the spiritual. Perhaps the world he rejected was a fixed-mechanical condition. This life to him was but a veil beyond whose obscurity lay the Real. He had observed the passage of the living into death, and had set himself to find a way of overcoming death. He found men dying in their striving for the sensuous, and urged them rather to seek out the spiritual. He found that man need not suffer even "though his body perish," for to him the *Tao* endures, and man returns at last to *Tao*. This to Lao-tze was not death, but life.

The *Tao* as Concept.—*Tao* is the key-word in Lao-tze's exposition. We have learned that in its simplest content it means "way, or path, or road." It means, also, "a manner of acting, a way of thought, a rule of life," and "nature, law, and reason." To Lao-tze and his school it means all this—and more. It is the ultimate explanation of the universe. It is the Ultimate, indefinable and indescribable. Lao-tze said he did not know its "name"; he simply called it *Tao*. When "forced to qualify it," he called it "reason, way, master, father, mother, carpenter." He named it by its qualities, which after all is description and not definition. We are reminded of the saying of Thomas Aquinas, that "we cannot so name God that the name shall express the Divine Essence as it is," and the saying of Augustine, that "God is ineffable; we more easily say what He is not than what He is." In Lao-tze's metaphysics *Tao* is primordial matter, formative principle, the self-existent, the self-acting, the homogeneous, the omnipresent, the intangible, the boundless, the inscrutable, the Real One, beside which the "many" are phenomenal and unreal.

Lao-tze's Reality was inherent in the Universal, and not in the particular. The *whole* and not its parts is real. The One is not merely the sum-total of the Many—it is more. "The several parts of the carriage are not the carriage," says the *Tao Tê Ching*.[9] The One, *i.e.,* the *Tao,* produces all, and by virtue of its very office of creator is greater than all its products, and is likewise independent of them. Yet the *Tao* is in all and through all—it *is* all. Unity itself is begotten of the *Tao*. In the beginning the *Tao* created the heavens and the earth, and then came "men and the ten thousand things" by the interaction of heaven and earth according to the operation of the *Tao* (by their *interaction, not* by the generation of heaven and the conception of earth, in an anthropomorphic sense).

This is a rather full description of "the indescribable"! But we have merely summarized what Lao-tze offers in the *Tao Tê Ching,* paragraphs 42, 10, 14, 22, 39, and 1,—save that we have phrased the summary *positively,* whereas Lao-tze characteristically described the *Tao* in terms of what it is *not*. William Hard said of Calvin Coolidge that "of all the politicians that have ever lived, he seems to be the one that has most grasped the fact that a negation may be action." Lao-tze taught through negatives, and

---

9 We shall encounter this idea again in Buddha's teaching.

advocated inaction as the true means of the realization of life. Some Hindu thinkers, also, trying to describe the indescribable, fell back upon an exposition of what it is not. For example, "Not earth, nor water, nor light, nor air, nor ether; not the senses, nor all things comprehended together by them; . . . the only, ultimate, imperishable [is] Shiva (*i.e.*, God)." If we should substitute, in a portion of Pope's *Essay on Man, Tao* for God, and It for Him, we might impute to this Western poet something of an unconsciously Taoist temper,

> "All are but parts of one stupendous whole,
> Whose body Nature is and *Tao* the soul;
>
> . . . .
>
> Warms in the sun, refreshes in the breeze,
> Glows in the stars and blossoms in the trees,
> Lives through all life, extends through all extent,
> —Spreads undivided, operates unspent;
> Breathes in our soul, informs our mortal part,
> As full, as perfect, in a hair, as heart:
> To *It* no high, no low, no great, no small;
> *It* fills, *It* bounds, connects and equals all."

And if we should put *Tao* in the place of *agapé,* or "love" (as in the Bible, I Cor., 13), we should find the Christian apostle Paul unknowingly setting forth something of the ethical qualities of Lao-tze's *Tao;* for example,

> ". . . if I bestow all my goods to feed the poor . . . but have not *Tao,* it profiteth me nothing. *Tao* suffereth long, and is kind; *Tao* envieth not; *Tao* vaunteth not itself, is not puffed up, doth not behave itself unseemly, seeketh not its own, is not provoked, taketh not account of evil. . . . *Tao* never faileth . . . the greatest of these is *Tao.*"

Such is *Tao* in Lao-tze's metaphysics. It is the symbol of the ancient Chinese mind seeking to understand the world of nature and to grasp Reality. Although this view was not entirely—or necessarily—one of world-rejection, it laid the ground for a later Taoist dogma of world-negation. Lao-tze may not have made a *dogma* of world-renunciation; his chief disciple, Chuang-tze, *did*. And the Taoist recluse—a Chinese contradiction in terms—of later times is a lineal descendant of this dogma.

What about religion? The great master shared inevitably the weakness of his land's religious sense. He has not left much, if anything, which bears directly on religion. He did use certain terms which even in China may have religious content, for example, *hsiao,* or "filial devotion," *shen,* "a spirit, or the soul," *kuei,* a "demon," *shê,* an "altar," *chi,* the "sacrifice," and *Ti* and *T'ien,* "Heaven." These terms were current in his day with at least a *polytheistic* connotation. Yet Lao-tze rejected the religion of his day! Of his predecessors, also. He seems at times to use these terms only to belittle them and what they stand for. *Ti,* "Heaven, or God," was used only once by him, and then he insisted that it seemed inferior to *Tao.* He intimates that *Ti* had sprung from *Tao,* although it represents a higher order than other creatures, such as men and the ten thousand things. There was no place in his system for the ancient Chinese God, whether *T'ien, Ti,* or *Shang-ti,* who was worshiped as the moral, loving, all-wise ruler of mankind, the very source and sustainer of life (*cf.* p. 57, above). *Tao* is not at all a name for God, not even the impersonal God of Pope, and not at all a synonym for St. Paul's *agapé,* or "love," and St. John's *lógos,* which in terms of Jesus Christ was "the light, and love, and life" of God. Lao-tze was a Taoist, not a theist.

The Higher Morals.—Lao-tze's ethics are most interesting. While his philosophy is hard to comprehend, his ethics are more tangible. He not only talked of the real nature of the universe and of the law, or reason, by which the world of change is governed, but he offered men a way of life, a method of realizing "the impartial, unstriving, spiritual *Tao,*" which is the producer, sustainer, and the end of all. In exposition of this way of life he used the ancient symbol *Tê,* or "virtue." In the *Tao Tê Ching,* twenty-five times he uses *Tê,* and thirty-two times he refers to the man who embodies *Tê. Tê* is the moral expression of the philosophic *Tao* and may likewise be inferred from several of the sixty-eight references directly to the *Tao. Tê* as a symbol is composite, the several parts of which together might be held to mean "the heart, or will caught in a net, advancing step by step to perfection." The net is the finite world into which *Tê* enters as an expression of the infinite *Tao.* Lao-tze does not say this in so many words, but it follows from such words as these, "the greatest virtue is simply following the *Tao,*" "the end of virtue" is the attainment of "vacuity's completion" in the *Tao. Tê* is most useful, as it is lost in *Tao.*

Tê operates as: (1) *goodness* ("superior goodness is like water, . . . benefits all things . . . does not strive . . . occupies the place which all men shun") ; (2) *humility* (the man of virtue "holds himself dear, but does not honor himself, knows himself but does not display himself"; "he beholds his smallness, and is called enlightened"; "he is not self-glorying, and he thus excels"; "he is lowly and therefore conquers, unlike those who render themselves lowly for the sake of conquest" [10]). (3) *quietude* (the woman always "through quietude conquers her husband, and by quietude renders herself lowly" and influential). Or we may comprehend *Tê* in its embodiment in Lao-tze's "virtuous, or ideal man." The "virtuous man" denies himself, divests himself of desire,[11] is indifferent to love and hate, gain and loss, favor and disgrace; he provides for the soul and not for the senses; he does not hoard, but rather gives away, thus acquiring the more [virtue] for himself, for "the empty find their fill"; he is truly rich, because he is rich in thought; he finds inexhaustible value in his emptiness, even as "the wheel's utility depends upon its hollow hub, and the clay vessel's usefulness depends upon its hollowness."

Man's sense of "nothingness" is the basis and the fulness of his morals, even as the "non-existence" or hollowness in things is the ground of their usefulness. A man's weakness is his strength and his strength is weakness, like the tree which "when it has grown strong is doomed." If a man have virtue he is safe, reptiles do not sting him, nor do fierce beasts seize or harm him; and if he come among soldiers, he will not fear their weapons. We may recall the Boxers' confidence in "virtue" when they rose against the "foreign devils." There is a passage in the *Gospel* of St. Mark, 16:18, with a similar import, "They shall take up serpents, and if they drink any deadly thing, it shall in no wise hurt them." The Taoist man of virtue acquires no common knowledge (*hsüeh,* in the sense of "schooling"), but aims at "simple development in all things"; he will deliberately divest himself of learning, that he may be rid of madness and weariness of the flesh. Instead of learning, whence comes "distress," he seeks "wisdom." The merely learned are not "wise." The more the man of virtue reduces "knowledge" and acquires "wisdom," the greater access has he to the *Tao.*

All this may seem very vague, intangible, and, perhaps, ridiculous. It is, at least, an exhibition of fine paradox at which Lao-tze

---

10 Is this a reflection on some of Lao-tze's contemporaries?
11 *Cf.* Jonathan Swift's facetious observation, that "the Stoical scheme of supplying our wants by lopping off our desires is like cutting off our feet when we want shoes."

was a master.[12] But the general tenor is quite clear. It may be summed up in three symbols, *wei wu wei*. *Wu-wei*,[13] or "inaction," is a dogma, if Lao-tze ever was dogmatic ("to do nothing," "to remain passive," "not to interfere" is the fundamental, indispensable approach to *Tê* and *Tao*). "With *wu-wei* there is nothing one may not achieve"; the *Tao* always practices *wu-wei*, and there is nothing that remains undone; "the highest virtue is *wu-wei*"; "the virtuous man does not strive," for "he that makes mars, he that grasps loses." "Rest is master of motion," "the farther one goes the less one knows," and "without opening one's gate, one may know the world."

Over against passivity, subjectively, and individualism, there is the virtuous man as a unit in the family, the social, and the political order. His asceticism has regard for others. He may marry and be virtuous, for virtue does not depend on celibacy. The good man has a duty toward the bad, to pay him good for evil, to teach him, and to save him. Apparently evil was real; indeed, Lao-tze draws a clear line between the evil and the good, as if they both were real. The good man has a duty toward the state. He does not reject the state, nor deny the Emperor. The ideal ruler is a man of virtue. However, Lao-tze seems opposed to government as such, there were better ways than politics. He was not a nationalist or patriot (the present nationalistic Kuomintang could not tolerate him). Patriots appear, he said, when a nation is filled with strife. He was opposed to war, pointing out that the good are not contentious, and that a truly great conqueror does not win by war. He considered weapons a "source of unhappiness" and famines an inevitable consequence of wars. They who have the *Tao* "enforce submission without resort to arms." The nation has its place, but the virtuous man in office "governs by ignoring distinctions of class,[14] by preserving the people from a knowledge of evil and hence from desire, and by making those who have evil knowledge afraid to use it." He rules by lack of ostentation, by moderation, and by non-assertiveness; and, of course, he does not levy heavy taxes! He does not multiply statutes, for "the more prohibitions, the poorer grow the people; and the more laws, the more thieves and robbers." He would banish war, suppress disorder, wipe out distress, and make government unnecessary, all by reformation of the human heart. Let men be men of *Tê* and *Tao*.

---

[12] He remarked, "True words seem paradoxical."—*T. T. Ch.,* 78.
[13] Giles, *Dictionary,* Nos. 12,753 and 12,521 respectively.
[14] Lao-tze thus denies a fundamental principle of later Confucianism.

It is plain that the Taoism of Lao-tze is something different in Chinese thought and life. It actually runs counter to much which China in her practical worldliness has considered wise and good. The teachings of Lao-tze and of Confucius ofttimes may not be reconciled. What the Sage would cultivate, namely, loyalty, duty, justice, benevolence, wealth, learning, propriety, and filial devotion, Lao-tze would ultimately, if not at once, abandon. The latter's virtue of humility, unlike the humility of the Sage, is valid only in *inaction*. His silence was deemed better than Confucian caution when one speaks. Confucian benevolence was at its best an evidence to Lao-tze of the absence of both *Tê* and *Tao*, for "Heaven and Earth exhibit no *jen* (benevolence)." To him only the spiritual, not the "natural," can exhibit *jen;* and the rules of *li* (propriety) are not the semblance of loyalty and faith; they are actually the beginning of disorder!

The Taoist Disciples.—Among the most conspicuous disciples of the higher Taoism are Lieh-tze, Mo-ti and Chuang-tze (Mo-ti was a convert from Confucianism). Lieh-tze lived a shadowy existence sometime during the fifth century B.C. We have his *Works*, but no other record of his life. In his writings we may find perhaps the clearest statement—in the Taoist view—of the origin and character of the universe. Lao-tze had only hinted at the origin of things. Origins in any system are a problem which arises later.[15] Things as they are receive the first attention, along with what the future is to be. Lieh-tze accounted for the origin of things in this way: In the beginning there was *chaos*,[16] an unorganized mass with potentiality. There was no ultimate Non-existence, and there was no *unnameable Tao*. Back of all, of course, was *Tao*, but it was not distinct from the nameable universe. Lieh-tze identified as one the knowable and the unknowable, thus modifying his master's uncritical view. There was in original Chaos a mingled potentiality of (1) *hsing*, or "form," (2) *ch'i*, or "spirit," and (3) *chih*, or "substance." Movement and change lay inherent in potentiality, along with reason whereby form, spirit, and substance might be realized. *Tao* is this guiding reason, the uncreated, passive, changeless, and eternal *Tao*, through whose *wu-wei*, or "non-activity," the universe once formed keeps running in a never-ending cycle of "coming and going" (*cf.* Lao-tze's saying, "The Departing I call far away, the Far-away I call the Coming Home"). Change took place in Chaos, and movement toward *hsing*, or

15 *Cf.* The Greek *genesis*.
16 Lao-tze had mentioned the "Abyss-mother" in *T. T. Ch.*, para. 6, from which Lieh-tze gathered synonyms for *Tao*.

"form," began. Out of this moving change was *ch'i*, or "spirit" generated,[17] and, likewise, *chih*, or "substance." From the evolution of these three came this material world of man. There was behind this evolution no personal, directive will with its conscious plan. Rather, the development was of the very nature of the potentiality of substance, form, and spirit. Potentiality possessed the power of evolution and realization. And this material world of man and the ten thousand things is the merely *phenomenal* realization of the various potentialities within original Chaos. In its eternal round of "coming and going" are heavenly souls and earthly bodies, creation, procreation and annihilation, life and death. Yet to Lieh-tze, who repudiates all distinctions, life and death, good and evil, here and there, coming and going, are in every instance one. To the wise man there is indiscriminate serenity amidst this world of change and revolution; the wise man lives "as if not living." Practically, this means that a living man is in this world a tenant marking time, while the true self is being realized. His true abode is elsewhere. While here, such characters as absent-mindedness, indifference, and ethical aloofness are virtuous and blessed. His philosophy is that of absolute identity, he is uncompromisingly monistic, an absolute idealist, a transcendantalist. Not illogically, it has been claimed that he had the power of riding on the wind.[18] Without doubt, his head was always in the clouds. Such was his attitude toward the world, his explanation of the universe, and his conquest over matter. He outdid his master.

Chuang-tze.—The most brilliant Taoist was Chuang-tze (*c.* 350–275 B.C.). He glorified his master, and gloried in attacks upon Confucianists. While in the first objective he was preeminently successful, his attacks upon Confucianism failed. No Chinese has yet been able to transform the higher mind of his countrymen from moral, optimistic monism to metaphysical idealism. Chuang-tze took his cue from the later theories of Lao-tze, and followed the "Old Boy's" example of denying himself the service of the state. Invited by a Duke to be his Prime Minister, Chuang-tze declined, with the remark that in such an office he would be like the sacrificial ox about to die, and that he would rather be a common turtle alive in the mud of its own local pond. Following the Master—more directly than did Lieh-tze,—Chuang-tze's central concept is the *Tao*. He, however, interpreted it as

---

[17] *Cf.* The Theory of Chu Hsi that movement generates *ch'i*, p. 106*f.*, above.
[18] The *Hsien-ching* says that a Taoist practitioner of the first class raises up his body and mounts into the void and is called a celestial Genie.—J. R. Ware, *JAOS*, 53–3, p. 216.

something yet more empty and transcendental. The Master talked of *wu*, or "non-existence," but Chuang-tze talked of *wu-wu*, or "nonexisting non-existence"!

Chuang-tze's Tao.—There is nothing positive in his *Tao*, yet the *Tao* is the essence of all things. It is an *empty Tao* which is the essence of all things. Therefore, this phenomenal world is ultimately unreal. At best, it has *now* only a relative reality. It is a world of appearance only. There appear to be individuals and differences, but these are but illusion. All experience is illusion, and there are no criteria by which truly to discriminate. The real cannot be distinguished from the unreal. Existence is relative, and there is no value in discussing such things as colors, sounds, and individuals. No good can come of this in a realm of relative existence. Each apparent object obeys its own nature under guidance of the *Tao* residing in it. It is the *Tao* within which is real and worth knowing. If one truly knew the universal *Tao*, he would have no sense of difference, individuality, and the like.

The *Tao* does nothing. It has no bodily form. It cannot be perceived by the senses. It only can be apprehended by the mind, which is the undifferentiated, self-directing, and self-recognizing *Tao*. In the beginning was the *Tao*. From it, by no exertion of its own, came God, and Heaven, and Earth, and "the ten thousand things." It was before the Ultimate, and yet is not old; it is timeless. The mind may seem to apprehend it, and yet the mind by striving can neither define nor express it. "Think not and you will know the *Tao*; abide nowhere and you will rest in the *Tao*; go nowhere and you will obtain the *Tao*." *Tao's* creation and *Tao's* creatures have no means of knowing it; it must be *immediately* perceived.

This is pantheistic mysticism of a sort, or the mystical, immediate perception that all is One, without discrimination and division. This is a philosophy of absolute identity within the *Tao*. With what results for morals and religion? It breeds indifference to all forms and transformations. It obliterates all moral distinctions. There is no separableness of good and evil. Self is ignored and action is condemned. Common opinions are always wrong, or unreliable, and duty must give place to destiny. Man does not aim to live. He aims to nourish his soul with the *Tao*. His ultimate ideal is a dreamless sleep in an absolute state beyond this phenomenal world of relativity, motion, and illusion.

This systematization by Chuang-tze is high doctrine indeed. Few can attain unto it, only those few ethereal and unusual souls whose natural food is ambrosia. To the many it is baffling and vexatious. Some, however, have found it valuable as a ground of moral laxity and self-indulgence—for does it not teach there is no evil! While all the greater Taoists were themselves ethically above reproach, it may not be ethically sound to obliterate distinctions,[19] between good and evil, by which all evil may be good. While the higher Taoist mysticism stresses sincerity, the very suppression of the self in the interest of its union with the *Tao* paves a certain way toward insincerity, the insincerity inherent in a doctrine of illusion. The higher Taoism seems colorless and empty, although it does insist that the true life of man must be a spontaneous expression of the universal nature, *Tao,* within him, and it discounts mere conformity to custom, ceremony, and legislation. It strips man to less than nakedness and emptiness, for it cuts him off from many wider areas of reality (while professing to make it known to him!) and robs him of his very soul while professing to preserve it. The higher Taoist seems to ride upon the wind, like Lieh-tze, in serene comprehension of vacuity, or, else, like Chuang-tze's pupil, to hop about as any bird, enjoying himself in the mood of one who thankfully "does not know."

Nevertheless, the higher Taoism has held an honored place. Great thinkers have been among its close adherents. It has enjoyed royal patronage, having been for a while from 212 B.C. the state religion. As early as 156 B.C. men began to worship Lao-tze as a god. In the seventh century, A.D., he was officially canonized as "Emperor." A century thereafter copies of his *Tao Tê Ching* were distributed at the Emperor's direction. On the other hand, Taoism has been often persecuted, whether by the state or by the masses,—in testimony to the normal Chinese sense that it is somehow different. And yet it lived and lives—due doubtless, in part, to its lofty mysticism, and, in part, to the magic of its later, lower form. It brewed itself the potion which has kept itself alive.

An Apostle of Human Brotherhood.—Now what of Mo-ti, Mo-tze, or Meh-tze? He may be placed between Confucius and the Taoist Chuang-tze, nearer probably to the former, possibly from 470 to 390 B.C. He may have lived even earlier and have known Confucius. In point of view he falls somewhere between the two, making for some slight uncertainty as to the place to

---

[19] There is a Taoist expression, *ling hun,* which indicates the power of distinguishing conveniently between right and wrong.

give him as a thinker.[20] He seems actually to have been reared in
the Confucian "school." It is, however, clear that he became dis-
satisfied with Confucian doctrine and swung away—shall we say
toward Taoism? He is undoubtedly "Taoistic" in many of his
major theories. However, if he and Lieh-tze were contemporaries,
the two were representing divergent views of Taoism, Lieh-tze
with his abstract emphasis on Chaos, Potentiality and Change,
and Mo-ti emphasizing ethics and religion.

Wherever we may place Mo-ti, we gather that he was the most
religious of all the ancient thinkers. Perhaps he is the most religious Chinese thinker of all time. He linked his thought directly
with the theistic tendencies of pre-Confucian China, and indirectly
indicates in what he taught, what progress China might have made
in matters of religious faith, had not Confucius put his dominating
stamp upon it. Mo-ti emphasized the commonly accepted virtues
of *jen,* "benevolence," and *hsiao,* or "filial devotion," and went
beyond all other Chinese teachers, before or after, with his
doctrine of universal love. Mo-ti was a native of the state of Lu,
and may have served in several states as a political advisor. He
seems not to have been merely a theoretical recluse. We know
little, however, of his life beyond the meager note in Ssu Ma
Ch'ien's *History*,[21] that he "was an official in the state of Sung,
skilled in the art of defensive warfare, and a stern ascetic," that
he lived simply in a modest house, ate the coarsest food, dressed
in skin or grass clothing according to the season, and at death was
buried in "a plain coffin of thin boards." This, after all, is a
revelation of him, even to the *thin* boards of his coffin.

Mo-ti's writings have preserved a full account of his position
on matters moral and religious. After centuries of neglect they
are enjoying today the interest and the favor of a growing circle
of Chinese and foreign students, as if his teachings still have value
long denied them. He reacted against the elaborate ceremonials
of Confucian orthodoxy, against the extravagance and ostentation
of funerals, in particular. He considered such funeral ceremonies
by the rich a waste of money which might be spent to better purpose
on the living poor; when the poor had costly funerals, they
merely forged the chains of debt and poverty. He caustically remarked that the time and money spent seemed strangely inconsistent with Confucian *scepticism* in religion. To which the Confucianists replied, that Mo-ti was disregardful and disrespectful

<hr />

[20] Hu-Shih,the leading Chinese scholar, insists that Mo-ti was virtually the founder
of an independent school. This issue is not important for our present purpose.
[21] Ssu Ma Ch'ien (died 86–74 B.C.), the Chinese Herodotus.

toward the proper claims of "filial devotion." Mo-ti criticized the
place Confucius gave to music, taking issue with the ancient theory
that music was efficacious in good government. He attacked Confucianists for their frank materialism, for their undue application
to affairs of politics, and for their crass uncertainty about the
world of spirit. He believed in spirits, their existence, and their
usefulness. But he seems to reason merely from the *universal* faith
in spirits, and men's testimony that they have seen and heard
them. He supports this argument by recourse to the records of the
ancients who knew the spirits and revered them. He attacked the
fatalism of Confucianism, holding it to lead to the "overthrow of
righteousness in the world." He meant that fatalism leads to in-
dolence, acquiescence in conditions essentially evil, and the sub-
missive acceptance of preventive ills. Rather than submit to fate,
Mo-ti would take the will of Heaven as his *standard,* and
coöperate creatively with Heaven. "When I do what Heaven
desires, Heaven will also do what I desire." "Heaven desires
righteousness . . . likes to have the world live and not die, to
have it rich and not poor, orderly and not disorderly." He thought
of "Heaven" as creating, owning, nourishing, and loving all
beings, a personal view characteristic of Sinæan times, which
Confucius minimized, if not rejected.

Mo-ti was inspired by the "will of Heaven" and the "love of
Heaven." He was eager to do "what Heaven desires," and to
avoid "what Heaven abominates." And "the will of Heaven that
is to be obeyed" is none other than "to love all the people in the
world universally." He gave his thought to an all-inclusive
universe: to Heaven above as God, to the middle realm of
spiritual beings, and to the world of men and things below.
For the world of men he had a message for the individual, the
family, and the state.[22] His great doctrine is universal love (*jen*).
If everyone were to practice and coöperate, all the evils of the
social order (such strife and confusion) would disappear. Universal love is in harmony with: (1) the spirit of the universe;
(2) the teachings of the ancients; and (3) human experience at its
best, *Jen,* into which he reads the quality of "love," was to him a
quality of nature in itself; it was the one effective method of the
ancients; it is the key to human happiness on earth and eternal
blessedness beyond. He once was criticized for saying that *jen*
is "profitable," but he was no materialist. When he said "love

22 *Cf.* J. Witte, *Mê Ti, der Philosoph der allgemeinen Menschenliebe* (Leipzig, 1928),
esp. pp. 33ff.

pays" he did not have material gain in mind; he thought of human welfare. In like manner, he pointed out some things which did *not* "pay," such as war.

He urged men to cease from strife on the ground that they were all sons of Heaven, and strife was something Heaven abhors. Aggressive war did not pay, because it was contrary both to the will and to the love of Heaven. His pacifism was neither sentimental nor æsthetic. Probably it was frankly *utilitarian*. He was, as Ssu Ma Ch'ien has said, an expert in *defensive* warfare. He wrote a treatise on fortification for defense. But aggressive war failed utterly in gaining any good end, whether to the victor or the vanquished. Aggressive war was "mutual hate" and "murder." To his credit, he actually prevented several wars. He held that "teaching which cannot be put into practice is not permanent."

Mo-ti was no quietist, but rather approved a strenuous life as contributing to the advancement of the race. In this he was no true Taoist. Nor was he truly Taoist in his failure to obliterate distinctions; he was Confucian in his willingness to *make* them, although he felt the making of them was a cause of evil. He was not indifferent, nor was he ethereally a mystic. On the contrary, his intense concern for human life lead him to formulate economic theories which have been criticized as faulty.[23] He was possibly too sternly an ascetic, and thus too much a *negative materialist*. He had a certain economic motive which may have gone far to destroy for the time, the obvious good of his moral and religious teachings. There is evidence that he held the theory, amazing for his day, that the earth rotates! But this is incidental to his more serious discussion of alchemy and the manipulation of the "five elements," in the truly Taoist vein. This may be why the Taoists preserved his writings and included them within their catalogues.

Now that China is in a certain revolutionary mood, with many Chinese leaders interested favorably in "heretics," Mo-ti the ancient heretic is coming into prominence.[24] This early powerful but unsuccessful rival of Confucius may yet find a place above the ancient Sage, although till now too "high" for popular acceptance. It were better to have Taoism prevail in such a form, than as a system catering to human weakness and credulity, even as love is more than magic.

---

[23] *Cf.* L. Tomkinson, *Social Teachings of Meh Tse,* in the *Transactions of the Asiatic Society of Japan,* December, 1927.
[24] *Cf.* "The Religion of Motze," in the *Chinese Recorder,* September, 1931, pp. 557ff.

CHAPTER VI

JAPAN AND RELIGION

The Japanese, both rulers and people, are displaying today [1] many signs of interest in religion—even to the point of controversy. Religion is reviewed along with changes taking place, not by revolution but by development, in government and in society. The "spirit" of Japan persists—the spirit by which she is peculiarly distinguished among the nations, and by which change in government, society, and religion, has always been controlled, if not initiated. This spirit is her life, and without it she would find it hard, perhaps impossible, to live. In so far as her spirit is religious, for Japan to live means, also, that Japanese religion will endure.

Much reconstruction in religion has been accomplished during recent years. Some old religious influences have waned, and certain old forms have decayed—it is as well for religion as for the economy of the natural order that forms decay; constructive forces bring about decay and thus renewal. The definitely anti-religious movement, however, begun in the spring of 1930,[2] seems to have spent itself or taken to cover. Many of the ceremonies once religiously inspiring to university students and intellectual leaders have lost their appeal; yet here and there some ancient forms of faith have been revived among them. Men and women in their prime in the rural sections, where life is burdened with excessive toil, pay scant attention to religion; yet the Christian "Kingdom of God" movement [3] has spread from the civic centers to the villages and the countryside. In 1929, Shinto "god-shelves" were officially installed in all public schools in the prefecture of Shiga for the pupils' use in worship. Immediately, the Buddhist Shin sect (*Shinshu*), alleging state discrimination, began an aggressive campaign against this action. Shinshu has campaigned also against the policy of the Imperial Government in supporting "State" Shinto shrines, yet Government has continued to sup-

---

[1] They are calling the times *hijoji*, the "extraordinary period."
[2] By a Japanese Marxian educated in Russia.
[3] A movement lead by the famous Japanese Christian, To'yohiko Kagawa.

port them. Christians have raised the issue of religious toleration and "disestablishment," and have implored the Throne to declare neutrality. Buddhists, Christians, and members of the Shinto *sects* unite in their desire for governmental tolerance. The Government appointed in December, 1929, a Commission of thirty representative men to study the problem. This Commission has so far made no report.[4] Rumor says the members have been unable to agree whether State Shinto is religion or not. The problem is perennial.[5]

The Government once indeed declared that State Shinto is not religion. The Department of Education has recently announced that certain State Shinto ceremonies of respect, required of students before certain State shrines, are not religious, but national. In August, 1899, the Department had issued a regulation that "it shall not be allowed in government and public schools and in schools conforming to the curriculum ordained by law, to conduct religious ceremonies even outside of the regular school curriculum." The departments are not at one, however, in the matter. Among the masses it appears that State Shinto is a real religion, and that at the State shrines religious exercises are performed. If governmental support of State Shinto has, therefore, the connotation of religion, how may *sectarian* Shinto, Buddhism, and Christianity rightly be denied their program of religious exercises in schools which they maintain according to the law? They are not strictly denied; officials have been lenient!

Interest in Religion.—To what extent this controversy is deeply and truly spiritual, rather than political, whether on the part of Government or the religious bodies, is not altogether clear. There are surer signs, however, of religious interest. There was held in 1928 a conference called by Shintoists, in which at least sixteen hundred delegates participated, including 550 Buddhists, 260 Shintoists, 150 Christians, and 640 "scholars" (Confucianists, etc). Their aim was a common understanding and the discovery of methods of religious coöperation. Among the "findings" of the conference were these: (1) that religion should have a place in public education; (2) that the religious bodies should prosecute programs of service among the people, emphasizing the dignity of life and labor; and (3) that the three leading religions (Shinto, Buddhism, and the *Ju-chiao*) should strive to eradicate from their beliefs and practices all elements of "superstition."

4 It had not reported before the close of 1933.
5 See *Japan Christian Quarterly,* July, 1931; *Japan Christian Year Book,* 1929, pp. 49–54; 1931, pp. 39–96, 127; 1933, p. 4.

The spirit of goodwill exists, but the "superstitions" have not all disappeared. There are priests who owe their influence to superstitious fear, worshipers who seek ceremonial purification in ancestral temples, and intelligent men who pay their vows at old fox-shrines. In May, 1931, there was held in Tokyo a "National Conference for the Promotion of International Peace through Religion." Among the delegates were 128 Buddhists, 107 Shintoists, and 75 Christians, all leaders of religion in the country. Each group set forth the possibilities of their faith for (1) justice, (2) patriotism, (3) international goodwill, and (4) peace. This conference admitted the rôle of the national spirit in matters of religion.

Since the Enthronement Exercises in the fall of 1928, the State cult of Shinto has enjoyed revival. This has stimulated lively activity among the various religious orders and has renewed the emphasis upon the "spirit of Japan." They designate this spirit *kokutai,* "the genius of the country." The Japanese have ever been a virile people. For many centuries they have exhibited an unusually compact social order and a common consciousness— a consciousness of unity and national character. The form of government has often changed throughout the centuries, sometimes it was feudal, sometimes clan government. Emperors [6] have changed, sometimes deposed, sometimes assassinated. This seems to contradict the theory that the Emperor is sacrosanct. It does not, in reality, any more than for a Japanese to kill himself means a denial of his own divinity. The Japanese have a profound conviction of divinity: in themselves, their islands, and their institutions. This "fundamental character of the Empire" has expressed itself in various forms, such as the Imperial *dynasty* and a long dynastic succession from the gods. The essential is not government, nor religion, nor any form. *Kokutai* is the essential. *Kokutai* is the *solidarity of the nation* persisting through the centuries. Parties, clans, and tribes may fiercely contend, the sects may brawl, but *kokutai* outlives contentions, indeed modifies and softens them, and directs the nation toward its destiny.

Japanese Character.—The Japanese have been a docile, teachable race, knowing how to make the most of their resources, whether of the islands or the mainland. Their culture without doubt is foreign (see the next chapter). *They* may be foreigners, having come from an original South Sea island home, bringing

6 Mikado, a term not now used. If the Emperor is spoken of, he is, *e.g., Tenshi Sama,* Son of Heaven.

their "chief-right" and "tabu." [7] But in Japan they have absorbed many diverse elements—except the aboriginal Ainu.[8] Peaceful Chinese and Koreans came and were assimilated. Culture and religion entered, and were welcome. But in the complex process something more than insulation dominated. There was a predisposing racial element, and a dominating spirit. The "Yamato" men formed the nucleus of the social order, and engendered *Yamato-damashii,* or *kokutai,* the dominating spirit.

The Yamato men gathered power first in the central region of the main island, Honshū or Hondo. They had vigor and docility, capacity for conquest and administration, and they gradually unified the 150,000 square miles of grass-clad, flowery islands washed by protecting waters, and comparatively easy of defense from foreign foes. They breathed the spirit and generated the religion which went to make the national genius. In *Shin-koku,* the "country of the gods," *Shin-to,* the "way of the gods," was promulgated. Shinto is a compound and a distillation of the beauty visible in Japan's blue waters and gorgeously tinted sunsets; her broken lines of sea-shore, quaint lakes in woodland stretches, and the gentle, fertile slopes of scattered mountains; her mild climate which favored life in the open; and her people's own qualities of mind and heart, responsive to the advantages of their situation.

Religions.—Three religions are officially recognized today: Shinto (in several forms), Buddhism, and Christianity. Confucianism is a leaven, rather than a body. There are scattered representatives of other faiths. Buddhism came in the 6th century, A.D., from Korea, bringing its arts and literature, and quickening the native religious impulses. It brought in priestly morals with religious institutions. It came in an idealistic, peaceful, even receptive, mood.[9] Its membership today is nearly fifty million. Forms of Confucianism may have come prior to the Buddhists' entrance, but the *Ju-chiao* as such came as part of the general flow of Chinese culture introduced by Buddhism. It brought civic morality, legal institutions, and educational methods; it gave conceptions of ethical loyalty and filial piety. It cared little for religious dogma, and was willing to accommodate its practical ethics to Japanese requirements.[10] Christianity reached Japan in 1549

[7] *Cf.* N. Whymant, *The Chinese-Japanese Puzzle,* p. 82.
[8] The Japanese called them "dogs" (*ainu*) in the contempt, or else because of their *hairy* frame. The Ainu were largely unassimilable. There are few left.
[9] Pacifistic Buddhism contributed to Bushi-do, or the "Warrior-way," and soldiers have freely adopted Buddhist principles.
[10] For example, the Japanese would tolerate no doctrine of "recall" or revolution, in the Chinese sense, nor any impairment of loyalty to the state and ruler.

through Jesuit missionaries. Once it seemed opposed to *kokutai,* and it suffered thereby persecution and an Imperial ban.[11] The real motive of the ban may have been political, or social, rather than religious. Buddhism, also, has been persecuted on account of politics. Christians number about 200,000. In recent years they have taken a leading part in social reformation. Shinto *sects* are late phenomena, and all together have a membership of nearly twenty millions. All Japanese, however, are Shintoists, on grounds already indicated.

Toleration.—There is conditional religious toleration, both by law and in actual practice,—unless the Educational Act of 1899 be an exception. The Japanese have been tolerant in religion since the foundation of their civilization. Religious persecutions have been rare. Not only have foreign faiths brought welcome culture with them, but they have "caught" the spirit of the Japanese. The Government, however, keeps control of all religious institutions in the islands. It established in 1877 a Bureau of Shrines (Shinto) and Temples (Buddhist[12]). In 1900, this Bureau was abolished, and two others were created in its place: (1) the Bureau of Shrines (State Shinto), and (2) the Bureau of Religions (Buddhism, the sects of Shinto, and Christianity). Since 1913 the Bureau of Shrines has been under the Department of Home Affairs, and the Bureau of Religions, under the Department of Education.

The Government intended as early as 1871 to make the State shrines non-religious. This end, as we have seen, has not been realized. A recent visitor at a public shrine near Tokyo saw rows of boxes containing charms of every description for warding off disease, for success in business, for driving away rats, and so on. He saw pilgrims led by the priest (or officiant) through a ceremony intended to renew the power of their charms and to bless themselves. This is religion, both in form and purpose, although primitive. But one object of the act of 1871 was accomplished, the official severance from the public shrines of the religious organizations which had long been associated with them, the sectarian Shinto societies. These organizations, thus cut off from the official cult, at least one of which had been formed before 1800, have been recognized as "religions." New sects have joined the ranks since 1871. They all have their own places of meeting

---

11 The ban was imposed in 1868 and ran for five years.
12 Christianity was not then included, for, although tolerated, it was not yet "recognized." It has been recognized since 1900.

and of worship, apart from the Great Shrines which remain, in theory at least, symbolic of the national spirit.

The masses of the Japanese have to some extent a Chinese trait of tolerance. But while Shintoists, Buddhists, and Christians are usually mutually distinguishable, all must be loyal to the State, if they would share its *kwan-yo-sei,* or "tolerant generosity." A man may be born a Shintoist, and without violence to his Shinto heritage, live a Confucianist, and die a Buddhist.[13] There is a "double aspect" Shinto, as well as a sectarian form; that is, Shinto modified by Buddhist features, having many temples, portable shrines, and paintings representing it. There is domestic Shinto of the private "god-shelves" (*kamidana*), with both Buddhist and Confucian elements, including Buddha-images and ancestral tablets.

[13] Japanese Buddhism is reserved for treatment as part of the total movement of Buddhism. What Shinto has meant to Japan is the subject of the succeeding chapter.

CHAPTER VII

SHINTO

Shinto, the "gods' way," [1] is Japan's original, national religion —rather, the original religion of the Japanese developed in their present island home. It may be identified with *kokutai,* the "spirit of the land," or with *Yamato-damashii,* the "heritage of the Yamato men" who founded the Imperial dynasty. It shares the claims of *chugi,* or "loyalty" to all things Japanese, and of *aikoku-shin,* or "love of country (*koku*)," the "gods' country (*shin-koku*)." Certain foreign factors have been prominent, the "teachings" of Lao-tze, Kung-tze, Gautama, and Jesus, but they have been tempered by the indigenous spirit. The "way of Buddha" dominated *conscious*-religious devotion for a thousand years (from the sixth to the sixteenth centuries, A.D.), but Shinto endured *sub*consciously during the entire millennium, subtly forceful, and ultimately consciously triumphant once again through official and popular revival. Shinto is scarcely yet a system—it never had a "founder." It is, as a religion, of the very nature and processes of Japanese mentality.

How then does this spirit bear a *foreign* name? It is the Chinese *shen-tao,* "spirits' way." After the *Butsu-do,* the "Buddha way," had reached Japan, the designation "Shinto" was given to the native cult to distinguish it from Buddhism. The term thus came in with continental culture, with the movement which ultimately gave Japan her written language with many foreign words imbedded in it, her initial literature, and many novel institutions. When the Japanese, obedient to their national consciousness, began to use their own indigenous expressions, *kami-no-michi,* the "way of the gods (*kami*)," came to stand along with *shinto,* or to take its place. The *kami* were with certain minor variations in the meaning of the word the Chinese *shen,* and *michi* was the Chinese *tao.* The "way" of the *kami* of the 6th century, A.D., was analogous in its simplicity to the way of the *shen* of the sixth century, B.C. In contrast with the *Butsu-do* (the Chinese *Fo-chiao*), the *kami-no-michi* has retained through the centuries comparative

[1] In Chinese, *shen-tao.*

simplicity both in ritual and creed, whether in formal, temple worship, or in the worship of the home. Shinto—we shall consistently call it such—met alien Buddhism in friendly struggle, asserting its self-consciousness passively but effectively.

Torii.—The casual observer of today may find on every hand the distinctive outward symbol of the *kami*-way, the *torii*. The *torii* is as conspicuously the Shinto symbol as the pagoda is for Buddhists, or the minaret for Moslems. It is, however, specifically a plain-timbered gateway which stands alone, generally above the path of entrance to a shrine. It is made of two large, equal, upright pillars, connected just below their upper ends by a horizontal cross-beam, and having a second, longer, horizontal beam laid across, and projecting beyond, the upper ends. Perhaps a block is fitted in at the center between the horizontal beams. The design of many *torii* (the word itself is either singular or plural) has varied from this simplest, original pattern under the influence of the ornate, Chinese *pailow* or memorial arch, and the elaborate Buddhist *torana*[2] or gateway to the *stupa* or funeral mound with its relic of the Buddha. Under such influence the upper cross-beam sometimes curves as if sagging on its two supports; or, if it lies straight between the pillars, its two ends curve or roll upwards. Sometimes, unusually, the wood is colored; at a shrine of the Shinto Fox-god, the *torii* is often red with paint or lacquer. Sometimes the *torii* is made of stone, or metal,[3] instead of wood—this, also, under foreign influence.

The original *torii* may have been a roost for fowls, in preservation of an ancient legend: A tradition says that fowls were set crowing on a roost outside the cave into which the national Sun-goddess had retired in petulance. Men wished to convince her that the dawn had come in spite of her own failure to appear! According to another view, the first *torii* may have been used for suspending the birds offered in sacrifice to the Sun-goddess and the gods. The arch was placed at first anywhere about the shrine. Its regular position is today at the front, due, perhaps, to Buddhist influence. A *torii* stands at every entrance gateway to a Shinto shrine; there may be many in a row along the way which leads from court to court through many of the larger sanctuaries.

What now of the Shinto shrine? There is a variation in size and rank among the many thousand shrines. There are modest, officially "unrecognized" shrines to the number of fifty or sixty

---

2 Whence *"torii."*
3 The main *torii* at Kidzuki is bronze.

thousand, scattered along the roadsides. There are over forty thousand *village* shrines, and in the larger *towns* about forty-five hundred shrines of higher grade. There are nearly two hundred *state* or provincial shrines. Greatest of all are the *national* shrines of Idzumo at Kidzuki [4] (at the northwestern edge of the main island of Hondo, or Honshu), and of Isé in Yamada, near the southern coast of Isé Bay, off the Inland Sea. The Isé shrines are the most pretentious, extensive, and revered, although those at Kidzuki rest upon a far more ancient site of worship, and still vie with the two at Isé in their claim to sanctity. All these types of shrines are "public." As for purely "private" shrines, called *miya,* their number is incalculable. They are of the household, and are often portable. They vary in design and size from the small *miya* of white wood in the humble laborer's hut to the beautiful, miniature temples in the residences of the wealthy. Many *miya* are carried in processions and otherwise displayed on Shinto holidays.

Types of Shinto.—As there are grades of Shinto shrines, so are there types of Shinto faith. Shinto is not exclusively a patriotic spirit. It has its definite, sectarian divisions, as well as its official, public character, and its domestic cult. Its *sects* developed during the latter days of Shinto's long subservience to Buddhism, and have served in competition with Buddhist sects. The three-fold division of Shinto into State, domestic, and sectarian cults, is not an absolute distinction, but it represents the wide range of the order from a national, non-religious (?) spirit to a religion with both creed and works. State Shinto and the domestic cult are the same in quality, save that, whereas the latter is an unorganized complex of primitive beliefs and offices, the former represents the national centering of traditional elements in the Sun-goddess as the Supreme Deity of Japan. The State cult has provided a place of extraordinary merit and of conspicuously high regard for the succession of rulers, or Mikados, as the Sun's divine descendants. In this way Shinto has expressed itself in relation to the social and political development of the national life, and in reaction against the presence and effects of foreign (especially Chinese) institutions. In its *sectarian* character, it claims the allegiance of nearly twenty millions, who find in it the satisfactions of religion.

The State Cult.—What Shinto is as *Yamato damashii,* or *kokutai,* or the national spirit and cult, may be understood by a

---

[4] See *Transactions of the Asiatic Society of Japan,* XLI, Pt. IV, pp. 495–554; L. Hearn, *Glimpses of Unfamiliar Japan,* I, pp. 172–210, 244–275.

visit to the shrines of Isé.[5] These stand—two groups of buildings
—four miles apart, at opposite ends of a straight boulevard.
At one end lies the park in which the *Geku,* or the "Outer Shrine"
is situated, dedicated to the Food-goddess (*Toyo-uke-Daijin*),
daughter of *Izanagi* and *Izanami,* the divine parents of things
Japanese. At the other, rises in its ampler park the holier *Naiku,*
or "Inner Shrine," dedicated to the Sun-goddess (*Amaterasu*)
and the divine ancestors of the Emperor. Each park contains a
wood of aged and lofty evergreen cryptomerias, in which the
simple buildings stand in perfect harmony with their setting.
The buildings are extremely simple, in striking contrast with the
sacred structures of several other faiths, including Buddhism,
which have indulged in costliness of materials and magnificence
of design and workmanship. In fact, they are so perishable that
they are renewed every twenty years. Each building is rectangular,
stands on pillars driven directly into the soil, is made of white,
unpainted cedar (*hinoki*) wood, and roofed with a thatch of
rushes, or of cedar-bark.[6] The simplicity of each is broken by
no decorative effects, unless by means of outer railings which
enclose verandahs, by the projection above the comb of the roof
of the two pairs of end rafters, and by little logs resting horizontally at short intervals at right angles across the comb. These
simple shrines, built in natural, wooded places, preserve the atmosphere of the primitive religion. At both Isé shrines are buildings
of various, even non-religious, purposes, but in each group the
holiest structures is the house of the Deity, whether the Sun-
or the Food-goddess.

The sanctuary of the Sun-goddess is a four-fold inclosure
within a 164-acre park. In this park are many impressive objects,
including grim memorials of Japan's struggles with the Russians, and the Chinese. There is a tall shaft in the form of a shattered cannon commemorating the battle of the Japan Sea, and a
Krupp gun taken from the Russians at Port Arthur. Such relics
within the sacred area are suggestive of the nationalistic quality
of Shinto. Through the first inclosure of the shrine runs a stream
in which devotees and pilgrims may attend to their ceremonial
ablutions. In the second compound stand a stable for the sacred
horse,[7] a booth with a stock of charms, amulets, and mementoes
for sale, and a hall for sacred dancing. In the innermost, which

---

5 Whither Shinto pilgrims go with such devotion as Hindus go to Benares or
Moslems to Mecca.
6 See Genchi Kato, *A Study of Shinto,* for illustrations.
7 *Cf.* sacred horses in ancient India, Greece, and Rome. In Greece a horse was
sacrificed to the sun.—Frazer, *Golden Bough,* I, 315; II, 229; IX, 122.

is a double inclosure, stands the holy place of the Goddess herself, accessible to none but priests and properly authorized officials and notables. This is Shinto's holy of holies, in whose veiled interior the Goddess dwells with her *holy relics,* the "divine imperial regalia." [8] These are a mirror, a sword, and a string of jewels. There is no image of her Majesty; Shinto has never been idolatrous. The mirror, round, metallic, and highly polished, is her peculiar symbol. It is kept wrapped in silk in a casket of flawless *hinoki* wood. It is the dearest relic of Japan: it has come down out of a remote, mysterious past,[9] bestowed by the Goddess herself upon an early ancestor of the race. It symbolizes the unbroken succession of divine rulers descended from the Goddess; it reflects the likeness of the Goddess; it is the reflection of her very soul; and it is protective of the nation.

Symbolism.—This mirror at Isé is reputed to have been enshrined there by the Emperor Suinin in 4 B.C. He brought to Isé the sword, a fabulous weapon found by the storm-god, *Susano-wo,* in the tail of a destroying dragon which he slew. This dragon-sword, however, did not remain at Isé. It was borrowed by a famous princely hero sent by the Emperor Keiko Tenno about 100 A.D., against some "eastern barbarians." This heroprince took the sword for his own protection on the hazardous journey, and for the sake of victory. When he returned, safe and victorious, he entrusted it to the custodian of the Atsuta shrine in Owari.[10] Once thereafter it was taken back to Isé, where it wrought many miracles for those who prayed to it, but afterwards it was deposited permanently at Owari. In its place at Isé rests a *replica,* which is venerated—as is the original weapon at Owari—as the symbol of the "severe spirit" of the Goddess, whereas the mirror, and its replicas [11] elsewhere, represent the "gentle spirit" of the Goddess. The third of the "divine relics," the string of jewels, is represented at Isé in replica. The original set rest at Tokyo in "The Sword and Jewel Room" of the Emperor's palace. They are rounded, kidney-shaped objects (*magatama* or "curved jewels") of precious stone, such as the ancient Japanese delighted to use for personal adornment,[12] and which

---

[8] *Cf.* the Scotch Imperial Relics at Holyrood, and the relics in the Sikh temple at Amritsar.

[9] It is probable, however, that the Japanese first learned mirror-making from the Chinese at the dawn of the Christian era, using an amalgam of copper, tin and lead. Later, they used iron. Glass mirrors came first from Europe.

[10] Owari is near Nagoya, north of Isé and beyond the Isé Bay.

[11] The most venerated replica of the mirror is that which has reposed since the ninth century A.D. in the Imperial Palace at Tokyo, along with a replica of the sword, and the *original* jewels.

[12] The Japanese early used agate, jade, amber, and amalgam objects for adornment.

they fancied were used by their deities, also. The "ancient" records mention the gods bedecked with "jingling ornaments." These Regalia jewels were handed down from "the age of the gods." They were bestowed upon the Goddess in the beginning by *Izanagi* himself, the sky-father. She, in turn, bestowed them, with the mirror and the sword which were then in her possession, upon her "august grandson" Ninigi, the founder on her behalf of the Japanese Empire. They are now kept "in a marked casket as a talisman to protect each generation of sovereigns" of Japan.

These Regalia objects of Shinto belonged originally to powerful deities. They were full of the potency (*mana*) by which these deities ruled the Plain of Heaven and all else besides. Having been bestowed by the gods upon the emperors, their creatures and descendants, they have since symbolized divine authority in government. They represent the attributes of rulers by divine right. The mirror stands for purity, righteousness, integrity, and wisdom. The jewels stand for benevolence, gentleness, obedience, and affection. The sword is symbol of valor, sagacity, firmness, and justice. Thus the "fetishes" of ancient times survive as tokens of enlightened government.[13]

To return to Isé. The Regalia in the Inner Shrine, the mirror, the sword, and the jewels, are deemed endowed with miraculous power to heal the body, to purify the mind, and to bestow on men prosperity, happiness, and peace. Therein is the shrine possessed of most unusual sanctity, especially through the sacred mirror, the very "presence" of the Goddess. In the Outer Shrine, seat of the Food-goddess,[14] are her own peculiar symbols. She holds her seat by invitation of the great Goddess herself (for so it was revealed to the Emperor Yuryaku in a dream) who long ago summoned her to Isé. She dwells in her own holy place, a spacious park with its gateways, groves, inclosures, and buildings only less pretentious than the sanctuary of the Sun, whose brightness she has shared. There are other deities as well at Isé, but we will view them later in the general Shinto pantheon. The other symbols at Isé we may notice now, for they fill out the essential Shinto situation. On the altar tables, and elsewhere, stand *gohei* or *nusa,* upright wands, sometimes tufted, representing branches of the sacred *sakaki* tree (the *cleyera Japonica*). Strips of notched paper usually hang from these *gohei*. These strips are modern,

---

13 For a full description of the origin and meaning of these relics and for an account of their use as royal symbols see D. C. Holton, *The Japanese Enthronment Ceremonies,* Tokyo, 1928.

14 There are other food-goddesses elsewhere, for example, *Ukemochi* (*Ukemuji*), and *Inari.*

conventionalized substitutes for the bast cloth (cloth made of the
inner fiber of *sakaki,* or other bark) which was hung in ancient
times on the boughs of sacred trees as offerings to the gods. The
sakaki tree, especially dear to the Sun-goddess, is associated
directly with her in myth and worship. In one version of the hidden sulking of the Goddess, the scene enacted by the gods before
the cave into which she had fled includes this sacred tree. According to this version, the deity *Ame-no-Koyane* dug up a five-
hundred-branched "true *sakaki* tree of heaven," and hung on its
higher branches the string of "curved jewels," on its middle
branches the mirror, and on the lower branches strips of bast
cloth. The company then recited a liturgy in honor of the Sun;
Ame-no-Koyane arrayed herself, kindled a fire, danced, and gave
forth inspired utterances; heaven shook; all the deities laughed
loudly; and the Sun at last peered out in curiosity and wonder
—and was captured! Thus the myth of the coming of light to
the world, whose glory and beneficence are symbolized in the
sacred mirror.

The use of symbols rather than graven images prevails throughout Shinto shrines and ritual. These symbols, whether the "divine
regalia," or the *gohei,* or the plain tablets which one often sees,
are called *shintai,* or "god-bodies." These *shintai* do not necessarily indicate mysticism, or any high conception of spiritual
religion. They rather represent the low state of culture prior to
the advent of Chinese and Indian influence. And they represent
something of the "spiritual" resistance offered by indigenous
Shinto to alien forces.

Ritual.—Let us look at Shinto ritual within the sanctuary of
Isé. There are generally daily offerings of uncooked food, and
drink: saucers of rice and salt, and trays of fish, birds, fruit,
seaweed, and vegetables; and cups of *saké* or rice-brew. The
deities delight in gifts of what is necessary and pleasing to mankind. The offerings are a service of thanksgiving, rather than of
supplication. Through its appointed servitors the State expresses
its gratitude to the gods for their aid. At certain times the services are in expiation of the national guilt. While the gods have
often saved the nation in extremity, they have also sent down
calamity as a punishment for national sin. How often indeed has
Japan met with calamity, with earthquake, tidal wave, or fire!
The ceremonial is simple. The offerings are brought forward,
one after the other, a ritual is recited, and the offerings are removed. The priests who bear them glide in and out with noiseless

steps. On occasion, dances are performed within the inner shrine to the accompaniment, in a separate building, of song and instrumental music. The dance is always a simple, rhythmic glide; the music is that of chanting. The ceremonial of the State cult is always marked by grave solemnity, although sectarian Shinto may at times include some noisy rites. State Shinto never uses fireworks as the Buddhists often do.

The Great Purification.—On great festival occasions the ceremonial is quite elaborate, although even then remarkably pure, in strict solemnity, and with motives such as characterize the daily rites. The most solemn ceremony of State Shinto is the *Ohoharáhi,* or Great Purification, a national atonement for "sins and pollutions," and for the cleansing away of "old shapes of foul disease." It is celebrated at Isé, Kidzuki, and elsewhere [15] twice yearly, and in connection with Enthronement exercises; and all Shintoists, in fact, all members of the several communities, are expected to attend. The rite is performed in homage to the gods, especially the Sun-goddess. It includes a water-sprinkling, the waving of the *gohei,* and the use of human effigies made of rice-straw. These effigies, representing the sinful worshipers, are thrown at last into the stream, the lake, or the ocean. While the whole ceremonial is marked by an impressive, archaic sobriety, it is in essence and motive an annual purging such as the *Apo* ceremony of Ashantiland (*cf.* pp. 24f., above). Shinto teaches by the *Oho-haráhi* the consciousness of communal guilt and the social obligation of repentance. The Emperor, by virtue of the authority descended to him from the Goddess, himself pronounces during the *Oho-haráhi* the absolution of the impurities and sins of his ministers and the people. The *Ritual* reminds one that when "the mighty words of the celestial rites" are recited, and the gods have heard, "all offences whatsoever will be annulled." It sounds like magic, but we are assured there is a moral connotation. As cleanliness of person is a habit of the Japanese, so their cult of Shinto enjoins purity of heart. One writer in the "Shinto Pentateuch" has said that "what pleases the Deity is virtue and sincerity, and not any number of material offerings." The author of the *Shinto-Shoden-Kuju* declares that ablution is "not merely the cleansing of one's body solely with lustral water," but "following the moral way."

[15] See L. Hearn, *Glimpses of Unfamiliar Japan,* I, 182–191, 198, 208–210, and *Transactions of the Asiatic Society of Japan,* XLI, Pt. IV, for the Kidzuki celebration. For ceremonial in general see Aston, *Shinto,* pp. 268–326. For the Purification Nakatomi ritual see Anesaki, *History of Japanese Religion,* pp. 44–45.

Shinto has an annual Harvest Festival held in the autumn, on Nov. 23rd, made all the more solemn by its celebration at midnight. The rice then offered has been grown apart in a special field, tended by hallowed virgins, and ceremonially sanctified. The occasion is one of profound thanksgiving to the gods.

Shinto has its various functionaries,—we may scarcely call them priests, save for convenience. Isé has its *shinkan,* "government ministers," who are under civil service regulations. The other large national shrines have their *shin-shoku,* "government officials," of a slightly lower grade. The lesser shrines of the State are attended by officials named by the local parishioners subject to government ratification.[16] The national "officials" of the larger shrines are virtually ritualists whose duty is attention to the regular, and the festival observances, and the upkeep of the shrines. They do no preaching, nor do they engage in religious propaganda; they are not priests in the strict sense of the term. The officers at the lesser, more numerous shrines are far more "priestly"; they carry on the ancient traditions of magic, exorcism, and the occult. They make use of various objects, spells, and prayers, mostly against evil spirits.

Shinto has many more gods than those mentioned—many *kami,* as the Japanese say.[17] A *kami* may mean anything from a natural object, or the "spirit" of such an object, to the gods of different ranks, including the Goddess herself, and even the "original spirit" itself. *Kami* is, in this respect, a wider term than *shen.* It is applied particularly to the various deities of heaven and earth mentioned in the ancient records, and to the spirits of these deities who reside in the sacred groves and shrines. But it is applied also to birds and beasts, fruits, personal adornments, mountains, and seas, and anything which is to be dreaded or revered for extraordinary and preëminent power. It applies to ancestral spirits also which came in time to be included by Shinto along with the primal nature spirits.[18]

Scriptures.—Shinto has its scriptures in which the stories of the *kami* may be found. There are two, in particular, the *Ko-ji-ki* or "ancient-time-chronicle," and the *Nihon-gi* or "Japan-chronicle."

---

16 *Cf.* the *Japan Yearbook* for the grades of shrines and functionaries. For a description of official costumes see G. Schurhammer, *Shinto,* p. 160; D. C. Holtom, *op. cit.,* p. 66.

17 The Japanese ideograph for *kami* is identical with the Chinese *shen*-symbol.

18 Original Japanese religion was nature-worship, and it is not possible to say precisely when ancestor-worship was begun—perhaps with the worship of the spirits of deceased *mikados.* When the mythology was first formulated in the ancient (?) records the royal dynasty had already been linked with the Sun as the Great Ancestral Goddess (*Amaterasu-o-mi-kami*), and a succession of heavenly ancestors who preceded the first earthly sovereign, Jimmu Tenno.

Both are filled with mythological lore, in spite of the fact that the former was compiled as late as 712 A.D., and the latter in 720 (the Japanese had first to learn to write before these "chronicles" could be composed). A third work, the *Engi-shiki* or "Origin of Rites," is later still, having been written in the 10th century, A.D. It records the details of ancient Shinto ritual, with prayers for various occasions. A fourth book, fourth in point of value, the *Manyo-shu,* comes from the 9th century. It constitutes the oldest collection of Japanese poems, with a few details of ritual, and some allusions to beliefs. These four are the Shinto sacred writings. They cannot be said to occupy a lofty plane, unless one deems their naturalism and realism lofty. The *Ko-ji-ki,* in particular, describes many "divine" activities in terms we might call obscene, in which respect it differs from the sacred canon of any other religion. Shinto scriptures and Shinto morals and religion are intimately related.

Theology.—We now return to the gods, the *kami.* Shinto has an interesting theology. There is not only "the Great Deity" of Isé, but myriads of gods besides. The *Engi-shiki* refers to "myriads." The 18th century reformer, Hirata, thought in terms of "the eight hundred myriads of celestial gods, the fifteen hundred myriads of gods" of various shrines, "the gods of branch-shrines," etc. Each region and community has had its own divinities. Frequently, one deity has gone by different names in different places. A few deities have been known and worshiped, each by its own proper name, throughout the whole "Great Land of the Eight Islands." All these deities were manifestly nature powers in their origin, but there is nothing to show that any confined itself to its primary nature function. One might perform the appropriate function of another. Among the "myriads," a small number of the gods were, of course, the most effective.

In early Shinto there seems not to have been one god who was supreme. Heaven itself was not a god, as *T'ien* was in early China. The Shinto heaven was but the region where the gods resided. The Sun-goddess was the most important deity, but her powers were not unlimited. There *is* evidence that there were gods before her. In fact, the myth accounts for several generations of celestial spirits which came spontaneously out of primeval chaos, and vanished later on.[19] The last of the series were *Izana-gi* and *Izana-mi,* male and female, but with a merely formal dis-

---

[19] It is probable that Chinese speculation affected the Shinto myth before it was recorded in writing.

tinction in sex, which plays no important part, either in the myth, or in the Shinto cult. These two powers descended from the "plain of high heaven," united, and gave birth first to many objects, such as islands, waters, winds, fields, food, and fire. All the things which they produced were *kami.* They produced, also, the "three noble children," the sun, the moon, and the storm. Or, as another version has it, *Izana-gi* alone produced these children: the sun from one eye, the moon from the other, and the storm-god from his nostrils, as he purified himself from the pollution of a visit to the underworld. Whatever their origin, these three stand at the head of the Shinto pantheon: the Sun-goddess *Amaterasu,* the Moon-god *Tsuki-yomi,* and the Storm-god, *Susa-no-wo.* The fire-god *Homusubi,* also known as *Kagut-suchi,* was born of *Izana-mi* who thereby lost her life. To the divine couple, *Izana-gi* and *Izana-mi,* were born the great earth-god *Onamuji (Ohonamochi),* whose shrine is at Kidzuki; the food-goddess *Toyo-uke* or *Ukemuji,* who shares the shrine at Isé[20]; and many gods of the sea, the rivers, the mountains, the fields, and the home. The greatest, however, of all the divine progeny, are *Amaterasu* (known today by her Chinese equivalent name of *Tensho-daijin*), and *Susa-no-wo,* the former presiding over all the realm of light, and the latter ruling over the ocean and the realm of hidden things. From the pairing of these two—or else by the spontaneous conception of the Goddess alone and by a sort of virgin-birth—came the "divine grandson" Ninigi, the immediate ancestor of the earthly Jimmu Tenno, and the succession of Mikados. Shinto myth has much to say about these two deities. They were often in conflict, but the Sun at last won the sovereignty of earth, as well as of heaven. She has thus assumed the leading rôle in Japanese religion. The affairs of earth she gave over to her august descendants, the Mikados, who, with their people, have since held her in the highest regard, both as Divine Ancestress and as Supreme Deity.[21]

Spiritism.—It is difficult to see less in this National, or Shrine Shinto, than a subtle union of politics and religion. The ancient tradition is in its own peculiar way markedly religious, and there is something religious still in the nominally non-religious concept of the divine nation. But Shinto is collective Japan, and the Japanese sould unalloyed. The gods, especially the Sun-goddess, and the land are inseparably connected. The story of Shrine

20 Who appears elsewhere as the god Inari, the rice-god, in the exceptional form of an image holding a head of rice, and with two carved dogs lying at his feet.
21 Thus the *one* head of nature- and ancestor-worship.

Shinto is not the story of theological creeds and priestly interpretations, but rather the record of "an indissoluble relationship between each individual and the Divine," too intimate for one man to interpret fully for another, too intangible for purely ecclesiastical organization, and yet withal a social and political force in the life of the entire people. Shinto affords an unusual example of the identity of man and nature. The Japanese had a dim recognition of the divinity of the universe, and a faint notion of all the divine aspects of the universe combining in one harmonious whole. They saw the divine *in* the natural, not above it and apart from it. Such a view lay behind the declaration of a 17th century Shintoist that "There is no deity apart from the human mind." In Shinto man was the center, and God was seen in man and his environment. The point of view is what we would call natural, rather than spiritual,—humanism, rather than a spiritism, in spite of what has been called in connection with Shinto the "doctrine of spiritism."

In harmony with the "humanistic" attitude, there is little place for prayer. Prayer, in any true sense, is almost entirely absent from earliest records until the present. An ancient Japanese poet of the 8th century, A.D., wrote,

> "Japan is not a land where men need pray,
> For 't is itself divine.
> Yet do I lift my voice in prayer."

This is somewhat in the mood of Desdemona when about to die,

> "Why I should fear I know not,
> Since guiltiness I know not;
> But yet I feel I fear."

Modern prayers are mostly for material blessings, whether prayers of thanksgiving, or of repentance and purification. The ancient records (the *Ko-ji-ki* and the *Nihon-gi*) contain no prayers, and only two references to prayer. The emperors seldom prayed, if the records may be depended upon. There are recorded prayers in the *Engi-shiki,* the book of liturgy, but they are, as in the case of Confucianism, chiefly announcements to the various deities, ascriptions of praise, and the rendering of thanks. Other than that, they are prayers, for example, for rain, food, children, health, protection from earthquakes, the success of the armies, and the welfare of the Empire.

The peculiar doctrine of "spiritism" is associated with the word *mitama,* or "august soul," for which "spirit" is the nearest English equivalent.[22] The Japanese today use this word for the departed soul. Shinto says that it is not the Sun-goddess herself who inhabits the shrine at Isé, but her *mitama,* an emanation or effluence from her, whose presence is symbolized by the several *shintai* or "god-bodies." The *mitama* is a kind of spiritual presence not unlike the *shekinah* of the Jews,[23] but no such comparison may properly be made between the Hebrew *Yahweh* and the Sun-goddess. *Amaterasu* has not the reality of *Yahweh,* although myth describes her as moving about in her real body, while being at the same time anywhere in her *mitama* presence. As might be expected, many Japanese have failed to distinguish between the *mitama* and the *shintai* itself, and honors are done to the *shintai.* Among the masses, the *shintai* have been worshiped directly, as if they themselves were the deities in the shrines, and not merely their symbols. Such worship is essentially magical, a dependence upon the magical efficacy of the *shintai.* It takes literally the reported saying of *Amaterasu* to her "august grandson," Ninigi, when she bestowed upon him the sacred mirror, "When you look into this mirror regard it as looking upon me, myself."

Morality.—Pure Shinto, as the old religious "spirit" of Japan, was simple in its ethics, as well as in ideas and in worship. The *kami-no-michi* was, ethically, the natural way, or the theory of life according to nature. Man, having an immediate perception or intuition of "spirituality," had *no code of ethics,* because he, being divine, needed none. "Being straightforward, they could do without teaching," said Mabuchi in the 18th century. "Because the Japanese were truly moral in their practice, they required no theory of morals," said Motoöri (d. 1801). Chesterton has said that "morality consists in drawing the line somewhere." The Japanese drew no line anywhere. Shinto has no written code of moral conduct, nothing to compare with the "Commandments" of the Hebrews, or with the prohibition of the Buddhists. Modern advocates of "pure Shinto" make a virtue of this lack: if man is good by nature,[24] he need not talk about goodness nor have a written guide.

While we may look in vain in the ancient Shinto books of "history" and ritual for a moral *code,* for any moral instruction, or for

---

[22] See Aston, *Shinto,* p. 26.
[23] *Cf. Habbakuk,* 2:20, "The Lord is in His holy temple." In the *Targums* this appears as, "Yahweh was pleased to cause his *shekinah* to dwell in his holy temple."
[24] *Cf.* the Confucian doctrine of human nature.

any moralizing reflections upon history, we may know that the ancient Japanese had a morality corresponding with their plane of culture. The Great Purification is sufficient proof. The earliest "great purification of the land," mentioned in the *Ko-ji-ki,* is at once testimony to the presence of a certain moral sense, and to the primitive quality of this sense. The "line is drawn" in a very naïve manner: "heavenly offences" and "earthly offences" are distinguished and enumerated.[25] Shinto commentators say that the former offences were so called, because first committed *in heaven* by the god Susa-no-wo. Among these offences were skinning alive, breaking down the divisions between rice-fields, filling up irrigation ditches, marriage[26] between unequals, and human intercourse with beasts. Among the "earthly offences" are listed the cutting of living, or dead bodies, the killing of animals, and the intercourse of a man with his mother, daughter, mother-in-law, or step-daughter. No gradations are observed; these are all equal crimes against both gods and men. As time went on, however, a process of development got under way, and a more acute and discriminating moral sense was generated.

Alien Influences.—Shinto has been subjected, from time to time, to higher influences from without. In spite of the resistance which these alien forces met, some modifications have been effected by them. Under the influence of Confucian, and of Buddhist morality, virtues and vices became more distinct, and "purification" became more than ceremonial; yet Shinto preserved even under Buddhist pressure a Confucian sense of man's innate goodness and self-dependence. *Three ideas* were prominent in old Shinto: (1) sacrifice and prayers, expiatory and in thanksgiving, in connection with the food supply; (2) concern for the government as identified both with the welfare and religion of the land; and (3) the dread of pollution which, if incurred, could be removed only through incantation and magical ritual. Civilizing effects came with the foreign religions. Buddhism alone brought highly developed doctrines, elaborate ceremonial, and art, whose effects were soon felt, although Shinto has scarcely kept pace with the progress of the resultant Japanese civilization. Under Chinese influence the utilitarian character of Japan manifested æsthetic qualities. The Japanese cult of the natural developed into a cult of the beautiful. Japan was more easily won to æsthetic than to moral standards of conduct, although it

---

25 Other faiths have had "great sins" and "small offences," *e.g.,* Islam.
26 Shinto has ever had, according to the records, a marriage ceremony.

cannot be said that she ever submitted to the dominance of the æsthetic to the extent China did. It has been inconsistent with Japan's prevailing mood to yield political place to music and art. Shinto's cult of beauty took its place *beside* Shinto's cult of loyalty, not instead of it. While Japan has given extraordinary expression to the artistic temperament, this expression has been for her a pleasure wholly consistent with her theory of the State. Japan has had her soldier-scholars and her soldier-artists.

Shinto has afforded *womanhood* a position higher than that which she has held in China. It is a corollary of the Japanese notion of divinity and of the moral sense that men and women should be equal. Women figure with unusual prominence in Japanese history, including many priestesses and many who have been Mikados. *Amaterasu,* of course, is female, usually. It is, however, a corollary, also, that there should have been a long-enduring phallicism. There was every inducement for the primitive Japanese to explain the mysterious growth of Nature by the analogy of human procreation. Not only has phallicism existed as a phase of agriculture, but also as an independent institution, and it has not yet disappeared altogether from the Japanese countryside.

Cult of Ancestors.—Old Shinto was, in the beginning, a comparatively primitive worship of the powers of nature as gods, who were humanized, and thought of in terms of human social experience; it became also *a cult of ancestral spirits*. This latter phase is a later development, and not an original element in Japanese religion.[27] There was in ancient Japan no sufficiently clear realization of the family to warrant an assumption that ancestor-worship was primordial. Worship of the *uji-gami,* ("guardian-gods"), the family, or clan gods, is not ancient, for the family and the clan are not ancient. The common people, at least, made in ancient times no pretence of divine parentage, and the peculiar form of the Japanese ancestral cult, namely the cult of the Sun-goddess as Divine Ancestress, waited upon the institution of the Imperial dynasty. There was no Mikado-worship in ancient times, because there was no Mikado in the later sense of the term, nor any central and supreme government. The history of the concept of *mitama* (soul?) suggests that the idea of "soul" is a comparatively late development. It seems fair to assume that the ancestor-cult is a direct result of Chinese influence.

Ancestor-worship was, however, readily assimilated with the

27 Lafcadio Hearn thought it original.

worship of nature-powers, whether with reference to the family, the tribe, or the Imperial dynasty, but the extent to which it developed as "Mikadoism" is peculiarly Japanese, distinct from Chinese theory and practice. The ultimate ground of the error which places ancestor-worship and nature-worship side by side as coeval in Japanese religion is the inference drawn from the character of the Sun-goddess as both natural object (the sun) and personified power (the ancestress of the race). The first Mikado was not "the heavenly grandchild" *until* the era in which the Shinto sacred books were composed in Chinese ideographs under Chinese influence. He had been before that scarcely more than what the poet Waller meant by his phrase, "the sonne of Heaven," applied to James II. The Chinese impulse, manifested then in the worship of Confucius and of Lao-tze, inspired the Japanese, also. The Mikado Ojin (3rd century, A.D.) became a deity under the name of *Hachiman,* the War-god whose symbol was the *dove.* The *Nihon-gi* declares the Emperor (any emperor) to be "incarnate deity." By the 10th century there were made to deceased Mikados offerings similar to those made to nature deities. The whole "eternally enduring dynasty" was linked at last with the divine Sun-Ancestress. As late as 1889 an article of the Japanese Constitution declares the Emperor's person to be "sacred and inviolable." Shinto today is a cult of nature and of ancestors, and to characterize it thus is to place it low in any list of religions arranged according to the standards of progress in religion.

In one sense, indeed, there is no longer any primitive Shinto. It no longer exists as a tangible, separate entity; it *is* a "spirit." The "Shintoist" is so by birth as a Japanese, being something else by virtue of his absorption of non-Shinto elements, or by adherence to another faith. We point to the overwhelming number of Buddhists [28] in Japan who are not without a proportionate influence. Nevertheless, *kokutai* endures. The paradox is well illustrated by two opposing opinions. In 1905, W. G. Aston, an eminent student of Shinto, remarked that "as a national religion, Shinto is almost extinct." In 1928, Genchi Kato, who holds the Chair of Shinto in the Tokyo Imperial University, said that "Shinto, as a national religion, never dies; it still is and ever will be." We ourselves have seen already that, in the words of E. Ryerson, "State Shinto is by no means moribund." We close our study of State or Shrine Shinto with this definition [29] by Dr. Kato,

28 About 50,000,000.
29 *A study of Shinto,* p. 208.

"The vital essence of Shinto manifests itself in an expression of that unique spirit of the national service of the Japanese people, which is not only mere morality, but is their religion, culminating in Mikadoism or their own peculiar form of loyalty or patriotism toward the Emperor, who is at once political head and religious leader in a government constitutional yet theocratic-patriarchal."

We need say little here about the *domestic* cult, little more than a brief description of its forms, for in essence it partakes of the qualities of the national cult.[30] The rites are very simple. In a room of each house is a "god-shelf," the *kami-dana,* on which stand tablets, or strips of paper, inscribed with the names of special deities, such as the Sun-goddess, the Food-goddess, or the god of a particular occupation, or locality. There may be the small shrine known as *miya,* containing a "presence" (mirror), along with pieces of sacred rice-straw, bits of rice-cake from a public shrine, holy texts, and charms. These are the stock of the domestic cult. Ideally, daily devotion is performed before the *kami-dana* by the offering of a prayer.

Hirata (b. 1776), the greatest expounder of Shinto and a leader in the revival of "Pure Shinto," after the passing of Buddhist dominance, recommended the following prayer [31] to be said daily before the *kami-dana* by every earnest householder,

"Reverently adoring the great deity of the two shrines of Isé, in the first place, the eight hundred myriads of celestial gods, the fifteen hundred myriads of gods to whom are consecrated the great and small shrines in all the provinces, all islands and all places of the Great Land of Eight Islands, the fifteen hundred myriads of gods whom they cause to serve them, the gods of branch-shrines, the protector of fields whom I have invited to the shrine set up on this shelf and to whom I daily offer praise, —I pray with awe that they will deign to correct the unwilling faults which, heard and seen by them, I have committed; and that they, blessing and favoring me according to the powers which they severally wield, will cause me to follow the divine example, and to perform good works in the Way."

[30] *Cf.* Hearn, *Unfamiliar Japan,* II, 396–403; *Japan,* 150ff; Aston, *op. cit.,* 44ff.
[31] Adapted from Hearn, *Japan,* pp. 150–151.

On special occasions little tapers, or lamps are lighted; sprigs of *sakaki,* a little rice-brew, and other articles offered with prayer, and the clapping of the hands, as usual. In some other room in the same household—in the "spirit-chamber"—may be tablets (*ihai*) to the family ancestors (the *uji-gami*). These are ordinarily strips of plain, white wood, bearing inscriptions, before which daily offerings are made of rice, flowers, etc. This aspect was introduced, of course, by Buddhism and Confucianism. Beyond these simple household rites (which have become perfunctory in many households, when not altogether absent) the religion of the individual Shintoist may get expression in daily visits to some nearby shrine, and, on festival occasions, in a pilgrimage to some distant shrine. Every Shintoist should make at least one pilgrimage to Isé, either in person, or by proxy, even as every Moslem should go once to Mecca, and every Hindu once behold the Ganges.

Revival.—In the 19th century the Shinto *sects* took definite form. There are now thirteen of them, each recognized by the national Government as "religions," and registered in the Bureau of Religions of the State Department of Education. Altogether, they maintain nearly ten thousand chapels and preaching-places, and have in great numbers their own ministers, or priests. Preaching and propaganda occupy a conspicuous place among them. Although it was not until 1871 that the Japanese Government drew the theoretical (or political?) line between Shrine Shinto as "non-religious" and Sect Shinto as "religious," thereby forcing the sects to stand apart and maintain themselves as independent bodies, sectarian Shinto arose first out of the eighteenth century effort to revive "Pure Shinto" as opposed to Confucian and Buddhist culture and religion. Patriotic scholars strove to revive interest in the ancient national literature, such as the *Ko-ji-ki* and the *Nihon-gi,* which had been for long neglected. This revival assumed under Motoöri (1730–1801) a religious character. He bitterly resented the presence of "Chinese" elements, oblivious, apparently, of the great value of many of them, and exalted the old deities and forms of worship in a spirit of ardent patriotism. He reiterated in emphatic terms the "divine" character of "the successive Mikados," and of "all things whatsoever which deserve to be dreaded and revered for the extraordinary and preëminent powers which they possess." He declared all foreign countries, especially China and India, to be outside the "special domain of the Sun-goddess," and fields where evil spirits operate that corrupt mankind. His pupil, Hirata (1776–1843), carried on with great effectiveness, writing hundreds of books and delivering innumerable lectures on behalf of old Shinto. He gave such prominence to the divine, sovereign rights of the Mikados that the Shogun or "General," who was *de facto* ruler,[32] banished him. It was fundamental with him that Japan is the Country of the Gods, and her inhabitants the Children of the Gods, that between the Japanese and other peoples there is a difference of kind, the Japanese being immeasurably superior to others in courage, intelligence, honesty, and uprightness of heart. Hirata's ardent nationalism did not prevent, however, his acceptance of certain foreign elements, such as belief in the immortality of the soul (Buddhist) and the duty of "filial piety" (Confucian). While this revival directed attention to indigenous elements in Japanese culture, the intellectual and moral poverty of primitive Shinto demanded further consideration of "foreign" values which had already served to enrich the common life.

Sects.—Against the background of this revival, and indirectly related to it, Shinto made many attempts to become a religion which would satisfy men's hunger of heart for personal communion with the Divine. Many sects arose with this end in view, and while they have been despised by Buddhists and national Shintoists alike, they have numbered their adherents by the millions. Some sects have come and gone with amazing suddenness; others have come slowly and slowly decayed; new sects have recently arisen; and a few of the older sects are influential still.

The Kurozumi Sect.—Consider the *Kurozumi-kyo* (the "sect of Kurozumi").[33] The founder was a man of many different names, according to the stages of his life,[34] but he was known at last as Munetada. He was a scion of the Kurozumi family of the related group of Fujiwaras, born Dec. 21, 1780, in a village known as "quiet hamlet two miles west of Okayama," a city near the Inland Sea. His family was listed from 1701 as among the *samurai* or warrior folk. Yet it was a priestly family. Munetada's father was the priest of the local Shinto shrine of *Tensho-daijin*, the Sun-goddess, and when the father ceased to serve, the son succeeded him.

Kurozumi Munetada's sectarian venture was a product both of the times and of his own experience. Chinese culture then pre-

---

[32] The actual administration of Japanese affairs was in the hands of Shoguns during modern times until the revolution of 1868.
[33] The Japanese *kyo* is the Chinese *chiao*, or "teaching."
[34] He had an "infant" name, another at fifteen, another in token of disaster in his family, another as a priest, and another still as the founder of a sect.

vailed throughout the circle of the leaders of Japan, while Buddhist influence dominated in religion. Many Chinese scholars and philosophers had emigrated to Japan after the fall of the Ming dynasty in 1644, and these had given impetus to a revival of Confucian learning. Perhaps the leading philosophy of the time was that of the neo-Confucianist Wang Yang-ming (1472-1528), called Oyomei by the Japanese. It emphasized dependence upon intuition, rather than on knowledge, in religious experience, and assured that any man might become a sage. Parallel with this, the influential *Shingon* or "True Word" sect of Buddhism was proclaiming the possibility of man's attaining buddhahood by thought and the power of the "True Word," even in the present life. This Buddhist sect had long been compromising with the Shinto cult by its declaration that Buddha and the Sun-goddess were one power. And it had built its temples on the sacred Shinto height, Mt. Koya.

In such an atmosphere of intuitionist philosophy and of the theory of the dependable immediacy of spiritual experience Munetada was born and reared. He knew something of Confucian philosophy and of Buddhist religion. He also doubtless knew something of the important third factor, which was combating alien elements. "Pure Shinto" (see above) was in process of revival. Munetada, under its influence, came to think that his own faith, despite its defects which he saw and understood, might enable him to realize what the foreign systems offered. His problem, therefore, was to become (or realize himself) a god, or *kami,* while yet he was alive. His becoming *kami* meant more than being Buddha or a sage. It meant the embodiment of the eternal spirit of his own country, and the realization of his own divinity.

In 1810, when his father stepped aside as priest, Munetada carried on the office. Three deities were worshiped at his shrine: (1) the Sun-goddess, (2) *Hachiman* (the deity of the *daimyos,* or rulers of Okayama), and (3) the ancestral spirit of the Fujiwaras. The crisis of his life came soon after he became a priest, rather, a series of crises set in. Both his parents died in 1812, within a week, and he mourned excessively. Soon he was ill with what the doctors pronounced an incurable disease. He sought comfort in religion, but prepared for death. He fasted one time for a period of twenty-seven days, and prayed constantly to the Goddess. On March 6, 1814, it occured to him that possibly he had brought disease upon himself by his excessive sorrow. With a different mind, therefore, he prayed for health. At dawn one day (December 22, 1814), while he was engaged in prayer, there came suddenly an experience of the Goddess which seemed to purge and brighten and restore him. He was then and there miraculously healed. He was possessed of *yo-ki,* the Sun-spirit. He had become *kami.* For fifty years thereafter he gave himself to the ministry of the majesty and power of the Sun-goddess.

Munetada's activities were many throughout the period of his ministry.[35] He made many trips to Isé. During one year (1825) he confined his devotion to one shrine only. During two and one half months of another year (1829) he repeated the *Oho-haráhi* ritual 46,900 times. In 1830 he began a ten-year visitation of shrines at the rate of one hundred every month. He often resorted to divination for instruction, using the Chinese hexagrams (*cf.* the Chinese *I Ching*). For example, once he learned that "in order to succeed, we must be at peace with our fellow-men"; and on February 4, 1839, he read the sign "to break a new path." He wrought many cures, sometimes by prayers to the Goddess, sometimes by his pilgrimages. At his death he was officially recognized by the Japanese Government as *Munetada-kami,* "God Munetada" (or, *Dai-Myo-Jin,* "great-shining-deity").

Munetada's Teachings.—His teachings centered in the Goddess, of whom he thought in terms of the "ancient" records. He neither ignored, nor denied, however, the "myriads" of lesser deities. He was virtually a *relative polytheist.* But he tempered his polytheism with certain philosophical tenets which he seems to have derived from the sixteenth century Chinese, Wang Yangming. He identified the Goddess with "sound wisdom," or "good knowledge," or "intuition," which he called *ryochi.* This *ryochi* is diffused in all beings and objects, which together make up the universe; in fact, *ryochi* is the universe, whose conspicuous central figure is the Goddess. It is she who fills all things, whether man or beast, fish or fowl, good or evil, and through whom all things are moved and guided. She is the wisdom which all men should desire, and which may be obtained by every sincere, devoted seeker. The Goddess in the heart of man is after all the great Reality. She *is* the "heart" or *kokoro,* "mind, soul, spirit." Kurozumi himself had found her on that Dec. 22, 1814. Her special seat was Isé, where he often went on pilgrimage. He had been healed and illuminated by her grace. Through her and in her

---

[35] For many of these details I am indebted to a former student, Mr. C. W. Hapner, of Japan, the author of a special study of the *Kurozumi-kyo,* based on original sources.

he had found the *Ten-Do-sama,* or "honorable heavenly way."
Her way is Truth. Such was his theology.

Kurozumi's *philosophy* was dualistic, in the characteristic vein
of modern China. Over against the "brightness" (*yo-ki*) of the
Goddess, is the "gloom" (*in-ki*), whence evil passions arise and
diseases spring.[36] He takes both *yo-ki* and *in-ki* for granted. Good
and evil are both "natural," but evil in man is due to man's self
(his *waré*), and to a certain form of illusion (*mayoi*).[37] It is
necessary to keep *in-ki* in subjection to *yo-ki,* if man have peace
of mind and health of body. If *in-ki* should prevail, man becomes
the victim of moral and physical ills. If *in-ki* does prevail, the way
of its subordination tò *yo-ki* is by the inducement of trance states[38]
and ecstasy, through which the sufferer may inhale the Divine
Spirit and realize his oneness with Divinity (the Goddess). To this
end he advocated breathing exercises, such as Taoists and some
Buddhists used, the repetition of a certain prayer to the Goddess
(and prayers, also, to all the gods of healing). To keep in health
of body and mind the devotee must rely upon "the cultivation of
the heart" (*yo-mu*), by which Munetada seems to mean in part,
at least, an identification of oneself with *Mu,* the Goddess as the
Ultimate. And the devotee must have the "heart of faith" (*shin-
jen*), a faith which clearly reflects the teaching of certain "faith"
sects of the Buddhists.

The *Kurozumi-kyo* gained great influence mainly through its
"healing" of the sick by faith and illumination. Kurozumi
(Munetada) himself had performed the "great incantation," and
had licensed several chosen priests for its performance. Each
head of the sect after him has performed this rite. The headquarters of the sect is Kurozumi's native village where a large
memorial to him was erected in 1880.[39] Since 1881 the sect itself
has been among those "recognized" by the Imperial Government,
but its best days seem to have passed. It claims today half a
million followers.

The Tenri Sect.—The *Tenri-kyo* or "heavenly reason teaching" reckons its followers as three and one-half millions. It has
been both prosperous and assertive during recent decades. Its
shrines, priests, and adherents are found throughout the Empire,
and it has looked forward to becoming the dominant faith. Its

---

36 *Cf.* the *yang-yin* theory of the Chinese.
37 *Mayoi* is the Indian-Buddhist *maya* or "illusion." Kurozumi's "faith" shows the
effects of Buddhist influence.
38 Munetada himself was evidently pathological, often experiencing trances which
he took to be an evidence of his possession of the *yo-ki* of the Goddess.
39 In 1862 a temple was built in Kyoto to his honor.

chief temple is situated in the village of Mishima, near Nara, an ancient Imperial capital. This sect came into the field during the early nineteenth century, when the common people had long been disappointed in other means of satisfying their hearts' hunger. By faith-healing and an energetic program of preaching it has gained public attention and won adherents. It has failed, however, to make a marked impression on the upper classes.

Omiki.—*Tenri-kyo* was founded by a woman, (Mrs.) Omiki Nakayama, born in 1798 of a peasant family in a village of the province of Yamato. At thirteen, she was married to one Nakayama, a farmer living in the neighboring village of Mishima. They were poor, but industrious, and frugal. She not only cared for the household and the children, but worked in the fields. Although she had little education, she seems to have gained the respect of the villagers by her kindness of heart and unselfish service. At the age of thirty-two, she was touched with pity for a poor mother of the village and made of one of the woman's children a foster-child, giving it equal attention with her own. One day, on returning from the fields, Omiki discovered her foster-child ill with small-pox in a virulent form. This she took to be a sign of her own neglect, and employed every means for the child's recovery. Medical skill seemed unavailing, so she resorted to the "higher powers." She visited the shrines of the gods, both Shinto and Buddhist, offered her gifts and her prayers, and even vowed two of her own children, if the foster-child be restored to health. The child was cured, but soon afterwards a natural daughter died—in partial payment of the mother's vows? Two years later, a second daughter was taken— to complete the vow? Omiki considered these events the work of the gods.

In her fortieth year, one of her sons was troubled by a painful ulcer on his foot. In this instance, the parents applied first of all to a minor priest, or exorcist, who brought some temporary relief through incantation. Upon the return of the pain, the services of the leader of a pilgrim society were enlisted, and he performed a *gohei* [40] ceremony of "bringing down the gods." The ulcer was cured, immediately, we may suppose, for the impression upon the mother was so pronounced that she went into trance for three days, and in the end was seized with a frenzy attributable to the gods alone. She deemed herself "possessed." This was the turning-

---

[40] See p. 143, above, for the meaning of the *gohei*. In this case the patient was inducted into a trance by the waving of the *gohei*.

point of her career. Soon thereafter *Kuni-toko-tachi-no-mikoto,* one of the ancient Shinto deities, spoke to her. A series of convulsions ensued, during each of which a deity was revealed to her. Last of all came *Izanagi* and *Izanami,* the divine parents. Ten gods in all revealed themselves. These she designated in the course of time the Ten Gods of the Heavenly Reason. They required the devotion of herself, her family, and all her possessions, upon pain of utter destruction. She came to be considered the special representative, indeed the incarnation of deity, and her words were taken as divinely inspired.

Omiki devoted herself thereafter to the religious life, giving forth her "revelations" in the form of hymns and sermons. She lived and taught for fifty years after her "call," gathering many converts, although she met with ridicule from both Shinto and Buddhist priests. In time an organization began to form as a means of preserving and extending the movement, and of resisting opposition. On her death in 1887, at the age of eighty-nine, an elaborate funeral service was performed, and her body was laid to rest on top of a low hill overlooking the village of Mishima. Six months later the sect received the official "recognition" of the Government. First a son, then a grandson, succeeded to the headship of the order, each living in state in Mishima. Omiki's teachings are preserved mostly in the form of manuscripts, including twelve hymns and reports of sermons. They are the irregular utterances of an untutored peasant speaking to the poor and uneducated, asserting her claims as a divine teacher, calling her hearers to accept her doctrine of deliverance from trouble and disease, and warning them vigorously to abandon sin and to lead upright lives as prerequisites to deliverance.

Omiki's Teachings.—Omiki taught that man's primary allegiance was to the moon and the sun. The words *Tsuki-hi,* "moon-sun," are her formula for God. It is a dualistic concept based upon the popular "Confucianism" of her region, which held the *yang-yin* theory of the universe. With her it is a naïve dualism, with neither theology nor philosophy. There were ten gods in all, but these two were the "higher possession" of her heart. They represented the male and female principles in the universe. Her Deity was the interacting Divine Parents who love and guard mankind, their children, and desire their purity of heart and happiness. Because of the desire of the Divine Parents for the happiness of their children, their children's worship is mostly praise and thanksgiving, with dancing and posturing, and with music from drums, cymbals, bells, and clappers of wood. In the house of worship are such objects as a mirror, the *gohei,* and the "god-shelves" for the offerings—such objects, in fact, as are common in Shinto shrines.

Omiki laid great stress upon *faith.* Healing could come by faith alone, and is actually hindered by physicians and medicine. "All disease is from the heart," she said, but the moon and sun are eager to make men's hearts "sincere"; therefore, have faith in them. Fertilizers were unnecessary for the fields; seed sown in faith brought the best crops. The doctrines about medicine and fertilizers have been modified in recent years by her followers, in deference to the Government and to reason. Trance states are doubtless still induced by the faithful for divine possession and revelation. But the ethical quality of the teachings continues fairly high. Duty is much insisted upon, especially the "five virtues" in the "five relations" (*cf.* Confucianism). Personal immortality was not emphasized; rather, Omiki said little about the future life, though she believed in it. Death was like "changing one's clothes," and then the good man would be reunited with the Divine Parents, moon and sun, in some realm whence his soul had originated as an emanation from them.

The Taisha Sect.—The *Taisha-kyo,* or "Great Shrine Sect," is the largest of the sects, claiming four and one third million members. It seems to have enjoyed its greatest prosperity during the years 1890–1895. It was established—some adherents say "revived"—in 1874, at Kidzuki, whence the name "Great Shrine," by a nobleman, Senge Sompuku, warden or "divine official" of the shrine. Under his direction the sect used the State buildings as their headquarters until the Government ordered it in 1879 to withdraw. Sompuku then resigned his State office in favor of his son, Takanori, and established the sect in his baronial mansion in Kidzuki. He continued head of the order until it was "recognized" by the Government in 1887, after which, giving way to a nephew as superintendent, he assumed the office of "chief preacher." The headquarters of the sect have continued in the Senge mansion, with the ancient guest-chamber as its main sanctuary.

To what extent is *Taisha-kyo* sectarian? One may observe that it follows orthodox Shinto very closely, especially the "Pure Shinto" of Hirata. It rests upon an ancient base, Kidzuki. It has no other cosmology than that of primitive Shinto. It regards as the chief deity *Onamuji* (or *Oho-Kuni-nushi*) the great earth-god of Kidzuki, who descended from the boisterous deity of storm and mystery, *Susa-no-wo*. *Onamuji's* shrine is second only to Isé in sanctity, and surpasses it in age. The Senge priests have claimed descent from *Onamuji's* first successor, and the *Taisha-kyo* shares this lineage through Sompuku. While still connected with the Great Shrine, the sect had worshiped other gods besides *Onamuji* in the Hall, where, according to an inscription, "the effulgence of the Deities is manifest"; had relied upon music from the flute and drums of the shrine; had made use of *gohei* and *sakaki*-branches bearing replicas of the "divine relics," the mirror, sword, and jewels; and had worshiped the ancestral spirits. It has continued ancient practices, such as intercessory prayers in prescribed forms, together with incantation by an authorized official. It has propitiated *Onamuji* as god of earth and Ruler of the underworld, in whose care are the souls of the dead. It has relied upon prayers to the Ruler to secure for the dead the rank of *kami*. It has a cult of ancestors. It puts high value upon pilgrimage to Kidzuki. Once pilgrims were attracted by prizes, but this practice has ceased. The sect has practiced ancient Shinto magic. Once Sompuku was carried after a ritual bath into the sanctuary of a meeting-place and enshrined, while devotees drank of the waters of the bath, and various amulets were consecrated through contact with his body. Such practices have long since been abandoned. In fact, the sect has combated the nonsensical belief in fox-possession. But wherein is it a *sect?*

Perhaps its official severance from the Great Shrine actually induced, or heightened, its sectarian character. It *is* a very completely religious organization, having its houses of worship, its places of pilgrimage, its objects of worship, its sermons, priests, prayers and catechism. Unlike the *Kurozumi* and *Tenri* sects, however, the *Taisha-kyo* was not born out of a great religious experience. It is a religious adaptation of the national cult. Lacking such experiences as Munetada and Omiki had, there is in it no theory of divine "possession," nor any extreme reliance upon "faith." The Government deprived the head of the order of the character of a "living *kami*," which has caused members to seek at times the prayers of the warden of the orthodox Kidzuki shrine. The members of the order are not distinguished by any sense of mission. The sect has no philosophy, or creed, which would challenge the more thoughtful Japanese. Perhaps it endures by reason of its "purist" qualities, its great numbers, its prestige as the *Great Shrine* sect, and its veneration of the Emperor.

How long sectarian Shinto can survive among the highly literate people of progressive Japan is a question. The thirteen "recognized" sects have a total membership of fifteen million, and there are many sects unrecognized. Mitake, Shinto-Honku, Shinri, and Shinshu, along with Kurozumi, Tenri, and Taisha, combined claim over twelve million adherents, but reason has demanded many modifications in their creed and practice.

CHAPTER VIII

INDIA AND RELIGION

India by the Map.—Many of us often yield to the fascination of detailed topographical and varicolored maps, and enliven the symbolism of cartography with historical and human episodes. Maps are more than charted lines and figures, as human episodes themselves are symbols. One line may be a boundary which divides two jurisdictions in defiance of the ties of kinship and community of interest. Another line may mark the place where jungles end the clearing. Here may be a range of mountains with their eternal, beneficent snows, and there a desert of arid sands eager always for refreshing rains. Here and there are routes and passes through which a conquering Hannibal, or a Timur rode. How many plains are sites where men of arms waged bloody war and changed the destiny of race, or state! There are also inconspicuous spots where some great man was born long ago, a Buddha, or a Christ, whose mark is still on living multitudes of men. Every line and color tells something of peculiar politics, and of the fate and temper of the populace. You cannot summarize a Nation's character.

India is a small, red and yellow portion of the map of Asia—red for the British, and yellow for the "Native" states. With all her 1,800,000 square miles of territory [1] India occupies only about one-tenth of Asia. But tenths do not constitute the relative importance of this land to Asia and the world, for if one appraises Asiatic *thought* and *institutions,* India is not the least of Asia; she may, in truth, be first! India might better be compared with Europe than with Asia, if the interest be *religious* thought and institutions. About the size of Europe, without Scandinavia and Russia, India is quite as complex, in any manner of accounting. For the study of religion, and of Christianity, in particular, India is indispensable. India is a peculiarly religious land, and a fitting field for the adequate study of the roots and fruits of faith.

If one would understand India, he must have due regard for

[1] *India proper* measures only 1,200,000 sq. mi.

the complexity which her map displays. There are complexities of temperature, humidity, and physical features; of political and economic history; diversities of language and social institutions; and variations of her peoples' outlook upon life. To an extraordinary degree, the country has determined the qualities of its inhabitants, her geographical isolation has been transmuted into a certain innate mental quality of seclusiveness. Indians are, to a remarkable extent, a self-sufficient people, with a mild disdain for other peoples, especially the "younger" races of the West. India is in some ways significantly different from other lands. We might cite the effects of Indian sunlight, her seasonal characteristics, and the socio-religious institution known as "caste." Nowhere else is the actinic ray so disastrously effective, the rainy season so influential, and caste so dominant and peculiar. Let us fix in our minds the wide *variety* in that region which goes by the simple name of India, or Hindustan. This is the first important fact to realize.

India is not so much a nation as a collection of separate states, and isolated communities. She is the home not of a homogeneous people, but of a congeries of ethnic stocks. To generalize about India is not merely unwise; it is impossible. She is at once a museum and a laboratory, filled with exhibits and experimental elements illustrative of the whole range of historical and contemporary life and religion, just as the quiver of a native Indian hunter was once observed to hold one arrow tipped with stone of the neolithic age, with another pointed with electric cable wire! At times she seems a people

> "Wandering between two worlds, one dead,
> The other powerless to be born,"

yet we are aware of many recent signs of progress, and of evidence on the part of millions of her people of the consciousness of unity. Efforts have been made toward a common language. It is suggested that *Hindi* now spoken in one form or another by a hundred millions would serve adequately as the common tongue. It has been pointed out that if British rule were sacrificed, the goal of unity might be served, a partial ground would be withdrawn on which caste has flourished in its present form.[2] There

---

[2] With reference to *Hindu*, see *Ind. Soc. Ref.*, Mar. 19, 1932: regarding British rule and caste, see *ibid.*, Nov. 1, 1930, p. 137. Indian national independence is, however, a story with which as such we have here no right to deal, in spite of certain of its forceful implications for religion.

is, indeed a certain unity. It is doubtless psychological,—or metaphysical? It has recently been expressed, somewhat extremely, "There is no difference (in the Indian view) between one place and another, one woman and another, one religion and another, one *guru* and another. The differences are the veils of *maya.*" *Maya* is "illusion" (we shall appraise it later on). Or in a similar vein, particles in time are sparks from the Imperishable, which beyond time return thereto. It is ignorance which beholds them differentiated. We must thread our way amid intricacies and apparent contradictions toward an understanding of essential India; incidentally, we shall expect to banish certain common misconceptions of Indian life and thought which the West has seldom satisfactorily understood.

Peoples and Religions.—Let us take a somewhat hasty view of India's *peoples*. According to the 1931 census, more than 350 millions live within the total area, including Burma and certain territories along the northeastern and the northwestern borders of India proper. The geographical basis, however, of our present study is *India proper,* the region roughly bounded by the Indus, and the Brahmaputra rivers, the Arabian Sea, and the Bay of Bengal. This is the setting not only of Hinduism, but of Jainism and Sikhism. It was the first home of Buddhism, now found in Ceylon, Burma, China and Japan,—save for 300,000 Buddhist still in India. On the Bombay side, most of the Parsis may now be found. There are five million Christians, and many millions "animists." There are seventy million Moslems. There are 320,000,000 people, two-thirds of whom are Hindus. These are the figures, although the census cannot segregate entirely the various faiths which have lived side by side for centuries: Hindus, 240 millions; Moslems, 70 millions; Primitives, 10–50 millions; [3] Christians, 5½ millions; Sikhs, 4⅓ millions; Jains, 1⅕ millions; Buddhists, 300 thousand; and Parsis, 100 thousand.

The population has been growing at a steady rate. Conditions have been favorable, including peace and the effective care of life, with fewer plagues and famines. Estimating the increase among the religious groups, it seems that during the decade (1921–1931) Hindus have increased by ten percent, Moslems by four, Sikhs, and Christians each by over thirty. It does not follow that all Indians are becoming Sikhs and Christians. The census, like maps, is more than its barest figures, and prompts such queries as, Is Christianity in India being Hinduized? Whence

---

[3] Ten million "animists," and forty million "outcastes."

come the extra Sikhs? and, Why do not "polygamous" Moslems grow as fast as "monogamous" Hindus? Indian Christians may have come mainly from the depressed classes and the primitives, but many were once Moslems, or Hindus of the higher castes. The modern Sikhs were once mainly Hindu, partly Moslem. The Moslems [4] are almost wholly of Indian extraction. Possibly the Jain community, which barely holds its own, owes its long life to the circumstance that it is typically Indian. One might affirm with confidence that India will remain religious, although he may not venture to predict what in the end the many households of the faith may be.

Races.—One faces the problem of dependence between races and religions. India is not a land of racially homogeneous peoples as is Japan,—or even China, meaning the basic stock. One can distinguish such peoples as the Gurkhas, Rajputs, Tamils, and Pathans, but there is for the masses a somewhat "basic" strain. There is the historically original deposit called "Dravidian," with its culture and religion. This stock is found today from the southern-most Cape Comorin as far north as the Tropic of Cancer. Once Dravidians inhabited the northern parts of Hindustan, but were displaced by successive waves of "Aryan," and Turanian im-migration. In the northeast they were pushed back by Mongoloids. The true Dravidian has very dark skin, although he is not a Negro type. He is short and squat in stature. His hair is black and straight, although a tendency to curl is not infrequent. His head is rather long than broad. His nose is broad, but neither it nor his face is flat. Such are the main distinctive features where this primal stock has not suffered alteration by admixture with Indo-European, Scythic, or Mongolian peoples. There are dis-tinguishable admixtures. The Bengali of today is Mongolo-Dravidian, with the cultural advantage of the Indo-European. The Maratha of the western, coastal hills is doubtless Scythic. The purest "Aryan" or Indo-European stock is Rajput, and the Rajputs have been at pains to guard it. In the Central and United Provinces especially, the masses are "Dravidian" mixed with "Aryan." These central portions are the seat of India's classic culture: of Brahmanism, Jainism, Buddhism, Indian Islam, and modern Hinduism. This is *madhyadesha,* the "middle country," the home of thirty centuries of Hindu culture. Here also is the seat of *Hindi* or *Hindustani,* the most widely spoken language.[5]

---

[4] Often designated "Mussulmans."
[5] *Bengali* is used by fifty millions, *Tamil* and *Telugu* ("Dravidian" tongues), each by twenty millions. In all India less than three millions are literate in *English.*

Proceeding from the southern cape to the mountains of the northwest border, there are gradations of stature from short to tall, and shades of color from black to white. We might trace along this route, successively, Dravidian, Aryo-Dravidian or Sanskritic, and Islamic or Perso-Arab-Indian, cultures.

We might include some *pre*-Dravidians, whose living representatives doubtless tell us what India's aboriginals were. There are Paniyans of Malabar, Santals of Chhota Nagpur, and hill and jungle peoples of the Central Provinces such as Gonds, Kols, and Kurkus. We may not rightly call them all "Dravidians," although topography may be the reason for their isolation. Four thousand years ago[6] there came into the midst of Indian aboriginals, and Dravidians, a fair-skinned people who had found their way through the hazardous defiles of the ranges of the northwest. They called themselves the *aryas* or "nobles," possibly on grounds of military prowess more than culture, for we scarcely believe that these nomads were highly cultured. The land first gained they designated *aryadesha*, the "country of the Aryas." They used other terminology for non-Aryan lands and peoples. In the north they made slaves of the indigenous peoples, and in time there developed a civilization which we know as Vedic.[7] The Aryas may have found in central and south India a greater culture than that in the north, greater than their own, perhaps. But they met no *physical* resistance. We have, from later *Sanskrit* literature, an ample knowledge of the commingling. This source contains much that for centuries had been orally handed down, and was written after *aryadesha* had extended into *madhyadesha,* including the region around Benares.

Along the eastern edge of the Sanskrit area, eastward of Benares, arose the Buddhist and the Jainist reformations of the 5th century, B.C., producing a *Pali* literature, akin to *Sanskrit*. Gotama, the Buddha, initiated a movement which shook the very foundations of Hindu culture. This movement was a major phase of the readjustment which is the proper measure of the heritage of India. Hinduism finally recovered from the Buddhist shock, with such resistlessness that Buddhism had to yield. It saved itself by emigration.

The Moslems intruded about the time the Normans were invading England, pouring in through several centuries, coming

6 We ignore, of necessity, the newly excavated evidence of culture in the Indus valley, at Harappa and Mohenjo-daro, in the third millennium, B.C. This early culture may have been Sumerian, but there is some suggestion of the Hindu god Shiva.

7 From *veda,* "divine wisdom" transmitted through the Aryas and finally recorded in the Vedas.

overland by way of Persia, and the northwest passages. They won dominion by warfare, commerce, and conversion. Not only to religion, but to art and the architecture of the land they made their striking contribution. Mughal art particularly was realistic, whereas the art of India until then was mystical, imaginative, and, at times, fantastic. Strictly Hindu art continued thus, for both painter and sculptor sought merely to suggest by symbolism the reality they saw behind appearance. Those who recall that Mohammed strictly forbade the making of any "likenesses," need but to know that to Indian Moslems pictorial art, at least, was not a sin.

After the Great Mughals the British came. Men had charted ocean routes, and several of the land routes to the East were closed.[8] The Mughals were in India when the English came, but were in decline. The Scythic-Hindu Marathas were then the rising power in western India. Most of southern India was held by independent princes, whether Hindu, or Moslem. *Sanskrit* was still the medium of culture. The great vernaculars, *Tamil, Telugu, Marathi, Hindi,* and *Bengali,* were still colloquial. But India's comparative isolation soon began to yield before the new pressure from the West. The English tongue came widely into use for politics and education. English literature was freely drawn upon. A hundred years ago Indians were zealous imitators of the West. Westerners—the British, in particular—had begun to examine with interest the great Indian stores of language, literature, art, and religion. Christianity as a phase of Western penetration is of great significance in India's *modern* life, but early Christianity, also, had spread directly into India, especially the south.

Indian Essentials.—India today is in a mood of strong reaction, the climax of thirty years of growing agitation spreading discontent among the masses. *Swadesha,*[9] or "self-determination," is their goal, and they are emphasizing all things Indian to justify their theory that they have at first hand all they need for independence. Certainly India has more regard than ever before for her own peculiar qualities of mind and heart, and is eagerly intent upon her just place in the world economy. There is as yet, however, no hearty unanimity on policies best suited to her. The situation is manifestly too old and too complex for speedy readjustment. Five peculiar qualities manifest themselves today:

(1) One quality is geographical—her *isolation*—which may be

8 Probably the opening of ocean routes took trade off the ancient land routes. It is not strictly true that the "Turks" blocked the highways.
9 One's "own country."

translated into *self-suffciency,* or *seclusiveness* of mind. Look closely at the map, and you will see this. There are nearly three thousand miles of shore-line, all fronting on wide seas. There are twenty-five hundred miles of mountain border, including fifteen hundred miles of stupendous Himalayas. These Himalayas are a multitude of interlocking ranges side by side, an impenetrable extent of untrodden and forbidding ways. Across the frontier on the northeast stretches a tangled mass of "jungly" mountains, through which no major thoroughfares have ever run. Only through the passes of the mountains of the northwest have there been avenues of contact with the outer world—until, of course, the ocean lanes were opened. India has probably been more self-contained than any other great region, and has perhaps come nearest of all lands to reaching judgments independent of the world.

(2) India is also more *acquisitive* than bountiful, more absorbent than generous, a quality which has enhanced her isolation. Outside elements have been welcomed not so much for what they were as for what India could make of them remolded. She has made them peculiarly her own. Within the range of history, India has displayed a power of assimilation much in excess of any susceptibility to change. This is impressive evidence that India possesses at least a passive principle of unity, whether geographical, psychological, or religious, to have so far taken care of foreign elements. The principle was effective even with the *dominant* Aryan culture, for it became *Indo-*Aryan ultimately. The Zoroastrians who fled to India when Islam first advanced on Persia (after about 650 A.D.) were not aware that they were "fleeing into the hospitable bosom of a people related to them by blood and language," nor were the Hindus aware that they were "receiving their very own kin." [10] The *ancient* Vedic Indians and the *ancient* Avestan Persians were related, but the evidence lay buried in their respective literatures, and had been to some degree obliterated by exclusive Indianization. It is not surprising that the London merchants sent by the English Crown to plant their "factories" in India, and to establish there a "nation," were not aware of blood and cultural kinship with the Hindus. It remained for Western linguists of the last century to discover through ancient literary records this Indo-European kinship. India, too, has shared the benefits of this discovery.

(3) India is *tolerant.* This is a different way of saying that she

10 M. Bloomfield, *Religion of the Veda,* p. 15.

is acquisitive. But not altogether. Sometimes her tolerance has been calm indifference. Sometimes it has meant the cordial welcome of new ideas (not *practices*), even prior to her own appraisal of their value. At times it may have indicated shallowness of mind, but often it has had the significance of ardent search for truth. India was tolerant toward the Jainist and the Buddhist reformations, but each submitted ultimates to general tendencies. The "Indian Idea" has prevailed with at least unconscious tolerance amid the conflicts of the centuries, although one might cite the apparent *in*tolerance of caste. Caste is after all an evidence of *fatal* toleration. Social segregation is a phase of Indian seclusiveness, and a temporal expedient in the consummation of the Indian Idea. India, therefore, may look on caste with tolerant indifference. Does not reality—in her view—lie behind, beyond, the processes and particulars of the here and now!

(4) India is characteristically *ascetic.* Her asceticism is both broad and narrow. In the narrow sense, it makes her crucify the body for the sake of the eternal soul. In the broader sense, it occasions the rejection of mere things as having value in themselves, and compels the conservation of all life, the non-human with the human. In the narrow sense, it creates a type of human individual, the ascetic *sadhu,* or *sannyasi.* In the broader sense, it builds up non-materialistic systems of philosophy. The majority of Indians, to be sure, are not ascetics in the narrow sense; on the contrary, hosts of Indians are practically materialistic. But India's temper is essentially ascetic, as is the goal, also, toward which both life and thought incline. She has sought ultimate Reality in preference to abundant life.

(5) India has peculiarly the quality of *abstraction.* She is *idealistic.* This is the thoughtful side of her practical asceticism. It applies, however, mainly to the higher types of people. The masses occupy their daily round with efforts toward a bare existence. The Indian ideal is not aggressive. It is more *taoistic* than Confucian. Ideally non-aggressive, non-assertive India stands in challenging contrast with practically assertive China, although both peoples are pacifistic.

These are five qualities of India. They stand either as causes, or concomitants of the process of assimilation, whose rate has heretofore exceeded the rate of change due to foreign influence. They are intangibles, perhaps, to Western thought, but India, especially in her religions, may not be understood without them. We cannot view India exclusively with our eyes of flesh—or, if we do, we shall often "want to shut them," said the Bengal Lancer.[11]

With the eyes of flesh we have too often seen areas of parched, cracked ground; innumerable animals, and humans repulsive in their sores and foul diseases; mouldy sanctuaries in their squalid courtyards reeking with the fetid odors of decaying, sacrificial flowers; for these are common sights in India. With the eyes of an understanding, sympathetic spirit we may see things strange but good; objects which are tangible, and thoughts which are elusive; all of which are factors of India's undying glory, and suggestions toward the final consciousness and life of man.

[11] Yeats-Brown, *Lives of a Bengal Lancer*, p. 125.

CHAPTER IX

Hinduism

Hinduism is the leading, the characteristic faith of India. It is the religion of the Hindu. But Hinduism is not reducible to any simple phrase, for it is as diverse as the numberless groups among the millions who profess it. As there is no *country* comprehensible under the simple designation "India," so there is no *religion* to be known as "Hinduism," if by religion we mean a system of devotion at once coherent, consistent, readily practiced, and easily understood. In Hinduism we find a faith more inchoate and intangible than any which we have thus far encountered, even as we find it in many of its forms a higher faith than these. Nevertheless, there are essential characters by which both the land itself, and its leading faith, may ultimately be known. As India may be called a climate, so Hinduism is an atmosphere.

Name and Form.—Sometimes we call the religion *Brahmanism*. We might designate it Brahmanic Hinduism, indicating the congeries of theories, and the medley of practices, amidst which the influence of the "Brahman" is predominant. But, while all Brahmans are Hindus, not all Hindus are Brahmans. There are groups who rely upon their own non-Brahman priesthood as authority in religion. However, we may say that all those Indians are Hindus who recognize, either directly or remotely, the dominance of Brahmans, especially the Brahman priests. By this they are distinguished from all others, not subservient to brahmanical tradition, *e.g.,* Moslems, Christians, and Parsis, and, to some extent, the Jains and Sikhs.

The word "Hindu" had its origin in *sindhu,* an ancient Indo-European term for river. The term survives, as well, in "Sind," and "Indus"—and in "Hindustan" or "river-land." India is the land of many rivers, especially the Indus, the broad, full stream, whose majesty impressed the early Indo-European immigrants to the Panjab, region of the "five waters," which finally converge in the main Indus channel. Northwestern India would be desert save

174

for these snow-fed water-courses. The designation "Hindustan" remained appropriate, as the immigrants extended their domain first into the Doab or region of the "two rivers" (the Jumna and the Ganges), and ultimately beyond the Vindhya mountains into southern India, watered by the Kistna, Kauvery, and Vaigai. *Hindu* rightly represents the cultural amalgam whose habitat is Hindustan.

Although Hinduism lacks any regular articulation as a system of *belief,* it is the very web and pattern of Indian life. While it contains all possible interpretations of religion, it is as a social scheme organized and articulate. It is reckless of creed, tolerant of religious rivalries, and patient with heresies; yet on the whole, it is all-powerful, and it has imposed upon men a way of life altogether unique in the history of religions. Hinduism is today the legitimate successor not only of its early self, but also of all antecedent, essentially Indian forms; yet it is something more than historical and sociological confusion. While Hindus have followed religious practices with a freedom not inhibited by any practical or speculative system, significant systems as such have been evolved by them. Something unitary, withal, has lurked behind the ways of the thoughtful, and the vessel of their faith has been molded upon a spiritual disc of speculative harmony, even as the village potter shapes the clay on his revolving wheel. Or, to change the figure, Hindus have been involved in the operations of persistent theories which have determined for them a *common state of mind.*

Definition.—The content of Hinduism has altered from age to age, and has differed according to community. Hinduism meant one thing in the early *Vedic* period (about 1200 to 850 B.C.), another in the time of the *Brahmanas* (writings of about 850 to 600 B.C.), still another in the subsequent era of the *Upanishads,* another in later *Epic* times, until today when it has a fuller content than previous centuries afforded. Nevertheless, we detect the processes of the varying ages. Hindus themselves are not agreed upon any thoretical definition of their faith; they agree only that there is *an essential Hinduism,* a "unity of spirit binding its different expressions and linking up the different periods of its history in one organic whole." [1] The problem reduces itself to the generalization that Hinduism is the religion of the Hindu; and that a Hindu is one who is born of Hindu parents; who marries a Hindu; who respects Brahman priests and depends more or less

1 Radhakrishnan, *Hindu View of Life,* p. 12.

directly upon their ministrations; who respects the cow as a sacred animal; who holds the ancient *Vedas* in reverence; who practices cremation; who accepts the distinctions of caste; who obeys the rules prohibiting marriage between persons of different castes, and dining with persons of inferior caste, and the eating of forbidden foods such as beef; and who believes in one imminent, all-inclusive Supreme Being, *Bráhman*,[2] and in the universal operation of *karma* and the transmigration of souls. A [Hindu] writer, Srinivasa Iyengar, while insisting that "Hindus have neither faith, nor practice, nor law to distinguish them from others," defines a Hindu as, "one born in India, whose parents, as far as people can remember, were not foreigners, or who did not profess foreign religions like Mohammedanism, or Christianity, or Judaism, and who himself has not embraced any such religion."[3] Another [Hindu] has identified a Hindu as, "one belonging to any one of the castes, or sub-castes recognized from times long past or in recent years; or any former caste man who has renounced the world; or anyone belonging to the depressed classes who has taken to worshiping Hindu gods."[4] He cites as Hindu a caste at Bassein composed of descendants of Christian converts readmitted to Hinduism, who marry only among themselves, and are served by Brahman priests.

It should be observed that a person may be converted to Hinduism;[5] that a Hindu may accept the ministrations of other than Brahman priests; that he may in effect reject the authority of the *Vedas;* that he may bury and not burn his dead; that he may on occasion eat and drink with men of inferior caste; *and* that he may be an "animist," or an atheist, or a worshiper of many gods, or a devotee of one only God. Nor do these statements contradict our definitions, nor impair the *fact* of Hinduism, however indefinable. Hinduism is a real and potent faith. India is so deeply religious that she is best understood through the religious approach. We are adopting no mere device, therefore, when we choose to observe Hindus at worship, and patiently inquire what it means in essential Hinduism, both contemporary and historical. We have in mind, first, the Central Indian villager whose tongue is *Hindi,* and who fairly represents, at its lower levels, the "Aryanized" civilization which flourishes between Bombay and Calcutta; and, second, the townsman of South Indian Madura,

---

[2] This form is neuter, and represents the impersonal.
[3] *Essentials of Hinduism*, 2nd ed., p. 9.
[4] V. M. Mahajani, *Essentials of Hinduism*, p. 76—not quoted altogether *verbatim*.
[5] Note several recent international incidents, including a tragic one.

where the "Dravidian" element is prominent in Hindu culture. Thereafter we shall make a pilgrimage, especially to Benares, *the* sacred city of all Hinduism.

Village Hinduism.—Lohári,[6] a village familiar to the author, with its varied population of one hundred and fifty souls, is situated some twenty miles north of Jabalpur, a city of the Central Provinces. It lies on the bank of the Hiran or Deer River which flows into the sacred waters of the Narbada, and thence into the Indian Ocean. In the dry season (our autumn, winter, and spring), the village has road connection with the main highway, two miles distant, but during the "Rains," it is inaccessible, save on foot. Its homes are thirty-five mud houses, with thatch or red tile roofs, clustered in irregular fashion about an open center. One house is larger than the rest; it is that of the head-man. Pillars of crudely carved wood flank his doorway, through which one enters an inner court. Color decorations of various designs adorn the walls. At the edge of the village is a glistening white temple, the most conspicuous village structure, and the pride of the inhabitants. The most interesting villager is the temple priest. He is a Brahman and the only Brahman. He must do his own cooking, and wash his own utensils and clothing. He may not risk defilement from the touch or even the shadow of those of lesser caste. He conducts worship for the inhabitants, mostly farmers, although among them live some brick and tile makers, and some fisher folk. At one side of the village lives a small group of *chamárs* or leatherworkers, outcastes who live their life apart and serve their own gods. Temple worship represents the higher order of religion in Lohári, but the villagers observe lower forms as well. Notice the iron spikes driven into the sacred tree, whereby man makes contact with the spirit of the tree. Notice also the stone symbols of *linga-puja,* the worship of the male and female organs of procreation. Upon the symbols of these organs in contact lie flower-tokens, and they are wet with libations of water which have been poured upon them. The chief god of the *chamárs* is a spherical, smooth, white stone resting on a mud base near their cluster of huts.

The visitor may see at a glance the primitive qualities of village Hinduism. He is in the midst of simple credulity, of the attribution of spiritual powers to natural objects and forces, of magic, and exorcism. Of course, there is no school. Scarcely more than five persons are literate, other than several boys attending a Govern-

---

[6] This village becomes typical by the inclusion of a few elements from nearby.

ment school nearby. It is the typical agricultural scene, and, be it remembered, India is essentially an agricultural country, for villagers make up about seventy percent of the population. But observe the Brahman priest. He represents the Aryanization of the community, with all that it means, socially and religiously. He is the apex of the social order and the spiritual arbiter of the community's conduct and destiny. He has some education, as it happens; although all Brahmans, whether priests, or of another calling, are not educated. He knows something of the history and literature of his faith. He conducts daily worship in his temple, and lives by the alms of his constituency. He is proud of his charge, and faithful in worship, although the visitor may wonder how this priest ministers to higher desires beyond the ritual.

The Temple at Lohári.—Peep into the temple interior; of course, you, a foreigner and, therefore, an outcaste, may not set foot within, or even on the outer threshold. There is a platform in the center, upon which rest certain emblems of the faith, chief of which is the short, smoothly carved pillar of *Mahadeva,* or the "Great God" *Shiva.* We shall learn more of *Shiva* later on, who is in direct succession from a pre-Aryan power of primitive India, such as the natural stone still symbolizes. Along with *Shiva* on the platform are other symbols; perhaps, a rudely carved head of *Shiva's* consort, and an image of the popular *Hanuman,* the monkey-god, the friend of *Rama.* Scattered about the platform are flowers, mango leaves, turmeric, grains of rice, and wheat, and fragments of cocoanut, the signs of priestly service. Here and there, especially in niches in the walls, are small clay lamps to be lighted on occasion. From the cross-beam over the doorway hangs a bell. This is the typical shrine of village Hinduism, save for the painted figure of a *clock* above the doorway! Neither the villager nor the temple ritual is regulated by a clock. Sunrise and sunset bound the rural day, with long repose at mid-day for man and beast. The priest performs his services mornings and evenings: prayers, gifts, and libations. He serves also on special occasions, in examining horoscopes prior to a marriage; fixing days for plowing, sowing, and the harvest; disclosing times when good stars smile on a journey; and conducting the annual ceremony for the dead. His services are indispensable, even as his very presence is a safeguard and a benediction. The women, who have no religious status apart from their husbands, carry on in their houses a daily worship with images from their own god-box.

Now and then a villager, or an entire family, goes on pilgrimage to some distant holy place. Occasionally a *sadhu* (holy man) passes by, feared, and frequently revered.

Hinduism in the Town.—In Madura,[7] we view a more imposing scene. This large city, situated beside the Vaigai River in the far south of India, was an ancient capital of a strong dynasty, and contains imposing temples of "Dravidianized" Brahmanism.[8] The great Temple is considered the finest, as it is the most extensive, example of Dravidian architecture in India. The style of the vast structure is most effective from a distant elevation, but the innumerable details of composition bear, upon close inspection, eloquent testimony to the skill and fervor of its builders. The general plan is a great square, about 725 ft. wide and 850 ft. long, inclosing a group of lesser squares. At the middle of each side of the outer wall rises a huge tower or *gopuram,* the tallest of which is 156 ft. high, and above various walls within the great inclosure rise five lesser *gopurams.* All nine of these are four-sided, truncated pyramids of stone, covered on every face with row upon row of carvings in infinite succession, and in a bewildering maze of color; for each carved image is painted, whitewashed or gilded, whether heroes, gods, goddesses, attendants, bulls, elephants, monkeys, or peacocks. Amidst this *primarily Dravidian* array, many of the deities of the Hindu pantheon find their place. Within the Temple area are many covered sanctuaries with their shrines and images, and many corridors bordered with elaborately carved pillars. The Hall of the Thousand Pillars (actually 985) displays carvings of heroic size in portrayal of fact and fancy in the religious life of South India,—figures which together with the sculptured reliefs of the *gopurams* are now monstrous, now graceful, now lewd, and to be understood, if at all, by the priests alone.

The Gods of Madura.—The most important shrines are those of the goddess *Minakshi,* the "fish-eyed" [9] consort of *Shiva,* and of *Shiva* himself under the title *Sundareshwara,* the "handsome deity." The two square sacred inclosures, of unequal areas, lie side by side; contiguous to both is the Golden Lily pool, surrounded by cloisters with ornate ceilings, and with their mural panels and their chiseled columns descriptive of many a mysterious episode. Within the pillared cloisters, Hindus devotees and students of religious lore

---

[7] Accent first syllable.

[8] For a just impression of the Great Temple of Madura one should refer to illustrations, such as those in *The National Geographic Magazine,* Vol. XXIV, No. 12, Dec., 1913, pp. 1322–1330.

[9] *Mina,* "fish"; *aksha,* "eye"—in Sanskrit.

may read, converse, and meditate. The sacred pool is handy for their ceremonial ablutions. Above the flat roof of *Shiva's* temple protrudes a golden pillar, his symbol. A curious female figure represents *Minakshi* in her own peculiar temple. In the story of *Minakshi* fact and fancy blend. She may have been a princess of an ancient Maduran line, esteemed for her chastity and charm. She certainly represents, as well, a female demon of the old Dravidian order; the two characters, however incompatible, have more than once united in one figure. It is said she had three breasts, and that if she met her lord, one would shrink away. She met *Shiva,* and her third breast vanished, whereupon she recognized her lord. Their marriage was at once arranged and duly consummated. This is clearly an aspect of the introduction of "Brahamanism" (by way of *Shiva*) into South India, and its mingling with "Dravidianism."

Minakshi was doubtless the leading deity of the early, southern demon-rites. To this day, every village of South India has its mother-goddess. *Shiva,* whatever he may have been originally, had been brahmanized. As he went about, he took local goddesses to wife. Through his bride Minakshi he established himself in Madura. Their marriage is celebrated annually with great pomp in the city and nearby, especially in the dry bed of the Vaigai. On the auspicious day, *Shiva* is brought from his shrine within the Temple, and placed upon a pedestal in the Temple marriage-hall, with *Minakshi* placed beside him, the priests of the deities reenact the impressive marriage rites, anointing the gods with oil, garlanding them with flowers, and exchanging presents. Next morning comes the great procession, with the people taking part, the Temple elephants leading. The gods ride in the enormous Temple cars, symbolically drawn by winged horses with forefeet aloft, but actually drawn by the people with long, cocoanut-fibre ropes.[10] Thus they are "given the air" to a nearby lake, and back again. At the lake they ride in a fantastic boat, which floats to the frenzied accompaniment of tom-toms and bagpipes. It is a gay, priestly festival.

In the Vaigai river-bed, where the populace gathers, honor is paid to *Allagar, Minakshi's* brother, who, by mischance, came late to the wedding, and has since been angry at his sister. The annual rehearsal of his anger affords occasion to all ranks and castes, especially the lowly,—for *Allagar* is very popular—for a riotous festival. The celebration might seem to any Westerner

10 *Cf.* P. Loti, *India,* pp. 113–130.

a combination of a religious camp-meeting and a better-class circus with its side-shows.

In Madura, as in Lohári, Hindu worship is, no matter how great the throng, *individual homage to the gods;* there is no "congregational" ritual. Into certain of the holiest places only the Brahman priests may enter and worship. Certain temple areas, especially in South India, are restricted to Brahmans, whether priests or laymen, but the corridors of the Madura temples are open to all, even to foreigners. Outcastes alone are forbidden. There are stated rituals to which the priests attend, in daily or seasonal routine, or on behalf of individuals who specifically commission them. Otherwise the faithful offer their gifts as they will, according to their power and their need, to this god, or another, at various shrines. Perhaps a rich merchant, bringing water from the holy Ganges, rides in state to the Temple; visits with offerings and prayers the greater shrines; pours out his holy water, prostrates himself and prays; bestows alms generously upon the priests; and finds some satisfaction for an agitated soul. The pleasant, poor in this world's goods, but with an urgent devotion, comes *afoot* and makes the temple rounds to the satisfaction of his own soul. The blind, the halt, and the lame, high and low, rich and poor, the well and the weak, throng the Temple corridors throughout the year, for Madura is a notable center of pilgrimage.

Benares.—To behold the very soul of Hinduism, or, better, the very soul of the individual Hindu, one must visit Benares. There are centers such as Madura, Srirangam, Kalighat, and Brindaban, where great temples dominate the scene, even when great crowds gather, but in Benares man is the dominating interest. He crowds every street, throngs up and down the steps at the river-side, bathes in the cleansing waters of the muddy Ganges, and joins the throng streaming incessantly past the innumerable altars. Benares is a city of 200,000 souls, seventy-five percent Hindus, including 30,000 Brahmans. It is the center of an ever shifting gathering of men, women, and children from every corner of Hindustan. It has 1500 temples and a quarter of a million idols. The soil it stands on, the waters that wash its burning- and bathing-ghats, and the very airs that blow upon it are all accounted sacred. This city stands in solitary supremacy, combining the virtues of all other centers. While it is a seat of all the gods of the Hindu pantheon, it is preëminently the *City of Shiva* whose followers predominate. The Golden Temple is his;

the Well of Knowledge is his; the so-called Monkey Temple is dedicated to his wife; there are temples to his son, *Ganesha.* The sacred bull is his, whether sculptured, or alive, and wandering freely among the temples. Most of the *sadhus* one meets are devotees of his, paying their vows of hunger, thirst, or what not.

One should approach Benares with a sense of the Hindu's other-worldliness, and his utter subjection to symbolism. Not otherwise may a Westerner escape offense at floors bespread with cow-dung, and awash with holy water; at the running sores on many a pilgrim; at the foul odors of decaying marigold, smouldering dung, and sizzling human flesh; [11] and at the dank dilapidation of muddy walls. There are other things which one should see: above all, the soul which in some sense has met God in the temple-round. He should view Benares as a symbol of Hinduism throughout more than twenty-five centuries. It is an ancient site; no doubt, of primitive religion. Some power antecedent to the more modern *Shiva* was doubtless worshiped there by "animistic," perhaps by orgiastic rites. In time came the martial "Aryans" of the north, and from the commingling in this "middle land" was born Aryo-Dravidian Hinduism under the priestly Brahmans. One should understand that with every dynasty and in every age, the chief significance of Benares has been religion, and that no other center has enjoyed equal eminence in the cure of souls.

The Ganges.—The religious character of the city is conspicuous along the two and one-half mile water-front of the sweeping curve of the left bank of the Ganges.[12] The opposite shore is barren—actually, mud flats. The sacred river is old in the thought of India, and is the holiest of all waters. In its heavenly form it sprang from the toe of *Vishnu* to purify the ashes of sixty thousand princes burnt by the angry glance of a holy sage. *Shiva,* to save the earth from the river's abrupt fall, caught the waters on his brow and checked its course with his long, matted looks. His act divided the flow into many streams, the Ganges being the chief. The earthly river flows in a course of 1500 miles from Gangotri in Garhwal state in the Himalayas to the Bay of Bengal. It receives on its way the waters of the Jumma, the Gumti and the Gogra, and every intersection, especially that with the Jumna at Allahabad, has some pretension to sanctity. The bed of the

---

[11] At the burning-ghat.
[12] The river runs northward beside the ghats.

stream near its source is divided into three basins, dedicated to *Brahmā*,[13] *Shiva,* and *Vishnu,* and the worshiper may at one pilgrimage avail himself of the cleansing power of the three great gods. Benares, however, is said to combine the virtues of all other places of pilgrimage, and if the weary pilgrim die within the *panch kosi* or "five *kos*" road (a *kos* is a mile and a half, or two) around the city, he is released immediately from the cycle of recurrent births, being transported directly to the heaven of his devotion. His body is burned on a burning-ghat and the ashes spread on the river. Every pilgrim—there must be a million of them, annually—is expected to visit various holy spots in the city and, certificated, to make the *"panch kosi"* circuit of the city, which may cover forty miles and occupy six days. The city, therefore, is crowded with earnest souls occupied with ritual: reverent men in prayer to the vivifying Sun; widows bathing carefully and devoutly; pilgrims from afar bottling holy water to take home with them; ascetics begging alms, or practicing austerities; hundreds of priests, bare of breast and arms, each sitting under his straw sun-shade and marking with the God-sign the foreheads of any faithful who resort to him.

The Ghats.—Especially serious is the group that comes for burning a body which they may have brought from a distance. The corpse bound in cloth is carried on bamboo poles. The bearers have come through the city streets crying aloud, *"Ram, Ram,"* *"Mahadeva,"* or some note of last appeal. Arrived at the burning-ghat they rest its feet in the river, while they gather the wood— at a price—and build the pyre. When the pyre is ready—*wealthy* mourners may make it of *sandal*-wood—the man nearest akin to the dead buys from a nearby temple the necessary sparks of sacred fire. The body is then placed on the wood and burned; what remains is thrown into the river. A jar of water is ceremonially broken over the place of burning, and the mourners go their way.

One may best see the ghats by a boat-ride (there are high-decked boats for the purpose), drifting with the slow current (slow, when the Rains have not begun). He will see an almost unbroken succession of steps along the river's edge, with masses of masonry, sometimes fallen awry. At the top of the steps of Janki Ghat are four temples to *Shiva,* with gilded pinnacles. He has a temple at the top of Kedar Ghat, where he dwells within painted walls, guarded by two doormen. At the foot of

13 A *personal* form.

the steps of Kedar Ghat is the well of *Gauri*[14] his wife, whose waters help cure fevers, and dysentery, and on the steps are many *lingas* (or *lingams*), emblems of *Shiva*. *Shiva's* dearest site is the Manikarnika Ghat, with its well at the top, into which the god once dropped an ear-ring, and into which, during eclipses of the sun especially, great numbers of pilgrims throw offerings of bel-tree leaves, flowers, milk, sandal-wood, sweetmeats, and holy water. At the second row of the Manikarnika steps stands a temple to *Ganesha,* "lord of hosts," *Shiva's* son, whose red-daubed image has three eyes, a silver scalp, and an elephant's trunk with a single tusk. He is here attended by a rat. Elsewhere, *e.g.,* at the Trilokam Ghat of the "Three Worlds," *Shiva* himself is the "three-eyed one."

At the Dasaswamedha[15] Ghat of the "Ten Horse Sacrifice," *Brahma, Vishnu,* and other deities are worshiped. *Brahmā* once offered here the ten-horse-sacrifice, and hither throngs of pilgrims come, during eclipses especially. *Vishnu* is here as the Trinity, and as the lion-man (*Narsingh*) "incarnation" (*avatara*). Here is *Sitala,* also, goddess of smallpox. The Panchganga Ghat of the "five Ganges" rests at the place where five(?) holy streams converge—celestial, terrestrial, and subterranean. Once at the head of the steps stood a temple of *Vishnu,* but now the Moslem mosque of Aurangzeb stands on the temple site, its minarets towering above the ghats, and its embarrassing presence a symbol of one Great Mughal's bigotry. But strangely enough, Hindu tradition, like the scent of the broken rose-bowl, clings to the spot and Hindus worship there. One ghat is sacred to the Jains who have built their temples on it; another is frequented by Gosains, persons of an ascetic order who having subdued their passions and renounced the world, are living a life of religious mendicancy; still another ghat is dedicated to the Moon-lord, at whose shrine every kind of disease is subject to cure; one ghat is given over mainly to burning. There are about twenty ghats of major importance, and no deity of any following is without symbol or commemoration.

Shiva's Special Seat.—Back of the ghats, sometimes deep within the city, are various shrines, chief of which are *Shiva's* Golden Temple, his Well of Knowledge, the temple of his wife, *Durga*[16] (the "Monkey Temple" of Western visitors), and the temple of the "food-full" goddess, *Annapurna.* The Golden

14 The "red"(?) goddess.
15 *Das-aswa-medha.*
16 The "remote" goddess, the counterpart of the "black" Kali in Bengal.

Temple is dedicated to *Shiva* as Lord of the Universe (*Vishveshvara*), and stands beside a temple to him as Great God (*Mahadeva*). Above it rises its conical stone tower, covered with copper plates overspread with gold-leaf (there are, in fact, several gilded towers and domes which rise together from a group of temples). The famous Well of Knowledge, sunk near the Golden Temple in a quadrangle of its own, is now protected by a high stone screen, and is covered over by a stone canopy—to prevent casting in offerings. Its water is available and is much desired—is it not the very sweat of *Shiva?* The *Durga* temple is dedicated to the darker side of *Shiva*. *Shiva's* wife in her terrible form is *Durga,* the inaccessible; she delights in destruction and in bloody sacrifices. Goats are slain for her here. Not far from the Golden Temple is that of the "food-full" goddess, *Annapurna,* the resort of beggars by the score, whom at *Shiva's* bidding she feeds (through the attendant priests, of course). This temple is symbolic of the variations in the Hindu cult, for within its compound are shrines of the Sun, of *Ganesha,* of *Shiva's* wife in the milder form of *Gauri,* the "brilliant," and of *Hanuman,* the monkey-god and friend of *Rama* who himself is an incarnation of *Vishnu.* For that matter, near the well of *Shiva's* ear-ring may be found two imprints said to have been made by the feet of *Vishnu,*—but had *Vishnu* when he made the imprints come to worship *Shiva?* [17]

The Pilgrim. Benares is Hinduism in epitome, and against the background of Hinduism localized in Lohári, Madura, and Benares, we shall be better able to understand the faith as a congeries of practices and doctrines. Follow, if you will, a pilgrim to Benares.[18] A young man goes at the behest of a mother too old to make the long journey. She would have him go, name her name to *Ganga-Ma* (Mother Ganges), and bring her sacred water to offer to *Shiva Mahadeva,* thus making her heart lighter for the long transmigration. She has him go in spite of his fears that *Ganga* may smite him for his own sins, as others have been smitten who dared bathe without repentance. He joins a company journeying by oxcart and afoot. They are all of a peasant caste, men, women, and children. They have bedding for the oxen, cotton quilts for themselves, flour and grains with vessels to cook them in, hookah pipes, and black tobacco, and jars for holy water. The menfolk carry bamboo lathis (staves) for protection

---

[17] Shivism and Vishnuism are, in a sense, *rival* sects.
[18] *Cf.* B. T. Badley's *India,* pp. 87–105.

against robbers, and perhaps swing their shoes on the lathi-ends across their shoulders.[19] They make slow progress, but are not impatient, so at last they reach the outskirts of the Holy City, where our young man leaves the company to go his own way into the bewildering city. The simple young villager mingles, in awe and amazement, with the multitudes come on a common errand. It is a new experience for him, with its results more or less problematical. He may fall in with the customary routine from temple to temple, to this ghat and that, and at last complete the circuit of the sacred city, thereafter making his way home again, empty of purse, but with his jar of precious Ganges water and a heart full of unquestioning satisfaction in his religious heritage. Benares may be not symbolism but magical reality: the Ganges itself a means of cleansing from sin, both root and fruit; the priestly mark on his forehead a seal of holiness; and the sacred water a cure for all ills and a magical protection. Or he may fall in with some who sow doubts in his mind as to what he will gain from external ritual. There have always been Hindus who question the efficacy of the rites; perhaps they are more numerous today than ever before, even within the Holy City itself. They would conserve the symbolism of essential Hinduism, both in the great centers and in the humble villages, but teach their co-religionists the supreme value of the devout mind. They openly condemn the primitive magic so widely current. There is no doubt, however, that the average Hindu pilgrim is still driven by a great compulsion: the sanctity of his shrines, the power of his priests, and the merit of his ceremonial. It is probable that our young pilgrim will return with a sense of merit, and with merit for his aged mother, also. So preëminent is Benares, the seat of all the gods!

Pilgrim Centers.—One may encounter pilgrims in all parts of India at all seasons, for holy places are many, and each has its auspicious time. There are, as well, periodic occasions of unusual importance. The native calendar lists several scores of festivals, most of which may be celebrated by the faithful at or near their homes. Some, however, call for a journey, if possible. At times (at all new moons and certain times of full moon) sea-bathing is especially meritorious, for example, at Somnath, on the coast of Kathiawar. Eclipses of the sun or the moon call for special devotion, often at special sites. And many a pilgrim seeks the

---

[19] Many men of the company carry each a pair of conventional, covered pilgrim baskets in bamboo racks slung at the ends of a shoulder bar.

merit of a tour to all the major holy places. Conveyances of all
sorts, including trains, are used, but the pilgrimage done on foot
brings the most reward. The follower of *Shiva* may go first to
Benares, then to Nasik (about a hundred miles northeast of
Bombay), where among the temples is one of extreme sanctity
marking the site where *Rama, Sita,* and *Lakshman* once worshiped *Shiva,* thence to the far south, perhaps to Madura, or
to further Rameshwaram which, although a Ramaite or Vishnuite shrine, contains a *lingam* placed there by *Rama* himself, and
which is daily washed with sacred Ganges water. From the far
south he may make his slow way to Kalighat, within the Calcutta
area, and there for the sake of inward power observe the outward
form of animal sacrifice to *Shiva's* consort *Kali.* Last of all the
pilgrim may cross over to Somnath on the Arabian Sea and gaze
—if he be of the twice-born,—on the well-guarded and highly efficacious *lingam* of the Great God. In the end he may return
permanently to Benares, "to live there in order to die there" with
the best prospects for the hereafter.

The follower of Vishnu may make the rounds of Muttra,
Allahabad, Dwaraka, and Jagannath Puri. Muttra is situated a hundred miles south of Delhi. It is the reputed birthplace and residence
of *Krishna,* an incarnation of *Vishnu.* Nearby is Mahaban, the
"great forest" where the babe *Krishna* was once hidden to save
him from death at the hands of an angry uncle. Nearby, also, is
Brindaban, where *Krishna* the Cowherd sported with the *gopis,*
the milkmaids, and stole their garments while they bathed. There
are many magnificent shrines in the Muttra area. Allahabad
(ancient Prayag) rests seventy-five miles west of Benares at
the confluence of the Ganges and the Jamna rivers,—and, they
say, a third river, the Saraswati, comes up here and joins these
two from its subterranean channel.[20] The conjunction of these
three(?) streams makes the site of Allahabad unusually beneficial,
and worship is rendered here to both *Shiva* and *Vishnu.* But to
Vishnu homage is done annually (about the middle of February)
in connection with the beginning of the Indian spring. It is a
time of rejoicing and of hope. *Vishnu's* son *Kama,* god of love,
is also worshiped then. It is an auspicious time for beginnings:
betrothals, marriages, and lessons. Dwaraka, by the sea at the
western tip of Gujarat, is one of India's holiest places and is

20 The Saraswati River falls from the Himalayas and is actually lost in the sands
of the desert. There is a legend that Saraswati, the "watery, elegant," was once the
wife of *Vishnu.* She is now the wife of *Brahmā,* is goddess of wisdom and patroness
of the arts and sciences.

especially revered by Vishnuites. It is the reputed royal city of *Krishna,* the "Lord of Dwaraka," and is a place of miracle. The shrine of *Jagannath,* "Lord of the World," is eastward a thousand miles from Dwaraka, at Puri, on the Bay of Bengal. *Jagannatha* is the god *Vishnu* in the form of *Krishna* (not the Cowherd, in this instance, but a nobler form); his image, although rudely carved, is said to have two eyes and a soul; the god is immensely popular because in his presence all castes are equal. The pilgrim may choose for his visit the time when the image of the god is bathed, or, preferably, the slightly later time of the Car Festival (June or July) when the image is taken, along with images of *Jagannatha's* brother, *Balarama,* and his sister, *Subhadra,* from their inner sanctuary on the "car-journey" to the Garden House a mile northward, where it stays for eight days until drawn back to the temple. After the elaborate ceremonies the pilgrim will bathe at the "door of Paradise," on the sea-shore, and crown the pilgrimage with absolution.[21]

Shivite pilgrims and Vishnuite pilgrims do not go separate ways and worship at exclusive shrines. Such exclusiveness is foreign to Hinduism. Centers of pilgrimage are places of common resort, even though tradition may assign, and practice preserve, something of sectarian character to each. In viewing Hinduism externally, we wish to comprehend what Hinduism is by seeing it in operation at particular centers, the process of acquaintance were we actually travelers in India.

Private Worship.—We should include private as well as public worship, for in family worship we may witness aspects of the ancestral cult which plays so large a rôle in Hinduism. Take the Brahman householder. The duties of religious exercise are his concern above all other men, unless it be the *sadhu,* the *sannyasi,* or the pilgrim. His morning ablutions are performed in the spirit if not in the form of worship at a stream, or a pond (*talau*), or the well in his garden, accompanied, perhaps, by an invocation to the sacred rivers to be present in the water he uses. He calls upon *Hari* (*Vishnu*) or *Hara* (*Shiva*), or both, and repeats the ancient *gayatri,* the prayer to the sun. He puts on his forehead the sign (*tilak*) of his god, and in privacy continues the morning ritual, with the recognition of various great gods, and the family ancestors, and the mention of the names of himself, his

---

[21] *Cf.* Yeats-Brown, *op. cit.,* pp. 258–263: Lowell Thomas, *The Black Pagoda,* pp. 305ff.; P. Loti, *op. cit.,* pp. 228–233.

family, and his clan. The Sanskrit prayer to the sun, the most
sacred of Hindu prayers, enters largely into the daily worship:

Ōm bhūr-bhuvah suvah
Ōm tatsavitur varenyam
Bhargo devasya dhīmahi
Dhiyo yonah prachodayāt [22]

Which means, in English,

Ōm, earth, atmosphere and sky;
Ōm, that desirable splendor of *Savitri* (*i.e.,* the sun);
May we obtain (or, meditate upon) that splendor of the god!
And may he inspire our thoughts!

Prayers are prescribed for the midday, and the evening, and
these, along with the morning prayer, are performed by all adherents of ancient Brahmanical tradition—either directly or by
proxy through a *purohit* or priest. Before taking food at midday,
the householder, or the priest on his behalf, does homage to the
family gods in what we should call the kitchen. In a Brahman
household the kitchen is as sacred as a private chapel. The images
are bathed, marked with sacred signs, and placed upon a low
stool. Little lamps are lit before them, camphor burned, a small
bell rung, and prayers offered; offerings of food are made and
sips taken of the water used to bathe the images. Evening prayer
precedes the evening meal, and the pious Hindu may pray again
before retiring. In the household of the pious non-Brahman
there are simpler and briefer, but none the less regular daily
rites,[23] to the more popular deities, and the spirits of dead ancestors. The Sundras, the lowest caste, do not neglect religious
observance, but both their notions and their practices are uncouth, being merely crude *linga-puja,* "worship of the *linga*"
of *Shiva,* with petitions to ancestral spirits and to various demons.

Women's Rites.—The woman of any caste, especially the
Brahman, has her own day of worship, including ceremonial
bathing, sun-worship, and worship of the *tulasi*-plant, or of a
pipal tree. She does homage to the family gods, possibly using
images of her own. She may worship the great toe of her husband's right foot, as if the husband were a god. However, in
late years the exigencies of newer ways of living, and the revi-

22 Cf. *Maitri Upanishad,* 6:6–7.
23 *Cf.* S. Stevenson, *Rites of the Twice-born,* pp. 207–251.

sion of traditional ideas have altered worship in many Hindu homes, whether of the higher or the lower castes. The current of Hinduism flows still with great force, but new occasions of human intercourse teach new duties to the gods, in domestic and in public life. The proverbial leisure of Hindustan has given way to activity that seeks world-favor, with less time for religion of the formal kind. There has been a shifting of interest from religion to politics, although here and there one finds a renewed emphasis upon religious forms as a demonstration of patriotism. There are indications in some parts of a violent revulsion against all religion, and a frank adoption of the spirit of materialistic progress. It is scarcely to be expected, however, that so great a religious heritage as that of Hindu India will yield its best features to decay and doom. That many aspects, including the *"sadhu* menace," will and ought to disappear, even the friends of India must concede.

India and America.—India today is very different from the West. Her ways are not our ways and our ways are not hers. Nevertheless, both Indian and Western cultures can be traced to a common source. The common culture flowing on the one hand into India, and on the other through Greece and Rome, became peculiarly adapted in each case to the particular region to which it spread. Linguistics readily shows the marks of kinship which bind India and America, which, although slight in themselves, suggest a possible basis of mutual understanding. Her *pitar* is our *father,* her *gaus* our *cow,* her *yugam* our *yoke,* her *pad* our *foot.* A community of religious interest is indicated by the connection of our word, God, with her *huta,* "sacrifice, worship, or calling upon." The Indian *Dyaush Pitar,* meaning the "sky" as god and father of mankind, was called *Zeus Pater* by the Greeks and *Jupiter* by the Romans. Yet, withal, the Indian mind refuses to be measured by the categories of Western thought. Its typical religious heritage is the gift of leisurely, tolerant centuries.

Caste.—Hinduism is not so much one religion as many religions. The designation is comparatively modern and is applied to a content which has altered from age to age, from community to community. An increasing complexity is noticeable throughout the centuries, a complexity of ideas and forms which defy exact description, even by Hindus. Legend accounts for many of them, but legends often vary, though the subject be the same. The social compartmentalization known as *caste* has serious re-

ligious significance, and figures largely, although it cannot always
be said whether caste is cause or effect. Certainly caste (Indian
varna), in its strict meaning, is something peculiarly and distinctly Hindu; it is essentially unlike any phenomenon elsewhere,
the classes in Chinese, Greek, or English society notwithstanding.
In theory, there are four major castes, but in reality there may
be three thousand lesser but mutually exclusive divisions. The
four are:

Brahman, or "priestly," although all Brahmans are not priests;
Kshatriya, or "warrior" and kingly;
Vaishya, or "vassal," the present mercantile groups;
Shudra, or "clean" (ceremonially), the present agricultural and
    artisan groups.

Members of the first three bear the designation of *dwi ja,* or
"twice-born," and wear, or are entitled to wear, the sacred
thread (*upanayana,* or *yajnopawitam*). For the Shudra there is
no initiation, or "second birth," and he wears no sacred thread.
The *sannyasi,* at the other extreme, does not wear the thread;
he has entered upon the last stage of existence in this life and
his own manifest character is his distinction. Ordinarily the
Brahman boy is invested with the sacred thread at eight years
of age, the Kshatriya at eleven, and the Vaishya at twelve. The
Shudra's only hope of investiture lies in a possible rebirth into
a higher caste in the next round of his existence.

The Brahmans, about one-third of the total number of *dwijas,*
or about 7% of the *Hindu* population, are the élite of Hinduism.
The priests of Hinduism are not all Brahmans; there are Shudra
priests who have a certain validity among their own. Of the
Brahmans, about seventeen millions, about one and one half million actually exercise the priestly office, not counting a million
Brahmans who are religious mendicants, attendants upon temples,
or occupants of minor religious posts. So there are about two
and one half millions of Brahman religious functionaries, or one
to every one hundred Hindus. In America we have one minister
or priest for every 575 persons, or one for every 250 Church
members, so India has, perhaps, an over-abundance of religious
leaders. The Brahmans who do not serve religion directly are
engaged in educational, administrative, and other higher service.
They may be land-owners, office clerks, in clerical service with
the railways, or teachers. They are widely distributed throughout

the whole social order. They have been dominant for twenty-five hundred years, since 500 B.C., approximately. When the Aryans came into India the warriors took the lead in conquest and in settlement. When their work was done, the Brahman as the minister of religion, the custodian of learning, and the teacher, gradually gained the ascendancy. He tended to keep his stock pure, whereas the other Aryan classes intermarried with the indigenous peoples. The Indian population became *brahmanized,* and the social classification prevails to this day. All Hindus have a Brahman consciousness. They recognize the privilege, priestly order, accept its superiority and its ministrations, and depend upon its leadership and authority in religious interpretation and cultural advance. This supremacy, arising first in upper-central India, in the *madya-desha,* spread into all parts of the land, notably the south, gaining unquestioned sway. In South India an extraordinary contrast between Brahman and non-Brahman developed. Over all India, but particularly in the south, the "outcaste" became conspicuously distinct from the non-Brahman, and has remained without the pale of the brahmanized order. Buddhism was, to a degree, a development out of, and a reaction against, Brahmanism, and carried on the conflict through several hundred years. Other movements, including the non-Brahman movement of our day, have throughout the centuries sought independence of the Brahmans, but Hinduism is still ruled by Brahman power.

It is the *fact* of caste, with a recognition of the Brahman's place in the system, which concerns us in our present survey. Nothing is more impressive than the fact of caste. Caste lines and caste consciousness are very tangibly in evidence. The Hindu gardener will milk the cow, but will not deliberately use a vessel tainted with beef; no Brahman will receive food or drink from a Shudra; the Hindu must have his bride chosen for him from his own traditional, hereditary group; no outcaste may draw water from a Hindu well, nor set foot within the precincts of a Hindu shrine, nor even, in some quarters, approach too near the person of an upper casteman. Each man is born to his station and career, and follows in detail the ways of his sires. It is assumed that caste is divinely appointed, and that man, by doing his own castework, not only meets his social and religious obligation, but fulfils his destiny. Although to many Hindus caste is a garment laid aside at death, if not before, to the masses caste is, for life, fixed and inviolable. The priest attends to prayer and sacrifice, the farmer tills his modest plots of ground, the potter tends his wheel, and so on.

Origins of Caste.—It took centuries and almost inexplicable circumstance for such a system to develop. One can point to a time in Indian history when there was no caste, probably three thousand years ago. When the Aryans came they found multitudes of people whom they called *dasyus,* evil beings, enemies of gods and men. Stand, if you will, in imagination, among the rudely built huts in an ancient Panjab village. About you are "mostly a comely folk, tall, and clean-limbed, and rather fair of skin, with well-cut features, and straight noses; but among them are not a few squat and ugly men and women, flat-nosed, and nearly black in colour, who were once the free dwellers in the land, and now have become slaves and serfs to their Aryan conquerors." [24] At the same time, far to the south, are Kolarian and Dravidian peoples, of whom no ancient descriptions are available. We know them through modern records alone, save as the Aryans noticed them in their early accounts. In general, we may ignore the Kolarian and equally primitive stocks which still number ten million, and dwell upon the interaction of "Aryan" and "Dravidian" in the making of Indian religion and civilization. Thus we may account for the continued importance of race, color, and religious consciousness in Hinduism. On the one hand, there were the "white-hued," straight-nosed, sacrificial, and godly Aryans, as they themselves said; on the other, were the "noseless" (*i.e.* snub-nosed), "black-skinned," "riteless," and "godless" *dasyus.* It need not be assumed that the "Dravidians" were so unlike the Aryans; at least the true Dravidian of South India had a culture of his own which still predominates. The Aryans who retained most nearly their own early character still survive in the warrior stocks of Jats and Rajputs of the Panjab, and Rajputana. In Central India, an Indo-Aryan culture formed under the leadership of the Brahman priesthood. The major elements were gradually classified, sometimes subtly, sometimes overtly; what did not yield to the common plan was left as "outcaste." Naturally the outcastes were left in the extremest possible isolation and oppression,—as pariahs. Caste is more than variations in geographical location, in language, in occupation, in color, or in religious heritage; it is a state of mind.

Hindu Classics and Deities.—The literary development of Hinduism may be more easily followed. Curiously enough the

[24] L. D. Barnett, *Hindu Gods,* p. 9.

Hindu has not been historically minded; story rather than history has engaged him. In tracing its literary development we may encounter in bold outline, at least, the progress of the faith itself. In terms of its writings, the story of Hinduism is, successively, that of the *Vedas*, the *Brahmanas*, the *Upanishads*, the *Law Books*, the *Great Epics* and the *Puranas*, to mention only the major units. The full account of the literature would require an encyclopædia; the units here named are each composite, a series of unique expositions of common matter. The original deposit is the *Vedas*, particularly the *Rig Veda*.

1. The *Vedas* are four in number: *Rig, Yajur, Sama,* and *Atharva.* They portray from the *Rig* to the *Atharva* the early orientation of the Indo-European cult to its Indian environment. The *Rig* may be said to reflect the religious ideas which the Aryans brought into India. They came in the freedom and vigor of pastoral peoples. They had domesticated certain animals, with the cow as the chief measure of economic value. Girls were early married by purchase or by capture; and sons were much desired for war, ritual observance, and the perpetuation of the family. Monogamy was the rule, with exogamy between the separate clans. They had a cult of ancestors: they burned or buried the corpse and purified themselves after the funeral; they despatched gifts with the deceased, sometimes offering human sacrifice at the funeral; and they worshiped the departed as the "divine fathers." They were polytheists: they worshiped the "heavenly ones" (the *devas*, or "shiners"), and the Sky itself (*dyaush, dyu,* sky) seems to have been their chief god. The Sky Father was called "lord" (*asura*), "encompasser" (*varuna*), "true" (*aryaman*), "friend" (*mitra*), and "generous" (*bhaga*); besides, there were *Indra* of the Rains, the *Nasatya* horsemen, *Yama* of the Dead, the ethical *Varuna,* with hosts of demons; they had their priests for various occasions, but priests did not monopolize worship.

Vedism proper is then a continuation of an older order with new contacts in a new location. The *Rig Veda* is a row of poetic lamps shining full and joyously upon the high gods, chief of which were *Indra, Agni, Soma,* and *Vishnu.* The *Atharva Veda,* the last of the four, often treats the gods with cringing fear, reflecting the common religion of the day. The *Rig* is the oldest Indo-European literature, and is likely the oldest surviving document among the sources of the *living* religions of the world. Its gods are not tribal or local, but nature powers protecting their people, rather than participating in their affairs. *Indra* is the favorite. He is the thunder-god primarily, armed with lightning and wielding the thunder-bolt, who sets free the all-important rains; he aids his people in battle, or in cattle-raiding; he is the gigantic drinker of *soma*. One-fourth of the thousand (1028) hymns of the *Rig* are inscribed to this almost national god. Next in order comes the fire-god *Agni;* one-fifth of the hymns are his. He has a three-fold origin: on earth he is "born of the wood"; in the atmosphere he is the lightning, and in the heaven he is the sun. He is a triad, the great priest, and the center of ritual. He has more power than any other to ward off from his people evil spirits and hostile magic. *Soma* is granted a whole book (No. IX) of the *Rig,* and is mentioned many times elsewhere, as well, for the *Rig* is mainly concerned with the *soma* sacrifice. He is god in his own right, and head of the *soma*-cult. Even *Indra* needed *soma* for strength. He is of both earthly and heavenly origin, even as the plant, his symbol. He is the great object of priestly interest and activity. Although Vedic ritual knew no national worship, no temple-service, nor any permanent place of sacrifice,[25] altars might be reared at any house or place. Perhaps a hewn, ornamented sacrificial post was set up, and offerings made of milk, butter, grain, cakes, a goat, a sheep, a cow, or a horse. Thrice daily, morning, noon, and night, the *soma*-sacrifice was performed, with pressings of juice mixed with water and with milk, and after each sacrifice gifts were made to the priests. While *Rig Vedic* sacrifice was essentially a gift-offering, there is also evidence of communion, wherein both the one on whose behalf the sacrifice is made and the priests eat of the food after the god has partaken,—or drink of the offerings, as in the case of *soma. Varuna* was somewhat ethically conceived. He is the god of explicit order, which may first have been implicit in the ordinance of the Sky Father, *Dyaush.* He is a holy god, both as cosmic and as ethical order, who witnesses men's deeds everywhere, who protects his own and dissipates their fears, who punishes (usually by disease) the wicked for their sins. He fills the rôle of a savior-god. These four gods are the chief of the "thirty-three." One goddess is important: *Ushas,* the dawn, fair and friendly daughter of the Sky, ever young and smiling, who visits daily every household. Two minor(?) deities, *Vishnu* and *Rudra,* loom large in the later story. *Vishnu* later embodies him-

---

[25] On the contrary, there was a locality (*vidátha*), a place of sacrifice, especially *soma*, which may have been fixed. See M. Bloomfield, art. in JAOS, 48–3, pp. 200ff.

self in various forms (*Krishna, Rama,* etc.) for man's good, and *Rudra,* often malevolent at first, becomes the "auspicious" (*shiva*) Great God Shiva.

The *Atharva Veda* portrays the religion of the fire-cult, the cult of the sacred cow, and tree and serpent worship. *Agni* is its leading deity. It has much to say of "breaths" and their uses; it abounds in charms to secure luck, love, and victory, or to ward off coughs, leprosy, foes, and death. Its magic eclipses the power of *Soma,* and the magician is often stronger than the gods. And yet there are a few lofty conceptions expressed in its hymns, carried over from purer(?) days. It has a beautiful hymn to *Varuna,* who beholds men close at hand, knows what they whisper together, counts the twinklings of their eyelids, and ensnares the men who lie. There is a noble hymn to *Skambha,* the "supporter" of order, faith, duty, and truth, and the Supreme God. The *Atharva* is what every subsequent composite writing is, a mixture of the lofty, the commonplace, and the absurd. One should not lose sight, however, of the lofty, which is the burden of our present task. All the *Vedas,* the *Rig, Yajur, Sama,* and *Atharva,* are regarded by pious Hindus as *sruti,* or truth divinely "revealed," or "heard," in contradistinction from the writings called *smriti,* or "remembered." Of course, the *Brahmanas* and the *Upanishads,* largely commentaries on the *Vedas,* or philosophical treatises based on Vedic concepts, are *sruti,* also.

2. The *Brahmanas* as ritual commentaries owe their origin to priests. The priests by that time (say 850 B.C.) had assumed the leadership in society and religion. A legend asserts that *Rama* of the Axe cleared the earth of Kshatriyas, and gave it to the Brahmans. More likely the Brahmans gained ascendancy through devotion to ritual and learning, and the favor which they found with both kings and people. Certainly the tradition grew of the magical powers of the priestly caste, and the *Brahmanas* are witness to the potency of sacrifice at priestly hands. The notion was held that priests through sacrifice might themselves become divine. One of the *Brahmanas* has it that there are two kinds of gods: the gods are gods; and the priests are gods. Many older elements were made over by the priests to reflect glory on themselves. Early Aryan nature-worship become "the religion of things done" (*karma-kanda*), and rites required meticulous performance. The *Brahmanas* set forth explicitly the details of the ceremonial. Each of the *Vedas* is commented upon toward this end, and its essence elaborated into intricate ritual, which only

a learned priest could control. While a few of the priests—so the records go—engaged in honest speculation about reality and the function of religion, most of them were a pampered lot who at best indulged in the formulation of new rules of sacrifice, deceptive and compelling plays around the sacrificial post.

3. The *Upanishads*—out of over a hundred a dozen are of real importance—are philosophical. Whereas the *Brahmanas* have to do with "works," the *Upanishads* have to do with "knowledge," the knowledge known to the inner circle of the enlightened few. This knowledge is exalted and expounded as a means to desired ends, and not of value in itself alone. As the priestly sacrifice had magical power, so also the right knowledge is magical. What is the right knowledge and what it gains remain for us to discover later. The goal of Hinduism is to be attained, so far as the philosophers are concerned, by knowing rather than by doing. The knower may ignore the gods, as well as the ritual, and in his wisdom become God. There is, therefore, apparent conflict between the *Brahmanas* and the *Upanishads,* although the latter reflect no such exclusiveness as the *Brahmanas.* The *Upanishads* seem to indicate that caste, as well as theology, was still in process of transition. Certainly the *Upanishads* insist that knowledge is not the exclusive prerogative of any group, whether Brahman, or other. There is not even, in the *Upanishads,* a philosophical point of view thoroughly systematized; there are only random speculations about the primal entity, the real, and the processes of life. We shall notice later the "six philosophies" which rest on these treatises.

The Golden Age.—4. The *Law Books,* the *Dharma-sutras,* or the *Dharma-shastras* (*dharma,* "law") originated in the dim period before the Christian Era. The *Great Epics,* too, come out of this age. It is the Golden Age of Sanskrit literature, although it is merely *smriti* in the religious view. The "Laws" of Manu form the basis of the curious system of Hindu jurisprudence observed still in the High Courts, although many scholars nowadays think that "Manu" has been taken much too seriously. The laws deal with every phase of life and conduct: the duties of caste, and caste insignia; the divisions, or *ashramas,* of life; students and their discipline; duties of the householder to his family and his guests; laws of inheritance, recovery of debts, the payment of taxes and rates of interest; punishments and penance for sins; begging and the distribution of alms; ascetic practices in relation to transmigration and the attainment of final bliss, etc. In this era the shudras, fourth caste, are an established order. Caste is complete, and one detects the beginning of the formal theory of defilement and untouchability.

5. The *Great Epics,* the *Mahabharata* and the *Ramayana,* purport to be history, and are therefore *itihasas;* but *itihasa,* the term for "history," means rather legendary history. The materials are first "history" (referring to about 600–400 B.C.) and later, "religion." As religious works they date from about the second century, B.C., to about 200 A.D., and include materials of various kinds as well as theology, a great deal of politics, for example. The background extends from above Delhi into the Ganges-Jamna intersection and on into South India. The works are of enormous size, the *Mahabharata* having 220,000 lines, and the *Ramayana,* 96,000. Obviously, the poems are of composite authorship. There is in neither one any consistent viewpoint; extremes of many sorts are exhibited: warfare is now sheer barbarism, now according to rules; the lusty warrior Bhima drinks blood from the skull of a foe, but many warriors are altogether anæmic; polyandry is a recognized institution, yet there is the noble and beautiful episode of Nala and Damyanti; caste is dominant, and the Brahmans fight; polytheism prevails, there are no sects; every man worships all the gods, and the gods are possessed of qualities both human and divine; action rather than thought rules the scene, although the famous *Bhagavad-gita,* the "Lord's Song," embedded in the *Mahabharata,* includes much philosophy. In both, the doctrines of *karma* and transmigration are assumed, but not developed. The plot of the *Mahabharata* is the war between the five sons of Pandu and the hundred sons of Dhritarashtra, his brother. The sons of Pandu win. *Rama* is one of the heroes. The *Ramayana,* the "adventures of Rama," celebrates the love of *Rama* and *Sita,* the exploits of *Rama,* the rape of *Sita* by a demon king, and *Rama's* recovery of her, with the final translation of *Rama* to heaven. Both epics have acquired a peculiar sanctity. He who reads, or listens to the reading of, the *Mahabharata* with faith may enjoy long life, an agreeable reputation, and ascent to heaven. Equal good may accrue to *Ramayana*-readers. The episodes, well-known and popular, are rehearsed nightly to listening millions. The chief characters are sculptured in stone about the temples, carved in the woodwork of houses, graven on metal household utensils, painted on the walls of houses and temples, and—in recent years—presented on the screen.

6. The *Puranas* are religious poems which share with the epics
the love of the common people. Tradition says there are "eighteen" *Puranas*. They are late, in spite of their general title (*purna*
means "old"); they presuppose the epics, at least. They, too, are
collections of diverse materials: creation stories, the "ages" of the
world, genealogies and legends of the gods, dynastic tales, sectarian dogmas, and ceremonial; philosophy, politics, medicine, gram-
mar, and art; descriptions of sacred sites and the pilgrimage, etc.
The *Vishnu Purana* is the scripture of the Vaishnava (Vishnuite)
sect. It is devoted to *Krishna* as *Vishnu's* representative, but
delights in erotic touches of *Krishna's* youth. It discusses the
earth, the duties of students, the virtues of the Ganges, Buddha's
false teachings, the four castes, the dissolution of the world, and
the true end of man.

Key Words.—This rapid, chronological view of the greater
works of Hindu literature has provided us the essential background for a comprehension of the long development of Hinduism
as religion. We do well to think in terms of Vedic, Brahmanic,
Upanishadic, legal-epic, and Puranic, which serve India in like
manner as Saxon, Norman, feudal, Stuart, and Victorian serve
England. However, as we have been at pains to show, Hinduism
is to an extraordinary and confusing degree the present fruit of
all those eras. Certain conspicuous words current in Hinduism
today might be cited in illustration of the development and
permanence of the main ideas. They are *key-words* to the situation, in spite of the fact that their meanings and their uses have
varied slightly from time to time. Here they are, in something
of verifiable sequence: *rita, veda, karman, brahman, sruti, maya,
prana, atman, ashramas, punarjanman, dharma, ahimsa, smriti,
yoga, shakti, avatara, mukti-moksha,* and *bhakti.* To commit them to
memory is as reasonable as learning certain mathematical tables,
or chemical formulæ. What do they mean, in ordinary usage?
When did they come into use? *Rita veda, karman, brahman* and
sruti, are assuredly Vedic. (1) *Rita* means "order": cosmic, ritualistic, and ethical. (2) *Veda* means "wisdom": divine wisdom which
the gods impart to man; and the primary Indian record of the gift,
its qualities, and its use, as in the four *Vedas.* Its further record
is found in the *Brahmanas* and the *Upanishads;* certain Hindu
sects have claimed that other writings, also, are really *veda.*
(3) *Karman,* or, more familiarly, *karma,* means "action, deed,
effect, or fate"; it is the mysterious power which produces action to
this or that end. (4) *Bráhman* (neuter) meant at first the "holy

power" within the universe, akin, perhaps,—but more generalized— to the *mana, orenda* of Primitives; it came to stand for "mind" (*cf. manas,* which refers particularly to mind in *man*), the cosmic principle which produces, organizes, and informs the universe. It absorbed the functions of other principles and the forms of many gods, and came to mean the All, the Absolute. (5) *Sruti* is what is "heard," or "revealed"; writings which contain *veda* are *sruti.* This theory is analogous to the doctrines of revelation, and inspiration in such religions as Judaism, Christianity, and Islam.

Maya, prana, atman, the *ashramas, punarjanman* (rebirth), and *dharma,* are at least Brahmanic. (6) *Maya* probably meant at first "mysterious power"; it came to have the philosophical connotation of "illusion," and "unreality," in which sense it differed widely from the holy "power," Brahman, Reality. (7) *Prana* is "breath, vital spirit, life," which plays a considerable part in later ascetico-mystical practices, such as *yoga.* (8) *Atman,* like *Brahman,* may be traced in a series of meanings, connoting "wind, breath, self, and essential nature." Soon the two terms were interchangeable. Later they became identical in idealistic philosophy (*cf.* "*Brahman* equals *Atman*), and *Brahman* did service for the two. (9) The *ashramas* were early established "stages" of human life, applicable especially to Brahmans, whereby education, the family, and the religious career were provided for each man. (10) *Punarjanman* means nothing more than "rebirth," a concept out of which grew the sweeping theory of transmigration, which when linked with *karma* took control of human life. Since Upanishadic times *karma* and transmigration have entered into every phase of Hindu thought. Involved in a recurring cycle of rebirth, one's destiny is fixed by *karma.* (11) *Dharma* has a wealth of meaning, but refers primarily to "duty," or a *code* of duty. Great stress is laid on duty (conduct), although much liberty of thought is tolerated. The *Gita* commends "the performer of the good, and not the believer in this or that view." *Dharma* is right action, virtue (*cf.* Chinese *Jen* and *Tê*), the path of discipline, the harmony which underlies life and things, the inner law for each man and group, and the very truth of things (how like the *Tao!*).

These eleven concepts form the ground of philosophy, especially Upanishadic, which carried further the early speculation involving Varuna, Agni, Prajapati, Purusha, and other powers and essences. In the Upanishadic era, also the time of the Jain and Buddhist "heresies," *ahimsa, smriti, yoga,* and *shakti,* became current.

(12) *Ahimsa* means "non-injury," or regard for the sanctity of all life. The concept entered prominently into the thought of the day. While the Jains, in particular, have pressed it *in extremis,* Buddha had a moral use for it, and it is a characteristic and compelling theory in Hinduism. (13) *Smriti* is "remembered," that is, tradition, in contrast with "revelation." Thus are designated, usually, the writings whose base is not strictly *veda,* such as the philosophies (the *darsanas,* "investigations, teachings"), epics, law-books, etc. (14) *Yoga* has a varied meaning, magic, spell, means, contact, propriety, mental concentration, the union of the soul and nature; and a system of philosophy and practice bears the name. (15) *Shakti* is a word for "power, energy, efficacy, the female energy" (*e.g.,* the wife) of a deity, especially *Shiva.* (16) In the legal-epic era the term *avatara,* a "coming down," or incarnation of the gods, came into common use, especially with reference to *Vishnu,* who chose this method of serving mankind. (17) From this era came the terms *mukti* and *moksha,* meaning "salvation, or release," *i.e.,* from *karma* and transmigration. In previous times men had relied upon "works," or "knowledge"; thereafter, they might avail themselves of more direct help of the gods. (18) In Puranic times the idea of *bhakti,* "devotion," flowered as a full-fledged theistic doctrine. It became a recognized way of *mukti,* or *moksha,* in the name of *Shiva,* or of *Vishnu* in one of his *avataras.* Into the conception was poured a content similar to the "faith, hope and love" of the Apostle Paul. These eighteen words are our irreducible, minimum vocabulary for knowing Hinduism, not the terms themselves, perhaps, so much as the ideas which they represent.

Modern Sects.—Modern Hindu theology (we are thinking of theology rather than of philosophy, of "gods" (*theoi, deva*) rather than of "wisdom" (*sophia*)) recognizes a great triad of gods, *Brahmā* (masculine), *Shiva,* and *Vishnu,* but we hear little of *Brahmā,* and we know *Vishnu* best through his *avataras, Rama* and *Krishna. Shiva* we know by his own name. *Brahmā* was early a personified power who in the *Brahmanas* was identified with the nature-father-god, *Dyaush-pitar,* and made the head of the priestly pantheon. He was a busy deity until the first centuries of the Christian era, creating, protecting, and destroying; but after all he was essentially a philosophical conception (his name is personalized from the same root as *brahman,* "power, breath, mind") which could have little bearing upon the practical affairs of men, so he has passed out of sight. In all India, *Brahmā* has not half a dozen temples, and it is doubtful if he is portrayed by image anywhere. He is one of the "high gods" to whom worship is no longer paid.

Shiva.—*Shiva,* on the other hand, is *Maha-deva,* "Great God." At first he was merely a name; the adjective *shiva* meant "auspicious." Many of the early gods were deemed *shiva,* productive and protective. *Rudra* of the braided hair, unimportant as a Vedic deity, in the Brahmanic era is a most "auspicious" god. Formerly, he was regarded as vengeful and terrible. Was he later called *shiva* in flattery, to make him so? He was the slayer of cattle, and prone to slay men. Even the gods feared him lest he slay them. He slew his father, *Prajapati,* for consorting with his own daughter. But with all his malevolence *Rudra* was a god of healing, and could restore what had been dissolved. He becomes *Shiva,* the most popular of all the gods, with his special seat at Benares, where he is worshiped under the name of *Vishveshvara,* or "Lord of all." He has his own particular abode, the celestial Mount Kailása, or is this a mountain of the Himalayas? In many homes and temples, brass representations of his heaven in ridged, conical form are found. There are many associates of *Shiva,* who are terrible and destructive; nevertheless, they, with himself, are looked to for salvation (*mukti*). Many are beneficent. Shiva's wife is *Devi,* "goddess," *Maha-devi,* "great goddess," *Parbati,* "mountaineer," *Uma,* "light," *Gauri,* "brilliant," *Durga,* "inaccessible" (the patroness, for example, of the Thugs), and *Kali,* "black" (the "mother" in Bengal). *Ganesha,* "chief of attendants," is *Shiva's* son by *Parbati* the Mountaineer. He is god of wisdom and the remover of obstacles; his symbol, the elephant-head (the elephant is both wise and powerful), is found in Shiva's temples. Nandi, chamberlain to *Shiva,* and the guardian of quadrupeds, appears in Shivite temples in the form of a bull, often milky white, lying prone. These are the holy family of Shivism, grouped in a temple with *Shiva's* pillar in the center of the altar: symbolized by the pillar; a head, or bust of his consort; the elephant-head; and the image of the bull. In thought and in writing *Shiva* is often represented as a fair-skinned man, his body smeared with ash, with a wealth of matted hair gathered into a coil on the top of his head; a third eye in the center of his brow; a collar of serpents and a string of skulls about his neck; holding a trident in his hand. He is occasionally represented with four arms, and, at such times, with five or six faces. The composite photograph speaks of universal power.

Shaktism.—One very significant association with *Shiva* is known as *shaktism*. *Shakti* is "power, or activity." In the popular mind, the vengeful, destructive qualities of *Shiva* have come to be exercised more by his consorts, *Durga,* the "inaccessible," and *Kali,* the "black." *Uma* and *Gauri* are gentle forms of his *shakti.* There is extensive worship of Shiva's female energy, especially in its baleful forms. "Right-hand" *shaktism* is comparatively decent, and by a purified devotion may become exalted. When *Kali*—or *Durga,* etc.— is taken as the "merciful mother," and the "savior of sinners," as she sometimes is, her worship exhibits elevation of mind and sincere conduct. Tagore wrote, "Mother, I shall weave a chain of pearls for thy neck with my tears of sorrow . . . and when I bring it to thee as my offering, thou rewardest me with thy grace" (*Gitanjali,* No. 83). Many modern poets, especially in Bengal, sing of the "mother of the universe," "*Shiva's* queen," "the happy one in my heart," "that *Kali* of the thought," "*Durga* whose name is the promised land of salvation," the "stony-hearted girl," "little mother *Uma,*" "*Durga* who feeds the world," and "*Kali* who drives man round and round the wheel of being." The burden of the poetry is that the "name," or the "feet" of the Mother (the prostrate worshiper humbly calling on the goddess) are more efficacious than austerities, or pilgrimages. "Left-hand" *shaktism,* however, exhibits much that is terrible and vile. In it the goddess is the energy especially concerned with sexual intercourse—*Shiva* is the god of reproduction, it is well to recall—and with magical performances and powers. At Kalighat, near Calcutta,[26] bloody sacrifice is offered to the goddess. Human sacrifices once were offered. At various shrines, indecent, orgiastic rites are observed in her name, as the "black" *Kali,* the "terrible" *Durga,* or the "great" *Maha-devi.* The barbarities of the annual *Durga-puja,* "Durga-worship," celebrate her powers and propitiate her favors. There are "rules" and a literature of this left-hand *shaktism,* known generally as the *Tantras.* It is a late, post-Puranic aspect of Hinduism, and is wholly inferior with five requisites: wine, flesh, fish, grain, and woman. Sexual intercourse, often promiscuous, is actual, not symbolical, in the ritual. Tantric shaktism is obviously a survival and a recrudescence of a phase of original Indian religion, a perversion of the view that divinity is both male and female. But on its higher side shaktism is a religion of the Motherhood of God.[27] Shiva's *shakti* claims the

---

26 "Calcutta" comes from "Kalighat."
27 Ramakrishna, one of whose disciples was Vivekananda, preached the higher shaktism. *Cf.* D. G. Mukerji, *The Face of Silence.*

worship of the majority in Bengal, but it is revered and feared throughout India.

Asceticism.—Shiva is *Maha-yogi,* the "Great Ascetic." He sits in age-long meditation; he haunts the burning-ghats; and wanders in the company of ghosts and goblins. He is god of the *sadhus,* a multitude which man can scarcely number. He is the god of "Works" and of those who depend upon works for peace of mind and final salvation. Several millions are completely devoted to religion; they have taken the religious way for life, giving themselves entirely to continual austerity, to forms and ceremonies. Many millions provide, with their worldly duties, for those ceremonies which promise peace. *Sadhus* and *yogis,* whose only pursuit is religion, are mostly followers of *Shiva Maha-yogi.* They are familiar sights. Here is a man measuring his length, his body the very measuring-rod, along a dusty, sunny highway to a holy place. There is a man buried up to his chin, enduring a stated period of penance. Yonder is a man seated devoutly within the "five fires," four heaps of burning fuel about him, and the burning sun pouring down its hot rays. One taking a vow of thirst sits tormented beside a river or a spring, or under a stand with its water-jar, which drips, drips, drips, on his head. Here is one sitting on his bed of thorns, or iron spikes; there, another walking on thorns, points up, made into sandals. All are seeking merit against the time of rebirth, hoping for passage on the "last journey." In *Shiva* is centered "the highest perfection of austere penance and abstract meditation, by which the most unlimited powers are attained, miracles are worked, the highest spiritual knowledge acquired, and union gained eventually with the great spirit of the universe." The common man may imitate *Shiva's* austere penance; the intellectual may meditate abstractly on the god. Both are intent on miracles. The common man may seek magical power; the intellectual, spiritual knowledge. Both seek union at last with the great spirit of the universe. What *Shiva* is might be shown by a mosaic of words from South Indian (Tamil) devotees; he is the ash-smeared and ever undefiled, lord of the burning-ground, both lord and lady, the pith of holy writ, the lord of wisdom, head of the heavenly ones, the forgiver of sin, the dispenser of grace, the lord of life, dweller in the thought of the good, the most real to man in the hour of death, the source of all, and, older than the oldest and newer than all that is new.

In modern Hinduism *Shiva* is virtually a sectarian deity, sectarian since as early as 300 B.C. During the Epic and Puranic periods his followers became remarkably exclusive. Such a phenomenon would seem to indicate, contrary to our previous remarks (Chap. VIII), a lack of tolerance on the part of Hinduism. Not so. Indian sectarianism, unlike that of Christianity, is an assertion of superiority of a religious order which *includes* rather than excludes details of other orders. In this sense *Shiva* is still the All-god of the early, Upanishadic centuries; but as modern polytheism developed, *Shiva,* to his own followers, remained "head of the heavenly ones"; and Shivism has not usually excluded anything not itself exclusive. Indian sectarianism is a matter of practice, and not of theory, which agrees with our observation that Hinduism is intellectually tolerant. A Hindu may *think* as he pleases, without disadvantage to his religious status, but is careful, possibly intolerant, with respect to religious *acts*. Yet within Shivism are many sub-divisions resting upon divergencies of, and often opposition to, formal observance. The million Lingayats, for example, who are the greatest Shivite sect of South India, are strict vegetarians, and total abstainers from spirituous liquors. They condemn child-marriage, and permit the re-marriage of widows. They recognize no caste distinctions, and they bury their dead. They reject the authority of the *Vedas* as *Sruti,* and the Brahman priesthood. On the side of theology, Shivism has allied itself more with systems of *dualism,* which accord reality to matter, than with idealistic thought which makes material unreal.

Vishnu.—The third member of the modern triad is *Vishnu,* the "pervasive," active deity. He and *Shiva,* in reality, divide between them almost the whole field; Brahmā, we saw, is negligible. While *Shiva* is the more popular and more widely recognized, *Vishnu* has more followers who are devoted to one god alone. But *Vishnu* is worshiped through his forms; in fact, more through his forms than in his own person. While *Shiva* has many names, many functions, and many associates, Vishnu has *avataras,* "descents, embodiments, incarnations," and has been worshiped mainly through them.

Vishnu was an Aryan solar deity in the Rig Vedic period. He seems to have filled a minor rôle; at least, he is not mentioned as often as *Indra, Agni,* and *Soma*. His importance increased, however, with passing years, and with the passage of the Aryans further into India. He comes to be identified with the increasingly prominent institution of sacrifice, and is at last elevated to conspicuous rank. In the Brahmanic era he assumes, along with

Rudra, the leading place in the living faith. Called *Naráyana,* "moving upon the waters," he was identified with the creator *Brahmā,* whose first place of motion was the waters (*nara*). His symbol is a fish, and the bird, *Garuda,* his mount. He was assigned a residence in heaven, designated Vaikuntha, a "penetrating spot," and given *Lakshmi, Saraswati,* and other wives. In this era he displays his peculiar power to "descend," or incarnate himself. In the Epic period he became the second member of the great Triad. He is at that time the embodiment of all-pervading mercy, and goodness; he is self-existent and preserving spirit; he was especially active when iniquity was triumphant, and religion was in danger. In these crises, he issued forth "for the defense of the good and the suppression of the wicked, and for the establishment of justice," as the *Gita* puts it (4:7–8), and his forth-coming was that of the *avatara.* Hinduism understands that this "incarnation" of *Vishnu* was not his mere self-manifestation in a human form, but a real incarnation, the god dwelling for the time within a human form. He was truly god and truly man at the same time, touched with the feeling of men's infirmities, and yet their savior from their distresses. This doctrine of the *avatara* was highly important for the development of Hinduism, both in its loftier meaning, and its less reasonable, as well. It not only brought god down to men, but it enabled Vishnuism to attach to itself a host of gods and demons as manifestations of *Vishnu,* even including forms of animal worship with the higher polytheism. In consequence, the divisions within Vishnuism outnumber, if anything, those of Shivism.

Vishnu is represented as having "descended" many times, as animal, or man. Once the number stood at ten, but additions have been made. In theory, the possible number is indefinite, if not infinite. Thus Hinduism claims Mahavira, who founded Jainism and Buddha himself among the later *avataras,* and no doubt Mahatma Gandhi will be so regarded. Of the *avataras,* however, two only are significant for current and modern Vishnuism, namely, those as *Krishna* and as *Rama.*

Krishna.—The Krishna-incarnation is possibly the older of the two; certainly it is the more popular. But there are *two* Krishnas which we must take into account, now separate, and again united into one. There is *Krishna* known as *Vasudeva,* and there is *Krishna* the Cowherd. Vasudeva may have been an early, religious reformer—a warrior-priest—whose son was *Krishna.* At any rate, long before the Epic period, there was a movement of monotheism carried on by *Vasudeva-Krishna* who sought to exalt God under the name of *Bhagavata,* "the Adorable." The reformer seems himself to have become the Adorable, the *Bhagavata,* the one God who loves mankind, by whose grace men may be saved. This *Krishna* is the *Bhagavata* of the original *Bhagavad-gita,* or "Song of the Adorable," a poem of the third, or possibly even the fourth, century, B.C., which commends faith in *Krishna* as the chief way of salvation. Says the *Gita,* "I, *Krishna,* am God; I am father, mother, the only lord and refuge; worshipers of me, when they worship, are in me, and I also am in them; he who worships me does not perish." Probably later additions to the *Gita* include: I am *Vasudeva,* I am *Vishnu* (and, even, "I am *Rama*"); at the end of many births the man of knowledge finds refuge in me, knowing *Vasudeva* to be the All." Toward the end of the Epic, and during the Puranic era, *Krishna* is thus identified with *Vasudeva* and *Vishnu* as the Supreme Being, the Absolute, and the source and essence of universal Being.

There is the other *Krishna,* the Cowherd, a musical, mischievous, amorous boy-god of a clan of herdsmen (the Abhiras, or the Yadavas, which?). In a manner difficult to explain, unless by the intermingling of clans, *Krishna,* the youthful lover-god, seems to have become associated with *Krishna,* the serious, gracious savior-god. The amorous *Krishna* has persisted, in spite of his austerer relative. This is the *Krishna* of the *Vishnu Purana* (written *c.* 400, A.D.), of the *Gita Govinda* (12th century, A.D.?), and of one book of the generally lofty *Bhagavata Purana* (9th century, A.D.). Herein he dallies with the cow-girls. Highly wrought passages tell of the power of sensual passion to stimulate devotion, much in the vein of *shakti*-worship in Shivism. There are many "Freudian" interpretations in terms of the erotic. Much development of sectarian Vishnuism is colored by this lower quality. In the twelfth-century *Gita Govinda* of Jayadeva, one of the *gopis,* or "cow-girls," *Radha* by name, a lower form of *Lakshmi,* is *Krishna's* especial mistress. She had won his favor by peculiar devotion in a previous existence. Her worship seems to have been first established about 1100 A.D. at Brindaban, on the Jumna River above Agra, whence it spread to Bengal. In Bengal, the climax came with the founding by Vallabha, sometime after 1500 A.D., of a new sect which held *Krishna* to be the eternal *Brahman* (Reality), *Radha* to be his eternal spouse, devotion to them the means of salvation, and the final goal of man to be living and sporting forever with *Krishna* and *Radha* in the glorious forests of a heavenly Brindaban. In actual practice this form corresponds with the left-hand *shaktism* of Shivism. The erotic aspects of Vishnuism, however, are confined to relatively small numbers, whose excesses are repugnant to most Hindus.

The higher *Krishna* is portrayed in the *Bhagavad-gita,* and the *Bhagavata Purana.* In the *Gita, Vasudeva-Krishna-Vishnu* as god is a personal, loving, savior, who offers men salvation through devotion to himself, and extends his divine grace to consummate their devotion. This is the emphatic theme which tends to make the composite *Gita* a spiritual unity. It portrays exclusively the higher reaches of Vishnuism. Lord *Krishna,* in the guise of a charioteer conversing *en route* with the warrior, Arjuna, is made to say—if the extracts be joined together: "I am the lord of born beings"; "I am indifferent to all born beings" (9:29) (he takes no account of caste, being universal savior). "Have thy mind on me, exercise devotion toward me, make thy sacrifice to me, do homage to me. To me thou shalt come. I make thee a truthful promise. Thou art dear to me" (18:65). "One attains by my grace to the everlasting, changeless region." "He who knows in verity my divine birth and works, comes not again to birth when he has left the body" (4:9). "Cast off all thy works upon me" (works are not the means of peace and salvation, save as they are done for *Krishna's* sake (9:27). "Abandoning all other religions, come for refuge to me alone." "The enlightened pay worship to me." *Krishna* extends salvation to all sinners, to women, tradesmen, and serfs (*shudras*), as well as to righteous Brahmans and devout rajas (4:36; 9:32, 33); devotion, expressed in the technical term *bhakti,* can break the round of births, and cancel all evil fruits. At one point in the dialogue, the warrior Arjuna is "smitten with amazement," bows his head, and, with hands clasped, gives expression to a passionate outburst of adoration of the all-sovereign, radiant, and merciful Lord" (11:15ff). On the whole, however, the *Gita* is a philosophical poem, not given to a display of emotion. It makes its appeal to the "enlightened," intellectually, and spiritually. The *Bhagavata Purana* displays more the intensity of Vishnuite devotion, and does so by resting upon and *idealizing Krishna* the Cowherd. It deals with the boyhood of *Krishna,* and his youth, and makes the love of the *gopis* (cow-girls) for *Krishna* symbolic of spiritual devotion. How often in religion has the love of God been expounded in the figure of earthly passion, and how often has God been made the sole object of such passion! The *Bhagavata Purana* gives expression to a new theory of devotion (*bhakti*), and contains utterances which, said Farquhar, "are worthy of a place in the best literature" of devotional mysticism.[28] He, however, qualifies this somewhat by saying, "Devotion" is "a surging emotion which chokes the speech, makes the tears flow . . . often leads to hysterical laughing and weeping by turns, to sudden fainting fits and to long trances of unconsciousness." All these effects are produced by gazing at images of *Krishna,* by singing his praises, by remembering him in meditation, and by mingling with his devotees, serving them lovingly, and hearing them tell of his glory and his love. By this new kind of devotion, release (*mukti, moksha*) may come speedily, independent of the long cycle of rebirth. The majority of *Krishna's* devotees follow the interpretation rendered in the *Gita* and the *Bhagavata Purana* at its best. There is no general thought or worship of *two Krishnas; Krishna* is one Lord with many qualities discriminatingly regarded by each sect in its own way.

Rama and Sita.—The *Rama-avatara* of *Vishnu* is more uniformly admirable than *Krishna,* even though the latter is more popular. *Krishna* is probably looked upon as more fully a manifestation of *Vishnu,* and as one with *Vishnu* himself, while *Rama* has a slightly more distinct personality of his own, and a more extensive life-career. We refer, in particular, to the *Rama* more exactly known as *Rama-chandra* (*chandra* means "moon"), and to the *Rama*-cult, which came into existence in the tenth, or eleventh century, A.D. However, there is indication that two thousand years ago *Rama-chandra* was deemed a full incarnation of *Vishnu* and called the eternal Real (*Brahman,* the philosophical Absolute of the Upanishads). On the whole, the same theological conceptions have been applied to *Rama* as to *Krishna.* The story of *Rama* is briefly told in a section of the *Mahabharata,* fully told in the *Ramayana.*[29] *Rama* may have been originally a hero of the northland, or a godling of some warrior clan, who through association with *Vishnu* became a universal god. He is never unchaste or impure, and his bride, *Sita,* is the very ideal of Hindu womanhood, matching with her womanly fidelity his own nobility. No story is so loved as that of *Rama's* trials, *Sita's* faithfulness, and the final triumph of their virtues. In the original epic of

---

28 Outline of *India's Religious Literature*, p. 229.
29 Composed in Sanskrit by Valmiki, who claimed he "saw" (*cf. sruti*) what he rehearsed, and was commanded by *Brahmā* to sing *Rama's* deeds. The popular Hindu version is by Tulsi Das.

Valmiki, Dasaratha, king of Ayodhya (which is Oudh today, with its capital Lucknow), had three wives, by each of whom he had a son. They were *Rama,* Bharata, and *Lakshmana,* with *Rama* his favorite, and the designated successor to the throne of Ayodhya. Bharata's mother plays a trick, unknown to Bharata, whereby *Rama* is banished for fourteen years; she planned to have her Bharata succeed, meanwhile. *Rama,* with *Sita,* and his loyal brother, *Lakshmana,* wanders forth an exile. The aged father, Dasaratha, dies of a broken heart, and Bharata, absent all the while from Ayodhya, was called to the throne. Bharata, loyal to *Rama,* refuses to take advantage of his mother's ruse, and sets out to seek *Rama* to persuade him to return as king. But *Rama* feels bound by their dead father's decree—it has the force of fate—and persuades Bharata to take the throne. Bharata rules as *Rama's* vicegerent, while *Rama* fulfils his wanderings.

The royal exiles wage combat in the forests with demonic adversaries. One she-demon, captivated by *Rama's* prowess and noble bearing, makes undue advances to him. Repulsed by *Rama,* enraged, she enlists her demon brother Ravana against *Rama,* inciting him further by describing the rapturous beauty of *Sita.* A decoy demon, in the form of a deer, lures *Rama* and *Lakshmana* to the chase. In their absence, Ravana seizes *Sita* and flies with her through the air to Lanka (Ceylon), his island fastness. *Hanuman,* the monkey-god, takes up the search and discovers the place of *Sita's* captivity. *Hanuman's* monkeys build a causeway over the watery expanse which he during his search had cleared with a bound, and *Rama* leads his forces over. Laying siege to Ravana's castle, *Rama* finally slays Ravana in single combat. *Sita* is rescued and by ordeal by fire proves her chastity. The triumphant, happy host returns to Ayodhya, where *Rama,* his exile ended, mounts his throne, with *Sita* as his queen.

The epic is little more than a hero tale like the Song of Roland or the Song of the Nibelungs. *Rama* is a prince of heroic proportions, not a god, not even a religious leader. Among the gods, *Brahmā* is the greatest, with *Shiva* and *Vishnu* playing leading rôles. With *Shiva* are mentioned his wife, *Uma* or "Light," a war-god son, and Nandi, his sacred bull. With *Vishnu* is named his wife, Lakshmi, goddess of fortune; and *Vishnu* rides upon the sacred bird, Garuda. Additions were made to the original story, several centuries later, and a newer theology introduced. The older polytheism is maintained, with *Brahmā, Shiva,* and *Vishnu* as the greatest gods, but with *Rama* as *Vishnu's* partial incarnation upon earth to punish Ravana. Ravana had abused the boon of invulnerability which Brahmā had granted him, and had done mischief on the earth. In modern times the person and adventures of *Rama* were further elaborated. In the version by Tulsi Das (a contemporary of our Elizabethans), *Rama* is a full *avatara* of Vishnu come to rescue men from their miserable estate in wickedness. Just as the original tale may reflect the conflict between Aryans and *dasyus* (especially, the Dravidians), so the *Ramayana* of Tulsi Das doubtless reflects the confusion of his own age. It was the time of the Great Mughal Akbar, and near the founding of European trading companies in the East. Hinduism had been much affected by Islam. Many reform movements were under way with many reformers abroad, both low caste and high. Tulsi gives a vivid picture of the sinfulness of the age: "No regard was paid to caste, or to the four stages of life . . . brahmans sold the Vedas, kings devoured their subjects . . . the right road was any that most took the fancy, the greatest pundit (teacher) was the one that talked the loudest . . . every boaster was thought a fine fellow, and every liar a wit . . . anyone with unkempt hair and long nails was celebrated as a model of mortification . . . the man was everywhere subject to the woman . . . everyone was addicted to sensuality, avarice, and violence, and flouted the gods, the brahmans, the scriptures, and the saints . . . married women appeared without ornaments, and widows were bedecked with jewels . . . Shudras instructed the twice-born in theology and, assuming the cord, received priestly fees . . . men are reckoned as theologians and philosophers who are merely covetous of their neighbor's wife, clever in trickery, and enmeshed in ignorance and selfishness . . . people of low caste, such as oil-men, potters, dog-feeders, and distillers, turn religious mendicants, and make brahmans touch their feet . . . any naked wretch is an ascetic . . . ascetics amass wealth and mendicants become householders . . . the world neither rewards nor even listens to the poet . . . everyone practices the duties of another station of life than his own, and the endless perversions of morality are beyond all description." [30] Not only has India listened to this poet, but the Gospel of *Rama* is a widespread influence in Hinduism today. Although there are no temple "clerks" to give us figures, there are probably a hundred million Ramaites, most of whom are in central and northern parts.

Amid the wickedness which Tulsi described, *Rama* is *Vishnu*

[30] From Growse's *Tulsidas Ramayana*, pp. 682–4.

fully incarnate come to save men and to bring in the Golden Age of purity, truth, and wisdom, with joy of soul. *Rama* is "of incomparable beauty; the bodiless, the embodied, the veritable source of every bodily element; the merciful, the mighty-armed, the dispeller of all life's terrors; without beginning, and unborn; the one, and indivisible; beyond the reach of all the senses; the friend of the unsensual, the destroyer of lust; at once inaccessible and accessible, the essentially pure, the unfailing comforter whom ascetics behold when they have subdued their mind and senses; the lord of the three spheres, the terminator of transmigration, whose praises make pure" (Growse, pp. 445–6). To this description of *Rama's* qualities, Tulsi adds, "By the grace of *Rama* every disease is extirpated, with a holy teacher for physician, faith for a prescription, contempt of the world for a regimen, devotion to *Hari* (*i.e., Vishnu*) for the life-giving drug, and a soul full of faith in the means of cure. . . . The *Vedas,* the *Puranas,* and all the scriptures declare that without faith in *Rama* there is no happiness; it would be easier for water to stay on the back of a tortoise, or for the son of a childless woman to be slain, than for any creature to be happy in opposition to *Hari*. Sooner shall thirst be satisfied by drinking of a mirage, and sooner shall fire appear out of ice, than for anyone to oppose *Rama* and yet find happiness. . . . Is there any creature, O dull of soul, who has worshiped *Rama* and not found salvation? . . . In this age of the world there is no other salvation, neither by means of abstraction, sacrifice, prayer, penance, the payment of vows, nor religious ceremonial. Think only of *Rama,* sing only of *Rama,* give ear only to *Rama's* infinite perfections" (Growse, pp. 707–13). Tulsi was not only a mirror of contemporary Hinduism, but an advocate of faith and morals of a high order. A philosopher, he wrote for the common man.

Among the important contradictions within the *Rama* Gospel, we should cite the debate between those who attribute to man free-will, and those who attribute all power to the Divine. There are the two schools. The northern thinks of man's relations to *Rama* as coöperative. They are the "monkey-hold" theorists; they believe that *Rama* saves only if man clings close to him, as the baby monkey clings to its mother in flight. The southern school minimizes man's part and magnifies *Rama's* part in salvation. They are the "cat-hold" theorists; man is like the kitten carried by the nape of the neck. Tulsi belongs to the northern school, which is in the majority. Note what responsibility he imposes upon man himself. His great theme is *man's* active devotion (*bhakti*) to *Rama.*

Salvation.—Vishnuism lays great stress upon *bhakti,* "devotion," as a way of salvation. With Shivism, the emphasis is laid upon "works," although the notion of *bhakti* is not altogether absent. In Vaishnavism there are works to be done, but both in the Gospel of *Krishna* and in the Gospel of *Rama,* works are minimized in favor of faith. This is the well-known *bhakti-marga,* or "faith-way" of salvation, as the characteristic Shivite way is the *karma-marga,* or "works-way." The *bhakti*-way presents a high view of God and man. God is personal and loving, and man is active and devoted. It is suggestive of men's service to their fellows. One *bhakta* poet has sung,

> "For men's saving I make known
>   These devices—this alone
> My desire.
> Can my *heart* unmoved be
>   When before my eyes I see
> Drowning men?"

Bhaktas rely upon faith, love, service, and God's grace, rather than upon vows, pilgrimages, and sacred rites. Discounting the *jnana-marga,* or "knowledge-way" [31] of the intellectual, they do not look forward to the final absorption of the soul into the All, or the identity of the soul with the impersonal Real. True, there is both high *bhakti,* and low, according to the thought of God's character. God, to *some* bhaktas, must be less than pure and holy, for he not only allows but entreats men to worship him through physical love and bodily excesses. To other bhaktas, God requires clean hands and a pure heart of those who seek him. These bhaktas sow to the spirit and of the spirit reap spiritual joy unsullied with carnal elements.

India has not only been religious; it has been *thoughtfully* religious. Many Indians have paid earnest attention to such matters as have exercised the thought of mankind everywhere. For example, Is there anything real amid the changing scenes of life? What and where is God? What are goodness, truth, and beauty? What are the sources of knowledge? What is the world? Is matter real? What is the relation of man to God? What is the chief end of man? Whence has man come and whither is he bound? Such

---

[31] The philosophies (*darsanas*) expound this way.

questions are more the prerogative of *thought* than of "works," or "faith." Many Hindus have not been content with *doing* things for *Shiva,* or with giving an *emotional* devotion to *Krishna, Rama,* or some other god. Rather, they have sought salvation by the *jnana-marga,* or "knowledge-way." They may have relied to some extent upon faith and works, for it is not always possible to discern consistent position on the part of a thinker.

Philosophy.—There are six so-called "orthodox" schools. They are orthodox because they seek to ascertain the nature of reality and of knowledge from the revealed texts (the texts which are *sruti*). The texts themselves are not systematized; their embodiment of spiritual experiences is not uniform. Seers wrote as the spirit gave them utterance, and their utterances disclose a variety of experiences, each purporting to be a "revelation." The texts are not always letter-perfect, for the early Vedic materials were composed and transmitted orally by priestly singers. Writing was probably unknown in India, or perhaps the *Vedas* were too sacred to be reduced to writing. At any rate, these "hearings" of the "seers" were not written down until the close of the Vedic era (*c.* 850 B.C.?). They have since provided the basic materials for Hinduism, and so have been systematized by scholars, who have made their own interpretations. No one school has been *scientifically* constructed; the scholars did not employ "pure reason," to use a Kantian phrase.

Once Buddhism proposed to seek knowledge apart from the sacred texts, and many Indians were attracted by the proposal; but when Buddhist speculation, rejecting metaphysics, was seen to end in agnosticism, India turned again to her original stores of wisdom, and gave diligent attention to expositions thereof. It seems, however, that the six "schools" developed out of Buddhist speculation, although the dominant Hindu system Vedanta was not fully formulated until the 9th century, A.D. It is not our purpose to examine all the schools; a technical discussion of philosophy is of itself, apart. It concerns us here merely as a means to comprehend the Indian religious mind. These are the "schools," or "demonstrations" (*darsanas*):

(1) Nyaya, the "logical," which arrives at conclusions by logical "analysis." It relies much upon the five senses, and treats the external world as substantial reality. It recognizes the Supreme Being.

(2) Vaisheshika (*vishesha,* "distinction, particularity"), the "atomic" school, which supplemented Nyaya. It maintains the

reality of the transient world, composed of differentiable aggregates of eternal particles. It, too, concedes a Supreme.

(3) Samkhya, a dualistic, atheistic philosophy of "synthesis." See below.

(4) Yoga, or "yoking," akin to Samkhya, but theistic—it holds that philosophy is not sufficient for "salvation." Yoga recognizes an all-pervading Spirit, not merely individual souls. The "yoking" of the soul with Spirit brings salvation.

(5) Purva-mimamsa, "former inquiry," an idealistic system, but ritualistic. It shares the fundamental theory of the Uttara-mimamsa (*q.v.*).

(6) Uttara-mimamsa, "latter inquiry," popularly known as Vedanta, the "end of veda."

These "demonstrations" come from an indefinite time, the legal-epic period and later, although their basic stock is Vedic, Brahmanic, and Upanishadic. They represent, in part, the re-thinking of problems raised by Buddhists. Several leading Buddhist thinkers were converted Brahmans. Of Sankhya and Vedanta, possibly the former is the older; the latter is more representative. They do not stand opposed in fundamental theory, but Samkhya is more truly philosophical; Vedanta, more mystical.

Samkhya.—Samkhya is built of materials from the Upanishads, as other systems, also, are, but it goes radically beyond such sources. Whereas the Upanishads are devoted to the discovery of the Absolute,[32] the Samkhya denies the Absolute—or, at least, excludes it, or minimizes its importance—and emphasizes the *individual soul,* in the world of the present. What Samkhya came to be during a long development may be seen in the *Samkhya-karika,* "Samkhya verses," a poem of the 4th century, A.D., consisting originally of seventy verses, and attributed to a certain Ishwara Krishna. This poem claims that it is consistent with scripture, with *sruti* materials. It is clear, nevertheless, that the poem's appeal to scripture is more formal than real, and that many of its leading ideas are derived not from the texts, but from independent thought. While it grants that there is some truth in the Vedic tradition, it insists that sincere philosophic thought is sufficient to achieve truth and salvation (*mukti*), without the aid of an inferential Supreme, whether the impersonal *Brahman,* or the personal *Ishwara.*[33] It assumes that the world is a place of misery, and that the soul is subject to transmigration. Un-

---

[32] *Cf.* A. B. Keith, *The Sankhya System,* p. 7.
[33] By an interesting perversion *ishwara* is ultimately derived from *asura,* which among the "Aryans" meant a demon, and among their Persian kindred a good spirit.

fortunately, however, it falls into a dualism with no provision for mediation between spirit and nature, or the *individual* soul and the Absolute. It is fundamental to Samkhya that the essential distinction be observed between the two, between nature and spirit. This is the knowledge (*jnana*) which saves! Samkhya cites the blind man who carries the lame man on his back (one being active, unconscious nature, the other, inactive, conscious soul), and thus gains guidance. This is clearly coöperation, for both men possess activity and so can coöperate. In the Samkhya view, however, the soul cannot act (as the lame man *can*), and nature is unconscious (while the blind man is *conscious*). If nature is unconscious, how can it be guided by soul? If soul is inactive, how can it guide and direct nature? This is the fatal dualism of Samkhya, in its exposition of the two eternal existences, nature (*prakriti*) and soul (*purusha*).

Samkhya directs men to fixe their gaze upon:

(1) *Nature (prakriti)*, the world as they see it. The world they see is real. They may not understand its origin, nor how it became active and productive from its original constituents of "goodness" (*sattva*), "energy" (*rajas*), and "darkness" (*tamas*); but they can perceive it through its products which differ according to the proportion of goodness, energy, and darkness. Nature is essentially other than soul, although somehow it was first stirred to evolution by union with soul. Nature is not, as in the Vedanta, the product of ignorance, being therefore unreal. Nature is as real as soul.

(2) Their own *souls (purusha)*. They may not comprehend how the principle of individuation operated to produce so many, individual souls, but here they are, conscious, endowed with mind (*manas*), the organ of apprehension, the channel of sense perceptions, and the agent of decisions. Here they are in a world of misery (three-fold: sorrows brought on them by themselves, those brought on them by others, and those inflicted by fate). They cannot remove misery by faith, nor by religious practices, but by knowledge. This knowledge (*jnana*) is gained from perception, inference, and the affirmation of tradition.

The Samkhya goal, won by the inactive contemplation of Nature and by the knowledge that nature and soul are eternally different, is isolation (*kaivalya*), not absorption, not identity. Freedom from misery, not any positive pleasure, nor any loss of individuality, is the ideal. One must realize his isolation from nature's three constituencies (*gunas*) of goodness, energy, and darkness. He is at last a passive spectator to the operations of Nature. Nature must continue to exist, in order that the soul may have opportunity to realize that he is free, inactive, isolated spirit. This is *atheistic dualism*. In the Samkhya, the knowledge which leads to *kaivalya* (beyond pain and transmigration) is offered to Shudras as well as to the "twice-born." Its theistic form, Yoga, recognizes all classes, even panchamas, or "outcastes," whereas Vedanta confines its benefits to the "twice-born." In the Yoga system it is not so much the gaining of knowledge as the practice of *yoga* in devotion to the Lord (*Ishwara*) that wins *kaivalya*. There is a proverb, "No knowledge equal to the Samkhya, no power equal to the Yoga." [34]

Vedanta.—The fundamental theory of Vedanta is that God (*Brahman,* absolute, or *Atman,* soul; they are both one) all-knowing and all-powerful, has created the universe by his will, and is the cause of all existence and dissolution. He is One, without another, and the end of all created things is resolution into Himself.

The Vedantic theory is old. It professes to have been originally Vedic; it contains ideas not unlike elements in such Vedic hymns as those of Creation (*Rig Veda,* Bk. X, No. 129), to the Golden Germ (*RV,* X, 121), or to Skambha, "the earth's upholder" (*Atharva Veda,* Bk. X, No. 7). As a system it represents, rather, a definite gathering up of the chief philosophical doctrines of the Upanishads. It attempts to be inclusive of all orthodox systems. This definite gathering up may have begun in refutation of Buddhism, Jainism, and other contemporary systems of "materialism," but it remained for Shankara, a Shivite reformer and the most important figure among Vedantists, to expound the full reaches of this philosophy. [35] We may call it pantheism, or monistic idealism (technically, advaita, or "non-duality") ; "All is God," or "only the One is real, the many are illusion." It is possible that we have never fully understood it; many of its terms, *maya,* "illusion" for instance, have not always had the same meaning. It has also used terms of other systems but with different connotations. It is difficult for us, as for many Indians, to see in it anything warm and inspiring. It has, perhaps, seemed to blur reality, including the distinctions between good and evil. Many have failed to gain from it any strong incentive for aggressive life and true worship.

[34] For Yoga see S. N. Dasgupta, *Yoga.*
[35] The reputed founder of Vedanta was Badarayana, to whom the *Brahma Sutras* or *Vedanta Sutras* are attributed. There are certain differences of view between Badarayana and Shankara, but the latter may be nearer the Upanishadic meaning.

Tulsi Das deemed it virtual atheism, and offered instead *bhakti* to *Rama,* the dispeller of ignorance and the lord of illusion. The *Gita,* also, while antedating Shankara himself, embodies nevertheless in its doctrine of *bhakti* to *Krishna* a milder, philosophic protest against Vedanta. In these days Shankara's Vedanta is being restudied with diligence, and many profess to find in his exposition God in terms of personality, and the individual self by no means empty and unreal. This, of course, is a modification of the general impression of Shankara held by the West.

Shankara.—Shankara[36] was born about 800 A.D. (788?) in the south of India, on the Malabar coast near Cochin. He came of the Nambudri caste of Brahmans. His father died in his childhood, and he was reared by his mother. He had a fair training in the *Shastras,* or sacred writings. He was inclined to study and religious meditation, disinclined to marry, and desirous of entering upon an ascetic career. He persuaded his mother to release him from the marriage she had arranged, and to let him become a *sannyasi.*[37] Forthwith, Shankara set out upon a pilgrimage to the north, to study with a famous *guru,* Govinda, at his hermitage on the Narbada River, who had been the pupil of the greater *guru* Gaudapada, an influential teacher of *advaita* Vedantism. After several years of study with Govinda who made him a full-fledged *sannyasi,* he went to Benares, where he taught and wrote for many years. He wrote commentaries on the *Vedanta-sutras,* the *Gita,* and the chief *Upanishads,* in formulating his system of Vedanta. In time he went on tour to teach, engaging extensively in controversy with many opponents. He founded a temple to the Goddess of Learning, at the mouth of the Tungabhadra river, east of Goa, and established a hostel (*matha,* a "monastery") with his chief disciple, Mandana, in charge. He visited his aged mother at the end of her life, and broke the rules of *sannyasa* to perform for her the last rites. He toured North India from Ujjain on the west to Assam on the east, and passed away somewhere around fifty years of age at Kedarnath in Garhwal, in the Himalayas, a renowned seat of *Shiva's* worship. He was a brilliant scholar, and his writings, in *Sanskrit,* are characterized by great intellectual capacity and an unusually fine style. The tradition of his teaching is nation-wide. As a life-long celibate he idealizes in his own person the true, philosophical *sannyasi.*

In his teachings, especially upon religion, he was altogether

---

[36] An assumed name meaning "Beneficent," and referring to *Shiva.*

[37] *I.e.,* one who has "separated" from the world, and has laid aside the sacred thread of the Brahman.

an orthodox Hindu. He accepted all the main features of orthodoxy: the inspiration of the *Vedas, Brahmanas, Upanishads,
Puranas,* etc.; the presence of all the traditional gods, of God.
His higher teachings may be indicated in brief outline:[38] There
truly exists only *Brahman,* who (which) is One, without a
second; spiritual, and unknowable; that is, unknowable through
the direct perception of the senses, or through any knower but
itself; it (he) is "that which is in itself, and conceived through
itself." The material world (of perception) is *maya,* "illusion."
The human soul (*atman*) and *Brahman* are in reality one. Since,
however, the identity of the soul and *Brahman* is contrary to
immediate experience, and since man lives in the world of experience, a distinction is made between ultimate truth, and the truth
of experience. Shankara distinguishes between *Brahman* as he
truly is (*para-Brahman, "supreme Brahman"*), and *Brahman*
enwrapped in attributes and limitations. This latter *Brahman* is
the same, but "lower" (*cf.* Chu Hsi's distinction between *li* and
ch'i in "dignity"), is the *param-atman,* "world Soul," and may
be termed *Ishwara,*[39] God.

Shankara distinguishes between higher, and lower knowledge.
To the "higher knowledge" (*jnana, vijnana*), beyond sense experience, *Brahman* is the one, unknowable Reality; all else is
maya, illusory, unreal, an inference from "lower knowledge"
(*avidya*). To *avidya,* within the realm of sense experience, is
a world, which, though phenomenal, is knowable. That is, in
contradictory(?) phrase, one *knows* the immediate world through
"ignorance" (*avidya*).[40] One cannot know what is altogether
unreal; the phenomenal world is not absolutely unreal; its reality
is, however, only relative, impermanent. It is the realm of time
and space, of *personal* experience; it is a confused world of confusion, which cannot be resolved into a *whole.*

Shankara refrains from pushing his interpretation to an obviously absurd extreme. He would not completely flout experience,
would not obliterate all distinctions (*cf.* the higher Taoists, on
the contrary), would not leave so abstract a conception of the
One, that man could disregard experience, or be antinomian.
Shankara left a place in his philosophy for ethics and religion.
He posited the Real and the Phenomenal, and urged that man
attain a union with the Real, that is, that the *real* self of man

[38] *Cf.* Farquhar, *op. cit.,* pp. 171–2.
[39] Shankara's *Ishwara* is the *vishisht-rupa,* "special form," of *Brahman.*
[40] *Vidya,* "knowledge"; *a-vidya,* "ignorance." *Cf.* the Apostle's words, "If the light
that is in thee, be darkness, how great is that darkness."

know at last Reality. Actual man would realize his possibility, would discipline his impulses through reason. Shankara puts on man a measure of responsibility, after all; responsibility for his own deeds (*karma* is not wholly impersonal?). Man may observe his acts, and by intelligence distinguish the supreme good from the worldly good [41] and from evil—but what is evil? Is there *positive* evil? Shankara's system would seem to leave no place for positives (positives are real—only Brahman is real!). At any rate, Shankara teaches that there is an End to which *jnana* will lead by breaking at last for the self the bonds of *karma* and rebirth in the "lower, phenomenal" world (*samsara*); that there is a *Dharma* with its prescriptions and prohibitions, which if man observe, obey, he qualifies himself for saving knowledge.

Shankara's goal [42] is the cessation of the *idea* of separateness, distinction, duality, and the consummation of the *idea* of the unity of all. *Mukti, moksha,* "release," comes for the man who rises above the world of the transient into the truth of *Brahman* (*para-Brahman*). It seems that true knowledge may be obtained in this realm of *samsara*. Then at death, *Brahman* insures the man of *jnana* final release from *maya, karma,* etc., into the stillness, peace, and completion of the Absolute.

Ramanuja.—Some eminent Indians have criticized Shankara's teachings as defective. Their criticism has been directed both at theory and practical application. Ramanuja, a Brahman of the twelfth century, A.D., proposed a "qualified non-duality." He wrote extensive commentaries on the same books which Shankara had interpreted. He rejected the distinction between the higher and the lower Brahman, and that between the higher and the lower knowledge. He rejected the absolute identity of the individual and *Brahman;* and, he qualified the doctrine of *maya,* as he thought Shankara had used it. He had little use for *maya,* since he granted the world (*samsara*) something of a *real* existence of its own; he used *maya* to mean the will of the Lord (*Ishwara*) by which he chooses to be born among men. Ramanuja is decidedly a theist; *Vishnu,* and not *Shiva,* or *Brahman,* is his God. *Vishnu is Brahman!* Ramanuja rests his faith in *Vishnu* as a personal God with attributes; *Vishnu is Ishwara,* the Supreme Lord. *Vishnu* pervades all, both souls and matter. All things are emanations from him. He expresses his interest in creation and his concern for mankind by manifestations of himself from time to time (a

---

[41] *Cf.* K. Sastri, *Advaita Philosophy,* pp. 191, 208.
[42] *Cf.* S. Radhakrishnan, *Indian Philosophy,* Chap. VIII; S. Dasgupta, *Indian Idealism.*

vague doctrine of salvation through incarnations). The life of man is determined by the principle of *karma,* and the soul is subject to transmigration. But good works and sound knowledge—and faith, also, to some degree—will nullify *karma* and bring cessation of rebirth. Man's ultimate end is not identity with, nor the realization of identity with, an impersonal *Brahman,* but continued existence in the loving presence of *Vishnu* in *Vishnu's* heaven, Vaikuntha. Release is possible not only to the "twice-born," but to Shudras, and to outcastes, also. They can all avail themselves, each in his own station and in his own way, of the fruits of devotion to *Vishnu.* Ramanuja sought, through his great *Commentary* and by pilgrimages of instruction throughout India, to link Vishnuism and the Vedanta. He himself punctiliously observed caste rules regarding food and intercourse with other castes, but sought to provide a cosmopolitan Gospel by a union of all the major elements in Hindu religious tradition. Tulsi Das got his Gospel through the line of Ramanuja, and did for the common people what Ramanuja had attempted for the more thoughtful of all classes. To the Western mind this modified Vedantism of Ramanuja is probably the nearest approach to a warm and inspiring theology.

The Basic Common Elements.—We now have before us two of the "six schools" of Hindu thought, all of which emphasize "knowledge" (*jnana*) above works (*karma*)[43] and devotion (*bhakti*) as the means of salvation. While Samkhya and Vedanta have many common qualities, it is not difficult to discern major differences. Samkhya is dualistic and would have man attain to a final *distinction* between the two eternal and real entities, of nature and spirit, to the exclusion of God apart from either (unless in the Yoga form of Samkhya, which personalizes spirit into God). Vedanta would have man realize his *essential unity* with God, and the unreality of all else but God and the soul of man, which are essentially and eternally one (unless in the "modified" Vedanta which is somewhat like Yoga, with an emphatic doctrine of *bhakti* "faith, devotion," etc., added). All six of the schools have many things in common, which, if we cite them, will tell us in conclusion what Hinduism is, in general: (1) The common emphasis on "knowledge," which is particularly true of the "schools" as such; they commonly refer, also, with varying emphasis to the values inhering in "works," and "devotion."

---

[43] *Karma* in this usage means the results, or examples of works, rather than the operating law as *karma.*

(2) The theory of *karma,* the inexorable law of the deed, which is possibly the most striking characteristic of Hinduism.

(3) Transmigration, or rebirth of the soul, with the world as the sphere of the soul's repeated "entanglement" (*samsara*).

(4) The eternity of the soul, although with difference of opinion as to the eternal "supreme soul" (*paramatman*) and the eternal "individual soul" (*jivatman*).

(5) A theory of the eternity of matter, but with the differentiation as to just what "matter" is (to the Samkhyist, for example, matter is something gross and real, and to the Vedantist it is something subtle or illusory which overlays the soul until the soul's release).

(6) The soul as caught in a bondage of misery (this is the chief ground for our calling Hinduism "pessimistic"), from which escape is sought.

(7) Mind (*manas*), the only expression of consciousness; that is, that *thought* is the only real expression of the soul's active and willing consciousness.

(8) The Ultimate is beyond the Present, however the Ultimate may be conceived. Bliss is not of this changing order of the world. There are no orchids blooming on the dead limbs of space and time.

Conclusion.—It occurs to the Westerner that Hinduism "satisfies the mind with shadows when it cannot enjoy the substance," as Bacon said of fiction, and that it offers little substance to enjoy. However, Hinduism in its "unscientific" way seems to have arrived at some valuable conclusions on life. Was there not a time when the earth was destitute of life? When it was a hot, cooling ball? Did it not then seem incapable of producing anything conscious? Consciousness, nevertheless, appeared! Was there not, therefore, consciousness before its appearance, in a form possibly not recognizable as such? Although the typical Hindu view of creation is that it began with "nothing," there was, even so, an initial process. Dare we say that, when "all is over," there is final *un*consciousness? If you say that consciousness was a new thing at the beginning, is it not possible that, after death, still newer forms of consciousness may arise? Who can draw the line at which consciousness began? Or the line beyond which it ceases? Is there consciousness in the vegetable? If there is, then why not in the mineral also? Samuel Butler once observed that "the hen makes the shell in her inside, but it is pure pottery." The Venus Flytrap closes on *nothing not good* (has it a sort of biological, or at least,

mechanical consciousness?). Hinduism has consistently held to
consciousness as the irreducible quality of existence. It has exalted
Mind. It is amazing, however, that it has employed the mind not
to use, renovate and glorify the world, but to reduce it to neglect.
Or, is this altogether so? Hinduism has an interesting solution of
the relation of man in his life-span to the world, and to religion.
No other faith has formulated so definite a program. We refer
to the four *ashramas,* "stages" of life. The scheme seems to
place more value upon *life* itself than upon the relations which
it sustains, and to dispense with any need of historical background,
or physical perspective. By the scheme of "stages," the Hindu may
be (1) the pupil, learning the ways of the fathers, according to
the station into which he is born; (2) the householder, married
and rearing a family, and engaging in the work of his station;
(3) the anchorite, dwelling apart to learn completely the life of
self-denial; and (4) the *sannyasi.* But, again, this is Hinduism's
ideal program for a few, namely, the privileged Brahmans, although, in effect, the lower classes may observe the routine and end
as *sadhus,* those who are "on the way," or have "reached the
goal." Yet even *sannyasis* and *sadhus* rejoice most in their isolation from the "world," and not in the recollection that they
sought in their proper "stage" to make the world any less miserable as a dwelling place. For them the soul is more than the
processes of sun or moon, more than the fire on hearth or altar.
"When the sun is set, and the moon is set, and the fire is gone out,
the soul is the light of man," said an ancient Indian sage (Yajna-
valkya). But the beauty of this lofty conception pales somewhat
by the very quality of its abstractness. Leaving Hinduism now,
with what meat we have been able to put on the dry bones of the
key-words once suggested, but not withdrawing from India herself, we turn to Jainism.

CHAPTER X

Jainism

More than a million Jains are found in India, representing an ancient and honorable religion. It was first a "heresy," but its very title, Jainism, connotes "victory,"—or the "faith victorious." Jains seem to have their own peculiar confidence in their peculiar way of life. Jainism, they say, is a religion of deliverance already demonstrated by many "victors" (*jinas*), and available today to all who follow their example. The Jains have not only offered their religion to their own countrymen, but even to us of the West. When, however, Westerners comprehend its discipline, they find it difficult even to imagine its effectiveness. It is almost inconceivable that this faith should find a footing in the West, or prove of value. What then is this Jainist "victory"?

Having endured through twenty-five long centuries, Jainism must have value of a sort. We have said it was at first a heresy; it was one of two. Buddhism was the other. Both arose at the same time and within the same territories. While Jainism cannot convincingly be compared with Buddhism in its central concepts, in variety of development, or in the extent of its history, it has managed to survive in its Indian environment, while, in the same environment, its rival met its doom. Yet one might say with justice that this survival is as much a sign of weakness as of strength, an evidence that Jainism has endured by accommodation. The small community of Jains, however, exerts an influence out of proportion to its numbers. In districts and towns where the Jains are found to any extent, they take a leading place as bankers, lawyers, merchants, and proprietors of land. They are not tillers of the soil, for a cardinal doctrine of their faith has kept them out of agriculture. On the other hand, all trades and occupations are open to them, save brewing, fishing, butchering, or any livelihood which involves "injury" (*himsa*) to a living being. Of course the Jains abstain from eating meat.

The Jainist Habitat.—Although the Jains arose in eastern India, whence Buddhism also arose, they are today, with slight exception, a western Indian people. If you take the train at Bangalore, in Mysore State, and travel northwards twelve hundred and fifty miles to Bikaner, in Rajputana, by way of Bombay, Baroda, Central India, and Gwalior, your trip will take you through the midst of the modern Jain communities. Twenty-five percent live in Rajputana, where lies their holiest temple-city, Mt. Abu, in the Aravalli Hills. Forty percent live within the Bombay Presidency. The remainder live further south, or else above Bombay, in Baroda, Gwalior, and the Central Indian states,—or on the eastern side of India, in and about Calcutta. On this trip from Bangalore to Bikaner, one will see many Jainist merchants and traders, especially the Marwaris, whose traditional home is Marwar (or Jodhpur) in Rajputana. These Marwaris are found in all the great trading centers, often as brokers and money-lenders. But their reputation is not always enviable. Much of the economic embarrassment of the peasantry has been laid to their charge. There is a slighting proverb, "The three-tufted ones (the Marwaris with their three-pointed *pagris* or head-pieces), the red-faced ones (Europeans), and the cactus-plant, cannot live without *increasing.*" According to another proverb, "Marwaris, crows, and Parsi liquor shops are everywhere."

The Jains are enterprising and well-to-do, even wealthy. They pride themselves on the absence of religious mendicants, or common beggars. They provide schools and orphanages for their children, homes (*ashramas,* or "retreats") for their widows, hospitals (*pinjrapols*) for their defective animals, and rest-houses (*dharmshalas*) for their pilgrims. For the conservation of communal interests they hold periodic conferences, and maintain associations in their larger centers. However, they seem to have suffered, during recent decades, a gradual decrease in numbers. Among the causes are these: Jainism exalts the ideal of celibacy; the remarriage of its widows has been prohibited; many marriageable men have been restrained from marriage because Jain women are too few, a scarcity made the more distressing by the marriage of Jain women to Hindus of the closely-allied Vaishya, or "merchant" caste.[1]

Templed Hills.—To see the Jainist faith in action, let us go on tour to Parasnath, Satrunjaya, Girnar, and Abu, four centers of Jainist pilgrimage. They are memorial sites, and shrines to *jinas,* and are seats of common Jainist worship. Throughout

[1] A Vaishya Hindu may marry, under certain circumtances, a Jain wife without breach of caste, some indication, at least, of Hinduism's attitude toward Jainism as a sort of Hindu *caste.*

the Jain community, there are forty thousand temples, many of which are among the choicest of India's gems of architecture. Often these temples lie in groups. The Jains, more than any other faith, have grouped their shrines in veritable "cities," especially on prominent mountains. Parasnath, Satrunjaya, Girnar, and Abu are lofty cities of clustered temples on conspicuous mountain-tops.

Mt. Parasnath (more accurately Parshva-nath) is a famous seat of worship. It rises, two hundred miles northwest of Calcutta, above the Grand Trunk Road, and supports an interesting group of "them Injian temples to admire when you see"—as Kipling's British Tommy said while "route-marchin'" on the Grand Trunk Road. It is the reputed place of burial of the twenty-third *jina*,[2] Parshva, who died in 776 B.C. Parshva was the immediate predecessor of Mahavira, the actual "founder" of the order. At the foot of his mountain lies the village of Madhuban, where one discovers at once evidence of a thorough going sectarianism which has tended to disrupt the modern Jain community. You find in Madhuban the local headquarters of the rigidly ascetic Digambara, "nudist, or sky-clad," sect, as well as the local center of the Shvetambara "white-clad" sect.[3] These divisions came many centuries ago in this very neighborhood. Some of the images in the temples are clad and some are nude, and it may be that Parshva's image, also, is sometimes nude and sometimes clad.[4] But this divergence in practice is not a source of bitterness.

The ascent of the five thousand foot elevation follows a winding way some twenty miles in length through thick woods, with large clumps of feathery bamboos. The ridge is sparsely covered with gnarled trees, amidst which at points of vantage are small temples commemorating the attainment of *kaivalya* (the Jainist goal) by various "saints." The chief temple, venerable, but not ancient, to Lord Parshva stands below the saddle of the ridge, in a hollow facing south, surrounded by a grove of plantains and fig-trees. It looks out over the sunny plains bordering the Damodar (Damodha) River as it flows sluggishly eastward to the Hugli and the Bengal Bay. The temples on the summit look Hindu from without, but unlike Hindu shrines, each contains *usually* only the "footprints" of a *jina,* who is known also as a *tirthankara,* or "ford-

---

2 There are twenty-four, in all.
3 There is a third sect, the Sthanakvasis, "those who worship everywhere," who have no temples, nor even images for public worship, although they have their private ritual.
4 von Glasenapp, *Der Jainismus,* appendix, p. 28, pictures Parshva's image as nude.

finder," and an image, also, of him only. The chief temple contains the foot-prints of the "lord" (*nath*) Parshva,[5] with an image of him, and, strangely, some marble figures of the *Buddha,* wearing the cord about his neck of the "twice-born" Hindu.[6] In the lesser temples, are idols of various Jainist saints.

The temples have their ministrants, and their ritual of worship. At the shrines of the "white-clad" sect, the priests are robed in a special garb. They wash the images of the saints, and dry them, and mark them with auspicious marks. They tender offerings of flowers, fruit, and rice. They make confession of sin and vows of consecration. Perhaps they mark on the temple floor in rice-grains the dot-and-crescent sign of "release" (*moksha*), the three dots for the "three jewels" (*tiratna*) of doctrine, and the *swastika* for the soul in process of rebirth. They may also offer worship on behalf of the pilgrims. The pilgrims, men and women, may worship in ordinary dress in the temple's outer court, waving sticks of burning incense, or a lighted lamp, saying their prayers and making offerings of sweetmeats, or fruit. At the shrines of the "sky-clad" sect, the officiants are nude, but their worship accords with the common ritual. Women, however, do not appear in the temples of the "sky-clad."

Parshva.—According to the current legend, Parshva was of the eighth century, B.C. After nine preëxistences he was born at last to queen Vamadevi, wife of king Ashvasena, of Kashi (Benares). One night during her pregnancy the queen saw a serpent by her side, and in deference to this portent she named her child *parshvatah,* whence Parshva, "by the side." Prince Parshva married in due time the "perfect" daughter, Prabhavati, of king Prasenajit. The crisis in his life came when he was converted by a picture of Nemi, the twenty-second *jina,* or *tirthankara,* of the Jains. He decides that he will become a world-enlightener. He gives his goods in alms, takes refuge in a hermitage, and at the foot of an *ashoka* tree renounces power and wealth, plucks out his hair, and acquires the knowledge which perfection brings. He is then thirty years of age. Thereafter as a "saint" he takes to wandering. He often fights the *asuras,* or demons, victoriously. Once to protect him from the burning sunshine, the serpent-king did him honor, holding an umbrella above his head (did a cobra

---

[5] The Western visitor may be reminded by these symbols of the "foot-prints" of Jesus in the floor of the church of *Domine Quo Vadis* along the Appian Way near Rome.

[6] The traveler in India soon becomes accustomed to the apparently inconsistent furniture in Hindu, Jain, and Buddhist temples.

spread its hood above him?[7]). In time, at Kashi, Parshva attains Kevalin (*kaivalya*). After a further term of wandering, he retired to Mt. Sammeta (modern Parasnath), where he practiced a month's asceticism, and destroyed the last vestiges of *karma*. At "death" his soul went heavenward and was adorned with divine jewels. Even his wasted body went to heaven, where it was duly burned. And over the bones was raised a mound, a *stupa*, in his memory. The gods set up (in heaven?) an image of him underneath a *chaitya*,[8] to which the power was given of granting one's desires who prayed to him, and of warding off evil influences from his devotees. Such are the virtues of Parshva at his seat on Mt. Parasnath, although according to the strictest Jainist theory he is not a god, but only an *example* of the life victorious.

Satrunjaya.—The holy mount Satrunjaya rises near the town of Palitana in western India, in the peninsula of Kathiawar. Its twin ridges, each a thousand feet in length, are closely covered with imposing temples in the characteristic Hindu design of northern India, with white walls, weathered domes, and gilded pinnacles. A massive battlemented wall, well fitted for defense in former days, entirely surrounds both ridges and the valley between. Within this wall are nineteen lesser, walled compartments, each with its own gate, and its group of temples about the major shrine. There are five hundred temples on these twin summits, including the nineteen major structures. All are built of stone elaborately carved.[9] Within are the symbols and imagery of the faith, the foot-prints and the figures of the saints. In several of the larger courtyards are small, ritual reservoirs.

Glassy-eyed images of the many *jinas* peer out from their cloisered cells, while priests and pilgrims go leisurely and devotedly in and out. Many of these *jinas* attained *kaivalya* on this "hill of the perfected," but the peculiar sanctity of Mt. Satrunjaya was imparted by the first *tirthankara* Rishabha, or Adinath, the "original lord," who is especially revered by the white-clad sect. His ample image sits in the chief temple, lavishly bedecked with jewels, including ear pendants and a crown. It gazes, wide-eyed, solemnly, and almost fiercely, into the heart of every worshiper, reminding all who revere the *jina* of the long-deferred yet hoped-for victory. It is a quiet place, this holy city. There is little demonstration as the pilgrims go about the well-kept, terraced streets, the neat passageways, and airy porches. There are

---

[7] At Parasnath he wears on his hand a cobra crown.
[8] A memorial tomb, surmounted by an umbrella.
[9] *Cf.* J. Burgess, *The Temples of Satrunjaya.*

no rude noises such as strike the ear at many Hindu shrines. Occasionally a bell is gently rung, or a drum softly beaten. On holidays there is chanting in the larger temples. Green parrots abound, and squirrels scamper freely about the precincts. Doves whir from temple to temple. On the wooded slopes, "there's the peacock round the corner, and the monkey up the tree." The setting is worshipful.

The Ninety-nine.—The greatest of the rites is called the "Ninety-nine." It takes three months to perform it. A devotee, when he undertakes this rite, is bent upon it for himself alone. There is no special season for it; it is done at any time the pilgrim may desire. He begins it at the bottom of the mountain. He ascends by leisurely stages the thousands of well-worn steps that wind about the hillsides, often stopping for prolonged rest at appointed places by the way. At the summit he makes the worshipful circuit of the central shrine of Lord Rishabha, and then leisurely descends again. Ninety-eight times this journey is made, up and down, after which he prepares himself for the final details of the rite. He fasts strictly· while he makes the last ascent. At Rishabha's shrine, he performs eleven times over all the varieties of worship, according to the local ritual, with each interval filled with chanting by singers accompanied by harmoniums, who are secured for a proper fee. On the completion of the worship, the custodians of the temple place—for another fee—the image of Rishabha in the courtyard of the temple, on a silver throne beneath a silken canopy. In the open court, the pilgrim pays the Lord Rishabha his final tribute of reverence, perhaps in silent meditation. He then sets out for home.

Girnar.—Seventy-five miles west of Mt. Satrunjaya rises Mt. Girnar above the town of Junagarh. The summit stands out above surrounding peaks. Its temples are among the most ancient in India, for many Jains in the early centuries fled westward from persecution into the comparative peace of remote Kathiawar. Sixteen temples are built upon a cliff beside the central summit. The largest and the most imposing belongs to Neminath, the twenty-second *tirthankara-jina*. It thrusts up a central pinnacle amidst a cone-like cluster of lesser pinnacles. It stands in a spacious quadrangular court bounded on every side by a high stone wall. On the inner side of the wall are seventy cloistered cells, each with a marble image shielded by a perforated marble screen. In the central shrine Lord Nemi is represented by a large black stone image adorned with jewels and massive ornaments of gold.

Round his figure are ranged many white marble images. In the outer hall toward which he faces, are slabs of yellow stone with representations of the 1226 pairs of feet of the first disciples. From the courtyard a passage leads to a low, dark temple, through which one may descend into a curious cave, where a marble image rests, an object of peculiarly superstitious veneration. It is said that the hollow in one of its shoulders is worn by "nectar" dropping from its ear. What faith, after all, is entirely free of grosser, miraculous elements caught up and carried along as its tides have swept over old foundations! The precincts of Neminath are simply and austerely impressive in the stillness of the lofty setting, with the cleanliness which is a Jainist virtue. It is impressive, too, to watch the sober pilgrims wind through the sacred halls, each conscious of his own great responsibility in patterning his life after the example of the "heroes" who have found the way before him.

A Hill of Wisdom.—Mt. Abu, the "hill of wisdom" (*arbuddha*), is the best known and the most frequented holy place. It is a high, extensive plateau, broken off from the ancient Aravalli Hills, less than two hundred miles north of the Gulf of Cambay. Within a broad grove of mango trees lies the "place of temples" (*devalwara,* called "Dilwara"). There are five temples, two of which should have our best attention, being, in many respects, unrivalled in all India. One is a temple of the eleventh century, A.D., dedicated to Rishabha. The other is of the thirteenth century, and dedicated to Neminath. They are built of white marble, and carved with all the delicacy and variety of ornamentation which the rich resources of Indian art could devise. The interiors are executed with a finish which defies description. The more recent of the temples—it is a shrine of the "white-clad"—is slightly more elaborate. The central shrine, terminating in a squat, corrugated, pyramidal roof, is surrounded by porches and pillars, with the whole inclosed in an oblong courtyard. Groups of monasteries and rest-houses are nearby. The central room of the temple, lighted only from the doorway, contains the image of "lord" Nemi seated cross-legged upon his "throne." In the outer court are fifty-two ornate cells, each with its image of a saint. The elephant room contains ten marble elephants, which, with their trappings, were carved with exquisite care. Mothers who were to bear *tirthankaras* saw "elephants" in their dreams, and thereby learned their secret. The ceilings and pillars, especially within the central shrine, are profusely ornamented with delicately traced human, plant, and animal figures. The rafters and struts are covered with geometric designs, while images are chiseled in the capitals. The domed ceiling of the central room displays the choicest carving, with its concentric circles of lotus-flowers, twenty-four in a circle. Eight of these flower-circles, from larger to smaller, and each in its own interval, hang as a cone, point downwards. The images of eighteen guardian spirits (*yakshas*) look down from the walls on Neminath. It took fourteen years to build, and they say it cost eighteen crores of rupees (about $60,000,000). It is the costliest setting for Jain worship, but it exhibits only the forms familiar already.

Ford-finding.—What is Jainism on its theoretical side? What ideas are embodied in the stones and images on the holy mountains? What faith is shown by the various ritual acts? Of what stuff is the Jain mind made? The Jains are counted heretics by the Hindus, but we suspect that the "heresy" is today less pronounced. In any event, we see in Jainism the last direct representative of the great movement of philosophic speculation and religious quest, which flourished in the valley of the Ganges during the 6th and 5th centuries, B.C. Jainism then, with Buddhism and lesser parties, voiced its protest against the thought of Brahmanism, but for several centuries the Jainist planet was dimmed by the splendor of the Buddhist sun. Not until after the Buddhist "light of Asia" passed beyond the land of its rising, did Jainism assume the leading rôle of heresy.

Jainism as a religion is more easily understood, if traced historically. We have already encountered several of the twenty-four *jinas,* or *tirthankaras* of the faith. They are honored as those who found passage through the "dark waters" of this life, who subjected themselves to the discipline necessary to achieve the true and final goal of existence. Jainism does not hold that they help men directly, save as they are examples and reminders of what can and should be done by all the faithful. Vardhaman *Mahavira,* the "great hero" Vardhaman, is considered the last and greatest of the line of twenty-four. We shall use the title and not the name when referring to him, this being the universal practice with reference to the great religious leaders. He is a somewhat shadowy figure of the sixth century, B.C., one of those vague personages that stalk across the stage of history without once turning their faces full upon you. Indeed, we must rest content with some conjecture in connection with all the early "history" of Jainism, nor can we honestly say that important new facts have been discovered during recent decades. There is a fairly substantial tradition which we may follow without undue risk of error, thereby avoiding tedious controversy. We may assume that Parshva, as well as Mahavira, was historical, and that Parasnath mountain is Parashva's chief memorial. Thus Jain origins are somewhere about 800 B.C., although the Jains, by means of their prophets, seek to establish the fact that their religion is as old as the human race. What had been gathering momentum before Mahavira was given by him something of definite form. He is, therefore, the "founder" of the faith.

Marhavira.—Mahavira was born about 540 B.C., in a village at the edge of the city of Vesali, the capital of Videha (in modern Bihar). His native state was the most powerful single principality among the nations in the valley of the Ganges. His father, Siddharta, was a wealthy nobleman of Videha, and chief of a warrior clan. His mother, Trishala, was related to the ruling house of Videha and was a sister of the governor of Vesali. His father was, perhaps, a lay disciple of the *jina* Parshva, and of his mother the legend is told that during her pregnancy she had dreams portentous of the coming of a hero. The child, however, did not take at once to religion; he seems to have had first the training of a warrior's son. In due time he was married to a certain lady Yashoda, of noble lineage, by whom he had one child, a daughter. We recall that the time of these events was one of unusual fertility for the discussion of religion, and for the rise of religious orders. A widespread reaction against Brahmanism had been gaining force during several generations. Many religious teachers had preached in conscientious and determined revolt against the sanctity of the *Vedas,* the power of the Vedic deities, the sacrificial prescriptions of the Brahmanical ritual, and the assumption of spiritual superiority by the Brahman priests. The center of Brahmanism at the time was west of Videha in the region of which Delhi is now the chief city. Sanskrit was in process of forming as the classical language of Hinduism. The immediate neighborhood of Mahavira, along the Ganges, was only slightly Brahmanized, and Pali was the language of the people. The two great Jainist and Buddhist "heresies," therefore, sprang up off-center; they were, in a measure, revolts against Brahmanism, but, in another sense, they were spontaneous local quests of truth. Both movements adopted in their ascetic mode of life the rules which had been already fixed by Brahmans.

Mahavira, in time, took to religion as a life career, the definite step being taken when he was thirty years of age. There is some ground for believing that he earlier considered the step, but delayed it in deference to his mother's wishes. He may even have been averse to marriage, if the ascetic instinct was thus early strong in him, but consented to marriage by his parents' arrangement. In any event, at thirty, after the death of both parents, he left his home, and set out as a wandering ascetic. He may have considered himself a member of Parshva's order, in which his father had held membership, as we are told. Tradition says that he, like Parshva, was borne from home in a palanquin to the shade of an *ashoka* tree, where he discarded his ornaments and fine raiment, donned a simple robe, plucked out his hair, and abstained from food and drink for two and one-half days. Thus prepared, he undertook for thirteen months a regimen of strictest self-denial, discarding all clothing, and counting nudity essential to true asceticism. For twelve years he went about, usually without shelter, enduring affront and injurious treatment at the hands of some of the inhabitants everywhere he went. "By uninterrupted meditation, unbroken chastity, and the most scrupulous observance of the rules concerning eating and drinking, he fully subdued his senses; nor did he in the slightest degree hurt or cause offence to any living being." When he was forty-two, he found the earthly end of his mental quest. He was in a field near an old Hindu temple, not far from a *sal* tree, squatting in deep meditation with knees high and his head low between them, bathed in the brilliance of a burning sun. Here he achieved the state known by various names, "cessation" (*nirvana*), or "isolation" (*kevala, kaivalya*), and became a *tirthankara* or "ford-finder," *jina* or "conqueror," and *arhat* or "blessed one." Thenceforth he was a recognized religious teacher. He seems to have identified himself shortly with an order then existent and known as the *Nirgranthas,* men who were "fetter-free." With him as their head, by a gradual transformation *they* became the order of the *Jinas,* or Jainists. This identification of Nirgranthas and Jains is open to question, but no essential of our present story depends upon this identity.

Possibly psychology, for want of exact historical data, can tell what happened to Mahavira in the sun-stricken field. What we know of the experience of many modern ascetics may be relied on for an explanation. He had long been under rigorous discipline of body, had meditated deeply upon aspects of the world and human life, and had discussed in current terminology the major theories of the day. He came, therefore, to realize something of a state which to him, at least, was new. Having failed to realize through others the true knowledge that he sought, he took as immediate revelation the climactic experience, and its knowledge-values, which visited him in the open field. Newness in religion is a relative term; what has lain long in the sub-conscious may bubble forth as *revelation*. Mahavira rejected much of the world he knew, and in the place of the discarded ideas and practices he put as his unique contribution the substance of his new experience. His clay became a pot by losing some qualities and by gaining others. No god spoke to him there in the open. Mahavira had to a peculiar degree the sense that what he got was somehow his own achievement. He himself had become as God, knowing good and evil. He was spared for thirty years to spread his teachings. His ranks were swelled not only by the former Parshva's followers, but especially from the highest grades of Hindu society, also. Instead of reproach and harsh treatment, he was given honor by hosts of pious householders, and he won the patronage of kings. What more was needed to confirm the freshness of his message! He elaborated during his wandering ministry the simple items of his original "knowledge," but he never forgot the method whereby he gained his goal, the way of nudity and mortification. Perhaps he was too austere.

Jainist Theory.—We cannot always say what is of Mahavira himself and what is due to subsequent development. In what field of faith can we ever be sure of the separate strands? What follows is, in the main, what may be with good reason attributed to Mahavira. His fundamental tenet is that all nature, even that which seems the most inanimate, possesses life and the capacity of re-animation. This theory is merely primitive man's consistent reaction to the world about him; the whole world is alive, and every object in it is alive. Can it be that Mahavira's theory of nudity is merely primitive? Nudity is deemed by the savage valuable in connection with magic rites; clothes are likely to convey "pollution" (the *mana* of others); it is a savage notion that the removal of clothing at times of worship is the extreme token of submission [to deity]. Mahavira may have thought that clothing might harbor insect or animal life, and be thereby the means of unpremeditated injury. Certainly the *animistic* theory of Mahavira is primitive, and he might not thereon build a reputation for high thinking. He went beyond this, however, as the records clearly indicate, and thoughtful Jainists have, until the present day, consistently and inflexibly held to his fundamental view as the most distinctive aspect of the faith. Its corollary is *ahimsa,* or "non-injury."

Mahavira's theory of "animation" is not altogether primitive, nor is it Hindu (in the sectarian sense); nor yet Buddhist. It is altogether different from Buddha's view of life, and more extreme than any Hindu view. It is based upon the dualistic proposition that there are in the universe only eternal souls (*jivas*), and eternal elements (*a-jivas*). He held no notion of the world as illusion (*maya*), as in the later Vedanta philosophy. He was "realistic," somewhat in the manner of the later Samkhya-Yoga. To Mahavira the soul (*jiva*) is real, it acts, and is affected by acts. There are innumerable *jivas;* each is conscious, and each is intelligent. The *jiva* is the knowing self; it perceives and it conceives. One may directly perceive his own *jiva* by introspection, and come thus to true knowledge, which is, in part, the distinction between *jiva* and *ajiva,* the self and the not-self. The *ajiva,* or "non-soul," is something atomic. It is a thing, unconscious, and without knowledge. *Ajivas* are innumerable; they are real and eternal and are not the product of thought. They are without size, and are immeasurable, yet they have "body" and the qualities of touch, taste, smell and color. They exist in various relationships, and in combination make up what we call "matter" (*pudgala*). *Pudgala* is what is perceived by the senses; and every "object" is a collection of *ajivas,* in addition to at least one *jiva* somehow enmeshed within.

Man, as a "living" object, is composed of *jiva* and *ajiva,* spirit and matter, correlated in a sort of parallelism. Both, remember, are eternal, uncreate and unending. The *jiva* is fettered by what its own activity (*karma*) has gathered about it. It has enveloped itself in numerous sheaths spun from *false* knowledge and *evil* deeds; it has defiled itself by unwholesome contacts. It must extricate itself and purify itself by true knowledge and strict isolation. Or, thinking in terms of any sort of *jiva,* human or otherwise, life must ascend in the scale of existence from lower to higher, gaining by gradual evolution freedom from gross matter, the senses, and the disastrous fruits of *karma* and previous re-births, breaking ultimately the sullying contacts and meshes of *ajivas.* It is to rise *above* qualities, relationships, motion, time and space, and to emerge finally disembodied and actionless. This is *Nirvana,* or *Kaivalya.* The *jiva* must free itself. In terms of man, he is his own savior. Said Mahavira, "Man! Thou art thine own friend! Why wishest thou a friend beyond thyself?" This means, more immediately, man's rise caste by caste. For any high caste man there are exactly fourteen stages in the process of his evolution.

Non-injury.—It is obvious that, in such a view, *ahimsa,* "non-injury," to any *jiva* is a cardinal virtue; *himsa,* "injury," a major evil. If the Jain be reminded that *jivas* are *in*destructible, he replies that if one injures another he causes pain to both and inhibits the process of release. If one kills another he deprives the one slain of an opportunity to work out his destiny. If the Jain be reminded that cases of suicide are approved by the order, he will reply that only certain forms of suicide are approved. If an ascetic starve himself to death in accordance with a holy vow to abstain from food, it is a worthy suicide, and the deceased has furthered his own good cause. At certain stages in his progress toward *Nirvana,* a man may deliberately limit by his suicide the remaining activity of *karma* and the opportunities for sin. But the doctrine of *ahimsa* seldom allow such exceptions. Rather, it has been carried to unusual extremes in the preservation, or prolongation of life. The Jainist *pinjrapol* is a place of suffering for the animals there, a means, as it were, for the brute creation to gain the merit of the way of pain. In its high regard for life, Jainism has strangely erred, even to the extreme of indifference to suffering in both the human and the animal world. Such is one of the long issues of Mahavira's theory of animation.

Yes-and-No.—There are intellectual intricacies (Mahaviran eccentricities?) in Jainism which need not long detain us here. We cite merely one, the baffling theory of "yes-and-no," or "maybe" (*syad-vada*),[10] which makes for extreme uncertainty in the realm of knowledge. This theory is all the more amazing in the light of the emphasis Mahavira placed on knowing. By it, one says "yes-no" to almost every proposition, for a thing may be viewed in many aspects, with no absolute judgment possible from any one.[11] All affirmations are true only in a limited sense, and everything possesses an infinite number of qualities, each of which can be affirmed only in a particular sense. What should you expect a Jain philosopher to do with our modern "true and false" questionnaires? His doctrine, in any case, gives him an uncertain philosophy. He deals with many kinds of "knowledge," but the test of the validity of "true knowledge" is that it helps man get what he wants (knowledge is not good for its own sake). It

[10] *Cf. syat,* "it may be"; *syad asti, syan na-asti,* "maybe it is, maybe it isn't."
[11] "A man must be a tyro in the arts of Erewhonian polite society, unless he instinctively suspects a hidden 'yea' in every 'nay' that meets him."—Samuel Butler.

reveals the *jiva* as the knowing self, and identifies the objects (*ajivas*, perhaps) that are known. It knows that permanence is involved in change, and that there is an Ultimate. Perfect knowledge (*kevala*) comprehends totality, not parts and relationships,[12] and is possible only to free and purified souls. It supersedes all lesser knowledge which is unable to get beyond relations, and which must say to most propositions, "maybe." The example of true knowledge is Mahavira in the open field where he attained *Kaivalya.* He spun his own philosophy out of the belly of his own experience.

Asceticism.—Along with the intellectual uncertainty which the Jainist heritage has fostered in its way, there is the practical certainty expressed in the ideal of *asceticism.* If the problems of the earth, man, and the universe will not respond to "maybe," they may be solved by discipline. There are "three jewels" of the order, right faith, right knowledge, and right living (conduct); all three abide, but the greatest "jewel" is right living; the other two are incidental accompaniments. One may have *faith* in the teachings of the *jinas,* but a *knowledge* of reality as it is, and the final entrance into reality, comes by way of *conduct,* "doings" (*charitra*). The Jain would cease to do evil and learn to do well, to avoid pain and to find happiness. The way thereof is the discipline of vows, "doings" in accordance with his "vows," after the example of the *jinas.* He does not pay his vows to "the Most High," as did the Israelite, for there is no God to the Jain beyond the deified Mahavira. He swears solemnly to himself, save that the layman takes his vows before a *guru.* There are three sets of solemn pledges, the "twelve," the "eleven," and the "five." The layman ordinarily takes the "twelve," and the ascetic the "five." The "eleven" provide the layman, if he wishes, a preliminary preparation for the "five" of strict asceticism. First, there is "renunciation." The candidate renounces such faults as doubt, any desire to join another faith, any questioning of *karma,* and any inclination to praise or associate with "hypocrites." The "twelve" vows taken thereafter are: (1) never intentionally to take life (*i.e.,* to destroy a *jiva*); (2) never to lie, or to exaggerate; (3) never to steal, or to take what is not given; (4) never to be unchaste (this includes fidelity to wife, or husband, and purity of thought and word); (5) to curb desire, limiting oneself to a reasonable amount of wealth, giving away all in excess (at least, at the end of one's life); (6) to limit the

---

12 Buddha's "knowledge" did not deal with *totals.*

motives for sin, *e.g.*, by regulating travel; (7) to limit the number of things used; (8) to guard against unnecessary evils; (9) to keep stated periods of sinless meditation; (10) to observe special occasions of limitation; (11) to spend occasional days as a monk; (12) to give alms, and to support the ascetic community. Such a special rite as the "Ninety-nine" at Mt. Satrunjaya finds place in this scheme. As death approaches, the layman is urged to take the vow of "non-attachment," to dispose of all his goods, and to refrain from food. There can be no doubt that the "twelve" are a wholesome discipline of life. The proportion of Jains convicted of civil and criminal offences is the lowest of all in India.

The five great vows of the ascetic (*arhat*) are virtually concentrates of the layman's twelve. They carry moderation forward into the strictest self-denial: (1) non-injury (*ahimsa*), (2) truth in speech, (3) non-stealing, (4) chastity (no thought, word, or act of sex),[13] and (5) the renunciation of attachment for any person or thing. We realize something of the rigor of the "five," if we consider at how many points the Jainist universe is "alive." With reference to all the vows, it seems not unfair to say that Jainism is too strenuous (certainly for modern times), is too self-centered (even their self-denials aim at "merit"), misrepresents sorrow and pain as evil and evidence of sin, and stops far short of a solution of caste and the goal of human brotherhood.

Sects.—A word about the sects. Circumstance as well as theory took part in their formation. Mahavira had organized an order with its various "heads." After his death, one of these "heads" took full charge, the office passing from head to head for several generations, until a time of joint-rule (two heads), about one hundred and seventy-five years after Mahavira. There came a famine at the time. One head (Bhadra-bahu), with many monks and laymen of the community, migrated to South India. After many years most of them returned to rejoin the northern community. But cleavage had set in, and by the first century, A.D., the division into two chief branches ("white-clad" Shvetambaras and "sky-clad" Digambaras) was complete. The former had remained at home; the latter had migrated. They differed with regard to dress for monks and had opposing views of sacred scripture. The "sky-clad" have never accepted in full the *Canon* which an early Council adopted under "white-clad" influence. This must be considered the most authentic of all Jain canons, although Jains have, as a rule, little use for scripture. The "nudists" (Digambaras) seem

---

13 Mahavira added this to Parshva's four.

to be the true heirs of Mahavira. They have consistently held womanhood in low esteem as "the greatest temptation in the world" [14] and "the cause of all sinful acts." They have never admitted women to the ranks of the *arhats* and nuns, nor agreed that they may win *Nirvana*. They even deny that Mahavira was ever married, and have no hesitation in forsaking living parents. They are to be found today mainly in South India. The more numerous sect of Shvetambaras admit women to full membership in the monastic order as candidates for *Nirvana*. Their monks and nuns forsake the world only *after* their parents' death. They use images in worship, but clothe them, and have remonstrated against what they took to be idolatry and polytheism, including the deification of Mahavira and other *jinas*. They are the prevailing sect of North India. There is yet a separate sect of non-idolaters, the Sthanakvasis, or those who worship "everywhere."

Conclusion.—Jainism has been subjected not only to internal division, but to forces from without. It has been favored by a few rulers, and persecuted by many. In its original seat in the eastern Ganges valley, Brahmanism gradually attained supremacy, pressing out all heresies. The Jains went westward. Although surrendering its native soil, the faith was compact enough, and conservative enough, to withstand its severest persecutions in the twelfth century by the Brahmans, and from the thirteenth century by the Moslems, by both of whom many temples were demolished, and many of the faithful slain. In South India, the Digambaras were argued into silence by the great Vedantist Shankara. Jains have never recovered temporal power since the Moslems came, but they have remained an effective religious community by reason of their solidarity, their business and commercial enterprise, their wealth and munificence, the comparatively high degree of literacy among them, their tenacious adherence to the theory of "animation," and their code of moral and religious discipline.

[14] *Cf.* Mohammed, "Woman is man's chief calamity."

CHAPTER XI

BUDDHISM

Buddhism has affected large sections of humanity, especially in Asia. Compared with it, Hinduism and Confucianism are provincial; they have served men merely where they arose, with only nominal effects beyond. But Buddhism was a moving current whose force was felt not only in India, its place of origin; it imparted its peculiar character to peoples elsewhere, and remolded many of their institutions. It has demonstrated greater qualities of growth than any of the faiths we have so far considered. Buddha was a son of Mother India. While he could not keep his hold upon his fellow-countrymen, his teachings were popular and impressive for many centuries in his own land, and his spiritual descendants flourish today in Ceylon, Burma, Siam, China, and Japan, with Tibetans representing him afar off. Yet he was not concerned with world-extent! He addressed himself to men about him. The faith he founded became worldwide, because men of many countries found it valuable. It is still worthy of men's thought, who seek the higher things of life. It has relevant suggestions about personality, knowledge, conduct, destiny, and the God-idea.

The Buddhist World.—Buddhism holds a high estate in China and Japan. It seems in India but "a dying echo from a falling wall." India considers it a failure. But Christianity, by the same token, is a failure to the Palestinian. Within less than a century, it lost control of Palestine; within less than a thousand years, it lost control of all the lands which it first conquered. It moved, however, to greater triumphs elsewhere. Buddhism has enjoyed victories similar in kind, if not in quantity; and even numbers do not measure its exact influence. There are today about one hundred and forty million Buddhists—maybe more; but we have no figures for many Buddhist areas. There are nearly 50,000,000 in Japan. There, with their twelve sects, 100,000 temples, and 55,000 priests and priestesses, they make up three-quarters of the population. They are the most active and progres-

sive members of the Buddhist Order. In Burma, 12,000,000
make up the bulk of the population; pagodas (*dagobas*) dot the
land, with more than a thousand in Mandalay alone. Pagodas and
monasteries are the chief objects of interest. With an average
of two monasteries for every village, the total number of the
monks accommodated is over 70,000. The faith holds unrivalled
sway over the masses, and enters deeply into the national life.
Burma is more truly, although conservatively, Buddhist than
any other land. The nine million people of Siam are mostly
Buddhist. The present ruler, King Prajadipak ("World-light"),
although he has become a constitutional monarch, regards himself
as king partly by "apostolic" right; he is the only independent,
royal representative of the Order. Buddhism is virtually the state
religion; Siam is the only country where the faith is thus established. It has 16,000 temples, and 130,000 priests and priestesses. Every layman serves as a monk for at least a brief term.
Most of the village, and more than half of the Government
schools are located in the *wats* or "temples," education and religion being thus identified together. In Ceylon, 2,750,000 Buddhists comprise more than half the population. Their faith is the
dominant, if not the national religion. It is kept alive by 8,000
monks, and many nuns. The Order owns a third of all the
fertile lands. In Tibet, Lamaism must be accounted Buddhist. The
Order includes the entire population of 2,000,000. Lamaism is
highly mixed with demon-worship, and stands, therefore, in marked
contrast with the Order elsewhere. Although the Burmese and
the Tibetans are kindred peoples, their countries differ greatly.
Their religions vary, even as the forbidding plateaus, gloomy
precipices, and dark abysses of Tibet differ from the dense,
voluptuous forests, and the watered, joyous plains of Burma.
The lamas of Tibet—there are several hundred thousand, in
3,000 spacious lamaseries—have played, often unscrupulously,
upon their peoples' fears. The Burmese monks are gentler, better educated, and more earnest. In India, mostly in Kashmir,
Sikkim, Assam, and Bengal, there are less than 400,000 Buddhists. East of Benares, in Bihar, the original home, there are
one thousand.

We have accounted so far for hardly more than 75,000,000.
The other half is found mainly in China, where it mingles with
the other cults, where, through compromise, it often becomes
somewhat indistinguishable from them. The Buddhist *monks* and
nuns of China can be identified; they play an important rôle in

the common life, reciting sacred scriptures, and advising the people about the gods and the sacrifices. Buddhist laymen are less conspicuous. But while Chinese Buddhism is apparently Chinese, the bulk of the people, in so far as they are at all *religious,* are essentially Buddhist. Although often a strange medley of worthy and unworthy elements, with forms both foreign and indigenous, the Chinese Buddha-way (*Fo-tao*) maintains itself in the complex fabric of the vigorous, practical Chinese situation.

Two Vehicles.—There are other differences than race and country in the Buddhist world. There are two main "schools," or "vehicles," the *Hinayana,* and the *Mahayana.* The former happens to be predominantly "southern," and often bears that name, while the latter is predominantly "northern." Hinayana claims twenty millions, mostly in Burma and Ceylon. Mahayana claims one hundred and twenty-five millions, mostly in China and Japan. But the schools are not geographically exclusively divided; there are Hinayanists in China and Japan, and Mahayana elements in Burma and Ceylon. The division is all-important on higher grounds: the "southern" school assumes that it has preserved the teachings of the Buddha himself, as he gave them to his first disciples; the "northern" school is manifestly a broader interpretation. Both have ample scriptures, including a common literature, but in general the *hinayanist* writings are in *Pali,* Buddha's own vernacular, while the *mahayanist* writings are in *Sanskrit,* the language of Brahmanical Hinduism. Even so, the two are kindred tongues, differences in terminology consisting often in varied spellings, rather than in separate meanings; although, at times, Buddhism has one definition for a term; Hinduism, another.

Mahayana is more alert today than Hinayana, especially in Japan. Japanese docility and Mahayana philosophy combine to afford accommodation, in Buddhist thought and practice, to Christian competition and Western science. Mahayana has never been essentially dependent upon an historical Buddha. Dates and documents have never mattered much to this Idealism. Never altogether lacking in "social" outlook, Mahayana is peculiarly able, through its profound philosophy, to prosecute modern education, and even to revive its ideal of world-dominion. Hinayana, also, has been astir in Ceylon, Burma, and Siam, although it has been dependent upon dates and documents, and must adapt them by means of new interpretations. Both schools are conscious of their relation to the present world. There is a thoroughgoing Buddhist philosophy of mind and conduct, which may have a further value for those who seek the sounder ways of living in a world where failure and frustration have often been man's lot—even though *we* may never don the yellow robe, with staff and begging-bowl, and join the Buddhist monk in his quest of the jewel in the heart of the lotus.[1]

Buddhist Idols.—Buddha-images are everywhere, especially in Buddha-lands. Perhaps we are familiar with them as we have them in America: small, brass, bronze, or gilded figures of the Buddha, gracefully clad in a flowing robe, seated and serene, legs crossed and the soles of the feet upturned, arms resting on the thighs, parallel with them or maybe crossed, with the palms of the hands upturned, typical of indifference to the world about, of the mastery of self, and of peace of mind. We may use such an image as a paper-weight, or ink-stand, with never a thought of the meaning in terms of long days and lingering nights spent in abstract contemplation, of fleshy passions cooled, earthly desires eradicated, and mighty, human conflict won. If the image is a work of art, not a caricature, it will give us this deeper meaning. The Buddha-images are, of course, of all sorts, especially where the faith is of long standing, as in Ceylon, Burma, China and Japan. Sometimes they seem mere milestones, memorials of times that have passed. Some of them, however, lodge where multitudes of worshipers are wont to gather, and are emblems of a living faith. Near Anaradhapura, in Ceylon, in a wild and secluded situation, there is an enormous, standing figure carved from the solid rock, rising some forty feet in height, with the right arm raised as if bestowing a benediction, or pointing the upward way. Near Rangoon, in Burma, is a huge reclining figure built of stone, the head, however, resting bolt upright. This image is so large that two or three persons could squeeze into an ear. At Kamakura, on the south shore of Japan, is the *Dai-butsu,* or Giant Buddha, a bronze casting of 1252 A.D., representing the Buddha seated in contemplation. This image is commonly reproduced in miniature for the trade. The *Dai-butsu* is fifty feet in height, and thirty-six from knee to knee. The eyes are of pure gold, and the symbol on the forehead is wrought of thirty pounds of silver. The figure sits upon a lotus-blossom pedestal, in one side of which an entrance gives access

---

[1] *Cf. Om mane padme Om, "Om, the jewel in the lotus, Om,"* the common formula of Buddhists.

to a ladder, by which one may climb through the figure to its
shoulders, and look about him upon beautiful stretches of land
and sea. This work of art, most imposing, is suggestive of perfect
repose and passionless calm. In addition to such heroic images,
there are innumerable smaller figures in the temples. Often there
are rows of them, each carved in the likeness of the one traditional form, all showing the one goal of the Buddhist quest. In
the carvings of the temples there is wider variety. In the chisel-
ings and etchings are portrayed the major phases of the Buddha's
life, who being first a Hindu passed in the grip of *karma* through
many births, and appeared from birth to birth in many forms.
The "birth" stories bulk large as temple decorations in wood and
stone. These stories gather up a wealth of legend and folklore, which have attached themselves to the Buddha tradition in
its national settings.

Pagodas.—Even more suggestive of Buddhism is the *pagoda,*
the tall, many-sided, and many-storied tower standing conspicuous, beside a temple, or else quite alone, in every Buddha-
land. The word pagoda is literally *būt-kādah,* "idol-temple." But
the structure is not a temple, nor primarily a place of worship;
it rests, supposedly, above a relic of the Buddha, particularly
some part of his body, which has been carried abroad. Pagodas
are, therefore, symbols of the widespread faith, the most characteristic feature of Buddhist architecture. Several in China
are very beautiful; the largest one is in Rangoon. In Burma, it
is the custom to hang bells—"tinkly temple-bells"—from the
pagoda balconies, which murmur their soft music in the gentle
breezes.

The Temple at Rangoon.—The Shwe Dagon temple of
Rangoon is one of the most important centers of religion. It is
not only the most sacred, but also the largest and finest temple
in Indo-China. The pagoda, they say, contains not only relics
of the Buddha, but relics, also, of his three immediate predecessors. When the first missionaries came with their precious eight
hairs of *the* historical Buddha, they found, already interred in
the sacred mound, these relics of three previous "buddhas"! The
temple is a stately pile, standing on a mound of rectangular terraces, at the edge of the city, dominating the entire landscape.
The topmost level stands one hundred and sixty-six feet above
the open flagged space surrounding the lower terrace. This upper terrace, about nine hundred feet long, by nearly seven hundred wide, is reached by steps on each side, which ascend un-

der handsomely carved teak-wood roofs, supported on huge wood and masonry pillars. At the top, in the center, stands the towering pagoda, with a circumference at the base of nearly fourteen hundred feet, and a height of three hundred and seventy. Profusely gilded from base to summit, it is surmounted by a gilded iron *ti,* "umbrella," from whose rings hang great numbers of jeweled bells. Four chapels stand at the four cardinal quarters of its base. In the northeast corner, covered by a gaily-decorated wooden shed, hangs one of the largest bells in the world. Along the western edge of the terrace, rests, under its magnificently carved canopy, a colossal recumbent statue of the Buddha.

Carvings abound, representing Buddhist episodes. From them one may read much of history. Usually they tell the story of religion; but there is a curious, secular panel over the eastern chapel. It illustrates the capture of the temple by British troops during the First Burmese War in 1824, showing the foreign soldiers with their rifles, the officers with their telescopes, and, underneath, the conquered Burmans! The many features of the temple represent accretions during many centuries; the Burmans dare to say as many as twenty-five! The center is resorted to by worshipers from every part of Indo-China, but is especially dear to Burmese. The terraces are never vacant; somewhere a pilgrim is at prayer. The bells quiver on the high pagoda balcony, and those along the passages are ever testifying, as the pilgrims strike them, that worship is in progress, especially when midnight is bright with moonlight.

Among the worshipers the monk is most conspicuous, moving in their midst, at times entirely unnoticed. With shaven head, in his own peculiar garb, fingering his rosary, his lips moving without sound, he seems cut off from the world of matter, cherishing only deep, religious thoughts. Yet he may normally live in one of the monasteries not far from the temple, with boys in training for the priesthood, one day to be ordained by him. Having come to the temple, worship is his sole concern. He prostrates himself with dignity before an alabaster Buddha-image set with sparkling jewels. This attracts the laymen as they pass. They pause and seat themselves on the floor, ready to follow him as he prays. He, however, is oblivious of their presence; nor will he pray on their behalf. They may follow, if they will. He addresses himself to the image, but in reality, he, like the Ancient Sage,[2] is "brooding by the central altar in the temple-cave of [his] own

[2] *Cf.* Tennyson, *The Ancient Sage.*

self." He mutters *sabba duhkha,* "all is sorrow," and the people say it. He murmurs *sabba anatta,* "all is transient, or unreal," and this, too, the group repeats. He is sure that these are the very words which the serene image would recite, could it speak. They are the words of Buddha. They are, as we shall see, the central theme of Buddhist thought. As the monk and the people repeat them in the presence of the image, their minds are kept upon the goal. They are not idol-worshipers, least of all the monk. He is perhaps a learned man; probably, of the old or Hinayana school, which takes no stock in idols. Nor does the image *represent* to him a god. He has no God. The Buddha is merely the pattern of what he, too, would become. As the monk prays, his "prayer" is merely meditation on the "truths" the Buddha taught. As he turns his steps toward the temple, he merely follows still the "path" which brings release from sorrow and from change. He seeks deliverance, but his hope lies in himself and in his code.

But the people in the temple? What of them? They, also, look upon the image—and they pray. They may, perhaps, naïvely be idolaters. To many of them, the Buddha, doubtless, is of heavenly essence and a god. Most of them fix their thoughts on him as *God. They* cannot, like the learned monk, have recourse to abstraction, and thereby cut the ties that bind them to the world of sense and human action. Indeed, the monk himself may be an object of devotion. He is, at least, a good example. Once they may have known him as an ordinary man; now he has severed his "attachments," and they revere him. Then, beyond him, is his own pattern, the Buddha, whom they may see in him. We may call their reverence *worship,* especially if it be directed to the Buddha. Such is the quality of their prayers, prostrations, flower-offerings and lighted candles. They do not always worship with the monks; they engage in their devotions when and where they will.

The Burman Cult.—The popular Shwe Dagon cult displays always simplicity, beauty, dignity and reverence; although the people's worship may be formal, ceremonial, traditional and sometimes unintelligent. The Burmese, still in general on the lower levels of culture, have no historical perspective through which to view the rational background of the faith, and the higher traditions of the temple and its ritual. They pray long prayers, at times; often, without meaning. They may not know the meaning of the briefest formulæ. They repeat the "Refuge": "I take refuge in the *Buddha,* I take refuge in the *Law,* I take refuge in the *Order"*: but, after all, what are the Buddha, the Law, and the Order, as institutions, to the common villager? It is, however, a comforting committal, as if to God himself.

The Burman Buddhist prays—there is no doubt about it. He prays to Buddha; he prays to other gods, as well. He also prays to spirits. Thus does he unwittingly flout the atheistic Hinayana. He believes in spirits of the river and the wood; they are the spirits of the land. He seldom cuts a tree, without first propitiating the spirit which controls it. As a householder, he reveres the guardian spirit. At each of many festivals, he honors a peculiar spirit. He honors on occasion the "king of spirits." In the Shwe Dagon and other Buddhist temples, therefore, along with Buddha-images, appear symbols of the ancient spirits, which share the prayers and offerings with Buddha. Some of these spirits may themselves have been responsible for a note of gaiety sounded now and then in pessimistic Buddhist ritual. In spite of "sorrow" and "change," there is joy. Sorrow is not the Burman's unremittent lot; nor does change forever mock him. The indigenous *nats,* survivals of the ancient animism, hover still about the temples, hearing and answering prayer. In each of the four Shwe Dagon shrines, they linger among the many images of Buddha, the ornately carved pillars, the fluttering canopies, prayer flags, sacred toys, and tables spread with votive offerings.

Chinese Buddhism.—Passing now to China, the scene is somewhat changed. Chinese Buddhism centers in the monastery, with the temple buildings within the monastery courtyard. This arrangement reflects the manner by which the foreign faith secured its hold on China—by monks and monasteries. There was no general *lay* conversion. We have already seen (*cf.* p. 51f., above) that Chinese Buddhist laymen mingle freely with the populace. The monk keeps himself apart, and the monastery is the unit of the faith's corporate existence.

The Monastery.—The monastery stands usually upon a hill; a common term for the temple, is, therefore, *shan* (or "mountain"). Some of the "heights" were, doubtless, Taoist in the early days, and Buddhism has conserved their ancient sanctity. It served itself heir to what it could absorb. The hill, usually, is tree-clad, with water and a garden at the base. If it be a rugged mountain, the monastery buildings occupy a slope with venerable trees, a rock garden, and a clear stream with waterfalls. The building site is walled. Each structure it incloses is distinct. The monk's houses are separated from the halls of wor-

ship. The temple, within the courtyard proper, may be threefold:
(1) the Hall of the Kings of Heaven, the divine guardians of
the monastery, (2) the Hall of the Great Hero Buddha, which
occupies the center, and (3) the Hall of Law. The central Hall
of Buddha is the largest; its roof projects above the others. All
the roofs are curved, with overhanging eaves, as in ordinary
Chinese architecture, which form the principal external decoration. The interior of each Hall is plain; wall-paintings are very
rare. There may be lotus-symbols in the wooden floors. If it be
a Mahayanist monastery, the type commonest in China, the pro-
fusion of art is shown chiefly in the temple gods.[3]

Mahayana: Prayer for Rain.—The contrast between the
Hinayana Burmese and the Mahayana Chinese cult lies not only
in the monastery setting; the monastic functions differ. Take,
for illustration, a Chinese Buddhist prayer for rain, a ceremony
held in the Hall of the Law. The seasons in Burma are pronounced and regular. Burmese monks do not pray for rain; they
know about when to expect it. Furthermore, the Hinayana monks
are not supposed to *pray*. In China, prolonged droughts are often
unseasonable. In the midst of them, the distressed farmers may,
in the end, other means having failed, have recourse to the
monastery. The Mahayana monks are used to prayer. For the
rain ceremony, a green cloth is spread upon the altar (the color
in itself is magical), on which are images of the *Dragon King*
who controls the rain. Flowers, fruits and incense are spread
before the images. The monks may don green garments suggesting either rain or, in season, spring. They first fulfil a period
of abstinence and purification, similar to the abstinence observed
by a Roman Catholic priest before a mass. During the ritual,
some of them recite appropriate stanzas of scripture, while others
attend to the offerings, the incense, and the sprinkling of water.
If the ritual be prolonged from day to day, alternating groups
maintain the continuity.

The rite may open with this stately and effective chant:

"Pearly dew of the jade heavens, golden waves of Buddha's
ocean, scatter the lotus-flowers on the thousand thousand worlds
of suffering, that the heart of mercy may wash away our great
calamity, that a single drop may become as a great flood, that
a drop may purify the mountains and the rivers.

---

[3] *Cf.* J. B. Pratt, *A Pilgrimage of Buddhism,* Chapter XVI. L. Hodous, *Buddhism and Buddhists in China,* pp. 19–22, refers to the monastery of Kushan.

We put our trust in the *boddhisattvas* and the *mahasattvas* [4] that purify the earth."

A monk with a bowl of water then thrice repeats, "We put our trust in the great, merciful *Kwanyin boddhisattva*" (the Chinese *Goddess of Mercy*). Then may follow this chant:

"The *boddhisattva's* sweet dew of the willow can make one drop spread over the ten directions. It washes away the rank odors and the impure. It keeps the altars pure and clean. The mysterious words of the Law are reverentially repeated."

During further chanting by certain monks, others walk around the altar, while one sprinkles water on the floor. As the water is sprinkled, the chanting monks repeat,

"We put our trust in the sweet dew-kings, the *boddhisattvas* and the *mahasattvas.*"

Assuming that the spirits have now come to the altar, while the abbot offers incense, the monks repeat, three times,

"The fields are destroyed, and, with their gaping cracks, resemble the back of the tortoise. The demons of drought have produced calamity. The dark people (*i.e.,* the Chinese) pray earnestly even while their crops are being destroyed. We pray that abundant, flowing water may descend to purify and refresh the whole world. The clouds of incense rise."

This is followed by the invocation,

"We cast ourselves wholeheartedly to the earth, O Three Jewels, who dost exist eternally in the realm of the *dharma* (the Law) of the ten directions."

Thereafter, much time is devoted to meditation upon the drought and the powers of the saints to help. Attention is called to the fact that Buddha himself prayed for rain, and that the service follows his example. Lest any availing power be overlooked, stanzas are recited in honor of "the king of light," and various groups of "dragon kings." Magical formulæ are em-

4 "Spirits of wisdom and truth," and "great spirits of truth," respectively.

ployed, the monastery bell is rung, and the wooden fish-gong is beaten, along with drums and cymbals. The potent name of the *bodisat Kwanyin* is repeated thousands of times. . . . And so the ceremony goes on until the rain arrives. This is one of the many services which are the peculiar prerogative of the Chinese Buddhist monastery. They are examples of a far more objective and theistic religion than any monkish ritual in Burma. And, as for the people, also, we see nowhere in Buddhist China scenes like those we witnessed at the Shwe Dagon pagoda. The Chinese monastery is not a popular resort.

Buddhism in Japan.—And now we pass to extraordinarily enlightened Japan. A far cry from Burma to Japan, the differences between Japan and China are, in their way, momentous. Japan is a literate nation, alert and progressive. She is the greatest Eastern power today, with a genius of her very own, and a national character which has shaped to itself constructively every susceptible element which has come in from without. Buddhist temples of Japan stand in extreme contrast with those of Burma, both in atmosphere and ritual. Japanese Buddhism, like that of China, is mainly Mahayanist. There are contrasts, too, with China, but mainly in connection with the monks. The Japanese monks are a higher type—higher, also, than the Burman.

Temples of Nikko.—The temples of Nikko are symbols of Mahayana at its best. Imagine a spacious garden with a rustic gateway. Along the outer walls, old and decaying, cling hardy vines of purple cryptomeria. You pass along a green lane, with high, thick hedge on either side. Gnarled and picturesque pine trees tower above you. Clusters of scented ferns flourish in sheltered nooks. Along the lane, you approach the red walls of the temple courtyard, above which looms the great, curved, thickly tiled roof of the shrine. A massive gateway leads into the temple court, a graveled space with rows of "lanterns" made of stone and bronze, standing with their ashes as memorials of the dead. Inside the temple, are altars of rare beauty, images of chaste design; hangings of brocaded gold; censers with their smoking incense; deep-toned drums, and silver bells. Shaven-headed priests in their simple robes, and reverent lay worshipers move noiselessly. Ornamented tables are set about, with handsome vessels on them of various shapes and sizes. The floor is spread with matting. Huge vases, holding gilded lotus-flowers, stand beside the walls. Delicate carvings cover both the walls and ceilings. The setting is artistic, clean, and dainty. You say, per-

haps, that the power of Japanese Buddhism is æsthetic, inhering
in the arts, in the sense of mysterious beauty, and in the allure-
ment of a world of mystery, of which the shrine itself reminds
you. Perhaps you yield, in this environment, to contemplation
and repose. What a place in which to cast all cares aside!

Although no ritual may be in progress, ceremonies of all sorts
are held from time to time: matins, vespers, masses for the dead,
and so on. Worship is not congregational, but by groups of monks,
or by the layman independently. Perhaps the mood is much the
same as elsewhere in Mahayana temples. How much in worship
is intelligent, how much formal, how much falls below the common level, it is difficult to say. Who can say how much the common people understand? They bow their heads, and prostrate
themselves before the images; they mutter many conventional
prayer formulas, and bestow their offerings; they clap their hands
(handclapping in the temples is distinctive of the Japanese). On
the whole, we may suppose that Buddhism in Japan shares the
general temper of the land, and expresses itself in terms of the
common mind. We may suppose, therefore, that many of the common people pray with understanding, and find new power through
devotion. To many of the highly educated, Buddhism provides
a character and force beyond anything natively religious.

The Faith.—Having passed hastily from land to land, we turn
now to the faith itself, which we have seen exhibited. What are
its basic teachings? How did they take form? How have they
pressed their claims upon mankind in various countries? Are
there values for the world today? What, indeed, is Buddhism?
We have watched and overheard both monks and laymen at their
prayers. We have seen certain objects of their devotion, including
the Buddha, gods, and spirits. We know there are, at least, two
"schools" of thought. These are only clues, however, to an intricate, amazing faith.

Buddhism as a word means "wisdom, or enlightenment" (in
Pali, bodhi; in *Sanskrit, buddhi*). Although *buddhi* is not merely
intellectual knowledge, Buddhism is, in origin, something of an
intellectual faith. The "Buddha" is the intellectual who possessed
this "wisdom, or enlightenment," which he formulated for mankind. When, therefore, we look for Buddhist origins, we encounter first of all a person, one of the noblest of all the sons of men.
His figure happens to be much clearer than that of his contemporary, the Jainist Mahavira, and even more distinct than the
person of Confucius, although neither the year of his birth, nor

of his death, is exactly known. There are, in non-Indian history, no contemporary references to Buddha. There are no native manuscripts contemporary with him. In the *Dīgha-nikāya,* or "Long Collection," the oldest Hinayana source, there is not a single line from Buddha, or from one of his disciples. Nor are Mahayana writings more dependable as source materials. Yet we have reliable details about him; we may depend upon tradition. The 3rd century, B.C., supplies our earliest sources. These are chiefly inscriptions and relics of the renowned Emperor Asoka (Ashoka). They testify to the Buddha, his racial heritage, the time and place of his birth, the existence of a cult of "buddhas," and the major teachings. A commemorative stone pillar, discovered in 1896 by the British Archæological Survey, was erected by Asoka about 250 B.C. It bore the legend, *"Hida Budhe jate Sakya-muniti,"* or, "Here was born Buddha, Jewel of the Shakas."

The Founder.—Gotam (in *Pali,* Gotama; in *Sanskrit,* Gautama), the Buddha, was born about 560 B.C. in the Lumbini Gardens, near the town of Kapilavatthu, a hundred miles north of Kashi (or Benares). The town stood at the margin of the plain, where the slopes of the Himalayas level off. In the distance lies the long, high range of mighty, snow-clad peaks, including Chomo Lungma, which we call Everest. In a figure, another mighty range called Hinduism lay along the west. The Shaka tribe (not *caste,* for caste was hardly established in that region then) occupied a plain which Hinduism had not yet subjugated. Gotam's father was a ruling chieftain of the Shakas; his mother was a noble lady from a kindred tribe. At the time the babe was born, the mother was on her way to visit her parents in their own country. Pausing for rest among the *sal-trees* in the Gardens near her husband's city, the birth-pains came unexpectedly upon her. Sheltered by the trees, which, says the pretty legend, bent their branches all about her,[5] and shielded by the draperies of her female attendants, her to-be-famous son was born. While tradition has magnified the event, we may still believe that it was an occasion of rejoicing; warrior folk are happy when a son is born. Both families and the inhabitants of both cities, his father's and his mother's, celebrated. Legend adds, that gods as well as men acclaimed him, and that the babe, with his first breath, proclaimed himself "chief in all the world." Sculpture sometimes shows him taken from his mother's right side, the gods assisting, thus empha-

---

[5] A Kentucky mountain ballad tells of a cherry tree that bowed down, for the Virgin Mary to pluck fruit from its branches.

sizing his unique quality, and possibly his initial independence of
the law of *karma* and transmigration. It is well to know that it was
customary then in courts, on the eve of royal births, to fabricate
predictions that a son would become a "world-ruler," or a "world-
savior." What there is in Buddhist tradition beyond such a mere
prediction may be the fantastic results of development, of success
in annexing the culture and folklore of more picturesque religions. Original Buddhism must have been barren of portent and
miracle.

We may believe that the child enjoyed the advantages of a
raja's son, that he was attended by well-educated nurses, and
that "the future Buddha began to grow, surrounded by a retinue
and in great splendor." At sixteen, he seems to have been provided with three lodges of his own, each in its appropriate site,
one for each of the three seasons, rainy, cool, and hot. We may
believe that, in his earliest years, the "prince" was "secluded
from life's rougher realities," as one record says, but that, in due
time, he received the training proper to his station. Reared in
easy circumstances, he may have been inclined to pleasure; he
always had the means to gain it. One record says his relatives
complained that he indulged too much in pleasure, that his
father rebuked him for it, and for devoting too little thought
to his career as raja. Contradictions have crept into the story
through efforts to accommodate the early, normal facts to his
career as a teacher of morals and religion. In those days, it was
not "good form" for warriors' sons to manifest unusual interest
in studies of a literary character. Horses, chariots, and knightly
exercises were prerogatives of royalty. Gotam was a skilful horse-
man, and a good shot with the bow, having "a twelve-fold skill
such as no other archer then could equal."

He was married at nineteen to Yashodhara, a "princess" from
a neighboring state. After nearly ten years, their only child was
born, a son named Rahula. Meanwhile, we may suppose, some
alteration was occurring in his outlook; there were no *sudden*
changes in his life. Had he been more a Hindu, he would have
followed out the scheme of *ashramas,* or "stages," as the custom
was. He was a Hindu of a sort, and remained a sort of Hindu
to the end; but he was not a Brahman. He might have seemed
to his contemporaries to be following the normal program of the
"twice-born," but his followers understood that he had followed
through, perhaps at first unconsciously, a program of his own.
Ascetics must have had some influence on him. They were of

many kinds; he was familiar with them. He enrolled himself at last as one of them.

The Great Renunciation.—At twenty-nine, an early age for such a step, he undertook the Great Renunciation. Having taken serious thought of life, a revulsion set in against the fleshly passions; he had no wish to be a ruling chieftain. He would renounce his family and his kingdom—scarcely realizing he was bound to institute a world-religion. There is no evidence that before he was married he questioned the propriety of marriage. Was it an indication of a change of mind that he gave his son the name of *Rahula,* or "fetter," a tie binding one unduly to the world? Something positive, also, may have moved him. His eyes were opened to the misery in the world about him, and his heart assumed some obligation to dispel it. The *Dīgha-nikāya* compresses into the brief space of a pleasure-ride four experiences immediately responsible for Gotam's Great Renunciation. As he rode in his sumptuous chariot drawn by four blooded steeds "as white as the petals of the white lotus," he beheld four "signs" at intervals along the way: (1) "a decrepit old man, broken-toothed, gray-haired, crooked and bent of body, leaning on a staff, and trembling"; (2) "a diseased man, whom the gods had fashioned so," repulsive with running sores; (3) "a dead man, whose condition the gods had ordained"; and (4) "a monk, carefully and decently clad, in the form the gods had fashioned."

Thinking of the old man, Gotam was distressed that every man must face the question of old age and weakness. He saw, also, that men were subject to disease and death, baffled by disaster and decrepitude, from which even death would not release them—Gotam held the doctrine of rebirth and *karma.* Why disease? Must it be? Is there no cure? Is death inevitable? Can life be extended and death delayed? If a man die, shall he live again? To what degree are sickness, age and death compatible with *life?* Science in our day is working on prolongations and escapes, whatever be the motive. Gotam merely was a thinker on these problems, without a laboratory, and lacking scientific instruments. He would find escapes through reason! Yet, at first, he sought them by renunciation. The monk impressed him. Here was a "decently clothed" ascetic (therefore, not a "sky-clad" Jainist, common in that day), a holy man whose very mien betokened his "release." He may have been a *shramana,* a *paribrajika,* a *bhikku,* or a *sannyāsi,* living outside organized society. Were he a *shramana,* he was indifferent to caste, wandering homeless for the sake of some higher, spiritual existence. Were he a *sannyāsi,* he had entered the fourth *ashrama* of earthly life, and likewise had cut the ties with earth and men, awaiting his time of union with the All. Whoever he was, he seemed to Gotam the symbol of a true way of living. Gotam Sakyamuni Siddhartha determined to follow his example.

One night, in the cool of the year, "in the middle watch," he arose quietly from his couch beneath the parental rooftree, took a last look (without longing, probably) into the quarters where his wife and young son lay, and, deserting all his earthly kindred, left the palace. Mounting a favorite charger, with a trusty servant running by his side, he rode off to the edge of his father's kingdom. Beyond the river-boundary, he stopped, dismounted, doffed his costly robes, stripped off his ornaments, and cut off with his sword the flowing locks "not suited to the monk." Donning a coarse, yellow garb, and taking only two extra garments, a bowl for alms, a razor, needle, belt and water-strainer, he made his journey afoot and alone to Rajagaha, capital of the state of Magadha, there to begin the great Quest formally.

He who had renounced so much had two qualities, the records say, in unusual measure: compassion and intellectual skill. These, with fidelity to his own self, determined both the character of his quest and the goal he found. The citizens of Rajagaha merely noted that one more man, a chieftain's son and heir, had adopted the ascetic way. They knew him better later. His father's city noted his departure. Some people recalled that he had once extended mercy to a stricken deer. Others remembered his wisdom in the market-place. Some, including his son Rahula, were destined to become his followers. For six years, he followed a beaten trail across the world, where men often grieve in conflict of soul, and visit misery upon each other. He took the *karma-mārga,* the "way of works," by which many more had sought to rid themselves of conflict and a miserable existence. He might have taken the *jñāna-mārga,* or "way of knowledge," but this did not appeal to him at first. Had the *bhakti-mārga,* or "way of devotion," then been known, he doubtless would have avoided it, for it was too theistic. He took the plain, broad way of Works, the strict, ascetic way, on which one travels light, but strenuously. He followed it through towns and villages, and off into the deep jungles. He met many teachers of religion, and discussed his quest with them. He met ascetics and conferred with them. He disciplined his mind and body so severely that he finally became a shadow of his former vigorous self. Gradually he gained influence, if not satisfaction; his works made a deep impression on many whom he met. Some began to follow him about.

Five men, in particular, who figure prominently in the later story, were won to him by his "austerities." He was extraordinarily severe; he ate little, drank little; he exerted every effort to subdue the body and the senses, that his spirit might rise freely above the world of mere material things. These men approved his ways and sought to imitate them; but they soon saw fit to leave him, for another change occurred in him. He left the plain, broad way so familiar to the people of that day; he gave up the way of great austerity; it had not given him the sense of peace he craved. His active mind must have gone unsatisfied; it was restless still. He says the way of works became as futile as an effort "to tie the air in knots." His five disciples felt, then, that he had proved false to the great ideal; to seek merit by any other way was to them as futile as "bathing with a dew-drop." They withdrew; and he went on alone. He suffered some discouragement; his restlessness continued; he was weak, well nigh exhausted. But perhaps he had in mind the *jñāna-mārga*. Philosophic speculation had been current. Many thinkers were discussing problems of life, its origin, character and destiny.

Once he stopped to rest at a spot of destiny, near the town of Gaya, eastward a hundred and fifty miles from Kashi (Benares). He sat under a fig-tree, which from the event became one of the most famous trees of the world. Doubtless, it was a spot already dear to Hindus; perhaps the tree was sacred, with a shrine beneath it. Gotam may have been attracted to it by its sanctity. It became the place of his Enlightenment. It became the *Bo*-tree, "tree of wisdom." Gotam sitting under it, became the Buddha, "the Wise or Enlightened."

A Temptation.—As he sat reflecting on the change come over him, there came a man to do him homage, as if he were the spirit of the tree personified. Was this event an outward confirmation of what the inner mind of Buddha knew had happened in him? If so, it must have given him a new appreciation of himself. Later, he explained what had happened to him as he sat beneath the *Bo*-tree: that through meditation he attained concentration of mind; that through unity of mind he attained to insight, vision and enlightenment. He had found the "way of wisdom." To what extent was this unique? It seems a normal Hindu process. It reminds us of what had happened to Mahavira. But no two men ever have the same experience. At least, the ingredients are different. Yājñavalkya, Mahāvira, Buddha, each is himself. We must find out what Buddha meant by "wisdom." He himself did not know at first. Whatever part his former discipline may have played in his achievement, in giving him a keener mind, he felt that he had found new satisfaction, not through works, but by a mental process. He was returning to a more normal manner of existence; he would not abuse his body, but rather nourish it moderately, for the good of his soul. He was no longer travel-weary and downcast; he was alert; he sat and "never blinked his eyes." A tide of bliss set in.

Even as he sat there, he communed thus with himself, "Sure is my release; this is my last birth; there is no further birth for me." He was aglow with confidence that the law of *karma* no longer dominated him, that he was no longer caught in the meshes of an entangling world (*samsāra*). He had passed through storm and stress; but he had found calm. Into his calm, however, there came a surprising temptation. Often, "just when we think we're safest, there's a sunset touch." Buddha was tempted strongly to enter at once into complete retirement, and to enjoy his "wisdom" until his earthly end should come, and he should enter into *Nirvāna;* or, virtually, to enter *Nirvāna* immediately, and not be drawn aside by any other thought or aim. Had he no duty to his fellow-men? Did he hesitate about his power to communicate to others the methods and the fruits of his own search? Must not every man find, at last, his own way? However, Buddha triumphed gloriously over this temptation; he had "compassion on all be-ings," not merely on a stricken deer; he willed to spend his life that all others might find the way. For forty-five years afterwards he lived to expound his way of wisdom.

The *Bo*-tree.—The *Bo*-tree became the symbol not only of enlightenment, but also of temptation and its overcoming, the symbol of a *new* way opened up for every "wanderer and searcher for the peaceful state most excellent." In our day, pilgrims come to Buddh-Gaya (Patna) from Ceylon, Burma, and Tibet, especially, to visit it, assuming that they find the very tree under which the Master sat. The faithful fondly believe that cuttings from the original found their way to other lands where they are tree-shrines in their own right. There is one, they say, at Anaradhapura, in Ceylon, which was planted in 240 B.C. by Asoka's younger sister, Sanghamitra. If one doubts that the *Bo*-tree of Buddh-Gaya is authentic, he may still believe the Anarad-

hapura tree to be the oldest in existence. Who would deny the
faithful the satisfaction of so inspiring a fiction! Has not many
a Christian soul subsisted on the presence and the efficacy of portions of the "True Cross" enshrined in various holy places?
After all, the tree was once alive and real. It was the scene of
a world-transforming episode. Although it lives today merely in
literature, architecture and art, it is more than figure only.

The Sermon at Benares.—Buddha went from the *Bo*-tree to
Benares, where he met again the five disciples and persuaded
them to listen to his famous "Sermon." Maybe it was providential
that they had left him for a while. There was no room for them
under the *Bo*-tree. Buddha had to tread that way alone. Now
he could tell of his experience, and recommend it to them. They
sat together in the Deer Park, outside Benares, near the present
ruins of Sarnath. He spoke of the four "Certainties" which he
had formulated, including the "Middle Path" between the "two
extremes" of "devotion to the pleasures of sense," and "devotion to self-mortification." This middle way, he said, "giveth
vision, which giveth knowledge, which causeth calm, insight, enlightenment, and *Nibbāna.*"

The Four Certainties (or "Noble Truths") are: (1) *Sabba
duhkha,* "all is sorrow, pain, and suffering"; *sabba anatta,* "all is
change, impermanence, and unreality." This is a world of *duhkha,*
and man, especially, is unreal. Birth, growth, sickness, decay;
grief, tears, and despair; association with persons and things
which we dislike, separation from persons and things we like;
not getting what we want, getting what we do not want; death
and rebirth; all these are the painful lot of man. This is life, and
life is this way, because man lives in a realm of change. Through
change the world is undependable. Man, also, by change is undependable. Nothing abides. This is the first "truth" for man to
learn.

(2) *Tanhā,* "desire, craving, and thirst," is the *cause* of *duhkha,*
sorrow, pain, and suffering, which characterize this world of
change. *Tanhā* brings man to birth; merely being born is the
greatest of misfortunes. Man's own desire, or mankind's desire,
creates this world of unreality. Craving is at the root of all events
in life. Not merely "wishing," but a deep-running impulse, or
potent tendency, makes for sorrow, and holds men in its grip.
Men are in the grip of *karma;* the use of *tanhā* is one of Buddha's
ways of saying this. As long as men allow themselves to "thirst"

for mortal life, they move in the current of *karma. Tanhā* must be eradicated; this is the second "truth" for men to learn.

(3) To find release from sorrow, pain, and suffering; to escape from the world of change, impermanence, and unreality, man must get rid of desire, crush craving, and deny his thirst. This is a third "truth" in itself. More especially, one should take no thought at death of what he would like to become through rebirth; on the contrary, he should harbor no desire to be reborn. Only thus can he stop the flow of *karma,* and break the round of transmigration. By this "truth," Buddha adds a definite attitude to the fact of sorrow and the fact of sorrow's cause, desire.

(4) The Middle Way, specifically, is the means of getting rid of desire, of crushing craving, and of denying thirst; and of escape from the world of change, impermanence, and unreality. It is not the way of the man who eats, drinks and makes merry, indulging the flesh and the fleshly lusts. Nor is it the way of the ascetic who utterly denies the flesh, the bodily passions and material comforts. The body is neither to be abused, nor indulged. The mind is in control; let no one question its integrity. Wisdom will find the middle way. Not pure, intellectual desire is to be eradicated,—else how might man yearn for his highest good!— but such desires as spring from fleshly sources.

The Path.—The Middle Way is eight-fold; it is a progressive, cumulative, constructive way; one treads it step by step. He clears the ground before he finds it. If one thinks of these steps as rules of living, he obeys them singly until he can obey them all together. There are times when any candidate must follow several rules on one occasion. Obviously, the steps are slowly taken; years may be devoted to any one of them. They modify somewhat the Hindu *ashramas,* for example. Primarily, they apply to those who already have renounced the world. Buddha had undertaken the third *ashrama* before he found the Middle Way. His *Sermon* at Benares was spoken to men who had entered at least the third, perhaps the fourth, stage of existence. But the "Truths" and the "Middle Way" are for all sorts and conditions of men. Any man might undertake the discipline, after he had assented to the doctrine. After he had taken the fourth "step," or learned obedience to the fourth "rule," he enjoyed the designation *chela,* or "disciple," having demonstrated right view, high aims, discipline of speech, and proper action. After the fifth step, he was termed a *bhikku,* "brother," literally "mendicant"; he had then renounced the world completely. After the eighth and last step, he was called an *arhat* (*arahant*), "saint," or "venerable." Actually, there were two grades of *arhats;* the second, so free of human passion that when they died, they virtually ceased existence—they "came not to rebirth."

These are the steps or rules of the Middle Way, a series of "thou shalts," arranged in a constructive sequence:

(i) *Right view,* a generous attitude, a tolerant open-mindedness, especially with regard to the new teaching and the new teacher. This is both sound theory and indispensable practice. The Buddha had to create within his audience of five the open mind. He had to make them free to question the *Vedas* and Brahmanical institutions, and willing to discard old notions. Attention, reflection, scepticism, these are essential factors in conversion. The Buddha had decided to convert all creatures, and so he first commanded open-mindedness.

(ii) *High aims,* such as kindness, and the spirit of benevolence; willingness to do things helpful to others; contentment to get on without many things, and the resolve never to be resentful, nor harmful of manner.

(iii) *Discipline of speech,* right speech instead of lying, back-biting, and abuse; instead even of idle babble, which is forbidden. When men babble about unimportant things, they become indifferent to important matters. He thought the chatter that he daily heard unprofitable. He cautioned his hearers against talking angrily in wrath or pride; against taking delight in others' faults, and carping at others' failings. He commanded silence, which brings poise to the mind, and peace to the heart. He spoke of silence that takes no offence, although other men speak evil of you.

(iv) *Right action.* By this he meant never taking what is not given; abstaining from intoxicating drink, and avoiding drunkenness; holding the sexual passions in check, and committing no murder. Although he spoke of right action in terms of its opposites, he conceived of the virtue positively.

(v) *Right living,* or livelihood, or vocation; engaging in no trade or profession by which financial profit is made from men's distresses, from the slave-trade, for example; holding to the general doctrine of non-injury (*ahimsa*) to man and beast, or any living being.

(vi) *Right effort,* self-control; the will to prevent evil conditions from arising; the will to overcome and destroy evil conditions which have arisen; and the will to cause good to arise and be fulfilled.

(vii) *Watchful-mindedness,* that is, guarding the mind against desire, or dejection; being on the alert to prevent impressions which communicate desire, dejection, or other harm.

(viii) *Concentration* of mind, which, ultimately leads, "beyond the sphere of thinking"; that is, which leads into trance-states, in which there is the immediate awareness that all shackles have been broken, all desire crushed, and perfect poise and peace attained. This, of course, is the Buddhist *Nirvāna,* or "extinction" (of desire, that is).

These, then, are the four Noble Truths of which the Buddha felt "certain." He himself had experienced them; in his sermon he expounded in some detail his own experience. The five men were converted; they accepted the truths and the living illustration of the truths in the Buddha himself; and forthwith they rejoined the Master that they might walk the Middle Way and come at last by it to *Nirvāna.* They were the nucleus of the new "Order," to which the "Law" was delivered by the "Buddha." In a sense, they took "refuge" in the Buddha, the Law, and the Order, the first to do so of all the millions.

The Order.—The *Sermon at Benares* on the Four Certainties and the Middle Way was based upon the Buddha's own experience. It was sketchy, and pronounced to the ears of a small company; but it gave the gist of "Buddhism." No major alteration, but only detailed elaboration succeeded it. It was the basis of the *Law* (the *Dharma*), even as Buddha's own experience was the basis of his Wisdom (*Buddhi*). The five who listened and became converted were the nucleus of the new *Order* (the *Sangha* or "Association"). They were the first to take "refuge" in the Buddha, in the Law, and in the Order; the first to accept the "truths" and him in whom they were embodied, even though they did not at first fully comprehend. The record says that Kondanna, a Brahman, was the first to comprehend; he was therefor ordained a *bhikku,* "brother." He "saw the Law, understood the Law, plunged into the Law, crossed over beyond doubt, banished questioning, and reached independent certainty." In time, the other four, Vappa the Samkhyist, Mahanama and Bhaddiya, of Rajagaha, and Assaji, were ordained as "brothers." Vappa later on resigned, finding himself still Samkhyist in mind, believing in Man (*Purusha*) as *un*changing being. Monkish vows could be abjured, or revoked; a monk might return to the world. No one, however, of the first disciples holds such prominence in Buddhist circles as was attained by four others who later joined the ranks: Kassapa and Ananda, both of whom survived their Master; Sariputta and Moggallana. Ananda might be called "the blessed intimate" of Buddha.

Buddha's Wisdom gained an ever-widening hearing. There was a crisis at the time in India. Mahavira had sought to meet it. Many "heresies" were current. Both institutions and ideas were criticized. Buddha proved to be the strongest critic of his day. He gained adherents rapidly. He traveled extensively during the cool and dry seasons; for the rains he retired to accessible retreats, where he discussed his theories at length with the inner circle of his adherents. He patiently repeated all his fundamentals. Many things he taught were learned by rote; most of what he taught was orally transmitted through several generations. We may trust the records which were made two centuries afterwards to give us the essentials which for a while were orally transmitted. What are the scriptures which preserve the exposition of his teachings?

Scriptures.—The Buddhist *Canon* offers many problems. We cannot date the literature exactly. There is no dependable chronology before Asoka; and after him, literary dates are hard to reckon. There is, first, the major problem of the two "schools" of teaching. Ordinarily, we say that Hinayana is the older. Some would contend that certain Mahayana works are nearer to *original* Buddhism. They think of Hinayana as a *narrowing* development, for which the Buddha himself is not primarily responsible. Possibly it was not Buddha who developed Hinayana. Both sets of teachings may be divergent forms of the original. Hinayana has its likenesses to Samkhya and Yoga; Mahayana, to Vedanta. There is a Hinayana *Canon,* and a Mahayana *Canon;* both agree upon the main points of the *Sermon at Benares.* We are inclined to think that Hinayana lies closer to the *Sermon* and that its *Canon* gives us more faithfully a picture of Buddha, the Law, and the Order. This is the traditional view. We describe first the Hinayana *Canon.*

There are "three baskets" (*ti-pitaka*):

(1) The *Sutta-pitaka,* or "Teaching-basket," containing the "discourses" (*sutta, sutra*) of the Master. It embodies various "collections," or *nikāyas,* such as the *Dīgha,* "long," the *Majjhima,* "middling," and the *Khuddaka,* "short." It contains various verses (*gathas*) about monks and the nuns, and many birth-stories (*jatakas* or forms of birth) of the Buddha;

(2) The *Vinaya-pitaka,* or "Discipline-basket," containing five books of the rules of behavior for initiates of the Order. It is the ecclesiastical code by which the monks and nuns are governed; and

(3) The *Abhidhamma-pitaka,* or "Higher Doctrine-basket," containing seven books of expositions of the finer points of psychology and dogma. It is the higher (*abhi*) doctrine (*dhamma*) of the mind, as distinct from the *dhamma* as moral conduct.

The Mahayana *Canon* does not ignore these "baskets," but it includes elaborate writings of later centuries which embody "idealistic," and "theistic" views at variance with the Buddha's atheistic realism. Among these works may be mentioned the *Lotus of the Good Law,* and the *Paradise Scriptures,* much in use in China and Japan.

Buddha's Gospel.—Buddha's general position is expounded in the *Sutta,* and the *Vinaya* baskets, the former giving us his *Sermon* and many expositions, with discussions of entanglements, release, faith, blessings, goodwill, happiness, holiness, the self, causation, buddhahood, and *Nibbāna;* the latter providing light on matters ethical and ritual.[6] We shall examine Buddha's views of human personality (the "self" and consciousness), of the world-process (*karma* and the "wheel of causation"), and, incidentally, of *Nirvāna* (*Nibbāna,* in *Pali*), a term which Buddha may have coined. His doctrines are profound; but in thought as well as in conduct he sought a middle way. He avoided "higher doctrine" in the sense of metaphysics, as "tending not to edification."[7] He sought some middle ground between "being," at one extreme, and "non-being" at the other. He did not attempt cosmogony, and he lightly touched cosmology. On a middle ground, he probably would have held it wrong to say that if an object is not heavy, it is light; that if a surface is not rough, it must be smooth. He could not have declared *Nirvāna* to be annihilation, or extinction. He is a *kind* of dualist, who finds a measure of compatibility between the "unreal" and the "real." He may deny the "self," but he does not make it *māyā,* or "illusion." His "non-self" (*anatta*) is not non-reality. His materialism is not the sort displayed by Samkhya and the Jainists; it is less pronounced. He may have dodged some issues which he did not care to follow through. He offers no judgment as to whether the world is eternal, or not; as to whether the soul and the body are, or are not, identical; as to whether the "saint" continues, or does not continue, after death. His chief assault was

6 The handiest volume of sources is F. L. Woodward, *Some Sayings of the Buddha,* Oxford University Press, 1925.
7 Cf. "*Nibbāna* is the place where there are no theological discussions,"— *Mahāviyūha,* 16.

directed against the current doctrine of the "soul" (the *ātman*), whether of one school, or another. He countered with his own doctrine of *an-ātman* (*anatta*). However, he assumed the "world" (*samsāra*), and there was for him *something* involved in the process of transmigration. Furthermore, man to him was real enough, or the mind of man was strong enough, to release himself from the meshes of *samsāra*. Denying the Hindu theory of transmigration, he countered with another doctrine of his own; for he must account for *karma!*

Anatta, Impermanence.—Let us call *anatta* "consciousness," for want of a better term. Buddha substituted "consciousness" for "soul," somewhat as our own Wundt and James have done. He talked in terms of feelings, volitions, sensations, and ideas. We might follow him readily in his exposition, if he had not rejected the "person" as an historical individual; if he had not contended that individuality is merely a matter of experience, and that personality is impermanent and phenomenal, begotten of ignorance, and nourished by desire. He says the individual is unreal! It is, in our experience, composed of elements and complexes, not one of which is properly an *ātman;* not one of which has value of its own; nor may a value be assigned it, save as such value indicates what to be freed from. *Atman* is only a *name* for the elements and complexes of experience; it is not a designation of Reality. Yet the Buddha recognized Reality; he called it *dhammata,* or the continuance of the *dhammas,* the mobile elements, or atoms of existence. He was, therefore, not a nihilist; there was room for *dhammas* in his doctrine of *anatta.*

One catches a note of expediency in Buddha's argument; he had to take account of other theories than his own. A certain dialogue throws light upon his method; he desired to maintain his own position. Once a disciple asked him plainly, "Is there a self, or is there not a self?" Buddha declined to answer, and he went away. Then Buddha said to the "blessed" Ananda, "If I had said to him, There is a self, I should have been agreeing with the ascetics and the Brahmans, who teach everlastingness; if I had said, There is not a self, I should have been agreeing with those who teach annihilation." [8] He had to contend, also, with the Jains. He denied the eternity of the Jainist *jiva;* his moderation triumphed over the Jains' extreme austerities; and for their *syad-vad,* or "maybe" doctrine, he proposed his "certainties." The real force of his argument is that the data of experience are not the ultimate

[8] *Cf.* Woodward, *op. cit.,* p. 223.

realities. His philosophy in this form, without the handicap of metaphysics, could challenge both the thinker and the common man.

Buddha held a trilogy of matter, mind, and forces. His term for individual is "stream" (*santāna*), a stream of consciousness. This harmonizes with his doctrine, *sabba anatta,* "all is change." The particles of mind and matter are held together by a force, but their relationship is more coincidence and spontaneity than what we should call causation, or cause-and-effect. He hesitated to admit the validity of cause-and-effect relations. What then is the human person? In reply, we shall offer a sectarian (*Sarvasti-vadin*) interpretation of a realistic cast, which seems to us not far from what Buddha may have taught.[9] It accords with passages in the *Majjhima-nikāya,* including these words, "Whatever form, Rahula, be it past, present, or future; inward, or outward; gross, or subtle; low, or high; near, or far; every form must be regarded thus, as it really is, by perfect insight: 'This is not mine: not this am I: herein is not the self of me.'" It admits of illustration by his figure of the chariot (see below).

The Person.—The human person is an aggregate, *five* "grasping groups" of *skandhas* (in *Pali, khandhas*). The *skandhas* are bodily elements and psychical states, with some force, or forces, making and maintaining their aggregation. They are:

(1) The Body, that is, the more material elements, called as a unit *rūpa,* which present to us the phenomenal "individual." This "individual" is an aggregate of ten varieties of sense data: the five senses, touch, taste, smell, hearing, and sight; and five corresponding sensations, which "manifest" themselves to the senses. But no distinction is drawn between sense data in the physical world, and their appearance in the human person as sensations (we would say, no distinction of mind and matter). These elements, whether senses or sensations, are some of the impermanent, conditioned *dhammas* (*dharmas*) which collect and fall apart —by force of circumstance!

(2) Feeling (*vedanā*), one *dhamma* only. Although a single *dhamma,* it is treated as past, present, and future; it is continuous in three tenses. Feeling is the spontaneous concomitant of contact; contact is the "manifestation" of the union of an object and a sense, that is, sensation. This is the region of desire (*tanha*), for sense contacts are productive of desire.

(3) Idea, conceiving (*samjñā*), one *dhamma.* This one *dhamma*

9 *Cf.* Th. Stcherbatsky, *The Central Conception in Buddhism;* W. M. McGovern, *A Manual of Buddhist Philosophy.*

represents a totality of aspects, and is, therefore, treated as a composite. Many aspects of an object, or a process, enter into the idea of it; conception is a recognition inclusive of more than bare idea.

(4) Volition (*chetanā*), a group of many *dhammas,* fifty-eight, one analyst has said. These are mental faculties, and general forces beyond Feeling and Idea, volitions of all sorts, coördinated and bound together by the *force* of Volition; for example, the will to know, the will to do, the will for this and that.

(5) Consciousness (*vijñāna*), pure sensation; again, a single *dhamma,* but with a multitude of subdivisions. *Vijñāna* is the general consciousness which, in some form, arises first from the operation of certain "forces" (*sankhāras, samskāras,*) [10] "Dispositions," were themselves set in motion by "ignorance." This *dhamma* comes of ignorance, and may be dissolved only by wisdom—Buddha's wisdom. A consequence of ignorance, it is also in itself a cause; it is productive of potential individuality, or the mind-and-matter mould into which the individual-of-experience is run. *Vijñāna* is more than mere sensation; it might be called awareness. It is more than feeling; it is without feeling. It is beyond either mere idea, or the conceiving faculty. It is a functional force, whose function may be better understood with reference to the "Wheel."

The Wheel.—The human person, this self of many *skandhas,* is bound upon (within?) a Wheel. We might say, with caution, it is produced and held together by a process, or a movement in the likeness of a wheel. The wheel is a common Indian symbol of man's life; the Buddha made particular use of it. By it the Hindu represents the reality of the *Whole,* whose parts are *un*real. The dominant Vedantic Hindu theory is that of the reality of the *One,* or the *oneness* of Being, and the illusory character of the many; diversity, in this view, is unreal. On the other hand, with the Buddha, wholes or combinations are merely *names;* there is no reality in a name; what there is of reality inheres in the elements alone, which bear a name. He uses the figure of the Wheel to account for the *relations* of the elements, to explain how all the *skandhas* come to be in the phenomenal human person, and in the world of experience.

He called it a *Bhavachakra,* "Wheel of Existence," and a process of "dependent-simultaneous(!) arising." He hesitated to use the cause-and-effect category, although his simultaneity includes

---

[10] These are possibly akin to the "volitions."

a measure of dependence. Buddha had no place for God as cause;
he describes existence by enumerating its constituents, and ex-
plaining them. Destiny for him is dissolution. But for the Wheel:
imagine twelve sectors in it, each with its portion of the hub, its
share of spokes, its portion of the rim—thus it appears in Buddhist
art; sometimes the Wheel is clutched in the four claws of a
tortoise, and embellished with intricacies of symbolism beyond
Buddha's own conception. The sectors do not represent real causes;
only relative moments. They are connected in the figure, not
causally, but as simultaneous manifestations in time and space.
The figure does not represent a process of evolution, wherein one
element arises from another. Actually, when the first moment of
life in the human person appears, all other moments are *immediately* present. How, then, does this differ from the nihilist's for-
tuitous concourse of particles, by which life is germinated? But
we have said that Buddha was no nihilist; he has a constructive
philosophy in explanation of man, and of the universe. And there
is at least this much causality in Buddha's scheme—he recognized
the law of *karma;* although he distinguished carefully between
"dependent arising," and the current conception of *karma* as an
efficient cause. To the Hindu, *karma* was the only cause; to
Buddha, it was one of the many causes—or occasions.

The Wheel [11] consists of:

(1) Ignorance (*avijja*), the fundamental "cause." There was
a fateful moment of *ignorance,* which may repeat itself, whether
in the history of mankind or in the individual man. When Buddha
taught, he addressed immediate audiences, accounting for how
things came to be at the given moment. Practically, ignorance
meant to him the absence of true *knowledge,* more particularly
the knowledge of the "four noble truths." He was not so much
expounding origins in the history of humanity, as accounting for
the state in which men found themselves. He was concerned, also,
with the presence of ill-conceived ideas, such as the view that
life is a fact, and not a changing process. *Avijja* was the presence
of false knowledge, and the absence of true wisdom;

(2) Forces, dispositions (*sankhāras*), which arise from Ignorance, or in conjunction therewith. *Karma,* for example, is one of
the many forces set in motion by *avijja.* These forces predispose
the production of all beings;

(3) Consciousness (*vijñāna*) is a product of the various
sankhāras. It represents the first moment of *life,* awareness and

11 *Cf.* Woodward, *op. cit.,* pp. 37–40.

recognition. In illustration of the motion whereby predisposition became conscious, Buddha used the figure of the ocean tides; he held the theory that the level of the rivers, lakes, and ponds was affected by the ocean;

(4) Name-and-form (*nāmarūpa*), mind-and-matter, potential individuality, incipient self-consciousness; the embryonic sense data, and the tentative sensations;

(5) Organs of sense (*āyatanas*), or "entrances." There are *six:* eye, ear, nose, tongue, skin, and *mind* (there are *five* in the *skandha* known as *rūpa*), and six elements for which they serve as "entrances" (one cannot *see,* for example, what is not *visible,* nor *hear* what is *inaudible*);

(6) Contact (*phassa*), the union of senses and their objects. For example, the eye, having seen what is visible, is joined in a union with its object—a "fetter," as it were, is forged out of the contact. This is the moment in the Wheel when coördination arises between the Inner and the Outer spheres, both of which have had a previous and corresponding development;

(7) Sensation (*vedanā*), the stimulation of the senses. This is the causal moment, or occasion, of desire;

(8) Desire (*tanhā*), burning, thirst, and craving. This moment is the ground of explanation of the sorrow of the world;

(9) Becoming (*upādāna*), grasping, attachment, holding fast. Here the "grasping groups," or *skandhas,* first arise, out of which the potential individual is produced. Here is formed the germ of personality;

(10) Coming-to-be (*bhava*), the imminence of existence, the moment prior to full birth. The Inner and the Outer have had further simultaneous development: the individual-to-be-born, and, in corresponding measure, the process whence the birth arises;

(11) Birth (*jāti*), the moment of aggregation of all the *dhammas* which produce the human person. Now appears the individual-of-experience, more fully conscious of the world about him, of which he is a part. *Jāti* is the interval from birth to death, during which the individual may acquire wisdom toward the cessation of the process, toward the breaking of the Wheel. If, however, during *jāti,* man does not acquire this wisdom fully, comprehending the "truths" and walking in the "Way," death takes him once again to the beginning of the Wheel.

(12) Death (*jarāmarana*). Being born means in itself that one must die; the *skandhas* will be separated—but not permanently, if ignorance remains. Every *dhamma* tainted with *avijja,* every re-

lationship tainted with desire, keeps the Wheel revolving. Get wisdom, eradicate desire; thence comes Release. Then one does not *die;* he gains *Nirvāna.* Otherwise he dies, and his *anatta* continues transmigration. In practical illustration of the theory of simultaneous continuity, compare the manner of selection of a new Dalai Lama, or Living Buddha of Tibet. He is the one born at the exact moment that the Living Buddha died.

Buddha's Contribution.—Buddha sought to free himself, and to induce other men to free themselves, from the Wheel. *To what* would he and they be free? He did not say, beyond his undiscussed *Nirvāna;* they did not know. He had no *philosophy* of freedom, no theory of immortality. He spoke of calm; but he seemed not to desire freedom from motion, nor to desire cessation of motion. Practically, and not speculatively, he would have men find happiness in the midst of the world of sorrow, and calm in the midst of change. His method of escape was *ethical.* Man was the captain of his fate; his mind could find the necessary knowledge; his mind could "slay craving"; it could acquire wisdom "beyond the sphere of thinking." "Verily, Rādha, the destruction of craving is Nibbāna." "Scatter consciousness . . . break it up." After all, he modified his theory of *Nirvāna.* Negative and selfish, it may be; but solitude and quiescence were to be earned by high intention and good conduct in the world. And in the world, men were counselled to seek purity of heart, and the establishment of universal friendship through self-effacement and compassion.

Did Buddha teach new truths? He *formulated* many things anew; but the newness was essentially his person. He was an attractive, forceful personality; herein lay his success and popularity. Individuality was prominently recognized in his day among the higher classes; there was ample opportunity for leaders. He became the greatest person of his age. His following was personal, and grew steadily through the loyalty of his followers. He extended himself through his disciples (*chelas*). When he had won sixty, he sent them out—one by one, to wander lonely like the rhinoceros—to preach "the glorious doctrine," and the "pure and perfect life of holiness." He was worthy of a following; during his whole Mission, he was a consistently moral person, preaching and practicing love to mankind, with unremitting fervor. His system may have been defective, incoherent philosophically, but his own sincerity and moral character were compelling. He was, if anything, greater than his teachings. Before his death at eighty, upwards of five hundred "brothers" were about him, many of them to be famous through their devotion. He did not mean to found an Order on himself; but the Order found in him its chief essential. When his end was near, he spoke these last words, "Behold now, brothers, decay is inherent in all component [or compounded, associated] things! Work out your own salvation with diligence." But they worked upon the pattern which he furnished.

With reference to society and politics, Buddha was conservative. He seems to have assumed the validity of caste, *until the time* when a man went "forth from home to the homeless life under the Law-discipline."

As the great rivers renounce their names, he said, when they flow into the ocean, so men of all the four castes are "reckoned just as recluses," when they join the Order. He did not talk with rulers about government, as Confucius did. He had no theory of state. He organized his own "societies," and laid down regulations for them; but he seems to have desired that they "assemble in harmony, do business in harmony,[12] and disperse in harmony," introducing no "revolutionary ordinance." He was tolerant toward other men, and other cults. He was humble; he had a "robe of rags." He was experimental, but agnostic; there were some things which he knew he did not know—they lay "beyond the realm of thought." He was an atheist. In his day many thinkers discredited the gods; he did so, sincerely. He could not oppose the Brahmans and *yogis,* and still accept their God, the *Brahman,* or the *Ishwara.* His denial of God rested fundamentally on the ground of his denial of the soul; *all* is change. The concepts of God and soul connoted something permanent—entities quite different from the permanence of change. He could not even have held the idea of the permanence of change, for his mind refused to dwell on general principles of a speculative character.

Beyond himself, his contribution to religion was almost wholly ethical. He proposed a moral training far superior to that of any other system until then; mainly, he taught men to be "full of a really affectionate interest for their brothers, human and nonhuman." [13] And "he inculcated that devotion to man that leads to self-sacrifice." He inspired his disciples with a missionary zeal previously unknown and inconceivable in India. Its basis was the

12 *Cf.* Woodward, *op. cit.,* p. 102.
13 E. W. Hopkins, *Ethics of India,* p. 137.

actual misery of the world, which needed immediate and serious attention; suffering was real, not theoretical! He proposed a cure. Did he have a cure for all? Having turned from "works" to "knowledge," he seemed to find in "knowledge" a remedy for the few, for those who could understand. Did he think there were some who "never could know"? He must have held that in some birth, however distant, there would be a chance for every creature. Meanwhile, the mills of the gods grind slowly. Naturally his mind dwelt most upon his monks; and, naturally, after him, monkish experience tended to outweigh the welfare of society.

The Cult.—Buddha did not organize a separate, thoroughgoing cult; he did not found an Order, as we know it; he instituted no symbolism; he left no *Canon*. Likewise, he left only bare suggestions of things spiritual, and only intimations of philosophy. A cult, however, was inevitable, if the missionary program was to be successful; if the teachings were to permeate the masses; if the thinkers were to be supplied with a philosophy; if the faith were to hold its own amidst absorbent Hinduism. In the Master's own time, the teachings spread throughout the kingdoms of Magadha and Kosala (roughly, modern Bihar and Oudh). In 259 B.C., the Emperor Asoka was converted, and the Golden Age of Indian Buddhism began. The faith completely triumphed for a time through Asoka's vast empire. He sent embassies on its behalf to Syria, Egypt, Macedonia, South India, and Ceylon. Although his messengers were not successful in the West, they laid firm foundations southward. What they established in southern India and Ceylon was essentially the Hinayana system, which the Emperor had decreed in a general Council. Further conquest northwards came rather indirectly, subsequent to Asoka. Greeks and Scythians penetrated the Northwest; hordes of Mongolians came in. Many of these accepted Buddhism—with alterations! Kanishka, a Scythian king in northwest India in the first (perhaps the second) century, A.D., became an active patron of a type. Under his patronage, it extended into Kashmir, Khotan, and Chinese Turkestan; and through the Indus-Ganges valley into the heart of the former Hinayana empire. His type was a curious assortment of Greek, Zoroastrian, Turanian, and Indian elements—a lax and tolerant form. He called a Council at Jalandhar, in Kashmir, as Asoka had done at Patna, and attempted a reorganization of the cult. The Hinayanists sent official delegates, but it was apparent that the "Great Vehicle," Mahayana, was forming.

Hinayana.—Let us follow more closely the variations in the two main "schools." Hinayana has, in general, kept the teachings of the Buddha, at their face value, with no desire to push inquiry into the realm of pure philosophy. A recent visitor to Ceylon, Burma and Siam, has observed in these lands that "cosmic questions are still in theory taboo and not even in symbolic form are they answered." [14] The realistic Hinayanists are more concerned with the immediate situation and the original doctrine. Incidentally, devotion to the latter has tended to prevent the absorption from the former of many lower, non-Buddhistic elements of creed and practice. But Hinayana, intellectually, has remained conservative, holding no theory of God, worshiping no God, revering but not worshiping Buddha, emphasizing salvation for the few by self-effort, and exalting the ideal of the self-centered *arhat* in his quest of *Nirvāna.*

Mahayana.—Mahayana is in every sense a "greater vehicle," having incorporated in unusual measure the beliefs and customs of the Hindus, Chinese, Tibetans, Koreans, and Japanese. It is thereby more manifestly a system of *religion,* with worship for all; divine personalities and many gods, inspired scriptures, salvation for the many; ministering *bodisats* instead of solitary *arhats;* miracle, incarnation, *bhakti,* and transfer of merit; and Heaven (heavens) and Hell (hells) as places of ultimate abode. The earliest Mahayana impulses were Indian. The two "schools" contended quietly for centuries in India. Hinayana then withdrew entirely, and Indian Mahayana was merged with Hinduism. The surrender came mainly between 400 and 650 A.D. When the Chinese Fa-hsien made his memorable pilgrimage (399–414 A.D.) westward, to the south of the Gobi desert, through Lop-nor to Khotan, across the high Pamirs to Swat, Taxila, Peshawar, and India, returning by sea, by way of Ceylon and Java, he found both schools strong and prosperous. But when another Chinese, Hsuan Chwang, himself a Mahayanist, visited (629–645 A.D.) India, he found both types already in decay. He found many who "had no faith in Buddha," and some who "adorned and sacrificed to *devas*" (Hindu "gods").

Early divisions in the Order, and consequent diversities of thought, seem to have arisen over monastic discipline and administration. The monks were uncertain about the rules; some were for stricter, some, for easier observance. In time doctrine was involved; there was no *official Canon.* There were sometimes

[14] J. B. Pratt, *op. cit.,* p. 96.

bitter quarrels. The "Elders," the Theravadins, formulated some decrees, rejecting what they deemed laxities in discipline. Some monks resented these decrees, and, forming an assembly of their own, made their own rules. The majority, it seems, withdrew and formed the Mahasangha, "Great Assembly," leaving the "little society" of Theravadin Elders to themselves. Out of these monastic groups the Schools developed, first debating rules, and then discussing principles of dogma. The Buddha himself probably had no *rules;* he treated isolated cases. But we find in the later *Discipline-basket* an infinitude of rules: a monk might not wear shoes with many linings; blue, black, yellow, red, brown, or orange colored shoes; shoes made of wood, or bamboo leaves; shoes ornamented with the skins of animals. Monks were puzzled to know what shoes they might wear. They could not dispense entirely with shoes; "foot-coverings" were required in the open, and "when ascending a couch." Were shoes a form of *mental* discipline? Hardly; not according to the Buddha. The Elders had gone, with reference to many questions, far beyond the simple rules he had laid down. A priestly code was forming from a *Decalogue.* Various prescriptions ultimately affected the monastic *mind,* as the activities of the Order multiplied. There were daily prayers and readings; short tours for collecting alms; a noonday meal; an afternoon siesta, or a time of meditation; an evening chapel ritual; occasional days of abstinence; and periodic days of fasting and confession. There were problems relating to the nuns, their dwelling, their training, and their services. Monastic properties, lands, and endowments accumulated, bringing their peculiar problems of administration. There were questions relative to laymen, whether permanently or temporarily in attendance on the monasteries. There were intellectual problems. All this, as usual, was fruitful soil for sectarian development.

Underneath *all* the theories propounded at the time in India, there prevailed the conflict between "realism" and "idealism." The thinker must define his general thought and attitude. There were Samkhyist, Yogist, Jainist, and Hinayana realists. There were Chārvakas who insisted that all they *knew* was food and eating; man is an "eater." The Lokāyats considered matter the ultimate reality. There were idealists, also: Brahmanical, "Vedantic," and Mahayanist. Buddhism split on the hard rock of contrast. The Elders, whence Hinayana, figured on the reality of external objects. They insisted that "all things exist" (*sarvasti*)

in the past, present, or future; that there is no such process
as evolution; that consciousness is a continuing current; that
matter is a "collocation" of the senses, which somehow ob-
structs the mind; that if a *self* exists, it does so only in *name,*
unless it is something entirely inefficient; that the individual
is an impermanent phenomenon. All this sounds similar to
Buddha.

The Mahasanghikas, whence Mahayana, held many views at
variance with the Elders'. They insisted that the whole body is
suffused with mind; thus scant room is left for matter in any
realistic sense. This makes corporeality something mental. This
view gained ground; Buddhist Idealism flourished. Mahayana
tended to free itself of rigid monastic regulation, to become free-
thinking, even emotional, to indulge in sympathy and charity, to
be more artistic, to believe in evolution and development. It
challenged Hindu speculation; in fact, may have induced it to
formulate its various "philosophies" (*darsanas*). In time, it felt
the force of both "Vedantic" idealism, and of the newly developing Hindu theism (we might say, the newer *poly*theism).

Indian Mahayanists.—Mahayana produced in India a number
of competent exponents: (1) Ashvaghosha (*c.* 100 A.D.) was
the most conspicuous early idealist. He had been a Brahman opponent of Buddhism. Converted, he brought with him his Brahmanical philosophy. He began to talk of Thatness (*tathatā,* from
tatha, "thus or so"), a condition without attributes of any sort,
whether existence, non-existence, or any other. Thatness was to
him the totality beyond qualification, designation, individuality,
or plurality. Apply this to the concept of the soul. The "soul" or
self, is "thatness," involved in the entanglements of *samsāra,* the
"world." It imagines itself something individual; but, if memory
could only be suppressed, it is aware of its real, absolute, un-
conditioned quality. Memory entangles it; it needs enlightenment,
or freedom from memory. It is the victim of ignorance; it stands
in need of wisdom. This is both Buddhist and Vedantic, possibly.
Ashvaghosha held, not that "all things exist," but that all things
from eternity abide in *Nirvāna,* and that their *appearance* is somehow due to ignorance. Knowledge, wisdom, restores things to
their original bliss, buddha-body, absolute, or void—whatever
Nirvāna was. His terms are Buddhist; his mind is Brahman.
After him came Nāgarjuna, Asanga, and Vasubandhu, to emphasize "emptiness," or the reality of "knowledge," and so
on.

(2) Nāgarjuna (2nd century, A.D.) seemed a nihilist (Shunyavad, from *shunya,* "empty").[15] He advanced the theory that nothing exists; that a "thing" has no existence, or essence of its own; that what appears to exist comes from nowhere, goes nowhere; that process, progress, cannot be affirmed; and that *Nirvāna,* to which men should aspire, is the absence of the essence of phenomena. Would he make the *dhammas,* Buddha's only realities, altogether unreal? Does he reduce *Nirvāna* to an utter void? Not exactly, but near it. He desires to emphasize wisdom and enlightenment. Existence is a continuous, imaginary procession of unreal *dhammas;* ignorance alone gives them reality. Knowledge of their fundamental unreality will stop their flow. "O, to be nothing, nothing," is his intellectual goal; this is vacuity's fulfilment. Is this not virtually an extreme use of *maya,* without its Hindu counterpart of *Brahman?*

(3) Asanga and Vasubandhu (*c.* 400 A.D.) were brothers, with similar points of view. Take Asanga. He sought to reduce all phenomena to mental states, to *mental* reality. He said that the mind revealed several types of consciousness: at the base, a receptacle consciousness, which contains all the seeds of phenomena; and various types arising in connection with the development of the various seeds. These seeds germinate through ignorance; there then appears unrest, the delusion of subject and object, and so on. Wisdom (*vijñāna,* "knowledge," whence Vijnanavad, the designation of his school) is the cure for delusion, unrest, and the like. True knowledge is that *nothing exists but mind.* Such wisdom transforms consciousness into enlightenment, and insures the knower's entrance to *Nirvāna.* Asanga is closer than Nāgarjuna to Hinduism; he is less tolerant than he to void; he lays more stress on knowledge. He was quite as atheistic, however; if, in his idealism, he was false to Buddha, he was true to him in atheism. And he was un-Hindu, likewise, in his atheism.

It was merely a matter of time for Mahayana in India to be lost in the jungle. Atheistic idealism could not survive; its chief foe was pantheism. Indian pantheism has never tolerated either a religious atheism, or a philosophic void. As *religion,* Mahayana had no place in India. It had developed as religion, distinct from speculation; the laymen and many of the monks had deified the Buddha, and a full-fledged ritual had been developed. But

---

[15] He thought, however, that he occupied a "middle" (*madya,* whence *Madyamika*) ground.

this is a sign of what was taking place in India: Hinduism incorporated the Buddha of Mahayana as an *avatara,* "descent," of *Vishnu!*

Buddhist Missions.—Fortunately for Buddhism, especially Mahayana, the door had long been open into China. Hinayana entered first, perhaps as early as the second century, B.C. Mahayana followed, with incomparable success. The earliest verifiable date in Chinese Buddhism is about 65 A.D. At that time, the Emperor Ming-ti sent emissaries to India to bring him Buddhist teachers for his court at Lohyang,[16] in western Honan. The foreign faith gained great influence through royal patronage. When, from about 335 A.D., monks and nuns began to be recruited from the Chinese, the faith was gradually established. It provided, especially as Mahayana, something of religious warmth instead of the cold, formal piety of China. Confucianism had become official, formal, and burdensome. Degenerate rulers had incurred the resentment of their subjects; with hatred toward the rulers went disregard of the state religion. Some rulers may actually have encouraged as a policy of state the introduction of a new religion. Taoism, also, was at low ebb. It had become a jumble of magical rites administered by ignorant and selfish priests, while the people languished. Thoughtful men, especially, were in revolt against Confucian rigor and Taoist superstition. In North China a sect of "Purists" had arisen, advocating the renovation of religion, and the simple life of virtue and reason. When the Purists and the Buddhists met, eventually, both recognized that they had many things in common. Many Purists became Buddhists, devoting their religious zeal, and their literary skill to their new-found doctrine. Many of the common people everywhere gave the first Indian monks a kindly welcome, and after the Chinese Order was established, the new faith gained favor rapidly. It is said that by 381 A.D., nine-tenths of northwestern China were Buddhist.

By the fifth century, A.D., Buddhism was flourishing in South China, also. Fa-hsien was only one of many pilgrims who by that time had made the trip to India. By 500 A.D., hundreds of Buddhist writings had been translated into *Chinese*. In 518, the first Chinese edition of the Three Baskets [17] was collected. In 500, we may say, Buddhism was indigenous to China. In India, the Golden Age of *Hinduism* had dawned; in China the New

---

[16] Lohyang was again the Chinese capital in February, 1932 A.D.
[17] A dozen collections, in all, have been made of the Chinese *Ti-pitaka.*

Era of Mahayana was begun. Meanwhile, Hinayana had become indigenous to Ceylon, Burma, and Siam. Against the background of the wide world, the ageless drama of religious movements was in progress.

While Hinayana entered China early, this form was out of harmony with the Chinese disposition. Notice the major contents of the earliest Buddhist scriptures which reached China, the Hinayana *sutras of the Forty-two Sections:* their ideal is the *arhat* (the Chinese *lohan*), who is the antithesis of the Confucian "sage or superior man," (although much like the mystical Taoist man of virtue and reason); they expound the dogma of the sanctity of all life (China has never stressed a doctrine of non-injury, as India has done); they hold the theory of *karma* and rebirth, contrary to any major Chinese theory of human life; and they emphasize the practical good of meditation, in contrast with Chinese practical activity. Their ideal of asceticism was far more vivid and compelling than any such Chinese ideal. Again, the *arhat* ideal struck at the very roots, not only of the Chinese family, but also of the theory and practice of filial piety.[18] Only impossibly extreme accommodation could reconcile such divergent attitudes toward life and the world. Meanwhile Indian monks took up their residence in monasteries, and the Chinese grew accustomed to them.

Mahayana was more accommodating. Its first literary appearance was the *Diamond Cutter,* translated by the Indian Kumarajiva, in the fourth century. It gave the faith a liberal character. Within a century, came translations of the *Scriptures of the Pure Land,* the *Lotus of the Good Law,* and Ashvaghosha's *Awakening of Faith;* and the purely Chinese *Sutra of Brahma's Net*—all Mahayanist, unless we call the Pure Land *Scriptures* more-or-less Mahayanist; they ignore the doctrine of vacuity, and cancel the long ages of *bodisat*-discipline and rebirth; they present a God able to save men from the one round of existence. With a full panoply of scriptures of its own, and a full regiment of its own monks, Chinese Buddhism was equipped for full independence; it set about perpetuating liberal Mahayana, and leavening the masses.

The Chinese monks, for the most part, have observed the rules of the Indian Order, as in the *Patimokkha,* the "moral code" for monks and nuns, translated in the third century. But their great ideal has been the *boddhisattva* (*bodisat,* for short; in

---

[18] It may be recalled that Buddha forsook his parents, wife, and son.

Chinese, p'u-sa), who outranks the *arhat*. It is embodied in the
Lotus, and *Brahma's Net,* especially, in association with doctrines
of vicarious suffering, Purgatory, Hell, and Heaven. Mahayana
has made some use of Chinese notions and devices, especially
magic, divination, and *fêng-shui* ("wind-and-water"). Pagodas
have been built where they might affect the weather! Monasteries
have often been supported because supposed to dominate *fêng-
shui.* Appropriating fully the virtue of filial piety, one of the most
important functions of Chinese Buddhism has been the funeral
ceremony. This has won the favor of the masses. The idealism
of Ashvaghosha, Nāgarjuna, and Asanga has been mainly for
the monks' consumption. Among the common people, emphasis
has been laid upon "heart-doctrine," and a form of *bhakti,* with
stress more upon the ethical than upon the pantheistic. The
Buddha has been presented more as an influence in men's hearts
than as a universal Spirit. For man's world-weariness Buddha is
the comfort. In some sects, he is God, with other divine beings
in his company, particularly the popular *Kwanyin,* Goddess of
Mercy. A corollary of Buddha's divinity is that man, also, may
become divine.

Chinese Mahayana: The Pure Land School.—Chinese
Mahayana [19] has emphasized discipline and morality, especially
for the monks, and for all, faith and meditation, above works.
One of the earliest sects taking definite form was the Pure
Land (*Ching-t'u*) school of faith, the flower of Mahayana. It
was established before 400 A.D. by a Taoist convert, Hui-yüan.
The former Taoist could accept much of the idealistic content,
even the moderate nihilism of Nāgarjuna (*Lung-shu*). He accepted Buddha's example of the postponement of *Nirvāna* for
the sake of compassionate service, and agreed to the *bodisat*-ideal.
He reconciled the inconsistent theories of the *bodisat* and *Nirvāna*
by modifying both considerably. He posited a Western Paradise,
where *Amitābha,* the Eternal Buddha, dwells; to which all men
may go who have sufficient faith in *Amitābha. Amitābha* had
transformed *Nirvāna;* in a previous birth, when he was Gotam,
he had vowed to do this, for the sake of salvation for all mankind. He set in the stream of life a veritable "Ark of Release," [20]
which any man could board with devotion (*bhakti*). The requirements of Pure Land salvation were: faith in *Amitābha,* prayers
to him, calling on his name. The prayer formula is *Namo Omi-*

19 *Cf.* K. L. Reichelt, *Truth and Tradition in Chinese Buddhism;* J. B. Pratt,
A Pilgrimage of Buddhism.
20 *Cf.* K. J. Saunders, *Epochs of Buddhist History,* p. 59.

to-fu, "In the Name of *Amitābha."* To utter the Name, with faith, wins remission of one's sins.

While the Pure Land theory minifies "works" as agents of salvation, its practice tends to magnify them; the common monk, or devotee, sees value in the repetition of the Name. It is not a far cry to the mechanical repetition of the Name; therefore, the Prayer Wheel in many monastries (lamasaries). At Jehol, near Peiping, there is a large, revolving cylinder—not a Pure Land instrument, but a symbol, nevertheless—on which the magical prayer formula is inscribed. Attendant priests keep it revolving for a fee. The better monks of the Pure Land sect have frequently protested against the formal repetition of the Name. They advocate some knowledge of the *Law,* learned through a teacher, as a sound practice of "remembrance of the Buddha." If man's faith, devotion, and knowledge should not avail, *Amitābha* is all-powerful, and may be relied on. How many "adherents" of this school there are is difficult to calculate; it has been, however, a leading sect for fifteen centuries. The Pure Land is attractive, and *Amitābha's* mercy, full of comfort and assurance.

The School of Meditation.—The Ch'an sect (the Indian *dhyāna,* "contemplation") is another influential body. It has cultivated the experience of immediate insight. In this it follows Buddha, who experienced at the *Bo*-tree *insight,* vision, and enlightenment. The sect was founded by a certain Bodhidharma, unknown in India, who claimed to be the 28th direct descendant and successor of the Buddha. According to the Chinese story, he came from South India, about 525 A.D., to Nanking by way of Canton. Meditation was then essentially a new idea and practice in South China, although Taoists were familiar with it. Bodhidharma's school appealed especially, but not exclusively, to Taoists. On the patriarch's arrival in Nanking, the Emperor Wu-ti, a Buddhist, who must have held a different type of faith, summoned him to court. Bodhidharma told him bluntly that benefactions, or other forms of works, were without merit; that readings, prayers, repetition of the Name, asceticism, all were vain. He had no use for scriptures, original or translation. His objective was the realization of the Buddha-nature in man's heart; this is man's salvation. Teaching had some value; it might give insight, and prepare the way for vision, and enlightenment. Instruction was indispensable; otherwise the doctrines of the school could not be spread; but the ideal program was the transmission of thought by means of thought; and beatific vision, thus induced, led to saving wisdom. Bodhidharma gave instruction, though he was wont to kick at those who came with idle questions. He pointed out that Buddha wrote no book, organized no cult, instituted no ritual; that what happened underneath the *Bo*-tree was psychical and instantaneous. This gave weight to meditation. However, he was inclined to minimize some aspects of the Buddha, the Eightfold Path, for instance, which gives more than transient value to *good conduct*. The school preserves a legend which supports its view: Buddha was once seated with his monks on the Peak-of-the-Vulture, in the Ganges River valley, when a heavenly king came, offering him a golden lotus-flower, and requesting him to give instruction in the *Law*. The Buddha, Blessed One, took the flower, held it in his hand, gazed mystically, and said nothing. No one in the party, except Kassapa, comprehended; he smiled with understanding of the Master's meaning. Then the Buddha said to him, "I have the wonderful thought of *Nirvāna,* the eye of the good *Law,* which I now give to you." This "thought," ineffable treasure, according to the school, came down to Bodhidharma through Kassapa, Ananda, Ashvaghosha, Nāgarjuna, and others. With Bodhidharma, the ideal of "Thatness" and "Vacuity" passed into China. The Emperor could not understand the "hidden teaching," so that patriarch, leaving Nanking, sat for nine years with his face to the wall, in a temple in Lohyang.

The Ch'an school found the *Buddha-nature,* not only in man's heart, but everywhere; Buddha is the All. The aim was the unity of Nature and human nature through the Buddha-nature. This was a peculiar accommodation of realistic pantheism (somewhat akin to Indian Vedanta, but lacking the Vedantic God) to Chinese monism and the prevailing theory of the essential unity of Man and Nature. One tendency of this mystic unity, as conceived by Bodhidharma's followers, was a blurring of good and evil; they counteracted this by what they drew from Nature of purity, compassion, strength, and peace. They promised that by the "hidden teaching" man might purify his mind alike from desire and the thought of "self"; that man might find health of mind and body; and that, in the end, he might enjoy endlessly the "presence" of the Buddha. This was the consummation of the Buddha-nature.

Comprehensive T'ien-T'ai.—The T'ien-T'ai, a third important sect, grew out of, and away from, the Meditation school.

It has persisted until the present with great power. The title came not from any form of doctrine, but from the monastery which the founder, Chih-K'ai (or Chih-I), built about 575 A.D. near Hang-chow in Chekiang. A monk of the Meditation sect, he came to emphasize the study of the scriptures as a means to knowledge, and an aid to faith. He took a comprehensive view of Buddhism as religion and philosophy, and impressed men with the fact that the faith is larger than any of its "schools." No one sect was custodian of the way of salvation; the sects should be combined, for the sake of a total view and program. He approved of scripture, discipline (for the monks, especially), ceremonial, and the ecstasy of beatific vision. He took account of the enormous variety of sacred writings, and the varying capacities of men. He evolved the theory that Buddha taught various truths at different times to various individuals; that he taught the absolute truth, during three weeks after the Enlightenment, to hosts of heavenly beings, and *bodisats;* that, during the next twelve years, he taught plain Hinayana and the *arhat* ideal to his earthly disciples; that, for eight years following, he taught them Mahayana and the *bodisat* ideal; that for twenty-two years thereafter he labored to reconcile the Hinayana and the Mahayana; and that, at the last, he taught the doctrines of the *Lotus of the Good Law*. The *Lotus* is, peculiarly, the scripture of the T'ien-T'ai school.

Chih-K'ai was, also, a philosopher. Accepting the doctrine of "vacuity" of Nāgarjuna, he sought to make it spiritual and less nihilistic. He blended the idealism of Ashvaghosha's *Awakening of Faith* with the teaching of devotion of the *Lotus*. He accepted the historical Gotam Sakyamuni, but made him the *Buddha*-embodiment of universal Reality. Gotam was the concrete human manifestation of truth (*tathā*), which, otherwise, is mere name and void. By a theory of three levels of truth, Chih-K'ai evolved a Gospel for every man: for the simple-minded living among material things which they hold real; for the higher-minded who, while living above the level of possessions, are yet confused about Reality; and for those who, professing to live far above the confusion of things and ideas, mistakenly put their trust solely in meditation. His creed amalgamated the three chief "ways" of Mahayana, knowledge, faith, and insight. The school promoted a remarkable spirit of tolerance and gave great impetus to learning. Nevertheless, it has continued as a *sect,* with its own scriptures, monks, and monasteries. A learned and able monk

of this order, T'ai-Hsü, visited America several years ago, in
advocacy of T'ien-T'ai as the universal Way. His visit aided
the just cause of tolerance and understanding.

Full Mahayana.—The "theology" (better, perhaps, the *poly-
theology*) of Chinese Buddhism should be better understood.
We have so far dealt mainly with the Buddha. All sects recognize
him, but with variations. He is, at times, an ample figure seated
serenely on a lotus. At other times, he is the gaunt ascetic (in a
mural design, or on a *kakemono;* otherwise, elsewhere, he re-
clines, "sleeping" himself away into, or in, *Nirvāna.* These figures
are historical. He is likewise deified, the incarnation of the *Law,*
or of the *Order;* and the God of boundless light (*Amitābha*).
As *Amitābha* (*Omito-fu*), he is, also, the compassionate Father
and Savior, dwelling in the Pure Land, or Western Paradise.
There are other celestial "Buddhas": *Yo-shih-fu,* the healing
deity, invoked by many in times of illness; *Vairochana,* the *Law*
incarnate; *Lochana,* the incarnation of the *Order.* These figures,
each with its own posture and symbol, are well known to their
devotees.

There are, also, divine *bodisats,* or *p'u-sas,* especially *Kwanyin,*
and *Maitreya,* or *Mi-lo-fu. Kwanyin* is, possibly, the most popular
deity in China. She is "Goddess of Mercy." Whence came she?
Obviously such a power is not entirely Chinese in origin. She
seems the female counterpart of an Indian god of mercy, *Ava-
lokita* (*Avalokitesvara*), who long ago heard the cry of man's
distress, and "bent low" to his assistance. At times she is connected with *Amitābha,* even as his "incarnation." In one account,
Amitābha sat on the golden lotus in his Pure Land paradise, looking over the world of men blinded by their evil passions, swaying
as if drunk with self, and groping in the darkness. He had compassion on them (he had vowed compassion), and faith in them;
so he sent them aid. That women, also, might be aided, who were
worse off than men, he was born a woman. He appeared on
earth as *Kwanyin.* Her very name means "one who hearkens
unto prayer." An ancient story (7th century, B.C.) may indicate
something of her Chinese origin: There was a maiden who refused to marry, fled her home, and became a nun.[21] Her father
was enraged and sought to burn the convent. Her prayers
brought rain which quenched the flames. Later, the father captured her, and took her home to marry, or to die. Choosing

---

[21] There *may* have been ancient *Taoist* nuns; but the tale sounds somewhat
Christian, if not altogether Buddhist.

death, she was tortured and strangled. Her body was thrown to the beasts, but carried off by a god in the form of a tiger. Her spirit took up its residence on an island off the coast of Chekiang, where its influence is available for men and women anywhere in need.

Kwanyin has shrines and temples of her own. Her likenesses are everywhere. She is everywhere implored. She is merciful, and answers men in the very voice of Heaven. She is a prophetess, and will reveal the future. Prayers are offered her, especially in times of crisis, including prayers for rain. She is worshiped regularly on the first and fifteenth of every month. She is a Madonna, with womanly grace and motherly tenderness. Young brides receive from their parents her image, with a censer and a pair of candlesticks. She fills among the Buddhists something of the place the Virgin Mary holds with Roman Catholic Christians, symbolizing the motherhood of God. Sometimes she is portrayed with a child in her arms. The place she holds might be illustrated by a lovely porcelain image of her in a Yale collection. It represents a comely maiden chastely clad in an ample, loose-fitting, figure-covered robe, which falls gracefully about her as she sits, serenely meditative, on a lotus-covered hill-top. On her topknot, on a lotus, sits a *buddha*-image, underneath a veil, which, caught mantilla-like, is draped on both her shoulders and falls full-length behind her. In niches in the rocks about her, are many other *buddha*-images. Jeweled pendants are suspended from her ears; she holds a tasseled rosary in her hands; and in the center of her placid forehead is the shining jewel of devotion.

Maitreya, or *Mi-lo-fu,* is the *Future Buddha,* dwelling in the Western Paradise, waiting to visit earth in the next great crisis, as another incarnation of the *Buddha.* Some day his day is imminent. He is an analogue of the *Old Testament messiah,* a reflection of the Hindu *avatāra,* and parallel with the Moslèm *māhdi.* He shares with *Kwanyin* the power of revelation; the Indian Asanga, for example, claimed special revelations from him. He was Indian before he joined the Chinese pantheon, always, however, the "coming" savior. Until he comes, he guides his chosen through the deepening gloom; he symbolizes hope. The *Laughing Buddha* seems, at times, to be his counterpart; he is a jolly comforter. The image of this *Buddha,* with wrinkled-fat paunch and a jovial countenance, sits often at the temple entrance-gate. His head is shaven, his legs crossed comfortably, with the upper part of his body carelessly exposed in a loosely-fitting mantle. He holds in his right hand resting on his lap a lotus, or a rosary; a bag of lucky gifts hangs from the left. If he does not carry on the tradition of the rotund, genial Hindu *babu,* he represents, at least, the well-fed, optimistic Chinese.

There is a full array of superhuman powers. Failing to compete with ultimate success in India, Buddhism took its congeries of gods and powers to China. Save for some similar Taoist and naturistic elements it met there, it found an open field, and has since preëmpted it. All told, along with *Buddhas* and *bodisats,* there are many tutelary deities, such as *devas,* heavenly kings, and angels; there are the "eighteen *lohan* (legendary beings fitted into historical theology), and the "five hundred *lohan"* (seen in some larger temples); there are patriarchs, of whom Tamo or Bodhidharma is the chief; and there are saints, including some of Gotam's first disciples (Kassapa, Ananda, and others).

Buddhism, especially Mahayana, became Chinese in China. It has shared the spirit and practice of toleration, and the theory that human nature was originally good. Many of its moral teachings conformed with those of China; others were adapted to the situation. But it emphasized consistently the idea that there is an insight and a wisdom which transcend morality. Its Order has been offered as a "refuge"; it is a way of salvation. It has been a religious way for many pilgrims. Families of all classes, especially those in straitened circumstances, have dedicated children to the monasteries, while adults, for various reasons, have "entered orders." Many monasteries are "universities," with libraries and curricula of studies, especially in Buddhist *Law* and *Discipline.* What the future holds for the faith is problematical, but time can hardly make all "its ancient good uncouth." Many monasteries and temples which had fallen to decay have been recently restored. Some of its institutions are now supervised by the national government. Reform movements have been organized by leading monks and laymen, with research, public lectures, and literary publication in their programs. Chinese Buddhism seems to be increasingly self-conscious, and to be, to some extent, aware of the pressing need of readjustment to meet present day demands.

Buddhism in Japan.—We must now look further into Buddhism in Japan, whither it went by extension from China. About 522 A.D., while the Indian patriarch Bodhidharma was finding footing in South China, a northern Chinese monk enshrined a Buddha-image in Yamato. About thirty years later, a Korean chieftain, a Buddhist convert, made a formal attempt to introduce his new faith into Japan. He sent an embassy to the chief of the Yamato-men, bearing a bronze-gold Buddha-image (probably *Amitābha*), some Buddhist writings, and a letter announcing the nature and notable achievements of the faith. The Emperor was pleased to receive the image, but dubious about the foreign faith. While a civil official dared suggest it would be well for Japan to profit by Chinese and Korean culture, the Emperor, following the counsel of his warriors, rejected the Korean embassy. Soon afterwards, a plague broke out, which was attributed to the presence of the image. So they threw the image into a canal, hoping to appease the evident anger of the *kami*.

Twenty years later, the Koreans sent another embassy, including monks, a nun, an image-maker, and a temple-architect, and bearing further scriptures. This time they won the support of the influential Soga family of the Yamato tribe, and were permitted to build a temple near Osaka, and to institute the *Order*. When a pestilence again broke out, soon afterwards, it was taken, not as a sign of the *kami's* wrath, but Buddha's warning of what might follow, if his faith were not heartily accepted. Whatever the incidents and omens, the faith was planted among the Japanese before 600 A.D. Its concomitants of continental culture may have weighed more with them than its essence. The new faith proved to be the means of breaking through the isolation of the islands, and to be a welcome ingredient of *Yamato-damashii,* or *kokutai,* the national spirit. It united with Shinto and became indigenous. A royal patron, Prince-regent Shotoku, nephew of the young Empress, espoused the cause, and gave it the prestige of imperial favor. He established a center at Horyuji, with a temple, monastery, study-hall, poorhouse, hospital, and dispensary. From this substantial base, the *Order* grew and permeated gradually the whole national life.

The Buddhist movement in Japan, compared with its Chinese antecedents, is more distinct, concentrated, and intelligible. It entered by one door, instead of many, as in China; and at a time which can be reconstructed from sound sources. Buddhism became, to a marked degree, Chinese in China; the Japanese became more nearly "converts." In China, the monk alone remained distinctive, while the layman included the Buddha-way in his "three religions." In Japan, the layman has been more exclusively a Buddhist, subject only to the higher claim of national loyalty. Even the Buddhist census of Japan is accurate. Buddhism reproduced in Japan the major forms it had acquired in China, but more concretely, by reason of the long Chinese experience. Its major scripture has been, from the first, the *Lotus,* with its simple but splendid ideal of the *bodisat,* a Gospel within the layman's comprehension.

The Major Sects.—Japanese Buddhism may be treated as six major sects,[22] showing its diversity, resourcefulness, and universal qualities. It has been other-worldly, and yet political; philosophical, yet practical; sectarian, yet dominated by a fundamental unity. The six great bodies enroll more than fifty million members, with 120,000 priests, 5,000 nuns, and 50,000 temples. The "True Word," and the *"true* Pure Land" sects comprise three-fifths of the grand total. The six originated at various times from the ninth to the thirteenth century. Before them, there were only "schools" of thought, especially among the monks, with various rituals. Some were reminiscent of Hinayana, some, of the stronger Mahayana. There were items of philosophy from Ashvaghosha, Nāgarjuna, and Asanga. After the ninth century, well-defined sects maintained themselves within the *Order.*

1. **Tendai** (the Chinese T'ien-T'ai) was founded by a noble, Saichō, later known as Dengyō Daishi (*i.e.,* Priest Dengyō). It has a membership to-day of 2,000,000. Careful lists are kept, for many lay memberships are *inherited.* Saichō, as a youth, had become acquainted with the *Lotus.* At nineteen, he withdrew from participation in affairs of state at Nara, and retired to a hermitage on Hiei Mountain, near Kyoto. Many came to get his counsel in religion. In 788, he built a temple at the hermitage. In 794, when Kyoto became the capital, he became conspicuous as chaplain of the inauguration ceremony. Later, the Emperor sent him about preaching the *Lotus* doctrines. In 804, Saichō, having realized how little he knew of Tendai doctrines, and desiring further commission for his ministry, visited the mother monastery on T'ien-T'ai Mount, in China. At the completion of a course of study in doctrine and administration, he was ordained as Dengyō Daishi. Returning to Japan, he founded the Tendai sect at Hiei Mountain; and, during his own lifetime, commissioned other priests to spread the faith.

---

[22] There are *three* "Pure Land" bodies, *one* "Contemplation" sect, *one* sect of Tendai, *one* of the "True Word," a group representing the "restoration" of primitive faith and ordinances, and others, altogether.

While Dengyō did not use the exact language of the mother sect, nor confine himself to the specific doctrines of its founder, Chih-K'ai, he advocated in general the same unifying Gospel of reason, grace, and beatific vision. He taught:

(1) That the gist of Buddhism is to be found in the *Lotus of the Good Law,* which shows that the Buddha-nature rests in all men, that the mind of any individual represents the whole Reality, and that all minds are really One Mind;

(2) That there are three primary truths in one, whereby *Buddha* is body, spirit, and reason; whereby all the *Buddhas,* although indistinguishable, are one, inclusive Reality;

(3) That the Buddha (Gotam) taught in periods, progressively, to prepare his hearers ultimately for the perfect idealism of Tendai; and

(4) That *Amida* (the Chinese *Amitābha*) is the supreme object of man's devotion; is the universal love-principle represented by Kwannon (the Chinese Kwanyin) and other *bosatsus* (*bodisats*); and is the One, into which every individual merges at last in the Eternal Peace.

2. **Shingon,** the "True Word" sect, has much the same philosophy as Tendai, but has offered the common man a more acceptable religion. It is more popular than Tendai, having over 16,000,000 members today. The founder, Kūkai, or Kobo Daishi, was one of the great minds of Japan. He began his career by comparative studies of Shinto, Taoism, Buddhism, and Confucianism; and early conceived the idea that religion, to be universal, must be based on universal truths. He thought there might be some "true word," through which universal religion might be understood and followed. Committed to Mahayana, and hearing of the "True Word" which had been brought from India to China in 720 A.D. (a similar teaching having been brought to Japan by a Chinese monk in 736), he crossed to China in 806, to study the tenets of the Shingon at Chang-an. At the end of three years he was ordained. Returning home, he established the new sect, with headquarters on Kōya Mountain. He wrought a new order out of a philosophy, a God-idea, secret formulæ, and a compromise with Shinto. He taught:

(1) A form of idealism, or pantheism, in the style of the Indian idealists, Nāgarjuna, and others. But he felt that com-

mon men could not be much affected by philosophy; he reserved this for the learned. By it he is able, ultimately, to identify all diversities in One, as Dengyō of Tendai had done.

(2) His God was *Vairochana,* the Great Sun [23] (in Japanese, *Dainichi*), the "body" of the universe, the *Universal Buddha.* He accounted for the earthly Gotam, Sakyamuni, as one of many manifestations of *Dainichi,* with all the *Buddhas* and *bodisats.* He recognized the various *Buddhas,* but only as they are included in the Universal. Dengyō had used the concept of *Amida* (*Amitābha*) to this same end.

(3) He emphasized a "secret," a "true word," which he claimed to have received from the Universal Buddha. The legend about it goes back to Sakyamuni, who taught *plain* truth during most of his life, but toward the last evolved a secret for those fitted to receive it. One of his disciples got it. Centuries later, Nāgarjuna, while in a Yoga trance, received it. Kobo Daishi got it. He had, therefore, two types of teaching: one for the plain man, another for the learned; and both from Gotam. Whereas the usual doctrines of the earthly Buddha are transmitted by tradition and interpretation, the "secret" is intuitive, immediate. "Thou canst not prove the Nameless, O my son." [24] It can be induced by Yoga, and learned while in a trance. If one knows the "true word," he realizes the hidden unity of all things in the Universal Buddha, and attains the true enlightenment. For the common man an elaborate ritual was instituted, with allegory and symbols; but since the ritual and the "true word" were in the keeping of the *Order,* the notion grew that to realize the full benefits of ritual, one should know the "true word." Magic thus crept into the ceremonial. Other words (*e.g.,* the mysterious syllables *abiraukein*) became efficacious. Salvation might be gained by thought, formulæ, and *yoga.*

(4) Kobo identified, further than any predecessor had done, the great Shinto *kami* and the *Buddhas,* making a dogma of this identity. Thus arose *Ryobu,* or "Two-edged" Shinto. It united Nature and the Buddha-nature, *Amaterasu* and *Dainichi.* It was Kobo's aim to conserve the values of Shinto natureworship under the efficacy of Shingon, but his compromise was not successful. Shintoists continued to hold communion with Nature in her visible forms. Both Shingon and Tendai

[23] Cf. *Amaterasu* of Shinto.
[24] Tennyson, *The Ancient Sage.*

were weakening when the Great Awakening came in the twelfth and thirteenth centuries.

3. **Jodo,** the "Pure Land" sect, is, to a degree, an extension of Tendai. It was founded in 1175 by Genkū, or Honen Shonin (*shonin,* "saint"), who was first a pupil in the Tendai monastery on Mt. Hiei. It has today about 3,000,000 members. Genkū studied the *Lotus* and other scriptures faithfully, and practiced *yoga* without finding the salvation he sought. But once he came upon a passage from a Chinese commentator, to the effect that if one would "only repeat the name of *Amitābha* (*Amida*) with all his heart, . . . and never cease the repetition for a moment," he would find the salvation, which "is in accordance with the vow of *Amitābha.*" [25] These words determined his career. Left hungry by the "rich butter of Tendai," and the "honey of Shingon," he found content in *Namu Amida Butsu* (*Nembutsu*), "Hail, Amida." His creed was: Have faith in *Amida,* and *Amida's* grace will save you. There was a tinge of "works"; the repetition of the *Name* was works. But Honen avoided the reduction to the simple repetition of the Name, which had happened in the Pure Land sect's career in China. Salvation came by man's faith, and the grace of God; if there is faith, there is no need of works.

4. **Shin,** the *"true* Pure Land" sect, developed from Jodo. It was founded by Shinran Shonin, the greatest disciple of Honen Shonin, and became immensely popular. It has a membership to-day of more than 13,000,000. Shinran went beyond the teaching of his master, holding that no merit was needed on man's part, except gratitude for the salvation which *Amida's* grace afforded. This is a logical conclusion of a theory of salvation by faith, without works; it makes even the repetition of the *Name* unnecessary. Shinran discovered various works unnecessary, including the usual monastic "work" of celibacy. He learned in a vision that monks might marry; he married in demonstration of the truth. Faith was his one essential; any person could thereby be saved. Shin advocates the worship of a personal God, *Amida.* It believes in personal immortality; such is the *true* Pure Land conception. It misses wholly the vague allurements of *Nirvana;* it personifies the Universal. And Honen insisted that these were the true teachings of the Buddha of the *Bo*-tree. As one might expect, without reference solely to numbers, Shinshu (the Shin sect) is the leading Buddhist body in Japan.

[25] *Cf.* J. B. Pratt, *op. cit.,* p. 480.

5. **Zen** (the Chinese Ch'an, the Indian Dhyāna), the "Meditation" sect, was introduced soon after the Pure Land sects were
founded, but Zen as a form of thought had long been current.
Bodhidharma (Tamo, in China; Daruma, in Japan) had long
been known. There were several founders of the sect: Eisai, in
1191 (in Kyoto); Dō-gen, in 1236; and Yin Yuen, a Chinese
monk, in 1654. The branches have a combined membership today of over 8,000,000. Zen has more temples than any other
sect; it has more nuns (naturally, the True Pure Land sect,
with its advocacy of marriage, would have few nuns!); next to
Shin, it has the largest membership of monks.

Zen, also, traces its origin from the Buddha. Recall, if you will,
the incident of the heavenly king, the golden lotus, and the
Buddha, on the Vulture Peak:[26] the Buddha merely meditated,
and said nothing; he could not *teach* the *Law* by words or acts;
the Absolute is above all distinctions and contrasts, such as one
may draw in earthly figures; it cannot be affirmed, nor yet denied;
it is a matter of *experience*. Zen lays its stress upon experience,
upon the psychical character of religion; religion is a matter of
the mind. A story might illustrate the theory: One day a Samurai,
or "warrior," layman visited a priest of Zen to ask about Heaven
and Hell, only to be answered calmly by a vituperation. The
warrior, angered, drew his sword to slay the priest, but paused,
as the priest—from a safe distance—spoke further, "Did you
ask about Hell? I see Hell in your face and eyes; your mind is
Hell." The warrior relaxed, put up his sword, and sat down,
together with the priest, in peace. Then said the priest, "Now,
your mind is Heaven." The warrior was content to learn thus
the hidden truth that a man makes "of his own mind a heaven
or hell." Zen is full of whims and paradoxes; of harsh methods
to shock unthinking men from religious indifference; of gentle
ways to satisfy serious, puzzled minds. It purports to aid men,
yet tells them no one else can really help them; they must find
their own enlightenment. It provides a setting and a secret, but
discounts the means to realize the secret from the setting. There
are books, images, formulas, and instruction; but they are of
slight avail. Even *thought* is not effective. Books may be read,
if in the proper spirit. One may study the example of great
masters, may meditate on Buddha and his *Bo*-tree experience.
These acts may help create the setting; but the ultimate is
knowledge of the Buddha within one's own nature, by intuition.

[26] *Vid.*, p. 280, above.

The quest is like a search for beard upon a stone; the realization is inaudible, like the rustling of the bamboo in a *kakimono*.

Zazen.—And yet, method has its value, if its setting be correct. As in Shingon, with its quest of the "true word," so, also, with Zen, something of *yoga* practice is employed. Zen calls it *zazen*, sitting in proper posture, in calm meditation, with the breathing regulated, intent on concentration. Through thought one comes to realize that thought is ultimately unavailing. One must consciously dismiss thought from his mind. Compare the Indian suggestion for concentration,—half humorously given, possibly, —the shaking of a pan of sand for a whole hour, without thinking "elephant." Zen proposes "problems," for the sake of demonstrating that solutions do not come at last by thinking. Thought is relative, and, therefore, irrelevant; one must not even think "the Buddha." Yet, paradoxically, Zen seems not to aim at world-renunciation; nor yet at the merging of the self and the Buddha-self. Let further details of *zazen* illustrate the method; *zazen* is the practice of Zen.

A quiet place, preferably a room, is indispensable. Use a thick cushion; keep wind and smoke from coming in upon you; keep out rain and dew. Have a place not too bright by day, nor too dark by night; warm in winter, cool in summer; and always immaculately clean. As you sit, give up such ideas as heat, light, will, and consciousness. Banish thoughts of recollection, perception, and contemplation. Make no distinctions between right and wrong. Have no desire, even to become a *Buddha*. Be eager, as though you were withdrawing your head from flames; yet become even as a dead tree. Do not doze. There is no need of burning incense, telling beads, reciting scriptures, making confession, or of calling on the *Name* of Buddha. Only sit in perfect meditation, until you win enlightenment.

There are two ways of sitting (according to one Zen monastery book): full cross-legged, and half cross-legged. In the former position, the right foot rests, sole upward, on the left thigh; the left foot, sole upward, on the right thigh. Your clothes are well arranged, but loosely tied about you. Your right hand rests, with palm upturned, on the sole of your left foot; the left hand, upturned, in the palm of the right. Both hands are kept close to the body in front of the navel, the thumbs touching at their tips. You keep your body bolt upright; the head erect, facing evenly forward. The tongue is held against the upper gums. Breathing is done through the nostrils. Lips and teeth are tightly pressed together. The eyes are kept moderately opened. One must, of course, find the right position; so you sway about, at first, breathing a few times through the open mouth. Once, however, in the proper posture, you begin the process of mental elimination, and of concentration upon emptiness. When you are ready to rise from contemplation, having made, perhaps, some progress toward enlightenment, place your hands upon your knees; move your body about, with gradually accelerating motion, breathing again, meanwhile, through the open mouth. Then, extend your arms to the ground; rise, stand, and walk, keeping your right side to the left wall, about the room—you were gazing, probably, at a blank wall. You turn to the right to emerge again into the world of common sense and things, purged somewhat of guilt, and fitter for the world. A private room is not essential; one may practice *zazen* in the temple, under a tree, among the tombs, or "on the dewy earth." One may not be alone; several may meditate together, if they do not sit face to face; there is some virtue in facing one's companion's back.

While Zen is notably a mystic way through the maze of transitory things, by which many types of men may flood their souls with peace, it has exerted an extraordinary influence upon the military classes of Japan. It flourished particularly when *Bushi-do,* or the *Samurai-no-michi,* the "Warrior-way," was popular. Its emphasis on self-discipline seemed to appeal to soldiers; self-control, in fact, is what all Japanese have valued most—coupled, of course, with loyalty. Its ethics were drawn largely from Confucian virtue, which emphasizes loyalty. Also, its disregard of temples, books, and objects of worship, in preference of individual observance, made it "portable." It is said that the Japanese capture of Port Arthur against tremendous odds was largely due to Zen discipline.

6. **Nichiren.**—This sect was founded in the thirteenth century by a monk named Nichiren,[27] it bears his name. It has today about 2,750,000 members. It was, at first, a restoration movement; the founder, thinking he had discovered original Buddhism, sought to restore it in Japan; but he knew only the *Lotus* Gospel. He had been a disciple of Shingon, and had studied Tendai. He had visited all the great temples, and had studied at the national Shinto shrine at Isé. A crisis came in the year 1253, when the young priest had ascended Kurozumi Mountain. There on a peak, facing the morning sun, he was inspired to cry out the

---

[27] Nichiren Shonin (1222-1282 A.D.).

simple salutation, "Hail, mysterious *Law* of the *Lotus.*" This was his proclamation of the discovery of the true *Law.* He took the name Nichiren, "Sun-lotus." The time was one of strife between the Emperor and the nobles (*shoguns*). The family to which Nichiren belonged stood with the ruler, sacrificing their castle for him; the Emperor was to them the symbol of the nation. The circumstance introduced a tinge of politics into Nichiren's reform. The *shoguns* were mostly *Amida* Buddhists. The Tendai monks of Mt. Hiei, particularly, did not support the Emperor. To Nichiren, *Amidaism* seemed both disloyal and heretical; he would found a sect both orthodox and loyal.

Knowing only the *Lotus of the Good Law,* he sought his orthodoxy therein. A self-appointed messenger of Gotam Sakyamuni, he deemed himself the one the *Lotus* had foretold.[28] His prayer, which became the formal prayer of his disciples, was *Namu Myoho Renge Kyo,* "Reverence to the Lotus of the Good Law." He thought he had rejected all sectarian "devices," false scriptures and impoverished ritual. He called simply on *Amida* of the *Lotus,* that is, Sakyamuni whom the *Lotus* reveals as Buddha, the original embodiment and revelation of the perfect *Law.* He retained the national *kami* within the range of *Amida,* whom he sometimes seems to link with the national Sun Goddess. He held the central concept of the One of reason. He offered no new doctrine to Japan, except the notion that he was an incarnation of the *Eternal Buddha*—and such a doctrine is not new in Mahayana. He may have seemed, at times, unBuddhist in his violence. He had "enemies," and he dealt with "enemies" of religion and the State. He risked his life sometimes, in furthering his cause. He went, at last, to Kamakura, then the seat of Government, where he built a temple, and organized a following. But for prophesying national calamity, he was banished. In 1270, with the Mongol invasion, his prophecy seemed verified and he returned, a hero in the public mind. He was conspicuously a "patriot"; he stirred his countrymen. Many have been attracted to his sect by its simple, dynastically nationalistic Gospel.

Conclusion.—Little has been added during recent centuries to what these major sects express, although Buddhism in Japan may not be called a fixed, conservative denomination. It is almost wholly Mahayanist, and mainly *Amidist;* but Mahayana has the germ of liberality and progress. Its philosophy is monistic, ideal-

---

[28] *Cf.* The *Lotus* (*Sacred Books of the East,* Vol. XXI, p. 564). Various Mahayana scriptures mention "coming" *Buddhas.*

istic; but there are degrees of reality and truth within the One. It holds the mystic idea of the Buddha-nature inherent in all things; and which reconciles diversities and contradictions. It retains the doctrine of impermanence (*anatta*), and a theory of rebirth; but little stress is laid on *karma*. Every household has its shrine; at the temples, services are carried on with regularity and devotion, attended by laymen in great numbers. While many elements in the *Order* need attention, it leaves wide opportunity both to priests and laity to bring about reform. There are many polytheistic elements, but somehow even these the people have transfigured by their extraordinary "power of religious sensibility," [29] where idealistic philosophy was lacking. At some risk, we might point to Shinshu as an indication of what the Japanese Buddhist Order may become. The interpretation of this sect seems to serve the needs of hosts of able, active, and progressive Japanese. Buddhism still contends with rival forces, Christian, neo-Confucian, and neo-Shinto, specifically. It came out of the Meiji Era (1868–1912) disestablished as the State *religion,* but it has continued to express the fundamental mind of the island empire. It continues public-spirited, cultural, and compassionate; it teaches men to *pray* in a land that is "divine."

[29] H. A. Keyserling, *The Travel Diary of a Philosopher*, p. 160.

CHAPTER XII

The Zoroastrian Parsis

Most Parsis live today in India, although their faith first grew in Persian soil, perhaps three thousand years ago. They are a remnant of the followers of Zoroaster, the Prophet of Iran. They are few in number, aggregating scarce a hundred thousand; but their faith, by reason of its age, its influence, and its qualities, secures attention.

Parsis have long been conspicuous in India, particularly on the western coast, where they are a most interesting community. In Bombay one soon observes them, and discovers their importance in trade, philanthropy, and the city's common life. He may have thought of them as "fire-worshipers,"—they have been mistakenly so called. He may have known something of their curious "towers of silence," where they lay their dead, where the vultures tear away the corpse's flesh. He may find there is a sober reason for the custom. To what extent the Parsis differ outwardly may be seen, in part, on a pleasant evening along "Back Bay." There one finds them among the crowds enjoying the breezes from the sea; dignified, well-clad men, wearing a distinctive head-dress, the shiny, black chintz *kokra,* not unlike a bishop's miter, and beautiful, unveiled women, attired in gracefully folded *saris* [1] of fine fabric and attractive colors. They differ from their Hindu neighbors; in many ways, they are manifestly an alien people.

Is it by favoring circumstance, or by essential character, that this small community still lives its own life in an absorbent environment? Both by extraordinary circumstance, and by the genius of their faith, they have preserved their own integrity. The circumstances constitute one of the most remarkable chapters along the rough way of human experience, some bitter and destructive, and some a favoring miracle. The Parsis, whether

---

[1] The *sari,* many yards of fabric three or four feet wide, made in many grades of quality, with variety in color and design, is the characteristic outer dress of Hindu women.

in India, or Persia, dwell alone amidst a multitude, no longer reckoned as a nation. Although distinct, and even clannish, they are held in high respect by those who know them. Wherever they find themselves they show ability to make themselves at home.

Parsis at Home.—In India, they are the most highly educated single group. They have been the most susceptible to the influence of the West. A strikingly disproportionate number of Parsis have risen to positions of public eminence. The Ready-money[2] family of Bombay early engaged in the China trade, and laid the foundation of great wealth. Dadabhai Naoroji (d. 1917), author and statesman, was the first representative from the East in the British House of Commons. Other Parsi names, including B. M. Malabari, are indelibly written into the record of Indian social reform. Many are permanently memorialized by gifts of public monuments, halls of assembly, and educational endowments. Some have made their mark as scholars, including B. T. Anklesaria. Their demonstrations of capacity and power may be a form of self-assertion, but are not ostentation. They are, in fact, conservative, yet the Parsi is not exclusive. One of their best Western friends, the late Professor J. H. Moulton, once said that "Parsi piety thinks it less blessed to give than to receive,"[3] but he had in mind their theory that charity begins at home. They take pride in their own community, but have proved to be good citizens. If they have seemed self-centered, this character may have been fused into them by a long career of hardship.

Half of the Parsis, approximately 50,000, live in Bombay. Several thousand live in each of these western India centers: Surat, Naosari, Karachi, Poona, and Broach. A thousand may be found in each of these towns: Bandra, Baroda, Ahmadabad, and Hyderabad-in-Deccan. There are several hundred in each group in Thana, Mhow, Nagpur, Jhansi, and Calcutta. There are four hundred in Yemen, in Arabia; and two hundred in London, England. Some have lived in America, including many seeking higher education. Their adaptability has been tested out in many lands and cities.

Gabars.—About nine thousand "Parsis" live in Persia ("Parsi" is etymologically *Farsi,* an inhabitant of Fars, a province of ancient Persia), in the towns of Yazd and Kirman, where they bear the name of "Gabars" (hard *g*). *Gabar* is of uncertain origin, but its

---

[2] This is, of course, an *English* term. Another family bore the name of Botliwala, from the source of their fortune in the bottle-trade.
[3] In his *Treasure of the Magi,* p. 209.

connotation among Persian Moslems is "infidel." [4] They are in short, a group of unbelievers living among Moslems (who, by the way, are "heretics"). They have often suffered persecution, but lately have enjoyed toleration. Moslems should *not* persecute them, for they are a "people of the book"; that is, they have their sacred writings, and, by the Moslem Prophet's own example and injunction, "peoples of the book" are tolerated. However, the Gabars have remained in the homeland of their faith, and taken their chances since the seventh century, A.D., at the hands of their Moslem overlords. The issue was debatable. While the Moslem often has respected the Zoroastrian for his abhorrence of idolatry, as well as for his confidence in "revelation," he has found these objections, namely, that the "magians" (priests) refused to concede that Allah was God, and the communal spirit of the people often made them seem disloyal to the Government. The Gabars have been compelled to wear, in token of their "infidelity," a dull, yellow garb, and have not been allowed—until recently, at least—to wear socks, or showy turbans, or to ride on horses. By leave of their governors, they have worn the sacred *kushti,* a three-ply cord, symbolic of the three fundamentals of their faith: good thoughts, good words and good deeds. Until a century or so ago, their Indian kindred regarded them with distinction, as occupants of the ancestral home. Deputations often came from India in quest of ancient lore and authoritative judgments on questions of faith and practice. One result, however, of this communication was that many Gabars migrated to India where they form, to this day, a slightly different group known as "Iranis," from the name of ancient Persia, Iran. They are more reminiscent than the Parsis of the common origin of ritual, dogma, and folklore. We may divide the living "Zoroastrians" into these *three* groups: Indian Parsis, Indian Iranis, and Persian Gabars.

The story of the Indian Parsis begins with their flight from Persia twelve hundred years ago.[5] The first fugitives landed at the little port of Sanjān, on the coast of Gujarat. Received hospitably by a Hindu raja, the strangers were not aware that they had found asylum among their kindred (see below). They brought to Sanjān, in perpetuation of their faith, the sacred fire from an ancient temple of Iran. This symbol of the original religion was relighted

---

[4] From Persian *gabar* came *gāwar,* and Turkish *giaour,* "infidel," or Christian. *Cf.* Byron's *Poems.*
[5] A Moslem historian records the campaign of the Saljuq Ibrahim in 1079ff. as far as the coast of India, where he found a settlement of Parsis at Nāvsāri (Naosari) in Gujarat. Another historian inaccurately called them "Khurasanis" deported by Afrāsiyāb.

amongst Hindus who still observed the rites to *Agni*, god of fire. One flame has burned in the Parsi temple at Udwada since 1742; it has kindled other altars as newer temples were established. In fact, once in the eighteenth century, fire was sent from India (Surat) to Yazd, in Persia. The Moslem poet, Sadi, noticed the jealously cherished holy fire of the Zoroastrian, but ridiculed it in his *Gulistan,* "Rose Garden,"

> *Agar sad sal gabar atish farozad,*
> *Wa gar ek dam daru uftad basozad.*

"Though for a hundred years the Gabar feed his flame,
Did he once fall therein, 'twould feed on him the same."

Other Parsis were doubtless drawn by trade and opportunity. There is no comparison between fertile Gujarat and the poor soil of southeastern Persia. While some Gabars resort to trade, most of them wrestle directly with the soil for sustenance. The Parsis, on the other hand, found ampler scope and surer reward for a natural aptitude in business. Moreover, they unconsciously enacted a drama of reunion between major stocks long separated.[6] Vedic Indians and Avestan Persians [7] were two branches of one racial and linguistic stem. One found a glorious home in India, prospered, and endured. The other had its day of glory closing with a bloody sunset. Each forgot the other, until tragic circumstance brings the Persian remnant to the hospitable bosom and the fertile soil of their Hindu kindred.

Not that the kinship was soon detected, nor that the reunion has ever grown complete! On the contrary, it seems that the fugitives, suffering from a persecution-complex, concealed from the friendly Hindus some aspects of their faith, and emphasized only such phases as might meet approval. There seems good ground to say that the Hindus expected their guests to conform as far as possible with the language, dress, and manners of themselves, and to leave their own behind. The Parsis may have found this expectation reasonable. But their faith they cherished secretly for many years. This was all the more possible by virtue of its extreme simplicity, both in doctrine and in ritual. Also, so-called "fire-worship" is common to Parsi and Hindu alike. Parsi worship did not arouse suspicion; rather, it tended to find favor.

---

[6] *Cf.* p. 171, above; also, M. Bloomfield, *Religion of the Veda,* p. 15.
[7] The later Zoroastrian priests, the Magi, were a different stock.

Hindus to this day perform the *Hom* ceremony, a sort of adoration of fire in the name of "blazing Agni" of the *Vedas*.

The Parsis lived in peace for about three hundred years. They multiplied, and founded settlements in various parts. At last the Moslems overtook them, bringing tragedy for Hindus and Parsis alike. At times, however, the Parsis again found favor with their Moslem conquerors, because of their reputed monotheism. The sixteenth century Mughal, Akbar, favored them and their faith; he established a fire-altar and its attendant in his inclusive "House of Faith." They have, of course, fared well under British rule,— save as they have been objects of "missionary" effort under "official" sanction, that is, Governmental patronage of mission work.

Religion.—What is the Parsi heritage? What, in particular, is the heritage of faith? We might examine first such outward signs as the "fire-temple," and the "tower of silence." These are merely symbols. When the Moslem, in contempt, called the Zoroastrian a "fire-worshiper," the latter properly replied that he no more worshiped fire than the Moslem worshiped stones, pointing to the Black Stone in the Meccan Ka'ba. The fire is to the Parsi what the Cross is to the Christian,—a symbol; it is quite as tragic, in its way. Take the Persian Gabar temple, sometimes called, in honor of his God, the "gate of Mithra." It is merely a small room, with a consecrated vessel resting on a tripod and containing the ever-glowing flame. The flame is guarded carefully from contamination, in spite of its conceded power to purify itself and the worshiper. Priests who are usually in the room droning sacred texts from the *Avesta,* veil their mouths, especially against a sneeze, or cough, lest their chanting pollute the fire. Take the Indian Parsi temple. It is more pretentious, although it is hardly to be distinguished from the outside from an ordinary residence. It may be one of the holiest temples, whose fire has been purified by the maximum of ceremony. The fire burns in the center of an inner room, in an ash-filled urn that rests upon a stone, four-sided pedestal. It is fed continually by its attendants, or the worshipers, with bits of sandal-wood. Worshipers come daily, especially on designated festal days. Men and women mingle freely in the temple, and perform alike the simple ritual.

Worship.—When one has come for worship,[8] he may recite, at the threshold of the shrine, the following *kushti* prayer of the "Girdle" ceremony:

[8] *Cf.* J. H. Moulton, *op. cit.,* Chaps. 3, 4.

The Omniscient God is the greatest Lord, *Ahriman* is the
evil spirit that keeps back the progress of the world.

May the evil spirit and with him all his helpers stay fallen
and dejected.

O Omniscient Lord, I repent of all my sins.

I repent of all the evil thoughts my mind has entertained,
of all the evil words my lips have spoken, of all the evil
deeds I have performed.

Praise be to *Ahura Mazda.*

Damned be the devil, *Ahriman.*

The will of the Righteous One is worthiest of praise.

He then passes through the outer hall, leaving his shoes, and
proceeds barefooted through an inner hall to the sanctuary with
its fire-altar. There stands a priest, a *mobed* (from *magupat,*
"head magian"), who receives his offering of sandal-wood and
money. After the offering the *mobed* gives the devotee some
ashes ladled from the urn. Applying the ashes to his forehead and
eyelids, the worshiper utters prayers in accordance with his
needs, and forthwith retires backwards from the chamber—he
may not turn his back upon the symbol of Lord *Ahura.*

The hour of worship is a time of worship only, not for education. That is, there is no combination of ritual, and instruction
in morals and religion. Such education is usually obtained by
readings in the sacred writings, and through discussions in the
family circle. The Parsi child imbibes the atmosphere, and
learns the rudiments of the faith, at home, while securing such
general education as the public schools afford. There is formal
training for the priesthood, both in creed and ritual. Modern
Parsi ritual, although comparatively simple, is more rigid than
the faith itself. The priesthood is an old order, well-intrenched,
with hereditary succession, whose leading office is the ritual. The
faith has long endured through ceremony, and differences of
creed(?) have been most often variations in the ritual.

Towers of Silence.—Consider now the "tower of silence," the
dakhme, where, as Strabo long ago observed, the dead are left
to be devoured by birds. There is a famous tower at Teheran,
conspicuously located on a mountain-ridge. It is a circular wall
of unbaked brick, without a gate, or door,—or roof. Ladders only
furnish access—a body must not be devoured by animals. The
floor inside is level, broken at intervals by rectangular pits. When
a Gabar dies, and the rites are said, his body is placed above a

pit inside the tower. When carrion birds have picked the bones, they drop into the pit and decay. This funeral custom is ancient, and well-adapted to its native habitat, where mountains are numerous, the air clear, and the sunshine strong; and where the land is thinly populated. It was not, however, Zoroaster's custom. In his day the ordinary dead were buried, the priests only being exposed to devouring birds. The custom would not do for a humid atmosphere in a flat, thickly populated country. What of India? There are in India long seasons, at least, of clear air, and strong sunlight; and many mountains. The Parsis themselves are few in number.

There are seven *dakhmes* in Bombay. One was first built, in 1786, by a member of the Readymoney family for the disposal of his own body after death.[9] It has been available since to others. Usually the towers serve the whole community. The seven conform in general with the traditional design, and serve the common purpose in the common way. Take a tower on Malabar Hill, a high-class, residential section of Bombay. A single opening midway up the outer wall gives access to the circular inclosure. The disc-like floor dips slightly toward the center, where there is a pit. Two low, concentric ridges, paralleling the outer wall, divide the radial area of the bowl in thirds. There are thus three circular rows, each with many compartments, the upper ring for male bodies, the middle for female, and the lowest next the pit for children's. A body is laid naked last of all in its appropriate circle. When the vultures have fulfiled their office, and the bones have bleached in the sunshine and the wind, the remains are thrown by gloved, professional attendants with tongs into the central pit, where as purified dust, they lose identity.

Many peoples, many customs. The Parsi funeral method is spectacular, but as commendable as any other for disposing of the mortal parts of man. Furthermore, the method meets for Parsis the dogma, developed after Zoroaster, to be sure, that the elements —fire, water, earth, and air—are sacred, and to be by man protected from deliberate pollution. The fire-temple is a symbol for the living, and the tower is a symbol for the dead.

Personal Devotion.—The Parsi ritual includes many elements. Prominence is given to initiation (the *naojote*), to marriage, special festivals, and the frequent *kushti*, "girdle" ceremony. The *joshi*, "astrologer," has long been used. The Magian has held office since the days of Zoroaster. Herodotus observed that "without

9 D. F. Karaka, *History of the Parsis*, Vol. II, p. 57, note.

a Magian it was not lawful for a Persian to offer sacrifice." Yet, the Parsi layman may be at times his own informal minister of worship. Often the Bombay Parsi resorts at evening time to some favorite spot along the beautiful Back Bay, where he may adore the Waters and do obeisance to the Sun. There he stands, a typical, lay devotee, on the hard sand at ebb-tide at the ocean's edge. His head is covered, for he is in the presence of Majesty, and he is bare-footed, having left his shoes as at a temple door. Facing the setting sun, he reads from a Gujarati edition of the sacred *Avesta,* and recites from memory a prayer he doubtless learned in boyhood, the Ardvisur Nyayish. The sun he faces, as it sets through the dust and mists hovering over Malabar Hill, and beyond the towers of silence almost hidden in their groves of palms, is the symbol of *Ahura Mazda,* his God. He prays to the sign of Mazda, closes the sacred page, kneels on the sands of the beach and bows five times so low that the ridge of his chintz hat touches the moist floor. Afterwards he advances to the brink, dips his finger-tips, touches his brow with the wet drops, as if ashes in the sanctuary, and prays again in humble thankfulness and earnest invocation. At last, he backs away up the beach, as the sun's rim dips beyond the Hill, his face toward the afterglow on the dark waters. He has worshiped simply, yet in how grand a Temple, whose music was the sound of moving ocean tides, and the murmur of the winds among the palms, and whose light was the candle of the Lord.

Zoroaster.—Zoroaster was a Persian of the noble family of Spitama, whose home was probably in northwest Persia, near Lake Urmiya. While we may never know exactly the time he lived, we must accept him as an historical personage, and we may as well accept his dates as 660–583 B.C.; they are tenable in the light of the evidence. The *Spend Nask,* which treated most fully of his life, was lost early, but there are scattered fragments in the later literature. The most we know is based upon the *Gathas,* a group of songs which are the oldest authentic portions of the sacred Zoroastrian scriptures, the *Avesta.* He himself may have written them; at least, he was their editor. According to the Gathic portrait, he was a man of stirring personality, filled with holy zeal, a veritable prophet, and a teacher of unquestionable power. It is a pity that later writings, which make up the bulk of Zoroastrian literature, obscured him with a veil of sanctification, and made him supernatural. They have him born of a virgin mother divinely set apart. They make him smile at birth in response to the laughter of all good creatures, and to the dismay of all evil forces, which flee in terror at his advent. They represent him as standing later before God himself (*Ahura Mazda*) to receive his divine commission as the reformer of his own day, and the forerunner of the savior (*Saoshyant*) who would come in the fulness of time to bring everlasting bliss to the pious, and to destroy utterly those who have opposed unceasingly "the holy creed which is the most imposing, the best, and the most beautiful of all religions."

The simple facts seem to be that Zoroaster early manifested a certain precocity, and as a youth determined to devote himself to the religious life; that at the age of twenty he left the house of his parents, against their will, and wandered forth in quest of truth and guidance. He devoted many years to wandering, observation, and study, and at the age of thirty received the first of the many revelations which made him the preacher, teacher, and reformer. He calls his various revelations "conferences" with God; there were eight, in all, the last of which came when he was forty-two, which gave him the confidence of a full, divine commission. Among his converts was a king, Vishtashpa. Others of the court embraced his message, lending high sanction to the new prophet of Iran. Success came slowly but surely, throughout wide areas, and at last a new, national religion was established on his message. He journeyed far in connection with his mission, through Media, and Bactria, as well as Persia. Perhaps the new movement actually got under way in Bactria, and, spreading westward into Persia, gained momentum through Vishtashpa's conversion. One of the prophet's several marriages was with a daughter of a royal councillor at the Persian court. The new religion met success, but it seems to have stirred up opposition. There seems to have been a religious war with the Turanians along the northern Persian border, during which Zoroaster lost his life at the age of eighty-seven. According to tradition, he was buried near the place of his birth, in the neighborhood of Lake Urmiya. Such are the simple facts of his life-story.

Zoroaster's Message.—What of his reform? What of the background of the prophet? What were the religious elements within the situation into which he came? There were, to say the least, Turanian, and Semitic, and Aryan factors. Southward, in Media, there was Magianism, a system of nature-worship led by "wise men" (*magi*). Northward and eastward, were regions of primitive shamanism under *shamans*. The priests of these cults were Zoroaster's most persistent enemies. In one direction or another, there were cults of sun, moon, stars, fire, water, earth, and tribal gods. Necromancy, sorcery, and the black arts had wide currency. The prophet's own religious background was "Aryan," or Indo-European. All the peoples of this stock revered the shining sky as God, and called him by various names. They revered, also, the sun-god, called in India *Mitra,* and in Persia *Mithra.* They worshiped, also, an august guardian of the moral law, known as *Varuna* in India, and in Persia *Mazda.* Both *Varuna* and *Mazda* were "Lord" (Persian *ahura,* Indian *asura,* whence *isvara*). They were supporters of all beings; they put fleetness and strength into steeds, milk into cows, fire into the waters(!), and intelligence into the heart. They placed the sun in the sky, and the sacred *soma*-plant (in Persian, *haoma*) upon the mountains. They had all knowledge and could not be deceived; they saw all the past and all the future. They were always present whenever two men met for any purpose.

In India the fortunes of *Varuna,* for want of a great prophet, waned; in Persia, *Mazda,* through Zoroaster, attained supremacy. *Mazda* became supreme, and other gods were forced into the rôle of demons, unlike their fate in India, where polytheism gave them place as gods. Zoroaster was a monotheist. He was *Mazda's* prophet; *Mazda* was the one *ahura,* or "Lord." *Ahura Mazda* was God, whose will was known through Zoroaster, and must be obeyed. His will was altogether good and for the good of men. This was the burden of the great reform: *Ahura Mazda* was both wise and good. By his wisdom he created Right. He was no mere nature-power, whether sky, or sun. He was Spirit only, and withal the spirit of truth, beauty, and justice. This expresses the great advance which Zoroaster made; he made religion *ethical,* and *spiritual*. He is perhaps the first reformer to achieve as much. He is "a monotheist of the strictest type," says one who knows. He was no metaphysician, nor theologian; he was a practical prophet, whose aim was, in his own words, to purify religion as he found it. He found much to modify, or to eradicate, in the old Iranian cult with its sundry elements. He stoutly opposed things which challenged the supremacy of *Mazda.* He seems not to have denied the existence of nature-spirits, but he did not care for them. He was interested alone in *Mazda,* whose *manifestations* were truth, purity, good mind, right order, and coming kingdom. Zoroaster was the first to pray, "Thy Kingdom come," the first to conceive of heaven and hell as mental states, and not locations somewhere in the universe. He was the first to proclaim the teaching that the "kingdom of God" is within man. He was first to teach that the world and man's own soul are fields of battle between good and evil and that the good must, and will succeed. God had no "chosen people," apart from those who made their wills conform to the will of God, and who gave themselves to true faith, and public service. Of necessity, Zoroaster gave large place to the freedom of man's will. Man is free to serve the Truth (*asha,* or *artha*), and to hate the Lie (*druj*). Man himself was first responsible for his own welfare; he was to ally himself with Mazda; and in the end Mazda would be victorious over all who had opposed him. Evil might powerfully contend in the night but Ahura Mazda is victor on the final morning.

Developments.—Somewhat in contrast with the doctrines of the founder, the new religion yielded to the dualistic implications of his teachings. It magnified the office of the Evil, and personified the Evil One. Zoroaster's Angra Mainyu, "evil mind," became the Devil, *Ahriman.* The Prophet himself may, indeed, have had a human, "evil-minded" enemy, who was the embodiment of *angra mainyu.* In any case, *ahriman,* derived from *angra mainyu* of the *Gathas,* becomes, in the later *Vendidad,* a proper noun. A certain form of monotheism, and a certain type of dualism are not incompatible. We speak of *ethical* monotheism, and a *subordinate* dualism. There is a problem. The eminent Iranian scholar of our day, Professor Jackson, thinks dualism "on the whole perhaps the most striking feature" of the ancient faith. But what of *Zoroaster's* view? He proclaimed *Ahura Mazda.* But he mentioned *Spenta Mainyu,* "Bountiful Mind," as *Mazda's* Holy Spirit. He mentioned *Angra Mainyu* as *Mazda's* Evil Spirit. We think that, with the Prophet, this was something psychological, not theological. He never seemed uncertain about the Lord's omnipotence, never despaired that Wrong would perish, and Right would be exalted. Practically, he made the world a battle-field, whereon good and evil were in constant conflict. Not that *Mazda,* both Lord and Creator, had created evil. He had created men, and given them their freedom, even to oppose their wills to his. They made evil for themselves; and the Lord, to test their souls, permitted evil to endure. This view gives point and ground to Zoroaster's ethics as a reformation. Before his day, there were many powers, some good, some evil, and some good-or-evil, according to their mood, or according as men thought they helped, or hindered. Zoroaster introduced the concept of *Ahura Mazda* as altogether good, as One who by his own nature always does good. Such is his *ethical monotheism.*

The religion, however, became organized on the basis of two great, rival camps, dividing men, gods, and the universe. There was the friendly *Ahura Mazda,* and his friends; there was *Ahriman,* the Devil, and his associates. Into *Ahriman* went, along with the Prophet's theory of "evil mind," his concept of the "lie." *Ahriman* is evil, and deceitful, a full-fledged Devil. Zoroaster had discussed the "attributes" of Mazda, the *amesha spentas,* "bountiful immortal" aspects of God's character: (1) *vohu manah* (good mind); (2) *asha* (right); (3) *kshatra* (power, rule); (4) *armaiti* (love); (5) *haurvatat* (health); and (6) *ameratat* (immortality). In the later development, these qualities of God became a hierarchy of heavenly powers—angels. They were the allies and servants of the Lord. Opposed to them were such personifications as falsehood, cold, disease, sexual sin, drunkenness, irreverence, and desecration, under the leadership of *Ahriman. Ahura Mazda,* and *Ahriman,* each became a *primal* spirit. God was good, the Devil evil; each was all-powerful in his own dominion. Man must throw in his lot with one, or the other. The Parsis are dualists, but, in their enlightenment, their dualism is not absolute. The Devil is real; but *Mazda* is supreme, and the victory in the end is his.

Other "personal" elements entered in, as time went on. The Prophet came to occupy more than his title rôle. He was so closely identified with *Mazda,* that to worship *Mazda* was to revere the prophet, also. He became "the chief of all things," "the incomparable among mankind," and "the completely good." In fact, the sinlessness of Zoroaster came to be a dogma. Likewise, there was added a doctrine of messiahs, or saviors, three in all, each to appear at an interval of a thousand "years." Each would be of the line of Zoroaster, born of a virgin mother. The third is *Saoshyant,* who will perform a *ceremony,* by which "all men shall become immortal for ever and ever," the living, if they are true to Mazda, the dead, if they have demonstrated their fitness by successful passage of the narrow Chinvat bridge of Judgment.[10] This bridge is as narrow as the edge of a keen blade, and passes over the fires of Hell. Those who make the passage enter Heaven, and for them the "Kingdom" has arrived; they await the final day. Others who fall are burned eternally. Need-

---

[10] *Cf. Yasht* No. 22, translated beautifully by J. H. Moulton in his *Early Religious Poetry of Persia.*

less to say, such elements as Heaven and Hell as localities, and such doctrines as the prophet's sinlessness, angels, demons, and successive saviors, are additions to the simple creed of Zoroaster.

Less noble elements, also, have crept in, such as distinctions between "cleanness," and things "unclean," the offices of the astrologer (*joshi*), and the magical potency of rites and formulas, elements which remind one of many things the Prophet sought to change, or banish.

Scriptures.—The original deposit of sacred writings was the *Gathas,* "Songs" (*cf.* the Indian *Gita,* "song"), of Zoroaster, seventeen, in all—at least, seventeen have been preserved. They are the basis of our understanding of the Prophet, whether he was editor, or author. Other writings were composed as time went on, for Zoroaster put no ban on scripture, in favor of his own person, or otherwise. Here is the final list:

(1) The *Yasna* or *Book of Worship and Sacrifice,* which includes the *Gathas.* As with the Vedic Aryans, so also with the Iranian, sacrifice was central.

(2) The *Visperad* or *Book of Liturgy* for use in worship.

(3) The *Vendidad* or *Book of Priestly Law,* with other materials, also. It represents a similar stage of theology and ritual to the Atharvan stage in India.

These three works are the *Avesta* proper (*avesta* possibly means "knowledge"), or the *Book of Knowledge.* There is, in addition, what is often called the "Later *Avesta,*" (Nos. 4, 5, and 6, below).

(4) The *Yashts* or *Book of Hymns and Invocations.*

(5) The *Khorda-Avesta* or *Book of Common Prayer.*

(6) Certain Pahlavi, and Persian writings, that is, works not in the classical language of the faith. There might be added such vernacular translations of the *Avesta* as exist in India.

The Parsis are heirs of all these elements, doctrinal, ritual, and scriptural. Some accept the body of tradition; others question much of it. There are two schools of thought, conservative, and modernist. All are proud of Zoroaster, asserting that he has made a permanent contribution to the ethical and spiritual interpretation of human nature and the universe. Many seek a revival of the "very simple creed" of the *Gathas.* A few are content to say the *Gathas* are *their Avesta.* The reforming Parsi is content with nothing less than a rationalized *Avesta;* but rationalization is, after all, not the final test of scripture. Zoroastrianism as a whole rests on more than *Gathas*. The "Later *Avesta*" might be ignored, and most of the *Avesta* proper might be renovated. But the situation in which Parsis find themselves is part of their religious problem. His three jewels might shine brightly there, or anywhere; *humata* (good thoughts), *hukhta* (good words), and *hvarshta* (good deeds).

These are the major assets of the faith: [11]

(1) Mazda (Ormazd), a personal, morally good, dependable, and helpful God, to whom all men, if they will, may turn.

(2) Man's responsibility, his duty to coöperate with God, not only for his own, but others' good.

(3) Coöperation with God includes animals, the improvement of the land, the raising of flocks, and the prosecution of business enterprise.

(4) A denial of the validity of asceticism as a means to moral and spiritual ends.

(5) Confidence in the final victory of goodness, truth, and righteousness.

This is the Confession of Faith of all good Mazdians:

I am a worshiper of Ahura Mazda.

I am a Zarathushtran worshiper of Mazda.

I agree to praise the Zarathushtran faith, and to believe in that religion.

I praise good thoughts, good words, and good deeds.

I praise the sound Mazdayashnian religion which allays dissentions, which realizes brotherhood, which is holy, which is the greatest, the best, the most excellent of all religions that exist, or will exist in future, and which is the religion revealed by Ahura Mazda to Zarathushtra.

I ascribe all good to Ahura Mazda.

This is my profession of the Mazdayashnian religion.

[11] As a commentary on the character of the community as a whole, we may be reminded that the Parsis are clannish, non-missionary (they covet no extension of the faith); have suffered much from the ravages of the "social evil" of prostitution, and intoxicating liquor. The Prophet denounced strong drink, and pointed out that Ahura Mazda is "never intoxicated."

CHAPTER XIII

The Sikhs and Their Religion

Sikhism, or more exactly, the religion of the "True Name" (*Sat Nam*), is of Indian origin, and of markedly Indian character. It arose four centuries ago as a quest for God. A "Sikh" is a "learner, or disciple, or, possibly, one who serves." The faith has had, as well, a distinguished political career, having become in time a nationalistic community. Sikhs (*sikh* is pronounced *seek*) are known as a people of military prowess; for warlike spirit some compare them with the Cossack and the Turk. Their martial exploits brought them fame in India, and have given them a name throughout the world. But their religion in itself is interesting. They have their own peculiar priesthood, Holy Book, lofty theology, code of rigorous morality, sacred ritual, and Holy City with its noble sanctuary.

The community numbers about four and one-quarter millions, of which about ninety percent live in their homeland, the Panjab, the northwest Indian region of the "five rivers." Although, in this region, they make up only about fifteen percent of the population, they have a prominence out of proportion to their numbers. The remainder of the Sikhs are found in various parts of India, and the East. In many provinces they serve as bodyguards to governors. There are several regiments of them in the British Indian Army, doing duty in widely separated garrisons. Small detachments are on military service in British possessions beyond India. Many are police patrolmen in India, or beyond, at Durban, Aden, Penang, Singapore, Hongkong, and Shanghai. Their service everywhere is valuable.

The Peoples.—Many tribes and castes make up the Sikh community. Half of the Panjabi Sikhs are Jats,[1] a stolid, sturdy, resolute folk, the best agriculturists in northern India. It is proverbial that "the Jat's baby is born with a plow-handle for a

---

[1] Many Jats are Hindus; some are Moslem.

plaything." The women and children work side by side with the
men in the open fields. They are a self-reliant stock, reserved in
demeanor, slow to speak, but often quick to strike. They may be
complacently disdainful, as a proverb shows.

> The Jat stood on his dung-hill as the Raja's elephants went
> by; said he to the *mahout*, "Prithee, whose *mice* may these be?"

Some have been drawn from the Arora tribe of merchants, or
petty dealers; others, from the Ramgarhia tribe, whose men are
principally mechanics. Some are Khatris, "warriors,"[2] from whose
stock Nanak, the founder of Sikhism sprang. There are Rajputs
among them, although the Rajputs are the proud, warrior race
of Hinduism, the purest-blooded "Aryan" stock remaining. Sikhs
and Rajputs are distinct. The Sikh Jat is rated lower than the
Hindu Rajput, for Jats have practiced window-marriage. While
Jats may rank as "warriors" in their own estimation, high caste
Hindus consider them as Shudras.

Their Character.—The Sikhs were first of all a convert people.
Anyone may yet join the faith who accepts the doctrine and the
baptism. The Panjab community has increased since 1900 by a
million, partly by conversion, partly by natural increase, and partly
by the reclamation of Sikhs listed with the Hindus by a former
census. Whatever their extraction, they are usually affected by
a common consciousness, which first developed out of differences
from Hindu and Moslem neighbors, and was later magnified by
wars with the Moslems, and the British. They are proud of their
career, and their inheritance. They are in theory a democratic
people, but dignified in bearing. What they have lacked in in-
itiative and dash, they have made up in hardihood, courage, resolution, and loyalty. To the temperament of the Jat, Arora,
Ramgarhia, and Khatri—often fighting-men by nature—Sikhism
has added the stimulus of a militant religion. While Sikhs were
not a great success in France, during the Great War, they are the
finest soldiery in their homeland, steady in victory; in defeat,
willing to die before yielding. Unquestioning loyalty to his leader
dominates the soldier; his heart does not quail before overwhelming
odds, because he deems death on the field of conflict an instant
access to the bliss of heaven. Witness the conduct of the Akalis,
"deathless ones," ten years ago in *passive* resistance to Government. Five hundred, including soldiers of the Great War, marched

---

2 *And* traders.

to the shrine at Jaito, near Amritsar, in defiance of official prohibi-tion.[3] Beyond a certain line they were fired on. They took the lead with heads erect and ranks unbroken.[4]

Or, witness the Sikh Wars, and the Mutiny.[5] During the years 1845 to 1849 the Sikhs fought two bitter wars with Britain. A large, well-drilled army had been formed under the redoubtable, one-eyed leader, Ranjit Singh (d. 1839). They made a bid for national integrity, having organized a *Khalsa,* Council, or "nation," of their own. Defeated in several hard-fought campaigns, their forces were shattered, and they lost control of almost all their territory; but they were shortly reconciled in a new national rôle as British allies. The last independent ruler, Maharaja Dhulip Singh, afterwards gave to Queen Victoria his famous diamond, the *Koh-i-Nur,* "Light of the World." The ninth Sikh *Guru,* Teg Bahadur, had foretold (before 1675) the British overthrow of the Mughal Empire, and the conquest of the Panjab. His prophecy may have eased the Sikh mind not a little. In the bloody Mutiny of 1857–59, when England might have lost her hold on India, the Sikhs proved themselves her best allies. Of late, how-ever, many have shared in the widespread effort toward *swaraj,* "self-rule," a newer type of nationhood for India, to which Indians in growing numbers have pledged themselves.

Amritsar.—Amritsar, in the Panjab, is the Holy City of the Sikhs. It is the seat of the Golden Temple, the *Darbar Sahib,* "Lordly House," which to Sikhs is what Mt. Abu is to Jains; Isé, to the Japanese; or, Lenin's Tomb in Moscow, to the Soviets. It is their Mecca, their Benares. The Temple is comparatively new, several earlier temples on the site having been destroyed by enemies. It was roofed a hundred years ago with copper gilt, and has since been called the "Golden Temple." The earliest shrine was built on the site toward the close of the sixteenth century, by the fourth *Guru,* Ram Das.[6] He transformed the humble village, with its healing spring, into a flourishing city, with its sacred lake, in the center of which he built the national sanctuary. The spring wrought miracles, and miracles have hap-pened at the lake: once a black crow fell in, and came out white; once a leper bathed there, and came away sound of flesh.[7] The

3 Government interpreted the movement as *political* and seditious.
4 See S. Zimand, *Living India,* pp. 230–243; W. N. Brown, *Asia Magazine,* Vol. 26, pp. 242–6.
5 See any history of India, *e.g.,* V. Smith, *Oxford History of India.*
6 Or, possibly the fifth *Guru,* Arjun, actually laid, in 1589, the first brick of the central shrine?
7 Possibly the leper bathed, instead, in a pool not far from Amritsar, where, legend has it, lepers can be cured.

name "Amritsar" means "water of immortality." Nanak, the
founder of the faith, had often visited the village, while on
preaching tours.

The lake, about 470 feet square, is surrounded by a broad
pavement along which are hostels, and chapels of chieftains who
come to worship. There are thirty acres of gardens round about.
The Temple is a square, two-storied structure on a platform 65
feet square. The flat roof is battlemented, with a kiosk rising
from its center, and a little cupola at each corner. The lower
half of the Temple walls are of glistening white marble; the upper
half, and the buildings on the roof are copper gilt. Inscriptions
from the Holy Book (*Granth Sahib*), in *Panjabi,* run round
the walls. Four silver-plated doors, one on a side, give entrance.
A marble causeway, 204 feet long, bordered on both sides by
rows of stone lanterns, connects the Temple and the massive
gateway on the shore. The Sikh enters the Temple by the western
door (Europeans may use the northern entrance). Inside, a simple
scene presents itself. There are no idols; neither are there murals
of the gods, but only flower designs. The *Granth Sahib* rests on
an altar on the eastern side. Perhaps a priest, a *mahant,* is standing at the altar reading from the Book, or fanning it ceremonially
with royal peacock feathers. A sheet may be spread on the center
of the floor to receive the offerings of the pilgrims; money, grain,
or flowers, may be offered prior to engaging in the ritual, or in
one's own devotions. Possibly verses from the *Granth* are being
chanted to the accompaniment of stringed instruments. The
pilgrims join in the chanting. Every twenty-four hours the Book
is read through by a relay of *granthis* or "readers of the
Granth." This is the chief aspect of the Temple ritual. At times,
the *Granth,* accompanied by sacred maces and a fan of peacock
plumes, is taken out and carried in procession, on its special,
cushioned platform, under its golden, jewelled canopy. In this
way, it is made accessible to multitudes at once. This processional
setting for the *Granth. i.e.,* the canopy, cushion, maces, and plumes,
is kept ordinarily in the Treasury on the second floor.

Origins of Doctrine.—We must now give some account of the
religion. Many antecedent factors lent it impetus. The faith is not
original. It had a nationalistic temper at the outset, for it arose
when the Mughals were vigorously enslaving the Panjabis. It
served itself heir to tendencies which had long been felt in
Hinduism, and Islam. There were many types of both of these
religions. The Hinduism of the masses was Puranic, with a

veritable riot of gods and goddesses. There were Sunni, and Shii Moslems, but among them were Sufis, also, Moslem *mystics*. And among the Hindus were many *bhaktas*, devotees of *bhakti* to *Krishna, Rama,* or some other deity as a means of salvation. The *Bhakti*-movement was affecting Moslems, also. Nanak, the first "Sikh," was in the line of succession with many *bhaktas*. There were Ramanuja, of the eleventh century; Ramananda, and Namdev, of the fourteenth, and Kabir, whom Nanak may have known in person.

Ramanuja was primarily a Vedantist, but he taught release through knowledge of the Lord *Vishnu*, by devotion (*bhakti*) to him, and by meditation on him. Ramananda worshiped *Rama* and *Sita,* and taught salvation through *bhakti* to *Rama*. Although he was a Brahman, and reserved the priestly function to his caste, among his disciples were a Moslem, a Jat, a Shudra, a woman, and an outcaste. Namdev, some of whose verses are included in the *Granth,* was a low-caste (tailor) poet of the heart, widely influential in the Maratha and the Panjab country. Kabir gave evidence of the interaction of Hindu and Moslem thought, of the interplay of Vishnuism and Sufism, in particular. In the *Granth Sahib* are 74 hymns, and 243 *slokas* or "verses," of his composition.

Kabir.—Kabir (1440–1518 A.D.) was a younger contemporary, and possibly a disciple, of Ramananda, a Hindu *bhakta* who taught in Benares. To what fold Kabir belonged by birth is still disputed. His mother may have been a Brahman. His name is Moslem (Kabir is Arabic for "great," the *Koran* applies the title *al-Kabir* to *Allah*). His father may have been a Moslem weaver. Legend says that at his death both Hindus and Moslems claimed his body, the one to burn, the other to bury it; that flowers were miraculously substituted and the body snatched away; that Hindus burned half the flowers at Benares, and the Moslems buried half at Maghar (where Kabir-disciples are still in charge of his tomb). Reared in a Moslem family of poor weavers in Benares, he was subject to the influences of both Islam and Hinduism. On adopting the religious life, he gave instruction to Hindus and Moslems alike. He gained admission once to a sect of Vishnuism, but he was much opposed to idols. He was affected by Sufi mysticism. He felt commissioned to a reconciliation of mystical Islam and non-idolatrous sects of Hinduism. In the end he was spurned by both parties, and became a free-lance in religion, establishing another sect, known as Kabirpanthis, "followers of the *way* of Kabir." There are 650,000 of them still, mostly in the Central Provinces, quite sectarian, and typically Hindu.

Kabir wrote in blunt, unpolished *Hindi,* but his ideas are susceptible of elegant translation. Rabindranath Tagore has beautifully rendered one hundred of his poems into English. The gospel of Kabir was universal. All men were brothers, and alike before God. Kabir accepted *karma* and transmigration, which makes him Hindu, and not Moslem, but he found release through the *love* of God. He was a rigid theist; denounced idols; questioned the validity of *Vedas, Puranas,* and *Koran;* urged men to an immediate apprehension of the Divine. He proclaimed that men might find God, the Real, in their own homes, in their own souls. He found God both in nature and in man, yet distinct from both. He was a *bhakta,* holding that religion without *bhakti* was no religion, whatever its asceticism, pilgrimages, almsgiving, or intelligence. Said he, "Utter the name of God: He extinguishes birth and death." "I utter his Name, and whatever I see reminds me of Him; whatever I do becomes His worship."

Nanak.—*Guru* Nanak Deva (1470-1540), the "holy teacher Nanak," was a disciple of Kabir. He may have met him in Benares at the age of twenty-six, when Kabir was an old man. He was born of Hindu parents in the village of Talwandi, on the banks of the river Ravi, thirty miles above Lahore; its name has since been changed to Nanakana. His stock, the Khatris, claimed to be of warrior rank, lower than the Rajputs, but higher than the Jats. But trading has been their occupation, rather than war—trading in a higher sense; they have not been petty shopkeepers. They are literate; many civil administrators have been drawn from their ranks by Mughal, and British rulers. They are staunch Hindus, but have furnished most of the *gurus* and priests of Sikhism. The leading *Gurus,* in succession, Nanak, Angad, Amar Das, Ram Das, Arjun, Har Gobind, Har Rai, . . . and Gobind Singh, the last, were all Khatris.

As a boy, Nanak's mind was turned to God. He thought that he might find God better through His mercy, than by a study of the Hindu Scriptures. He questioned the validity of the ceremonies of his caste. He was initiated at the age of nine (this is the customary age of *Brahman* initiates), and invested with the sacred thread of the "twice-born." Yet he wrote in verse that, if he could have mercy for the cotton, contentment for the thread, truth for the twist, and continence for the knot, he would have a sacred cord which would never break, or be soiled, burned, or lost. He pro-

tested caste restrictions, and the authority of the Brahman priesthood, taking eventually to private study, and to wandering about
interviewing various teachers and reformers of the day. Learning
Persian, he began reading Moslem literature (many of the Sufi
writings were in *Persian*).

Married in his youth, he kept his home until after his second son
was born. Thereafter he became a mendicant entirely devoted to
religion. Ordinary occupations had been distasteful to him; he
had an aversion to manual labor, and commercial activity. Once,
indeed, he had entered the service of a Moslem governor; but
ties were irksome to him. Both in private life, and in public service
he remained unhappy. He fulfilled the first two "stages"
(*ashramas*), according to the Hindu standards, those of student,
and of householder; but his soul was "athirst" for God, as he
conceived Him, and his spirit was in rebellion against the times.
As he wandered, he would often pause to say, "I am thine, O
Lord." He retired to the forest, or to the desert, spending day and
night in meditation, prayer, and vigil. He visited the holiest shrines
of India. Pious legend, however, has charted for him several
impossible itineraries. Perhaps he went on pilgrimage to Mecca.
If so, he must have been the first *Hindu* to enter that inviolable
Moslem sanctuary.

Hearing at last a definite, divine call, Nanak was commissioned.
He had disappeared again into the forest, was wrapped in prayerful meditation. He was carried in a vision to God's presence (had
he read the *Koran,* Chapter XVII?), and given a cup of ambrosia
to drink. He heard God say then to him, "I am with thee, I have
given thee happiness, and I shall make happy all who take thy
name. Go thou and repeat My Name; cause others to repeat It.
Abide unspoiled by the world. Practice charity, perform ablutions,[8]
worship, and meditate. My Name is God, the primal *Brahma*.[9]
Thou art the Holy *Guru*." Thus Nanak's quest bore fruit, at last,
and out of these ingredients sprang the Faith. He tarried in the
place of vision several days, and afterward went home to confirm
his renunciation, distributing his possessions to the poor. Having
sat a day in complete silence, he gave utterance to the startling,
revolutionary announcement, "There is neither Hindu, nor
Moslem."

Teachings.—The remainder of his life, some forty years, was

---

[8] This is striking, in the light of Nanak's disdain of ritual.
[9] *Cf.* "From the time of the *Upanishads* on, India is axiomatically monistic or pantheistic . . . the conception of the True One that hath no second, the Brahma."—
M. Bloomfield, in *Studies in the History of Religion,* p. 169.

spent projecting his vision into the "dark age" (*Kaliyuga*), which he asserted lay all about him. He went about in a religious habit of his own invention: the regular lower garment, *dhoti,* and sandals, to which he added a mango-colored jacket, with a white shawl thrown over it; a *qalandar,* or Moslem hat, on his head; a rosary of bones around his neck; and he kept painted on his forehead a saffron mark in the style of the Hindu's *tilak.* For a companion on his wanderings he had a former Moslem servant, Mardāna by name, who was skilful with the *rebeck,* an Arabian stringed instrument. Nanak made verses, through the chanting of which to Mardana's accompaniment he conveyed his teachings. In later years these teachings were assembled by him in a work of modest size, known as the *Japji. Jap* means "remembrance," or praise in remembrance of the Lord; *ji* means "honorable." This work is the nucleus, by many Sikhs considered the epitome, of the *Granth Sahib;* although the *Granth,* with added contents, attained huge proportions at the hands of succeeding *gurus,* and a host of bards, and saints.

From the *Japji* one may gather such elements as these in illustration of the character and teachings of the author: [10] "There is but one God whose Name is True [he is *Sat Nam*], the Creator devoid of fear, and enmity, who is immortal, unborn, self-existent . . . The True One was in the beginning . . . The True One is now also . . . The True One ever shall be. God cannot be described by words . . . Who can sing His power? How shall man become true before God? By walking according to the will of God as predetermined . . . All are subject to His order . . . In every age man subsisteth by God's bounty. By hearing the Name man becometh as *Shiva,* as *Brahma,* as *Indra.* By hearing the Name even the lowly become exalted . . . By hearing the Name man attaineth understanding . . . sorrow and sin are no more. Hearing the Name is equal to making the pilgrimage. By hearing the Name the blind may find their way. By obeying Him man knoweth all worlds, and suffereth neither punishment nor death . . . he attaineth the gate of salvation. When the mind is defiled by sin, it is cleansed by the love of the Name. God is ever True, He is the True Lord, He is the True Name (*Sat Nam*) . . . Hail to Him, the primal, the pure, without beginning, the indestructible, the same in every age."

Here are doctrines of peculiar force, although they were not

altogether original with Nanak; nor are they wholly monotheistic.
They repudiate most of the popular ideas and practices in contemporary Hinduism. They soften the rigor of Islamic monotheism.
They present a more spiritual and socially inclusive religion in
the name of one, all-powerful, loving God, who as Creator and
Supreme Spirit makes no distinctions of high and low, is ignorant
of caste, and looks upon the hearts of men. He may be called by
any name, *Brahma, Hari, Rama,* or *Allah;* but He is neither
Brahma, Hari, Rami, nor *Allah.* Nanak's faith was that of the
inner light, shining from inner truth and understanding. He
emphasized the unity of the Supreme. Yet he did not escape either
polytheism or pantheism. He practically assumed the Hindu
pantheon, and added *Allah,* to make them subservient to his God
of the True Name. He did not treat them as the fiction of man's
mind. There are implications of pantheism in the indescribable
unity of God. His virtual rejection of the world tended toward
the notion of the world as *maya.* Actually, he did not reject the
world; but his world-renunciation was not to be gained by
pilgrimages, ritual exercises, and solitary asceticism. He accepted
the doctrines of *karma* and transmigration,[11] inconsistent as
they are with true *bhakti,* and religious vision. He was both Moslem
and Hindu in his emphasis on fate: "The die is cast, and no one
can undo it." He is typically Hindu in the place he gives the *guru*
as man's guide in matters spiritual; although he exalted *guru*ship,
in un-Hindu fashion, above the scriptures (at least above all other
scriptures than his own). It seemed consistent for the Sikhs in
after years to hold the *guru* like an *avatara.*

Nanak's contribution was transformed. His brotherhood of
man became a brotherhood of Sikh believers, and, in the process,
introduced to India one of the most stirring periods in her history.
Nanak was more or less a quietist, and many of his later followers were "easy-going." Normally, the movement would have
lapsed back into Hinduism, or borne the character of Hinduism
under some sectarian name (there is, in fact, a sect of Satnamis).
But that it did not fade into the common Hindu day, is due to the
need which soon arose to support both separate existence and
peculiar tenets by appeal to arms. The militant, political development began under the fifth, and sixth *Gurus,* Arjun, and Har
Gobind, culminating under the tenth, and most powerful, Gobind
Singh.

11 The third *Guru,* Amar Das, built a well with 84 steps to the water, each signify-
ing 100,000 rebirths—8,400,000 in all, through which the soul must pass, if the cycle
be not broken.

Persecution.—The Sikhs had frequently been persecuted by the Moslems. The *Gurus,* especially, were objects of Mughal tyranny. There were questions of property, taxation, and fealty at stake. Nanak had once been a slave to Babur. Amar Das was often reviled by Moslem villagers, as he bore water from the Beas River; they often broke his water-jars. The Sikhs endured with forbearing for a while, resolved the more to organize in their defense. Ram Das and Arjun gave prestige to the faith by establishing the Golden Temple at Amritsar. Ram Das had made the *guru*ship hereditary. Arjun, an able leader, in some ways the most notable of the *Gurus,* made Amritsar the great Sikh capital, giving to Sikhism both a civil body and a political integrity. He collected the scriptures; Nanak's *Japji;* writings of preceding *Gurus* and his own; and other items of a kindred quality; calling the whole collection the *Adi Granth,* the "Original Book." Spiritual pontiff of the order, he made himself the civil executive; he instituted various measures, such as taxation, for the maintenance of a State. Mughal suspicions were ultimately aroused by the wealth, activity, and influence of the order. The Emperor Jahangir summoned Arjun to his Court, charging him with the propagation of a false religion, and with treason on the basis of aid which Arjun had once given Jahangir's son, the rebel prince Khusru. No compromise was possible. Report says that the Emperor—doubtless, seeking solid ground for action [12]—commanded Arjun to expunge from the *Granth* all passages at variance with orthodox Moslem and Hindu doctrine (Jahangir was a *Sunni* Moslem). This the faithful *Guru* declined to do, saying that he desired the dissemination of the truth. He was delivered to imprisonment, cruel torture, and death, although many Sikhs have believed that their beloved leader was rescued by God himself from the bonds and wounds of his tormentors, and taken bodily to heaven.

It was said of Arjun that "his necklace was his sword-belt," but the *Gurus* after him relied on more than necklaces. They kept a body-guard, and maintained an army. Every Sikh became a soldier, a *sepahi* ("sepoy"). The ninth *Guru* Teg Behadur (1664–1675) had opportunity to take sides with the Hindu victims of the bitter persecutions of the Mughal bigot, Aurangzeb. In a true sense he became a martyr to the cause of freedom in religion and in thought. Captured by the Mughals, charged with blasphemy

---

[12] The ground he found was untenable from the strict Moslem point of view, for the Sikhs were a "people of the Book," and as such were entitled to religious toleration.

and rebellion, he was tortured for a while, and finally beheaded. This *Guru,* standing once on the roof of his prison, gazing off toward Bombay, prophesied the conquest of India by the British. His martyrdom redoubled the growing warlike tendencies of Sikhism, and afforded his son, Gobind, who as a lad of fifteen, succeeded him, both reason and occasion to organize the *Khalsa* or association of the "Pure," and to institute the Baptism of the Sword.

The Khalsa.—The times of Gobind Singh (1675–1708) were full of trouble. Aurangzeb, the zealous Sunni, was bent upon the extirpation of the rival faith. At first young Gobind retired out of range, while his people met the fury of attack. With strength of years and mind, he ventured forth, called his men about him, and bound them to the *Khalsa* and himself by an impressive rite, initiating them into a substantial fellowship of suffering, and triumphant devotion. In the center of the camp he put volunteers to the test. He asked for five willing to die, then and there, for him and the cause, saying that God had demanded a blood-sacrifice in payment for His favor. From those who willingly responded, he chose five, and took them one by one into the tent. Four times he emerged with a sword-blade dripping blood. The fifth time— he brought out all the men alive; a goat had been substituted for the sacrifice. Following the ordeal, the ordinance of Baptism (*pahul* or "gate") was administered first to the five, then to the multitude, and to all recruits thereafter. With daggers (two-edged for the man; one-edged for the woman), sweet water was stirred in an iron bowl; and with this water, this *amrits-ar* or nectar, each person swearing fealty was anointed. Each man thereafter took the name of *singh* or "lion." Each *singh* has since adorned himself with the "five *kakkas*":[13] the *kesha,* a top-knot (his hair is never cut; he is a *keshdari,* "hairy one") ; *kanghi,* a comb (usually worn at the back of the head) ; *kará,* an iron bracelet; *kirpan,* a short sword; and *kachá,* "shorts." These are the marks of "pure" Sikhs, whom one need not mistake for other Indians.

Fiery souls flocked to the banners of Gobind. Soon he had an army for offense against his enemies. He was not always successful in battle with them; in fact, he was often in sore straits, at times near death. His sons were captured, and slain at Sirhind, near the city of Ambala; Sikhs, as they pass the fateful spot still cast stones of revenge and scorn. Gobind escaped capture by the Mughals, but fell victim to an enraged Pathan whose father he

13 *Kakka* is *Panjabi* for the letter "K."

had slain. Before he died, however, he had enspirited his countrymen for exploits later on.

Gobind Singh ordained that, after him, there should be no *Guru,*
but only the *Khalsa,* and the *Granth Sahib.* He made over the
Khalsa to God, he said, and the *Granth* alone might serve as
head of the community. Unable to secure an authentic copy from
its custodians, he composed a Book of his own from the best
materials available. He took the *Japji* without alteration, nor did
he alter the essential teachings of the line of *Gurus.* Sayings of
his own are included in the volume, laying stress upon the welfare
of the nation. Sikhs, said he, should continue the worship of the
one, invisible, true God; should honor the memory of Nanak and
his successors; but should bow to naught save the *Holy Book.* "He
who wishes to behold the *Guru,* let him search the *Granth.* The
Guru will dwell with the *Khalsa* . . . Wherever five Sikhs are
gathered together, I am also there with them . . . Consider the
Khalsa as the *Guru."* He bade his people ignore temples and
shrines, except the *Darbar Sahib* in Amritsar; to discard the
sacred thread of the Hindus; to ascribe no special sanctity to
the Ganges, or any water, save the nectar of the Baptism; to confine their ritual bathing to times of worship at the Temple. He
reëstablished the ban on caste, throwing the ranks open to all.

Later Sikhism.—Sikhism has experienced during the last two
centuries certain doctrinal modifications, and has suffered from
sectarian division. It has yielded much to the pressure of Hinduism.
The *Guru* has become an *avatara,* like *Rama,* and *Krishna* to the
Hindus. Nanak is no longer a wandering minstrel singing of God
in the hearts of men; he is no longer man's guide in the darkness
of *Kaliyuga;* he is an incarnation of God. "*Guru* Nanak is God,[14]
the Supreme Brahma," one Sikh writer has said. An inscription
on the Golden Temple proclaims Nanak the incarnation of *Rama.*
Many Sikhs believe that he worked such miracles as the cure of
leprosy, the drawing of water from dry ground, and the restoration
of the dead to life. In the same vein, every *Guru* is an incarnation;
each successor was an incarnation of Nanak; all together are a
ten-fold manifestation of the Divine Spirit. The *Granth Sahib*
has become an idol, itself a symbol and manifestation of Divinity;
it is Revelation. The Sikhs are afraid of *Maya:* "Illusion hath
reduced the world to subjection," but "*maya* approacheth not him
whom God mercifully associateth with the saints." The common

[14] He is called today Nanak Dev. "Deva" is "God"; although *deva* and *devi*
(fem.) are often used by Hindus as merely honorific titles.

people have never questioned the validity of *karma* and trans-migration (nor did Nanak escape these theories). The *Granth* says, "Impute not blame to anyone, but rather to thine own *karma*," and "This soul hath dwelt in many wombs"; "The un-grateful shall wander in transmigration." Caste has been allowed to reassert itself. Sikhs discriminate between those who, though equal by religion, are unequal socially. The Mazhabis, of outcaste, or Moslem origin, are Sikhs only by religion; yet the *Granth* pro-claims that "he who knoweth God is a Brahman"; and Gobind said, "The four classes shall be one, each calling on the *Guru*." The faith has yielded much to Hinduism, and very little to Islam. It is Hindu both in its virtues and its weaknesses. Its *bhakti* is Hindu. While man's "body is the field of his acts," salvation is by the mercy of God. Monogamy and sobriety are commended. Early marriage (cohabitation) is forbidden, and the injunction is, "If possible, drink not at all." Some Sikhs, however, consume large quantities of *bhang* or Indian hemp. Sikhs usually burn their dead, as Hindus do. They are creatures of their environment.

Sects.—It is natural that the "easy-goers" have yielded more than the "singhs." There are the two main groups today:

(1) The Sahajdaris, "easy-going" followers of Nanak, chiefly. They are not distinguished by peculiar outward signs. They shave their heads, much in the manner of the Hindus (are often called "Monas" or "shaven"); and, like the Hindus, they indulge freely in tobacco. They have little interest in Gobind Singh. They differ little from unwarlike Hindus.

(2) The Keshdaris or Singhs. They are the major strength of Sikhism today; perhaps they are in the majority. They stand distinct from their neighbors, and constitute the party of progress and reform. They revere all the *Gurus,* but Arjun and Gobind above others. While the two groups have never been antagonistic toward each other, the Keshdaris, since the recent Sikh revival, have declined to give their daughters in marriage to "easy-going" husbands,—unless they would first submit to the rite of *pahul*. The Singhs have lately sought to revitalize the faith, to redeem many of the shrines from careless administration and corruption. The most energetic reformers of the lot have been the Akalis, "the deathless ones," or Nihangs, "those free from care." They are the bravest of the soldiers. They eat no meat; they drink no spirituous liquors; but they do eat bhang. They are bitter toward the Moslems. They are, in their own view, the true warriors of *Akál Purukh*, "Immortal Spirit," their designation for *Sat Nam*.

They salute one another with the Sikh war-cry, *"Wah Guruji
ka Khalsa, Wah Guruji ki Fatah,"* or, "Hail, the *Khalsa* of the
Guru; Hail, the Victory of the *Guru."*

It is one of the strangely heartless turns of time and circumstance, that Hinduism should take unwittingly heavy toll of Sikh
vitality. Perhaps the historian of religion will recognize that the
Sikhs did something to save India from Islam. They were an
obstinate bar, at a critical time, saving much of Hinduism from
the common enemy. We might express the hope for every
energetic, reforming member of the Sikh community, who adheres
to the religion at its best, shorn of lesser elements, that his "time"
(*kál,* "death") may not come soon; that he may be in truth
a-káli.

CHAPTER XIV

The Hebrew-Jewish Faith

Modern Jewish religion has an ancient Hebrew ancestry. The Jews were nourished in the "House of Israel," and represent a noble lineage of at least three thousand years; the actual beginnings are conjectural. The general background is "Semitic," the common soil of Judaism, Christianity, and Islam. We are, at last, therefore, on more familiar ground, with greater need than ever of impartiality. We are now concerned, at least indirectly, with *our own* traditions. It will be interesting to learn how three great, enduring faiths sprang from the narrow, common soil; and no less interesting to discover how and why these three have been antagonistic.

The Jews most nearly represent the ancient, common heritage. Their movement has shown marvellous endurance. All the world is conscious of it. Jews have, in a peculiar measure, the title of the universal people. Their story is, unquestionably, the most dramatic of all the records of popular religious movements, which linger in world-history. For downright human interest there is nothing to excel the story, scene by scene, among the nations. Despite their wide dispersion, and notwithstanding the fact that in their movement all types of thought and every form and feature of religion are combined, there are certain signs and habits which classify this people as of one peculiar stock. Perhaps it was ironical, that within one year (1933) there could be held a pageant of the Jew in history,[1] showing something of his contributions to the world, and that the Nazi Germans could remind the nations of an essential conflict between Jewish and nationalistic aspirations.

Population.—The Jewish population of the world today is over fifteen millions. The total is an estimate, for many lands have never had a census; and some figures are not up-to-date. Recently, here and there, the distribution has been again dis-

---

[1] Such a pageant was held at the Century of Progress Exhibition, in Chicago, in July, 1933.

turbed by politics and other factors. In fact, the disturbance incidental to the World War, whereby millions of these "wanderers" were set in motion, has not yet subsided. There were nearly seven million Jews in pre-War Russia,[2] but the number now is less than half of that; and traditional Jewry has fared scarcely better under Bolsheviks and Communists than it did in earlier, frightful Tsarist days. Perhaps, they will fare better in the territory recently assigned them by the Soviets for the building of their own "republic."[3] The fifteen hundred thousand in the Soviet Ukraine may have been augmented recently. There are about three million Jews in Poland; about one million in Rumania. There were 500,000 in Germany before Hitler came to power; but, since then, there has been an exodus, especially to Poland. There were half a million recently in Hungary, and about 300,000 in Czecho-Slovakia. Within the British Empire are 725,000, including 300,000 in the British Isles; in the French Empire, 750,000. Altogether, there are about 9,000,000 in Europe, 5,000,000 in the Americas, 1,000,000 in Asia, and 500,000 in Africa. Except for Tanganyika and Bolivia, no important state or community in the world lacks its Jewish representative. There are small groups in such widely separated places as Alaska (500), Surinam (750), the Belgian Congo (175), Hong Kong (150), Hawaii (75), the Virgin Islands (70), Malta (35), and Panama (25). There are 12,000 in China, and 1,000 in Japan; 4,000 in Spain, 40,000 in Persia, 25,000 in Moslem Arabia, 82,000 in Turkey, and 165,000 in Palestine. The American Jews are mainly in the United States, half the total living in the State of New York. The New York metropolitan area, with nearly 2,000,000, is the largest Jewish center in the world. This locality might be seriously referred to as the Promised Land, long sought by harassed Judaism. How long it may remain so is a secret of the coming years, a question which the Jew himself must answer. No other "promised land," Palestine, especially, has proved a permanent asylum. Jews have become peculiarly an urban people, and, on this account, may never have again a Canaan of their own. While some of their dispersions have been forced upon them, they have often scattered of their free will; and they have often held long residence in places of severest persecution. The "peculiar" Jew, whom the world has known for two and one-half millennia, comes of the tribes of Benjamin and Judah.

[2] Exclusive of Russian Poland.
[3] Biro-Bidjan. *Cf. New York Times*, Feb. 28, 1934.

The descendants of the other "sons of Israel" have long been "lost" among the nations. How the families of Judah and Benjamin have *preserved* themselves among the nations, and what the glorious heritage is, which these two sons of Israel transmitted, is the burden of our present chapter. We shall follow them not merely through the major channel of their historical migration.

Jews in China.—The chief community of Chinese Jews was located in the inland province of Honan, in K'ai-feng-fu. It was founded prior to 1100 A.D., and endured with varying fortunes until the nineteenth century. There was another early settlement in the port-city of Ningpo. To-day, the Jews of China live mainly in the trading-centers on the coast.[4] Most of them are late-comers, rather than descendants of any ancient colonists; many are transients "from every nation under heaven." [5]

Tradition records an *ancient* settlement in China. Possibly, Jews of Persia went thither overland before the Christian Era, engaging in the silk trade. Two Moslem Arab merchants, who were in China (having gone by sea) in the ninth century, brought the report that "Jews had been settled in the Empire from time immemorial." These Arabs may have encountered one of the many legends of the "Ten Lost Tribes." But that they actually found Jews in China, we must believe. They reported that the Emperor knew about Noah, Moses, and the Hebrew prophets; and that he had portraits of them.[6] No permanent settlement, however, can be dated positively earlier than the ninth century, A.D. They came by land. The immigrants of later centuries doubtless came by sea, from India, especially. The K'ai-feng-fu community maintained itself for over seven centuries, its fortunes, meanwhile, varying. It had its synagogue, and several times enlarged it. It was fashioned in the temple-style of China, but this was no more than the appropriation of a local setting for their own, peculiar ritual. They had their *Torah,* Law, and worshiped the One God, Yahweh. They must have held strictly to the Law, for their Chinese neighbors called them "the sect (*chiao*) which extracts the sinews," that is, of the meat they eat (*cf., Genesis* 32:33). They took on Chinese ways, including costume and language (but not for ritual); but they avoided pork, of which the Chinese are so fond. They did not hesitate

---

4 Harbin, in Manchukus, is one of the newer centers of the Far Eastern Jews.
5 *Cf.* S. Mendelssohn, *The Jews of Asia*, pp. 133–163.
6 We need not believe that he had merely learned of them through the *Koran,* which Moslems brought, or through the *Bible*, which Nestorian Christians may have brought. It is not always possible, however to sift traditions.

to intermarry with the Chinese, but they seem to have preserved their own peculiar features; a record says, "their look was quite different from that of other persons." Some ancient rites and customs were surrendered, as time went by,—*not* including the rite of circumcision. But throughout the centuries, they suffered no essential loss of their racial and religious character. They did not renounce their faith, and *live*. That is, the community as such, while it endured, was Jewish. This may be observed of the later communities, also, in spite of individual defections. And it is a question, whether the direct line of any Jew who has renounced the faith soon loses its peculiar ("racial"?) quality.[7]

Indian Communities.—The Jews of India have composed another fascinating chapter in the universal story. Tradition says they went there first in the days of the glorious King Solomon.[8] It is better to assume that they first went thither in the early centuries of the Christian era, fleeing from persecutions [9] in Persia and Arabia. Many of the Indian community live in Bombay City and the neighboring town, Kolaba, in Calcutta, and down the Malabar coast, in the native state of Cochin. The Kolaba and Cochin settlements are ancient, and fairly large. Other Jews, elsewhere, are few in number and comparatively late arrivals; they are Sephardi, sometimes known as "Spanish." [10] Many of them are not explicitly enumerated in the census; they have been, carelessly, at times, included with the miscellaneous "others," after Hindus, Moslems, Christians, Sikhs, Jains, Parsis, and "Animists" have been recorded. Nevertheless, they are well organized, and many of them are alike "remarkable for their wealth, their liberality, and their capacity for business." They are able rivals of both Parsis and Jains. These statements apply, also, of the larger groups of Cochin and Kolaba.

The Kolaba Jews are known as *Beni Israel,* or "Sons of Israel," which might indicate an early settlement. They are mostly agriculturists, oilmen,—and soldiers; a few are schoolmasters; some fill posts in the India medical service. On the whole, they are industrious and thrifty; many are landowners, and not one a beggar. They are not generally abstemious, as their Hindu

---

[7] There are many cases of "converted" Jews; for example, Samuel Isaac Joseph Schereschewsky, of the Chinese community. Born in Lithuania, educated in America, whither he came from China, and where he became a Christian, he was made a Bishop of the Protestant Episcopal Church of China, and founded St. John's College, a leading institution of Shanghai.

[8] "India," in this case, was probably *Arabia*. The two were frequently confused.

[9] Some Christians, and some Moslems, later, persecuted them.

[10] The other modern type, Ashkenazim, or "German," is not often found in Asia.

neighbors are; but, like the Hindus, they indulge in costly feasts and ceremonies. They were "discovered," in the eleventh century, A.D., by a Cochin Jewish traveler, who published an account of them. His curiosity had been aroused by reference to "Saturday oilmen" in the vicinity,—so called, because they did *not* ply their trade on Saturday. Upon further inquiry, he found them to be Jews holding fast to certain vestiges of Hebrew law and ritual, and preserving definite, plausible, but unreliable traditions of their origin. Many of their original trappings had been lost in migration, much of their old faith had grown dim in isolation; but their Jewish spirit lived within them in their "heathen" situation. The traveler testifies that an ineradicable minimum of distinction had endured. Like all the Jews of India, they have seldom suffered persecution; the chief exception was the "inquisition," in the sixteenth century, by the Catholic Portuguese, and this fell mainly on the Jews of Cochin. While the Jews of mediæval Europe were often living under iron rule, and often expelled, as from England, France, Spain, Holland, and Germany, their brethren in the East had peace. The Hindu attitude in matters of religion is tolerant indifference.

The Cochin Jews exhibit interesting phenomena, especially with reference to environment. They may have settled from Persia in the first Christian century, or from South Arabia (Yemen), in the sixth. It appears that they first occupied Cranganore, whither a certain Joseph Rabban [11] came, with "seventy-two families,"—from Persia (?); more likely, from Aden, in Arabia. There is evidence of a charter granted the colonists in the eighth century by native rulers—to the "white" Jews, in particular (see below). They were given rights of residence, organization, and trade; and of the undisturbed exercise of their religion. Their "head" was allowed the high privilege of riding on a horse, or on an elephant. They enjoyed for nearly a thousand years the status of a "state," increasing meanwhile in wealth and numbers, and multiplying branches on the Cochin coast. Their numbers may have grown to 80,000. Then came the devastating war (16th century) between the Dutch and the Portuguese. During a period of Portuguese ascendency, Cranganore was destroyed, and the Jewish state demolished. When the Dutch prevailed, the Jews, their allies, reëstablished themselves in Cochin town. Later on, they fared as well under the English East India Company, and renewed their strength. Their worship

11 Joseph may have been a *"rabbi."*

was conducted in their own synagogues, under the ancient *Law*, with the rabbinical *Book of Prayer*.

There have been two types of Jews in Cochin, "white" and "black,"—with some "brown" variations. The latter claim to have been the earlier in India; the former claim the higher rank. This evidence of caste consciousness need not surprise us. The two groups have declined to eat together, or to intermarry. The whites dress much after the fashion of the Brahman; the garb of the blacks resembles that of their Moslem neighbors. Do the colors represent light Persians, on the one hand, and dark Arabs, on the other? Or, is one the "Arya-color," and the other "dasya"?[12] The darker stock may indeed be the older on the scene, their color due to longer residence under the Indian sun and, possibly, to intermarriage with Dravidians. The "whites" may parallel their claim of superiority with that of the North Indian stock which "brahmanized" South India. Both types have made concessions to their environment: in language, costume, occupation, and marriage. Nevertheless, a Dutch admiral, who visited the Malabar coast in the eighteenth century, could bear witness that they had retained, "both men and women, those characteristic features which distinguish this peculiar people from all other nations of the earth."

Some notable additions to the Indian Jewish constituency were made about 1700 A.D., after the English East India Company had established control of the western coast. Coming from Baghdad, they settled in Surat and Bombay. The former city had been wrested from the Portuguese; the latter came to Charles II as part of the dowry of his bride, Catherine of Braganza (Portugal). Jacob Semah of Baghdad settled in Surat in 1680; others followed him; they built a synagogue, laid out a *bayt hayyim* (an "abode of life," *i.e.*, a cemetery), and organized the colony. Later, they moved to Bombay, where they were cordially received by the Beni Israel. One of the early settlers from Baghdad was David Sassoon, who built up an extensive business in Bombay, and dominated the opium trade with China. His family has constituted the most important unit in modern Indian Jewry, being noted alike for its wealth, philanthropy, and devotion to education and religion. They have been the benefactors of the Beni Israel, and of their co-religionists in Palestine.

Australian Jews.—What the "wandering Jew" may accomplish in little more than a century may be adequately illustrated

[12] Recall the color-line in ancient India.

from his experience in Australia. When the doors were opened to this virgin territory, Jews were among the first to enter, enjoying religious freedom and finding a hospitable home. Their numbers have increased to over twenty thousand, and they have had their conspicuous share in the development of the land, in agriculture, stock-raising, industry, and politics. Synagogues are established in all the major cities. Jews have been mayors of nearly all the capitals. Many have sat in the state parliaments. Some have founded public journals. And the Australian theater was established by a Jew. Jews have found opportunity for the exercise of all their talents, usually, however, with equality in social rank withheld.

In even the freest non-Jewish situation, the Jew has either not forgotten, or has never been allowed to overlook, the fact that he is judged "peculiar." Even where he has most completely adapted himself, he has not escaped suspicion. It may not be miraculous, but it is a mystery that the "chosen people" of Yahweh are "peculiar." A rabbi recently declared that "Israel still runs true to form as the riddle among the peoples of the world." [13] We may not finally understand them and their faith, but we must set about examining the facts as their ritual and their history disclose them. We may discover *how,* and something of the reason *why* the Jews, who have never been a "missionary" people, are spread abroad so generally, have retained their solidarity, and claim to have a universal faith.

Symbols.—First, let us look at certain outward symbols of the faith, especially modern ritual. Life is largely dominated by common practices sanctioned by tradition. There is no central, religious authority, no single, ecclesiastical dignitary who exercises universal rule. The order in each country is autonomous; every community and each congregation is self-governing. There is no longer a Jewish priesthood; the rabbis are laymen; Judaism is a lay religion. Creeds are foreign to the Jewish spirit, except one, the Shema, which is brief and commonly accepted: "Hear (*shema*), O Israel; the Lord our God is One Lord" (*Deut.* 6:4). The Jews have a theology, partly due to age, but more because of modern controversy, especially with Christians; they have, therefore, a statement of the faith. But ritual is more important. Judaism is a thoroughgoing, ritualistic system, with highly complex forms, embodying ancient mysteries.

The divisions among Jews are mainly due to ritual, rather than

[13] *Cf. The Atlantic Monthly,* July, 1933.

to creed. There are two chief divisions: (1) the *Ashkenazim,* including Russian, German, and American; they constitute ninety percent of the Jewish total; and (2) the *Sephardim,* including Spanish, Portuguese, North African, Near, and Far Eastern, Jews. Most Jews of both divisions are "orthodox." "Reform Judaism" is a very recent product of America, where its congregations number less than two hundred. It is an influential variation and development, enjoying wealth and educational prestige; but it represents an assimilationist minority, many of whose members ultimately may join mysteriously the ranks of the "Ten Lost Tribes." That is, a few may achieve complete acceptance among non-Jews. Since "reform" Jews tend toward dejudaization, this movement may be disregarded in our present study. The overwhelming bulk of Jews are orthodox, who look for their preservation to their own conservation of their traditional belief and ritual. Having been true to themselves and their tradition, they have survived, with no great loss of numbers, in the end, the sufferings and struggles of a wide dispersion. They hold themselves dependent still on their essential character. This is, virtually, the one and only dominant authority in the Jewish Church. Within the range of this authority, the two types of Jews exist. The distinction was unknown among the ancient Hebrews, but the types are recognized by anthropologists, and by Jewish usage and tradition.

The synagogue is the modern stronghold of the faith; the ancient *Law* is its foundation, and prayer has been for centuries the sacrificial incense which pervades the sanctuary. The religion of the Synagogue is a survival from the destruction, in 70 A.D., of the Palestinian state and the Temple in Jerusalem. It has conserved belief in both the early written, and the later oral, Law, as if revealed together at Mt. Sinai; and it has allowed for special institutions, which the prophets and the rabbis had begun. It has never lost the vision of the Restoration of the People (*cf.* Zionism), and has not consented to a program of "reform," by which to judaize the world. While cherishing its past, it has inspired piety independent of the ancient situation and broader than the land from which the people scattered. The local synagogue is not a place of sacrifice, nor even a place where merely the ancient *Law* is recognized; it is the symbol of the value of the ideal faith.

The Synagogue.—Synagogues have been built in no fixed form. Most, perhaps, have been rectangular, after the pattern of the Temple in Jerusalem; but some have been octagonal.

Their name is *Greek* for the *Hebrew keneset,* "assembly." The "house of the people," or the "house of assembly" (*bet ha-keneset*), was an ancient institution. There were many of these houses, according to the need, whatever the motive of assembly. Their use continued even after worship was centrally provided for in Jerusalem. After the "Return" (to Palestine from the Babylonian Captivity) in the sixth century, B.C., the Jews worshiped in these "houses" side by side with the cult of the restored Temple. Hellenistic Jews first called them "synagogues." After the destruction of the Temple (in 70 A.D.), and the Dispersion, these buildings multiplied, and have been the centers of the faith as it spread throughout the world. Each synagogue has been, usually, a unit within a group of structures, which includes the schoolroom (for children learning the religion, and adults who read the *Law*), the slaughter-house (to provide the *kosher* meat), and the *mikvah,* or place of ritual ablution; with a cemetery adjacent.

The synagogue [14] is the habitation of the Ark of the Covenant (*cf. Deut.* 10:2; *Ex.* 25; I *Kings* 8:1–8), which contains the scroll of the *Law*. This rests in the sanctuary (by the east wall, perhaps), covered by a drapery. Before and above the Ark hangs the perpetual lamp; and seven-branched candlesticks may flank it. The reader's desk, from which the *Law* is read, rests on the center of the floor before the Ark, and facing it. Along the side walls of the building, and in the balconies are rows of seats, or stalls. There is a women's gallery (which was once a separate court, for the synagogue was essentially an assembly hall for men). There is no imagery beyond the Lion of Judah, the six-pointed Star of David, and fruit and flower designs.

The Sabbath.—The day of public worship, which perpetuates the ancient "Sabbath," [15] is the Christian Saturday. It begins, more exactly, at nightfall on the Christian's Friday. Candles are then lighted by the mother in the home, while the men attend the synagogue, engaging in a service culminating in the blessing (*kiddush*) of the wine-cup. It closes on Saturday at sundown with the *Habdalah* ceremony, with its odor of spices, the sputtering of wine on burning tapers, and the blessing of the wine-cup of salvation. It is traditionally a day of rest and joy,—complete rest from all labor, and satisfaction in the care of God. To a degree, rest has been enforced by prohibitions; the *Mishna* (*c.* 200 A.D.) enumerates thirty-nine kinds of "work" which may not be done on

---

14 Our description is based upon the *conventional* type of building.
15 The term is derived from the *Babylonian shabatum,* the day of the full moon.

Sabbaths, including the lighting of a week-day fire. These prohibitions have been irksome in modern times, and devices have been
used to circumvent them. As with other faiths, the Jewish, also,
has had need of adaptation to a changing world.

Of the three services of Sabbath worship, the one held on Saturday morning is the longest and most important. It occupies, when
fully chanted, about three hours, lead by the minister (*hazzan,*
"cantor") and the rabbi. Certain parts belong by right and custom
to descendants of the priests and Levites—if there are such. The
cantor is a layman who leads the chanting, partly from the *Law,*
mostly from the *Psalms,* which form the groundwork of the
service. The rabbi is a layman who provides the sermon, if there
is one. Ordinarily, he is the teacher in the community, the
authority on matters of the *Law,* the ritual, and food. During the
Sabbath morning service, the scroll of the *Law* (the *Torah* and the
Talmud; see below) is taken from the Ark and carried solemnly
in procession through the synagogue and placed awhile upon the
reading-desk. The whole *Torah* (the "Pentateuch") is read each
year on Sabbath mornings.

The service may begin with the chanting of a psalm of praise,
or the singing of a hymn, to God. Prayers of thanksgiving may
follow, for the blessings of God in daily life; and a prayer for
guidance. Then come readings from the *Torah* and the *Talmud,*
with responses and doxologies, which culminate in the central
item of the liturgy, the Shema: "Hear, O Israel, the Lord thy
God, the Lord is One." After this comes the recital of the
"eighteen blessings" (*shemoneh esreh*) of praise, petition, and
thanksgiving, followed by a period of meditation. Then the men—
at least, a few of them who will—take part in the reading of the
Law, and in the further recitation of the "blessings." Prayers are
included for specific individuals and the whole assembly, with
the "mourners' response" in memory of the dead. The service may
end with the singing of a hymn.

The ritual preserves a note of tragedy. Whence came it? It is
not the solemn note of sacramental worship, for sacrifice in the
manner of the ancient ritual [16] has disappeared; not the burnt
offering of national repentance, but the sorrow of the broken heart.
It is the tragedy of Israel's very life career, symbolized, for
example, by the new synagogue at Rome—on the site of the
ancient Roman ghetto. One may breathe within the new structure

---

[16] After the Temple was rebuilt in 516 B.C., and worship had been centralized,
sacrifice was prohibited elsewhere. Synagogues were never centers of the sacrifice.

the mediæval atmosphere of persecution, suspicion, and slander, from which the Jew was wont to escape by refuge within his own quarters. He lived in European ghettos for five hundred years. There he lived by social pressure the life which centered in the synagogue; there he attained coherence and peculiar solidarity, and learned to love above all else the *Law* of Yahweh. The ghetto-vase is shattered, but the scent of the rose, and of the bitter rue it held, still lingers. The Jew's religion and his life are one; his ritual commemorates his life; hence the tragic note with which he celebrates his length of days at God's disposal.

The Law.—The *Law* is the foundation of the faith. "Law" has both a special and a general meaning. Primarily, it means the *Torah*, the "Law" of Moses (*c.* 1500 B.C.), who the first "law-giver." *Genesis, Exodus, Leviticus, Numbers,* and *Deuteronomy* are associated with his name. They compose the *Pentateuch,* or "five-fold" writing.[17] This is the essential *Torah.* It tells the story of the "beginnings" of the world: "In the beginning, God," and nothing else; creation came from nothing, by the "word" of God, and took form according to His will; He shaped a man out of the dust of the ground, and gave him for a "soul" His own breath; a woman was made from a rib of the man as he slept—they are the parents of the human race. It tells the story of the "fathers" of the House of Israel, Abraham, Isaac, and Jacob (Israel); of various institutions, such as sacrifice, circumcision, the Sabbath, priests, and kings; of the origin of envy and strife among the Chosen People, and their captivity in "Egypt" (Goshen). It recounts the plagues sent by God upon the Egyptians, forcing Pharaoh to let the People go; the leadership of Moses, and his reorganization of the nation under Yahweh and the *Law,* including the "Ten Commandments." It adds a *priestly* interpretation of the sacrifice, indicates the ritual for the consecration of priests and Levites, enumerates the laws against uncleanness and describes in vivid details the wanderings in the Wilderness. It recapitulates, in *Deuteronomy,*[18] the "repetition of the law," the details of the ritual of religion, and the rules of diet; establishes a calendar of festivals; gives laws for individual and social welfare; and expounds the "covenant" relations between Israel and Yahweh. Such is the substance of the *Torah,* in its special meaning.

The *Torah,* in a general way, is composed of many other writ-

---

17 Although tradition has attributed the *Pentateuch* to Moses, the form in which we have it was not complete before the fourth century, B.C.
18 *Deuteronomy* was actually formulated *c.* 700 B.C. Many of its items had, however, long been current.

ings, also. It may refer to the whole *Canon* of the Jewish Scriptures. This *Canon,* which took form as such about 100 A.D. contains: (1) the *Pentateuch,* (2) the *Nebiim,* or "prophets," and (3) the *Kethubim,* or *Hagiographa,* the "Writings." These are the Jewish *Bible;* Christians call them the *Old Testament.* They were inscribed in *Hebrew* and *Aramaic.* Later (3rd century, B.C.), a translation into *Greek* was made (called the *Septuagint,* or the "Seventy"). There are, in addition, about fifteen sacred writings, called *Apocrypha,*[19] or "secret," which are not included in the Hebrew *Canon;* they are not considered *Torah.* Obviously, the *Canon* assumed form slowly. There is no evidence of any *Scripture* recognized as *sacred* before the 2nd Temple (6th century, B.C.); simply "the Law" existed, divinely revealed. Many factors entered into the process which produced the *Canon,* not the least of which was the final need of Jewish defense against Christianity. The larger *Torah* was defined in contrast with the Christian *Gospels* and many hellenistic writings. The sequence of the writings in the *Canon* is no sure sign as such of the dates of composition; it is established, for the most part, by the sequence of *events* depicted.

The Prophets.—By the sequence of events, the *Nebiim,* or "Prophets," which were actually the first writings (after the requisite culture had developed) follow after the early history. The prophets themselves are fascinating and eternal figures; we should examine some of them:

(1) Elijah, *c.* 875 B.C., was the foe of Queen Jezebel of Tyre and her god Melkart; the champion of the cause of Yahweh against all the *baals,* or "powers" (gods) of Canaan.

(2) Hosea, *c.* 800, in Samaria, was the first prophet of the "love" of Yahweh, who expected Israel to be faithful to him as a bride to her husband. He warned the Israelites [20] of impending chastisement because of national sins; but he prophesied the redemption of the nation through the love of Yahweh.

(3) Amos, *c.* 800, in Judah, declared that Yahweh, disgusted with ritual, cared only for the "offering" of a righteous life, because the very character of God is righteousness. He preached the universality of Yahweh, yet declared that the Hebrews would be punished more severely than other peoples for their sins,— *because* their privileges as the Chosen People were greater. More

---

[19] The *Apocrypha* includes the Books of *Esdras, Tobit,* the *Wisdom of Solomon,* and *Maccabees.*

[20] Hosea prophesied in the "Northern Kingdom" of the Ten Tribes. A division between *Israel* and *Judah* had occurred in 975 B.C.

is expected of the privileged few. He prophesied definitely a judgment upon the nation, but announced that a Remnant would be saved out of the Captivity, and restored again to the Homeland.

(4) Isaiah of Jerusalem, *c.* 750, preached for forty years the majesty and holiness of God. When the Northern Kingdom ("Israel" proper) fell in 721 B.C., he declared to the King of Judah that Samaria's [21] fall was a just punishment for the people's sins, a confirmation of the predictions of Hosea, Amos, and himself; and that Judah, also, if she did not change her ways, was doomed. In obedience to Isaiah and under the wise guidance of other leaders after him, Judah paid attention to her ways, and forestalled her fate (she fell in 587). Inherent strength preserved her as a nation, while the indifferent Ten Tribes lost their identity, and were never reunited. Judah, with Benjamin, is the soil whence sprang the Jews of the Dispersion, and the Christian movement. Her prophet Isaiah crystallized the high teachings of his predecessors, and added a weighty message of his own. He emphasized God's interest in penitence and righteousness, rather than in heredity and ceremony. God had had enough of burnt offerings; considered incense an abomination; hated feasts. He would not hear the prayers of men whose hands were smeared with blood, and whose ways were oppressive of widows and the fatherless.

Isaiah looked for a King to come,—a Messiah,—whose wisdom, might, and beneficence would provide the people peace and plenty. He proclaimed a vision of the whole earth full of the "knowledge of Yahweh." He "saw" a glorious future for Judah —she would be exalted. Under the prophet's influence the worship of Yahweh, meanwhile, centered in the Temple (Solomon's Temple) in Jerusalem. He preached the comforting doctrine of the inviolability of the city and the safety of the people, *if only* the holy sanctuary were kept pure. Indeed, he seems to have believed in the Temple, whatever happened to the people, for it was Yahweh's seat. As if in confirmation of his confidence, when Sennacherib "came down like a wolf on the fold," an outbreak of bubonic plague among the enemy raised their siege, and saved the city. Thereafter the inhabitants believed the word of Isaiah that Yahweh dwelt on Mt. Zion and not on Mt. Sinai. He thought that Yahweh, dwelling within the Holy of Holies, would direct the sifting of the People until the Remnant was left from which the glorious, universal Nation should arise.

---

[21] Samaria was the capital, strongly built; it withstood the Assyrian siege three years.

(5) Micah, a younger contemporary of Isaiah, spoke boldly against idolatry and class oppression. He was not sure that God had any interest in the Hebrews' *material* welfare. He prophesied the ruin of the nation, but assured the people that they would be pardoned who had purged their guilt. He is the author of the famous words, "What doth the Lord require of thee, but to do justly, and to love kindness, and to walk humbly with thy God!" These are his summary of religious law and moral obligation.

(6) Jeremiah [22] c. 625, is the conspicuous and forceful religious guide of Judah during the last forty years of her independence. He leagued himself with the good King Josiah (641–610) to further a thoroughgoing reformation. The nation had sunk into idolatry and shame, under a former ruler. "High places" were rivals of the Temple. Josiah restored the Temple to its primacy, centralized religion once again,[23] abolishing the wayside shrines, destroying the images, and suppressing the pagan priesthood. But, unfortunately, he fell in battle at Megiddo, in a war between Assyria and Egypt (*cf. 2 Chron.* 35:20–25). Thereafter, Jeremiah tried, almost alone, to stem the returning tide of idol-worship, immorality, and false national confidence. He preached the inwardness of Yahweh, pleaded for reverence and devotion in the hearts of men, and emphasized the need of national regeneration. He laid unusual stress upon the value of individual religion, that is, the importance of the individual in religion. Religion formerly had been conceived almost politically. Social welfare was, indeed, religion's obligation, but religion's operation toward that end began within the hearts of individuals. He was confident that even though the nation perish, Yahweh's cause would prosper, if individuals were responsible and true. He had, also, a new idea of Yahweh in relation to all other gods. Yahweh was One, alone, and universal; and the other gods were simply "vanities," unreal. From Moses down, the power of Yahweh had been qualified; Jeremiah was the first unconditional Jewish monotheist.

(7) Ezekiel, *c.* 600, seems to have been a young priest held captive in Babylonia before the fall of Jerusalem—groups of "captives" often passed back and forth. After the great body of his people joined him, he began to inspire them with the hope of a Return; he actually drew up plans of organization, and a ritual of worship, for use when all were once again in Zion. Among

[22] Jeremiah is miscalled(?) the "weeping prophet," probably by having the *Book of Lamentations* associated with his name.

[23] This was accomplished on the authority of the *Law* ("Deuteronomy") which was "found" by the High Priest Hilkiah when the Temple was being renovated.

other things, he specified the dimensions of the Temple, and
provided for a class of Levites, distinct from the priests, for
Temple service. He, too, emphasized the individual's responsibility
before God; he denied that "the sins of the fathers are visited upon
the children," that the "fathers' sour grapes set the children's teeth
on edge." Each individual would be judged on his own merits,
chiefly. But Ezekiel's enthusiasm for the Return, the Temple, and
the ritual made Yahweh somewhat exclusive once again. Yahweh
became again the Jewish God; "foreigners" and the "uncircumcised" would be excluded from the Temple.

(8) "Second Isaiah," [24] the "Isaiah" of the Exile and Captivity,
began to preach in Babylon in 550, about twenty years after
Ezekiel died. A new Persian King, Cyrus, had arisen, and this
prophet counted rightly on his favor toward the Chosen People.
He discerned the monarch's strength and breadth of mind, and
proclaimed him God's "anointed," through whom the People
would be saved. Isaiah II, therefore, prophesied release from
bondage, the return to Judah, the rebuilding of the Temple, and
the exaltation of Yahweh "above all the earth." Cyrus would
conquer Babylon and set the captives free. The Persian captured
Babylon in 538, the prophecy was vindicated, and the Jews
obtained permission to go home. But all did not desire to return!
With tyranny removed, there were advantages of Babylonia. Many
captives had learned trade and commerce during exile; there was
desolation back in Judah. The prophet's message, therefore, took
account of these new facts. He urged upon his people, with im-
passioned words, the view that *they in themselves,* the nation as
a whole, were the Messiah which had been predicted, who would
come to make Yahweh known throughout the earth. Israel itself
was the "Suffering Servant of Yahweh," who had already borne
the chastisement due the nations, and who, by means of further
suffering, would save them, if they repented. Jerusalem, by this
program, would become the center of the world, and the Temple,
the "house of prayer for all the people"! He persuaded 50,000
to return to Judah; and this was half of all the captives. This was
indeed a "remnant"; a nation once 3,000,000 strong had dwindled
to 100,000. But the Remnant was Jewish gold burned free of dross
in the crucible of compromise and slavery.

We have traced, in terms of men, the major teachings of the
Nebiim. There were fateful issues in their times, and inspiration
in their messages. With what mingled feelings of despair and hope,

[24] Cf. *Book of Isaiah,* Chaps. XL–LXVI.

we all, especially the Jews, must recollect their words and deeds.
There are values still for all humanity in their sincere and anxious
"prophesies."

The Writings.—The third portion of the *Canon* is the
Kethubim, the "Writings," which include, with others, the well-
known books of *Psalms, Proverbs, Job, Ecclesiastes, Ruth,* and
Daniel. As compositions, they range from scattered psalms, written
by King David prior to 1000 B.C., to the heroic tale of Daniel,
written in the second century. The one hundred and fifty psalms
themselves as combined within the *Psalter* range through this
whole period. Nos. 13, 23, and 110 are among the oldest; also
Nos. 61 and 62. Some were composed by exiles in Babylonia; for
example, the 42nd, 43rd, and 90th. Some were written in the
enthusiasm aroused by Cyrus, the Persian "deliverer"; for example, No. 4. The 8th and 51st were written in the times of
Nehemiah and the restoration. They represent a wide variety of
mood and scenery, as one may see even upon examination. The
Psalter was the first of the *Kethubim* to find its place within the
Canon. It became the nucleus of the Temple hymn-book; the
psalms were used, also, in synagogues. *Proverbs, Job,* and
Ecclesiastes are writings of "wisdom" literature of the fourth
century, and later; although some proverbs were doubtless phrased
by Solomon. They represent Greek influences upon the thought
of the Jews in Palestine. *Daniel* was among the latest works composed, although in the *Canon* it is placed before *Hosea,*—because its "hero" is the Daniel of the Babylonian Captivity, who
interpreted dreams for the king, and who, when thrown into the
den of lions, was protected by the God of Israel. Thereby the
writer would inspire the Jewish Maccabees waging war against
the Hellenes.

The Talmud.—The *Canon* as such is not the Scripture upon
which the modern Jew relies *exclusively.* Teachings known as the
Talmud ("teaching") became current after the *Canon* had been
closed, and seem, at times, to have overshadowed the *Law,* the
Prophets, and the *Writings.* They come from the period of Roman
rule, and the early years of the Dispersion, after the fall of
Jerusalem. This *Talmud* consists of comments of the rabbis, and
their interpretation of the Law and the Ritual, being at first oral,
and later reduced to writing. There are two portions of it: (1) the
Mishna, "Repetition," and (2) the *Gemara,* "Completion." The
materials which form the *Mishna* dealt with all aspects of life, and
all branches of religious observance, with a view to making plain

the course of life amidst varying experiences, and reducing the probability of transgression. Back of it was the *Law* (the *Torah*) itself, but the interpretations varied, especially in the Jewish academies of Palestine and Babylonia. Therefore, the *Gemara* was composed in "completion" of instruction; thus usually do explanations multiply of things inexplicable. The result was a huge mass of traditional regulation and details of ritual, too large for ready reference, and unwieldy for the expert. Yet the *Talmud* actually shaped the course of orthodoxy during the early Christian centuries. The *Mishna* of the rabbis, *e.g.,* Hillel, Shammai, Judah, and Akiba, and the *Gemara* of the "Sayers" were immediate, real, and valuable. The voices of the prophets, including Zechariah, whom many took to be the last,[25] had long been silent. It seemed that God himself had ceased to speak to his own People. The battlements of Zion had been stormed effectually; the Restoration program had been ruined; the Temple had been desecrated and at last destroyed. But the Law remained! It was tangible; it could be worn about their necks, it could be inscribed by "repetition" on their hearts; it could be practiced in minute detail in daily life. The *Talmud* may not be inspiring reading, but it is a very human, very Jewish document.

The Talmud's size became embarrassing. Compare its bulk with the modest *Pentateuch*. It could not be read on Sabbaths in a single year, nor on the Sabbaths of a century, perhaps. It was at last reduced. A reduction called "A Copy of the Law" was made in the 12th century by Moses Maimonides, of Spain and Egypt. In the 16th century, the handy digest called *Shulchan Aruch,* "the Prepared Table," was arranged, which became the standard code of life and law. It has been the final authority for the orthodox Ashkenazim, especially in eastern Europe.[26]

Ceremony.—Judaism is preserved also in ceremonial. No faith survives without its ceremonies, fasts, and festivals. The course of Judaism has been, in these respects, spectacular. In the ancient days of her glory, Israel observed a Temple-ritual which may be compared with nothing less than the annual Temple- and Altar-services in ancient China. Many rites are still observed, which are of unusual interest and impressiveness. They indicate endurance on the part of Jewish temper; although, it is evident that ritual and religion are at present in decline throughout the

[25] Zechariah prophesied *c.* 500 B.C. But was not John a prophet?
[26] We may not ignore, however, those Jews who have taken their Bible *figuratively,* and have found law and life through gnostic, esoteric, kabbalistic signs (symbolic diagrams and numbers). There have been many forms of magic, mystery, and mysticism among modern Jews.

greater part of Jewry. On the contrary, there are some indications that the faithful are making a fresh start toward a revised theory of Jewish existence, which may hold fast to what is good in rites and theory, and may be equal to the growing need of general reconstruction in religion and the reorganization of world ideals.

The two great holidays are *Rosh Hashshanah,* the "New Year," and *Yom Kippur,* the "Day of Atonement," occurring in the fall of the Christian year, with ten penitential days between the two. In Palestine, for example, they mark the end of the drought and the coming of the rains, perpetuating the memory of early pastoral times. The New Year is also the Day of Judgment, when Satan makes his accusations, and when God opens the Book of Records, to decide who are worthy to live longer, and who may have to die within the coming year. On the Day of Atonement these fates are sealed. It is a solemn day, only less sacred than the Sabbath itself, although the latter may really be the later institution. But before men's fates are sealed, the guilty have a chance to claim forgiveness, and to make atonement.

Under the ancient Covenant, atonement was made by bloody sacrifices, both for moral and for ritual offences; the blood of the offering represented the surrender of the worshiper's own life to God. Many of the prophets, however, criticized the ceremony, when it became too formal. Hear the prophet Micah fulminate against it: "Wherewith shall I come before Yahweh, and bow myself before the high God? Shall I come with burnt-offerings, with calves a year old? Will he be pleased with thousands of rams, or ten thousand rivers of oil? Shall I give my first-born for my transgression, the fruit of my body for the sin of my soul?" Then he answers, gently, in the famous judgment, "What doth Yahweh require of thee, but to do justly, to love kindness, and to walk humbly" with him? In the modern ceremony, which has long lacked the bloody element, the worshiper depends for his forgiveness on his own forgiving spirit. As a man forgives his fellow he finds forgiveness of God. He must repent likewise for the wrongs he may have done. On the evening of the Day (*Yom Kippur*), the cantor chants in the synagogue the well-known prayer *Kol Nidre,* "All Vows," a plaintive penitence for wrongs done other men. But the genesis of this moving prayer, transposed later by easier circumstances, was the idea of "release" from the burdens which *others,* that is, their persecutors, had imposed upon the oppressed Jews! The whole Day is one of fast and expiation.

Succoth, the "Feast of Tabernacles," the most joyful of feasts, falls several weeks beyond *Yom Kippur.* It celebrates the ingathering of the crops, and commemorates the care of Yahweh, for his People which they wandered "forty years" in the Wilderness. In the Temple days, of old, many sacrifices were offered, while the Temple was illuminated. In the synagogues today, the occasion calls for decorations of plants and fruits, and a procession of glad men bearing citrons and palm branches bound with myrtle and willow. The close of the feast marks the conclusion of the annual reading of the *Pentateuch.* In the homes, in the diningroom, or in the private garden, are erected decorated booths (*succoth,* whence the title of the feast), made of tree-boughs. In these booths, reminiscent of the shelters in the Wilderness, festive meals are served, and special prayers of thanksgiving are pronounced. It is customary during this festival to give alms to the poor.

Pesakh, the "Passover," or the "Feast of Unleavened Bread," is notable, and of ancient origin. Traditionally, it celebrates the Exodus, but actually its history is more complex. Perhaps it first arose in Canaan, in synchronism with a Canaanitish festival of spring, which celebrated the release of man and beast from winter's bondage. It doubtless dates from the nomadic days, when the half-barbaric Hebrews roved hungrily, by tribes and families, from one oasis to another, fighting for water and pasturage. It was celebrated at the spring equinox, with bloody sacrifice, an offering of the first-born of flocks and herds (and man, also?). Since the Exodus, it has reminded men of escape from bondage, and of entrance into the Land of Promise, after "forty years." God's hand was seen in man's relief. In the later times, when Israel was in bondage to overlords in Palestine, the Passover was a time of possible disturbance on behalf of freedom. The Roman rulers, for example, were uneasy, when the people went up to Jerusalem "for the feast."

While the Passover is now duly celebrated publicly, in the synagogue, with hymns of rejoicing and prayers for freedom, it is peculiarly a *family* festival. As a domestic celebration, it is called by the Ashkenazim the *Seder,* simply "the Feast." It is usually the occasion of a family reunion, thus preserving in strength and beauty the Jewish home. In ancient times, each family slew a lamb in its first year, roasted it, and ate it with unleavened bread and bitter herbs. Since the destruction of the Temple, the lamb has not been eaten; a roasted bone is placed upon the table as a symbol.

The meal consists of unleavened cakes; parsley dipped in salt
water; watercress or horseradish tops for bitter herbs; nuts and
apples, and slices of horseradish. During the feast, each participant
sips, at intervals, four cups of wine: after the story of the
Exodus has been rehearsed; after the eating of the cakes and herbs,
and a general washing of the hands; after the recitation of various
psalms and benedictions; and during the final celebration. It was
an old custom to include a prayer in defiance of the Gentiles!

Such are the rites and properties which keep the Jew alive,
which preserve his history. What is the story of the Jew? What
is the essence of his enduring religion?

History.—Jewish history cannot be told in brief; its years
are three thousand five hundred, at least; its events, too numerous
to calculate. The story might be told in terms of patriarchs, kings,
prophets, priests, and rabbis; but Israel is more than individuals.
At any rate, we must include the common people. We must observe
the Nation. The People moved as a body, with peculiar solidarity,
with kinship of feeling, institution, and destiny. With something
of this solidarity, they move into view as many tribes, about
1500 B.C. We see them in the country once called Canaan, later
Palestine (*cf. Philistine*). Many different sources help us reconstruct the shadowy movement. They themselves tried to write
their history in the *Pentateuch,* I and II *Kings,* and I and II
Chronicles. But we have seen something of the uncritical manner
of their composition. Historians of religion are still trying to
reconstruct an easy flowing record of this People.

Before Moses, who may be as late as 1350 B.C., events are purely
conjectural; before David (*c.* 1000), all is tradition. Before David,
the times are veiled in mystery. The records of Egypt, Assyria,
and Babylon may be relied on only after David's era. No Egyptian
record mentions the "Egyptian" bondage,—although we must
assume there was a Bondage, in the time of Tutankhamen (14th
century, B.C.). The Hebrews were in *Goshen,* not in Egypt. Their
passage of the "Sea" was the crossing of an upper *arm* of it. The
"forty years" are merely recollection. The "wanderings" were
real enough. In fact, the substance of the flight, the crossing,
and the wanderings is all well-attested; and Moses must be treated
as historical. We may believe the vivid story of the pre-Mosaic
period. Babylon, Assyria, and Egypt were closed to nomads.
These tribesmen, some of Rachel, some of Leah, wandered in no
man's land, moving from oasis to oasis in a generally sun-smitten,
wind-swept wilderness, full of terrifying powers which they had

to placate or coerce. Meanwhile, the great nations, weakening, no longer fought back and forth in Syria and Palestine. Then these nomads, along with others, could enter in and occupy the land. There were several immigrations: (1) the Aramæans, on the north, and (2) the Hebrews (*Habiru,* from *'eber,* "beyond"), in Canaan proper. They were both Semitic. But there came in, also, the Philistines, uncircumcised Ægeans from Crete, especially, with whom the Hebrews had to battle for supremacy. The Semites gradually absorbed the aboriginals (the "Canaanites" and Amorites), setting up a kingdom of their own. Thereafter, the struggle, political and cultural, was with the strengthened powers round about, now Egypt, now Assyria and Babylonia, then Greece and Rome. In their "Promised Land," they brought to flower and fruit poetic imagination, prophetic insight, a moral sense, and a spiritual frenzy, which are invaluable possessions of civilization for all time.

Moses.—While the "patriarchs," Abraham, Isaac, Jacob (Israel), and Joseph, were before him, Moses is the founder of the Hebrew religion. Abraham may be the "father," and the Israelites, his "children," but Moses is responsible for the adoption, and the exclusive worship, of Yahweh as the Israelitish God. He it was who, as the Jews and Moslems have preserved the story, first "talked" with God. God "spoke" from the burning mountain to Israel through him. The God-idea he gave them was compelling and formative. When Moses first met Yahweh, he was a fugitive from the wrath of the Egyptian Pharaoh, sojourning in the country of the Kenites, in the neighborhood of Sinai (Horeb). He married, meanwhile, Zipporah, daughter of the Kenite Jethro, Yahweh's priest. At the Mount of Yahweh, he learned the divine majesty and power; in particular, the "Ten Words" were revealed to him,[27] and Yahweh promised to redeem the Hebrews from their bonds. On returning to "Egypt," Moses rallied his enslaved kinsmen, announced Yahweh, and arranged the Exodus. At Sinai, the People entered into "covenant" relations with Yahweh, and agreed to abide by whatever Yahweh would reveal from time to time. The revelations were the Law of Israel. The doctrines of *Revelation* and *Law* remained at the very foundation of the faith. Yahweh dwelt for long in the holy mountain, but his "presence" went with his people, symbolized by a sacred

---

[27] See Exodus, Chaps. XXXIV and XX, and *Deut.,* Chap. V, for the details of the *Decalogue.* There are several versions, because several sources were finally assembled independently. In one document, the mountain is called Sinai; in another, Horeb. There are other variations, also.

stone (the "tables of the Law") in a box, or ark (the "Ark of the Covenant") ! [28] And around the Ark of the "presence" the twelve tribes journeyed and were transformed. They began to formulate the theory, as they went on, that they were the peculiar recipients of God's Word.

Under Moses' successor, Joshua, they entered Canaan, seizing land for all the tribes. Outwardly, the ties were loose which bound them; their life was pastoral; there were chieftains, but no king. There was no hierarchy (priesthood) in control; affairs were in the hands of "judges," until Yahweh ordained a kingship. The shepherd Saul was at last anointed as King by Samuel. There was for long no capital—until David, Saul's successor, captured the stronghold of Jerusalem. It continued the capital, and is still the Holy City. It flourished especially under Solomon. For more than a century there was an undivided Kingdom, recognized by neighboring states. In 975 B.C., ten tribes seceded, to establish a kingdom of their own, with its capital at Samaria. With varying fortunes, they endured for two and one-half centuries. In 721, their city fell, and they became dispersed and "lost." Possibly, they had long been "losing" by amalgamation with the aboriginals, and by indifference to Yahweh. When Samaria fell, the country-side was by no means stripped of "Hebrews"; there were "Samaritans" aplenty left to annoy their southern kindred. The two tribes of Judah and Benjamin retained their kingdom until 587, furnishing, as we have seen, the pattern and substance of Judaism. It was the House of Judah, which was rebuilt after the Captivity in Babylon. Thereafter the people were no longer known as "Hebrews," but "Jews," a name derived from Judah by way of the hellenistic designations, Judæa and *Ioudaioi*. From under the Persian mandate, the Jews passed, in 332 B.C., to the Greek, and to the rule of Alexander's successors, the House of Antioch. For a brief space, in "Maccabæan" times, the Jews were independent; and then they passed to Rome. During Roman rule, Jesus, a Jew of Nazareth, was proclaimed Messiah by "John the Baptizer," and by the Galilæan fisherman, Simon Peter. The career of Jesus of Nazareth, "King of the Jews," was a source of worry to the Roman governors. After his death, there were several years of revolution; the people had been stirred by the ancient messianic hope, and the ideal of world dominion. Unfortunately, Jewish leaders inaugurated revolution at a time when universal order was maintained by Rome, and when her citizens had

[28] Centuries later, Mt. Zion and the Temple in Jerusalem became his seat.

unusual ground of happiness and prosperity. They lost their city, in the end, and the Nation was destroyed. Jerusalem fell to the troops of Titus in 70 A.D.

The Dispersion.—The *Diaspora,* or "Dispersion," followed, and the story of the Jewish faith thereafter is the story of the Jews among the nations, with all that this has meant for politics, morals and religion. They were thenceforth men without a country, but with all the world before them. Having no land, they still possessed a consciousness of solidarity; they were Yahweh's People; they had the Law, the Prophets, and the Writings. Having no Temple, nor priesthood, they had their synagogues and rabbis. The Star of David went before them, and rested where they found a habitation. Be it said to the credit of humanity in general, and of the Roman Empire in particular, they were allowed to settle and perpetuate their faith. They preferred the cities, but did not hesitate to occupy the soil. They had learned trade and commerce, but could be content, each by his own house and fig tree, or among his flocks. Although they scattered, they kept together through their common rites; they went where rabbis would accompany them, and where *kosher* meat could be provided. Some returned to Babylon, and some to Egypt; while some remained in Palestine. Many passed westward to Spain and France, where they have enjoyed centuries of almost uninterrupted prosperity. Often they had the official protection of Church and State, whatever disabilities they suffered from the populace. Pope Gregory (590–604 A.D.) forbade Catholics to molest them, unless by due process of law; his one restriction on them was, that they might not own Christian slaves. Spain supplanted Babylonia in the eleventh century as the center of Jewish life and thought. The Moors afforded them protection, when they acquired Spain; and Moslem Arab literature and science were congenial to their minds. They were expelled at last (1492) by Roman Christian bigotry. But, meanwhile, they had produced in Spain, in many types of intellectual activity, a succession of great names; the greatest, possibly, was Maimonides, or Ibn Maimun, the philosophic theologian. There were poets and philosophers. Perhaps, the poets were, to some degree, original; they often sang of wine and love, rather than about the majesty of Yahweh and the *Torah;* but wine and love are common themes both in Israel and Islam. The philosophers were borrowers; their type of specula-tion was not based on Jewish principles; it was Greek specifically neo-Platonic. Back of all mediæval Jewish speculation lay phi-

losophy purveyed by Greeks and Arabs. Maimonides set out to
reconcile the Hebrew Moses and Greek Aristotle, and that on the
basis of the Arab Aristotelianism of Ibn Sina (Avicenna)!

In contrast with the Jewish lot in Moslem Spain, there was
tragedy in Christian Europe, which had stemmed, to its holy(?)
satisfaction, the tide of Islam. While the rulers were often
tolerant, depending much upon the Jews for loans, and the
management of finance, the populace was generally hostile, indulging in outrage on the slightest provocation. When the
Crusades were under way, feeling was predominantly bitter.
Christendom sent, in blind fury, plundering legions against the
Moslem "infidel" in Palestine and Syria; and vented spite upon
the Jewish infidel at home. The Church was nervously alert to
every hostile tendency, and the life of every non-conformist was
in jeopardy. In 1290, every Jew was ordered out of England.
A century later, they were wholly driven out of France, exiled
from many towns in Germany, and, in Spain, subjected to
incessant persecution. In 1480, the (in)famous Inquisition was
established, a sorry confusion of ecclesiastical tyranny, the
subservience of kings to Church dictation, and an unholy bigotry
on the common Christian's part. The Inquisition worked its
greatest havoc in Spain, Portugal, Spanish America, and Portuguese India (Goa). Thousands of Jews were caught in its toils,
meeting death by burning, as the proclamation was enforced,
known in *Portuguese* as *auto da fé* (*Latin, actus fidei,* "act of
faith"). *Autos* were held in Spain until as late as 1826, and the
Inquisition lasted there until 1834.

During the Middle Ages, the Jews fled in great numbers again
eastward to Poland, Russia, Turkey, and the Moslem East.
Although, while in the West, some intermarriage had occurred,
with some modifications of thought and custom, the Jew was
still distinct, and bound by his Tradition. His existence and
distinction had been emphasized by the ghetto. By 1600 A.D.,
practically all the Jews of Europe were confined to ghettos. The
ghetto was, under the prevailing circumstances, a refuge and a
prison; residence within was both by Jewish choice and Christian
law. A ghetto pattern gradually appeared, made visible by the
acid of persecution and seclusion. Out of his own cabined life
the Jew spun for himself the only universe he knew. He lived
apart; the ghetto was his little world of home, school, synagogue,
shop, and cemetery. He might wander in the larger, outer world
by day, but at nightfall, the ghetto was his only place of safety.

While he thus lived intensively, he lived more peacefully than in the days of his wanderings. His culture was a concentrate, satisfyingly rich in the virtues of his faith, and of value to obscure the foulness, congestion, and stupid degradations of his residence. And still at the center of the community rested the Ark; above it flew the cherubim; and the people cherished hope and a sense of their eternal mission. Amidst the fires of freedom kept nourished in their bosoms, lingered the ancient hope of the Messiah; they stood ready, with pent-up devotion, to set out again under his leadership, when he should come.[29]

A New Dispensation.—Eventually, a change came suddenly for the pent-up Jew; he benefited greatly by a widespread revolution. When the Bastille fell on July 14, 1789, a new day dawned for the Western races, and for the Oriental Jew. It restored his larger universe, and gave him opportunity to enter it—when he had recovered from the shock! "Liberty, Equality, Fraternity," the watch-words of the Revolution, brought promise to the Jew of leveled mountains, paths made straight and smooth, and the salvation of the Lord. But anachronistic Judaism found itself suddenly in a world transformed; ghetto culture had lagged behind the progress of the world at large. When French armies of the Revolution broke down the ghetto barriers beyond France, the liberated Jew came into rights he had not fought for, nor anticipated. But he was quick to seize his opportunity in industry, science, and philosophy—and he entered offices of state. Manna once again fell plentifully in the wilderness.

It was a new Diaspora, this time one of eagerly claimed privilege, but with greater risk to Judaism than the scattering of 70 A.D. The peculiar Jewish culture-concentrate was threatened by dilution. The faith itself was threatened by the change. Tradition fairly staggered in its new environment, finding, for example, that Judaism held no monopoly on Revelation; finding that its orthodoxy was, to some extent, a liability. The Jewish social order itself once again collapsed; and the Jews have faced the old, persistent problem of their relation to the world. Many have become assimilationists, or internationalists, freely surrendering their orthodoxy for worldly place and power. Most have clung, for one reason or another, in love of *Yahweh* and the *Law*, to their reasonable rôle of a peculiar, Chosen People.

The Faith.—What is the essence of the Faith of this peculiar

---

29 It is not surprising that many "messiahs" took advantage of the expectation: for example, the false Sabbatai Zevi (1626–1676). *Cf.* J. Kastein, The Messiah of Ismir.

people? Having no Church, nor a Creed, nor even a strictly uniform Code of any kind, it is difficult for one to generalize on their morals and religion. There is often no clear line between the "orthodox" and the "reform" branches of the Ashkenazim majority. Sometimes, there is little difference between the Ashkenazim and their Sephardi brethren.

Between "Reform" and "Orthdox" the difference is often one of *mission,* rather than of ideology. Between the "German" and the "Spanish" Jew the difference is especially *ritualistic.* Judaism is much like Sunni Islam and Protestant Christianity in this, that the individual believer is his own authority; the individual has the right of private judgment; he is his own priest; he confesses to God himself. He is, in this respect, unlike the "Greek" and "Roman" Catholics. In Greek and Roman Christianity the priest and the layman are distinct; and the Church is the authority, with its pronouncements *ex cathedra* binding on the individual.

We might attempt a summary of Judaism in terms of these five items:

God.—1. *God is One.* The *Shema* is the glory of Israel, as the similar assertion is the glory of the kindred faith, Islam (*cf.,* the *Koran, sura* 112). Such is the basic principle of true religion. Jesus the Jew built upon it his conception of the Father. There is One righteous, loving God. This is the most precious and most comforting aspect of man's conception of the *Universe.* It is said that the Rabbi Akība (d. 132 A.D.), while under torture of the Romans, breathed the word "One" and found sufficient peace. Unity came to be the great conception in the life of Israel. It represented God, the corporate life of the people, the nation's mission to the world, and, above all else, that singleness of purpose and devotion by which the individual and the nation worshiped God, who alone was, is, and evermore will be.

God's unity was an achievement—and the gift of "revelation." Or, we might call it *realization,* or discovery. The Jewish doctrine is, that the One God was "revealed" to Moses at Mt. Sinai. The idea is not, however, out of harmony with the concept of progress. The Jews did not learn all about the One God through Moses. They learned more through the later prophets. Moses did not know his name; he said to his kinsmen in Egypt, "I AM hath sent me unto you" (*Ex.* 3:14). A certain passage of time is indicated in one of the records: *"Then* began men to call upon the name of YHWH" (Yahweh—*Gen.* 4:26; but *Genesis* was written *after* Moses). While, in Moses' view, the God of Moses was not exclusive, except for Israel (*cf. Ex.* 20:3), the later theory of God's exclusiveness was traced back to him. Moses became by tradition the founder, in every major sense, of Hebrew religion. The higher doctrine of Yahweh is, nevertheless, the contribution of the prophets, in the era of the kings. To them, Yahweh was not merely *one* of many names for God, nor yet merely a *name;* Yahweh was *the* name of the *only* God. To them, also, Yahweh was a righteous God. Ethical monotheism is a realization of prophetic insight.

Even so, the prophetic doctrine of One Righteous God did not carry far, at first. The Nation was slow to comprehend it. Many of the people never understood it—they followed their own gods. They were not truly Yahweh's people who did not recognize and worship him. Perhaps, the Ten Tribes could not weather the severe Assyrian storm because they were not Yahweh's people. They had not understood his unity, his justice, and his love. Nor did all of Judah seem to comprehend, for only a Remnant was preserved, those who put their trust in Yahweh. Moses and the prophets had another view of Yahweh which many of the people could not understand. They conceived of God as *near* his people, in the burning bush and otherwise, "revealing his secrets unto his servants the prophets" (*Amos* 3:7), while the people were inclined to think of Yahweh of the burning mountain, ruling from his mountain-height, or from some distant Heaven. While the prophets, therefore, knew that Yahweh, of necessity was one, good, true, holy, and near (the "beauty" of the Lord was not thus early emphasized), the populace was not so sure that God's morality was essential to his divinity and power; nor did they feel his presence near.

When Judaism as such (differentiated from the Hebrew faith) took form upon the basis of the priestly law (the priestly interpretation of revelation, ideas, and institutions), God became transcendent and "deistic." That is, Yahweh became a *deus,* or "high God," whose seat was Heaven, whence he ruled the life and ways of men, his creatures, whom he had made in the likeness of himself. He had revealed his *Law;* men must obey. In the time of Jesus, the faith was highly legalistic. The Pharisees, for example, insisted on the *Law* and its fulfilment. It remained for a philosophy of the Yahweh-concept to modify or to supersede the theory of God as Law. This was initiated by hellenistic Judaism, that is, by Judaism after it became engulfed and gravely challenged by Greek thought, near and after the Diaspora.

The Jewish Philo (d. *c.* 40 A.D.), of Alexandria, attempted, in the manner of his day, to account for God as the Absolute, who revealed himself through the scriptures to the common man and through Reason (Logos) to the thinker. But Philo had no Jewish disciples, nor any influence on the later faith; his interpretation was more effective in Christianity. Jewish scholastic, or hellenized, theology may be better seen in Moses Maimonides (1135–1204).

Times were different in the Middle Ages. Judaism, Christianity, and Islam, all had to face the problems of philosophy. Each evolved its own more or less influential "scholasticism." What Ashari had accomplished for Islamic thinkers, and Aquinas was soon to do for Christianity, Maimonides accomplished for the Jews. He was a Spanish Jew born in academic Cordova; but, swept out of Spain by a conservative reaction against philosophy, he spent his life in Egypt, as court physician to the Saljuq Saladin. He sought to show that there is and can be no essential contradiction between philosophy and religion. He would establish Judaism upon a philosophic basis; he would make God reasonable, and not merely the object of man's faith; he would show that man's mind and man's heart can both agree on God. To this "second Moses," man's *mind* is, therefore, a medium of Revelation! He strenuously opposed: (1) all anthropomorphists, those who believed that God made man "in his own image," and that, therefore, God may be understood by reference to his creature; and (2) all attributists, those who attributed to God corporeal or psychic qualities, such as hearing, seeing, and the like.

He held God to be One, with "no Unity like unto him in any way"; Incorporeal, not having "any corporeal qualities"; and Incomparable, like unto nothing else at all [30] as an object of man's devotion—"There is none other than He to whom it is proper to pray." He exalted faith. He preceded many philosophic statements by the phrase, "I believe with perfect faith . . ." He thus reconciled faith and reason. He made a careful study of the scriptures, his very method making this essential. But he took all anthropomorphisms (*e.g.,* references to God's hand, throne, etc.) to be figurative. He could say no more of God than that he *is*. Therein he employed Aristotelian argument which led from contingencies back to necessary existence, from motion to a primal, unmoved mover. God was ultimate Reality. God, however, was Creator: "He alone was, is, and will be, the Maker

---

[30] This view is practically Mohammed's, "There is none like unto Him."

of everything." By what process? In Neo-Platonic fashion, Maimonides interposed between the Absolute God and the material universe a series of immaterial intelligences which emanated from the Absolute, ten in all; through the last the world was "actualized." Matter was mere potentiality, which did not appear as "things" until the "actualizing intelligence" operated on it. The human intellect (a system of ideas, the highest of which exist as pure form, therefore imperishable) is thus actualized from potentiality; as is prophecy, also (the highest stage of human attainment). The soul is pure form, and, therefore, is eternal. The prophets stand upon the plane of pure intelligence, and, therefore, speak truth. Moses, especially, was a prophet. As for man, he does not represent God's highest purpose; he has no guarantee as such of immortality; his destiny lies in himself, not in his stars. Man needs for his effective guidance to God's ends which are inscrutable the *Law* as given to "our Teacher Moses." Rewards and punishments are shown therein; man may obey and live, or disobey and die. A Messiah will appear, in the commonly accepted form of a personal deliverer, to remind men of their dangers and their opportunities. And "at the time when it will please the Creator," there will be "a resurrection of the dead." Maimonides believed in Yahweh, Moses, the Law, the Prophets, and the Writings! He sought to reconcile them all with Unity. God remained the fundamental concept of the Jewish faith.

Law.—2. The *Law* is paramount. It involves both the *Torah* and the *Talmud,* with often no clear line drawn between the two. Particularly, it represents an attitude which fails to separate the truth from the Law by which to realize it. Some Jews have contended that "all the *Torah* was given unto Moses . . . that this *Torah* will not be changed, neither will there be another *Torah.*" Maimonides detected this opinion in his day. In practice, however, the Jew finds himself in modern centuries the heir of a voluminous accumulation of Pharisaical and rabbinical statutes and regulations impossible wholly to comprehend or to practice. Maimonides strove heroically to find the true Moses and the essential *Law,* but was unable to ignore completely the accretions of the *Talmud.* The Jew is legal-minded; but his Law has drooped beneath the burden of the letter. By all the circumstances of long tradition, there should never be a lawless Jew.

The Jew has held himself to be the creature of God's Law. God early said to him, "I am the Lord, thy God. . . . Thou shalt

. . ." (*Ex.* 20:2ff.),—or, "Thou shalt not." While God's com-
mands were positive and negative, no negatives applied to men
who gave obedience to the first command, "Thou shalt love the
Lord, thy God, with all thy heart" (*Deut.* 10:12). Man has known
that his behavior was a prime concern of Yahweh's, for Yahweh
had bestowed his nature on him, had made him a moral creature,
and properly expected him to do what was required. It was
hard, however, to obey the first command; and hard to know
what to avoid in changing circumstances. Laws forever tend to
multiply; life tends to be reduced to rules of conduct. The
Talmud went on multiplying statutes, although reiterating the
essential truth that God looks upon man's heart. Is it possible to
obey in form and not by heart? Yes, but this obedience is good
for Law and not for Life. God and Life and Law are one.
Reverence and morality are not possible without Law. Man is
not God; he has eaten no fruit of any tree, which has made him
wise as God. Jewish Law has aimed to emphasize the fact that
man lives by the breath of God, that piety is nourished by man's
obedience to divine commandment.

Ritual has its rightful place, and may be ignored by man only
to his own hurt. There are many rites which, in essence, God
ordained. But the Jew has often lapsed back into magic, mis-
taking the identity of God and Law, or misunderstanding both.
He has employed the primitive's coercion, thinking God could be
controlled by ritual. Or, take the Jewish Sabbath, for illustration. In terms of the true *Law* the Sabbath had a moral connotation; it was a day of rest and restoration, following an inexorable
principle of God and Nature: "God rested on the Sabbath day"
(*Gen.* 2:3). But many Jews have often made either too much of
the Sabbath, or nothing at all, without reference to its moral
quality. Take another aspect of the Law, the race's health. The
early dietetic regulations were properly referred to God. While
based upon some physiological or economic requirement, to observe them "in the name of God" recognized their moral character. If man would live, neither his body nor his mind may be
abused; they must conform to Law. Jewish orthodoxy, on the
whole, has never disregarded Law; but its observance has been
legalistic. Legalism has been to orthodoxy, during all the Christian
centuries, its very nationality.

Sin.—3. *Sin* is an act more than a condition. By this "legalistic" view, righteousness, also, is an act, primarily. Obedience to

the laws of Yahweh is a virtue; disobedience is sin. A proverb says, "Atonement is reversion to obedience." This accords with the prophetic judgment, in contrast with the former Covenant, that repentance and obedience bring the restoration of God's favor; under the old Covenant, it required sacrifice. In the Temple there was bloody sacrifice, but never any subsequently in the synagogue. Repentance was thus moralized.

Sin is more the act of the individual than of the People; nor is the quality of his act determined by heredity. The emphasis which Judaism has usually placed upon the freedom of the will has tended to exclude a doctrine of hereditary evil. "In Adam's fall we sinnèd all," as a Christian catechism put it, is contrary to Israel's mature experience, and her ablest prophets' judgment. One is not sinful by nature, in the sense of being "conceived and born in sin." The "iniquity of the fathers" is visited upon the children only when the children themselves "hate" Yahweh (*Ex.* 20:5). Children may follow the evil example of their parents, and yield to hereditary disposition, but, if they do, the blame is theirs; nor do they sin, if at all, by some special, inner compulsion. Sin is an indulgence of the flesh in selfishness, a yielding to the fleshly nature, an overt act against the social order.

Conversely, atonement, restoration, and salvation are an individual concern. One may not atone for the error of another; this kind of atonement is as contrary to Jewish as to Chinese thought, although both have held to forms of public worship by the ruler or the priest on behalf of all the people (see p. 61, above). The Jew could not conceive of the efficacy of the apostle Paul's assurance, that "as in Adam all died, so in Christ shall all be made alive." The death of Jesus had no salutary meaning to the Jew. In the Jewish plan, a man must find his own way to life and God. The "return" (*teshubah*) to God is the sinner's own free act.[31]

Jewish tradition has its own peculiar view of sin and evil, along with what it holds in common with all faiths of higher quality. Among the acts which have been, from time to time, prohibited are the worship of any god but Yahweh, bowing down to images, "taking the name of God in vain," misuse of the Sabbath, disrespect for or the dishonoring of one's parents,

---

[31] Mohammed's judgment was, "To God is our return," but the Arab prophet put less emphasis on man's freedom in this life, and more upon God's omnipotence hereafter, than the Jew did.

murder, adultery, theft, false witness, and covetousness. The very order in which these fundamental "Ten Commandments" are listed is itself suggestive—if there was any meaning in the sequence, beyond the priority of the first. These commandments came by "revelation"; but, also, certain other acts, or practices, were long legitimate, such as polygamy, concubinage, prostitution, the father's right to put his child to death, and slavery. These were outgrown through further revelation. Or, is the very ardor and insistence of the ancient prophets' utterances against these evils an indication that they were not outgrown? Idolatry, adultery, and fraud are frequently the major grounds of the prophets' condemnation. However it may bear upon the social question, it is every woman's duty to bear children; celibacy is sin. The use of alcoholic liquors is traditional, especially on festivals and Sabbaths; although the Jews have not been prone to drunkenness. A Jew would be, consistently, an anti-prohibitionist.

Prayer.—4. *Prayer* has long since held the place of sacrifice. It was the only worship which the prophets sanctioned. It came into general use among the Hebrews during their captivity in Babylon. Sacrifice could not be reconciled with a conception of a moral God. Sacrifices were by their very origin unethical, arising from the worship of the dead; blood was shed as nourishment for the spirits in the Underworld. Or, sacrifice was magical and impudent. Read what Isaiah thought of the killing of sheep, the drinking of wine, and other acts, to save the holy city from Sennacherib (*Isa.* 22:1–14; *cf.* 1:11–17). When the prophets realized that Yahweh would not countenance the worship of the dead, they knew that the major motive of the sacrifice had been removed. The one object of true worship was the living God himself.

Prayer is individual, subjective, but may influence God. Man is thereby his own priest in God's presence; the old priesthood has disappeared. Man prays in the faith that God hears him and will answer. While the "reform" Jew deems prayer entirely subjective, its value inhering in the act and attitude themselves, the "orthodox" has held that prayer moves God and may alter his decrees. He holds that not only may prayer itself transform the worshiper, but may be the means of freeing him from guilt and retribution. This is the common Talmudic attitude, and unquestionably the rabbinic point of view, although the *Talmud* itself contains this prayer of pure submission, without appeal, to God:

"Do thy will in heaven above, and grant contentment of spirit to those that fear thee below; and that do which is good in thine own eyes. Blessed art thou, O Lord, who hearest prayer."

The Future.—5. A Hereafter and a Judgment, merging into Immortality, have always been included in Hebrew theology, although with a significant variation. The hope of continuity has varied according to the conception of the Nation and the individual, but a final termination, whether by loss of identity or through annihilation, has been abhorred. God is "from everlasting to everlasting," and man continues forever as an object of the Lord's regard. He will not leave his creatures in the dust; "the dead shall be raised up," but he will judge them according to their deeds. God is ever ready, in fact, to reward goodness and to punish evil, here and hereafter.

Among the early Hebrews man was regarded both as flesh (*basar*) and as breath (*nefesh*). At death, his flesh returned to the dust, but his breath persisted as a disembodied spirit, haunting the place of the body's burial, with many of its former powers retained, and with some new powers added. Although, for example, the disembodied breath was "feeble," it was freer and possessed of greater knowledge. The living kept the spirits nourished by offerings at the graves. Under Babylonian influence, long before the Babylonian Captivity, there developed the theory of Sheol, the place to which the dead "go down" (*cf. Ps.* 28:1; *Isa.* 14:19, for later reflections of this notion), and the idea of Death as the ruler of Sheol (*Ps.* 49:14). Sheol was the last abode, from which there was no "return." The cult of the dead, based on these conceptions, was really the chief hindrance to the Yahweh-reformation. During the Captivity, Zoroastrian influence gave the Hebrews a theory of the bodily resurrection for all who were accounted worthy at the bar of judgment. You will recall that Zoroastrians were judged at the last day according to "good thoughts, good words, and good deeds." There came also the expectation of a restoration of the Nation and a Golden Age on earth, as one may observe in *Ezekiel* 18:5–9; 32:21; and especially Chapter XXXVII. After the Jews returned from the Exile, they conceived a resurrection for *all* men, and a last day when all should rise to receive judgment. This is the doctrine of the Pharisees and of the *Talmud*. From Greek influence after the time of Alexander, there came into Judaism the doctrine of the immortality of the soul. The soul is inherently divine, a spark from the divine fire; man's birth is a fall, the body his prison-house; death is his release, and then he passes, not to Sheol—unless to just punishment—but to the heaven of God. His body, being evil, is left among the universe of things; the soul, because it is divine, is immortal. The net result for doctrine was an ultimate adjustment of these varying theories. A combination of Platonic and of Pharisaic thought, uniting spiritual immortality and a resurrection, found great favor in rabbinic Judaism, in opposition to the Sadducees' denial of any conscious existence after death. The school of Sadducees soon ended—there was no conscious existence for it after the destruction of Jerusalem! The school of the Pharisees became rabbinic Judaism; and their views of the Hereafter prevailed. Centuries later, Maimonides declared his "perfect faith" in "a resurrection."

The Messiah.—The messianic hope has been persistent. Or-thodox Jewry has looked for a Messiah, while Reform Judaism, with its "prophetic universalism," has thought of Israel itself as the Messiah. There has been an expectation of the "rule" of God (*cf. Isa.* 11:1-9). In the early days, the Hebrews held the notion that they were Yahweh's Chosen People who would realize under him a world dominion, with glory and peace for the nations. Soon there developed the expectation of a unique person who would lead them to their destiny of universal sway. He would be "the Lord's anointed" (*messiah*). *Isaiah* prophesied the coming of a wonderful, mighty, eternal Prince of Peace, through whom a perfect social order would be achieved on earth (*cf. Isa.* 9:6; 10:2ff). Micah heralded the ideal one who would "feed his flock in the strength of Yahweh." Jeremiah foretold the coming of a king of the line of David, who would "deal wisely and execute righteousness in the land." Ezekiel spoke of a Shepherd who would feed the house of David. Then Isaiah II, under the inspiration of a new situation, offered the conception of the Chosen People itself as the Messiah to usher in the Kingdom. But the Nation perished, and the hope has centered on an In-dividual. The Messiah has never come, but many messiahs have appeared, including Theudas (1st century, A.D.), Bar Kochba (130ff. A.D.), Serenus (720), Ibnu'l-Ruki (1160), and Sabbataï Zebi (d. 1676).

A recent collective interpretation of the messianic hope is Zionism, the restoration of the Jews to Palestine under their own government. It revives the earlier nationalism, which great masses of the Jews have never given up, and lays stress upon their need of a religious homeland. Zionists have taken the Dispersion as an evidence of national sin, and their wanderings among the nations as a means of penitence. At last their penitence should be rewarded; they should be allowed to "go back home." Once again political history seems to be repeated—the English Cyrus has espoused the cause of restoration. Lord Balfour promised a Return, and reconstruction has been under way for many years, with notable accomplishments in irrigation, trade, and education. But there are still "Samaritans," we mean Moslem Arabs, to delay proceedings. Palestine has long been Moslem territory. Many empires have included it. There are no inherent rights by conquest. And Jewry is divided on the venture. "Reform" Jews especially are indifferent. While the present waxing mood of anti-Semitism in certain portions of the Gentile world is turning the thoughts of many Jews toward Zion, *Palestinian* Zionism has grown static. Most Jews are content, either to swear allegience to existing nations under whom they dwell, or to wink at national boundaries, and to pursue their own ends through international propaganda. The hope of an individual Messiah wanes, while the Jewish people continue to preserve their own identity, chiefly through such peculiarities as inhere in their ideas of God, the *Law,* Sin, Prayer, and the Hereafter.

Reform.—A century ago, among the Ashkenazim of Germany, the party of "Reform" began. It has been remarkably successful in America, especially among Jews of German origin. It aimed primarily at a reformation of the ritual (and brevity in worship has been a virtue in America) ; but back of the movement lies an era of emancipation, which began with Moses Mendelssohn (1729–1786), or Moses III, called the Emancipator. He aimed at intellectual liberation, primarily, realizing that the isolation of the ghetto was harder on the Jew than legal disability. *Hebrew* occupied a still center in the whirl of *German;* he rendered into *German* many portions of the *Torah.* Ghetto culture was a concentrate in isolation; he established a Free School in Berlin, for instruction in religion, and in general culture. While he prosecuted reformation for his people, he was at heart a faithful Jew. Judaism was to him a revelation of the *Law;* this was its sole distinction. He was a man of the broader culture, believing in religion, but he saw no peculiar doctrines in his own faith; to him the Jewish mission was the conservation of the *Law* revealed by Yahweh to Israel alone. This was an historic circumstance in the

life of this peculiar people. Religion was one and universal, but
for Jews the *Law* of Yahweh was perennially binding; it was
their chief glory. Mendelssohn, we may remember, was a friend
of Lessing. The poet portrays his Nathan the Wise in quest
for the truth beneath all creeds; makes a plea for kinship among
all men despite divisions of religion; advocates *love* as the chief
virtue in the thought of the Divine. Mendelssohn would have all
who are "born within the house of Jacob" stay loyal to their
natal hearth,[32] but welcome truth wherever they may find it. He
was an advocate of separation between Church and State. He
would keep men mindful of religion, and would preserve the
Law for its moral implications, also. He strove to save morality
from being wrecked by "business."

The Reform movement has modified some of Mendelssohn's
ideas, and initiated details of its own. It has shortened the ritual
of worship, *e.g.,* the *Yom Kippur* festival; it uses *German* (*English,* in America) instead of *Hebrew* or *Aramaic* as the ritual
language [33]; it includes congregational hymns sung to the accompaniment of instrumental music; employs mixed choirs; confirms girls as well as boys; seats the women and the men together; and has the men remove their hats in synagogues. It
formulated a new "benediction" in recognizing sex equality, to
take the place of the former, "Blessed be Thou, O Lord, King
of the world, who hast not made me a woman." It distinguishes
between morality and ritual, and changes both ceremonial and
dietary laws according to conditions. It has disregarded *kosher*
regulations. The men have shaved their beards and sideburns;
women no longer hide their tresses under wigs. This represents
the "scientific" view, "reform" having arisen under the impact
of modern "science," with its theory of "evolution," its historical
criticism, and its new philosophy.

Jewish Reform considers Israel a messianic people, with an
obligation to instruct the world in true monotheism and in
genuine (or specious?) internationalism. Without a priesthood,
it considers every Jew a priest. Already, however, some disaster
has accompanied the reform. There is danger that with every
Jew a priest, the time may come when no Jew is a priest. There
are many Jewish radicals and atheists, who, although they are

---

[32] Many Jews have turned Christian, whether in fact or in name, *e.g.,* the Maranos
of Spain. Some have given up religion, altogether, to become the "suffering servants"
of Karl Marx, instead. Many early Christians were Jews at heart—there were
"Judaizers" in the apostolic Church.
[33] From this use of *German* came *Yiddish,* which is *German* written in *Jüdisch* or
Hebrew characters.

the same "peculiar" people, lack the fervor of inspired prophets of religion. Dilution and desertion cannot be the means of world conversion. In contrast, Orthodoxy may preserve itself among the nations, holding up the beacon of the *Law*. Perhaps the heritage of Moses I, preserved by the rabbis and by Moses II, and enlarged by Moses III, with a renewal and a newer application of the message of the Prophets, is after all the shining glory of the Jew, the just ground of his loyalty, and the basis of coöperation in the progress of mankind.

CHAPTER XV

THE RELIGION OF JESUS AND CHRISTIANITY

Christianity is at once a modern, an ancient, and a timeless faith. In numbers and their distribution, it is, in extraordinary measure, a world religion, the most extensive which the world has ever known. By ordinary reckoning, it was founded twenty centuries ago by Jesus, the son of Joseph, a citizen of Nazareth, in Palestine. But by Hebrew-Christian genealogy, Jesus was "the son of David, the son of Abraham" (*Mt.* 1:1) who, as Mohammed said, was neither Jew nor Christian, but a "seeker" after God.[1] "Abraham, rightly or wrongly, is by the writers of the *New Testament* regarded as the founder of their religion; to them the appearance of Christ is not its beginning but its climactic point."[2] The Christian tradition is even more inclusive, for Abraham was "the son of Noah, the son of Adam, the son of God" (*Lk.* 3:34, 36, 38), and Jesus is the "Son of God" (*Mk.* 1:1). The Christian *Gospel of John* expands the meaning of a phrase of *Genesis,* and "In the beginning, God" (*Gen.* 1:1) becomes "In the beginning was the Word, and the Word was with God, and the Word was God" (*John* 1:1). In John's interpretation, Jesus was "the Word." All this establishes a timeless lineage. Yet, by another mode of reckoning, Christianity is, with two exceptions, the Moslem and the Sikh, the youngest of the living faiths.

Diversities.—Christianity is infinitely varied, especially in its historic aspects. Fortunately, it is possible for the student to trace with accuracy most of the variations, for the strictly Christian records are abundant. Many early documents, especially, are precise and easily intelligible. It is *not* so easy to determine which is the fundamental theory or institution, and which the variations. We shall find it somewhat difficult to answer, at any stage of our investigation, the question, "What is Christianity?" or to say to what extent this or that *form* may be Christian. But we have an obligation to the former, which the present chapter

[1] *Koran,* 16:121.
[2] B. H. Streeter, *The Buddha and the Christ,* p. 117.

360

strives to meet. We have no desire to press the latter issue, nor to be dogmatic on it, although it proceeds inevitably from even the most objective interest in the former. Let the leaders of the many sects themselves tell us wherein they are Christian. Often, we need not contradict them; we may, at least, agree that they represent—or represented—aspects of the *essence* of the faith, and called attention to some values other sects have disregarded, —perhaps had not discovered. We may rightly be disturbed when any one division claims possession of the *whole* of truth for any age, or for all ages. Truth has been too broad for the comprehension of any individual, or for any fellowship, in a given time and place. Christianity is a multitude of elements in one.

The geographical extent of Christianity. is at once suggestive of its wide variety; it shares the varied qualities of the whole world. Nothing but a Pentecostal demonstration (*cf. Acts,* chap. 2) would harmonize the world's diversities of race, or make the many tongues of men intelligible to all. There would still remain the varied climates, skies, and scenery. There are probably more than 650,000,000 Christians in the world,[3] a total so great as to be of little value as a commentary on the faith itself; for generalization is inadequate, if not impossible, on institutions and ideas so scattered, even though they bear a single *name.* In such a total there are, also, at least three types of individuals: the genuine, loyal members; nominal and indifferent adherents; and many actively antagonistic, who prefer another name. The complexity is greater both in quantity and quality than it is in Hinduism, but Christianity has the more coherence; its tangible qualities are more conspicuous; it is more historical.

Christians fall mainly into three divisions: "Roman" Catholics, about 325,000,000; "Protestants," about 200,000,000; and "Greek" (or "Orthodox") Catholics, about 125,000,000. In addition, there are 800,000 "Syrian" and "Romo-Syrian" Christians in India, 1,000,000 Copts in Egypt, and 5,500,000 Christian Abyssinians. Differences are based on theories of the relationship of Church and State, on methods of internal jurisdiction, on accommodations to the local situation, and on subtle changes in the common consciousness; but, in particular, the differences inhere in ritual and creed. It is a question of authority, whether resting

---

[3] This figure includes: Europe, 455,000,000; N. America, 115,000,000; So. America, 62,000,000; Asia, 34,000,000; Africa, 8,000,000; Oceania, 7,500,000; and more particularly, India, 6,300,000; Abyssinia, 5,500,000: China, 3,250,000; Egypt, 1,200,000: and Palestine, 90,000.

upon Jesus, the words of Jesus, the "Church" he founded, the words of his apostles, statements of Christian councils, or interpretations by the individual. Christianity is vaster, more elaborate and formal than the faith of Jesus.

Externals.—Christianity may be viewed externally; it has its outward forms and symbols, which represent the inner faith. There are places of public worship: "meeting houses," chapels, basilicas, and cathedrals. They have their spires, towers, cupolas, and domes. The building may be cruciform; but whatever the ground plan, the crowning symbol is most frequently a cross. In outward form, the "church" may be readily distinguished from an Oriental temple, a Moslem mosque, or a Jewish synagogue. Its furnishings, also, distinguish it: the altar, font, figures in stained glass, icons, mosaics, images, scenes and "stations" from the life of Jesus, and quotations from the Scriptures. Public worship is participated in, or performed by, congregations of the faithful, as in mosques and synagogues. There is a "service" or a ritual, with psalms, hymns, and spiritual songs; litanies and other prayers; chants and processionals; and usually a sermon or address. All of which will indicate in some way the "Christian" heritage. Like those of all other faiths, the Christians have their days of public worship. Like Jews and Moslems, they have a special weekly day of prayer. Like mosques and synagogues, the church has been peculiarly the center of "activities" for its constituency; recently, also, like them, it has been a center of formal religious education. Whence came the churches, their furniture and ritual? Whence the ministers and priests? Whence the scriptures and statements of the faith?

The House of Worship.—It has been a current theory that the church was patterned on the Roman house or *domus*. In reality, it had an Oriental derivation. "The type of the Christian basilica goes back to the sanctuaries used by the adherents of oriental cults," says Laing;[4] perhaps to the sanctuaries of the "mystery" religions. Such a sanctuary contained an entrance space, an eastern door, a central hall (with columns), and an apse (the altar end, usually semicircular) at the western end, with an image of the god. St. Peter's Church in Rome thus has an eastern entrance and a western apse, with the altar; but very early a change of custom ordained a western entrance and an eastern apse and altar, in the manner of shrines of the sun-cult—and possibly under the influence of sun-worship. There

[4] G. J. Laing, *Roman Religion*, p. 189.

were analogies between Christ and the sun; in the figure of the sun, he had "risen with healing," had shed "light," etc.; and the Nativity fell on the date of the festival of the sun-god of Rome. Cathedrals, the "seats of bishops," have followed this west-east orientation; but many other houses of worship are indifferently located, perhaps with some deliberate aim at "non-conformity." Cathedrals have followed, also, the pattern of the cross, representing the nearest approach to uniformity among the many later types of Christian churches. The basilica, in the early days, usually had: an open court, with a fountain in the center and colonnades along the sides; a transverse corridor of entrance; a wide, central aisle flanked by columns to set it off from narrower side aisles; a transept across the eastern ends of the aisles, forming the arms of the cross; and an apse beyond the transept, commonly semicircular and extending the central aisle. The Church of St. Paul, in Rome, about a century old, represents faithfully this early, longitudinal plan. The basilica roof, early made of wood, was later made of stone, and notable developments occurred in vaulting, in the Romanesque and Gothic manner. In England, Gothic became the national style. With the centuries, the basilica grew in size and acquired additions. The clergy growing in numbers and importance, the transept was increased, and a choir was interposed between it and the apse. For the cult of the saints, chapels were built around the sanctuary proper.

In the Christian East, especially Armenia and Byzantium, the "Byzantine" style developed, with the dome the most conspicuous feature. Retaining the western entrance and the eastern apse, the body of the structure was a huge central hall covered by a spacious dome. The Church of San Sophia, "Divine Wisdom," in Istanbul (Constantinople) is the great example of Byzantine style,—although it has been, since 1453, a Moslem mosque. St. Mark's in Venice echoes the eastern style, and the cathedral at Moscow,[5] with its towering height and eccentric decoration, is dominantly Byzantine.

The parts of the early buildings were variously used in public worship. In the open court or in the entrance-corridor, the penitents and new converts would assemble. The congregation stood within the sanctuary proper, the women by themselves, in the left aisle or in the gallery above it. The clergy occupied the transept, in the center of which then stood the altar. At one

5 The Union of Soviet Republics has transformed the uses of this building.

end of the transept was a pulpit; at the other end, a lectern. The bishop's throne (*cathedra*) was in the apse, raised above the benches of the lesser clergy. Adjoining the church were a baptistry and the clergy's houses. In Western churches today, the sexes intermingle, but in the Eastern, they sit apart. Penitents and recent converts are everywhere admitted to the sanctuary.

Many of the early churches had been pagan temples. Christianity inherited and appropriated many elements of paganism. Among the converted Italian temples were: a shrine of Apollo at Nola; a temple of Hera, near Croton, in South Italy, which had become the seat of Juno Lucina, made into a church of the Madonna; the temple of Augustus, which Tiberius had built in Rome; and the famous Roman Pantheon, or "Temple of All Gods." Many sites were renovated; on Monte Casino, Benedict drove out with holy water the false god Apollo and established St. Martin in his place. Many of the rites of the Roman goddess Juno were continued in the worship of the Virgin Mary.

Meanwhile, ecclesiastical architecture, with its ritual and symbolism, developed somewhat independently. Or, breaking away from the pagan heritage of Greece and Rome, it developed forms in other lands in harmony with local situations or doctrinal requirements. The Baroque style, for example, was sponsored by the Jesuits for the church in Mexico. There have come to be many "national" types of building. While the Protestant Reformation was, in many places, a revolt of creed and polity, which did not greatly alter architecture, it was, in its "nonconformist" aspects, a thoroughgoing revolution. By choice and by necessity, there arose the chapel and the meeting house. In America, save for the uniform New England meeting house, and the reproductions of cathedrals, there are countless churches without special form,—whose variation may be in itself a monument to independence and to the right of private judgment! Where Christianity has gone in recent centuries in the furtherance of "missions" in India and the Far East, the churches have followed lines familiar to the missionaries. It is probable that, if the faith continues in these lands, the newer buildings will accord with Oriental patterns. Already there are churches in the style of mosques and temples. By similar suggestion, alterations will occur in ideas and ritual.

Leadership.—Leaders and officials of the Church [6] are vari-

---

[6] We now capitalize the word, and use it thus hereafter to designate the body of believers, their beliefs and practices; *any* body, for we do not raise the issue of the *"true"* Church.

ously known as apostles, presbyters or elders, pastors, prophets, bishops, ministers, priests, deans, deacons, friars, rectors, vicars, curates, teachers, and readers; and presiding elders, district superintendents, secretaries, arch-deacons, arch-bishops, cardinals, patriarchs, and popes. Each office has its own history, and represents a special function of the incumbent. It may represent some theory of the Church, its character and jurisdiction. There is a view that the ministry is a priesthood, that the priesthood is an office, and that worship may be properly conducted only through the ministry. Or, it may signify the priesthood of all believers, with no recognition of indispensable, fixed orders of the clergy. Among some, the layman is equal with the clergy in esteem.

Origins.—How did the Church begin? Of what elements was it early constituted? What goals were set for it? What character conditioned its development?

Only informal groups followed Jesus during his brief ministry. Being mostly Jewish, they did not attempt to organize themselves in separation from the Temple and the synagogues. Jesus himself took advantage of the Jewish institutions and read the Jewish scriptures, although the burden of his message was an other—, or an un-worldly Kingdom. Following the brief career of Jesus, a movement in his name got under way; independence of Judaism was inevitable and expedient. Societies were formed, composed of those who accepted his Gospel, professed faith in him, and were baptized. For administrative purposes and the general oversight of these believers, Jesus had left a band of personally selected apostles. The societies may have chosen their own "elders," or "bishops"; but in some instances the leaders were appointed by apostles, thus establishing an unpremeditated continuity. The early . "racial" uniformity was soon altered; Gentiles as well as Jews became converted. With the growth in membership, a combination of various social, economic, and religious elements developed; and gradually the "bishop" attained preëminence as the administrator of the order and the guardian of true teaching. Thus did the Church take form.

The faith, spreading at first around the Mediterranean basin, naturally followed, as an order, the pattern of the Roman imperial administration. The Church societies were administered from the larger civic centers, whose bishops rose thereby in power and dignity. The sees of the leading metropolitans were Antioch, Alexandria, Jerusalem, Ephesus, Constantinople, and Rome. In the third century, the imperial idea of a "Catholic or universal" Church appeared, connoting the whole body of believers. But when, in the fourth century, the Emperor transferred his seat from Rome to a city of his own foundation (Constantinople), the line was faintly drawn between a Western and an Eastern Church. Meanwhile, the Roman bishop assumed the leadership of the "universal" Church; but Eastern Catholics have never recognized his primacy. In the eleventh century, there was decreed a formal separation between the Western and the Eastern Churches, the Patriarch assuming full authority over Eastern "Orthodoxy," and the Pope retaining his authority at Rome. There were further preparations, as political and other circumstances altered in succeeding centuries.

Church Theory.—Four theories have prevailed with reference to Church polity (*i.e.*, the character and function of the Church):

1. The *World or Universal* Church. "The Church is the Kingdom of God on earth." There is a Catholic Church, which is coextensive with Christianity. Both the Roman Catholic and the Eastern Catholic Churches have claimed to be *the* Universal Church, although other Churches have held as strenuously the theory of "apostolic succession" in their ministry. Perhaps the recent reorganization of the Eastern Churches on a national basis has modified the theory of their character and function. But for many centuries the Eastern Church has shown few signs of universalism. The World Church theory has identified, whenever possible, the Church and State as one; it has made the Church the State. Kings have often tried to use the theory toward political consolidation, possibly relying on religion as the means to unity. Akhenaten of Egypt devised a "reformation," joining within the "horizon of the disc" [7] the altar of *Aten* and his own council-chamber. Moses, Mohammed, Akbar and Elizabeth are among the rulers who have experimented with religion as an aid to politics, each of them desiring unity of rule. The Churchman Augustine proposed a Roman ecclesiastical State, the "City of God." Christianity was to the Romans the one amalgam of the many elements within the Empire, as Hellenism had been to the Greeks the culture which might bind such different areas as Athens, Alexandria, Syria, Parthia, Persia, and Bactria.

The World Church theory magnifies the priestly office, makes it indispensable. In consequence, the office is above the man who holds it. The man becomes, by ordination, the priest or

---

[7] Amen-hetep IV (d. 1358 B.C.) called himself "Akhen-aten," "God-satisfied," and proposed solar "monotheism" for the state.

minister; not in himself, therefore, but in his office, he finds power. All offices are joined in a system of succession, whether of rank or time. The humblest, duly consecrated officer is linked ultimately with a Patriarch, a Pope, or some official head. And by a theory of "apostolic succession," through the "laying on of hands," the connection is maintained presumably with Jesus, and certainly with "the inspired apostles, with Peter at their head."

2. The *National* Church. All Church members within a nation are subject to a national administration. It amounts to a close association of Church and State, differing little from the identity of the two in the World Church view. But the Church is purely national, even though the State be an empire with colonies, or a federation of independent states. The Armenian (Gregorian), the Abyssinian, the English, the Lutheran, the recent Welsh, the Czecho-Slovakian, and the very recent German Christian Churches are examples. The National Church considers itself in direct succession from the early apostolate, tracing the rights of its clergy through the deacons in the Church at Jerusalem, and the bishops ordained at other centers. Strictly speaking, the theory of the National Church is qualified when there are organized and recognized dissenters. Certain Churches, for example, the Methodist and the American Protestant Episcopal, are of "national" descent, although in no sense National. These two descended from the Established Church of England. The Methodist, although "episcopal," has its own distinctive government, but the Protestant Episcopal is governed like the Church of England.

3. The *Presbyterian* Church. The entire Church is a single entity, and should function as a whole, even as the membership of any local Church should function. The "Presbyterian" theory posits a middle ground between episcopacy and congregationalism, between the government of the bishop and the independence of the local congregation. Government is representative, by election, in which laymen have equal rights with ministers. Local churches are united in a Presbytery. Presbyteries are associated in, and governed by a Synod. Over the Church as a whole the General Assembly has jurisdiction. The local church is organized with presbyters or elders, and deacons. Local affairs are controlled by the Session, composed of presbyters. The pastor is a presbyter, but not a member of the local congregation; he is a member of, and responsible to the Presbytery, which instals him in his

pastorate. The Presbyterian Church has no fixed orders of officials beyond its presbyters and deacons. The influence of the minister follows more from his own character than from his ordination. He is officially not unlike the Jewish rabbi. The system itself is democratic, but with an aristocratic touch. The Church of Scotland is Presbyterian. The system is extensive, flouishing especially in the United States and Canada.

4. The *Congregational* Church. The local congregation is self-governing, in the manner of early apostolic times. Emphasis is placed upon man's right to worship God directly without priestly intervention; the priesthood is dispensable. The Church arose from "Puritan" and "Separatist" movements in Great Britain, in protest against Episcopal Establishment, and in doctrinal and governmental deviation from Presbyterianism. Congregational-Christians, Baptists, Disciples of Christ, Unitarians, and Universalists are examples. There are no fixed orders, save as certain customary proprieties are observed in the administration of the "sacraments" (Baptism and the Lord's Supper). Each congregation is democratic and autonomous. The minister may be inducted into office by a vote; he may be "installed" by an invited Council; but he is responsible directly to his own people; his character is the test of office.

While these four theories are chiefly governmental, they involve a great variety of doctrine. There are many views with reference to the character of Christianity, its scope, and the operation of the Christian spirit. We shall view such questions in a later setting. Political theory and doctrinal position are by no means always one. Doctrine cuts across the four divisions. For example, Disciples of Christ and Methodists emphasize the individual's own immediate concern for the welfare of his soul, while Baptists join with Presbyterians to emphasize God's part in man's salvation.

Sacraments.—Christianity, like other faiths, has dramatized or vitalized its doctrines; it has its "sacraments," especially Baptism and the Lord's Supper. This sacramental aspect is original, with two qualities inherent: (1) pure symbolism, and (2) magical potency. They lay in the Jewish background, and were naturally perpetuated as Christianity became a formal institution. The Jews had often thought of sacrifice as wonder-working, as in itself effective toward national safety or the destruction of their enemies. They often gloried in the spectacle, as if God were pleased and made favorably disposed by it. Their prophets denied this theory and condemned this sort of sacrament, insisting that "God looketh on the heart." Jesus preached a spiritual Kingdom of the heart, but recognized certain outward signs of it and instituted certain rites in aid of it. He "suffered" himself to be baptized by John, because it "thus became him to fulfil all righteousness" (*Mt.* 3:15). He also baptized (*John* 3:33). He "sacrificed the passover" (*Lk.* 22:7) and instituted a memorial supper (*Lk.* 22:13ff). Christian ritual thus began with Jesus, by his qualified extension of accepted rites.

The early Christians, Jews and Gentiles, observed the "sacraments"; but there were differing views of their significance. Often wonders were expected of them; at least, they were relied on for the bestowal of an inward "grace." Some thought the rite of baptism to be a cleansing of the mind and a means itself of spiritual renewal. Some thought of the "supper" of bread and wine as magically beneficial. Others, more truly, it seems, considered baptism to be the outward sign of inner consecration, a public demonstration of the conversion which had already taken place within. These understood the supper to be purely a memorial of the Christ, and an occasion of the fellowship and communion with him. Baptism was performed once only for each convert; the Lord's Supper was eaten frequently—weekly, as a rule—by all members of the Church.

Seven sacraments, in all, came gradually into use, in contrast with the simple rites of Jesus, and in extension of early apostolic practices. Each has been variously interpreted, whether as magic or as symbol. They had assumed a formal character by the third century, at the latest. Each had its character either as material or activity; and each acquired in practice, at the hands of various officiants, a peculiar inner quality. These are the seven: Baptism, the Lord's Supper, confirmation, ordination, penance, marriage, and extreme unction. The Roman Catholic Church observes them all. The Eastern Catholic Church has five, excluding marriage and extreme unction *as sacraments*. Protestants—except the Friends, who have none—have only two, Baptism and the Supper. A sacrament, in whatever Church, is properly administered only by a duly qualified official, someone "in orders." The propriety of this is evident, even to "non-ritualists." Christianity as a spirit does not live effectively without its formal agencies.

The death of Jesus became the one great sacrifice in Christianity. All Christians might appropriate its virtue. Since he had eaten the "Last Supper" with his disciples before his death, this meal, in perpetuity, has memorialized the great event. It has gone by other names, also: the Eucharist, Holy Communion, and the Mass. In a non-ritualistic sense, the Lord's death upon the cross represented his complete spiritualization, and the sharing of his presence with all believers. In like manner, the Supper as a formal rite is a sharing of his presence.

His baptism could have been, at most, symbolic, an assent to John's announcement, and an outward sign of the inner sense of mission. The believer's baptism is the formal mark of entrance into the household of faith. One apostle designated it a burial with Christ and a rising with him to newness of life. If one were baptized without faith, as in infancy, the rite was not complete. And the fact that it was only *once* administered caused some to doubt whether its efficacy persisted. On various grounds, new sacraments developed.

Confirmation is an initiatory ceremony administered to the individual: by the Eastern Church, following his baptism; by the Roman Church, about ten years afterward; and by certain Protestant Churches—although it is not a "sacrament" in their view—after one who has been baptized as a child has arrived at adolescence with instruction. It consists of the laying on of hands, and prayer, and, in the Roman and the Eastern Churches, of anointment with a balmy oil, the holy *chrism*. It implies—or else *imparts,* according to the view—a strengthening by the Holy Spirit, and thus prepares the candidate for full communion.[8]

Ordination applies, in particular, to the Christian *ministry*. It is the rite of formal appointment by which a person is authorized to perform public religious acts on behalf of the Church. In the Roman, Eastern, Anglican, Methodist, and certain other Churches, it obtains for the candidate entrance into the holy order constituted by the grace of apostolic succession. In the Roman Church, the succession follows from the apostle Peter who, it points out, received the primary of office from Christ himself (*cf. Mt.* 16:18). In non-episcopal bodies, ordination is simply the solemn introduction of the candidate into the office and the duties of a minister. In Catholic theory, the rite distinguishes the subject as a priest by an indelible distinction. In any Church, it is performed but once upon any individual. There is, however, no common recognition among all Churches of the validity of

---

[8] Christian confirmation is analogous to the assumption of the thread by a higher caste "Hindu," who then becomes a "twice-born."

the act of any of them. The chief office of the ordained minister, or priest, is the consecration, or the administration of the Lord's Supper.

Penance is an act of punishment for sin, preceded by confession, and followed by absolution. In fact, this sacrament, according to the Council of Trent (1545–1563), consists of contrition, confession, satisfaction, *and* absolution. It rests within the authority of a bishop or a priest, and has something of the force and precision of the ancient Jewish sacrifice—the steps of recovery from sin are well defined, and reassuring to the offender. By Christ's own decree the Church has power to forgive sins (*Mt.* 16:19, 18:18), except a mysterious "unforgivable sin" against the Holy Spirit. Grievous sins, such as murder, adultery, and fornication, were at first deemed unforgivable, but penance ultimately provided their forgiveness. Nevertheless, degrees of sin have been established by the Church, with lines drawn between ritual offences, moral evil, and moral turpitude.[9] Penance removes the immediate guilt and the eternal punishment which the sin would have incurred. It will be seen, in consequence, to what natural proportions the Confessional has grown in Catholic churches, and what influence is exerted by confessors.

Marriage, as one of the seven *Roman* sacraments, signifies a durable union between one man and one woman, established by an appropriate ceremony performed within the Church, that is, by someone in holy orders in the Roman Church. Divorce is, normally, not allowable. No priest may marry, and no married man may be ordained. In the Eastern Church, celibacy is the rule for priests of the highest rank, but a married man may be ordained to the ordinary priesthood (if his wife die, however, after his ordination, he may not remarry).

Extreme unction is administered to persons dying. As in the case of the Eucharist and penance, this ceremony is performed by someone of the rank of priest, or higher. Through it forgiveness is mediated, even without penance, and recovery, if possible, is aided. The Eucharist may be administered; or, in emergencies, merely parts of the body may be anointed with consecrated oil (usually, the eyes, ears, nostrils, lips, hands and feet). Burial always, if possible, is in consecrated ground and under the full direction of the Church.

Worship.—Public worship may be free, with an order of services locally arranged; or, may be ritualistic, with a ritual

9 *Cf.* the two kinds of sin, mortal and venial, of the early Churchmen.

prescribed by an authority. Naturally the Christian, with his peculiarly spiritual religion, seeks to perform, in public, acts which God delights in, such as hymns, and prayers, and recitations from the sacred scriptures. Not unnaturally, many Christians have believed that God has prescribed certain forms whose observance wins his favor. At any rate, a ritual was devised in accordance with the various needs of worship (inclusive, in some instances, of the various "sacraments"). It was not possible for the Christian Church to escape the need of ritual. On the other hand, circumstances have allowed for the accumulation of spectacular and elaborate forms. They have become to many Christians what the *Law* has been in Judaism, objects of supreme devotion. The non-ritualist, with his spontaneity, may find peculiar satisfaction in the very directness and freedom of his worship. The ritualist, with his prescribed formality, may be equally as certain of divine favor. Some branches are highly ritualistic, notably the Roman, the Eastern, and the Anglican, while others, including Presbyterian and Congregational bodies, are notably informal. Differences of opinion have prevailed as to what constitutes true worship, and what its value is to worshipers. Historically, worship was at first comparatively simple. Jesus himself was devoted to the Temple and the synagogue. Early Christians met for worship in any place available, including private houses. Justin Martyr (martyred between 163 and 167) has described the important early elements: "On Sunday, a meeting is held of all who live in the cities and villages, and a section is read from the memoirs of the Apostles and the writings of the Prophets, as long as the time permits. When the reading is finished, the president in a discourse gives admonition and exhortation to imitate these noble things. After this we all arise and offer a common prayer. At the close of the prayer . . . bread and wine and water are brought, the president offering prayer and thanks for them according to his ability, and the congregation answering 'Amen.' Then the consecrated elements are distributed to each one and partaken of, and are carried by the deacons to the houses of those absent (from the meeting). The wealthy and the willing then give contributions according to their freewill; and this collection is deposited with the president, who therewith supplies orphans and widows, the poor and needy, prisoners and strangers, and takes care of all who are in want." This is merely one report, and may not tell the whole story, but its simplicity inspires our imagination. We see the major elements of worship: a Sunday meeting, Scripture reading, a sermon, common prayer, communion, a freewill offering, and gifts to dependents and the needy. The only officers named are the "president" (doubtless an "elder," or "bishop"), and the "deacons." From other accounts the more complete development may be reconstructed.[10]

Scripture.—Let us follow Justin's reference to "the memoirs of the apostles and the writings of the prophets," that we may get more acquaintance with the Christian Scriptures, especially the *New Testament*. We have said that organization and creed have been the two separately controlling factors in the history of Christianity. We might now say the Church and the Bible, although the Church by means of its councils and its creeds has constituted itself the interpreter of the Scripture. In the long history of Christianity the ultimate authority has rested now in the Church and now in the Scripture.

As Justin indicates, the nucleus of Christian Scripture was apostolic literature. In the time of Jesus and amongst his people, the Jews, the authoritative scriptures were the *Law,* the *Prophets,* and the *Writings.* Jesus on various occasions referred to these scriptures, sometimes with approval, but usually in contrast with his own teachings. He preached his own Gospel. He himself wrote nothing which endured, being more intent upon the spirit than upon the letter.[11] His sayings were remembered in men's hearts, and they interpreted them "as the spirit gave them utterance." The writings of the apostles Paul and John (after 50 A.D.) constitute more than one-third of the entire canonical *New Testament;* although some of them were lost. The "gospels" of Matthew, Mark, and Luke made up another third. By about 350 the Canon was fairly permanently defined, with the line drawn, for the most part, between the authentic compositions of those who had "seen the Lord" and later writings which claimed authority.[12] An established Canon was indispensable to combat the "heresies" which were springing up on every hand and to provide a scriptural basis for the faith. Since the Canon formed, writings by Christian authors have been confined to interpretation (a method analogous to the Jewish *Talmud*).

For the very earliest Christians, as for Jesus himself, the

---

10 Concerning "holy water" and its uses, see G. J. Laing, Roman Religion *Survivals from Roman Religion,* Chap. XXIII.

11 His writing in the sand might be taken as an ironical demonstration of the imperfection of the written word.

12 The book of *Revelation* was admitted because attributed to the aged apostle John, who recorded herein his "visions" of Jesus and the future.

Old Testament was "Scripture." The words of Jesus came, however, to have an authority equal, at least, to the Jewish writings. His teachings were orally preserved. Had the disciples thought of reducing them to writing, they would doubtless have said there was no need, for he would be "coming again" so soon,— to establish the Kingdom of God on earth, and to be its King. The apostles taught orally at first. Their written teachings came as letters to distant churches concerned with various issues of organization and doctrine. Sometimes discussions were carried on by letter; for example, with the Christians in Thessalonika, who, with others of their co-religionists elsewhere, were looking for the "second coming" (*cf. 2 Pet.* 3:10), and were troubled about the fate of several of their number who died meanwhile (*cf. I Thess.* 4:15). There were such problems as: the relation of the Gospel to the *Law* (*cf. Gal.* 3); the relation of Jewish and Gentile Christians;[18] the propriety of eating meat slaughtered with a pagan ceremony (I *Cor.* 8); Paul's claim to apostleship (I *Cor.* 9); conduct at the Lord's table; the character of the resurrection; women's place in the Church (I *Cor.* 11, 15); the dangers of heresy and apostasy (*Col.* 2:8; I *Tim.* 4:1; I *Jno.* 4:1); the relation of "faith" and "works" (*Jas.* 2:26); and many more besides—for a new spirit and a new movement must wrestle with many immediate and practical impediments, both without and within. Both as human documents, full of local color, and as religious treatises, these apostolic writings are of perpetual interest.

The day came when the earthly career of Jesus increased in vital and doctrinal significance in the mind of the Church, and, in response, the *Gospels* were composed. That is, "Lives" of Christ were written in exposition of what must actually have happened. We have the books of *Matthew, Mark, Luke,* and *John,* written sometime between the years 75 and 95, in Jerusalem(?), Rome, Antioch(?), and Ephesus, respectively. *Mark,* in fact, represents the basic account, with *Matthew* and *Luke* representing selections and revisions of *Mark,* along with additions of their own. They are "historical" writings; and so is *John,* but *John* emphasizes doctrine to a greater degree. Mark tells the story simply and directly, although his order of events is more topical than chronological. He wrote for the information of the Romans, and dwelt much upon the *acts* of Jesus. Matthew wrote a Palestinian, and Luke, a Gentile record. Both include

---

[18] This Jewish-Gentile problem is discussed in the *Epistle to the Romans*.

much "discourse" [14] material in amplification of Jesus' acts. There were already various written sources back of these Gospels, upon which the writers could—and did—rely. John adopted an outline of his own, varying much from the "Petrine" tradition followed by Mark and others, and emphasized facts and ideas which he wished to impress upon the Christians of Asia (Asia Minor) in his time. We have, therefore, in the *New Testament* three prominent strains of tradition: the Pauline (as in the numerous letters of the apostle Paul, written while on his missionary journeys, and while he was a prisoner in Rome); the Petrine (as in the *Lives* by Mark, Matthew and Luke, and in sections of the *Acts of the Apostles*); and the Johannine (as in John's *Gospel* and in his *Epistles*). Three strong personalities set in motion three persistent currents of tradition.

Each exhibited his own peculiar tendency in the interpretation of the person and the ministry of Jesus. Paul emphasized experience, and Peter, miracle; while John developed the view of Jesus as the Christ, the "Word," and the "Son" of God. These differences of emphasis do not, in any case, represent the whole interpretation, nor are they mutually contradictory with reference to Jesus' person, acts, and teachings. It can be seen, however, that thus early the foundations were laid within the accepted Canon itself for variations of structure, and for divergencies of theory within the Church.

In addition to the *Epistles* and the *Gospels,* there are other writings in the Canon, for example, the *Acts of the Apostles*. It represents a second volume by Luke, written to meet the need of an authoritative record of the apostles' work. The prominent figures in the *Acts* are Paul and Peter, with emphasis, perhaps, on Peter, although the exploits of both are often paralleled. In the sequence into which the various writings of the Canon finally fell, the *Acts of the Apostles* forms the bridge between the historical *Gospels* and the interpretative *Epistles,* and is itself the key to an understanding of the idea of the Canon.[15] If you would know the full list of the twenty-nine books of the *New Testament,* in their canonical order as representing a certain relativity of religious importance, you may take up a copy of the *Bible*. The *New Testament* came to occupy a place with the *Old* as the fundamental Christian Scripture. Between the facts and the truths of the *Old* and of the *New* are indissoluble bonds.

---

[14] *I.e.,* sayings of Jesus.
[15] *I.e.,* the conception of the Canon as a full account of *apostolic* Christianity.

Indeed, one may discover by an association of the two an amazing narrative of progress in the history of religion. In the *Bible* as a whole one finds many persistent currents of tradition, such as the legal and the priestly (Moses, Ezra, and Peter), and the prophetic and the theological (Amos, II Isaiah, Paul and John). The *Bible* is in itself a complete source-book for Religion. The Christian, therefore, has at his disposal, in his home and in the Church, an incomparable volume which in its account of the Hebrew-Jewish-Christian faith *more* than typifies the results of the general quest of man for God and the religious life. The extent to which the *Bible* is used by the Church, especially in services of public worship and for purposes of religious education, has varied from time to time and in accordance with the comparative value placed upon it as authority. During the second and third centuries, the growth of the Church may be largely attributed to the uses made of the *New Testament* writings which were in the way of acquiring a divinity of character. In fact, one of the principles operating toward the formation of a Canon was the general *acceptance* of the writings (other writings which to some churches seemed worthy of recognition were ultimately excluded because all would not agree upon them; sometimes purely local considerations entered in).

The Canon.—While we speak of a Canon of Sacred Scripture, we should not be unmindful of the fact that after all there is no universally accepted form. There is, in reality, a Protestant canon of today, and a smaller, or a larger collection used by certain other branches of the Church. The Syrian Church omits 2 and 3 *John, 2 Peter, Jude,* and *Revelation.* The Coptic Church omits the book of *Revelation.* The Eastern Church includes in its canon many apocryphal, or "doubtful" writings (*i.e.,* doubtful from the point of view of the Hebrew and the Protestant Scriptures), such as the *Wisdom of Solomon, Judith,* I and II *Maccabees,* etc. The Roman Church uses the *Vulgate,* and includes, by a decree of the Council of Trent, *Judith, Ecclesiasticus, Baruch,* I and II *Maccabees,* and III and IV *Esdras.* No formal, official decree of the Roman Church had earlier (than Trent) fixed the limits of its *Bible,* this Church having had a yet more urgent interest in its welfare as a *body.* In actual practice, no Church ever uses its entire Scripture. No Christian ritual has ever included the requirement, or the customary procedure, of a periodic public reading of the *Book,* as does Judaism for its *Law,* and Islam for its *Koran.* Also, a lingering disposition has been shown to assign unequal values to the various contents. While some Churches and individuals have believed, in theory, that "all Scripture is inspired of God" (nevertheless, without the actual use of all of it), others have reserved to themselves some right of private or communal judgment. Martin Luther utterly rejected *James*. Alexander Campbell, one of the founders of the Disciples of Christ, believed that revelation could come only through the written Word (the Protestant *Bible,* he meant), and yet gave the *New Testament* a practical preëminence, at least, over the *Old*. And among Christians, there have always been many to take literally what the Scriptures say, making them not only an ultimate external authority, but an authority to be precisely understood and followed. Other Christians have sought to understand the "meaning" and the "spirit" of the Scriptures. There have been many versions and translations, a translation being in the nature of the case something of a commentary. The *Old Testament* was composed in *Hebrew,* and the *New Testament* in *Greek*. There is a *Greek Old Testament* (the *Septuagint*), a version in *Syriac,* and another in *Latin* (the *Vulgate*),—all made from the *Hebrew*. There are *Syriac, Latin, Coptic,* and other versions of the *New Testament* made from the original *Greek*. There is an interesting series of illuminating English versions of the *Bible* as a whole, including those of Wycliffe, Tyndale, and Coverdale (particularly the *Great Bible* of 1541), the *Geneva Bible* of 1560, the *Bishop's Bible* of 1568, the *Rheims* and *Douai Bible* of 1609 (the first Roman Catholic *Bible* in *English*), the *Authorized Version* of 1611, the *Revised Version* of 1885, and th *American Standard Revised Version* of 1901. During recent years, several versions of the *New Testament* have been made "in modern speech," and even in the colloquial. If it has been impossible for the Church to reach complete agreement on the problem of the inspiration of the Testaments in their primary tongues, it is even more impossible to decide about the *inspiration* of the versions. One version very convincingly makes Paul refer to "the sacred writings which are able to make you wise unto salvation through faith which is in Christ Jesus," and to add, "Every scripture inspired of God is also profitable for teaching, for reproof, for correction, for instruction which is in righteousness: that the man of God may be complete, furnished completely unto every good work" (II *Tim.* 3:15–17). This is a careful statement, with several instructive qualifications. Paul wrote before certain writings appeared which came to be held sacred, or inspired. The problem is not only one of inspired scripture, but one of inspired persons. God early inspired persons who had not the ability to write; they *spoke* in the power of his spirit. The writings of inspired apostles were naturally thought to be inspired. No one, however, will claim that God has not inspired persons since, even though it were for no more than interpretation. The Catholics established the theory of the inspiration of the *Church*. The Protestants, in their turn, established the theory of the inspiration, therefore the infallibility, of the *Bible*. Both theories have of necessity been affected by dynamic and historico-critical views of all the facts in either case,—for example, various discrepancies in the text, and many doctrinal inconsistencies, of the *Bible*. If the study of the *Bible* has modified the theory of its literal inspiration, it has exalted the Book as a stupendous human document, inspired *per se* and by no means uninspiring. It has related it to man's continuing quest for God.

Prayer.—Justin made reference to "a common prayer," or a prayer in unison. The Church believes in prayer and makes use of formal prayers. Justin referred also to the prayer of the president (the "presiding" elder, or bishop) made "according to his ability," probably *ex tempore*. Both ritual and spontaneous prayer are recognized. Prayer has been an indispensable part of Christian self-expression; it has been at times the expression of an even more elemental mood. Jesus himself prayed. The apostle Paul commended prayer "without ceasing." To Jesus and usually to the early apostles, prayer was "spiritual" rather than "formal"; it was an act of fellowship with God, prompted by some need of power, peace, or happiness in God. It assumed that God was "nigh unto all who called upon him in faith," and was more anxious to bless men than they were to be blessed. The individual, confronted by his own peculiar need, might pray spontaneously in words of his own selection, or he might appropriate a commonly accepted form. The "Lord's Prayer" whose words are ascribed to Jesus in his *Sermon on the Mount* represents the earliest of such forms (*cf. Mt.* 6:9–13). During common worship, the use of formal prayers came to be the custom. The Lord's Prayer has been used extensively, and books of common prayer have been formulated. Many Church "fathers" composed prayers for the various congregations. The Catholic Church developed the elaborate ceremonial of the Mass, in which was provided a large place for formal prayers. The *Roman Missal* contains the liturgy of the Mass, standardized in the sixteenth century by the Council of Trent. The Mass is always celebrated in *Latin,* but the layman may follow it in translations in his own tongue, joining from time to time in common prayer. The Church of England has its *Book of Common Prayer,* finally revised in 1662. It includes the order for daily morning and evening prayer, with prayers and thanksgivings for various occasions. The Protestant Episcopal Church has used since 1789 a modification of the Anglican *Book of Common Prayer,* omitting the Athanasian Creed, and modifying certain portions of the ritual. The Presbyterian Churches have their *Book of Common Prayer,* formulated first by John Knox in Scotland in 1562, and amended in 1661 by the Westminster Assembly. American Presbyterians use at their own option a *Book of Common Worship* published in 1905, which includes forms of morning and evening prayer, and forms for use in connection with baptism, communion, marriage, and other services. The Methodist churches use a modern service book—at their option,—including a form of Sunday worship prepared by John Wesley on the basis of the Anglican *Book of Common Prayer,* with omissions, abbreviations, and modifications. Many American denominations use books of worship with prayers for regular and special occasions. Many ministers of so-called "non-liturgical" churches freely appropriate for their public worship the significant expressions used by gifted souls before them, lending to their own order the impressiveness of age. Original, inspired utterance is rare, although Carlyle once said, "Prayer is and remains the native and deepest impulse of the soul of man." One of the most impressive common prayers of the Christian Church is this prayer of St. Chrysostom (344–407), the greatest of ancient preachers,

"Almighty God, who hast given us grace at this time with one accord to make our common supplications unto Thee; and dost promise that when two or three are gathered together in Thy Name Thou wilt grant their requests; Fulfil now, O Lord, the desires and petitions of Thy servants, as may be most expedient for them; granting us in this world knowledge of Thy truth, and in the world to come life ever lasting. Amen."

There is in the phraseology of this prayer nothing that is exclusively Christian. It rather represents an even wider faith, save as it is the prayer of a particular Christian preacher, and is used exclusively in Christian worship. The Christian Church was heir of the noble prayers of the *Old Testament* and of the *Hebrew* liturgy which was peculiarly prayerful. The prayers of the Church are basically Biblical, as is indicated by several phrases of St. Chrysostom; the historical connection cannot be denied.

Hymns.—Hymns also are characteristic elements of worship. Although Justin did not mention them,—for, in days of persecution, worship was often quietly conducted to avoid detection— the use of hymns was common from the first, both in public and in private. They were not only a natural expression of the Christian spirit, but also a method of doctrinal instruction. A history of Christian theology might be written from a study of the Church's hymns. The *hymnos* of the Greeks was a festival song to the gods or heroes. The term came to be applied to the Jewish *psalm*. In early Christian writings the *Latin* term *hymnus* covered all "songs with praise to God." The *Psalter,* the Jewish *Psalms,* was the Church's first hymn-book; some sects have steadfastly refused the use of any other. From the fourth century, metrical hymns have been written; in due time many were admitted to the liturgy. Since the Reformation, hymns have been composed in great number for congregational singing, although in "Calvanistic" circles, psalm-singing only was recognized in worship. From about 1700, *English* hymns have been written and used in the Protestant churches of England and America. These hymns are expressive of Christian experience and social obligation. They are expressive of theology, although some have been used by congregations fundamentally opposed to their inherent doctrine; in the ecstasy of song, doctrine has been ignored! A standard collection of hymns may contain the compositions of Eastern Orthodox, Roman Catholic, German Lutheran, Scotch Presbyterian, English Wesleyan, Southern Methodist, Unitarian, and other Christian writers, so cosmopolitan at last is hymnody.[16]

The Mass.—No form is so distinctive of the Christian Church as the sacrament or "mystery" of the Lord's Supper. It has held the central place in worship from apostolic times. Justin mentioned the "Eucharist," with its elements of "bread, and wine with water." The *Greek* term *eucharist* remains the normal name for the sacrament throughout Catholic theology, but is gradually superseded by the *Latin missa* for the whole rite, especially in

---

16 "Poetry is more philosophic than history," said Aristotle.

the Roman Church. At first, the rite concluded a Church *agape,* or "love-feast"; but in time, it came to be, as now, a daytime, more or less elaborate ceremony, the center of the cultus. It is most elaborate, especially in the form called "high Mass," in the Greek and Roman Churches. In the Roman Church, the Mass is both a mystery and a sacrifice, particularly the latter, representing Christ's *atonement.* It provides for penitents forgiveness of sins committed after baptism. Baptism was especially important in the early Church, when converts chiefly came from heathenism. It is important still in conversion "from the world." But the Mass supports the Christian; it is the sign that Christ continually suffers and atones for weak humanity. This doctrine of atonement served itself heir to the Jewish theory of sacrifice, and its ministers assumed succession to the Jewish priesthood. This Judæo-Roman theory is the very core of Roman Catholic doctrine, somewhat in contrast with the Greek's central doctrine of the Incarnation. It keeps men reconciled to God.

The Mass is very complicated, with minute rubrics (liturgical rules) to be followed by the celebrant and his ministers. The high Mass may be sung by a priest at a consecrated altar on any day except Good Friday. Normally, it is celebrated every Sunday morning and on feast days. The celebrant must be in the state of grace, fasting from midnight, free of censure; and he must observe the rules concerning the elements (unleavened bread and fermented wine), vestments, vessels, and ritual. At the time of the ceremony,[17] the procession comes to the altar, at whose foot the preparatory prayers of contrition and supplication are said. The altar is incensed and the choir sings the prayers. If the *"Te Deum"* is said, the celebrant intones the *"Gloria,"* which the choir continues. After the responses, "The Lord be with you," and "And with thy spirit," the collect of the day is chanted, followed by the *Epistle* read at the south side and the *Gospel* read at the north side of the altar. Thereafter, the deacon, with the subdeacon, goes in procession to the north of the choir to sing the *Gospel.* A sermon may follow the *Gospel,* followed, in turn, by the singing of the Creed. This ends the portion known as the "Mass of the Catechumens." Next comes the "Mass of the Faithful," introduced by the Offertory. The bread is offered to God by the celebrant, with prayer. The deacon pours wine, and the subdeacon water, into the chalice, which is then offered

---

[17] The description offered is very brief, seeking to indicate merely some of the essentials of the service.

to God, with prayer. The offerings, the altar, the celebrant, ministers, and people are all incensed; and the "secrets" are said. The priest then bathes his fingers and recites the Eucharistic prayer in preparation for the solemn Canon of the Mass. This is the Communion, in particular, including the Lord's Prayer, the kiss of peace, the *"Agnus Dei"* (the "Lamb of God that takest away the sins of the world"), the elevation of the bread and of the wine to signify their transubstantiation into the body and the blood of Christ. The Communion of the people follows, through partaking of the bread, if there are any who desire it, with absolution. After the choir has sung the Communion, there are further "greetings," and the deacon sings the dismissal. After a blessing, a prayer, and the Last *Gospel* (the first chapter of *John*), the procession returns to the sacristy.

History.—We ask now more directly, What is Christianity? What is the faith embodied in these many forms? We must find the essence living in the forms it vitalizes. What is Christianity as a movement in world history?

Christianity, whatever its present claim may be on men so widely scattered, whatever the influences it may have exerted during nineteen centuries, rests primarily upon an historic person, Jesus Christ; it must be understood with reference to his life and teachings. It is one of nine religions living still, each founded by a person. This historic fact need not detract from spiritual reality; but it qualifies it. We happen not to have complete accounts of Jesus' life and teachings; the various fragments which we have are sometimes contradictory. His "life" was not set down in writing, until years after the earthly phase of it had closed. Meanwhile, some impressions of the many who had been with him had altered, and some of those who wrote about him had various motives. Biographical details are mainly found in several *Gospels,* chiefly those of Matthew, Mark, Luke, and John. A "gospel" is a "God-story," a "good message" (*euangelion,* "evangel") concerning the dealings of God with men through Jesus Christ. Additional facts of Jesus' life are found in some *Epistles;* but first-hand materials are meager. A few hours would suffice to read them all. Yet, far beyond the miracle of the loaves and fishes, the volumes written on the basis of these fragments are impossible to number. The biography of Jesus has been ever in the making, including men's devotion and experience in every age.

Jesus (4 B.C.–30 A.D.), the son of Joseph and Mary, was born in Bethlehem, a village of the Roman Palestinian province of Judæa (Judah). The name Jesus, which his father gave him (*Mt.* 1:25), was not uncommon. It is the *Greek* form of Joshua. As something more distinctive, he was called by many Jesus of Nazareth. His parents were Jews of Nazareth, a village of the northern Palestinian province of Galilee. At the time of his birth, they were visiting in his mother's ancestral home in connection with the taking of a census. Bethlehem was the "city of David," from whom Joseph was descended. While Jesus was inconspicuously born of humble parents, and among a subject people, he came of the noblest Hebrew stock. This descent was emphasized by the records made when he attained distinction. It was further pointed out that he was not only nobly, but uniquely born—his mother was a virgin. This statement was, at the time of record, readily accepted. It represents, at least, a justifiable attempt to demonstrate the uniqueness of Jesus' life and character. He came as the long-foretold Messiah of the Jews and the Savior of the world.

He was reared in the faith of his fathers, which then centered in the synagogue. He spent his early years in ways normal to Jewish life in the small village, learning, in particular, the trade of his father, a carpenter. But there dawned in his youth the strange, sweet consciousness of a peculiar mission. Luke's *Gospel* (2:41-51) recounts this experience. He became, somehow, aware of a relationship to God, which surpassed the ties of home and kinsfolk. He felt himself, to an unusual, unsurpassed degree, the "son" of God, and bound to the doing of his heavenly Father's will. This God-consciousness meant the giving of himself in a spiritual ministry to mankind. Coming gradually, it did not disturb him; rather, he maintained a growing confidence; but it puzzled his own people, and aroused suspicion in the village. His mother seems to have been the only one who understood him. He did not forsake his home in immediate response to the inner vision. He dwelt among his "brothers," but went often to the "Father's house." At last a crisis came, after which he gave himself exclusively to his "Father's business" (*cf. Lk.* 2:49-52).

The Ministry of Jesus.—When Jesus was about thirty years old he attended the preaching of John "the Baptiser," an earnest Jewish prophet who had come with a message of repentance. It was a time of national despondency; the people were on edge. The words of the prophet struck home, and a movement got under way. Jesus joined it and was baptized at once by John in the river Jordan. This was the seal of his own mission, and John, apparently realizing the significance of the ceremony he had performed, drew away from the public scene in Jesus' favor. Thenceforth, Jesus gave himself to his active program of reform, offering men "salvation" and declaring himself to be the "way." It is now common knowledge to us that he made a tremendous impression upon the people of his land, especially upon a chosen few who gave themselves entirely to serve him. They surrendered themselves to *him,* catching something of the power of his spirit and the scope of his mission. He became the "Way" of their devotion, and they in their turn announced him throughout a widening world as the Way for all mankind.

Jesus spent two or three years in a public ministry, before his death at the hands of the Roman government. The common people heard him gladly. His was a new voice in evident opposition to the old oppressive order. But many Jewish and some Roman leaders came to think him dangerous; representing either the synagogue or the state, they were uneasy over things he said and did. Jesus placed his emphasis on life itself and on its spiritual expression, indifferent to the government, and in opposition to the Jewish, especially the Pharisaical, emphasis on the *Law,* the Sabbath, and ceremonial cleanness. Although he declared plainly that he came not to destroy, but to fulfil, his teachings were held inimical to the Jewish faith; and the Romans failed to understand the proclamation of his kingship. As he became increasingly aware of his technical Messiahship, the Romans were correspondingly aroused against a "king of the Jews" in Palestine. Nor were the Jews then looking for the kind of a Messiah Jesus was; they wanted not a spiritual, but a worldly, agent to win freedom for them, and to reëstablish Israel as an independent kingdom (*cf. Isa.,* chaps. 11 and 52).

Jesus announced his Messiahship first to his own disciples, requesting them to guard his words in secret. (*Mk.* 8:27–30). His public bearing and his deeds, however, proclaimed his character; and he, at last, confirmed his office in the synagogue of Nazareth (*Lk.* 4:16–21). In John's version of the Master's life, the cleansing of the Temple is Jesus' public demonstration of his office (*Jno.* 2:13). It is possible that this "cleansing" in Jerusalem, rather than the notice in the synagogue, represents the climax which lead directly to the Crucifixion. By entering the Temple on such a mission, Jesus invaded the stronghold of the *Law* and ceremony, greatly angering the custodians. The incident led shortly to the Roman court, for there was connected with it and with him a popular uprising against the government; Rome could tolerate "no king but Cæsar."

In reality, the force of Jesus' messianic office was spent in "doing good." He was intent on life and love instead of law and force. While the records represent him as performing miracles, they indicate that he deprecated all such evidence of his Messiahship. He wanted faith, not wonders. Once he could work no miracle because the subject had no faith (*Mt.* 13:58). The apostle Paul did not rely on miracle as a proof of Jesus' power; he does not mention miracle in this connection. While the common people heard him gladly, often following him to see some "mighty work" performed, insight and faith achieved the messianic climax. By his own immediate followers he is called "the Christ," the *Greek* for the *Hebrew* word Messiah, meaning "the Anointed," or "the Consecrated." It came at Cæsarea Philippi, in Galilee; Simon Peter was the spokesman; through him the chosen group acknowledged Jesus as "the Christ, the Son of the living God" (*Mt.* 16:13-20). This testimony and confession, not publicly disclosed for many days, became the test of men's discipleship. It identified him as "Son of God," in a peculiar sense. His followers had realized at last what he had felt in Nazareth. The issue was essentially his relationship to God the Father. The charges which the Jews and Romans might later lodge against him were incidental. The character of "Christ, the Son of God" was to the high priest "blasphemy" (*Mt.* 26:65), as his "Kingship" was to Pilate treason (*Lk.* 23:3). But this was true faith to his followers. It was man's own way to "sonship." Men could become the "sons of God," who believed in Jesus, the "only-begotten Son." "Whosoever believeth that Jesus is the Christ is begotten of God," says an *Epistle* (I *Jno.* 5:1). Jesus made an inspiring, transforming impression on his disciples, and in the midst of his impressive and yet tragic ministry, wisdom grew indelibly in their devotion.

The Apostle Paul.—The apostle Paul, while not one of the Twelve,[18] was probably the first disciple to understand the true character of Jesus, and to comprehend the uniqueness of his teachings. He was the first to write an interpretation of his life and work. Paul had been a typically legal-minded Pharisee.

---

[18] The Twelve included Simon Peter, Andrew, James the son of Zebedee, John, Philip, Bartholomew, James the son of Alphæus, Thaddæus, Simon the Canaanæan, and Judas Iscariot (*Mt.* 10:2-4). Matthias was later elected by the group to fill Judas' place (*Acts* 1:26).

He had not even been directly associated with Jesus during his lifetime. But he claimed "apostleship" through having "seen" Jesus in a vision which totally transformed him (*Acts* 26:12–19). This was an *experience,* rather than a miracle, through which his Jewish prejudices were gradually uprooted; for example, Paul the Jew was ashamed of the Jesus of the Crucifixion (Jesus had died disgracefully). But he saw the "Christ" even more clearly than the disciples had seen *Jesus;* he saw the Risen Lord beyond the brief career of Jesus' earthly ministry. Jesus had become the divine Son of God, the Redeemer of mankind. He had become the very "Word" of God, through whom God would speak to men of every race. Paul is one of the most remarkable examples in the world of spiritual transformation, combining with peculiar balance the historical sense and the psychological experience. His conviction of the Resurrection, which he felt so profoundly, became the very foundation of the Christian Church.[19] Jesus was the Christ, the Son of God, through resurrection. This is the testimony of the angels and the disciples at the open tomb (*Mk.* 16:6; *cf. Jno.* 20:18). Members of the Eastern Church still greet one another on Easter morning with the salutation, "Christ is risen."

Jesus' Teachings.—In time, the details of the life and work of Jesus were reviewed and put on record in the form of *Gospels.* Here we may discover what he taught, especially in *Matthew, Luke* and *John,* where the *Logia,* or "sayings" of Jesus may be found. The *Gospels* vary in their emphases on the works (miracle), teachings, and character of Jesus. *Mark* emphasized the works; he seems to have furnished the outline of Jesus' active ministry, which *Matthew* and *Luke* filled in with details of teaching from a lost *Aramaic* book of "Sayings." *John* has some things all its own, *e.g.,* chapters 7–10, and 14–17. *Luke* also has some independent materials, *e.g.,* chapters 10–17.

Jesus' teaching was plainly Jewish. He was devoted to the essence of the *Law,* by which he had been reared. He declared the greatest of all commandments to be, "God is one; and thou shalt love the Lord thy God with all thy heart, and with all thy soul, and with all thy mind" (*Mt.* 23:37). He was an uncompromising monotheist, with the Jewish awe of a transcendent God to be unquestioningly obeyed; but God was also a loving Father. Between Moses and Jesus, seers and prophets had learned much about God; they had learned his Fatherhood. But

---

[19] See a further reference to Paul, p. 389.

God to them was peculiarly the Father of the *nation*. To Jesus, God was the Father of mankind, his Father, the Father of all, even of those who were "unthankful and evil." The *fact* of God's Fatherhood was absolute. Theologically, Jesus fulfilled the *Law*.

He greatly modified his Jewish concept of the world, so greatly did he love the natural order. To the Jews, as to the Hindus and the Buddhists, the world was evil. The Jew, in particular, distinguished between the good God and evil Nature. All things physical were evil to the fellow countrymen of Jesus, especially when they made distinction between consistent Judaism and stray bits of hellenistic love of Nature, which were then in circulation. Man's spirit was caught in a prison-house of matter, from which some means was needed for escape. Strangely enough, this notion of the "world" has been the general Christian view. The "world" means contamination; one must deny the world and cleave to God. Jesus seems to have thought somewhat otherwise. To him, creation was the work of God; God "saw that it was good" (*cf. Gen.* 1:31). He saw God in the material and the beautiful; creation was an extension, as it were, of God. Men's bodies were the temples of God's spirit, through which the spirit might be effective in the world. Not everything in the world was good; but men should strive to make it good. Men should *overcome* the world, should make it spiritual. Jesus did not condemn men merely for living in the flesh; he was himself God manifest in flesh. He came not to condemn the world, but to offer men abundant life. Men walked in spiritual darkness; he would give them light. They lived in the shadow of death; he would show them how to live forever.

While at heart a Jew, he was a moralist; although he had no thoroughgoing program of reform—nowhere, according to the records, does he explicitly condemn slavery and war. It was clearly his intention to put meaning and value into a man's life: "Are not ye of much more value than" birds? "Be not anxious. . . . Seek ye first his kingdom" (*Mt.* 6:26, 31, 33). Man is not a pilgrim and a stranger on the earth, as the *Epistle to the Hebrews* has it (11:13), looking to some distant heaven for his only satisfactions; he is God's noblest creature, the crown of the Father's loving workmanship. Jesus healed men of their diseases; he was anxious for sound minds in sound bodies. He took interest in their daily toil, in fishing and sowing. He enjoyed the fireside, and would perpetuate the family and the home. Men and women were partners in the world's work, equal in origin, value, opportunity, privilege, and duty; he put new meaning into woman's life. His love of children is proverbial. He offered a full Gospel as leaven to make a good life in an improving environment.

His view was ethical, not legalistic, nor ritualistic, although he was instructed in the synagogue, studied with the rabbis, and disputed with them. He was not interested in institutions, but in attitudes, especially men's attitude toward God. The people had long fondly hoped for a new order, or "kingdom," whether coming by transformation or a cataclysm. What would he do? He knew the old tradition of the coming "reign of God." He knew the common hope of force, catastrophe and reconstruction. The Jew was "worldly" to this extent, at least; he coveted an independent Jewish state. The lingering Jewish hope in Jesus was in vain. His "kingdom" was not to come by observation; it is "within you." He defined the "reign of God" as God's will done on earth as it was in heaven. He preached to the crowd a kingdom composed of godly men, free from nationalistic and ritualistic limitations (although not destructive of worthy national and ceremonial elements), operating by its own spiritual principles, destined to be inclusive and eternal. He could not have denied that his kingdom, although spiritual, might consistently assume a wide variety of forms before its consummation.

What would he have men do about the kingdom? Enter it. He mentioned some requirements for admission. Men must forsake some things, as he had forsaken some; otherwise they were not worthy of him. He told a wealthy man that what he lacked was to sell his goods and give the proceeds to the poor. He told a woman that her *faith* had "saved" her. He spoke of "wholeness," safety, peace; such are the other side of his Gospel of the Kingdom. The oft-repeated question of the *Book of Acts* is vital, "What must I do to be saved?" Jesus expected the transformation of society through saved individuals. Each individual meets his own requirements; there is not a common way for all. This is a moral, rather than a ritual, interpretation. From his day, salvation was the burden of the Christian message; but the Church developed a *technique*. The term and the process, with Jesus, were untechnical. It included one's "release" for sins (moral evils), such as insincerity, self-seeking, dishonesty, impurity, and evil-mindedness. He would have men true to *him;* he and the Father were one. He did not hesitate to offer his example; and the disciples were quick to appropriate it. The central theme of the apostles' preaching was Jesus as the Savior. Rites were less essential than the imitation of Jesus and the surrender of the will to God. Paul had not become a follower of Jesus by way of ritual.

The Church.—With Jesus what he was, simple, moral and untechnical, how did the order of the *Church* arise? We do not draw a line of demarcation between him and it; we are concerned, however, to adopt some device by which the organization of the Church and the development of Christian doctrine may be accounted for. We must understand the formal order and the major differences within it.

While Jesus lived, there was thought of him alone; he was the dominating personality. His presence assured accord among his followers, often in spite of individual rivalries. When Jesus was removed, and as opportunities arose, the zeal, ambition, and ability of his many followers were manifested. The Diaspora, which involved the Christians with the Jews, was the sort of "scattering" which called for special leadership. Two men become conspicuous as leaders, Paul and Peter; and on these two basic rocks the Church was built.

Paul, the Churchman.—Paul was unquestionably the foremost teacher of the early Church, although Peter is the "key" to the major doctrine of "apostolic succession." Paul was a Jew, born at Tarsus, in Cilicia, before the birth of Christ; he suffered martryrdom in Rome, perhaps in 64 A.D. His family were Roman citizens. He set out to be a rabbi, and pursued a course of study to that end. As a Roman Jew he was doubly hostile to Christianity, and had some share in the early persecutions of the Christians. But he became a convert in the manner vividly described in *Acts,* chapters 7–9, and spent thereafter thirty years in missionary service, in Syria, Asia Minor, Greece, and Rome. His theology was primarily an interpretation of his profound experience (*Acts* 9:4–19, especially) ; but to him is due the recasting of the faith in terms of rabbinical and hellenistic speculation. Through him, Christianity shook off the Jewish *Law,* and, in spite of Rome, [20] became a world religion. He established many churches, and instructed them. He wrote at least eight, or ten Epistles to them, wherein we may find these points in his theology:

---

[20] When Christianity dared to stand alone, it was proscribed by Roman edict. Paul himself lost his life in defiance of the state.

(1) Jesus is the risen Lord (*Kurios*), rather than the Messiah in the Jewish sense. He is the Spirit (*Pneuma*) of God, which fills the believer, and through which the believer may be one with Christ. The risen Lord reveals the Spirit of God. Not so much the earthly life and words of Jesus, but the revelation of the Spirit, is important.

(2) The death of Jesus is the most important earthly incident; it is the central fact of Christianity. The Cross is the great symbol of the faith. Christ died for all, an *atoning* sacrifice for man's shortcomings. God himself presented Jesus as a sacrificial gift (*Rom.* 3:21), by which men find it possible to be reconciled to God; or, else, Jesus, in obedience to God, offered himself as atonement for the sins of men.

(3) Jesus has fulfilled the *Law;* the *Law* is abrogated. Henceforth, God keeps no books of debit and credit, not dealing with men according to their transgressions, nor rewarding them according to their righteousness; he is bountifully merciful. The "righteousness which is of faith" supersedes the "righteousness which is of the law" (*Rom.* 10:5-10). Man is justified by faith. There is no *code* of regulations for human conduct.

The Apostle Peter.—Simon Peter was the leader of the Twelve, originally a fisherman of Bethsaida, on the Sea of Galilee. He may have been a Gentile; his name, at least, is *Greek.* He lived at Capernaum. While not the first disciple to respond to Jesus, he first acknowledged Jesus as the Messiah (*Mt.* 16:13-19), and was first to believe after the Crucifixion that Jesus had risen from the dead (I *Cor.* 15:5, a Pauline testimony). Rallying the disciples and the scattered followers, he became the leader of the larger Church. According to one interpretation, Peter had been commissioned by Jesus as the foundation "stone" of the new community (*Mt.* 16:17-19). He became a missionary in Syria, and suffered martryrdom, perhaps in Rome in 64 A.D.

Peter was unwilling to break entirely with the Jewish *Law,* but he favored the extension of Christianity among the Gentiles; his faith was Græco-Jewish. There were defects in his education; he had to be instructed in the matter of "clean" and "unclean" foods (*Acts* 10:9-16). He emphasized the office of the apostles and the function of the Church, in contrast with Paul's emphasis on "the Lord" as "Spirit" and on Christianity as experience. Thus arises the theory of apostolic succession. This succession of apostles, bishops, and so on, became the guarantee of the purity of doctrine in the Church, and an indication of things required for salvation. It was, further, an effective device against heresies, and against the dilution of the faith by speculation. It lent itself eventually to the establishment of a hierarchy, or an episcopal organization of the Church. In other words, the Church became custodian of the faith. When the congregation at Rome, which Peter founded, acquired primacy in Italy and the West, Peter received the title of its first Bishop. The Pope is his successor.

St. John.—There is an early "Johannine" strain, also, although it is not always clear who "John" was. He was more a thinker than an active leader; he is the author of several writings. The Church father, Irenæus, identifies the author of the *Gospel of John* as none other than John, the disciple of Jesus; but Papias says that the disciple John was martyred *early* with his brother James, before the book of *John* was written. We may believe that the disciple John wrote the *Epistles of John,* and that he lived awhile at Ephesus, where he suffered martyrdom at an advanced age. We may assign the *Gospel* to him; but it is difficult to believe that he wrote the book of *Revelation,* which belongs to an entirely different school of thought.

The "Johannine" theology, in any case, is a comparatively late development, based presumably upon "history," but flavored, possibly, with extracts from the Grecian mysteries. It establishes the thesis that the historical Jesus and the Christ of faith are one and the same, although not dwelling so much upon the *man* as the *Gospels* of Mark, Matthew, and Luke do. It, however, takes into account more of Jesus' life than Paul's epistles do. It emphasizes fully Christ's divinity. The Johannine interpretation saved the faith from any wholly mystical interpretation, on the one hand, and from the current "gnosticism," on the other. There were many Gnostics—a motley crew, in fact—who proposed salvation by *gnosis,* mystical enlightenment, by way of the sacraments in secret; not by man's rekindling the divine spark within him, nor by a Savior. By *gnosis* could man be saved from the sensuous, the sensual, and all cosmic evils; man's soul was held in prison in an evil world. There were "gnostic" Christians who sought to universalize the faith through an eclectic philosophy which made "knowledge" uppermost, with Christ in the mythical rôle of an "enlightener." They thought of God after the *Old Testament* Jewish fashion, set over against an evil world. John countered this by his exposition of Christ as light, love, and life; and by developing further Paul's concepts of Christ as the Wisdom (*Logos*) and the Love of God.

The Building of the Church.—Christianity as such began to form within the second century, although the disciples were "called Christians first at Antioch," in Syria, in the previous Century. Its form and scope as a "universal" Church represent the reconciliation of many strains. It arose, in fact, from the crucible of a "world with fierce contestants filled," including Jews and Judaizing Christians, pagan philosophers and sceptics, initiates of the Greek Mysteries with their own "salvation," Gnostics, and adherents of the cult of Emperors. Its compactness was increased by severance from Judaism,[21] which had official standing; but it put itself thereby "beyond the law"; it had no standing in the courts. A long season of bitter trials followed. But by the fourth century the Church had both a body and a soul, with which to grow and carry on in a hostile world. Its soul was a quenchless yearning for a life distinguished from the world—it could not look with favor on a situation fraught with persecution, and it could not yield the doctrines for which it had to suffer. It gradually became ascetic, although preserving its high doctirne of Jesus as the Savior of the world. Its body was a huge establishment with friars, priests, bishops, cardinals, and Pope. It accumulated wealth, mostly property. It gained at last official recognition by the State. Many brilliant apologists and leaders were produced in these centuries, including Justin Martyr, of Samaria and Rome (*c.* 100–165); Irenæus, of Smyrna and Lyons, in Gaul (*c.* 135–200); Tertullian, of Rome and Carthage (*c.* 150–225); Origen, of Alexandria and Cæsarea (200–250), who made the first critical edition of the *Bible;* and Augustine of Italy (354–430). We must soon refer to them again. With Augustine, the firm foundation of the Roman Church was laid. The East won prestige through the Councils. At one great Council (at Nicæa, 325), the Emperor had presided, a creed had been adopted, and the troublesome Arian controversy had been settled(?) for a while. We must trace the development of "orthodoxy."

The Person of Jesus.—The major issue between the Christians and the Jews was Jesus. It remained the major issue in the Church. For the first disciples, Peter met the issue squarely by declaring, "Thou art the Christ, the Son of the Living God." [22]

---

[21] The Jews rejected Jesus as the Messiah, laying the ground for the long discussion of his person. *Cf. John* 12:48.
[22] See also *Acts,* Chapter II. Peter's sermon on Pentecost in Jerusalem.

But the question everywhere persisted, "What think ye of Christ? Whose son is he? (*Mt.* 22:42; Jesus puts the question). Whose *son* is he? The title, "son of God," had several connotations in the days of Jesus; it was broader than the later Latin dogma of the "virgin birth," for instance. It might imply some "godly" quality; it was applied to the Jewish nation, and to Jewish kings as objects of God's love and power. The disciples used the term to mean Messiah, with a more ethical and religious connotation. Jesus was the "Son," who inaugurated the Kingdom of the "Father." Under Greek influence the "Son" became the *Logos,* "Word" of God, with a metaphysical quality beyond the figure, indicating that Jesus was begotten before time, and had appeared by birth from a virgin mother. On Italian soil, the virgin birth was emphasized; there appeared the cult of the Madonna, analogous to, and perhaps dependent on, the veneration of Diana, a Roman virgin goddess. But not until 431 A.D., in Ephesus, was the virgin Mary designated as the "Mother of God."

Judaism was not a fertile soil for the larger theory of Jesus' person; but Greece and Italy were ready ground, each with its own content to bestow. The movement on behalf of Jesus the Messiah acquired a philosophy (or, shall we say theology?) under hellenistic influence. It won for him an Empire in the West, where Peter had implanted in practical and legalistic Rome a loyalty to Christ as the suffering Son of God.

Creeds.—The first official settlement of the controversy on the person of the Christ was made in Asia Minor, at Nicæa. The Emperor had become a convert, making possible an ecumenical, "universal" council. Bishops assembled at Nicæa from all parts of the empire, 308 from the East and 10 from the newer West. They were to pass judgment as a body upon the "heresy" of Bishop Arius of Alexandria. Alexandria was a university center, a cosmopolis of intellect. It had thinkers of renown and gloried in their controversies. There were Stoics and Sabellians, Jewish rationalists and Pharisees, Christian Montanists and pagan Gnostics. Arius (256–336) had been expounding "heresy." He assigned to Christ an office and a character subordinate to God; the Son subordinated to the Father. Jesus was of a "substance" similar to, but not the same as God. He acclaimed Jesus as the Son of God, but in the sense of having been created; Jesus, therefore, was a creature and not God. He insisted that Jesus was the very "first" of creatures, but he held the philosophic notion that there was (a time?) when Jesus "was not." Nor did he accept the Neo-Platonic Christian theory of Jesus as an "emanation" of God the Absolute, by which the "Word" (*Logos*) became manifest in flesh. In a situation teeming with ideas, Arius represented the belief in a unique God above the world, separated from it by an impassable gulf. He ranged the *Logos* and the Christ, who was the *Logos* incarnate, on the side of the world, apart from God. Alexandrian Christians, for the most part, however, were more "orthodox" than he. They believed in the one nature of God the Father and of the Son, Jesus, and in their identity of substance. This made clear the office of Jesus as their Savior. Jesus was divine, and the incarnation of God; he was the symbol and expression of the immanence, or indwelling, of God in all creation. These Alexandrians seemed to be outdoing even Paul who believed in Jesus as the Messiah, the Son of God, preëxistent in association with God, the agent of God in a cosmic redemption, and himself the archetype of redeemed humanity.[23] They were even more "Johannine" than John, and beyond any Petrine stage of dogma. Jesus was himself the uncreated God, the Son, of one nature with the Father, and therefore with absolute power to save men from decay and to give them immortality. The Alexandrians, when they realized what Arius was preaching, could not tolerate him. They called a local synod and condemned him. But since he represented a more than local heresy, the Council of Nicæa tried, condemned, and banished him. Thenceforth, his theories spread among the pagan Goths and Vandals, for the early Unitarian Aryans were enthusiastic missionaries. Indeed, several times the views of Arius prevailed at the imperial Roman court, and he would have been restored to honor had he not died the very day before the one set for his restoration.

Athanasius (293–373) happens to be famous as the champion of orthodoxy. Arius' chief opponent at the Council of Nicæa. While actually present at the Council, he was then only a deacon.[24] He has been called "the first ecclestiastical Prince of the grand style"; but his name is inaccurately associated with the well-known "Athanasian Creed." *After* the Council of Nicæa, while Bishop of Alexandria, he became conspicuous as the leader of the party which professed belief in the anti-Arian doctrine of Christ as "of one substance" with God the Father. But he held no easy sway, nor an uninterrupted term of office. He was expelled

---

[23] *Cf.* B. W. Bacon, *New Testament Introduction*, p. 118.
[24] He was thirty-two and Bishop Arius was sixty-nine.

five times, and five times reinstated by an Emperor whose own orthodoxy was never certain. "Orthodoxy" had *not* fully been established. The "Athanasian Creed," which represents the trinitarian position in its most uncompromising form, came later, apparently reflecting the theological opinion of the Latin churches in Gaul, North Africa, and Spain.

The controversy over the person of the Christ was not effectually adjusted until the Council of Chalcedon, in Asia Minor, 451 A.D., which added certain phrases in elaboration of the "Nicene" creed, making clear that:

(1) Christ is fully God, and fully man, of the *same* nature with God, both in his humanity and in his divinity;

(2) He is divine, begotten of God; he is human, born of the virgin Mary;

(3) He was begotten before all ages, and in these later times, for man's salvation;

(4) He is like men, save that he alone is sinless;

(5) He is to be acknowledged in two natures, distinct, yet indivisible, inseparable, and not to be confused or changed;

(6) Mary as his mother is the "Mother of God."

While this Council met on Greek soil, its six hundred bishops mostly Greek, its findings were accepted, East and West. The Church assented generally, also, to its condemnation of the "heresy" that Jesus had one nature only, after his birth or incarnation. The heretics (Monophysites) themselves disagreed about this single nature, whether it was human or divine; the controversy lingered for a century and a half.

The Eastern Church.—The unity of Christian order and belief was destined to disruption. There were fundamental differences between the East and the West. It was not a matter of geography, although this entered in. Many differences were circumstantial; but there were fundamental differences of mind. There are "Eastern" and there are "Western" modes of thought, although one may detect *three* currents moving in the early centuries in the Church at large, each playing an important rôle, the mystico-historical, the metaphysical, and the sacramental-mystical. The first two flourished in the East; the last prevailed in Rome.

The Eastern Church (Greek, Armenian, Syrian, Balkan, Palestinian, Indian, and Russian) is directly apostolic. Its branches sprang from the original soil; it was one in the beginning. Its congregations have descended from churches founded by Apostles, or visited by them in connection with administration. Its tongue was Greek, the language of the eastern Mediterranean; its documents were Greek; its great theologians wrote in Greek; its members were imbued with hellenistic culture. It passed on the bulk of its theology to Rome; the Western Church counts among the "Fathers" Polycarp, martyred at Smyrna, in 155, and among the "saints," John of Damascus, who died in 754. The early, "universal" Councils were held in Eastern territory, dominated by Eastern bishops. The early trials and bitter persecutions occurred on its soil. It has accounted itself custodian of orthodoxy; it calls itself "The Holy Orthodox Catholic Apostolic Church."

On the other hand, the Eastern Church was the scene of almost all the early heresies; the Eastern mind is highly controversial. Its theology developed out of controversy. It persisted in debate in spite of violence and ridicule, and won for speculation through the categories of Greek thought an honored place in Christianity. Yet, having passed on priceless gifts, it fell into inertia. By rejection of the growing claims of Rome, and through a final separation, it fell into isolation, without an independence of its own; it has been subservient to the State, its Patriarch taking orders from emperor, king, czar, sultan, and president, in succession. While it has maintained a peculiar unity of faith, its moral character has waned, and its organization has been rent by politics.

The Eastern ritual is lengthy, varied, and elaborate, with preaching of a controversial character. Worship centers in the Eucharist, or Mass, in connection with which the Church holds the doctrine of transubstantiation; the "substantial" body and blood of Christ, along with his divine spirit, are present in the bread and wine of the Supper, after their consecration at the altar. Except for the icon or crucifix, no images are used in worship; pictures are much used, instead, offering no such possibility of spiritual embodiment, they say, as a rounded image does. The *Bible* is an open book, much used, and recommended to the laity; but prevalent illiteracy among them has prevented its wide reading or close acquaintance. Monasticism is maintained, and the bishops are chosen from the monasteries. Celibacy is required only of the bishops; to become a bishop, one must never have been married. Celibacy is the rule for all clergy *after* ordination, save in the case of priests and deacons married before admission to the order.

The Eastern Church has not been "missionary"; it has been content, usually, to maintain itself by natural extension; it has never sought, for example, the conversion of Islam. The one notable extension beyond the Near East—and Russia—into India came early amidst the general spread of Christianity. In South India, some "Thomas Christians" still observe the forms of thought and ritual which characterizes the mother Church.[25] The Doukhubors of Russia and Canada are an "Eastern" sect of puritans who rejected the episcopacy and sacramentarianism. The fortunes of the major branches have varied. The Church in Russia and in Turkey has suffered much from Soviet and Kemalist iconoclasm.

The Western Church.—Western, or Latin Christianity rests upon the common base, but may be traced as a distinctive movement. Its separation from the East began in doctrine and was confirmed by political expediency.[26] As early as 190, the Roman Bishop Victor excommunicated the Eastern Church, because of controversy over the time of the Easter festival. In 1054 came the final, embittered separation, when the "Universal Archbishop" (Patriarch) of the East closed all churches of the Latin rite within Greek territory, making it impossible for marriage or funeral services to be performed among them. The Roman Pope in turn excommunicated once again, and finally, the Eastern Patriarch. The divided jurisdiction has since prevailed, although recently certain cordial greetings have been exchanged between the Churches.

Latin Christianity began in North Africa, at the opening of the third century, with Tertullian (c. 150–225). He was a Roman lawyer of Carthage, a convert to the faith, for which he composed a brilliant apologetic. At first he was a "Montanist," or follower of the monk Montanus, an Asia Minor prophet of the "second coming" of Christ. Montanus proclaimed himself the "Spirit of Truth" (cf. John 16:13), emphasized the practice of asceticism, and was the first to distinguish between venial and mortal sins. Tertullian was the head, for a while, of the Montanists of Carthage, independent of the Church. Later he became a Church-

---

25 The South Indian Christian community is mixed, including not only the descendants of the early "apostolic" Church holding the tradition of St. Thomas; there are Nestorian "heretics" ("Jacobites"), and many Roman Catholics. The Thomists and Jacobites use *Syriac* in their ritual, and deny allegiance to the Roman pontiff.

26 In 395, Theodosius, of Constantinople, died, the last ruler of the united Empire. Thereafter, the Western and the Eastern Empires were ruled separately.

man. As a Roman, he knew Stoicism, but the only Stoic tinge to his theology seems to be the idea that the soul of man is corporeal, and is procreated. He was far from hellenistic, on the whole. Christianity was not a theory of Jesus' person, his nature, or his Incarnation; it was a change of heart, and an absolution from one's sins. He did not dwell upon the escape of a man's soul from the prison of an evil body, or from death, but on man's escape from sin. He was legalistic. He emphasized the heinousness of sin, and the need of divine grace for its forgiveness and man's redemption. Sin was a quality of man's original nature—man was born in sin—which must be eradicated by the grace of God, and man's own good works, including confession and self-mortification.

Tertullian thus anticipated many of the doctrines of the Roman Church, even using the term Trinity in its later sense. His exposition had special influence upon Augustine, who gave to Latin Christianity its formal character.

Augustine.—Aurelius Augustinus (353–430), the son of a pagan father and a Christian mother, was born in Numidia, Roman North Africa. He became one of the most influential men of Christian history; he established the Church of Rome on its firm, never-yielding foundation; he supplied interpretations to the later Protestants. With his name are associated the familiar doctrines of original sin, predestination, divine grace, and the Trinity; and the seven sacraments. He passed three crises, two intellectual, and one moral, on his way to eminence. He was for ten years, while in the higher schools of Carthage, an "auditor" of the Manichæans,[27] whose faith had reached the West. But, baffled by their subtleties, he became a sceptic. He went to Rome, where he encountered Neo-Platonism;[28] thence to Milan, as a

---

[27] Mani (216–276) was a Persian prophet of eclecticism and a universal faith founded upon Zoroaster, Gautama, Jesus, and himself. He based his gospel upon the Zoroastrian dualism of light and darkness, good and evil. He established two orders: (1) the "elect," who followed the strict and austere articles of faith and discipline, and (2) the "auditors," or novices. Among his injunctions were marriage, sensual indulgence, and the eating of animal food. His worship consisted mainly of prayers, chants, confessions, fasts and festivals, and almsgiving.

[28] *Neo-Platonism* was founded by Plotinus (205–270), of Alexandria and Rome. It is a "Platonic" philosophy coupled with religious mysticism. Plotinus made God the Absolute without self-consciousness, but a Being absolutely good who could be directly apprehended, in spite of being above knowledge and reason. He is both the first and the final cause of the universe. There are various "emanations" of Divinity, in a sequence of Intelligence, World-Soul, individual souls, and Matter (the realm of sense which is irrational and evil). Through ascetic exercise the individual soul may recall its divine origin, may learn to cherish and revere the things of the spirit, and at last return to God.

Man's soul by nature is divine. It fell, and has been taking pleasure in its sensuous experiences. Through ecstasy a spark of recollection is rekindled in the soul. Through ecstasy, also, it gets foretastes of its primal nature and cultivates a desire to return to God. Salvation, in other words, comes by turning from matter and sense through

teacher of literature, retaining his interest in Neo-Platonic speculation. This philosophy freed him, at least, from any vestige of
Mani, save sensual indulgence—he kept a concubine. He became a
pupil of Bishop Ambrose of Milan, learning morality and Christian
doctrine. Through Christian Neo-Platonism he banished sensuality
and scepticism, finding peace and an undivided will. His conversion to Christianity included celibacy. He returned to Africa
in 390 as a "presbyter," and from 395 he was Bishop of the
Church in Hippo. The Roman Church enjoyed then renewed
prestige, for in 380 the Emperor Theodosius (in Constantinople)
had declared the Roman faith the test of orthodoxy.

Augustine's theology came mainly from the *Epistles* of St. Paul,
although the "predestination" which his legal mind found in them
did not fix itself upon the Church, until emphasized by Anselm
in the eleventh century, and John Calvin in the sixteenth. He
was at first inclined to think that man and God coöperated in
man's redemption; but, remembering his own crises, he came to
assign all power to God. He even held that the faith needed for
redemption came from God. God is the only independent Being,
altogether good. He creates and maintains [29] whatever goodness
is in man. Man is born in sin, and lives in sin, if he lives apart
from God; evil is separation from the good. Man is saved by
God's election and God's grace; divine election is the only ground
of individual salvation. The sacraments of the Church, however,
are the channels of God's grace. Original sin in infants and non-
Christians must be purged by baptism. The Mass maintains the
Christian life. The Church alone administers the sacraments;
salvation, therefore, is proved through the Church alone. The
Church is the divine Empire, the City of God; human empires
rise and fall, but the Church endures. In 445, fifteen years after
the death of Augustine, and nineteen after the publication of his
City of God, the Emperor recognized the Pope as not only first
in ecclesiastical honor, but also supreme in civil jurisdiction.

By the fifth century, Christianity, having achieved notable
success throughout the Roman world, was conscious of the
fallow fields of barbarism. Having triumphed in the realm of

---

ecstatic contemplation, and, through supersensuous channels, finding one's way back
to God.

It can be readily seen, therefore, to what extent such a philosophy as this would
free Augustine from the bewilderment of Manichæan dualism, especially since his
Roman mind could take it literally. Neo-Platonism was, indeed, a very precise scheme
of salvation. It was a mystical, idealistic monism, with a place for man's intelligence
as an agent in salvation,—through intelligent contemplation to self-forgetful ecstasy, and
complete knowledge in union with the divine and Absolute God.

29 The "elect" must be given grace to endure, or they are ultimately lost; they are
not predestined to salvation.

pagan culture, it would wrestle with the pagan peoples who from every side were penetrating Rome. There would be one Christian culture, whatever happened to the Empire. The sturdy pagans would serve the Church; the doom of Rome would be the Church's opportunity, for Christians had declared "a war in which there should be no compromise and no peace, until Christ was Lord of all," until the gods of Rome, and the emperors *as gods,* were vanities. The passion of the Church for the triumph of its Lord had sent its members everywhere, among the high and low, into palaces and military camps, to slaves and temple-women. They faced angry mobs without fear, at peace with God. It was a glad, even an "hilarious" spirit, said Augustine, which bore them on, even the clean, conquering spirit of Jesus. Now they would face with confidence the new tide which surged upon them. In spite of peril, fire, and sword, the Church assumed with notable success its obligation to the material conquerors of Rome. By the fifth century, it was an institution in its own right, brooking no interference from the State, imbued with an imperial ideal, inspired by the theory of universal rule. It had served notice, even in Augustine's *City of God,* that temporal rule would be subjected to the Church. This is the fundamental theory of the Papacy; this dictated the Church's policies as it made its way through confusion to consolidation and reform. The World Church was in process of actualization. The pattern had been cast for the resolution of the Middle Ages.

But the task was staggering for a thousand years, whether struggling with earthly potentates—for the State continued— or leavening the masses of "barbarians." There were "dark" centuries; from the fourth to the fourteenth, the Church extended its dominion throughout Europe, establishing new channels of grace, yet suffering inevitably—although not always consciously—a certain slow dilution of many of its higher doctrines. The year 1000 was a special trial; there was a widespread notion that the world was coming to a tragic end; this sort of notion runs in cycles everywhere. The terror passed; it may have added fervor to religion. There had been an early European base; the faith had been established, within "apostolic" times, tradition says, in Britain, Spain, and Gaul. In the fifth, sixth, and seventh centuries, the "Arian" Goths and Vandals, who had overrun the West of Europe and North Africa, were reclaimed (converted to the "Athanasian" faith); Burgundians, Franks, British Celts and Saxons, and the Swiss became converted.

In the centuries succeeding, Irish and English monks crossed as missionaries into Friesland, Saxony and Bavaria. Northward, the faith soon spread among the Danes and Scandinavians; eastward, among Moravians, Bohemians, Hungarians and Poles. During the twelfth, thirteenth, and fourteenth centuries, the eastern Baltic peoples were converted, Lithuania being the last European country officially to announce its conversion, in 1386.

A thousand years were time enough for complete conversion, but it does not appear that the masses were wholly spiritually transformed; they accepted their new faith largely at the dictation of their rulers. Popular Catholicism, therefore, embodied many theories and practices presumably discarded, for example, the cults of St. Nicholas and St. George. Indeed, the converting agencies had brought with them many elements derived from Oriental, Greek, and Roman paganism; witness the stream of holy relics which poured in from Italy. In these areas of ruder culture, the legalistic, dogmatic, and sacramentarian character of the Church found ready nourishment. Meanwhile, the extension was consolidated and maintained by rites and sacraments, especially from the sixth century on, in charge of many monkish orders. In all strategic centers, cathedrals, churches, chapels, and monasteries were built; and daily the sacrifice of the Mass and prayers and readings were performed. These tended to develop a monastic ritual of perpetual prayer; and the litanies of the saints and of the Blessed Virgin were elaborated, and responses, hymns, and chants were freely introduced. An elaborate calendar was formulated, of holy days, saints' days, feasts, fasts, and confessions. The procession of the consecrated bread and wine was instituted (in the eleventh century). A liturgical unity and a common mind were gradually developed throughout Europe. It was a notable achievement.

Monasticism and the Friars.—Monasticism played a leading rôle. Having flourished in the East during the third and fourth centuries, it was introduced at Rome about 340. It caught the West's imagination. Jerome, editor of the *Latin Vulgate Bible,* one of the four "doctors" of the Roman Church, wrote glowingly in praise of it, while Bishops Ambrose of Milan, Martin of Tours, and Augustine of Hippo constructed monasteries. The movement seemed providential; with worldliness in the Church, increasing wars under the leadership of Churchmen and the allied nobility, and disorders multiplying everywhere, many Christians renounced the world, finding refuge in the monasteries.

As the Church expanded into Europe, the monks became the bulwark of the faith, many of them becoming as conspicuous in their active ministry among the people as certain Eastern saints were famous for their isolation. The Western monk renounced the world but labored in it; the crown of Eastern monasticism was the hermit, observing labor, fasting and prayer in solitude. Among the noble host of Northern brothers "of the Rule" were Martin of Tours (d. 396), Patrick of Ireland (d. 461), Cuthbert of England (d. 687), and Boniface of Germany (d. 754).

The Rule was founded by Benedict of Italy (480–542), who built a monastery at Monte Cassino. By the tenth century, the Benedictine order was dominant throughout the West, with 37,000 monasteries. It imposed a lifelong vow of poverty, chastity, and obedience; limited the daily round to the monastic precincts; proscribed the use of meat, except in case of sickness; provided a daily round of manual labor, a daily period of public chants and prayer; and it encouraged learning. It was an extraordinary demonstration of world-renunciation, which in time acquired control both of the Church and of the world; it supplied the Church its bishops, cardinals, and popes. But in the end, its very *worldliness,* coupled with its communal isolation, brought about its fall. Other orders were established, for the sake of *un*worldly participation in the Church's work; for example, the mendicant friars, the Franciscans and Dominicans, of the thirteenth century, and the Jesuits, of the sixteenth. The grey Franciscans were bent on practical helpfulness; the Dominicans were zealous to defend the faith; the Jesuits were organized to combat the "Protestants." Other orders had preceded them, some to make monastic ideals chivalrous; for example, the twelfth century Bernardine "poor soldiers of Jesus Christ," the Knights Templar, defenders of the shrines and pilgrims in Palestine, and the Augustinian Knights of St. John, established from among the Hospitalers. With such orders, monasticism had "passed out of the cell forever." We are yet to see what wealth of resources and power in politics and religion they acquired in their day.

In contrast with monasticism, the Church itself continued its direct assault upon the world; through the Pope, especially, it kept up its contest with the State. The object of the struggle was, ostensibly, reform; in reality, the goal was Church supremacy. In the tenth century, both the Empire and the Papacy were established institutions, but neither had then its own clear field of jurisdiction. Paralleling the Orders of the Church, through which the Church survived, Feudalism came, in time, to aid the State. While it represented social segmentation, gave power to the usually brutal few, and reduced the masses to despair, its individualistic aspects saved the State.

From 1000 A.D., the burning question was, What can the Church accomplish for mankind and governments? The social situation called loudly for reform; the masses needed safety from disorder and relief from servile toil; rulers too readily engaged in devastating wars; the private wars of Christians not only were embarrassing, but their drain on public morals was appalling. The Church alone could be the means of reformation,—if it would likewise set its own house aright. It represented the only comprehensive order of the day; there was no other voice to which the whole of Europe might attend. It had ventured to interfere with wars; in 990, in connection with the anticipated Day of Judgment, it had proclaimed a "Truce of God," first in France, then in Flanders, Germany, and Italy. But to be effective, the Church must be supreme; the Churchman of the hour was Hildebrand of Cluny; he would be the agent of reform, consolidation, and supremacy.

A commoner, Hildebrand was sorely troubled by the chaos in society, by the tyranny of the nobles, and by much corruption in the monasteries. The Benedictine monasteries, in particular, had grown immensely wealthy; amidst luxury, the Rule was scarcely kept. As early as 910, the monastic House of Cluny had been established in protest against these evils; Hildebrand became a member in 1047. Two years thereafter he was called to Rome, to be associated with the popes, before whom he resolutely championed Cluny principles. Becoming Pope in 1073, after having served as cardinal, he carried on reform for a dozen years. As a cardinal, he had procured legislation whereby popes were nominated only by the cardinals. As Pope Gregory VII (1073-1085), he added dignity and power to his office. He opposed the investiture of the clergy by the Emperor and feudal lords; many bishops and archbishops were vassals of the kings, landed proprietors through royal generosity. He opposed simony, so-called from Simon Magus (*Acts* 8:9-24); many Churchmen had *bought* their offices from kings. Gregory issued, in 1075, a decree that feudal investiture and ecclesiastical simony should cease. He opposed indulgences; but they were not checked until 1562, and have never been abolished altogether.

Papal Sovereignty.—Further, Gregory aimed at sovereignty;

he would establish "the principle beyond dispute that the pope, as viceroy of God, was above all earthly rulers." Issuing a decree to this effect, Henry IV of Germany, the Holy Roman Emperor, treated it with scorn. The Pope summoned the Emperor to Rome, but the latter, although somewhat weak at home, resisted. The Pope banned him, and deposed him; and, when he came submissively to Canossa, restored him. But the tables were soon turned, and Gregory, humiliated by Imperial decree, died an exile in Salerno. The dispute, however, was not settled; it was later compromised at Worms (1122), after which the popes, exclusively, bestowed religious offices, and the kings, the rights of property and office in the state. Nevertheless, Gregory had put new life into the Papacy, extending its prerogatives, and marking the path by which it reached its zenith under Innocent III (1198–1216). He had been more immediately successful in clerical reform. He decreed that all clergy should be celibate; he banned their marriage as a sensual entanglement; since his time, celibacy has been the rule with clergy, as with monks.

Innocent III was able to make a political reality of the papal theory of both temporal and spiritual supremacy; yet within the Church itself were many, notably the friars, who realized that power as well as wealth were dangerous. The ideals of the "begging friars," Franciscans and Dominicans, ran counter both to material worldliness and political imperialism. The Papacy had gained ascendancy, because of the obvious need of the control of social forces. When the so-called Crusades [30] renewed the intermittent struggles between Europe and the East, the Church with its prestige became their sponsor. Individual independence, once manifest, was no longer tolerable. Even the new social movements, such as merchant guilds, commercial leagues, and universities had need of, and assented to the Church's moral leadership. But still another factor was emerging, the middle class, somewhere between the haughty noble and the grovelling serf, somewhere, likewise, between temporal authority and ascetic isolation. The friars may be viewed against the background of the middle classes, and the scenes of common life.

The Friars' motive was not so much the good of their own souls as the nobler aim of service to their fellowmen. They were not interested in the prelacy nor in the nobles, but in the common man. Yet they were true Churchmen, defenders of the faith. The Dominicans especially strove for doctrinal purity among the

---

[30] Wars of the Cross; yet some were frankly mercantile.

masses. Oddly enough, the Inquisition was entrusted to them, and they became *oppressors* of the common man; there is often much confusion between heresy of doctrine and heresy of heart. Dominic (1170–1221), a Spanish intellectual, was commissioned by the Pope (Innocent III) to preach among the Albigensian heretics of southern France.[31] Convinced that ordinary parish priests, and monks in their seclusion, could not deal with living heresy, Dominic organized his black-robed friars. They went about barefoot, in utter poverty, preaching informally, teaching the earnest, and confounding heretics. He trained many good preachers and skilful controversialists, of whom Thomas Aquinas (1227–1274), the great Schoolman, was perhaps the most distinguished. Many teachers in the universities were recruited from the order, which was composed generally of members from the higher social classes.

The Grey Friars, or Franciscans, followed more closely the ideal of life found by losing it in service. They were more "spiritual" than their black-robed brothers. They, in particular, became the foreign missionaries of the Church. As an order, it began with the Italian monk John Bernadone, better known as St. Francis of Assisi (1182–1226). Born in Assisi, of a rich father and a noble mother, he was, in his youth, a prodigal, given to indulgence, fond of wine and war. Overtaken by illness, his mind was wholly changed; he had "visions." He had not liked his father's business; he may have come under the influence of Peter Waldo [32] who renounced great wealth, adopted poverty, and preached among the masses; his visions may have been the climax. He took literally the command of Jesus to surrender goods, and to preach to those in poverty and need. He became the symbol and exemplar of rigorous asceticism, joyous mysticism, and self-denying service. He tried to reënact the life of Jesus. Like-minded idealists attended him, serving the lepers by the city walls, tramping through the countryside, ministering anywhere to the sick and sorrowful. He believed that laymen sworn to poverty, chastity and obedience, living by alms and manual labor, might be the saviors of society. For a while, St. Francis was averse to any formal order, but soon saw that, if the move-

---

[31] The Albigenses were Manichæan in theology, as Augustine once had been, emphasizing the dualism of light and darkness, God and Satan. They followed Mani also in forbidding marriage, private property, and meat. They rejected the *Old Testament* as the work of Satan. They would not baptize: baptism was not a purely Christian rite. They taught transmigration until the final state of bliss. They were almost exterminated by Crusaders and the Inquisition.

[32] The Waldensian sect was founded in 1177 by Peter Valdo of Lyons. It was theoretically orthodox.

ment were to be effective, it should be organized. The order was recognized in 1209 by the Pope. While many of the early "brothers" were humble, even ignorant, men, the Order ultimately included many intellectuals, among whom were Roger Bacon (1214–1292), the English *doctor mirabilis,* and Duns Scotus (1255–1308), of Oxford, Paris, and Cologne. Franciscan influence was enduring. Thomas à Kempis' *Imitation of Christ,* written in 1441, is in the mood of the simple-hearted saint of Italy. His ideals opposed the Pope's ambition for worldly glory, man's greed for power and gold, and the Churchman's narrow bigotry that heresy is of the creeds. In a day of brutal hypocrisy, ecclesiastical concern for orthodoxy, the masses' eagerness for peace, and many restless movements of reform, his ideals, through the figure of a "beggar," focused human thought upon Reality. It is said that in his old age, St. Francis, sick and broken, saw from the mountain-top a vision of the Crucified Redeemer, and felt thereafter in the palms of his hands and the soles of his feet, the *stigmata,* the burning wounds of Jesus.

The Schoolmen.—Scholasticism is another major aspect of the Middle Ages, the most important, with respect to *thought* within the Church. It was a movement in theology, which paralleled the Renaissance; it represents the rationalization of theology. While popes and emperors were struggling for supremacy, while the common man was criticizing privilege, the thinker in the Church was scrutinizing dogma. This thoughtful process gathered impetus from the tenth until the fifteenth century. It lost its vogue—beyond the bounds of the orthdox Church—when scientific and humanistic inquiries developed; then reason interfered with dogma. But until about 1200, reason was employed to vindicate the Church's doctrines, not to shatter them. The sum of rational religion, in the view of the Roman Catholic Church, was arrived at by Aquinas. Leo XIII commended his work as sufficient for Catholics for all time. Let us scan the process of his *Summa Theologiæ*.

The scholastic movement deals with faith and reason, and establishes the fact that they are two pathways to one goal. The spirit of speculation has always lingered in the Church, especially where it might feed on hellenistic theories. Augustine had sanctioned inquiry; he was liberally dogmatic; he once believed in freedom of the will; but tradition has emphasized his legalism. Anselm of Canterbury (1033–1109) *explained* many things in legalistic fashion; for example, the death of Jesus (the

Atonement) was a satisfaction of God's injured honor; men's sins had outraged God; the innocent Jesus died on men's behalf; in return, God rewarded Jesus by granting believers absolution from the penalty of sin; Jesus had satisfied God's sense of justice.

Aquinas found that men may not speculate too freely; reason had its limitations; while there is in Christianity nothing *un*reasonable, there is much which outreaches reason. Natural religion may be fully understood by reason, but Christianity as revealed religion must be understood by faith, God enabling man's naturally weak intellect to be the means to things transcendent. Reason and faith are both divine, but must be kept distinct and separate. There was special need of this sort of demonstration, for Hellenism, once overcome by Latin legal-mindedness and ritual, was renewing, through Jewish and Arabian philosophers,[33] its attack upon the West. It brought in theories of social ethics; the disciplines of psychology, epistemology, and metaphysics; and such terms as form and matter, potentiality and actuality. Latin theology could not survive without considering these elements; nor without a willingness to use Greek categories. Aquinas was the champion of the faith in this emergency. He was an heir of Aristotle, whose works he edited, and of Neo-Platonism. He recognized two sources of religious knowledge: (1) the *Bible* and apostolic tradition (the works of the "Fathers"), and (2) Platonic and Aristotelian writings. Both sources came from God and must agree, when adequately understood. Consequently, Aquinas taught that men may through reason know God as the Absolute, the First Cause; we may perceive "cause" by noting its effects; we may perceive such effects as men's bodies, and men's souls which are "forms" of bodies. We know God the Absolute through what he has created in exposition of Himself. But God as the true Object of devotion cannot be known through reason, save as reason is extended by our faith; we know him through revelation, especially through the *Bible,* which is truly the record of his revelation, and through the Church, by which his revelation was confirmed. For perfect knowledge we must accept the doctrines of the Scriptures—he laid great stress upon the doctrine of the Trinity—and depend faithfully upon the sacraments. Natural reason demonstrates God's existence, and man's moral obligation to the right; faith

---

[33] The Spanish Moslem philosopher, Ibn Rushd or Averroes (1126–1198), had been very influential with his interpretation of Greek philosophy. See Chapter XVI.

agrees with this, but goes further, and finds through unquestioning obedience God the Redeemer of mankind.

The Church is the perfect earthly channel of God's grace. The state has merely transient validity; it is a stage of life leading to its own completion in the Church. The world is not altogether evil in itself; it is preliminary to the kingdom of God's grace. There is temporary good and temporary evil, natural right and natural wrong. There are prohibitions; these are absolute. There are counsels, which are relative. There are grades of social ethics; morality may be qualified; natural right may at times be wrong, and natural wrong may at times be right; the Church is the final arbiter.

The Church, during the fourteenth, fifteenth, and sixteenth centuries, suffered a series of disturbing, if not shattering, shocks, including Protestant dissensions. We shall not follow her history as such beyond the sixteenth century, for our aim is characterization and not history; but we must yet include in our survey the means by which she met the shocks. Her responses were mainly two: (1) the founding of the Jesuits, or Society of Jesus, in 1540, and (2) the decisions of the Council convened from 1545 to 1564 at Trent in Germany.

The Jesuits.—The Society of Jesus was a spiritual army of the Pope, a major agency for extending his dominion. They established missions in all parts of the globe, making converts and reclaiming many Protestant dissenters. They specialized in education, founding many secondary schools and universities; their methods were entirely scholastic. In both theology and ethics they were exponents of Aquinas. They held Aquinas' theory of qualified morality, permitting probability and mental reservation,[34] although the charge that they ever formally taught that the end justifies the means cannot be proved against them. They magnified the fact that the priest in the confessional is the expert on the moral quality of specific conduct; and they emphasized the primacy of communion, the Mass.

Their founder was a Spanish nobleman, Ignatius Loyola (1491–1556), who, recuperating from a wound received in battle, was converted to the religious life, as he read the lives of various saints. He hung his weapons on the altar of the Virgin, and, eager to convert the Saracens, undertook an arduous

---

[34] Mental reservation allows one under duress, or in emergencies, to qualify his verbal statements for the sake of some justifiable objective. *Cf.* the Moslem Imamites, with their doctrine of *taqiya*, allowing them in time of stress to dissemble their religious views.

pilgrimage to Palestine. Induced by Franciscans in Jerusalem to prepare himself for missionary service, he studied from 1528 to 1534 at Salamanca and at Paris. In 1534, he organized at Montmartre the Society of Jesus, including Francis Xavier, the famous apostle to India and the East. The Jesuits put themselves directly at the Pope's disposal. They rose to temporal power in France, Spain, Portugal, and Austria; their influence was pervasive. While they lost political prestige eventually (after 1759), they continued to enhance the Papacy. They have been particularly active in the Western Hemisphere.

Trent.—The Council of Trent (1545–1564) remained officially in session during eighteen years, working at its problems through two commissions. Decisions were valid, if the Pope approved. It clarified many issues, modified some, and sought to establish the details of Church authority. Its decrees were not accepted universally by the Catholic states,[35] but they served generally to stiffen clerical morale. According to the Council:

(1) The *Latin Vulgate* was the sacred Canon, and Church Tradition was coequal with it as Scriptural authority, the Church having the right of Scriptural interpretation. This gave papal usages apostolic warrant.

(2) The sacraments were further validated, being defined as symbols of sacred reality, visible forms of invisible grace, containing and bestowing grace on those suitably disposed.

(3) Justification, *i.e.*, being "made just," from the natural state to the state of grace (*cf. Rom.* 3:20–31), does not rest upon faith alone, but upon works also. It embraces the remission of sins and sanctification, forgiveness and grace coming *at once*. God's grace is not given for man's merit, but through the merit of the death of Christ.[36]

These few items may serve as indication of the Council's disposition. Church organization, management, and discipline were considered. Steps were taken to regulate indulgences, whose abuse had led to public scandal,[37] toward the regulation of the calendar of saints and holy days, and toward the education of the clergy. An *Index,* censorship or blacklist, was provided for

---

[35] The German states had the right by a ruling of the Diet of Augsburg (1555) to choose for their people between Catholicism and the Lutheran *Augsburg Confession.* This Roman tolerance was merely for the princes, not the people. The Peace of Augsburg, ordained while the Council of Trent was in session, could not possibly be kept. The stage was set for war.

[36] The Protestant reformers were emphasizing justification by faith; faith made it possible and sure: but forgiveness was the act of God, who alone could forgive sin.

[37] The method of indulgences imposed pecuniary fines instead of penances for mortal sins, especially among Germanic Christians.

offensive publications. The Council recognized, by implication, the primacy of the Pope; but not until 1870 was the doctrine of the Pope's infallibility (when speaking *ex cathedra*) promulgated. With the decrees of Trent, the *Index,* the Jesuits, and the Inquisition, the Church was prepared to crush the Protestant Reformation. Although Trent's decrees were deliberately vague on issues which divided Catholics, they were characteristic of the Roman Church; they removed all hope of reconciliation and reunion with the Protestants.

The Roman Church continues to enjoy unusual power; it rests still in the ascendency in the West. Papal policy is definitely seeking to increase the sense of Catholic solidarity, to create an international consciousness; the Pope would be the interpreter of international law, and of the conscience of humanity. Although this policy has failed on several conspicuous occasions, the Church is showing new signs of solidarity and world influence. Perhaps its power still rests on these three factors, chiefly: the traditional, the legalistic, and the sacramentarian. The Catholic individual takes comfort in the Church and finds assurance in the sacraments. He finds in it the idea of the Holy; he lives under the spell of blessed relics. He believes that works are meritorious; that the good deed brings somehow its own reward, and the evil deed, its dire consequences, unless it be forgiven. He is assured that God can be prevailed upon by his doing the works which God has appointed. The lives of the saints provide accessible example; the rules of holy living are explicit; the works enjoined are tangible. He experiences through the Church something of the ripeness and completion of the ages. His guides, the clergy, are in apostolical succession, linking him with the fountainhead of faith. He finds in his Church sufficient breadth; it is the true, the universal, Church, whose foundation is divine, whose plan is heavenly, whose character is revelation. There is no salvation for him otherwise; and, after all, his Church is lenient; he has a certain freedom of belief; and there is a lengthy list of pardonable sins. What more could he desire? His Church is practical, visible, adaptable, and durable.

Protestantism.—Protestantism as a conspicuous movement emerged comparatively late; it arose in the sixteenth century. But it was inevitable, taking human nature as it is; it was inherent in Christianity from the beginning; Jesus was himself a protestant. Dissenters, including "heretics," of various sorts appeared in every century of the Church's history, but at last a crisis came which introduced a permanent division, a "third estate" in Christendom. Protestantism itself assumed many forms, but essentially it represents an extension of the spiritual and Scriptural character of Christianity, in contrast with the formal organizational. Protestants and Catholics are fundamentally related, but the two bodies are historically distinct. The term "Catholic" has been limited unduly throughout the centuries by Roman—and Greek—usage. Protestants, however, have been equally restrictive in their uses of "true" and "universal."

"Catholic Church" was first used by Bishop Ignatius of Antioch, about 115 A.D., in a letter which he wrote to the church at Smyrna from Troas, while *en route* to martyrdom at Rome. His simple meaning is inspiring, ". . . wherever Christ may be, there is the Catholic Church." And he was still as simple in his reference to the fact that a bishop's presence is the visible test of the presence of the Lord, the invisible head of the Church. By definition, "Catholic" means "universal"; by implication, unity and uniqueness; the unity of the Body of Christ, the uniqueness of the Truth of Christ. But history preëmpted for it the meaning of the visible Church. In Roman Christian usage, it represents an exclusive Body, and exclusive Teachings, a hierarchy, with its offices and creeds, at whose head stands the Pope.

The supreme issue between "Protestants" and "Catholics," in a restricted sense, is papal; witness the Protestant references to their Catholic brothers as "papists." Pius X (1903–1915) decreed categorically that "all those who do not acknowledge the Roman Pontiff as their Head, do not belong to the Church of Jesus Christ." This confirmed the issue of several centuries, in which the Protestants cannot concur. They, rather, hold it true, as Ignatius wrote, that "wherever Christ may be, there is the Catholic Church." The original Protest, the basis in action whereby the separation came, was issued by five princes and fourteen free cities of Germany against the action of the Diet of Speyer in 1529, which *revoked* the decree of 1526 that each German prince should determine the religion of his state.[38] The following year the Augsburg Confession was drawn up, and the Catholic Church decided that all who subscribed to it would be considered Protestants. Theology thus joined with politics to bring about the Reformation. In practice, the term Protestant was shortly used in Germany, to cover "Lutherans"; in England and elsewhere, all opposed to Rome. Many dissenters adopted

[38] The Peace of Augsburg, 1555, renewed the decree of 1526.

the term officially, and used it until they came to realize that they, too, were Catholic, having their spiritual origin in the religion of Jesus, as transmitted by the first apostles and their successors. The day may come when all Christians realize, through world experience, the primacy of the Christian spirit; when all men know that unity transcends locality, class, nationality, race, and dogma.

Luther.—Martin Luther (1483–1546), the son of a miner of Eisleben, a Saxon village between Wittenberg and Erfurt, became virtually in 1517, at Wittenberg, the first Protestant. He had attended the University in Erfurt, to complete his training for the law, but at the age of twenty-two he had suddenly become a friar, instead, in an Augustinian monastery. He had become distrustful of "the world"; in a state of restlessness and dimness of soul, he sought salvation. He fasted in the monastery until he fainted, scourged himself until he bled, and nearly wrecked his constitution by asceticism,—without relief of mind and peace of soul. After two years, he began to read the Scriptures; while reading Paul's *Epistle to the Romans,* he experienced conversion. Reading that "the just shall live by faith" (*Rom.* 5:1), he began to question the great emphasis which the Church had put on works. He weighed the "justification" to be found by the believer through faith in Jesus Christ over against the "merit" of ceremonial observances. He found satisfaction in the *Bible,* beyond the Church itself; it became the source of his authority; personal experience became the test of his salvation. He had gone back of post-Augustinian works to Augustinian and Pauline faith.

To divert the friar's mind from his own immediate concerns, his superior secured for him a post as teacher in the University in Wittenberg. But there he became involved in the controversy which raged about indulgences. A Dominican friar, Tetzel, came to Wittenberg with indulgences to sell, and Luther filed a protest; he nailed some theses on the door of the church, Oct. 31, 1517. While, at first, the public thought the move another fight between monastic Orders, it appeared through Luther's continued protestations, that there was something more afoot. He was forthwith haled before his Order, at the Pope's direction, and indicted on a charge of heresy. He was tried at Augsburg, in October, 1518, before a papal legate, but asked for trial before a general Council—which popes were not willing to attempt to call in those days. Six months later, in a debate in Leipzig with

John Eck, the most eminent Catholic controversialist, Luther was forced into a damaging admission, that he agreed with John Huss, who had been burned in 1415 for heresy! Unperturbed, he carried on the contest, issuing many articles in German, proclaiming that all true believers, as well as all true priests, are priests of God. He was shortly excommunicated (1520), but burned the bull defiantly. Half the states of Germany refused the publication of the bull,—here was a national issue! While he was condemned at the Diet of Worms, in 1521, where he declined retraction, he was permitted to withdraw in safety; there were many of his countrymen then ready to lay down their lives for him. Had he died then, his triumph would have been complete; he had established the cause in terms of: Biblical authority, distrust of "holy works," personal experience of salvation, and the rights of nationality.[39] Subsequent interpretations were based substantially on these elements. His reformation was in part political, sharing the impetus toward the nationalizing of the German and Scandinavian Churches, beginning with Saxony in 1525; although for a century there was devastating civil war. Theologically, he was conservative; he was more Catholic than most of the reformers; the "Reformed Churches" went beyond him. His position, that of orthodox Lutheranism, is this:

(1) The *Bible* is the inspired and infallible authority in all matters of faith and life.

(2) Good works are the fruits and evidences of faith.

(3) Salvation comes by faith.

(4) Two sacraments, Baptism and the Lord's Supper, are real channels of grace, not mere symbols; Christ is really present in the bread and wine.

(5) The believer is predestined to salvation, but the condemnation of the non-elect is not necessarily eternal.

Lutheranism in America, in spite of having lost much of its nationalistic character, remains as conservative, sectarian, and diversified as its prototype in Europe. It ranges all the way from personal piety to the efficacy of "works." There are four millions of "Lutherans" in the United States; perhaps 75,000,000, altogether, in the world.

Protestant Episcopalians.—The Protestant Episcopal Church is essentially a national type which sprang directly out of Ref-

---

[39] Luther's record was, however, somewhat clouded by the Peasants' War. He unwittingly aroused the peasants to rebellion, and urged the princes to crush them ruthlessly, "to merit heaven better by bloodshed than by prayer."

ormation soil. It originated, politically, in England, by the Act of Supremacy of 1534, which constituted Henry VIII "on earth the Supreme Head" of the Church of England. Protestant theological elements were later introduced; but today there is an increasing tendency among Episcopalians to regard themselves as Catholic, as representatives of the universal Christian Church, and as true agents of saving grace, of which the sacraments are channels. Long prior to the Act of Henry, John Wycliffe (1320–1384), a contemporary of the Bohemian John Huss, had kindled in England the fires of reform,—by his translation of the *Bible* into *English,* by his writings, and by the ministry of his "Poor Priests." After him came John Colet, who used the *New Testament* as the basis of his lectures at Oxford; and William Tyndale, translator of the *Bible* and champion of religious liberty. Luther's writings found their way to England. Meanwhile, there was gathering discontent; popular dissatisfaction with greedy bishops, careless friars, and immoral priests. The times were ripe, at last, for Henry's assumption of self-rule. Yet he did not reject the spiritual authority of the Pope; his confiscation of monastic properties was greed; he merely nationalized the English Church, made it independent of the Pope as worldly sovereign. To deny to Henry the headship of the Church was treason. In turn, a papal bull delivered Henry's soul to the devil and his kingdom to the first invader.

By the "Six Articles" of 1539, Henry gave the Church a creed, essentially papal, with the Pope left out; for example, the bread and wine of the communion were the blood and body of the Lord. His son Edward's Act of Uniformity of 1549 obliged all churches to use exclusively an English *Book of Common Prayer*. It was followed shortly (1552) by certain *Articles* of Religion. But the country was divided, and Edward's sister Mary was a Catholic, who repealed the former legislation, restored the *Latin Prayer Book,* and persecuted Protestants. Elizabeth seems to have had no deep convictions on these matters; in her own life she kept many Catholic forms, praying in her private chapel to the Virgin. The nation seemed of two opinions. But the Reformation had set in, and England would have her own interpretation of it. Another Act of Supremacy (1559) reaffirmed the separation, and restored the English *Prayer Book*. Elizabeth appointed new bishops where necessary, and named as Primate of all England her own Archbishop of Canterbury. The *Thirty-nine Articles* (1563ff.) established the details of creed in conjunction with the

Prayer Book, and the Church of England was at last a fact. It was wholly national; no worship was allowed other than what the law prescribed; but the Church remained episcopal, although the exact authority of the episcopate was difficult of settlement.

The Anglicans, like the Lutherans, occupied a middle ground, not so far away from Roman doctrine. Their *Book of Common Prayer,* containing creed and ritual, was largely drawn from the *Latin Book of Prayer.*

(1) The episcopacy is based, in theory, upon the *Bible;* but "high" Churchmen have claimed divine right for it, a certain confusion with reference to the character of the Church issuing from this contrast of divine and Biblical authority.

(2) The clergy are in apostolical succession (this is essential doctrine), and non-episcopal orders are not recognized as valid. There are, in theory, no monks; but there are corresponding "fathers." There is no rule of celibacy for the clergy.

(3) Worship is liturgical, but less elaborate than the Roman Mass. In 1928, an unsuccessful attempt was made to revise the *Prayer Book* in the interest of a greater sacramentarianism. "Communion" is used instead of "mass," and "table" instead of "altar." Independent of the special ritual of "Holy Communion," there are regular services of Morning and Evening Prayer. There are no images, but, in a minor way, there is veneration of the saints. There is, in general, no confessional; but many "high" churches use the office. The congregation participates largely in the services, by responses, confessions, psalms, and hymns. In the days of Queen Elizabeth, the novelty of psalm-singing in the open air turned many people to the Reformation.

(4) Two sacraments are recognized: Baptism, and the Lord's Supper, which Protestants generally retained. But the Anglicans expressly rejected the Lutheran opinion of the Supper; they denied the "real presence," by transubstantiation, of the blood and body of the Lord in the bread and wine. These elements were to be taken and eaten, "with faith and thanksgiving," as symbols, "in remembrance that Christ died" for men.

(5) There is wide freedom of theological interpretation, especially among the "low" churches. Much of the "Calvinism" (*i.e.,* predestination) of the *Articles* (Article XVII) has been softened, or forgotten; the perseverance of "the elect," rather than of all believers, is adhered to. Man must share responsibility

for his own salvation. The Church has recently discussed all its major problems of belief and ritual, and has undertaken to carry on its work in accordance with the newer personal and social needs. It has continued an original interest in the union ("high" Churchmen call it "reunion") of the Churches. It has discharged its reasonable share in the modern missionary enterprise.

The disestablished Churches of Scotland and of Ireland, and the American Protestant Episcopal, carry on the tradition of the mother Church of England; they are autonomous branches. The American episcopate is in apostolic succession, although certain English laws had to be repealed in colonial days, so that American bishops could be consecrated in the mother country. Churches had been organized in all the colonies, before the Revolution. By 1789, the American Church had been reorganized somewhat after the national Constitution, with a House of Bishops and a House of Deputies, the latter representing "dioceses." There are now two million members. Each diocese has its own convention; since 1913, they have been grouped into eight provincial units. In doctrine, discipline, and worship, the Americans follow closely the English *Book of Common Prayer,* with the "Athanasian" creed omitted, and the *Thirty-nine Articles* not required. The *Apostles'* and the *Nicene* Creeds are emphasized. The liturgy is fundamentally "Catholic." There are "high" Churchmen, who preserve the Catholic sacramentarian heritage, not without an intimation of transubstantiation in the eucharist, and with insistence on the divine episcopate.[40] There are "low" Churchmen who have adjusted themselves more nearly to the "democratic" mood; and some *very low,* who since 1873, have carried on the Reformed Episcopal Church. All have been anxious for the restoration of the undivided Catholic Church, as expressed in the *Declaration on Unity,* 1886, "the return of all Christian Communions to the principles of unity exemplified by the undivided Catholic Church during the first ages of its existence."

Further diversity in Christendom is easily exemplified; Protestant denominations have been numerous, based on doctrine, ritual, and organization. Catholicism has managed either to annihilate, or to assimilate, its major "heresies"; but among Protestants are Lutherans, Anglicans, Calvinists, Puritans, Dissenters, Separatists, Presbyterians, Baptists, Congregationalists, Disciples of Christ, and Methodists, representing geographically, or doc-

---

[40] Two "high" Church parties, the Oxford Movement (Keble) and the Anglo-Catholics (Pusey), have celebrated their centennial (1933).

trinally, independent areas of revolt. We are not here concerned with them all, but only with the major types.

Methodism.—"Methodism," a system followed by a number of denominations, arose in England. Its "method" is episcopal; but in fundamental doctrine, it is "Arminian," with stress upon the freedom of man's will; it is "evangelical," with primary loyalty to the *Evangel* or *Gospel* of Jesus, in contrast with ecclesiastical or rationalistic types of Christianity. Its background is the Church of England; its motive was to stem the tide of irreligion, to which the Anglicans were paying little heed. The Elizabethan settlement survived almost unchanged until the eighteenth century. All free spirits in the Church, and, on the outside, "non-conformists," were vigorously suppressed. Worship was predominantly formal. The clergy were incredibly lazy and indifferent. "Reason" had its vogue as the highest of the human faculties; "enthusiasm" was condemned as foolish and indecent. The morals of society were low; gambling, cockfighting, bear baiting, profanity, drunkenness, and degrading theatrical performances exhibited the common weakness. Gin shops agreed to make a man drunk for a penny, and dead drunk for tuppence. Licentiousness accompanied inebriety.

The Wesleyan revival began in 1729 with the "Holy Club," so nicknamed for its piety, a group of dons and students in the gay, port-drinking University of Oxford. Among the sixteen members, John and Charles Wesley and George Whitefield were the leading spirits. The Wesleys, High Churchmen, of an ascetic and somewhat legalistic temper, directed their attention to what we now call "social service." When the Club disbanded in 1735, for want of a definite objective, John Wesley went as a missionary to America, but no immediate success beyond encountering a band of "Pietists" (Lutheran Moravians), with whom he found a sudden, assuring joy of his own salvation. Returning to England, he found that Whitefield had also "experienced" salvation, and was preaching with amazing power among the Bristol miners. Wesley caught new fire from Whitefield; both were bent upon a sweeping, evangelical revival. Whitefield was of humble birth; Wesley was a scholar and a gentleman. The former was a "Calvinist"; the latter, an "Arminian." Wesley took the lead; he was an organizer; he instituted "methodism," scrupulous observance of religious practices and principles of reform. For fifty years, until he died at eighty-seven (1791), he went about, chiefly on horseback, throughout all the English and Scotch countryside, holding "meetings," and organizing "societies." Warmth, vigor, and evangelical teaching characterized his ministry of the love of God in Christ. He preached the common virtues to the underprivileged poor and to the rich, alike. Before his death, tens of thousands had turned "Methodist," and an independent Church under its own bishops had been started in England and America (1784). Himself an ordained clergyman of the Church of England, which he never left, he passed on to others the succession of the apostolic office. The "societies" received no recognition from the Church of England; an independent movement was, therefore, contrary to Wesley's judgment, expedient and necessary. The total membership today is at least ten millions, eight of which are found in North America. Operating as a Church, and not as "missions," Methodists have been conspicuous in foreign service.

Methodist ritual is simple as compared with Wesley's, which the societies rejected as too Anglican. It is Biblical, and rich in hymns, especially of Charles Wesley's composition. Doctrine is not easily summed up, for there are episcopal, protestant, primitive, Calvanistic, and Arminian elements involved; but as a Church there is a substantial unanimity of Arminianism. Man himself must seek salvation through "perfect love," and "entire sanctification." If he backslide, he must seek the mourners' bench to be restored. He is free to sin, if he falls from grace; grace is not persistent; but he can recover and be saved.

Presbyterianism.—Presbyterianism, as a type of ecclesiastical administration, falls midway between episcopacy and congregationalism; it is a revival among certain Protestants of early apostolic practices. As doctrine, it emphasizes apostolic elements as formulated and expounded by John Calvin, a contemporary of the Jesuit Loyola. As a movement, it arose in France and Switzerland, extended into Holland, Poland, Hungary, England, Scotland, and America; and elsewhere during the modern missionary crusade. It was more independent of the Roman Catholic Church than Luther's movement. "Calvinism" had, in fact, permeated for three centuries the growing Reformation, before Calvin led it in rebellion against Rome. It was Calvin's special task to provide the distinctive pattern of the anti-papal revolution

Calvin.—John Calvin, or Jean Couvin (1509–1564), a Frenchman, born at Noyon, Picardy, was a lawyer's son, and himself trained for the law. Severe and censorious, he nevertheless objected to the Church's persecution of the French reformers, and published an edition of Seneca's *De Clementia* (*On Mercy*), hoping to mitigate injustice. His body was weak, nervous, and dyspeptic, but his mind was keen and logical. He was a religious genius, a strong, if not original thinker, and a dominant personality. Through unknown influences (in an atmosphere of Humanism) he became a Protestant. In 1536, at the age of twenty-seven, he published his monumental *Institutes of the Christian Religion,* comparable, but more coherent, with the work of Augustine, and similar in doctrine. Composed in defence of French reformers, it came to be the ablest and most comprehensive statement of the Protestant position. He took the *Apostles' Creed,* clause by clause, to show that Protestantism was its true expression. His theology was based ultimately upon the *Bible.* Finding it expedient to withdraw from France, he took refuge in Geneva, where Farel, a young reformer, persuaded him to tarry. The citizens already having declared their freedom from the Pope, welcomed the fugitive.

Although once expelled for possibly forgivable harshness, he returned in 1541, to remain the balance of his life, and to establish a theocracy, or "rule of God." In effect, it was a local Protestant autocracy. "His practical interpretation of civil liberty was that the Church as the oracle of God should control the State and that John Calvin should control the Church." There was small room for liberty, civil or religious, under Calvin, and yet Geneva became the center of the Reformation movement. "The spiritual indebtedness of Western Europe and America to the educating influence of Calvin's theology is well nigh measureless." He must be measured by the standards of his day, whereby we adjudge him memorable for his intolerance of *unethical* behavior. He put morality back into religion. He felt himself to be an instrument of God, and God was, to him, nothing if not moral. But it was left for doctrine to be the ground of Calvin's severe intolerance, when in 1553 he allowed the Unitarian Servetus to be publicly burned for his heretical attack upon the Trinity.

Calvinism made itself heir to Luther, whom it honored. It shared with Luther an Augustinian emphasis upon the doctrine of free grace, that God gives to man an inner power without which he could not attain salvation. Paul, Augustine, Luther, and Calvin agree on grace as an agent of salvation. In Augustine, grace is associated with the Church, perhaps dependently; in

Calvin, grace is free from ecclesiastical control, and is the only source of efficiency which enters into salvation. The sacraments to Calvin are symbolical, the Lord's Supper being a solemn privilege from which moral offenders were excluded. Grace cannot be earned; when it comes it is wholly undeserved. God gives it to a chosen few. Man is naturally evil, totally depraved, and salvation is the gift of God. Calvin's teaching emphasized two aspects of religion: man's absolute dependence upon God; and a life of active service to the glory of God. All things are included under the will of God; man has no freedom of will whatsoever. The *Bible,* the *Old Testament* as well as the *New,* is the record of God's will. Predestination was the central dogma. Calvin and Luther both believed in predestination, that events are predetermined by the will of God, but Calvin did not emphasize, as Luther did, justification by faith, remission of the punishment of sin, as a working out of God's predetermination. To Calvin, consciousness of "election" was man's assurance that his sins had been forgiven. The Church is not a human institution, subject to change at man's direction, but is divine: it is the Kingdom of God on earth, and as such is the medium of man's salvation. On the other hand, the State is human and humanly ordained. Church and State are separate, independent entities. Calvin, however, had attempted in Geneva to establish a holy commonwealth, under the rule of "presbyters" elected by the citizens. It did not succeed, for the line could not always be clear between the "presbytery" and the secular authorities. In any case, the divine Church is above the human State. Calvinism was once summarized during its controversy (1618–19) with the Arminians in the famous "five points," or theses: (1) absolute predestination (no freedom of the human will); (2) particular redemption (only the "elect" are saved); (3) total depravity (man's innate sinfulness); (4) irresistible grace (God cannot be resisted by one whom he has chosen); and (5) the perseverance of the saints (if "elected," man is sure of being saved). While these five theses cannot properly be taken out of controversy as an exact statement of the Calvinistic faith, they may serve not altogether inexactly as a summary.

Calvinism became a movement and a spiritual tradition, taking form in accommodation to its new surroundings. In France, the Huguenots perpetuated it. In Scotland, John Knox (1513–1572) and the Covenanters were Calvinists. In England, Calvinism split into Puritans, Presbyterians, and Congregationalists. Everywhere it ill agreed with monarchy. In England, there were political reverberations, in which Presbyterians were involved. Although the Westminster Assembly (1643–1648) failed to formulate the unity of the national churches of England, Scotland and Ireland, according to the best "Reformed" tradition, the debates bore fruit. The doctrinal statements consisting of the "thirty-three articles" have stood as the "Confession" of the Presbyterian Church; were for many years accepted "for substance of doctrine" by Congregationalists; and were included in the Philadelphia *Confession* of the Baptists. The name Presbyterian in America is borne only by those presbyterian churches which derive their origin from Great Britain, and are thus distinguished from the Reformed Churches (presbyterian) whose origin lay in Europe. Throughout the world there are seven million members of the "Presbyterian" faith, including three million in America. While Presbyterians have fallen somewhat sharply into two groups, fundamentalists and liberals, Calvinism as a creed sits rather lightly on them. They are, however, faithful children of the Calvinist tradition.

Congregationalism.—In the "congregational" type, the local congregation is autonomous, but in fellowship with sister churches. Among the "congregational" bodies are the Congregationalists, the Baptists, the Disciples of Christ, the Unitarians, and the Universalists. They represent, however, some diversity of doctrine. Their general background is English "Puritan," or "Separatist." The Puritans at first accepted the Elizabethan settlement, although they maintained their ardent aim of purifying the Church's forms of worship. They discounted the authority of the hierarchy and tended to find religious guidance in the Scriptures. They not only demanded formal independence of the Papacy, but the elimination of all "popery." They attacked the use of the cross in baptism, the ring in the marriage ceremony, the cleric's wearing of the cap and surplice, and the veneration of the saints. About 1570, they strove for a reorganization of the Church, some desiring a presbyterian organization, without such names as "arch-bishop" and "arch-deacon," which, they said, were "drawn out of the pope's shop." Some went so far as to suggest actual separation from the Church of England.

In 1580, Robert Browne organized a separate congregation in Norwich, the first Independent, or Congregational, Church in England. Queen Elizabeth turned upon the Separatists, and upon the Presbyterians, with as much severity as she meted out officially to Catholics, and Separatism disappeared, until the later Puritan Rebellion. Meanwhile, some dissenters, with no standing in their own land, exiled themselves to Holland (1606ff.), where they laid the foundations of "Congregational" theology and organization. Many of them crossed in 1620 in the *Mayflower* to America, and renewed their movement in New England. Entrenching themselves in Massachusetts and Connecticut until the nineteenth century, they have since spread throughout the states. Congregationalism is an interesting phenomenon; it seems to be the extremity of anti-hierarchical revolt, unless the milder Friends or "Quakers" are at the extreme, rejecting practically all religious institutions for guidance by the Inner Spirit. It represents the Church's primitive democracy and independence. It has never had a rigid creed; its theology is liberal, and easily revised; it is only faintly "Calvinistic." Its worship is scarcely to be distinguished from that of other non-episcopal communions. It has been generously coöperative, especially with the Presbyterians and Unitarians, the former being early kinsmen, and the latter, extreme separatist brothers of a century ago. Recently a union with the "Christian Church" was consummated (1933). It has cherished the open mind and education, and has a worthy record in philanthropy. It was the first among American Protestants to organize a foreign missionary society. The body is chiefly held together by the pride of heritage, but since 1871 its affairs have been administered by a National Council. Since the merger with the "Christians," the membership has reached about one million.

Baptists.—Baptists are non-conformists, or Separatists, who put special emphasis upon the sacrament of baptism, the rite being by immersion for adult believers, and having no sacramentarian or magical efficiency. They refuse to practice infant baptism. Doctrine has been with them of greater moment than the form of government. Remotely, they are apostolic; for baptism by immersion was doubtless the practice of the early Church. In succeeding centuries, the mode had varied, and the meaning had been much debated. More immediately, they were heirs of "Anabaptists," a sixteenth century group who baptized again (*ana*) those who as infants had been "christened" by the Church. They were "heretics" both to Catholics and to Protestants; many Protestant reformers wrote against them. Luther turned opinion against them in 1522; they were driven out of Switzerland to Moravia, out of Italy to Poland. Persecuted in Holland, they reorganized under Menno Simons as Mennonites, and formed associations with anabaptist brethren in other nations. The Baptists sprang from Anabaptist Separatists sojourning in Amsterdam from England. These Separatists in 1609 had repudiated their baptism as infants, had been immersed, holding that baptism is not valid, unless *faith* precedes it. From 1612, Baptist congregations multiplied in England on the strength of their protest against infant baptism.

Baptists have a varied creed. Generally, they are Calvinistic, but, unlike Calvin, they insist upon the complete separation of Church and State. Each local congregation is autonomous; there is tolerance of creed, but emphasis on "experienced" conversion. Close communion has been a common practice, the admission of none but their own members to the Supper. In addition to the ties of believer's baptism and close communion—both of which have loosened slightly, recently—the main body of Baptists is knit together by various "associations" and a general "Convention." The name covers a wide variety of religious opinions, educational enterprises, and philanthropic activities. Although English Baptists number only half a million, the movement gained remarkable impetus in America, totaling eight millions. They organized at Providence, in 1638, under the leadership of Roger Williams, an English Separatist, banished from Massachusetts in 1636. The movement took special hold in Pennsylvania and the southern states. Not long ago, there were four million "Baptists" in Russia. All of the larger Christian Churches tolerate immersion, but few have made it the exclusive mode of baptism, as did the early Church. The Disciples of Christ are peculiarly an American immersionist body, emphasizing faith and repentance before baptism. Without a creed, they have taken the Scriptures as authority, including the weekly observance of the Lord's Supper as thus warranted.

Conclusion.—We may rightly deduce from many of the foregoing materials that the Christian Church of the last three hundred years has made its greatest progress in America, a conclusion based not merely on the obvious fact that America was a virgin area, but on the fact also that experimentation of unusual significance has been carried out. Both Protestants and Catholics came freely to the Western Hemisphere. In the United States alone are roughly 20,000,000 Roman Catholics and 35,000,000 Protestants.

In Europe, Catholic and State Churches have had the right of way. While American Christianity has been denominational, its spirit has developed peculiarly *inter*denominational and *un*denominational activities, which have had their reflex influences on doctrine. The Roman Catholic Church of America has developed as a unit, showing no disloyalty to Rome, but conscious of a somewhat national character and an American destiny. Protestant Churches have long sustained a Federal Council through which interchanges of opinion might be registered and coöperative social enterprises undertaken. Most recently, they have undertaken through Commissions of their mission Boards a thoroughgoing inquiry into the aim and scope of their missionary ventures of a century. Problems purely domestic seem now to catch the imagination and to enlist the generosity of loyal Christians, Protestant and Catholic. There is a growing sense of obligation to the underprivileged, the duty of benevolence toward their minds and bodies, and a lively interest in the principles by which a sound society is built. But there are no essentially new problems beyond those we have discovered by our total survey. Familiar problems persist under new conditions and new designations, and the loyal Christian seeks to meet them by renewed applications of the pure spirit and sound morals of Jesus. If there is a major problem and incentive for the Christian Church today, it is the secularism manifest within and all about it. It must meet it as such dangers have been met before, by a just blending of virtue and religion, a kindling of devotion to the good, an impression of the idea of the holy, and an appreciation of the majesty and love of God.

If we venture to ask, at last, What is Christianity? we might answer by this summary. Christianity is:

(1) The person and the teachings of Jesus. He is a sufficiently distinct historical character. He may be known in comparison with other men. He may be experienced, even mystically, as the Friends have known him. He may be idealized as the incentive to high thinking and clean living. He warrants the highest we can think of him.

The substance of his teachings is available. They are simple and practicable, whatever we, with some freedom of selection, may discover them to be. A modern scholar has reduced the authentic "sayings" to these nine: *Mk.* 10:17–18; *Mt.* 12:31; *Mk.* 3:21; 13:32; 15:34; 8:12; 6:5ff; 8:12–21; and *Mt.* 11:5. One need not accept this judgment, altogther, but yet might find therein such items as the goodness of God, a fatal form of sin, the divinity of Jesus, a final judgment, the humanity of Jesus, popular credulity, the need of faith, the efficacy of spiritual nourishment, and love for the poor and needy. It would be difficult to assemble other passages which are more comprehensive and impressive in essential meaning. One may choose others for his own good, however.

(2) The *New Testament,* which every Christian Church accepts, whatever its evaluation, whatever portions may be emphasized. It confirms the *Old,* and the *Bible* as a whole is a progressive revelation, not yet closed. It furnishes a concrete standard of appraisal of the views and practices of any age. Being the basis of the creeds, it might serve the common good without the creeds. Textual and critical difficulties are involved, but are not insuperable barriers to individual interpretation.

(3) Tradition made by Councils, and resulting creeds. They supplement the Life and the Book, and may not rightly displace them. They are common property to Christendom, for example, Nicæa, Chalcedon, Trent, and Westminster. The Eastern Church has accepted no Christianity but that of the Councils prior to 1000, but later Councils produced nothing which was not related to earlier fundamentals. The Roman Church includes pronouncements of the Pope with findings of the Councils. The national Churches have had their Statements and Confessions. Many Reformed bodies have had their creeds. Something essential might be discovered in all of them. Altogether they elaborate Tradition, and are inextricably woven into Christianity.

(4) Christians, members of the Churches. They have made the faith. They represent the informal elements, perhaps, but they make up a "goodly company," with prophets, priests, apostles, saints, scholars, workmen, and the varied types of the many ages. Something of common humanity affects the Church through them, and they become in any comprehensive view the body of the Lord. They with their devotion constitute effective catholicity, which may not be constricted by official definitions.

These are the four ingredients of Christianity, illustrative of its complexity, yet evidence of its development and of its comprehensive value, and proof of its continuance.

Here is a device of words, by means of which the thoughtful

reader might reconstruct the constitution and the movement of the Christian Church:

(1) God: Yahweh of Sinai transferred to Zion, by way of Moses, and the prophets; gods of other nations, vanities; ethical monotheism develops, with Yahweh as Father of Israel, becoming in Jesus, Father of men; Truth, Light, Love.

(2) Revelation: through Law, prophesy, the Son, Scriptures, and the Church.

(3) Jesus: Son of man, Son of God, Messiah-Christ, the *Logos,* Life, Savior by incarnation and atonement.

(4) Disciples: apostles, "Christians."

(5) Church: Kingdom of God, societies, apostolic succession, episcopate, Councils, creeds, Papacy, Catholic.

(6) Scriptures: Law, Prophets, Writings, Epistles, Gospels, Apocrypha; Inspiration.

(7) Salvation: Faith, repentance, baptism, works, grace, atonement, predestination, etc.

(8) Sacraments: Baptism, Lord's Supper; confirmation, ordination, penance; marriage, extreme unction; eucharist, mass, communion.

(9) Reformation: Authority, priest, minister; Protestant, progress.

CHAPTER XVI

The Moslem Religion

While popularly, but inaccurately, known as Mohammedanism, the religion of the Moslem is Islam. The differentiation is at once important. "Mohammedanism" is derived from a title of the founder, *Muhammad,* "the one worthy of continual praise." But he called the faith *Islam,* "submission," or "peace won by submission," to God, emphasizing its divine, rather than its human origin. He said that he was "only a man," a "warner," an "apostle"; that "there is no might nor strength but in God," to whom all men "return." It is a fundamental error in Islam to reflect upon the sovereignty of God. The *Muslim,* "he who has given himself over to God," claims no merit of his own.

Islam is the latest of the great "world religions." Sikhism, the last in time of the twelve living faiths, rests properly against its Indian background; but Islam follows naturally our consideration of Judaism and Christianity, for it rests upon the Semitic basis common to the three. A reformation of Arabian paganism, its positive qualities, beyond the personal, are partly Jewish, partly Christian.

Islamic culture is largely present in the whole world today; Christendom especially stands deeply in its debt. Among Islamic cities there are Cordova, Granada, Cairo, Istanbul, Baghdad, Samarcand, Agra, and Delhi, every name suggestive of some glory in the earth. Among famous Moslem rulers must be numbered Omar of Madina; Walid of Damascus; Murad, and Sulayman of Istanbul; Harun, and Mamun of Baghdad; Salah-ud-din (Saladin) of Syria and Egypt; and the immortal Akbar of Delhi. Each of them represents some lasting contribution to mankind. Masters of poetic form and sentiment have put us in their debt. Omar Khayyam is possibly (thanks to Edward Fitzgerald) better known in England and America than in his native Persia. Europe has freely levied toll on Moslem literature of earthly love. The *Arabian Nights* (the *Thousand and One* tales) have ministered to our spirit of adventure. We enjoy hearing the poet Rumi (Jalalu d-din, "ornament of religion"), talk of worldly things,

"Poor copies out of heaven's original,
Pale earthly pictures mouldering to decay,"

and are stirred by his hopeful query,

"What though thy frame be withered, old, and dead,
If the soul keep her fresh, immortal youth?"

In Sadi of Shiraz, "a deep interpreter and master sage," is "matter for every taste." Says he, as warning,

"Can wise hearts ever take the world to wife?
Can pure minds linger in th' embrace of life?

. . . .

Who eats his corn whilst yet the blade is green,
At harvest-time a crop of husks will glean."

What of such philosophers and guides as al-Ghazali, Ibn al-Arabi, and Ibn Rushd (Averroes)? Among the words we use are many laden with connotations of trade, science, and learning: saffron, asparagus, muslin, gauze, and taffeta; orange, palm, and lemon trees; admiral, alcove, alcohol, and sofa; algebra and cipher. The Renaissance, with its universities of Padua and Paris, was inspired by Islam. Our academic gown suggests the *abba* of the Arabs. Moslems are world figures, the makers and carriers of culture.

Numbers.—Moslems today, in this year of the *Hijra 1353* (1934),[1] may number nearly two hundred and forty millions.[2] There is a belt of them, more or less continuous, from Gibraltar (*Jabal-Tariq*, the Rock of Tariq) eastward to the Philippines, containing upwards of 200,000,000, including Moors, Algerians, Egyptians, Arabs, Persians, Afghans, Panjabis, East Bengalis, Javanese, and Moros. In India alone are seventy millions; in the Dutch East Indies, thirty-six; in French Africa, twenty-five; in Afghanistan, twelve; in Egypt, twelve; in Persia, ten;

[1] The Moslem calendar reckons in lunar years from the Christian solar year 622 A.D.,—or, more exactly, from the year of the "Journey" (*hijrah*), or transfer from Mecca to Madina, which fell in the Christian year 622.
[2] This is an estimate, including uncounted populations.

in Arabia, ten; in Turkey, nine. Elsewhere are unnumbered millions, including China, South "Russia," and the steppes of Turkistan. In many Moslem lands there is no enumeration. "Allah knows," and man need not concern himself to no good purpose. Within the belt, which may be called the Moslem World, Moslems are in an overwhelming majority—except in India, Burma, and Siam; they dominate thought and conduct. The strip occupies one-third of the earth's tropics, extending into the warmer edge of the north temperate zone. This has meant simple, but not always easy living. In many sections there is constant drought. Save in certain luxuriant islands, and fertile river valleys, physical resources have been meager, compared with many other regions of the earth. Mineral wealth is scarce. The nomads have depended on their herds, and all settled stocks depend on agriculture and the manual trades. Railroads are few. The horse, the camel, and the donkey furnish transportation. And yet the peoples of these regions moved the world. The crescent may all too truly symbolize them now, but their moon was full for centuries. The student of culture and religion must reckon closely with their demonstration of simplicity as power, and with their forceful theory of God.

Symbols.—Islam today is indicated by such familiar symbols as the mosque and minaret. Tall towers rise over all, beside the domes of mosques. They are "pillars" of prayer (*manar,* "pillar," or "light-house"), appropriately conspicuous since about 700 A.D., in every Moslem center. On the balcony the *muezzin* (*muadhdhan,* "he who utters the call" to prayer) has daily "kindled the fires" of devotion. Five times a day the "call" (*adhan*) floats out over the community, spoken in the Arabic.

Allahu akbar, Allahu akbar, etc.,

"Allah is great, Allah is great. . . .
There is no God but Allah.
Muhammad is Allah's apostle.
To your prayers! To your devotions!
Allah is great; there is no God but Allah."

This has been the public call for many centuries, expanded from the simpler, original, many times repeated "Allah is great; come to worship." It has been sounded from the earliest days by the human voice, not by trumpets (they were Jewish), nor by bells (they were Christian), nor yet by pagan conch-shells.

The Mosque and Prayer.—The place of meeting (*jami*)[3] is the mosque (*masjid*). The Arabs called it the *masjid* or "place of prostration"[4] before Allah, referring especially to the place of public, congregational worship. Often the larger mosque is simply *jami,* the place of Friday meeting. The traditional form of the house of prayer is that of a square, walled-in, roofless court,[5] with a fountain, or a pool, of water in the center. On two, or three, sides of the court are colonnades, or cloisters for shelter—often used by students of the "sciences." Across the side toward Mecca stands a domed structure, with floor above the level of the court, in which the worship centers. Every mosque is so constructed—or adapted, as in the case of churches taken over from the Christians—that when the faithful pray, they face the direction (*qibla*) of Mecca. There is a niche, or alcove (*mihrab*) which indicates the *qibla.* What a vast wheel is the immediate Moslem World at prayer, the faithful bowing along the spokes that point to the ancient Meccan *Kaba!*

Mosques are plain, often bare like the Shinto shrines in their simplicity; quite unlike the bizarre temples of the Buddhists and the Hindus, or the sumptuous cathedrals of the Christians. They may be richly adorned by mere geometric lines, carved capitals and arches, flower-tracery, and Koranic texts chiselled in the artistic *Arabic.* There are no images, no human or animal figure designs (except in mosques of the heretical Shiis in Persia, and elsewhere), no pews, no chairs. There are reading racks; jars by the pool, or in the cloisters for use in the ablutions; mats and carpets on the floor; and near the alcove which points toward Mecca is a pulpit (*mimbar*), with its steps and canopy. This is the setting and the furniture of Islamic public worship.

Friday is the special day of prayer (*salat*),[6] when congregations of the faithful assemble in the mosque. While one may pray in private, and often does, he bears in mind the Prophet's words that prayers said in the mosque, especially in one of the holier mosques,[7] is more notably rewarding than the "prayers of a man in his own house." One may join in the mosque with those who follow the leadership of the *imam*[8] at any designated hour, such as sunset. While the call is sounding—from the

---

[3] Mosques have been meeting-places for men only; although in some lands, veiled apartments were provided for the women.
[4] Prostration in worship is practiced by Hindus, and Buddhists, also, praying individually.
[5] The entire mosque is often under roof in Turkey, Syria, and Egypt.
[6] *Cf. Koran,* 2:239.
[7] The *Kaba,* and the Madina *masjid,* especially.
[8] "Imam" means "in front of," or "leader." It came to represent an influential office.

minaret, or the wall—the faithful congregate. On passing an
inner entrance, one leaves his shoes, or sandals. At the particular
place he chooses for his prayers, he may leave his outer coat,
sometimes his turban. He repairs then to the pool, or fountain,
or uses one of the water jars, for his ablutions (*tawaddu,* "washing"). Many ceremonial "washings" are prescribed: of hands,
mouth, nostrils, face, fore-arms, neck, and feet. While bathing
he may whisper to himself, "I cleanse my body to be fit for
prayer, to draw my soul near the most high God," and "O Allah,
examine my accounts with favor." After he has bathed he
may sit awhile with a group assembled about a "reader" (*qari*)
intoning passages from the *Koran.* If he is able, he may read
directly from the Book. In time, the *imam,* the leader of public
prayer, appears (probably from a side room off the court), and
the worshipers take their places for the common ritual, each on
his own mat of "prostration" (*sajada*).

The ritual is picturesque, and, when understood, impressive.
With the motive of "submission," there are many postures to
assume, culminating in "prostrations." A full *salat* ranges from
the initial standing posture, hands folded before one, through a
dozen attitudes in which one kneels at last, and bows his forehead to the floor. This is a *rakah,* a "bowing down." For a
service, a minimum of *rakahs* is prescribed. There are prayers of
sunset, dawn, etc.; prayers of "watering" (in time of dearth),
of sickness, travel, and rest; prayers of necessity, and of praise.
The "prayer of assembly" is held on Friday, at midday, consisting of two *rakahs.* With the *imam* leading, all perform the
prayer in unison—a most impressive ceremony in such a great
mosque as that in Delhi, India. On Friday, after prayers, the
imam may preach a sermon from the pulpit, somewhat in the
Christian manner.

There is responsibility, as well, for private prayer, or "supplication" (*dua*),[9] as distinguished from *salat.* Moslems are
encouraged to present to God, whether in the mosques, or in
their houses, their own peculiar needs. Mohammed once declared that "supplication is the heart of worship." Prayer in
one form or another is a "pillar" of religion, second only to the
"witness" that "there is no God but Allah." The true Moslem
is a man of prayer. What it means to him, a "wisp of mist" in
God's sight, appears in the familiar picture of the solitary but
never lonely Arab traveler on the sand-swept desert, who, as the

9 *Cf. Koran,* 14:42.

evening shadows settle rapidly in the hollows of the ruffled sands, slides from his kneeling camel—hobbling his mount—and spreads his rug to pray. Whatever his "supplication," he recognizes the omnipotence and providence of God.

Pilgrimage.—The *Hajj* or Pilgrimage, in the twelfth month of the year, is yet another well-known symbol of Islam. The rite affects, in reality, or in imagination, the whole Islamic world. Mohammed first performed the *hajj* as a *Moslem* office [10] in the last year of his life (February, 632), thereby epitomizing theory and practice. In readiness for the pilgrimage, the pilgrim discards his common garments to don the *ihram,* a white, pilgrim robe. He dismisses for the time the world and the things of the world, to devote himself completely to the praise of God. He joins in Cairo, or Damascus, the multitude which annually sets out for Mecca in pursuance of the solemn ritual whose minutest detail Mohammed ordained by word and by example. There are "stations" where one rests; prayers, bathings, fastings, and sacrifices to perform; and the inspiring circuit to be made of the Holy House, the *Kaba,* with its precious black stone.[11]

Pilgrims gather from all lands, from all walks of life, speaking various tongues; but in the *hajj* they meet as one community. The high and the low, the wealthy and the poor, the learned and the ignorant, tread the common level under the pilgrim robe. They resume the primitive simplicity which the isolation of Arabia has preserved throughout the centuries. In the sacred city they surrender to the common consciousness, and renew the vows of brotherhood. Mecca, whose political fortunes have varied with the years, has remained religiously the dearest spot in the Moslem world. If the faithful find it possible once to obey the Prophet's injunction to make the *hajj,* he considers the rare privilege the "perfection of his faith." Mohammed "perfected Islam," as he said, when he made the pilgrimage, for it was witness that he had conquered all his enemies, and had established the fundamentals of the faith. He had labored long, had prayed *toward* Mecca; now, at last, he prayed *in* Mecca, at the Holy House.

Islam is, on the whole, a simple faith, but it has a history which shows diversity and change. Whatever the force of its austere essentials, its major contributions to the culture of mankind

10 Mecca had been a pilgrim center in pagan times.
11 *Cf.* R. F. Burton, *A Pilgrimage to al-Madina and Mecca.*

have been the fruit of change. Its own life has been enriched by many variations wrought by contact with a varied world beyond Arabia. We must follow these two phases of its history, what we may call traditionally: (1) the *Sunna,* the "Way" of Mohammed, which is the *essence* of Islamic orthodoxy; and (2) the *Shia,* "sectarian divergence," with its heresies of head, and its heresies of heart. First we follow *Sunna,* from Mohammed on.

The Prophet.—Mohammed (570–632 A.D.), next to Allah, is the potent name throughout Islam—potent still among one-seventh of mankind. It has been the inspiration of the hero, and the martyr; lives, goods, households, and dynasties, have been gladly risked on its behalf, often with success and empire as rewards. While the grandeur of world-dominion is no more, the Prophet's name is held in honor by his people.

Mohammed was an Arab, born in Mecca, in "the year of the elephant," as it was reckoned; that is, in the year made memorable by the appearance of an African elephant in an army that beleaguered Mecca. The enemy had come from Yemen to avenge an alleged violation of a Christian shrine in South Arabia, by some relative of a pagan Meccan tribe. It was a futile demonstration; they withdrew—put to flight, the Meccans thought, by the Meccan god. Mohammed later said it was "the Lord" that caused their stratagem to miscarry, by sending birds with claystones to hurl upon them.[12]

The child, whatever his name then was, was humbly, inconspicuously born in this memorable, auspicious year. He was humbly reared, his parents, Abdullah and Amina, being in meager circumstances, although related to the ruling tribe, the Koreish (*Quraysh*). Abdullah died before the child was born; Amina, when the lad was six years old. The orphan went first to live with his father's father, and then, with his father's brother, Abu Talib. As a youth he was a shepherd and herdsman in the neighborhood; later on he took to caravanning. Once on a journey he got as far from home as Syria, traversing the region known today as Transjordania. He rose to be the leader of a caravan, entrusted with the goods of a wealthy Meccan widow named Khadija. He was successful on the venture, doubly successful— he became the husband of Khadija. This gave him his own house, and heightened reputation. It gave him ease of mind. It gave him opportunity to satisfy a longing for religion. From twenty-

---

[12] *Cf. Koran, sura* 105.

five to forty his commercial interest and activities slowly waned, while he became a "seeker" for the one God. There were *hanifs* or "seekers" among the pagan Arabs of those days; there were Jews with their creed and ritual of Yahweh, the One God; there were Christian monks, and anchorites. All these had their influence on Mohammed.

The times were ripe for reformation, and a major Arab prophet of reform was in the making. He seems to have begun with the assumption that there is and can be only one true God. Having heard of prophets of this God among the Jews and Christians, he began to wonder at the lack of any prophet of the Arabs. Would he be the Arab prophet? Many factors, psychological, and objective, entered into his transformation. He mused, he prayed. At last a crisis came. Once as he prayed, as his custom was, in a cave beyond the city's rim of hills, the "Lord" (*Rabb*), whom he had sought, announced himself, and gave the seeker his divine commission.[13] He did not learn at this time the Lord's name, but he felt his sovereignty. The prophet of the Arabs then emerged. Mohammed's humble branch was destined to become exalted, to be like the lowly bramble in Jotham's fable, to which all the lordly palms and cedars said, "Come and rule thou over us." [14] This happened in our year 610, Mohammed's forty-first. For twenty years thereafter, he filled the increasingly comprehensive rôle of prophet,[15] pattern, and builder of a state.

At first, however, he moved cautiously. He was not altogether certain of himself. He harbored for a while the thought that maybe he was mad (*majnun,* "bejinned"). Also, he was aware that Meccan paganism was deep-rooted, and violently jealous of its institutions. His confidence returned through renewed "revelations" from the Lord; but he did not abandon caution. He practiced patience; patience was a virtue which the Lord explicitly commended. He carried on his mission secretly, winning converts to "Islam" both in Mecca and beyond, establishing connections with other tribes than the Quraysh, especially in Yathrib, later called Madina. At last his mission was suspected by the Meccan tribesmen, and the issue was forced into the open. The line of cleavage then was drawn between Islam and paganism. The resentment of the pagans burned hot against their reforming kinsman, and their hostile pressure grew dangerous and intoler-

[13] *Cf. Koran,* 96:1–5; 74:1–7.
[14] *Bible,* Book of Judges, 9:5f.
[15] *Cf. Koran,* 48:29; 33:21.

able. For a while the ties of blood preserved his life; but Islam had severed blood connections! Mohammed and the Moslems fled (622 A.D.), to be cordially received in Yathrib, where many influential converts had been won, who felt highly honored by the Prophet's presence.

The Hijra.—Mohammed's "flight" (*hijra,* "journey") from Mecca to Madina marks the transition from the old Arab pagan era to the new Islamic. It marks, also, a further transformation in the Prophet's office. In Mecca, Mohammed was the simple, earnest messenger of Allah. He had learned the Lord's true name. He came to know that Allah tolerated no "association" of any other name or power with his own. In this respect, the Prophet of Arabia came to view the other gods as "vanities," as the Hebrew Jeremiah at last had done. Mohammed knew there could no more be two Gods in the world than "two hearts in one man." *Koran, sura* 112, proclaims this as revelation, "Say: He alone is God; God is eternal; He begetteth not, and is not begotten; and there has been none like unto Him." This is the gist of the *Koran.* The Moslems rate these fifteen *Arabic* words as "one-third the value" of the whole Book![16] Mohammed challenged Meccan and Arabian paganism (polytheism), denounced specific gods by name, and prophesied hell-fire for all their worshipers.

In Madina, "the city" (of the Prophet), Mohammed lived ten years. He sat as judge, as well as prophet, under Allah's guidance. He adjusted feudal differences among the citizens; he substituted Moslem brotherhood for blood-ties; he established a municipality, and prosecuted "hypocrites"; he annihilated groups of enemies; he instituted rites, including the postures of *salat,* for various occasions of worship; he learned what God would have men do in various situations and relationships. And from the point of vantage in Madina he laid his plans for winning Mecca. He never lost his Meccan heritage. That is, the *Kaba*[17] was "the House of Allah"; the waters of Zemzem were holy—they burst forth first at God's command to quench the thirst of Ishmael, son of Abraham, the "first Moslem", and the "father of the faithful." Mecca was beloved of Allah; was his peculiar seat. Mohammed, therefore, would not rest until he had purged it of non-Islamic elements, and had made it the capital of Islam. Although, during the first years in Madina, Mohammed

---

[16] There are 77,630 *Arabic* words in the *Koran.*
[17] *Cf. Koran,* 5:98.

had directed prayer toward Jerusalem, he had turned about; for many years Mecca had been the *qibla*. He had sought to make the Meccan pilgrimage, before the city was his, and had been allowed by an armistice to do so. Then in 630 Mecca fell —by capitulation. The *Kaba*, the Black Stone, and Zemzem, were purged of pagan connotations; the "days of ignorance" were gone; Allah was sole Lord in his own House. In fact, the *Kaba* became the symbol of the larger house which Mohammed had built, the *Daru l-Islam*, the "House of Islam." [18]

Sunna: Brotherhood.—Look now at this larger House, the home of *Sunna*, built of the "words" of Allah, and of "sayings" of the Prophet, on certain "pillars" of the faith. It is an exclusive House, excluding all save those who have "submitted." Those who have not submitted—or who do not enjoy some special privilege—live in what the Moslem call the House of War (the *Daru l-Harb*). The *Daru l-Islam* is a house of brotherhood—a fraternity, more than a sorority—in contrast with the tribal system it displaced. In pagan days, a man acted with his tribe. "The strength of the pack was the wolf, and the strength of the wolf was the pack," as Kipling phrases it. Morality was tribal; each member conformed with the customs of his tribe in dealing with other tribesmen. A double standard was maintained, save that there was, of necessity, a certain common chivalry: it was "unlawful" for any tribe to foul wells, or water-courses; certain "truces of God" were to be observed. Morality was feudal. It demanded an eye for an eye, or a life for a life; but it might allow settlement on an economic basis, say ten camels for a man.

Mohammed's brotherhood abolished tribal, and feudal morals; but it may remain a question as to whether he precluded the application of a double standard. His brotherhood was *religious*. Loyalty to Allah was supreme, exclusive. Morals were what Allah enjoined. But the innovation was not mere speculation; it emerged from a concrete situation, shaped by common sense. The Moslem "fugitives" (*muhajirun*) from Mecca were taken in as *brothers* by the Yathribites, sharing bed and board; they had cut the ties of tribalism, and had forged new ties of faith. Later they actually slew in battle (Badr, 624) members of their own immediate families, and thereby sealed the innovation. Allah revealed a new order, which won the day. After Mohammed, the Moslems came to know by "experience" that Allah would

---

[18] This Moslem "House" may be compared with the *Dharma*, which represents the Hindu's total round of life.

tolerate no caste, no color-line, no inequalities in *religion*. Witness the Pilgrimage throughout the centuries. As the House
expanded through foreign conquests, it came to hold a wide
variety of peoples: not only fair Arabs and their black-skinned
slaves from the Sudan, but, also, dark men of Syria and Egypt;
yellow-skins of Turkestan and China; fierce-eyed Afghan moun-
taineers; pale-faced, tall Circassians; wiry, nut-brown men of
Hindustan; and brow-hued Moros of the Philippines—all brothers
and equals in the sight of Allah. Slaves have been kings; women
have been sultanas. Intermarriage is a common practice. Mohammed said, "Moslems are brothers in religion; they must
not oppress each other, nor fail to assist each other, nor hold
each other in contempt," and, "No Moslem has perfectly believed until he wishes for his brother what he wishes for himself."

It may be no special condemnation that a "House of War"
is recognized, and that the rights of brotherhood do not apply
therein. Russian Christians held "pogroms," in which the Jews
were mercilessly slain. Jews at one time "had no dealings with
Samaritans." The Sikh *Khalsa* rid itself of Moslem enemies.
Nor has Islam extended its dominion by the sword alone. It
has "tolerated" Christians, Jews, and Sabians, as "peoples of
the Book." It has been a "missionary" faith, winning converts
by force of doctrine, social pressure, economic privileges bestowed, and the satisfaction of human aspirations.

The Pillars of the House.—Mohammed built the House upon
five "pillars." These represent five obligations incumbent upon
every loyal adherent. Whatever freedom a Moslem has enjoyed,
or may enjoy, in the "sciences," he remains bound by "duties"
whose discharge display his faith *in action:*

(1) The "Witness," or confession of the Faith, "I testify
that there is no God but Allah; I testify that Mohammed is the
Apostle of Allah." One must ever be ready to give witness,
not only daily at the hours of prayer, but at any time, especially in an emergency. It is the pledge of loyalty. The
Moslem merchant-missionary may use it to confirm a convert
(in the presence of two witnesses). If the faithful warrior
utter it with his dying breath, it becomes the seal of martyrdom. It veils no speculative subtlety; it represents a plain,
indisputable assertion, the fact of God, his sole reality, and
the fulness of his power.

(2) Prayers (*salat* and *dua*), formal prayers at five ap-

pointed times [19] each day: in the early morning at sunrise; at noon when the sun has crossed the zenith; in mid-afternoon; in the evening at sunset; and when the night has fallen. The posturing itself is prayer, but it may be accompanied by recitation, or readings from the prayer-book. *Salat,* especially, is the "pillar," being seen of men.

(3) Fasting, at any time, but particularly in the month of Ramadhan.[20] In this month, no food, nor drink may pass one's lips, from sun-up to sun-down. Fasting always gains one merit; it may atone for sin.

(4) Almsgiving, of two sorts. *Zakat,* "purification," is legally imposed, a sort of income tax, as in the case of "booty." [21] Save for the "fifth" of the booty, no rate is specified by the Prophet. He did not think in terms of taxes, having no thought of Islam as an organized political state. Other alms, known as *sadaqa,* "righteousness," are recommended.[22] "What you expend of well-gotten goods shall be paid to you again, and you shall not be wronged." "Allah says, Be thou liberal, thou son of Adam, that I may be liberal unto thee."

(5) Pilgrimage [23] to Mecca once in a lifetime, either in person, or by proxy. Mohammed spoke more of this than of prayers, alms, and fasting. He had it in mind as a means of unity among his people, scarcely realizing how widely the faith would spread. Making the pilgrimage is impossible for most, even by proxy. Prayer toward Mecca has largely taken its place, and has supplied the unity of consciousness which the Prophet sought. Nevertheless, Mecca itself is the goal, if possible, and distinction attaches to all who make the journey.[24]

These are the minimum requirements, upon which all doctors of Islamic law (*fiqh*) agree. They are simple enough for every man to understand, and for the most part capable of execution. The Moslem may, therefore, always know the tests of his religion. These "duties" were not ordained *as such* in any rounded program of obedience, but each detail is based on some prophetic

---

[19] These five times daily are nowhere mentioned together in a single passage of the *Koran.* They come of piecing together various references.

[20] The month of Ramadhan perpetuates the pagan Arab custom of a "holy truce" each year, on economic and religious grounds. At times the fast is a severe test of faith, for on a luma calendar, it falls sometimes in midsummer. See *Koran,* 2:179–183.

[21] *Cf. Koran,* 41:6; 19:56.

[22] *Koran,* 2:280; 4:114; 9:58; 8:42.

[23] *Koran,* 3:90f; 2:153.192.

[24] On arrival the pilgrim becomes a *hajji.* He thereafter wears some mark of his performance, perhaps a piece of the discarded *Kaba* covering in his waistcoat.

revelation. Some doctors have included "holy war" (*jihad*), making a list of six. But Mohammed did not clearly designate *jihad* a "pillar," for it operates from a different motive—the *five* are explicitly imposed on all believers. Each of the "five" applies to individuals, primarily. *Jihad* represents Islam at war; it became a social obligation. Mohammed set the precedent for martial action. Once, using the sanguinary term *qatilu*, "killing," he bade his people, "fight until there be no other faith than Allah's"; but he gave example, also, of tolerance toward non-Moslems whose religion was contained in scriptures, and modified the duty of unremitting warfare. *Jihad* is "defensive war," by definition of the doctors; the Moslem need not fight unless the Faith be threatened from without.[25]

The Koran.—Hear now the "words" (*kalimat*) of Allah found in *al-Quran*, the *Koran*. The *Koran* is like the "roll of a book," which Jeremiah had from Yahweh against Israel and Judah (*cf. Jeremiah*, chap. 36). It is a "Reading" [26] from Allah. It contains Mohammed's "recitation" of what Allah enabled him to "read," when he needed guidance, or when Allah had some burden to lay on him. "Allah it is who hath sent down the Book" (*Koran, 3:4, 5*). It is genuine—"no imposture," said Mohammed to his critics. It is the only body of authentic "revelations," and is, incidentally, the one trustworthy source of our knowledge of the Prophet's life. It is the record of his earnest quest for God and true religion.[27] The earlier chapters, in particular, show sincerity on his part; although, some later passages disclose the opportunist, and the politician.[28] No parts may rightly be considered the fruitage of a disordered brain, or the by-products of an abnormal personality. Mohammed's own doubt when his career began is evidence that he was sincere; he suffered in agony during a cessation of "revelation." Naturally the passages vary with varying circumstances. The "readings" were received throughout the twenty years of his active mission, under manifold conditions.

The Koranic materials were not written down by Mohammed. He spoke them; [29]—although there is no good ground for saying he could not read or write—and they were orally transmitted for a while. Some persons who heard them committed them exactly, or recorded them on palm-leaf, parchment, or the bleached

25 An "offensive" war may be undertaken to prevent *attack. Cf. Koran,* 60:7,8.
26 The same word is used in *Nehemiah,* 8:8.
27 *Cf. Koran,* 3:17, "The true religion with Allah is Islam."
28 *Cf.* 58:13,14; 5:94: 4:29,102.
29 Many early chapters open with the word "recite" (*qul*).

shoulder-blades of animals. There came to be many "readers" who knew the *Koran* by heart. After the Prophet's death, when readers were dying and records liable to perish in the confusion of the times, the readings were compiled into a single volume. They were arranged in *suras*, "rows," [30] but not in order of either time or topic. There are 114 *suras*, each with a title, which may or may not represent a main idea, ranging as a whole from the largest to the smallest chapter—save that the *Fatiha*, or "opener," contains only seven verses. The second, the *sura* of the Cow, contains 286, and the last has six. Actually the 108th is the shortest, with only ten words in three verses. The whole *Koran* is the smallest basic scripture of any great religion; is scarcely two-thirds the size of the *New Testament*. It is also, possibly, the best authenticated, for it was arranged so early that it must contain the *ipsissima verba* of the Prophet; it has come down almost unaltered. That its terms have proved, at times, to be obscure is not due to alteration in transmission, but to lack of understanding of their ancient connotations; they are often variously interpreted.

The little Book cannot be summarized in brief, for it covers a wide range of subjects. As it stands, it lacks coherence. It must be rearranged, if anything of sequence be discovered in it.[31] The casual reader of it finds it dull. The serious student may misunderstand it, for lack of knowledge of Arabian psychology and history, and because of its confusion. One encounters, also, the baffling theory of "abrogation," by which a "later" revelation has rescinded an "earlier," without expunging the latter from the Book (*cf. Koran*, 2:100). Moslems all together admit 225 abrogated passages. See 2:109, which says, "whichever way ye turn, there is the face of Allah," and 2:139, which bids men pray toward Mecca. Other abrogations often do not operate so clearly. Then, too, the serious student finds himself involved in the science of theology (*al-Kalam*), if he would know the Book. But there are several passages which might be taken as the gist of what Mohammed taught directly from Allah. Take, for example, *sura* 17:23-40:

"Put no other god with Allah. . . . Thy Lord hath decreed that ye bow down to none except himself, that ye show

---

[30] The use of the term *sura* has since been restricted to chapters of the *Koran*.
[31] This has been done by Noeldeke and others, with what result one may see in J. M. Rodwell's translation. Palmer's translation adheres to the order of the *Arabic Koran*; it is excellent, however.

kindness to your parents . . . speak to them respectfully,
and defer to them humbly in tenderness. . . . He is gracious
to those who render their due to kindred, the poor, and the
wayfarer, and are not wasteful. . . . Let not thy hand be
tied to thy neck, nor yet open it completely, lest thou sit thee
down in beggary. . . . Kill not your children for fear of
want: God will provide for them and you. . . . Be not
adulterous, for it is foul and evil. . . . Slay no one whom God
hath forbidden you to slay; whoever is slain wrongfully, his
heir shall be recompensed. . . . Touch not the substance of
an orphan, except rightfully. . . . Give full measure when you
measure, and weigh with a just balance. . . . Walk not proudly
on the earth, for thou canst not rend it, nor canst thou be in
size a mountain: these are evils, hateful to thy Lord."

Or, *sura* 5:39ff.:

"Fear Allah. Desire union with him. Strive earnestly in his
way, that ye may prosper. . . . If a man or woman steal,
cut off the hands in recompense. . . . We have sent down
the Law (*tawrat*) [32] wherein are guidance and light, and whereby the prophets prophesied who professed Islam. . . . We
caused Jesus, son of Mary, to follow in the footsteps of the
prophets, confirming the law which was before him, and we
gave him the evangel with its guidance and its light. . . . If
God had pleased he would surely have made you all one people.
. . . To God shall all return. . . . Be on your guard against
(Jews and Christians), lest they beguile thee from God's precepts. . . . Take not Jews or Christians as your friends. . . .
If any of you believers should desert his faith, God will then
raise up a people loved by him and haughty toward all infidels. . . . On whom God wills bestows he grace. God is
vast, omniscient. Your protector is God and his apostle, and
those who believe, who observe prayer, and pay the legal
alms, and who bow in worship, are your friends. . . . They are
truly the people of God; they shall gain the mastery. . . . God
guideth not the unbelievers. . . . Be not troubled for Jews
and Sabians and Christians who believe in God and the last
day and do what is right. . . . They are infidels who say 'God
is the Messiah, the son of Mary,' or who say, 'God is the third
of three'. . . . There is no God but the one God. . . . Be
faithful to your engagements. . . . Avoid wine and games of

---

[32] *Cf.* the Jewish *Torah,* "Law."

chance, and statues, and divining-rods, which are the work of Satan who would thus sow strife and hatred in your midst. . . . Kill no game while you are on pilgrimage; eat fish. . . . God hath appointed the Kaba an asylum for mankind. . . . Unto God belonged the sovereignty of the heavens and the earth, and of all that they contain, and he hath power over all things."

The Reformation.—These two statements are not comprehensive, nor are their items quite consistent; but they illustrate the social and religious program of the Prophet. They illustrate his dependence and his originality. He drew on many sources for his message, but his own experience and insight moulded them. He was reared a pagan, and frankly admitted the retention of pagan elements (*cf. Koran,* 3:90; 22:30); but he learned about the customs and the teachings of the Jews and Christians. He knew Abraham and Jesus, but the former was his ideal. He drew more on Jewish than on Christian sources. He uses many Christian terms, such as satan, hell, evangel, idol, pulpit, and apostle, and through Christianity got his ideas of the resurrection, and the judgment (*cf.* the "last day"). He uses many Jewish terms, such as law, ark, paradise, fasting, prayer, and angels, and the bulk of his tradition is primarily Semitic. The Christianity he knew was heretical in doctrine, and low morally. He turned against both Jews and Christians for their drunkenness.

As the statements indicate, these were among his accomplishments: a general elevation of prevailing standards of life and thought; advocacy of a redistribution of wealth, and the elimination of poverty; restriction of murder, the prohibition of the killing of female children "for want"; the regulation of polygamy [33] in a land where women were often in the great majority; provision for a regular procedure in divorce. He put a ban on gambling, on commercial interest (Moslems later resorted to "discount" instead of "interest"),[34] and on alcoholic drinks. But the motive of reform was God. His God-idea was a bold assumption. He insisted that men accept it without question, "without

---

[33] He failed, however, because of "special privilege," to make his public policy and his private practice coincide in this regard. After the death of Khadija, he took at least ten other wives, distinct from concubines, while permitting other Moslems only four at one time. Eight of his wives—nine, with Khadija—were widows, and one, a divorcee. He had two sons, and four daughters, not including his favorite Ibrahim, son of Mary, the Coptic concubine. But several of his marriages were prompted, probably, by political motive, or sheer benevolence.

[34] Muhammad Abduh, a Hanifite doctor, ingeniously justified savings-bank accounts with interest, on the ground that the depositor was really a shareholder in the enterprise.

how," or why. He pointed out God's manifest omnipotence and providence, and refused to speculate about them. He talked of God's omniscience, God "knowing what is in men's heart's." It is not surprising what Islam says about a "foreknowing" and a foreordaining" God. But the Prophet was not predestinarian, or deterministic, unreservedly,—he was not so speculative. In practical vein he attributed to man some freedom, some control over his own acts, "following his own inclinations."

The God-idea, more than the moral reformation, constituted the innovation, the chief disturbance of the Meccan situation. It has ever since brought Moslems into conflict with other faiths, not only "infidels" ("associaters"), whom it is right to slay, unless they "turn," but, also, Jews, Christians, Parsis, Hindus, and all non-Moslems. In fact, Mohammed was opposed to Christians for their "three gods" (God, Jesus, and Mary). Islam is most insistent on the dogma that Allah brooks no rivals.

Creed.—The Creed, formulated mainly on the basis of the "words" of Allah found in the *Koran,* has consisted of six items:

(1) Belief in Allah, such is God's "essential name," for whom the witness must be given; Allah who rules from afar (20:4; 13:2), encompasses all (41:54; 17:62), is personally near to every believer (96:16; 11:64), dwells within men's hearts as His own inner witness to Himself (51:21; 96:13);

(2) Belief in Angels, especially Gabriel, the angel of revelation, through whom Mohammed heard God's utterances (Gabriel read from the heavenly tablet on which God's words were inscribed);

(3) Belief in the *Koran* as the Word of God, taken as it stands, and in its clearly indicated meaning;

(4) Belief in prophets, especially Mohammed. There are twenty-eight in all, but six are worthiest, each with a special name: Adam, the "chosen of God"; Noah, the "preacher of God"; Abraham, the "friend of God"; Moses, the "converser with God"; Jesus, the "spirit of God"; and Mohammed, the "apostle of God," worthiest of praise.

(5) Belief in the Judgment, whose issues mean Heaven for the worthy, and Hell for the unworthy, both places being regions of permanent abode in delight, or torment; and

(6) Belief in the Omnipotence and finality of Allah.

Hadith.—We come now to the "Sayings" of the Prophet, as distinguished from the "Words" of Allah. They are called "Traditions" (*Hadith*), and have had far-reaching influence. The Prophet gave them as opinions on all kinds of themes—and the faithful have added to them freely. The Sayings altogether are innumerable; but the doctors have segregated those acceptable as "genuine" (*sahih*). One of the best editions is, however, three times the size of the *Koran*. Mohammed the man talked on far more topics than Mohammed the Apostle. Various factions have followed various *hadith,* and have freely fabricated them in support of positions, political, or religious, unless some plain meaning of the *Koran* prevented. Many *hadith* are elaborations of Koranic verses; for example, the Koranic curse on those who trade in wine is applied to ten specific persons from producer to consumer. Others are less directly related to anything Koranic; for example, "The holder of a monopoly is a sinner," "A martyr shall be pardoned every fault but debt," "Pay the laborer before his perspiration dry," "No judge shall decide between two persons when he is angry," "Woman is man's worst calamity," "God dislikes divorce," "Fear God in respect to animalism," "A king is God's shadow upon the earth," "Government is a trust from God," "He is strong who withholds himself from anger," "A bell is the devil's instrument," "The calamity of knowledge is forgetfulness," "The best person near God is the best amongst his friends," "The best of men is Ali," "The hearts of men are at God's disposal," with many trivialities, as well as mingled wit and wisdom.

The Law.—If we turn now to religious law, we shall complete our survey of the *Sunna.* There are four accepted "schools," each of which worked over the mass of materials at its disposal, and composed a system of rules and regulations. These regulations have applied in various regions throughout *Sunni* Islam, where strictly civil codes were not relied on. This law was final in the early days when religion and the state were one. Varying emphases on constituent materials brought varying interpretations of the Law. One school conservatively held to Koranic exposition; others found authority in *hadith,* also, even venturing beyond *hadith,* and adopting such principles as the Roman Catholic Church has used, namely, agreement, analogy, and opinion. While Islam has never held "Church" councils, nor adopted an elaborate creed, religious Law has claimed to represent authority in faith and practice.

The four schools had become established within two centuries after the Prophet's death. We know them by their founders, Abu Hanifa, Malik ibn Anas, as-Shafii, and Ibn Hanbal. They lived in the golden period of empire. During these centuries Eygpt, North Africa, Spain, Asia Minor, Iraq, and Persia, were added to original Arabia. In consequence of this expansion, social, political, cultural, and religious changes had occurred. The schools of Law sought to provide procedure for the conduct of affairs in accordance with religion.

(1) The Hanifite, founded by Abu Hanifa (died 767 A.D.), a Persian who wrote in *Arabic*. He accepted the *Koran*, but as a non-Arab, he had little interest in *hadith,* or in Madina, the home of *hadith*. He extended the *Koran* by means of analogy (*qiyas*), and opinion (*rai*). If he found for a case at law no exact precedent in the *Koran,* he drew an agreeable analogy, whether from the *Koran,* or from the local situation. If need be, for lack of precedent, he resorted to opinion in the light of local circumstances. He even ventured to run counter to the *Koran,*[35] if his ruling "seemed better" (*istihsan*) for the locality. Among adherents to his interpretation have been the Abbasid rulers of Baghdad, the Osmanli Turks, and many chieftains of North India, and Central Asia. The Hanifites are liberals.[36]

(2) The Malikite, founded by Malik ibn Anas (d. 795 A.D.), an Arab judge of Madina. To the *Koran* he added the *Hadith*— he lived amidst *hadith*. He proposed, also, "agreement or consensus of opinion" (*ijma*),—the *ijma* of Madina, naturally. He found use for analogy, and opinion, but relied on *Koran, hadith,* and *ijma,* especially. If analogy and opinion were in conflict, he would base his judgment upon "public advantage, or the common good" (*istislah*). His system has prevailed in Arabia, Upper Eygpt, among the Berbers of North Africa, and in Spain. The Malikites are liberal conservatives.

(3) The Shafiite, founded by as-Shafii (d. 819 A.D.), an Arab of Persia. He was more liberal than Malik, but less so than Abu Hanifa. He accepted *hadith* as equal with the *Koran;* in fact, he might prefer some *hadith* above *Koran,* if the *hadith* with reference to the case in hand were later than the *Koranic* reference. He would "abrogate" *Koran* by *hadith;* he was a liberal "traditionalist." He used analogy, and agreement, but rejected opinion in any form, whether for "better," or for the

---

35 He would not have the hand cut off for theft.
36 *Cf.* his *Hedaya* or *Commentary* on the *Koran.*

"common good." He found freedom of interpretation through employing the "agreement" of any time, or place, not merely that of early Islam in Madina. Among his followers have been the lawyers (*qadis*) of Syria, Lower Eygpt. and South India.

(4) The Hanbalite, founded by Ibn Hanbal (d. 855 A.D.), an Arab of Baghdad. He was once a pupil of as-Shafii, but reacted against liberalism, both in thought and conduct. He is an arch-conservative. His time was one of liberality, even laxity. He was reared in the days of the Khalif Harun, which closed characteristically in "Arabian nights." Abu Nuwas, who drank and jested with Harun, had sung of four things which "banish grief and care, . . . water, wine, gardens bright, and faces fair"; had impudently called for wine at times of prayer,[37]

> "Whilst the flask goes twinkling round,
> Pour me a cup that leaves me drowned
> With oblivion, ne'er so nigh
> Let the shrill muezzin cry!"

And Mamun, a successor of Harun, had declared for rationalism, and the Shiite heresy. Against these heresies of doctrine and of life Ibn Hanbal waged a strenuous battle. He was often persecuted and imprisoned; but he won a following, although the smallest of the schools. He confined his usage to the *Koran,* interpreting it by letter. His chief followers have been the Wahhabis of Arabia, who now control the Kingdom of the Hijaz, with the two holy cities (*Haramayn*) of Mecca and Madina. Conservatism scored again in terms of isolation.

These schools of Law show concretely the variations which accompanied the growth of Islam as a state. Comparatively early, the state has recourse more and more, however, to civil law, leaving the schools to guide religion, when their rulings did not controvene the civil code. Religious Law is still influential in religion, but has little power in politics; it is scarcely more potent than Roman Catholic Canon Law is in Roman Catholic nations.

Shia: Ali and Others.—The other main division of Islam is *Shia,* with its 20,000,000 "heretics." *Shia,* "sectarian divergence," consists mostly of ten million Persians, six million Indians, some East Africans, and others. They hold Mohammed

---

[37] The wine-sellers of the day were, of course, "infidel" Christians, Jews, and Zoroastrians. Retailers in modern times are Christians.

in sincere regard, but consider him the *nabi,* "prophet" of Islam, while revering Ali, his cousin and son-in-law, as *wali Allah,* "friend of God," and the *Imam* or "Pattern."

Ali was the son of Mohammed's uncle, Abu Talib, who gave him a home in his youth. The cousins were friendly playmates, and adult companions. Once Ali saved Mohammed's life, when an assassin came seeking him in his father's house. Ali later married Fatima, the Prophet's daughter by Khadija, his sole surviving child. He had two sons, Hasan and Husayn, through whom a line of blood-descent was established from the Prophet. Further prestige was accorded Ali by his election to the Khalifat (Caliphate), fourth in succession to Mohammed. These offices came to be referred by his partisans to certain passages in the *Koran,* thus claiming for him the favor of Allah and Mohammed. The Koranic *wali,* "friend, or one who is very near" [to God], is found in *sura* 10:63. The word *imam* occurs in *sura* 2:118, "I [Allah] am about to make thee [Abraham] an *imam* ['pattern, or leader'] to mankind." The word *ali,* "high, or exalted," occurs in several passages, *e.g.,* 4:38; 42:51, in connection with God himself; and while they do not refer to Ali, they provide excellent materials for legend. Alid partisans went even further; they fabricated an *hadith,* making Mohammed say on his return from Mecca to Madina, after the Farewell Pilgrimage, "I shall soon be called back to heaven; I leave you two important bequests, the *Koran,* and my family." The reference, say to the Shiites, is to the family of Ali; they point, also, to *Koran* 33:33, with its reference to Mohammed's "household."

The Alid legend refers to the Prophet's going "back" to heaven; time and circumstance had combined to generate the theory of Mohammed's divinity, or to allow the Prophet's "family" a peculiar spiritual quality. With Ali as *Imam,* he joins the line of Abraham; becomes "exalted" (*ali*). This is germinal divinity for Ali, if no more; and it is not far to the establishment of a divine Imamate in contrast with the obviously human Caliphate. Mohammed made no such provision for the government after him—a "succession" was merely the natural outcome of events. But political contingencies, combined with the raw materials of the *Koran,* and with fabricated "sayings" of Mohammed, created for Ali through his partisans a strong case for him as the rightful leader of Islam. Deprived(?) of his rights until after Abu Bakr, Omar, and Othman, in suc-

cession, had filled the Caliphate, his friends grounded his claims
not on election, but on blood and spiritual relation. They declared the first three Caliphs spurious. Alids have held that
there has been but one duly qualified Caliph, Ali. After him,
also, have been interlopers, with the rights of true succession
in the office never recognized. Instead, the Imamate has represented true religion. Shiism is a combination of political
ambition and religious fervor, based upon the *imam*ship of the
divine Ali and his descendants.

Shiism did not grow directly out of Arab soil. Its fundamental
doctrine of divinity, Mohammed's, Ali's, and others', is manifestly contrary to original Islam, and to the Arab mind. It was
first conceived by Abdallah ibn Saba, a Jew of Yemen. According to a "saying," he once remarked to Ali, "Thou art God."
This saying may be only a garbling of *sura* 4:38, *inna Allaha
kana aliyyan,* "Verily Allah is exalted," making it, "Verily Ali
is Allah." Abdallah was a malcontent in the days of Othman,
Ali's predecessor, finding political capital in such doctrines as
the return of Mohammed (*cf. Koran* 28:85), the sanctity of
Ali's family, and Ali's apostleship, and a kind of transmigration
theory which he derived from Hellenism(?). Ali in the end,
while Caliph, objected to the veneration of himself, banishing
Abdallah to Persia, where the exile transferred his allegiance
from Ali in particular to Shiism in general, as the opposition
movement. Persian Shiism was taking on a character broader
than merely Alid. Particular Alids and general Shiites have
often been at variance.

Shiism in general is largely Persian, representing the perpetuation of a pre-Islamic heritage. Persians before Islam had
long believed in the divinity of kings, and in kingship by divine
appointment—"royal" and "divine" were synonyms. Aliism was
bound to thrive in Persia. The divinity of Ali, and of his line,
was ultimately accepted as a fundamental dogma by all Shiites
—*ultimately,* we say. The dogma had little chance to win the
Caliphate while Baghdad was the imperial capital, while the
Abbasids (Abbas was Mohammed's uncle) ruled successively
by "election" (by election, in theory; by descent, or usurpation,
in practice). During the Abbasid days the Shiites nourished the
divine Imamate. Inevitably, however, there were dissensions
among them, and rival candidates for power. Each organized
his propaganda, and, with opportunity, fomented a political disturbance. The nearest Shiites came to government in Abbasid

days (till 1258 A.D.) was through certain favored ministers, or through such action as that of the orthodox(?) Mamun, who declared for rationalism, and adopted Shiite green as the color of the state. The Imamate eventually divided into two: (1) the "Seveners" insisted that the *visible* line of "leaders" ended in 770 A.D., when the *seventh* rightful Imam died, without the appointment of a successor, and (2) the "Twelvers" maintained the legitimacy of the line [38] until 870 A.D., when the *twelfth* Imam mysteriously disappeared at Samarra. The Twelvers constitute the great majority of living Shiites. The Shahs of Persia have been representatives of the invisible Imam. In the absence of a visible Imam to whom allegiance could be sworn, the theory of an invisible Imam to come in time of crisis prevailed. Crises have been numerous, and many messianic Imams and Mahdis have appeared. A certain Obaydallah claimed descent from Fatima, the Prophet's daughter (rather than from either of her sons by Ali), and announced himself the Mahdi. His dynasty, the Fatimid, ruled in Africa and Eygpt from 909 until Saladin supplanted it in 1171. Lord Kitchener of Khartum fought a later Mahdi in the Sudan. The Syrian Assassins (from *hashish*, a hemp concoction) were a sect of Shiites. The Indian Ahmad-iyyas produced a Mahdi recently. Shiism has honeycombed Islam, whether as religious, or political propaganda.

Karbala.—Perhaps an illustration may help us understand the genius of the "heresy." There is a village, Karbala, fifty miles southwest of Baghdad, the center of Shiite devotion. It holds the tomb of al-Husayn, younger son of Ali, who fell a martyr at a time of crisis. He was the third Imam, after his father, and his brother al-Hasan. In the Moslem year 61, with sixty-five adherents, he set out for Kufa in Iraq, once his father's capital,[39] intent upon establishing himself with Kufan aid as Caliph in opposition to Yazid, the rightful Caliph seated in Damascus. Yazid sent an army to Kufa, who quieted the city, and planned to intercept Husayn in the neighborhood of Karbala nearby. Peaceful overtures met with obstinate resistance from the party of Husayn, with several skirmishes resulting. On the evening of the ninth day, following evening prayer, the Kufan forces closed in on Husayn. Shiite tradition makes the night one of bitter trial, and sorrowful tears on the part of Husayn and his little company, and one of violent abuse and sacrilege on the

---

[38] Through an eighth Imam, Ismail, son of the seventh, who had disinherited him, according to the Seveners.

[39] His father, Ali, was assassinated in the Kufa mosque in A.H. 40.

part of their "enemies",—sacrilege, for the very blood of Mohammed flowed in Husayn's veins. Next morning, Husayn, realizing the hopelessness of his position, bathed, and anointed himself with musk, and made ready for his "martyrdom." In the fighting, Husayn's little son [40] was slain by a flying arrow, a nephew was mutilated by swords and daggers, and he himself, even while his sister shielded him (a sign of her devotion rather than his cowardice), was wounded in the mouth by a well-aimed arrow. At last the enemy pressing in furiously, Husayn fell with many wounds, his body to be mangled shamelessly by the horse of one relentless rider.

This tragic episode has been amplified by details of fact and fancy into a stirring drama, which has taken hold of the imagination of half the Moslem world. It is more than Shiite, since it concerns Mohammed. Into the warp of the bare incidents have been woven timeless details of angels, kings, prophets, revelation, the preëxistence of Mohammed, the divinity of Ali, the saviorhood of Hasan and Husayn, vice and virtue, the resurrection and the final judgment, and the sole reality of Allah and Islam. In the Shiite world this drama is more or less extemporaneously enacted every year, during the ten closing days of the month of Ramadhan. The scene wants nothing to make up a powerful passion play. At times it has engendered religious fervor boundlessly fanatical, and political outbursts of unprecedented fury. Its theology, on the other hand, is simple. Ali was the divine afflatus, the very glory of Allah which first shone in Mohammed who transmitted it to Ali as his successor and the rightful leader, through himself and family, of Islam. Husayn was not only a martyr; he was the divine *Imam,* and the savior of his people. By his death he atoned for mankind's sin, and became man's avenue of access unto God.

The more thoughtful Shiites have been liberals, theologically and philosophically. They have not believed the *Koran* "eternal." They have assumed some freedom of the will, and of action, on man's part; for they have deemed God "just;" he punishes men only for the sins for which *they* are responsible. They have believed the unity of God, but have not been averse to reason as a means of understanding him, and they have emphasized the mystical experience of God.

The Development of Islam.—The *development of Islam*—and its character today—as religion, theology, ethics, and philosophy, might be more comprehensively portrayed through

40 His mother was a Persian royal princess.

a description of the course of three effective principles which have operated from the early days: *naql,* the "traditional," *aql,* or the "rational;" and *kashf,* the "mystical." These three [41] have operated both in orthodoxy and in heresy, although the first is strictly orthodox, and the other two have given rise to heresies.

Naql, or tradition [42] was preëminent in two early periods: from the death of Mohammed until about 785 A.D.; and from about 850 to 900 A.D. While it has endured since then, it has been disputed by the advocates of *aql* and the devotee of *kashf,* especially from 785 to 850, when *aql* was preëminent; and from 1000 until 1500, when *kashf* as well as *aql* enjoyed great influence. The latter era might be called the golden age of Moslem *thought,* as distinct from empire.

Little more need here be said about tradition (*naql*); it was summed up, in essence, while we studied *Sunna.* Something more is necessary, however, to understand the "scholastic" adaptation. There occurred a movement comparable with the movement headed by Aquinas. This movement, both in Islam and in Christianity, sought to reconcile religion and philosophy, or the traditional and the rational. In Islam the scholastic theologian was Ashari.

Reason and the Rationalists.—Ali ibn Ismail al-Ashari (*c.* 873–941 A.D.) was an Arab born in Ashar, a part of Basrah, in Iraq. He later made his home in Baghdad. In Basrah [43] Ashari first attached himself to a rationalistic group under the master al-Jubbai. Such groups had flourished for a century in Iraq, Syria, and elsewhere (but not in the Hejaz!). They were called Mutazilas, "separatists," or "come-outers." They were rebels against orthodoxy and tradition. While Mamun was Caliph (813–833) in Baghdad, their system was adopted as the state religion. Both hellenistic and Persian elements, especially the former, appear in it. How "lax," and "revolutionary" were these Mutazilites, to whom Ashari was at first attracted, will appear from this hasty summary of their ideas:

(1) They were the leading Moslem rationalists, employing *aql* as a proper source of religious knowledge along with revelation. In fact, they made *aql,* or reason, the final standard

---

[41] Another sort of triangle has figured also recently in political affairs: Islam, Pan-Islam, and Nationalism.

[42] The term here refers to the traditional, conservative view of things religious, and is not to be confused with the term *hadith* as "tradition."

[43] The port on the Tigris River whence Sindbad set out on his marvellous voyages, as described in the *Arabian Nights.*

of their judgment in matters of religion. They held that there is both a natural, and a revealed knowledge of God; that the natural knowledge may be ultimately obtained apart from revelation; and that, if Moslems stay in ignorance, it is because they shut their eyes and minds to nature.

(2) They insisted on the Unity of Allah, and denied whatever infringed upon his unity, claiming in this manner to be truly Moslem. They rejected, as applied to God, all the man-like figures of the *Koran*. They denied that God sits upon a "throne," or in any manner occupies a "place," being thus dependent. They denied that God has hands, feet, eyes, and a body of flesh and blood, being thus dependent for his works, his motion, his sight, etc. They insisted that God could be seen everywhere, as Mohammed had once said, and need not be worshiped in any one direction, as Mohammed later said he should be.

(3) They accepted the *Koran* as revelation, *but* they held to their own view of it, interpreting its "words" in harmony with reason (*their own* reason). The essential *Koran,* they said, is the very "word of Allah" (the *kalam Allahi*). They did not believe in the "eternity" of the Book, in its co-existence with Allah himself. Their view was that in a sense the *Koran* was created, and that it consisted of sounds, letters, etc., which were "revealed in time." They clearly saw that any notion of the *Koran's* "eternity" demanded a literal interpretation of the Book. The *Koran* was not that sort of *kalam Allahi*. The *Koran* was the "word of God" in somewhat the same fashion as Christians spoke of Jesus as the "word (*logos*) of God." They did not think God's words could be fully written in a book.

(4) They insisted upon God's "justice," outraging orthodoxy by saying that God *must* be just. The orthodox insisted that God had the *right,* and the power, to do as he pleased with men; in the phrase of Burns' Holy Willie, "to send ane to Heav'n and ten to Hell a' for his glory." They held that God made man for himself, to enjoy immortal blessedness, and that God, therefore, must make salvation possible. They accepted Mohammed the Prophet as God's Apostle to mankind. They held that God at all times serves the highest ends of men, and they insisted that men accept the world for what it is, and take events as best for them (this was Greek, even Stoic).

(5) They assumed that man is possessed of freedom of will and action, that he has "power," or *qadr*. Since he can discriminate between evil and good, he must accept responsibility for wrongdoings. They refused to lodge in God's will the distinction between good and evil. They combated the doctrine of predestination as an obstacle to progress, proclaiming that such a doctrine would be proof of God's injustice.

Perhaps they pressed their rationalism to extremes. Or, possibly, reactionary persecution (under the Caliph Mutawakkil) sealed their doom. Someone said, "They went with their heads up till such a time as God produced Ashari." But even before he joined them they had lost prestige. Smarting under popular disfavor, they took more earnestly to speculation, and in Ashari's time they were discussing such abstractions as "thing," "existence," and "qualities." He found this idle exercise, and revolted from it. In contrast, he grew practical, and became the champion of a reasonable orthodoxy, which, after him, withstood the attacks of pure speculators. He represented Arab stock against both Greek and Persian. He is the final architect of Arabic Islam, composing over fifty volumes on behalf of it.[44]

Scholasticism.—Ashari's separation from his master, al-Jubbai, and the Mutazilas took place publicly in the Friday mosque of Basrah. A stock question had arisen: Can a believer (Moslem) commit a "great sin" and continue a "believer"? The case in point was that of three persons who had died, a believer who had sinned, a sinner who had not repented, and a little child. Whither had they gone, etc? Al-Jubbai contended (the reports are somewhat garbled; at least, there are two versions of the episode): (1) that a Moslem may become, by reason of a "great sin," unworthy of honor and of heaven; although, if he had previously given the "witness" (of allegiance to Islam), he is no unbeliever; he will not be fully punished as a *great* sin deserves, if he repents; (2) that an unrepentent sinner goes, undoubtedly, to hell, being worthy of hell-fire for his failure to repent; and (3) that a little child, neither sinning nor sinless, goes neither to heaven, nor to hell, but to a mid-region, where there is neither reward nor punishment; God may take

[44] Especially the monumental *Book of Explanation and Exposition*. He enjoyed the proceeds of an entailed estate (*waqf*) left by an ancestor for the benefit of his descendants.

a young child, if he knows that the child by growing up would become an unrepentent sinner; God thereby enables some to escape punishment for sin. The group around the master in the mosque was thrown during this argument into some confusion by an inevitable question by Ashari, Why had not God taken the *sinner* young before he had had opportunity to commit the sin by which he lost the reward of heaven? Ashari contended that God were really *unjust* to deny anyone the reward which he might have merited, that it were unjust for God to send a child to some intermediate condition (*cf.* purgatory in the Roman Catholic doctrine), who might have grown up to be a *believer.* Ashari parted from his companions on the ground of "Allah's justice." [45]

His full position, developed in succeeding years, which stands as scholastic orthodoxy, may be summarized as follows:

(1) God is one and all. He is the one fact, the one reality. There is no nature as such belonging to men and things; all nature in them is God's. The life, the knowledge, the power, the will, the hearing, the seeing, the speech, in man are the divine qualities of God. God must be assumed, not questioned. Mohammed had said, "Think of God's gifts, not of his qualities." "He is the self-subsisting," and "He is not subject to question regarding what he does." That God is "not subject to question" (*cf. la yusalu,* 21:23) becomes a major plank of orthodoxy. Ashari phrased it, *bila kayf,* "without how."

(2) Being is one and all. There is a universal entity, a *primum mobile,* and certain qualities manifested in existence. A thing is both substance and quality, and existence is the very essence of it. The Mutazilas held, on the contrary, that a thing does not become a thing *for us* until God has bestowed upon it the quality of existence. Ashari admitted the reality of the two categories of substance and quality, and considered all other "attributes" of Being, or Existence, subjective aspects within the knower's mind. This was Ashari's method of establishing the relation between the knower and the thing-to-be-known, between knowledge and the thing-in-itself. He thus offered an answer to the question, How can, or does, man know God? Man does *not* acquire knowledge of God through *aql,* or "reason," but by the recognition of God who

[45] He organized the "Party of Unity and Justice."

is already in existence, even in man's mind itself. Man, therefore, knows God directly, and not through the processes of reason.

(3) The anthropomorphisms, or "man-likenesses," in the Koranic accounts of God must be accepted, but taken *bila kayf,* "without question," and without the thought that these "qualities" or "attributes" of God, such as hands, feet, etc., may be compared with the actual hands, feet, etc., of men. They are essential qualities which are a part of God's very being, not agencies upon which he depends for his existence, or for his operation of the universe. He takes the *thoughtful* view of God as personality, having life, knowledge, power, will, hearing, seeing, and speech.

(4) The *Koran* is the Word of Allah (*kalam Allahi*), existing from the beginning. In the beginning was the *Koran* and the *Koran* was with Allah, and the *Koran* was Allah, etc. Man had no part in its creation; in fact, it was *not created;* it is eternal. Mohammed was the medium through whom the divine spokesman Gabriel reported to mankind what was inscribed on the "heavenly plates."

(5) Man himself can produce no action; God alone can produce an act. What power man has (and he is allowed some power of his own) does not, and cannot affect his acts, for God creates within man both the power *and* the act. Man has some freedom and, therefore, some responsibility, but *man cannot create* anything. He is endowed with the power of choice between acts, between good and evil, but God himself creates the act, or the result to correspond with man's selection!

Such is Ashari's *Kalam,* his reconstruction in theology, a revised connection between reason and religion. He banned philosophy as such, to turn men's minds to God directly. He did no violence to the orthodoxy of even the illiterate conservative; but he gave the *thoughtful* conservative a defensible system of theology. Coming out of the camp of the radicals, he turned against them the edge of their dialectic. Well he knew the uses of their weapons; with them he refashioned and revived original Islam. While his monumental *Book of Explanation and Exposition* itself stands in need of some reduction to consistency, it met to the satisfaction of orthodoxy every challenge from the liberals of the time. Unfortunately, the note of bitterness appears occasionally in it. Although the author, by natural disposition, was "strongly inclined to gaiety and humor," his kindliness was eaten up by dogmatism; he died with a curse upon his lips for the advocates of daring rationalism. It remained for the third great strain of thought to emphasize the gentler side of faith, and to generate a kindlier scholasticism. Mysticism (*kashf*) found its great exponent a century or so later.

Mysticism.—In the year 1000 A.D. the Moslem empire had lost cohesion. A dozen dynasties rivalled the Abbasid, including the Zayrid in Tunis and Granada; the Fatimid in Syria and Eygpt; the Ghaznavid in Bactria, Afghanistan, and upper India; and the Buwayhid all around Baghdad—with the Saljuqs near at hand, and ready later to attempt a new consolidation. But culture often disregards imperial foundations; this was a golden age of culture; life and thought were ripening in freedom from entanglements of state. Moslem thinkers levied toll on wider territories, and spoke to remote distances. As Goethe spoke from Weimar to the world, so Rumi, from Tabriz and Koniya, has touched the hearts of mankind everywhere. In the eleventh century, this sort of universalism was in evidence. Many Moslems looked to Islam to become the common faith of men. Ghazali was their spokesman. *Mysticism asceticism too.*

Ghazali and Sufiism.—Abu Hamid Muhammad ibn Muhammad ibn Muhammad ibn Ahmad al-Ghazali (1058–1111 A.D.) was a Persian, born in the Persian village of Tus. He became "the most original thinker that Islam has produced and its greatest theologian." He is called the "example of Islam," and the "ornament of religion." He was a Shafiite in Law, a "liberal traditionalist." He studied many years in Naisabur, in Khorasan, under the Imam al-Haramain. Before he was thirty he went to Baghdad, welcomed there by the Nizamu 1-Mulk (Secretary of State), famous patron of culture in the Nizam's *madrasa,* or university, whose general character was Asharite. After a decade in the *madrasa,* his professorship was interrupted by political disturbances. He withdrew to Syria, made the pilgrimage to Mecca, wrote a number of books, and wandered widely; taught a while in the *madrasa* at Naisabur, and finally retired to his native village, Tus, in charge of a *Sufi* monastery. He died at fifty-three.

Ghazali completed what Ashari had begun. He took Islamic dogmatism, legal, logical, and philosophical, mixed with it mysticism, intuitional, and transcendental, and renewed the *life* of

Islam with a new theology. It was not pure theory with him; what he accomplished came out of the anguish of his own soul, in strenuous adjustment to reality. His theology sprang peculiarly from his own personal, spiritual experience. In early youth he disengaged himself from dogma based upon external authority; he could not agree with the scholastics, nor approve of those who insisted that religious truth might be known only through some infallible guide and teacher. The immediate alternative was Sufiism; but he could not accept it at the time. He became a *sufi* outwardly, perhaps; he was at heart a sceptic. His scepticism deepened, aggravated by a nervous temperament, as he continued his studies, and took to teaching. He came to think that certainty of knowledge was utterly impossible of attainment. He tried philosophy, the way of logic and of reason; he entered into heated controversies with members of the sects, especially Shiis. But philosophy, intellectualism, failed him. He was in despair, when upheavals in the state brought on a crisis. Then he turned to Sufiism with devotion, the way of the ascetic, and of religion as *experience*.

Sufiism is not extraneous to Islam. Ascetic elements have inhered since the beginning of the faith. Sufiism capitalized them. Mohammed was at times ascetic. The fast is an ascetic symbol. Mohammed also was a mystic, as suggested in the *Koran,* chapter 94.[46] The Sufis utilized Mohammed's mysticism. "Sufiism" began about 750 A.D., in Syria, and spread widely, finding congenial soil throughout the empire. On Greek and Persian soil, especially, many Moslems turned away from luxury and the world, imitating Christian and Manichæan monks and anchorites. Like the *hanifs* of the Prophet's day, these *faqirs,* "poor men," and *darwishes,* "mendicants," were unrelated individuals on a common quest. Ultimately a *sufi* theology developed, culling ideas everywhere from Greece to India. Seeming too individualistic, the Sufis were considered first as heretics. Their asceticism and their mysticism seemed at variance with orthodoxy for about two centuries. The *sufi* poet, al-Hallaj, was put to death as a heretic for saying *ana l-haqq,* "I am truth," although he had said, also, that the "true lover of God" was one who "bestows on none other a thought, from the moment when he sets forth to seek until he hath found what he sought." It happens that *al-Haqq,* "the True," is a Koranic name for God. Al-Hallaj, however, was merely expressing his opinion that man, made in

---

46 *Cf.* the author's *Mystical Elements in Mohammed,* pp. 41f.

God's image, is essentially divine. But he was put to death as a heretic and a blasphemer!

Sufiism has never been a sect; it is, rather, a suffusion, and an eclecticism. In general the *sufi* fundamentals are as follows:

(1) God alone exists; all else is illusion. God is mysterious knowledge, or reason (*aql*); but He is unknowable-in-himself. *Aql* is not the means of knowing the rationally-unknowable God.

(2) God can be known only through intuition and ecstasy. These agencies operate mainly through the exercise of "remembrance" (*dhikr*), whether of the quiet, meditative type, or through action, such as the whirling of certain darwish orders.

(3) God is Goodness. Evil has no reality of its own; it is the negation of good.

(4) The goal of man is union with God. Man seeks the shrine where he is one with Deity, as al-Hallaj has said. Man's soul seeks loss of identity in the consciousness of unity with God as reason, goodness, and reality.

Sufiism is "spiritual," not formal. It disregarded the ordained "prayers,"—which gave semblance to the charge of heresy; its *dhikrs* took their place. Extreme *sufis* have over-emphasized reliance upon God—they have disdained property and work of any sort.[47]

Ghazali Makes Sufiism Orthodox.—To return now to al-Ghazali. He became a *sufi* in principle. As a wandering ascetic, in flight from Baghdad, he sought peace for his soul within his own mind. He found both peace of mind and certainty of knowledge through a remarkable conversion. His theology is this conversion, with the insight it afforded into mysteries which had baffled him, and doubts that had assailed him. By formulating his experience he revivified Islam.

He altered *sufi* theories and practices; divorced them from their heretical associations, especially with Shiites; and gave them, revised and perfected, a place in orthodox Islam. As Ashari had established a metaphysics for Tradition (*naql*), so Ghazali propounded a philosophy of Mysticism (*kashf*). He found himself at variance with canon lawyers and speculative

---

[47] Shaykh Abn Said said Sufism required one to "put away all that thou hast in thy head, give all that thou hast in thy hand, and shrink from nothing."

theologians. He despised the casuistry of canon law,[48] and went far toward relegating it and legal casuistry from religion altogether. He opposed the rationalists, for their atheism, their intellectual intolerance, or their lack of an ultimate ground for their philosophy. He criticised the orthodox *kalam* (*i.e.*, the scholasticism of Ashari) for its intellectual subtleties among the learned and its tendency to make religion for the masses a scheme of logically articulated articles of faith. He demonstrated the main, broad principles of Islam upon which all could take their stand as true believers; by consensus of opinion (*i.e., ijma,* or "agreement") his program was adopted by the great majority. While he found certainty in experience and ecstasy, he pointed the faithful back to their early sources in the "Word of Allah" and the "Sayings of Mohammed." He reintroduced the element of fear in faith, even as Mohammed had counselled men to fear God and remember the last day, for fear had been a factor in Ghazali's own conversion. But he put a wholesome emphasis on love, the love of God and man, whereas Sufiism had often made that love unearthly and fantastic. All these things he not only preached with eloquence, but wrote with scholarly acumen. Not his least interesting teaching is that all men may become believers, not all by the same process, but each in his own way: the thoughtful, through reflection, discussion, and interpretation; and the masses, through obedience to literal demonstration.

More Intellectuals.—The list of thinkers, theologians, writers, poets, and religionists of the Golden Age would certainly include the Arabian al-Kindi (d. 873 A.D.) the Arab Ashari, the Turk Farabi (d. 950), the Persian Ibn Sina, or "Avicenna" (d. 1037), the Persian, al-Ghazali, the Spanish Arab, Ibn Rushd, or "Averroes" (d. 1138), the Eygptian Arab, Ibnu l-Farid (d. 1235), the Persian Rumi (Jalalu d-din of Rum, or Iconium, d. 1273), the North African Arab, Ibn Khaldun (d. 1406), and the Persian Jami (d. 1492). Al-Kindi was a rationalist who, having studied Greek, introduced the thought of Aristotle and Plotinus—as if it fitted in with the *Koran!* The Turk Farabi studied *Arabic* in Baghdad, and took up the exposition of Plotinus—in the name of Aristotle,—as if his man of "reason" (*aql*) were a *Koranic* character. Ibn Sina, also, was an "Aristotelian," who realized at last that Greek thought and Islamic could *not* be reconciled, and—

[48] Islamic canon law had developed intricacies and subtleties in a quantity and manner similar to the details of the Jewish *Torah* in the days of Jesus.

unwittingly?—became a heretic through his devotion to philosophy. Ibnu l-Farid, Jalalu d-din, and Jami were great poets and great mystics, who through no want of true devotion included in their verse ideas much at variance with traditional Islam. Ibn Khaldun saw Islam as history. His interest was the civilization of the world. He is one of the great philosophical historians of all time. But we turn to Ibn Rushd in more detail, because he may be taken as the representative of Islamic philosophy as such, and as the typical medium through which the Islamic version of Greek thought was introduced to Europe.

Ibn Rushd.—Ibn Rushd, "Averroes" (1126–1198 A.D.), was born in Spanish Cordova, where his grandfather and his father had been *qadi*. He studied law and medicine. At forty-three he became the *qadi* of Seville, and two years later, *qadi* of Cordova. At fifty-six he was appointed chief *qadi* of Andalusia, the Spanish dominion of the al-Muwahhidun, "Almohades" or "Unitarians," whose *mahdi* had gained control of Morocco, and parts of Spain, in 1130. The Almohad chieftains, Yusuf, and his son and successor, Yaqub,[49] extended him their generous patronage.

Ibn Rushd turned his attention—mainly through *Arabic* translations, for he did not read Greek—to the Greek philosophers, especially to Aristotle. He aimed to clarify and expound them. He wrote important philosophical treatises of his own, after Greek patterns. He commented upon Ashari and Ghazali, adversely on the latter, calling him "that renegade." Spanish Islam, however, was no proper soil for free discussion. He aroused the opposition of the theologians (the *faqihs,* or Canon "lawyers"). He fell into disfavor at the court.[50] He was branded "heretic." His "heresies" were based upon: (1) the question of the eternity of the world. He had been asked (by Yusuf) whether the world (the universe) was an eternal substance, or had had a beginning in time; (2) the question of the nature of God's understanding; (3) the problem of the universality of the soul; and (4) the nature of the resurrection. These were "live" issues at the time, not only in Islam, but in Christendom.[51]

Ibn Rushd's solutions may be deduced from the following outline of his theology:

---

49 Yaqub (Jacob), a contemporary of the famous Saladin, who sought his aid against the Crusaders, was a patron of arts and letters, as well as a warrior of renown. He built the Giralda, Seville's well-known observatory.

50 A possible contingency was that Yaqub needed the *faqihs'* support in his war against the Spanish Christians.

51 Ibn Rushd's "heresies" were condemned a century later by the Christian bishops of Paris, Oxford, and Canterbury, who knew his writings through Latin translations.

(1) There is one God; he knows all things, past, present, and to come. He is creator; his knowledge was the agent of creation. His knowledge is not universal, nor particular, as man's knowledge is. Man's knowledge is derived and speculative; God's is absolute. Man is a knower, but not on a plane with God.

(2) Man is part of God's material creation, endowed with soul and intellect. The soul is something subtle: in the form of the body, independent of the body, eternal in its individuality.[52] It is the energy, the driving force, of man. It is the *life* of man, which energizes his material body *in association* with it. The intellect of man is immaterial and abstract; its existence in reality is dependent on association with the universal Active Intellect of God.[53] It is man's [passive?] means of grasping the ideas derived from God. When man's intellect is merged into the active intellect of God, it becomes eternal. As for man's body, it obviously decays, but is reborn in a higher, heavenly form.

(3) Philosophy does not contradict religion; it approves. God meant man to be a *thoughtful* creature, a philosopher. Philosophy, knowledge, intelligence, these are the means to life and immortality. Ibn Rushd looked to a future life, incomparably superior to this, but not to be comprehended now by any anthropomorphisms. He opposed Ashari in this regard—and in others, also.

(4) Religion is valid, *if* in agreement with philosophy. Both are avenues to truth, if both agree. The true prophet with revelation, and the true philosopher with knowledge, cannot disagree. There is place in religion for the true scholar, with the fruits of his research. If a passage of the *Koran* seems to contradict philosophy, there must be some "higher" meaning in the passage—seek it. Truth reveals itself in many forms, according to the recipient. Religion has two aspects: an outer and an inner. The common man must take the *Koran* in its literal sense, such as he can grasp by "observation" (*zahr*); the learned man must use "interpretation," and seek the "inner essence" (*batn*). Let religious truth be taught according to the capacity of the learner. Let the masses believe upon authority. The learned are not obligated to communicate to them the fruits of research.

[52] He leaves, however, the *proof* of the immortality of the soul to revelation.
[53] *Cf.* Aristotle's Reason. He would relate through it the world of sense and the world of thought. His realism is a monism of substance, but a dualism of body and soul. Individuals are the key to universals.

Thus speaks the *qadi*-philosopher. His *Commentaries* aroused great admiration, especially in Christendom; but he did not reconcile effectually the Law and Reason. He was not original; he was a Spanish Arab Hellenist, much in debt to Aristotle. As al-Kindi, al-Farabi, and Ibn Sina (Avicenna) had done in the East, Ibn Rushd hellenized Islamic thought in Spain and Africa. He was in debt to his Spanish predecessor, Ibn Bajja (Avenpace), who, in the Greek tradition, had thought of God as Active Intellect, of Reason as man's guide in all affairs, of truth as something to be found by abstract thinking, and of immortality as the union of man's intellect with God's. Ibn Rushd, however, was the thinker-in-public-life, seeking to reconcile practical Islam and abstract thought. He opposed Ashari's *Explanation*. He opposed Ghazali's way of ecstasy and contemplation. His views did not prevail; they are still heretical. His honor rests in Europe, not in the Moslem World. Already, in his century, Islamic power in the West was in decay (it lost its hold on Spain in 1498); but the gift of culture was permanent; and none did more than Ibn Rushd to this end.

Islam in Modern Times.—Little that is really new has happened in Islam since 1500. The Osmanli and the Mughal dynasties were demonstrations more of power than faith. Moslem empire has long since been disintegrated; many portions of the House have been dismantled. Islam as politics has waned; the religion of Islam endures. There is need of reconstruction; perhaps a new apologetic is developing. But as yet no prominent interpreter has appeared in succession with Ashari and Ghazali, no thinker worthy of Ibn Rushd,—unless it be Muhammad Abduh of Egypt.[54] No new principles of reconstruction seem available; in Islamic religion, as in others, there is really nothing new. It is a question of adjustment.

Many things have happened to arouse Islam. Political, economic, social, philosophical, and religious ideas have crowded in upon the people from the ends of the earth. When the French, for instance, entered Egypt, they introduced many European institutions. Throughout the Near East, magazine and newspaper materials have served as leaven. Turkey has a western code of law. Nationalism is pronounced in Turkey and in Egypt. Pan-Islam is kept in mind in several quarters; but there seems no prospect of renewal of political solidarity. Shiite Persia has been independent

---

[54] *Cf.* C. C. Adams, *Islam and Modernism in Egypt.* London, 1933. This work, however, may overrate him.

several centuries. Increased independence for India will enhance *Hindu,* not Moslem power. Islam must rest content to be a spirit, a religion. As Abu Bakr said at the Prophet's funeral, "Mohammed is dead, but Allah lives," so we might say, The Caliph and many sultans are dead, but Islam lives. Spiritual solidarity is possible.

One old principle that seems new has been established, namely, that the faith is independent of the state. Islam does not depend upon political control within its own household. It flourishes where British, Spanish, Dutch, Russian, French, Italian, and American rulership prevails. Moslems have learned, also, that the Caliphate is not essential. There are claimants to the Caliphate in the Hijaz, Morocco, and Afghanistan; but they arouse no general acclamation. When the Turks banished the last Caliph, "the shadow of God on earth," the shadow of the theory vanished, also. Long before that the Moslem world had been content with a non-Arab incumbent of the office.[55]

Mohammed is still the Prophet. The *Kaba* is still the symbol of religious unity,[56] and of the common consciousness. All Moslems swear by Allah. The faith still is conservative; but there are liberals in the fold—not to mention freethinkers, atheists, anarchists, libertines, and communists (whose antecedents have been known to us as Zindiqs, Ismailians, Assassins, Mutazilas, etc.). There are many advocates of social reformation in Turkey, Syria, India, and Egypt. The veil has been discarded in polite society. The desire for education grows among the liberals. They have added to their "sciences." Some have undertaken a reëxamination of the faith, new Koranic exegesis, for example. The radicals will not affect the future, constructively; the conservatives cannot. The fortunes of Islam lie with the liberals. They are finding in the faith itself the essential principles of "progress." They have shown how Islam first developed from tribal to national, to international, proportions. One has found in Ibn Rushd the doctrine of creative evolution. They show what rôle *ijma,* "agreement," has played in progress—the system of Ghazali was accepted *by agreement.* Public opinion, they assert, must be developed to care for the newer needs. They would discard excrescences, accumulations, non-essentials, and employ effectively the *vital* principles by which the faith has lived. They talk about the "spirit of Islam," but

[55] The theory long held that only an Arab of the tribe of Quraysh might properly be Caliph.

[56] There are many sects—*ex post facto hadith* accounts for 73 with *Sunna*—but all are Moslem. The "schools" of Law, though differing, are Moslem.

are aware that sheer idealism without reference to the past is futile. They rely upon such demonstrations in the past as brotherhood, democracy, and tolerance, and would raise up leaders in succession to the conservative *faqihs,* and *ulemas,* who would take a "modern" view of things. *Allahu akbar!*

CHAPTER XVII

CONCLUSION

COMPARING RELIGIONS

No religion has lived long, if at all, to itself. Its origins have usually implied antecedents. The activities of its adherents have brought them face to face with opposition and the need to justify themselves. Sooner or later, other faiths have been encountered, and comparisons have become inevitable. Never before in the history of religions has comparison been quite as much resorted to as recently. Judaism, Christianity and Islam have been compared for many centuries by theologians and statesmen. Constantine hesitated long between Mithra and Jesus. The Great Mughal Akbar, in the sixteenth century, ventured to compare Islam, Hinduism, Jainism, Zoroastrianism, Christianity, and others.[1] All faiths today may be brought to view by the serious student, for their scriptures may be found in all the larger libraries, and their adherents intermingle in unwonted measure. Many students have resorted to first-hand investigation among the peoples in the lands of the various living faiths. We, at the conclusion of this course, are somewhat better prepared to answer the many questions propounded at the outset (see p. 4). Further, we may venture to indicate certain general aspects of the situation.

Religion is not to be confused with culture. It is not fully to be understood in terms of culture. It is not necessarily of low quality in low society, nor of high grade among the civilized. Some "intellectuals" have eschewed religion, as if irreligion were a consequence of cultural development. Many truly inspired men have been "unlettered." There is a "wisdom" not the product of the schools. "Revelation" is not altogether subject to man's own con-

---

[1] *Cf.* "To gather here and there
From each fair plant the blossom choicest grown,
To wreathe a crown not only for the king,
But in due time for every Mussulman,
Brahmin and Buddhist, Christian and Parsee,
Through all the warring world of Hindustan."

trols. God is not the creature of men's imagination. He is not excluded by the boundary of world society; he is not merely *of* the social order.

A religion must be understood, in part, in terms of culture. Its forms take shape in its environment—Yahweh was a mountain deity. It speaks the language of its people, and loses prestige otherwise. It reflects political and social institutions; God may be "the Lord," *or* a great "Deliverer." It is colored by man's own experience; the "visions" and "dreams" of its prophets are a priceless heritage. It is practical, thoughtful, mystical, according to prevailing moods of its adherents. Its ideas fit the world it moves in. The process of *a* religion begins for man within his own locality, describes his situation, discovers a Beyond whence help may reach him, and provides escape for him in the last extremity; it is the way from the immediate to the hereafter, from bonds to freedom.

Religion is conservative, but not only so. It inculcates fear of innovation, especially in ritual; but it is productive of its own forms; it has inspired reformation. In times of social revolution, it has provided checks and continuity, lest human institutions be utterly destroyed. Hammurabi, Zoroaster, Krishna, Buddha, Jesus and Mohammed offered the substance of religion for the reconstruction of society. Religion is the one effective means of progress in the midst of man's vicissitudes. It preserves the quality of hope, and rebukes man's arrogance; it reveals God who as ultimate goodness and truth is the same yesterday, today and forever. It posits faith as the very evidence of things unseen, and assures men that love is the greatest virtue.

A religion must be studied *in itself*. Although as an historical movement, it may not easily be separated from other faiths, it has, psychologically, an essence of its own. For the consciences of its adherents its values may be absolute. Psychology is, at least, more indispensable than history in the study of religion. History is often reconstructed in large measure out of the experience of the present. Psychology, rather than history, defines the *goal* of faith. The adherents of a faith must be its first interpreters. Its origins and values *are* what they are to them. Because religion is native to the human mind, its special forms must be described by those who molded them. The faithful must explain the acts and symbols of their faith. By such means we understand particular religions.

Religions are inevitably and profitably subjected to comparison. The method in our day is mainly due to increased acquaintance with the sacred scriptures of religion and "the proper study of mankind." Among the commonplace results which have already been attained are these: various religions may not properly be classified as "true" and "false"; the historical origin of a faith is not exclusively determinative of its final value; ultimate truth is higher than any one religion, and all religions are like partners in the quest for final truth; and positive spiritual values with reference to progressive life itself are the test of faith. Our curiosity has already encountered amazing similarities among various religions. Further knowledge may teach us fundamental differences among them.

Three sets of problems emerge when religions are compared: (1) The problem of discovering what each religion is *in itself* and *as a whole*, before comparisons may be attempted for the sake of value judgments. This may be a long view, or a broad view, primarily. Preferably, it is the broad view; that is, the comparison of religions as they are at a given time, especially if they be then in contact; otherwise, the long view, to see what each has meant historically as times and circumstances varied. One may discover the varied ways in which the different faiths have met persistent issues among men, what the concepts, practices and attitudes of each have been. This is a search for "essence" in each faith. We may then compare the essences, possibly detecting certain "types" thereby.

(2) The question of similarities and differences. Similarities are most significant, if independent; we mean the similarity of particulars in different regions. One religion may seem very like another in detail. If so, the student may reserve his judgment until he learns the differences. He desires to know to what extent a given faith reveals religion as a whole. Similarities tend to indicate religion as a whole; differences between faiths may establish grades of quality. One may not be too theoretical. He should keep in mind such factors as development, the relation of ideas to practices, the influence of politics on theology, the effects of syncretism, the racial mind, and changes in the body due to converts.

(3) The question of "stages" in development, if there are such. To the anthropologist, religion is a phase of human culture, obedient to the same laws which govern human progress in society. He sees a movement from low and crude stages to higher and more refined. Does this tell the story of religion? It ignores the "high gods" of early cultures, and fails to account completely for the "survivals" of crude forms in higher cultures. Are there "cycles"

both in social institutions and in religion? An archæologist[2] has discovered that "the government [of ancient Egypt] moves from autocracy to democracy until the democracy eats up everything and a stronger power starts the cycle over again." We may review each of the great religions as an historical movement, to discover what evidence each may offer. Further, we may reach by such consideration some conclusion with reference to religion as a whole. We may decide, in view of the evidence, that men early thought of a Power (not merely powers), a monistic, or possibly a monotheistic, conception, known among various peoples by different names; and that with the expansion of culture "monotheism" expanded. In such manner we may account for unifications of religion, often through some priest, king, or theologian. This amounts to the reconciliation of practical "polytheism." Thereby the many gods, who were nature, functional, or abstract powers, become identified in the One, or are transformed as attributes of the One. On the other hand, we may think the evidence confirms the evolutionary theory of the anthropologist, with powers (or, perhaps, an all-pervasive energy, *mana*) to begin with, and the One God a long-delayed achievement. One's judgment may be swayed by "science," or by traditional theories of "revelation" and of the "inspiration" of holy scripture.

Comparative studies throw light on many problems besides God, revelation and inspiration, including holiness, miracle, human nature, distinctions of good and evil, succession in the priestly office, authority, sacraments and salvation. While comparisons may tend to modify the orthodox interpretations of these aspects of religion in any given area or denomination, they do not provide a refuge for the unbeliever. Rather, they tend to show the essence of religion at its best. They indicate the principles and qualities through which religion must survive. Man may not permanently express religion in terms which do not meet the tests of mind, conscience and spirit. As an expression, in the qualities imputed to it, religion must be: (1) intellectually acceptable; (2) morally adequate; and (3) spiritually satisfying. It may do no violence to what the best *thought* of earnest men expect of it. It may not build its universe of intellectually impossible materials, giving way to myth and legend as substantial fact. It must command respect in thoughtful circles for its conceptions of nature and of human values. It must persuade the thoughtless and hold them when they learn to think. It must meet the temper of the changing ages.

2 Sir William Flinders Petrie.

It must meet the *moral* needs of men, not holding to a once effective code no longer applicable. If it operates at all by code, it does so for expediency, for it makes man's will the central factor in discriminations between the evil and the good. By this a man follows not a sanction altogether from without, but his own enlightened will. He that *willeth* with insight shall *know* what is needful for his good. In the realm of morals, inner compulsion is ultimately superior to legal imposition. Religion demands what life itself demands, if the race survive.

It must satisfy the *spirit* most of all: this is faith's chief function. It must feed the mysterious inner hunger of mankind, for few men have ever found for long their own sufficient nourishment. Religion postulates the origin and guidance of the world as spiritual, therefore intelligent and good. That only can be spiritually satisfactory which satisfies the human reason and the will. Religion as integral to human nature urges upon man the life of the spirit as the highest end. Not in opposition to the world, but in service to it; not in other-worldliness, but in joyous concern for man's perfection as a worldly creature. The negative results of extreme asceticism have become impressive. Every faith has had its ideal man, but too often on a pattern from another world. Those religious leaders are most worthy still of our attention, who have asked for perfect men in an improving social order, in a world transformed by man's remembrance of his neighbor. God works through good deeds even more than good ideas. He is revealed in Truth and Goodness, but if these are not embodied, they cannot be effective revelations. He is Spirit, the Father of men's spirits, and is served best by spiritual understanding and obedience. The great reformers have not taught a new religion; they have sought to deepen the spiritual life of men. They have imposed upon mankind no authority beyond the spirit.

We are children of the present day, followers of the living faiths, disciples of leaders of the past whose faiths are still alive. We weigh the past and wonder at the future. We run enormous risk, if we do otherwise; we dare not ignore the past. How may we of this day be at once loyal to ourselves and to past leaders? We must not see the present too immediately; it must not shine so clearly that it dazzles. Many men in other eras, say the Renaissance and the French Revolution, saw their own present so distinctly that most of the past escaped them to their hurt. Many today are disposed to draw a line across the past, to disregard it, to see nothing in historic faith. The honor that we do ourselves must perish, if it does not flow from reverence for our ancient leaders. Nor is that true honor to the present which tacitly insults the memory of the past. It is not modern to scoff at Shankara, Buddha, Jesus and Aquinas. It is modern, scientific and philosophical to be concerned about them, to be interested in the history of religion. Such curiosity becomes us. The historic, especially historical religion, is a tremendous force bound to surge creatively into the future; there is no separation of the present from it.

Human advance is in large measure an extension of the past. We profit by the race's long experience; time makes ancient *forms* uncouth, while ancient good is everlasting; we find new uses for essential values. We do not wish to perish when the present dies; we know we shall *not* die; but the honor that we do our forebears is a worthy measure of our memory. One may revolt against the past, but the best in it gets most of us eventually. This is a reassuring, hopeful fact with reference to religion, with reference to many differences among religions. As disciples of historic faiths, *we* have often made the differences! Mohammed, Buddha, Jesus and Confucius were not acquainted with each other. They never walked a common road, then parted. Had they trod the common way, they would not have parted. We speak, of course, in a figure. Their disciples have waged the conflicts in religion. Differences have been established by disciples. The fundamental emphasis of the leaders have had much more in common. To search for the simple gospel of the greatest men of insight is to find eventually the basic factors of religion. The disciples of all faiths *must* find the basis of agreement; otherwise their differences are futile contradictions. A faith may have peculiar *values* for its followers, but truth is one, and contradictions in essentials must appear unreasonable, immoral and spiritually deficient. Sentiment may not do duty as conviction; supposed conviction is mere sentiment when one aspect of the whole denies another. It is fundamental that the followers of any faith, if they would deal at all with the followers of any other faith, should first seek for their convictions. It is fundamental, also, that religion has to do with human welfare.

APPENDIX I

A STUDENTS' MANUAL

The contents of this volume, with the materials indicated in Appendix II, Bibliography, are intended for a full year's course, three hours weekly. The following topics and questions may be found useful for discussion as the course proceeds. They provide, incidentally, an outline of the course.

Chapter I. Introduction—See p. 4 for a set of questions intended for inconclusive discussion.
1. Is change consistent with belief? How may one distinguish between essential faith and incidental aspects?
2. Which tendency is more pronounced in a religion, conservation or innovation? Is religion essentially conservative?
3. What factors enter into definitions of religion? What conditions qualify the definition?
4. Is there an "Eastern" and a "Western" mind? Illustrate with reference to definitions of religion.
5. Compare the prophet and the priest.

Chapter II. The Religion of the Primitives
1. Distinguish between "primitive" chronologically and culturally.
2. Compare the anthropocentric world with the cosmocentric. What is the present relative importance of man in the universe? How large is the universe by present calculation? What bearing have these facts on faith?
3. Who is the Negro? What are his chief characteristics in Africa? Compare the African and the American Negro.
4. What "true" and what "false" elements characterize African Negro religion?
5. What objective has the primitive in the use of ritual?
6. Differentiate between magic and religion.

Chapter III. An introduction to Religion in China
1. To what extent are the Chinese "religious"?
2. What influences have affected the Chinese from without?
3. What have Chinese generally thought about the moral qualities of God, Nature, and human nature?
4. To what extent may ceremony be moral?
5. Are there necessary relations between religion and morality?

Chapter IV. Confucianism
1. See pp. 69–70 for many recent objections to Confucianism. What validity, if any, has each of them?
2. Are the Chinese "Classics" inspired? What has given them authority? What sort of authority have they had?
3. Was Confucius as an example of the scholar in politics a success? Should one be able practically to demonstrate his own theories? To what extent does the value of a theory depend upon applicability?

471

4. What is the ground of ethics in Confucius' view? How may one discriminate, in his view, between right and wrong? *golden Rule.*

5. What relation has knowledge to right conduct?

6. What relation, if any, is there between propriety (*li*) and filial devotion (*hsiao*)?

7. Are the "Confucian" distinctions in society at all valid?

8. Is the "ideal man" religious? Was Confucius religious?

9. Compare the teachings of Mencius and of Confucius. Did Mencius add anything?

10. Whose theories might serve China better today, those of Hsün-tze or those of Mencius?

11. Is there an essential Confucianism; are there permanent elements?

12. To what extent was Chu Hsi modern? To what extent "Confucian"?

13. In what respect, if any, are ancestors worthy of commemoration?

14. To what extent is the family a religious unit?

15. Is there any connection between Nature and the will of Heaven?

Chapter V. Taoism

1. What is "divination"? What is its objective? What its value? What abuses have resulted from its practice?

2. To what degree is mysticism compatible with the Chinese disposition?

3. What is "primitive" in higher Taoism? In what particulars are higher and lower Taoism similar?

4. Wherein lies Reality, in the whole, or in the individual parts?

5. Which is better for morals, higher or lower Taoism? How might mysticism be immoral?

6. What bearing has legislation upon the progress of morality?

7. Is higher Taoism religious?

8. Compare Chuang-tze and Mo-tze with reference to human conduct.

Chapter VI. Japan and Religion

1. What is the Japanese government's attitude toward religion? *Interest*

2. Does this attitude differ from that held by China?

3. Are religion and nationalism compatible?

Chapter VII. Shinto

1. In what particulars are the *kami* similar to the Chinese *shen?*

2. Differentiate the kinds of Shinto.

3. What "primitive" elements inhere in State Shinto?

4. Explain the lack of ground in Shinto for such religious elements as priests and prayers.

5. How has the idea of the Sun-goddess developed? What changes have occurred?

6. Have forces from without affected Shinto? How?

7. In what respect have outside forces failed to affect Shinto?

8. Compare the position of women in Japan with woman's lot in China.

9. Wherein is sectarian Shinto more religious than the State cult?

10. Is sectarian Shinto more patriotic than State Shinto? Is it more ethical?

Chapter VIII. India and Religion

1. What advantages and handicaps does nationalism naturally meet in India?

2. What influence, if any, has "race" upon religion? Have physical features of a land any influence on both?

3. Is India in any way peculiar? Have intruding elements been affected by any Indian qualities?

APPENDIX 473

Chapter IX. Hinduism

1. What is "Hinduism"? Why may it not easily be defined?
2. Compare Hinduism with the faiths already studied. Is it more or less religious?
3. Compare Madura and Isé as religious centers. What about their respective deities?
4. To what extent are faith and works necessary in religion?
5. By what signs can faith be known in Benares? What creed may be deduced from the works observed?
6. In what ways is the Golden Temple at Benares a symbol of the Hindu faith?
7. What symbols represent the many deities?
8. Is Hindu sectarianism intolerant? Wherein is Hinduism intolerant? Is intolerance essential to sectarianism?
9. Is caste inherent in human nature? What sanctions may it have from religion? What validity, if any, has it?
10. How does Hindu caste express itself?
11. What factors entered into the development of caste, which tended to make it peculiar to India?
12. Compare the religion of the *Rig Veda* with that described in the *Atharva*. Account for whatever differences appear.
13. How have religion and philosophy been identified in India? Wherein have the two differed? How have the objectives of the two compared?
14. What place has law had in Hinduism? To what aspects of life has law chiefly applied? Is law compatible with Hinduism?
15. What main concepts distinguish philosophy? What are the chief concepts of religion?
16. How does theistic Hinduism differ from pantheism?
17. How may Vishnuism be distinguished from Shivism?
18. Is asceticism necessary to religion? To morality?
19. How may the two types of Krishna worship be accounted for?
20. To what extent is the doctrine of freedom of the will true of Hinduism?
21. How does Hinduism make provision for "salvation"? Are the "ways" mutually exclusive?
22. How rigidly must the Hindu adhere to creed? Has he liberty of thought within the faith? Are there creedal tests of faith?
23. What manner and content of thought are typical of the Hindu Indian? Is there a Hindu-mindedness?
24. What is the Hindu idea of the good?
25. How large is the Hindu universe? What place has man in it?

Chapter X. Jainism

1. How may the decrease in the Jain community be explained?
2. Who is a jina? What are the means to such a state?
3. Are Jains idolatrous?
4. What place has prayer?
5. Comment on Mahavira's attitude toward his parents.
6. What is the highest goal of the Jain?
7. To what degree is non-injury required of humanity?
8. What validity, if any, has the "yes-no" theory?
9. How much alive is the universe? How much dead?

Chapter XI. Buddhism

1. Does *extent* suggest qualities of the faith?
2. Do the monk and the layman, in Hinayana, pray?
3. Differentiate between Hinayana and Mahayana.

4. Do Mahayanists worship? What and how?
5. What youthful experiences affected Gautama (Gotam) profoundly?
6. What value did Buddha attribute to asceticism?
7. Describe the "wisdom" which he attained.
8. Wherein is Buddha's a "middle" way?
9. What is the relation of selfishness to sorrow and satisfaction?
10. May one be happy without desires? Does the eradication of desire necessarily bring happiness? What of a "Laughing Buddha"?
11. What place has the will in Buddhism?
12. Are any Buddhist morals valuable today?
13. What bearing has law upon the freedom of man's will?
14. Did Buddha use the concept "cause"? In what sense?
15. Why and how did Buddha criticise the "soul" concept?
16. What place has "knowledge" in the Buddhist way?
17. Did Buddha, or does Buddhism, teach annihilation as the end of man's existence?
18. To what original elements in Buddhism could Mahayana appeal?
19. Was India congenial to Mahayana? What ground had it in competition with Hinduism?
20. How was monasticism possible in a Middle Way?
21. What views of the world were held by Mahayana?
22. Differentiate, if possible, between Buddhist and Hindu idealism.
23. Did India ever need Buddhism?
24. What has Buddhism had to offer non-Indian peoples?
25. What modifications were required of the faith in China? In Japan?
26. Compare Maitreya and the Hindu Krishna.
27. Compare the Hindu, Buddhist and Chinese doctrines of human nature.
28. Has Buddhism political and nationalistic elements? Could it be a national religion?
29. What is the Buddhist attitude toward war?

Chapter XII. The Parsis

1. How may we account for Zoroastrianism in Moslem Persia?
2. Why may Zoroastrians have had to flee from Persia?
3. Why is potentially destructive fire held sacred?
4. What similarities have existed in the Zoroastrian and the Hindu doctrines and practices? On what ground?
5. What have Parsis thought and done about religious education?
6. What bearing has religion on the disposal of the dead? Compare Parsi and Hindu customs.
7. What kind of reform did Zoroaster attempt? Did he succeed?
8. Explain his view of good and evil.
9. Was Zoroaster a monist? Was he a monotheist? Were his moral teachings in harmony with the idea of one supreme God?
10. Of what does salvation consist in the Parsi view? What must one do to be saved?

Chapter XIII. The Sikhs

1. Do Sikhs differ in stock from the Indian masses?
2. Distinguish the political and religious elements involved in the origin of the Sikh movement.
3. How did the movement become predominantly nationalistic?
4. Is the Sikh religion monotheistic?
5. What constitutes authority? Has the seat of authority varied?
6. Are the scriptures "inspired"?
7. What relation has the faith borne to caste?
8. Compare Nanak and Gobind Singh.

9. What Indian characteristics are involved in Sikhism? How has Hinduism affected it? *KARMA. PolyTheisTic*

10. What moral and religious values have Sikhs most emphasized? *AbsTenence FRom liquoR, Belief in God*

Chapter XIV. Judaism

1. To what extent are Jews a "universal" people?
2. What does Judaism connote to you, at first thought?
3. What has preserved some Jews? How have others been "lost"?
4. To what extent, if any, are Jews assimilable?
5. Why has the Jew called the cemetery the "abode of life"? Might an atheistic Jew properly use the term?
6. What is the relative importance of creed and ritual?
7. Compare the synagogue and the Temple, historically and ritually.
8. May one with due propriety work on the "Sabbath"?
9. What tragic aspects of life and history are portrayed in ceremonial?
10. What is the orthodox Jew's opinion of the Law? How, if ever, has he criticized it? Is he a philosopher?
11. What have prophets accomplished among the Jews? What is the function of a patriot? Can he be justified?
12. Compare the individualistic and the social interpretations of religion and of ethics. Which, the individual or the group, is the more sensitive to hurt and more responsive to good?
13. Explain the variations of the Jewish God-idea.
14. To what extent has persecution affected the Jews and the Jewish mind?
15. How has history been affected by concepts of deliverance and a deliverer?
16. How has the idea and practice of sacrifice varied?
17. What permanent elements inhere in the faith?
18. Was Moses a monotheist? What was he?
19. Explain the chief effects of the Dispersion.
20. Compare the Christian and the Moslem treatment of the Jews.
21. What is the doctrine of "revelation"? What persons were "inspired"?
22. How has philosophy affected Judaism?
23. Explain the views of sin and of evil.
24. Were there, or are there priests?
25. Trace the doctrine of the "Messiah."
26. What ground of hope has Judaism today? What prospect of realization?

Chapter XV. Christianity

1. How binding is one's birth into a religious order?
2. By what outer symbols may the faith be known?
3. Does Christianity contain pagan elements?
4. Did Jesus organize a "Church"? Did he reject Judaism?
5. Distinguish various theories of the character and scope of the Church.
6. With what theory of the Church is the priestly office most in harmony? Why?
7. What are the sacraments? How many?
8. Was Jesus a Christian?
9. What new elements did Jesus introduce? Was he a reformer?
10. By what titles was Jesus known? What did they signify?
11. What did Jesus' disciples think of him?
12. Compare his own and the popular views of miracle.
13. Compare his and the Jewish views of the world and of man.
14. What did Jesus think of law and ritual?

15. Differentiate between Christianity and the religion of Jesus.
16. Compare Jesus and Paul.
17. Compare Peter, Paul and John, with special reference to the development of ideas and practices.
18. What was the major issue among early Christians? How had Paul and John solved the problem of the person of Jesus?
19. What views on celibacy have been held by the Eastern and the Western Churches?
20. What early "heresies" appeared in Christianity?
21. What were Augustine's views of "the Church," "original sin," and the freedom of the human will?
22. Was the idea of a Savior unfamiliar to pagan Romans?
23. What essential differences were there between eastern and western monasticism?
24. How unworldly were the several great monastic orders?
25. What relative positions were held by the State and the Church until about the year 1000?
26. What is "simony"? What are "indulgences"?
27. Distinguish between the Black and the Grey friars.
28. How did Aquinas deal with reason and faith?
29. What political and moral issues came to a crisis in the Protestant Reformation? Was Luther a reformer or a revolutionist?
30. What are the major differences between "Catholics" and "Protestants"?
31. How did Protestantism become established in England? Through what persons, and by what acts?
32. Compare Anglicans and American Episcopalians.
33. How do Presbyterians and Baptists differ in polity and in doctrine?
34. What peculiar views of human nature and salvation did John Wesley hold? What is "methodism"?
35. Is Christianity democratic?
36. What kinds of "authority" appear in Christianity?
37. What is Christian tradition? Explain "apostolic succession."
38. What are the irreducible elements of Christianity? What makes a "Church"? What makes a "minister" (or whatever title)?
39. Distinguish between religion as dogma and as spirit. Are the two essentials? If so, in what proportion?

Chapter XVI. Islam
1. What makes a mosque? *Pillar of prayer.*
2. Is Islam democratic? *yes,*
3. Are there pagan elements in the faith?
4. What does Mohammed's "flight" represent politically and doctrinally?
5. What changes in the Arabian order did Mohammed accomplish?
6. What are the "pillars" of the House of Islam? Were they original with Mohammed? *Confession, Prayer, Fasting, alms, Pilgrimage.*
7. What is the theory of the Koran? *of Mohammed? Allah*
8. Describe the Moslem idea of Allah.
9. How has the Koran been supplemented in Moslem history?
10. Explain the character and cause of various interpretations of Canon Law.
11. What views of the Caliphate have been influential?
12. Compare politics and religion in Sunna and in Shia. *Shia-ali,*
13. How were Greek and Semitic elements reconciled in Islam?
14. What had Ghazali and Ashari in common? Did they differ? Is mysticism compatible with Islam? *yes with mohammed*
15. What were Ibn Rushd's heresies? *Eternity, first God, Resurrection*
16. Are there principles of change and progress in Islam?

Chapter XVII. Conclusion

1. What is profitable in a comparison of religions? What validity has comparison? *Find the ultimate truth.*

2. Why might Constantine have hesitated between Rama, Maitreya and Jesus as he did between Jesus and Mithra?

3. To what extent is sacrifice common in religion? *Most all love it.*

4. What other common elements have we discovered by this course of study? *Search for satisfaction, leader,*

5. What fundamental difference is there between monism and monotheism? *Monism - no devil,*

6. What is the difference between Religion and a religion?

7. How might the study of Comparative Religion affect belief, for example, a doctrine of the virgin birth? *So common among them*

8. What does Comparative Religion tell us of the theory and practice of prayer? *A universal practice*

9. What religious leaders have asked for perfect men in *this* world? How? Why?

10. What are the relations of religion, culture and nature?

11. What values inhere in sacred scriptures?

12. What bases of human progress are there in religion? *- Human life is an extension of the past.*

APPENDIX II

COLLATERAL READINGS

The following sources are selected with reference, mainly, to the topical headings in the chapters of this book. No attempt is made to indicate how much reading should be assigned for one class session. More materials are listed than can be used directly in course, including many biographies.

General works on the world's religions:

1. *Religions of the World.* By Carl Clemen, editor (trans. by A. K. Dallas). N. Y., 1931.
2. *Religion in Various Cultures.* By H. L. Friess and H. W. Schneider. N. Y., 1932.
3. *A Short History of Religions.* By E. E. Kellett. N. Y., 1934.
4. *The History of Religions.* By E. W. Hopkins. N. Y., 1918.
5. *History of Religions*, 2 vols. By G. F. Moore. N. Y., 1913, 1919.
6. *The Evolution of Ethics as Revealed in the Great Religions.* Edited by E. H. Sneath. New Haven, 1927.
7. *Treasure-House of the Living Religions.* Selections from their sacred scriptures. Compiled and edited by R. E. Hume. N. Y., 1932.
8. *An Outline Introduction to the History of Religions.* By T. H. Robinson. Oxford, 1926.

Chapter I. Introduction to the Study of Religions:

1. *The Birth and Growth of Religion.* By G. F. Moore. N. Y., 1923.
2. *The Coming Religion.* By N. Schmidt. N. Y., 1930.
3. *The Origin and Evolution of Religion.* By E. W. Hopkins. New Haven, 1923.
4. *Introduction to the History of Religions.* By C. H. Toy. N. Y., 1913.
5. *The Philosophy of Religion.* By D. M. Edwards. N. Y., 1929.
6. *The Origin and Growth of Religion.* By W. Schmidt (trans. by H. J. Rose). N. Y., 1931.
7. *The Quest of the Ages.* By E. Haydon. N. Y., 1929.

Chapter II. The Religion of the Primitives:

1. *The Religion of the Primitives.* By A. Le Roy. N. Y., 1922. Pp. 38–61 (the primitive in the presence of nature), 90–131 (belief), 173–215 (worship).
2. *The Soul of the Bantu.* By W. C. Willoughby. N. Y., 1928. Pp. 7–35 (the soul), 57–89 (spirits), 203–225 (rites), 298–328 (images), 328–361 (ancestor-worship).
3. *Primitive Man.* By J. Murphy. London, 1927. Pp. 136–163 (mana, animism), 211–241 (magic and religion).
4. *Primitive Religion.* By R. H. Lowie. N. Y., 1924. Pp. 99–134 (animism), 33–53 (the African Ekoi), 54–96 (Polynesia), 3–32 (Crow Indian).

5. *The Religion of Lower Races.* By E. W. Smith. N. Y., 1923. Pp. 1-64 (the Bantu and their religion).
6. *Religion and Art in Ashanti.* By R. S. Rattray. Oxford, 1927. Pp. 9-47 (fetishes, shamans, priests).
7. *Orokaiva Magic.* By F. E. Williams. Oxford, 1928. Pp. 7-66 (the Taro cult, ritual and doctor), 169-225 (magic).
8. *Sons of Africa.* By G. A. Gollock. N. Y., 1928. (Sketches of Negroes.)
9. *Robert Moffat.* By E. W. Smith. London, 1925.
10. *François Coillard.* By E. Shillito. N. Y., 1923.
11. *David Livingstone.* By C. J. Finger. N. Y., 1927.

Chapter III. Religion in China:

1. *The Soul of China.* By R. Wilhelm. N. Y., 1928. Pp. 50-95 (revolution), 115-128 (Mt. T'ai), 286-305 (occultism and religion).
2. *Modern Tendencies in World Religions.* By C. S. Braden. N Y., 1933. Pp. 87-135.
3. *China.* By Paul Monroe. N. Y., 1928. Pp. 1-19, 77-111 (changes, thought, religion).
4. *China Today through Chinese Eyes.* London, 1927.
5. *Chinese Recorder Magazine,* vols. 59-65 (various articles on revolution, rural religion, scholars and religion, the Kuomintang and religion, the conflict of cultures, etc.)
6. *San Min Chu I.* Trans. by F. W. Price. Shanghai, 1927. Sun Yat Sen's principles of government.
7. *The Religion of the Chinese.* By J. J. M. De Groot. N. Y., 1910. Pp. 3-48 (animism, spectres), 62-88 (ancestor-worship).
8. *Researches into Chinese Superstitions.* By H. Doré. Many volumes. Shanghai, 1917ff. Vol. IV, pp. i-xviii, 340-362 (divination). Vol. II (charms).
9. *The Foundations of Modern China.* By T'ang Leang-li. London, 1928. Pp. 235-278 (new social order), 116-142 (gospel of Sun Yat Sen).
10. *Making a New China.* By No Yong Park. Boston, 1929. Pp. 251-307 (freedom, revolt).
11. *A Short History of China.* By E. T. Williams. N. Y., 1928. Pp. 603-623 (nationalism, etc.), 629-652 (origins), 28-84 (ancient times).
12. *Chinese Religious Ideas.* By P. J. Maclagan. London, 1926. Pp. 15-43 (ancient God-idea).
13. *La Chine Antique.* By H. Maspero. Paris, 1927. Pp. 156-186 (ancient religion).
14. *A History of Religious Beliefs and Philosophical Opinions in China.* By L. Wieger. Peking, 1927. Pp. 73-124 (pre-Confucian).
15. *The Original Religion of China.* By J. Ross. London, no date. Pp. 107-138 (God), 185-225 (sacrifice).
16. *Folkways in China.* By L. Hodous. London, 1929. Pp. 1-40 (popular religion). 103-125 (sea-goddess, Mt. T'ai).
17. *Religion in China.* By J. J. M. De Groot. N. Y., 1912. Pp. 176-215, 285-319 (worship of the universe, fung-shui).
18. *The Chinese Renaissance.* By Hu Shih. Chicago, 1934.
19. *The Mind of China.* By E. D. Harvey. New Haven, 1933.
20. *The Chinese: Their History and Culture.* By K. S. Latourette. N. Y., 1934.

Chapter IV. Confucianism:

1. On Confucius:
   Confucianism. By H. A. Giles. N. Y., 1915.
   Confucius and His Quest. By M. Magre. London, 1929.
   Kung-tse, Leben und Werk. By R. Wilhelm. Stuttgart, 1925.

Confucius and Confucianism. By R. Wilhelm. Trans. by G. H. Danton. N. Y., 1931.
Konfuzius, sein Leben und seine Lehre. By E. Schmitt. Berlin, 1926.
Confucius. By J. Legge. London, 1875.
2. On the teachings of Confucius, in addition to the works cited above:
The Three Religions of China. By W. E. Soothill. London, 1913.
The Doctrines of Confucius. By E. Faber. Shanghai, 1902.
The Analects of Confucius. Trans. by W. E. Soothill. Yokohama, 1910.
Sacred Books of the East, Vol. III (Shu, Shi, etc.).
3. On great Confucianists:
Confucianism—Giles. Pp. 96–118 (Mencius, Hsün-tze).
The Life and Works of Mencius. By J. Legge. London, 1875. Pp. 14–37 (life), 37–76 (opinions), 123–385 (works), 77–88 (Hsün-tze).
Mencius on the Mind. By I. A. Richards. London, 1932.
The Mind of Mencius. By E. Faber. Boston, 1897.
The Political Principles of Mencius. By F. C. M. Wei. Shanghai, 1916. Pp. 35–80 (teachings, etc.).
Lao-tze und der Taoismus. By R. Wilhelm, Stuttgart, 1925.
Hsün-tze. By H. H. Dubs. London, 1927. Pp. 19–38 (life), 77–154 (nature, virtue, conduct).
The Works of Hsün-tze. By H. H. Dubs. London, 1928. Pp. 213–246 (rules of conduct), 301–317 (human nature).
Chu Hsi and His Masters. By J. P. Bruce. London, 1923. Pp. 56–96 (life), 99–125 (matter, law), 161–171 (moral order), 187–207 (human nature).
The Philosophy of Human Nature by Chu Hsi. Trans. by J. P. Bruce. London, 1922.
The Humanness of Chu Hsi. By J. P. Bruce. London, 1925.
History of Religious Beliefs—Wieger. Pp. 657–678, 715 (Neo-Confucianism, Chu Hsi).
Confucianism. By F. Starr. N. Y., 1930. Pp. 57–241 (Mencius, Hsün-tze, Chu Hsi).
The Story of Oriental Philosophy. By L. A. Beck. N. Y. 1928. 429 pp. Pp. 388–408 (Mencius).
The Political Philosophy of Confucianism. By L. S. Hsu. London, 1932.

Chapter V. Taoism:

1. On Lao-tze and his teachings:
Lao-tze und der Taoismus. By R. Wilhelm, Stuttgart, 1925.
Lao-tsze. By G. G. Alexander. London, 1895. Pp. 35–52 (life), 55–114 (*Tao Teh Ching*).
Lao-tseu. By H. Cordier. Paris, 1911.
Laotze: The Simple Way. By W. G. Old. London, 1922. The *Tao Teh Ching.*
The Canon of Reason and Virtue. Trans. by P. Carus. Chicago, 1913.
Laotse. By Oskar Ewald. München, 1928. Pp. 7–87 (Lao-tze).
The Rhythm of Life. By H. Borel. London, 1921.
Wu Wei. By H. Borel. N. Y., 1911.
The Teaching of the Old Boy. By T. MacInnes. London, 1927.
Three Religions of China—Soothill. Pp. 44–84.
Confucianism—Giles. Pp. 129–164.
History of Religious Beliefs—Wieger. Pp. 145–200.
Kritische Betrachtung über Lau-tsze und seine Lehre. By M. Chiu. Berlin, 1911.

2. On the great Taoists:
   Chuang Tzu. By H. A. Giles. Shanghai, 1926.
   Chuang Tsze. By F. H. Balfour. London, 1881.
   Dschuang Dsi. By R. Wilhelm. Jena, 1912. (Translation of Chuang-tse's works.)
   Taoist Teachings. By L. Giles. N. Y., 1912. (Teachings of Lieh-tze.)
   Taoisme. By L. Wieger. 2 vols. Paris, 1911, 1913. Vol. II, pp. 69–199 (Lieh-tze), 209–509 (Chuang-tze).
   Musings of a Chinese Mystic. By L. Giles. N. Y., 1910. (Chuang-tze).
   Mo Ti. By H. R. Williamson. *Tsinanfu,* 1927.
   The Social Teachings of Meh Tse. By L. Tomkinson. In *Transactions of the Asiatic Society of Japan,* Dec. 1927.
   Le Philosophe Meh-ti. By A. David. London, 1907. Pp. 17–56 (on universal love), 128–166 (man, morals, destiny).
   Les Philosophies de Lao Tseu, Khong Tseu, Mo Tseu. By Hoang Tsen-Yue. Paris, 1925.
   History of Religious Beliefs—Wieger. Pp. 207–213 (Mo-ti), 513–520, 573–588, 603–612 (developments).
   Short History of China—Williams. Pp. 81–83, 99–111, 189–192, 323–325, 353 (historical setting).
   La Chine Antique—Maspero. Pp. 486–507.
   Mythologie Asiatique Illustrée: Mythologie de la Chine Moderne. By H. Maspero. Paris, 1928. Pp. 227–362. (There is also an English translation.)
   The Ethical and Political Works of Motze. By Yi-Pao Mei. London, 1929.

Chapter VI. Religion in Japan:

1. *The Japan Year Book.*
2. *The Japan Mission Year Book,* especially 1931.
3. *Japan Speaks for Herself.* By M. Stauffer. N. Y., 1927.
4. *The National Spirit of Japan.* By S. Honaga. London, 1916. Pp. 88–104 (spirit, morality, religion).
5. *Japan in the World Today.* By A. J. Brown. N. Y., 1928. Pp. 24–51, 253–265 (people, religions).
6. *The Task in Japan.* By A. K. Reischauer. N. Y., 1926. Pp. 64–136 (Christianity and native religions).
7. *The Chinese-Japanese Puzzle.* By A. N. J. Whymant. London, 1932.
8. *History of Japanese Religion.* By M. Anesaki. London, 1930. Pp. 1–15 (the people, etc.).
9. *Modern Tendencies in World Religions*—Braden. Pp. 136–176.
10. *Whither Asia?* By K. Saunders. N. Y. 1933. Pp. 105–204 (Kagawa).

Chapter VII. Shinto:

1. *Japanese Enthronement Ceremonies.* By D. C. Holtom. Tokyo, 1928. Pp. 11–22, 55–67, etc.
2. *The Faith of Japan.* By T. Harada. N. Y., 1914. Pp. 1–72 (kami).
3. *The Shinto Cult.* By M. S. Terry. N. Y., 1910. Pp. 7–63.
4. *Shinto.* By E. Ryerson. London, 1924.
5. *A Study of Shinto.* By G. Kato. Tokyo, 1926.
6. *Nippon Shindo Ron.* By Y. Hibino. Cambridge, 1928. Pp. 36–49 (loyalty, filial piety), 66–75 (beauty, spirit), 147–165 (patriotism).
7. *Shinto.* By W. G. Aston. London, 1905.
8. *The Kojiki. Transactions* of the Asiatic Society of Japan, vol. 10.
9. *The Nihongi. Proceedings* of the Japan Society, vols. 1, 2. London, 1896.
10. *Japan, an Interpretation.* By Lafcadio Hearn. N. Y., 1905.

11. *Unfamiliar Japan,* 2 vols. By L. Hearn. N. Y., 1894. Vol. II, pp. 385–404 (worship).

12. *Development of Religion in Japan.* By G. W. Knox. N. Y., 1907. Pp. 45–113.

13. *Shin-to.* By G. Schurhammer. Leipzig, 1923. Parallel German and English. Handsomely illustrated.

14. *Le Shintoisme, Religion Nationale.* Ed. by J. M. Martin. 2 vols. Hongkong, 1924, 1927.

15. *Transactions* of the Asiatic Society of Japan, vols. 38, pts. 2, 4 (Food-goddess, ancestor-cult); 41, pt. 4 (Idzumo ritual); 49, pt. 2 (Shinto as religion).

Chapter VIII. India and Religion:

1. *The Indian Social Reformer* magazine, weekly, Bombay.

2. *The Power of India.* By Michael Pym. N. Y., 1930. Pp. 215–297 (diversity, revolution, princes and peasants).

3. *Voiceless India.* By G. Emerson. Pp. 3–20 (a northern village), 250–323 (barter, caste, etc.), 418–444 (God in the village).

4. *Living India.* By Savel Zimand. N. Y., 1928. Pp. 3–62 (people), 65–106 (Hinduism, caste), 126–182 (cows, mosques, the masses).

5. *Contemporary Thought of India.* By A. C. Underwood. N. Y., 1931. Pp. 95–130 (social elements).

6. *A Geography of India.* By G. Patterson. London, 1909.

7. *Economic Conditions in India.* By P. P. Pillai. London, 1925. Pp. 1–40 (economic evolution), 69–128 (agriculture), 233–266 (labor), 267–330 (industry).

8. *Young India,* By M. K. Gandhi. Second series. N. Y., 1927.

Chapter IX. Hinduism:

1. General, in addition to the references above:
Village Gods of South India. By H. Whitehead. London, 1916. Pp. 33–45 (the cult), 46–116 (Telugu and Tamil worship), 138–152 (origin of village worship).
Benares, the Sacred City. By E. B. Havell. London, 1905.
The Hindu at Home. By J. E. Padfield. Madras, 1896.
Seen and Heard in a Panjab Village. By M. Young. London, 1931.
India and Its Faiths. By J. B. Pratt. Pp. 15–33 (worship), 34–45 (the pilgrim), 140–165 (priests).
Purdah. By F. H. Das. N. Y., 1932.
Caste and Race in India. By G. S. Ghurye. N. Y., 1932.
Modern Tendencies—Braden. Pp. 20–86.
Whither Asia?—Saunders. Pp. 31–64 (Gandhi).
The Making of Modern India. By N. Macnicol. London, 1924. Pp. 37–84 (conflicts, ideals, realities), 85–153 (mysticism, devotion, the holy life, God).

2. The sects:
India and Its Faiths—Pratt. Pp. 46–189 (the many gods, duty and destiny, works, priests, reforms).
Rites of the Twice-born. By S. Stevenson. Pp. 368–417 (the worship of Shiva and Vishnu).
Religions of India. By E. W. Hopkins. Pp. 348–523 (Shiva, Vishnu, etc.).
Indian Theism. By N. Macnicol. London, 1915.
The Ramayana of Tulsi Das. By J. N. Macfie. Edinburgh, 1930.
Myths and Legends of India. By J. N. Macfie. Edinburgh, 1924.

3. Higher thought, ethics:
Ethics of India. By E. W. Hopkins. Pp. 1–134 (Hindu).

Hindu Ethics. By J. McKenzie. London, 1922.
The Hindu View of Life. By S. Radhakrishnan. N. Y., 1926.
The Evolution of Ethics—Sneath. Pp. 99–141.
The Religion of the Veda. By M. Bloomfield. N. Y., 1908.
The Religion of the Rigveda. By H. D. Griswold. N. Y., 1923.
Indian Philosophy, 2 vols. By S. Radhakrishnan. N. Y., 1927.
History of Indian Philosophy. By S. Dasgupta. Cambridge, 1922.
The Thirteen Principal Upanishads. Trans. by R. E. Hume. N. Y., 1931.
A History of Indian Literature. By H. H. Gowen. N. Y., 1931.

Chapter X. Jainism:

1. *Mahavira the Man.* By A. C. Sen, in *Calcutta Review,* May, 1932.
2. *The Heart of Jainism.* By S. Stevenson. Oxford, 1915.
3. *Der Jainismus.* By H. von Glasenapp. Berlin, 1925. With illustrations.
4. *Jainism in North India.* By C. J. Shah. London, 1932. Illustrated.
5. *Studies in South Indian Jainism.* By M. S. R. Ayyangar and B. S. Rao. Madras, 1922.
6. *Life of Parçvanatha.* By M. Bloomfield. Baltimore, 1919.
7. *Gaina Sutras.* Ed. by H. Jacobi. *Sacred Books of the East,* Vols. XXII, XLV.
8. *Cambridge History of India,* Vol. I, pp. 150–170 (chapter by J. Charpentier).
9. *India*—Pratt. Pp. 254–290.
10. *Indian Philosophy*—Dasgupta. Pp. 169–207.
11. *Treasure-House*—Hume. Pp. 463–4, citations to Jain scriptures.

Chapter XI. Buddhism:

1. The Buddhist world:
   The Pilgrimage of Buddhism. By J. B. Pratt. N. Y., 1928.
   Pp. 144–187 (external aspects in Siam), 305–416 (temples, monks, laymen in China), 503–566 (temples, laymen, etc., in Japan).
   Buddhism as a Religion. By H. Hackmann. London, 1910.
   Pp. 93–295 (modern Buddhism in Ceylon, Burma, Siam, China, Korea and Japan).
   The Story of Buddhism. By K. J. Saunders. Oxford, 1916. Pp. 76–98 (Ceylon).
   Buddhism, Primitive and Present, in Magadha and Ceylon. By R. S. Copleston. 2nd edition. London, 1908.
   Buddhism and Buddhists in Southern Asia. By K. J. Saunders. N. Y., 1923. (Burma, Ceylon, Siam).
   Buddhism and Buddhists in China. By L. Hodous. N. Y., 1924.
   Buddhism and Buddhists in Japan. By R. C. Armstrong. N. Y., 1927. Pp. 144. Pp. 15–30 (temples, priests), 50–96 (sects), 68–78 (social ideals).
   The Religion of Tibet. By Chas. Bell. Oxford, 1931.
   India—Pratt. Pp. 371–424 (doctrines and value).
2. Gotam and original Buddhism:
   Buddhism—Hackmann. Pp. 1–35.
   Epochs in Buddhist History. By K. J. Saunders. Chicago, 1924. Pp. 1–28.
   The Pilgrimage—Pratt. Pp. 1–91.
   The Life of Buddha. By E. J. Thomas. N. Y., 1927.
   The Life of Buddha. By A. F. Herold. N. Y., 1927. Legendary.
   Some Sayings of the Buddha. Trans. by F. L. Woodward. Oxford, 1925.
   Gotama Buddha. By K. J. Saunders. N. Y., 1920.

Hinduism and Buddhism. By Chas. Eliot. London, 1921. Vol. I, pp. 129–184 (life), 185–236 (teachings), 237–253 (monastic).

The Life of Gotama the Buddha. By E. H. Brewster. N. Y., 1926.

3. Historical development:

Buddhism—Hackmann. Pp. 36–92.

The Pilgrimage—Pratt. Pp. 92–115, 211–271 (Mahayana).

Buddhist India. By R. Davids. N. Y., 1903.

Asoka. By V. Smith. Oxford, 1909.

Epochs—Saunders. Pp. 29–104.

A Manual of Buddhism. By Mrs. R. Davids. London, 1932. Pp. 341.

Hinduism and Buddhism—Eliot. Vol. I, pp. 263–274; Vol. II, pp. 3–6, 63–82.

Indian Philosophy—Radhakrishnan. Vol. I, 589–605 (difference between Hinayana and Mahayana).

History of Indian Philosophy—Dasgupta. Vol. I, pp. 125–151.

Ashvaghosha's Awakening of Faith. Trans. by D. T. Suzuki. Chicago, 1900.

The Lotus of the Wonderful Law. Trans. by W. E. Soothill. Oxford, 1930.

4. China and Japan:

Truth and Tradition in Chinese Buddhism. By K. L. Reichelt. Shanghai, 1927. Pp. 330. Pp. 298–311 (today), 228–297 (monasteries, pilgrimages), 77–126 (masses for the dead), 127–170 (the Pure Land school).

Buddhist China. By R. F. Johnston. N. Y., 1913. Pp. 92–121 (Pure Land).

Hinduism and Buddhism—Eliot. Vol. III, pp. 244–280 (China). 281–302 (Chinese Buddhist literature), 321–335 (monastic life).

The Pilgrimage—Pratt. Pp. 352–416 (China), 436–502 (Japan).

Studies in Japanese Buddhism. By A. K. Reischauer. N. Y., 1917. Pp. 351. Pp. 1–50 (origins), 51–78 (Mahayana), 79–182 (Japan).

Essays in Zen Buddhism. By D. T. Suzuki. London, 1927. Pp. 299–346 (meditation hall), 26–148 (enlightenment and ignorance).

A Study of Shin Buddhism. By G. Sasaki. Kyoto, 1925. Pp. 97–139 (life of Shinran Shonin).

The Creed of Half Japan. By A. Lloyd. London, 1911.

Shinran and His Work. By A. Lloyd. Tokyo, 1910.

Development of Religion in Japan—Knox. Pp. 80–113 (general), 114–137 (Pure Land, and Nichiren).

Nichiren, the Buddhist Prophet. By M. Anesaki. Cambridge, Mass., 1916.

Chapter XII. The Parsis:

1. *Religions of the Empire.* Ed. by W. L. Hare. N. Y., 1925. Pp. 207–230.

2. *The Treasure of the Magi.* By J. H. Moulton. Oxford, 1917. Pp. 119–210 (the Parsis), 5–118 (Zoroastrianism).

3. *Zoroastrianism and Our Spiritual Heritage.* By P. A. Wadia. Bombay, 1923. (The Parsis, prayers, Gathas).

4. *The Religious Ceremonies and Customs of the Parsees.* By J. J. Modi. Bombay, 1922.

5. *History of the Parsis.* 2 vols. London, 1884. Vol. I, pp. 53–90 (Persia), 91–213 (India); II, 146–164 (Zoroaster), 165–208 (Creed).

6. *Early Zoroastrianism.* By J. H. Moulton. London, 1913. Pp. 343–390 (translation of the Gathas).

7. *Zoroaster, the Prophet of Ancient Iran.* By A. V. W. Jackson. N. Y., 1901.

8. *Zoroastrian Theology.* By M. N. Dhalla. N. Y., 1914.
9. *Zoroastrian Studies.* By A. V. W. Jackson. N. Y., 1928.
10. *Zoroastrianism.* By H. McNeile. London, 1915.
11. *The Teaching of Zarathushtra.* By J. H. Moulton. Bombay, 1916. Pp. 1–18 (God), 19–29 (evil), 39–44 (soul), 45–55 (future life), 56–68 (ritual), 69–80 (life of Zoroaster), 81–96 (the Parsis).
12. *The Ethical Religion of Zoroaster.* By M. M. Dawson. N. Y., 1931. Pp. 271.
13. *The Parsi Book of Books, the Zend-Avesta.* By R. E. Sanjana. Bombay, 1925.
14. *Sacred Books of the East,* vols, 4, 5, 18, 23, 24, 31, 37, 47.
15. *The Zoroastrian Doctrine of a Future Life.* By J. D. C. Pavry. N. Y., 1926.
16. *Our Perfecting World.* By M. N. Dhalla. N. Y., 1930. (A Zoroastrian view of progress.)

Chapter XIII. The Sikhs:

1. *The Sikhs of the Punjab.* By R. E. Parry. London, 1923.
2. *History of the Sikhs.* By J. D. Cunningham. Ed. by H. L. O. Garrett. Oxford, 1918.
3. *The History of the Sikhs,* 2 vols. By W. L. McGregor. London, 1846.
4. *The Punjab Peasant in Prosperity and Debt.* By M. L. Darling. N. Y., 1925.
5. *Northern India.* By W. Crooke. Oxford, 1926. Pp. 85–125.
6. *The Caste System of Northern India.* By E. A. H. Blunt. London, 1931.
7. *The Songs of Kabir.* Trans. by R. Tagore. N. Y., 1915.
8. *Hindi Religious Poetry.* By Ahmad Shah. Cawnpore, 1925. Pp. 43–50 (Nanak).
9. *Psalms of Maratha Saints.* By N. Macnicol. N. Y., 1919.
10. *Sikhism.* By E. Guilford. London, 1915.
11. *The Sikh Religion,* Vols. I–VI. By M. A. Macauliffe. Oxford, 1909.
12. *The Religion of the Sikhs.* By D. Field. N. Y., 1914.
13. *Critical Study of the Sri Guru Nanak Dev.* By S. S. Thapar. Rawalpindi, 1904.
14. *Journal of Religion,* vol. 9, pp. 281–290. *Art.* by A. Widgery on "Ethics of the Sikhs."
15. *Oxford History of India.* By V. Smith. Oxford, 1920.
16. *Memoirs of Babur,* 2 vols. Ed. by L. King. Oxford, 1921.
17. *The Adi Granth.* Trans. by E. Trumpp. London, 1877.
18. *Ranjit Singh.* By Lepel H. Griffin. Oxford, 1911.
19. *Asia Magazine,* vol. 26, pp. 242–246 (the Akalis).
20. *Living India.* By S. Zimand. Pp. 230–243 (the Akalis).
21. *The Sikhs.* By J. H. Gordon. Edinburgh, 1904.
22. *Religion and Short History of the Sikhs.* By G. B. Scott. London, 1930.
23. *The Book of the Ten Masters.* By Puran Singh. London, 1926.

Chapter XIV. The Hebrew-Jewish Faith:

1. Numbers, distribution, etc.:
   Jewish Life in Modern Times. By I. Cohen. N. Y., 1929. Pp. 1–14, 111–132 (racial characteristics), 214–222 (migrations), 277–290 (worship).
   The Jews. By M. Fishberg. N. Y., 1911. Pp. 1–20, 90–178 (types).
   The Jews of Asia. By S. Mendelssohn. N. Y., 1920. Pp. 1–51

(Turkey), 73–97 (Persia), 98–132 (India), 133–163 (China), 164–234 (Yemen, Iraq, Kurdistan).
The Jews of Africa. By S. Mendelssohn. N. Y., 1920.
The Jew through the Centuries. By H. L. Willett. Chicago, 1932. Pp. 23–70 (Palestine).
Cochin Tribes and Castes. By Krishna Iyer. Madras, 1912. Pp. 400–434 (India, customs).
Modern Tendencies—Braden. Pp. 272–327.

2. Ritual, scriptures:
Jewish Encyclopædia. N. Y., 1903–1925. Articles on synagogue, Sabbath, etc.; on the Torah, etc.; Passover, Tabernacles, etc.
The Old Testament.
Jewish Life—Cohen. Pp. 58–74 (domestic religion), 277–290.

3. Historical:
The Jew through the Centuries—Willett.
The Religion of Israel. By G. A. Barton, N. Y., 1918.
Pp. 56–75 (Moses and the Covenant), 94–126 (the prophets).
The Story of the Jews, or Stranger than Fiction. By L. Browne, N. Y., 1931. Pp. 22–47 (origins), 48–103 (David to the Exile), 104–135 (Persian, Greek, Roman rule), 151–267 (dispersion, wanderings), 294–350 (modern reform).
Israel among the Nations. By N. H. Baynes. London, 1927. Pp. 42–75 (Canaan, monarchy), 74–167 (captivity, Persia, Greeks, etc.).
A History of the Jewish People. By M. L. Margolis and A. Marx. Philadelphia, 1927.
The Semitic Religions. By D. M. Kay. Edinburgh, 1923. Pp. 1–110.
History of Religions—Moore, Vol. II, pp. 1–106.
The Jew and His Neighbor. By J. W. Parkes. London, 1930.
The Evolution of the Hebrew People. By L. H. Wild. N. Y., 1917.
Hebrew Religion. By T. H. Robinson and W. O. E. Osterley. London, 1930.
The Pharisees. By R. T. Herford. N. Y., 1924.

4. Theology, etc.:
Judaism. By I. Abrahams. London, 1907.
Jewish Theology. By K. Kohler. N. Y., 1918. Pp. 52–145 (God and His attributes), 231–260 (freedom, morals), 261–297 (prayer, immortality), 331–377 (the mission of reformed Jews).
Affirmations of Judaism. By J. H. Hertz. London, 1927. Orthodox.
Evolution of Ethics—Sneath. Pp. 159–232.
The Foundations of Jewish Ethics. By A. H. Kohler. N. Y., 1929.
History of Mediæval Jewish Philosophy. By I. Husik. N. Y., 1916.

5. Modern, reform, etc.:
Hear, Ye Sons. By Irving Fineman. N. Y., 1933.
How Odd of God. By L. Browne. N. Y., 1934.
The Reform Movement in Judaism. By D. Philipson. N. Y., 1931.
Dreamers of the Ghetto. By I. Zangwill. N. Y., 1898.
The Ghetto. By Louis Wirt. Chicago, 1928.
Frontiers of Hope. By H. Kallen. N. Y., 1929.
Atlantic Monthly, July 1933. Art. "How the Jew Does It."

Chapter XV. The Religion of Jesus and Christianity:

1. General:
Religions of the World. Ed. by Carl Clemen. Pp. 339–436.
History of Religions, Vol. II—Moore. Pp. 107–385.
Religion in Various Cultures—Friess and Schneider. Pp. 298–496.
Cf. pp. 533–556.

A Short History of Religions. By E. E. Kellett. N. Y., 1934. Pp. 168–563.
> *History of the Christian Church.* By Williston Walker. N. Y., 1918.
> *A History of Christian Thought.* By A. C. McGiffert. N. Y., 1932.

2. Early Christianity:
> *The Jesus of History.* By T. R. Glover. N. Y., 1917.
> *Jesus.* By W. Bousset. N. Y., 1906.
> *The Life and Teachings of Jesus.* By C. F. Kent. N. Y., 1913.
> *The Evolution of the New Testament.* By J. E. Symes. N. Y., 1922.
> *The History and Literature of the New Testament.* By H. T. Fowler. N. Y., 1925.
> *The New Testament.*
> *The Founding of the Church.* By B. W. Bacon. Boston, 1909.

3. Historical, etc.:
> *A Short History of Our Religion.* By D. C. Somervell. N. Y., 1922.
> *The Conversion of Europe.* By C. H. Robinson. London, 1917.
> *The Making of the Christian Mind.* By G. G. Atkins. N. Y., 1928.
> *Faith.* By Stewart Means. N. Y., 1933.
> *The Story of Christianity in Outline.* By C. H. Moehlman. Rochester, 1930.
> *Christianity.* By C. Guignebert. N. Y., 1927.
> *The Spread of Christianity.* By E. C. Moore. Chicago. 1919.
> *The Spread of Christianity.* By P. Hutchinson. N. Y., 1922.
> *History of the Christian People.* By H. K. Rowe. N. Y., 1931.
> *From Justinian to Luther.* By L. Pullan. Oxford, 1930.
> *Christian Epoch Makers.* By H. C. Vedder. Phila., 1908.

Chapter XVI. Islam:

1. *The Moslem World of Today.* Ed. by J. R. Mott. N. Y., 1925.
2. *The Arab at Home.* By P. Harrison. N. Y., 1924.
3. *Manners and Customs of the Modern Egyptians.* By E. W. Lane. Various editions.
4. *Hajji Baba of Ispahan.* By J. J. Morier. N. Y.
5. *Observations on the Mussulmauns of India* (by Mrs. M. H. Ali). Ed. by W. Crooke. Oxford, 1917.
6. *A Pilgrimage to al-Madinah and Meccah,* 2 vols. By R. F. Burton. London, 1913.
7. *The Legacy of Islam.* By T. W. Arnold and others. Oxford, 1931.
8. *Mohammed.* By D. S. Margoliouth. N. Y., 1906.
9. *Mohammed.* By Edith Holland. N. Y., 1914.
10. *The Koran.* Editions by Palmer, Rodwell, *et al.*
11. *Mohammedanism.* By D. S. Margoliouth. London, 1911.
12. *Mohammedanism.* By S. Hurgronje. N. Y., 1916.
13. *Aspects of Islam.* By D. B. Macdonald. N. Y., 1911.
14. *The Origin of Islam.* By R. Bell. London, 1926.
15. *Mohammed and Islam.* By I. Goldziher (trans. by K. C. Seelye). New Haven, 1917.
16. *Islam.* By H. Lammens. London, 1929.
17. *Muslim Theology, etc.* By D. B. Macdonald, N. Y., 1903.
18. *The Faith of Islam.* By E. Sell. London, 1907.
19. *Development of the Quran.* By E. Sell. London, 1909.
20. *The Preaching of Islam.* By T. W. Arnold. N. Y., 1913.
21. *Arabic Thought.* By D. O'Leary. London, 1922.
22. *The Sociology of Islam,* vols. 1, 2. By R. Levy. London, 1931, 1933.
23. *Eastern Poetry and Prose.* By R. A. Nicholson. Cambridge, 1922.
24. *Modern Movements among Moslems.* By S. G. Wilson. N. Y., 1916.
25. *Studies in a Mosque.* By S. Lane-Poole. London, 1893.

26. *Indian Islam.* By M. T. Titus. London, 1930.
27. *The Ahmadiya Movement.* By H. A. Walter. London, 1918.
28. *Whither Islam?* Ed. by H. A. R. Gibb. London, 1932.
29. *The Expansion of Islam.* By W. W. Cash. London, 1928.
30. *The Mystics of Islam.* By R. A. Nicholson. London, 1914.
31. *Evolution of Ethics*—Sneath. Pp. 329-356 (art. by J. C. Archer on Moslem Ethics).

INDEX

INDEX